歐亞學刊（國際版）

INTERNATIONAL JOURNAL OF EURASIAN STUDIES

新1輯（總第11輯）

余太山　李錦繡　主編

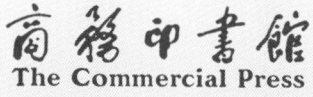

2011年·北京

First Edition

Copyright © 2011 by The Editors-in-Chief

All rights reserved. No part of this book may be reproduced in any form or by any means without permission in writing from the publisher.

ISBN 978-7-100-08518-2

I. International Journal of Eurasian Studies II. YU Taishan, LI Jinxiu

FOUNDED BY

The Foundation for East-West Understanding & Cooperation

Published by The Commercial Press
36 Wang Fu Jing Street, Beijing 100710, China
Printed in the People's Republic of China

Plate I-1
Image of riders from the Tomb of Horemheb, Egypt, (1322-1306 BCE), stone, Museo Civico Archeologico, Bologna

Plate I-2
Image of rider on pile carpet from Pazyryk, Russia, Kurgan V, wool (From Rudenko 1970)

Plate I-3
Reconstruction of the horse from Berel, Kazakhstan, Tomb 11, various materials including gold, wood, leather, iron. (From: Francfort 1999)

Plate I-4
Reconstruction of horse from Ak-Alakha, Ukok Plateau, Kazathstan (From: Polos'mak n.d.)

Plate I-5
Spindle whorls (clay and wood) and saddle pads (leather) from Zaghunluq, Phase II (*MXUAR* 2003: Pls. I, 3, drawings)

Plate I-6
Saddle cushions from Tomb 2 at Zaghunluq, Xinjiang, PRC, Tomb 2, leather. (After: *MXUAR* 2003: p. 92)

Plate I-7
Saddle cushions from Subeshi, Xinjiang, PRC, leather. (From: *Kaogu*, 2002/6; and Wang 1999)

Plate I-8
Clay seated Chinese riders—later Eastern Zhou. (From: 咸陽市文物考古研究所,《咸陽石油鋼管鋼繩廠秦墓清理簡報》, *Kaogu yu Wenwu* 考古文物, 1996/5)

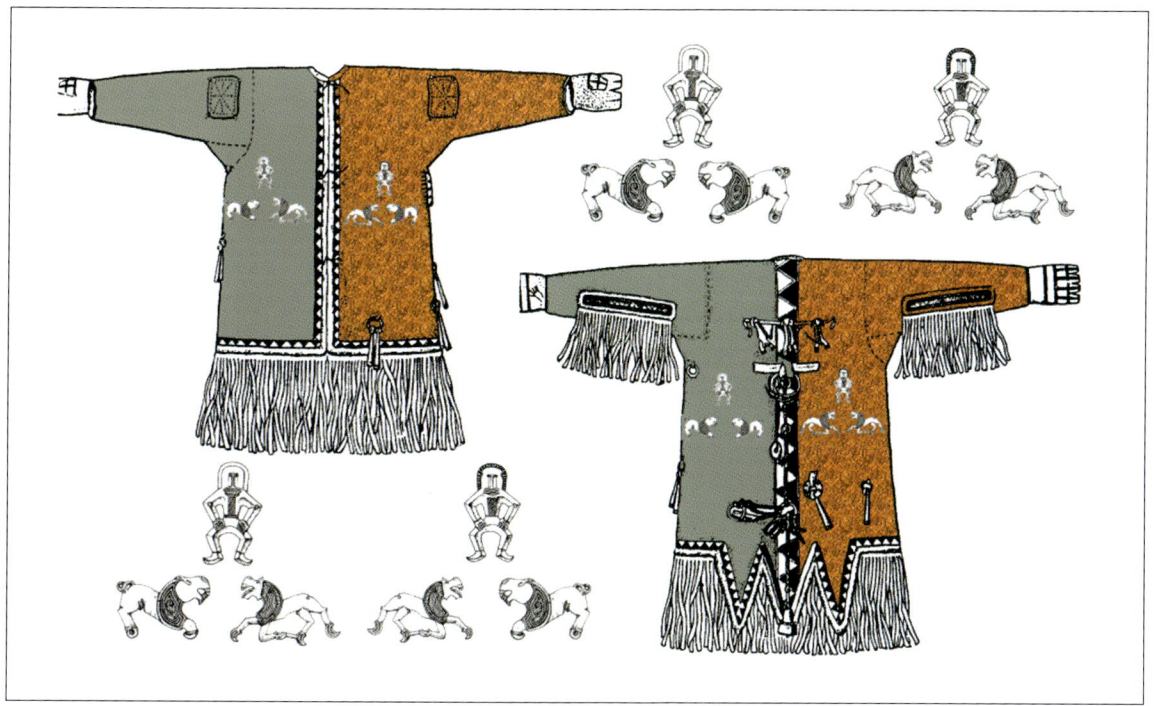

Plate II-1
Reconstruction of the shaman jacket (caftan) with Martynivka mounts based on W. Szymański's proposal. Shaman robe after Szyjewski (2001) with author's modifications

Plate III-1
Tell Khwaris, Sasanian (?) mosaic (Costa 1971: pl. XXXV)

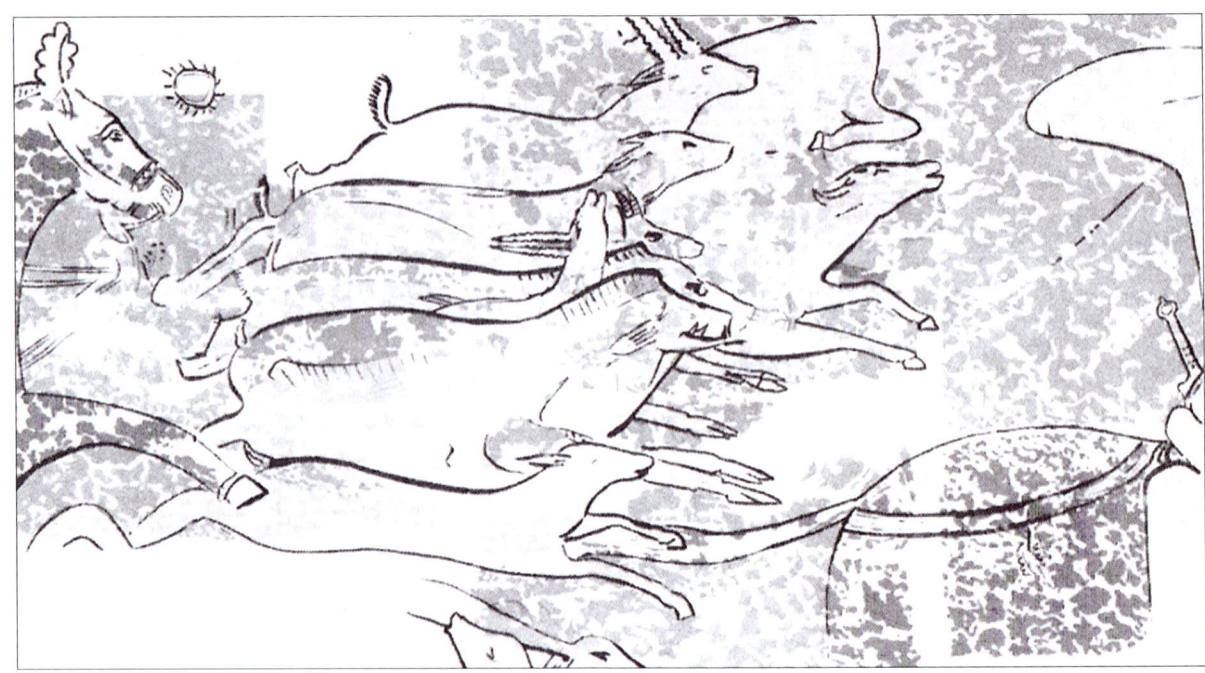

Plate III-2
Susa, mural painting, possibly late-Parthian (Ghirshaman 1982: fig. 224)

Plate III-3
Hajyabad, Sasanian mural painting (reproduction after Azarnoush 1994: pl. XXXV)

Plate III-4
Dome of the Rock, detail of the mosaic, intermediate octagon, inner face (O. Grabar, 1989: fig. 29)

Plate IV-1
Han mirror found under the wooden construction of Barrow No. 7

Plate IV-2
Decoration on the inner side of the chariot's canopy

Plate IV-3
Bronze axle caps and iron pins

Plate IV-4
A general view of Barrow no. 7

Plate IV-5
The intraburial construction of Barrow no. 7: wooden chambers inside large stone cist

Plate IV-6
The intraburial construction of Barrow no. 7 after clearing: the outside burial chamber, the inside burial chamber and the coffin

Plate IV-7
A lacquered vessel and birch bark boxes near Doll no. 1 in western outside corridor

Plate IV-8
Carved images on birch bark boxes: a nomad camp with yurts on wheels (left) and carving of a man's profile in a helmet on birch bark disk (possibly depicting a coin)

Plate IV-9
Fragment of a hieroglyphic inscription on a lacquered box with a name of Kaogong workshop

Plate IV-10
A disposition of finds in south-eastern corner of the inside corridor: a lacquered quiver, a lacquered stick, a lacquered cup, a braid, an iron spoon, silver phalars, bronze plate, and iron horse harness

Plate IV-11
Tubular gold pendants, a small gold vessel and fragments of ritual sword in lacquered wooden scabbards inside the coffin

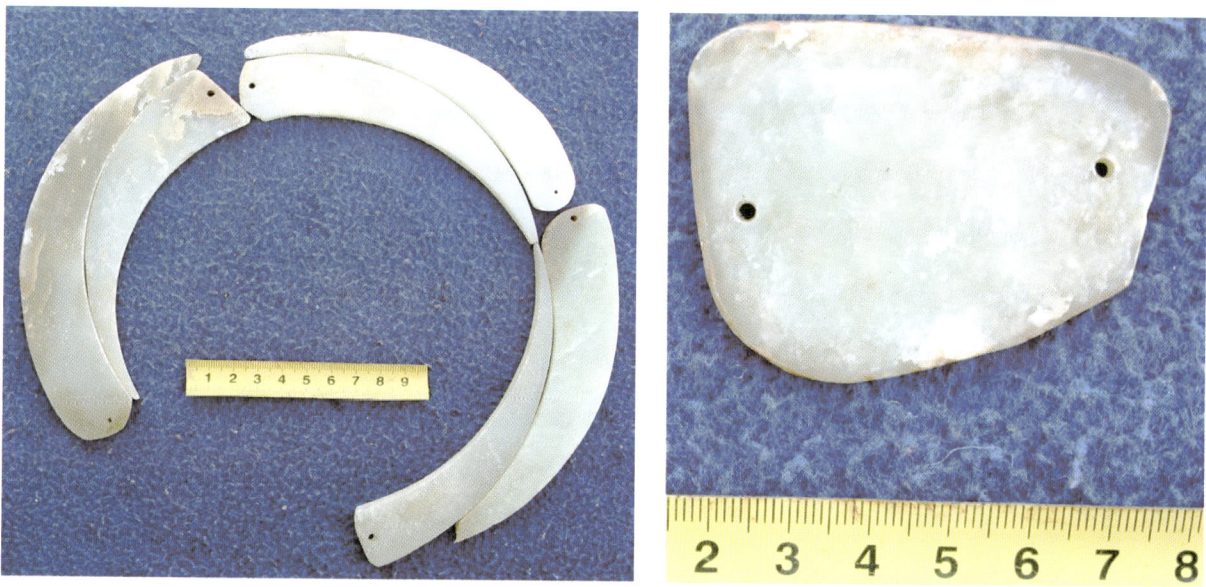

Plate IV-12
White jade plaques and diadem

Plate IV-13
Gold buckle shaped as a satyr's head

Plate V-1
Bugut stele with Sogdian inscriptions (on front and both sides) on stone tortoise (photo: H.T.)

Plate V-2
A she-wolf nursing a baby? Or only a dragon? (Small fragments are attached on digital photo) (photo: H.T.)

Plate V-3
Ruins of mausoleum at the Bugut site (photo: H.T.)

Plate V-4
Fragments of roof tiles between the strata (photo: H.T.)

Plate V-5
Bugut site. Row of 276 balbal-stones (L: 300m) (photo: H.T.)

Plate V-6
Ruins of mausoleum at the Tsetsüüh site. Stone tortoise is located in the foreground. (photo: H.T.)

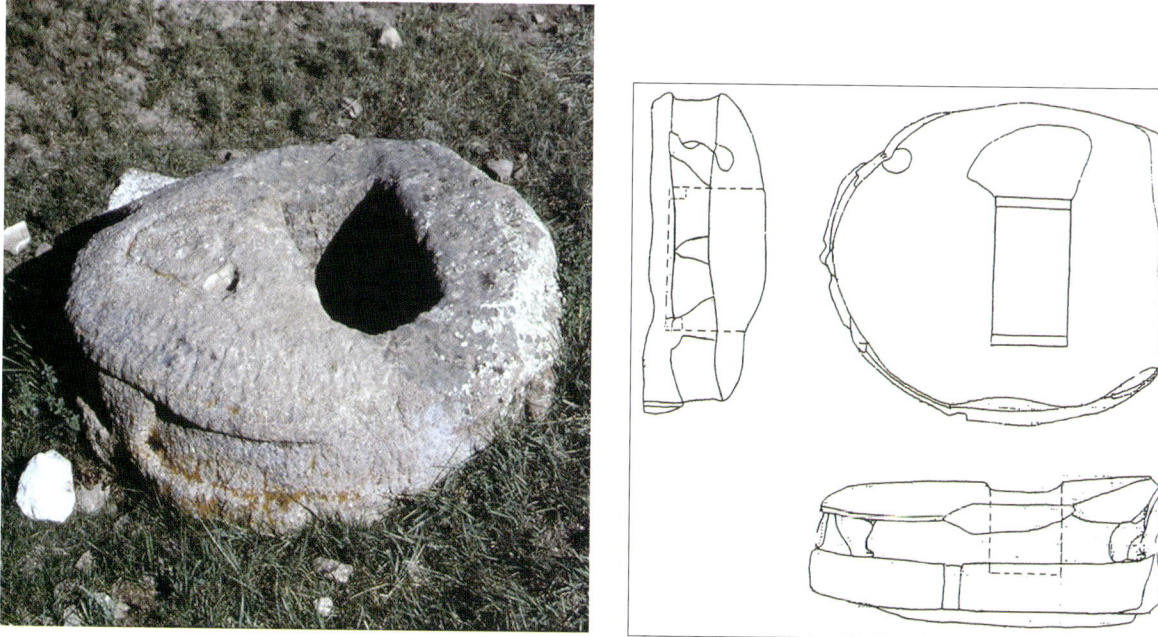

Plate V-7
Stone tortoise base for a stele without a head. The form and size are the same as the Bugut tortoise. The hole is a little larger than that of the Bugut stele. (photo: H.T.; ill.: Moriyasu and Ochir 1999)

Plate V-8
Row of 210 balbals (L: 308m), Tsetsüüh site. (photo: H.T.)

Plate V-9
Japanese archaeologists in 1999 surveying fragments of roof tiles which had been piled up by Vojtov's expedition. (photo: H.T.)

Plate V-10
Corner fragment of a square flat roof tile with a runic inscription, "i-l-l-k"＝illik? (photo and rubbing: H.T.)

Plate V-11
Sogdian inscription on the lower part of the stone statue in Zhaosu, Ili district, Xinjiang Uyghur Autonomous Region (photo: H.T.)

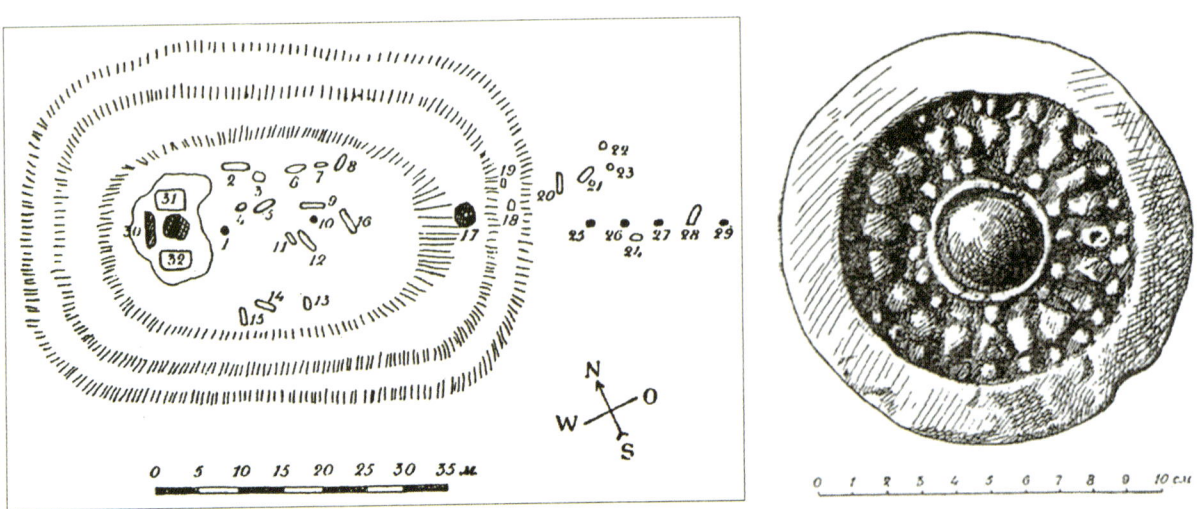

Plate V-12
Ungetu site, 100km west of Ulaanbaatar, near River. Tola. Roof tile-end with lotus ornament (Borovka 1927)

Plate V-13
Stone statue at Ungetu. (photo: H.T.)

Plate V-14
Stone statues, probably having a role as balbal beside the mausoleum of Köl Tegin, Mongolia (photo: H.T.)

Plate V-15
Civil official (left) and military official (right) from the tomb of duke Lu An 樂安, ca. 150 CE, Shandong. (Jinshisuo 金石索)

Plate V-16
A pair of guardians standing in front of the tumulus, 景陵 Jingling, of 宣武帝 Emperor Xuanwu（r.499-515）of the Northern Wei. One statue is a replica, and the head has been added as part of an imaginative rstoration. [photo: H.T.]

Plate V-17
Excavation site of the sacrificial altar 祭壇 of the Zhaoling 昭陵 mausoleum. Entrance is in the north.

Plate V-18
Stone statues with Turkic hair style, unearthed from site of mausoleum of Emperor Taizong. Courtesy of Dr. Zhang Jianlin. (photo: H.T.)

Plate V-19
Shiveet-ulaan site. (Photograph taken from kite and side view: H.T)

Plate V-20
Statue holds a vessel in front of chest. [ill.: Moriyasu and Ochir 1999; photo: H.T. and Ramstedt et al. 1958]

Plate V-21
Sitting stone lion at Shiveet-ulaan. H.: 82cm. [photo: H.T.]

Plate V-22
Stela with "70 tamgas", kept in Hairhan temple. [photo: H.T.]

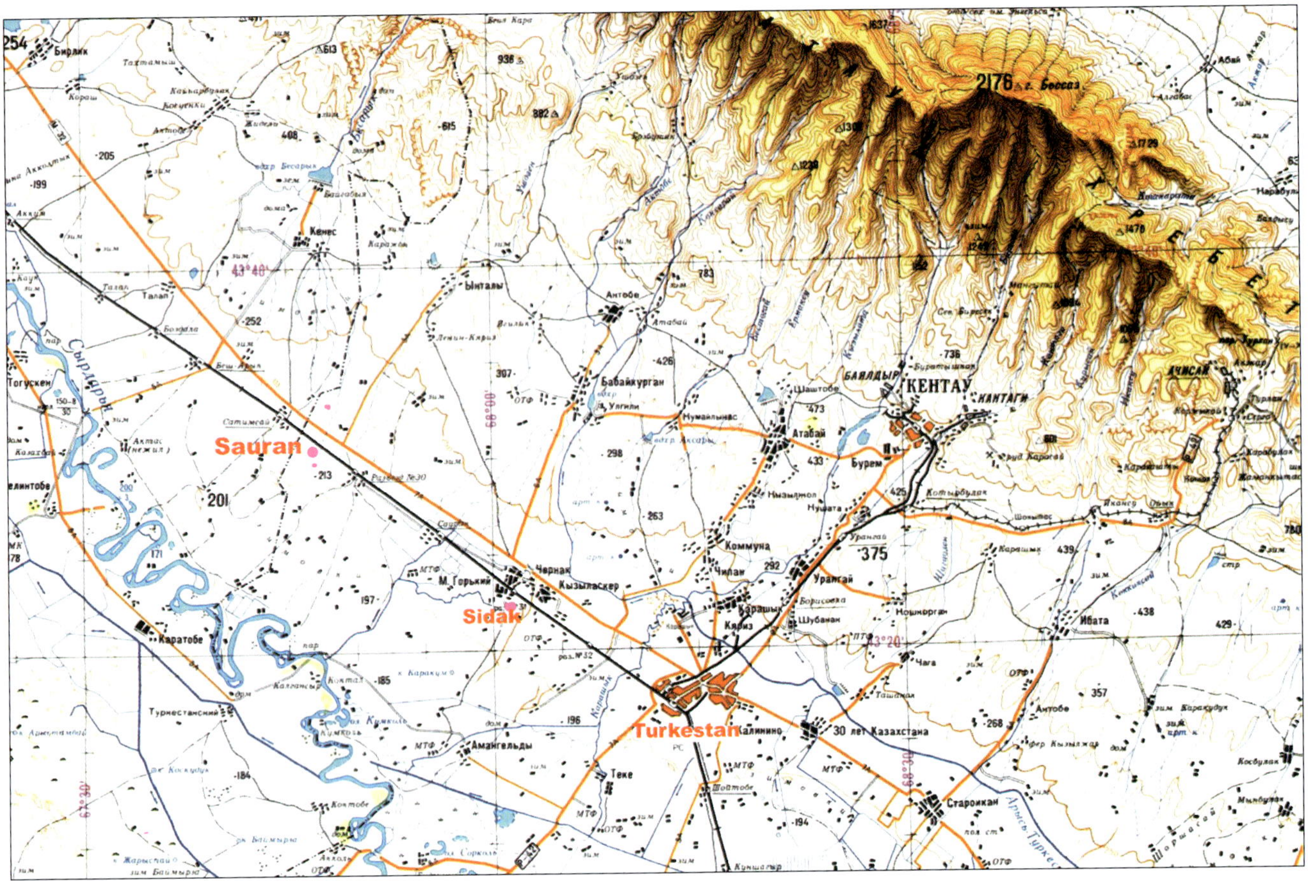

Plate VI-1
Map of "Sauran Archaeological Complex".

Plate VI-2
Central fort of Sauran. Major objects of archaeological studies of 2004-2009

Plate VI-3
Outward appearance of Sauran north-east wall segment.

Plate VI-4
Inner face of west wall segment. Structure of early wall under the later dated foundation.

Plate VI-5
Blockstone pavement at the entrance to *hanaka* (Dig3)

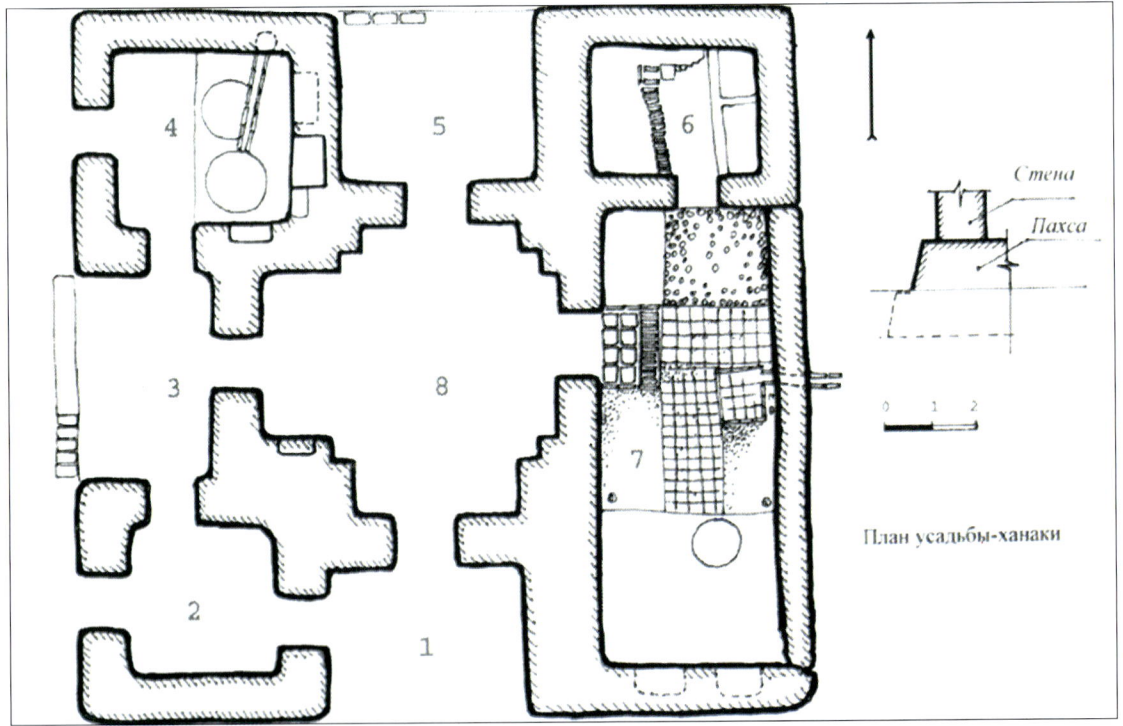

Plate VI-6
Plan of farmstead No.1 north of fortification

Plate VI-7
Ancient city of Karatobe – Ancient Sauran

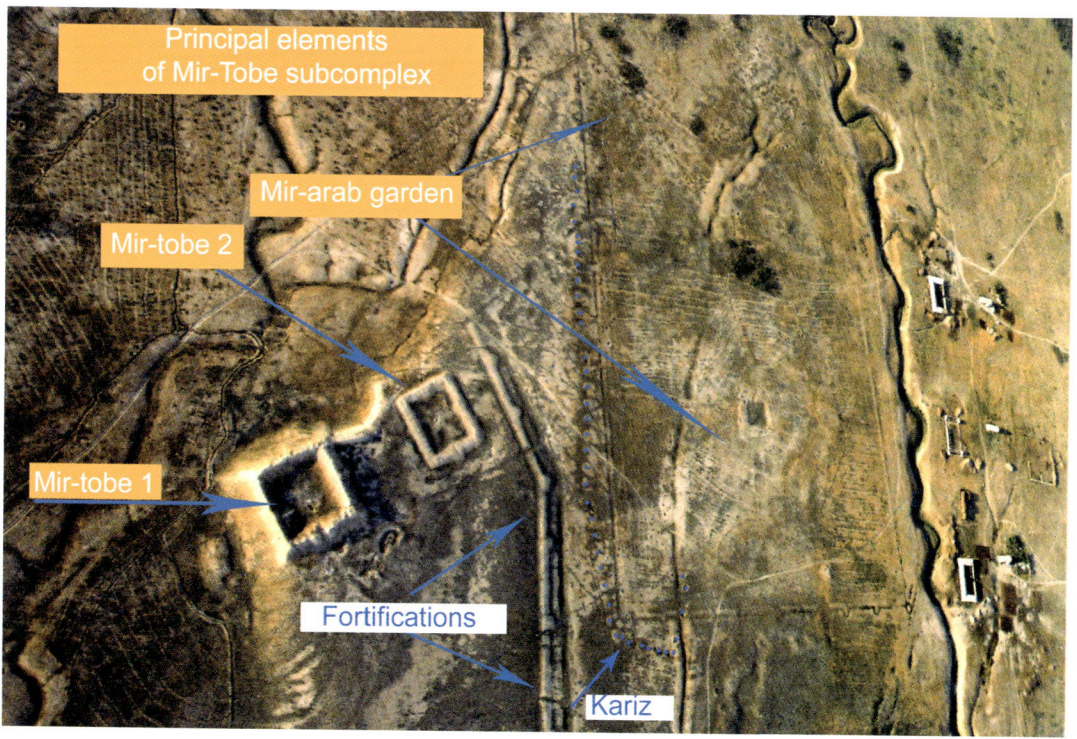

Plate VI-8
Mirtobe

Plate VI-9
Grand Sauran *kariz* running to north corner of ancient site

Plate VI-10
One of the kariz north of the later-dated site of Sauran

Plate VI-11
Dig No.1 in Karatobe citadel south corner

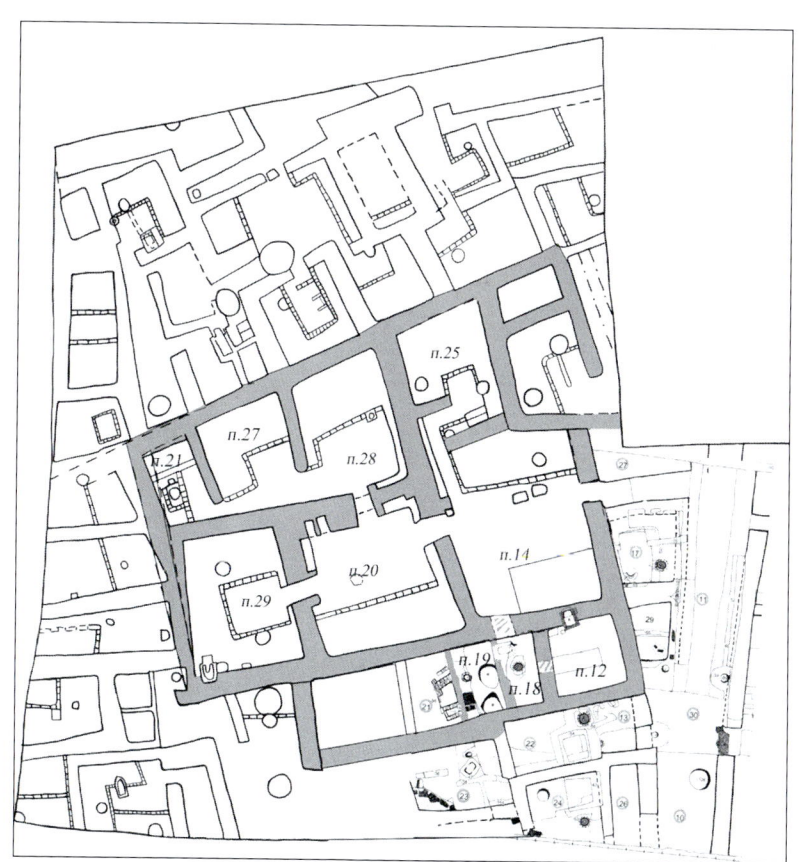

Plate VI-12
Plan of the "house of the well-to-do local" of the 12th–13th cc. in a block of urban housing

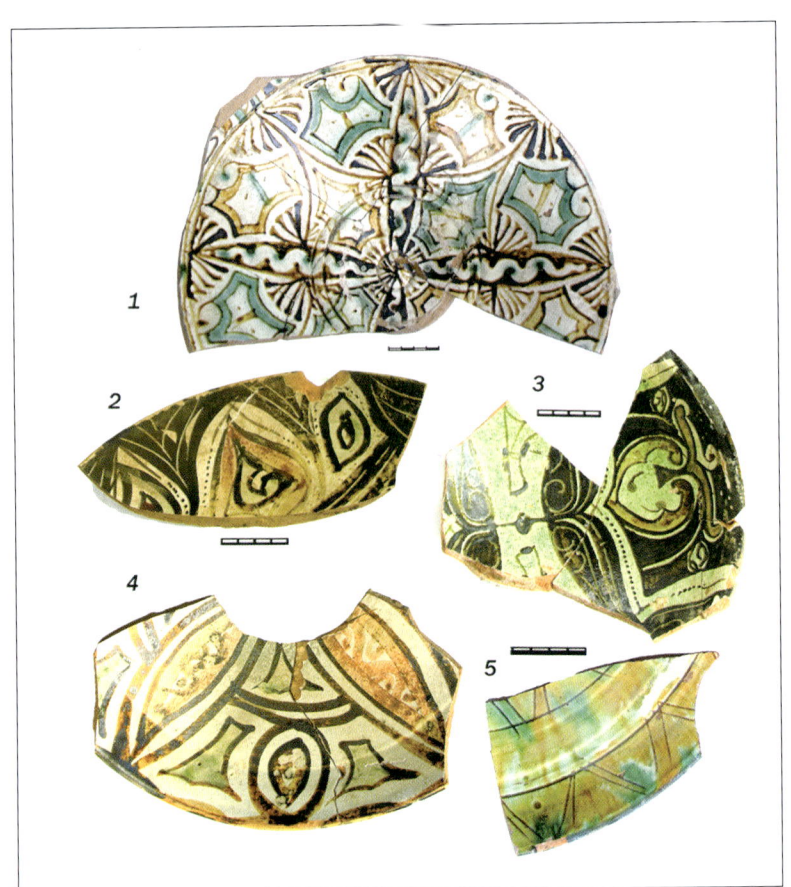

Plate VI-13
Representative range of colors of glazed ceramic of the 13th century

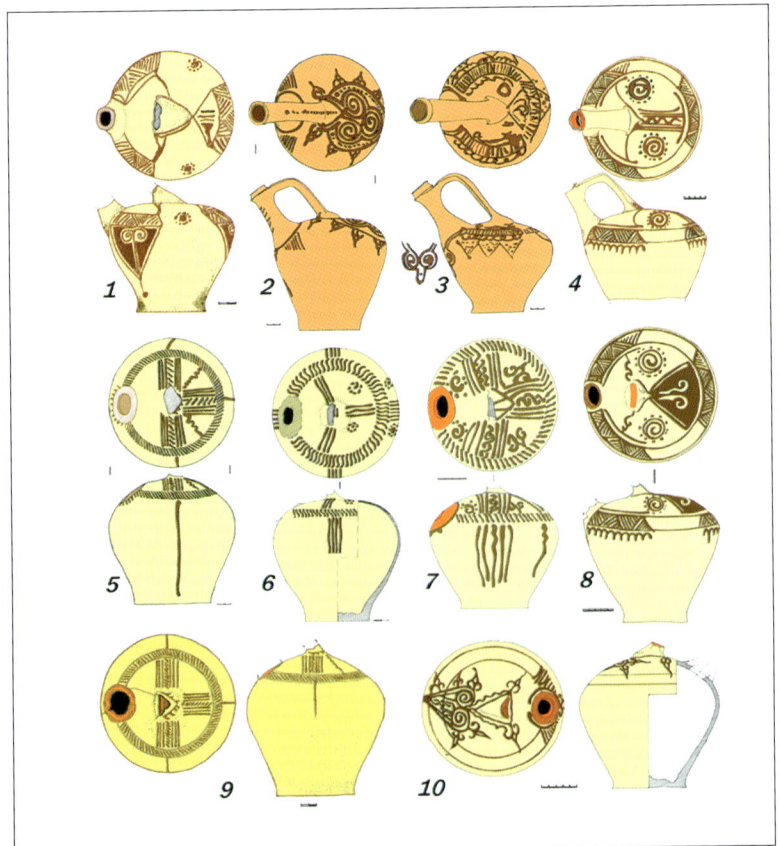

Plate VI-14
Engobe painting on jugs of the 12th – 13th cc

Plate VI-15
Ceramic altar in house of 11th century

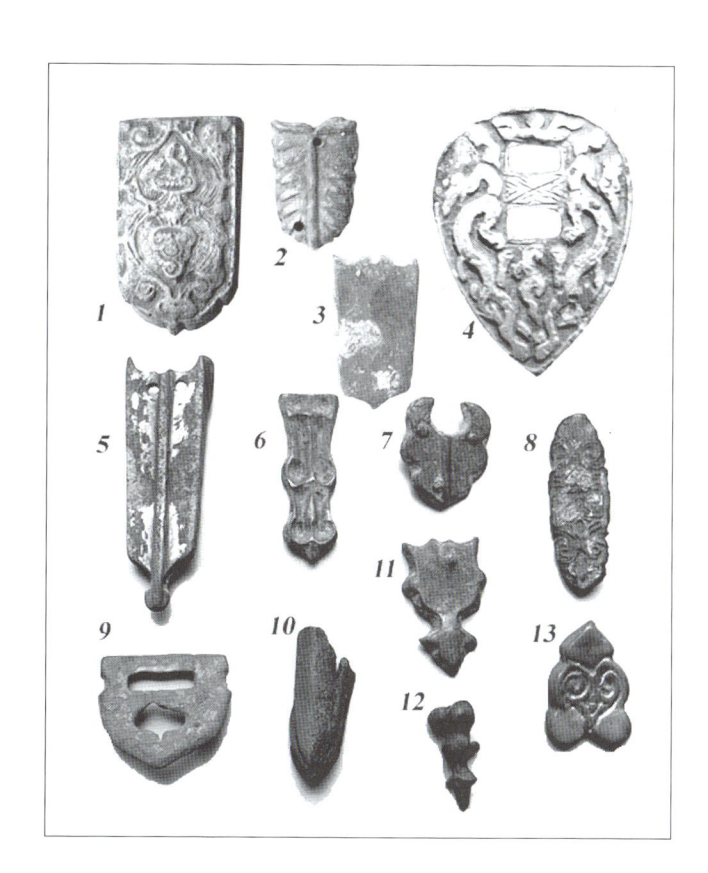

Plate VI-16
Belt buckles of the 12th – 13th cc. from upper layers of Karatobe, bronze

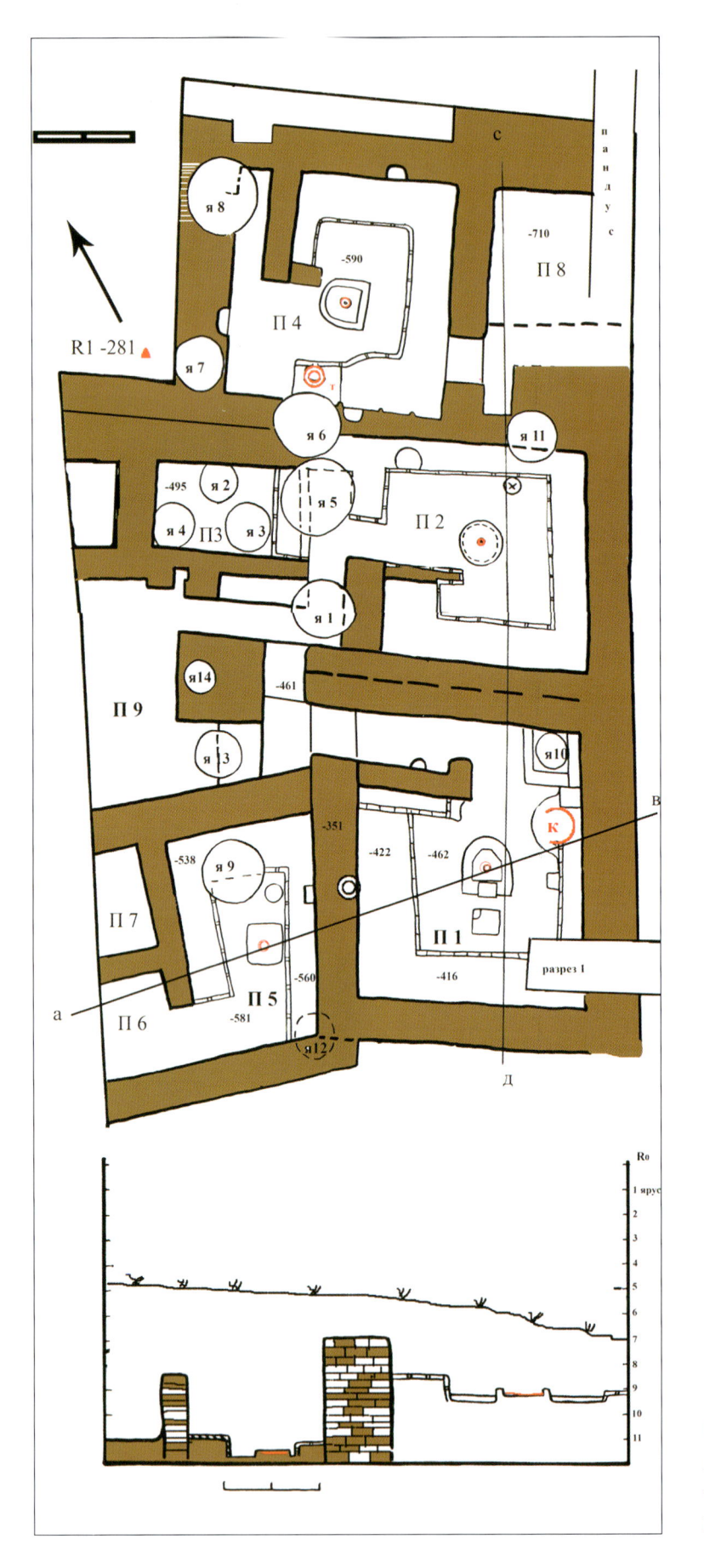

Plate VI-17
A site with rooms for public worship at the occupation layer of the 8th– 9th cc.

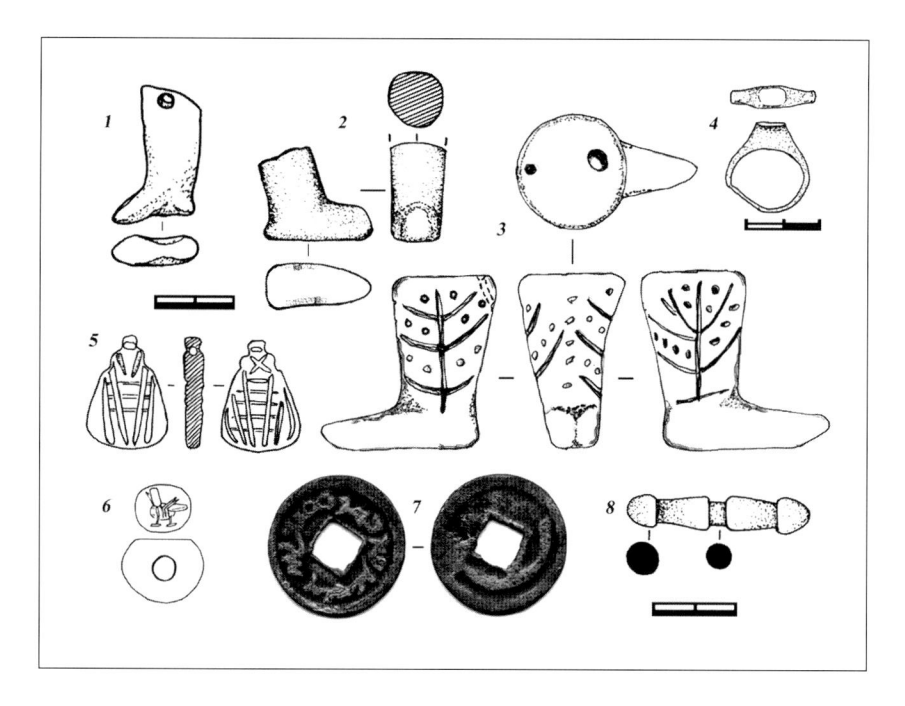

Plate VI-18

Some artifacts from Karatobe occupation layers of the 8th–12th cc.: 1-3 ceramic; 4,7,8 – bronze; 5- turquoise; 6- chalcedony

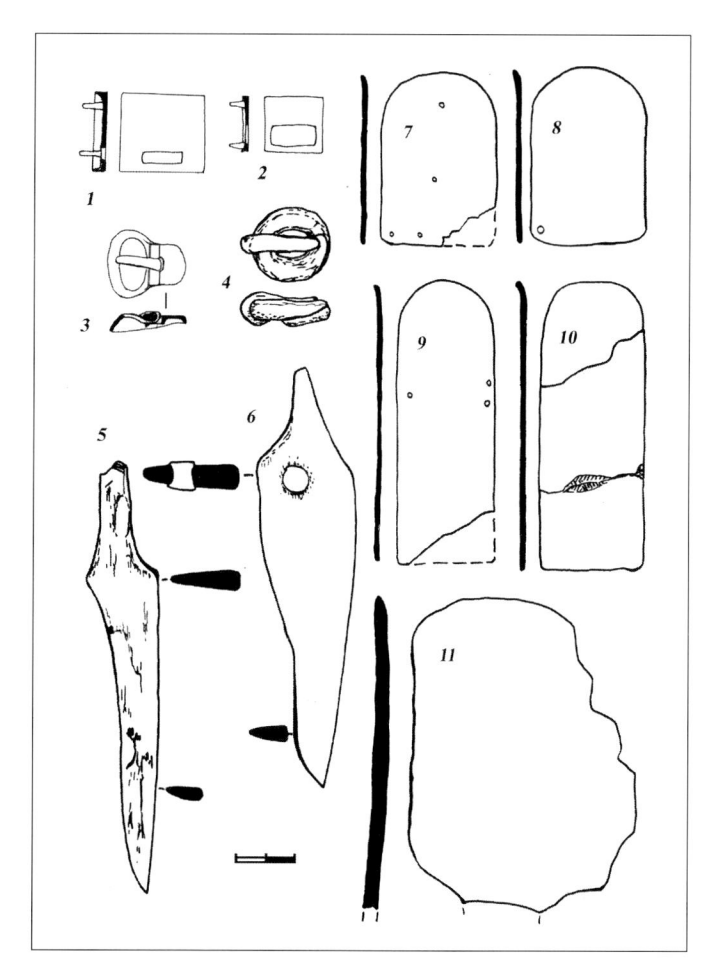

Plate VI-19

Finds from the floor of the construction horizon of the 8th–9th cc.: 1-3 – bronze; 4-11 – iron

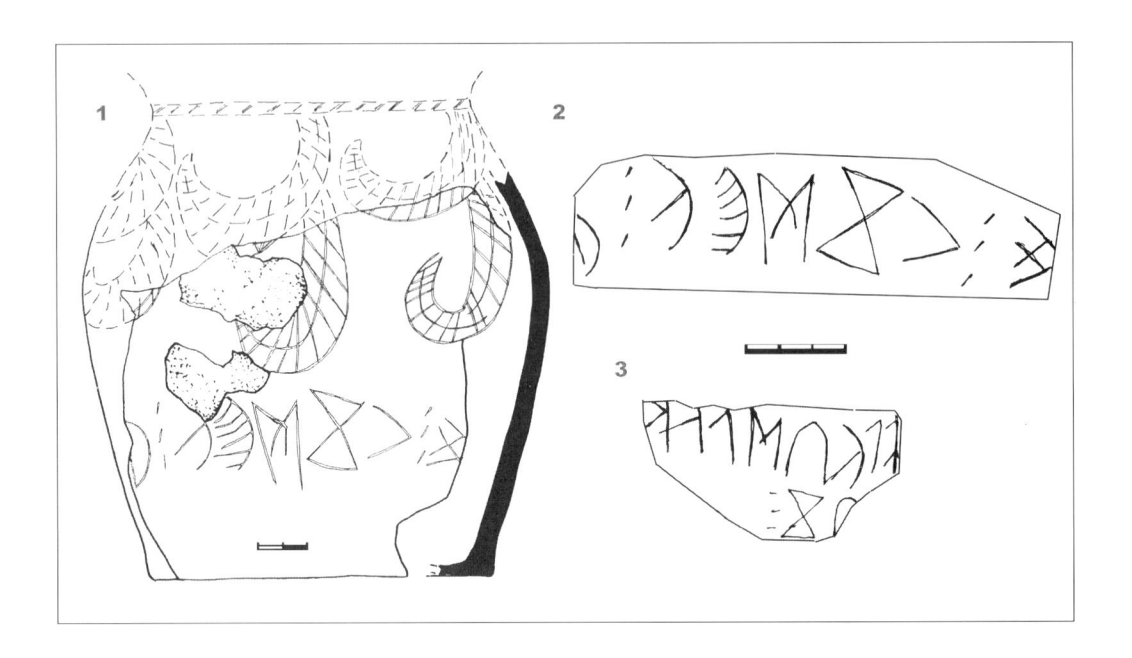

Plate VI-20
Reconstruction of black clay pot with a fragment of runic inscription of the 9th century

Plate VI-21
Plaster pattern remaining on wall of room 4 (CH3)

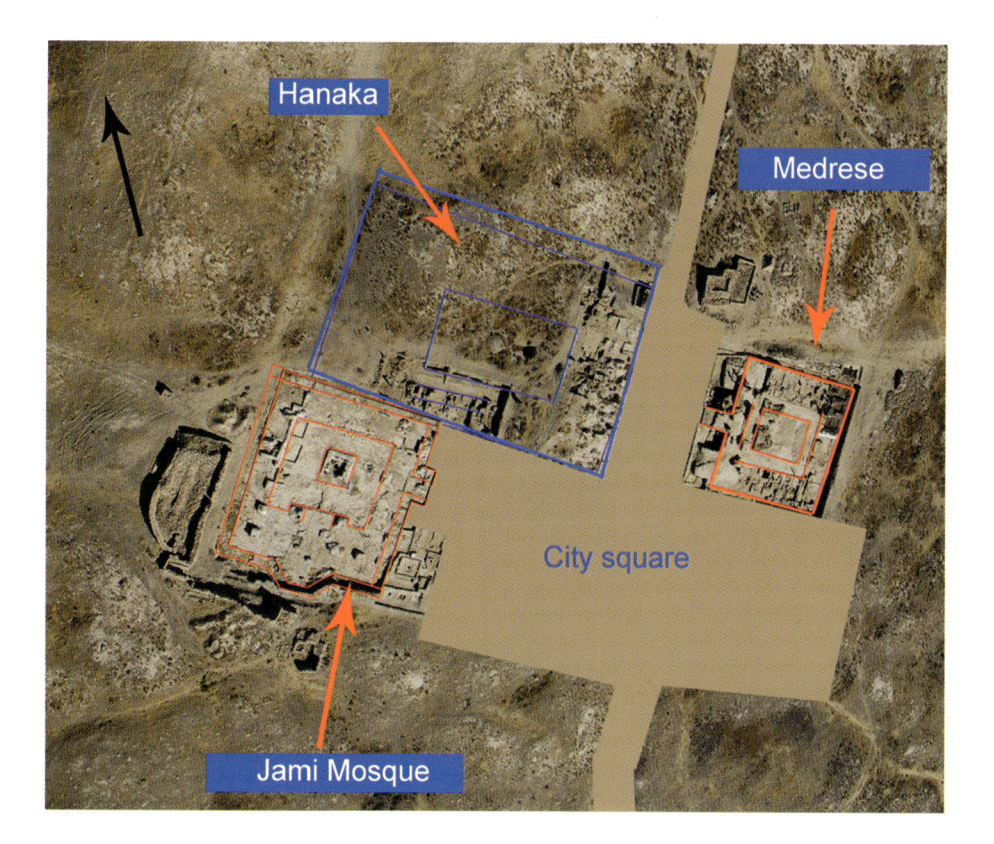

Plate VI-22
Principal sites excavated in the central square of Sauran

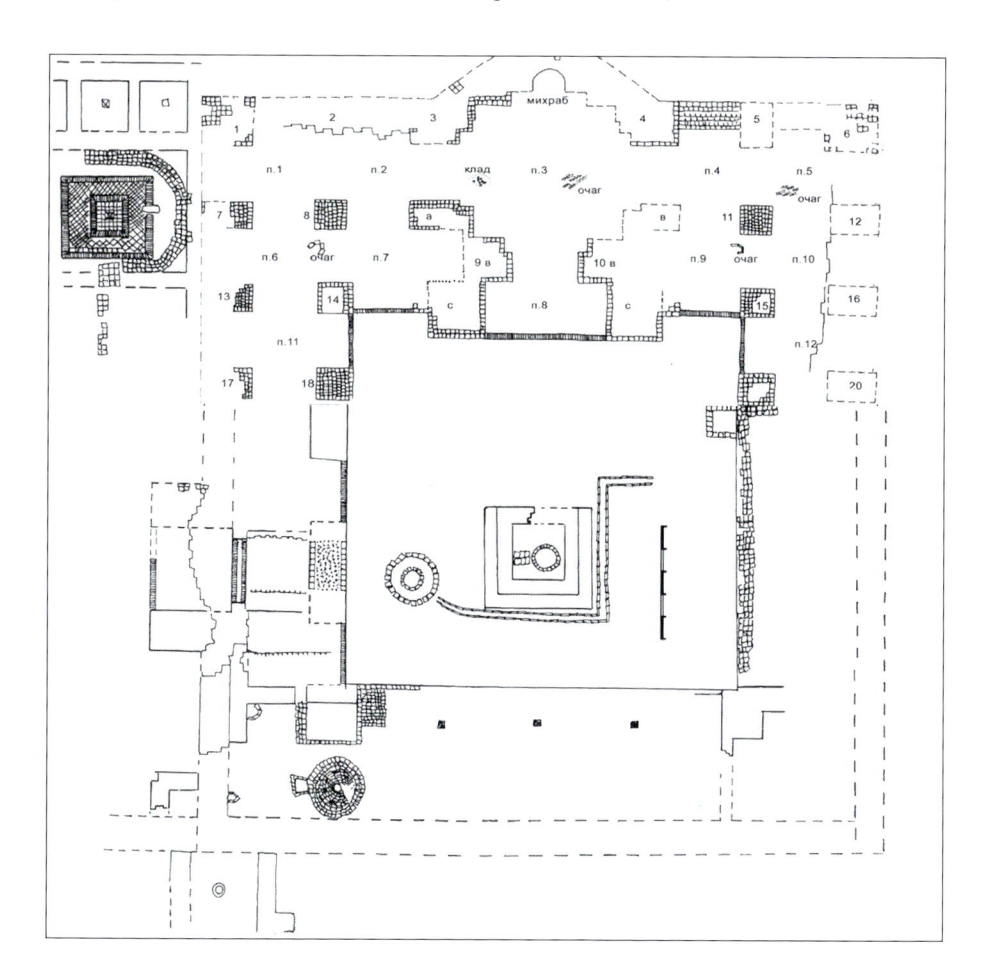

Plate VI- 23
Plan of Jami Mosque of Sauran

— 37 —

Plate VI-24
Alternate reconstruction of Sauran Mosque

Plate VI-25
Front staircase and ruins of the front portal of Sauran Medrese

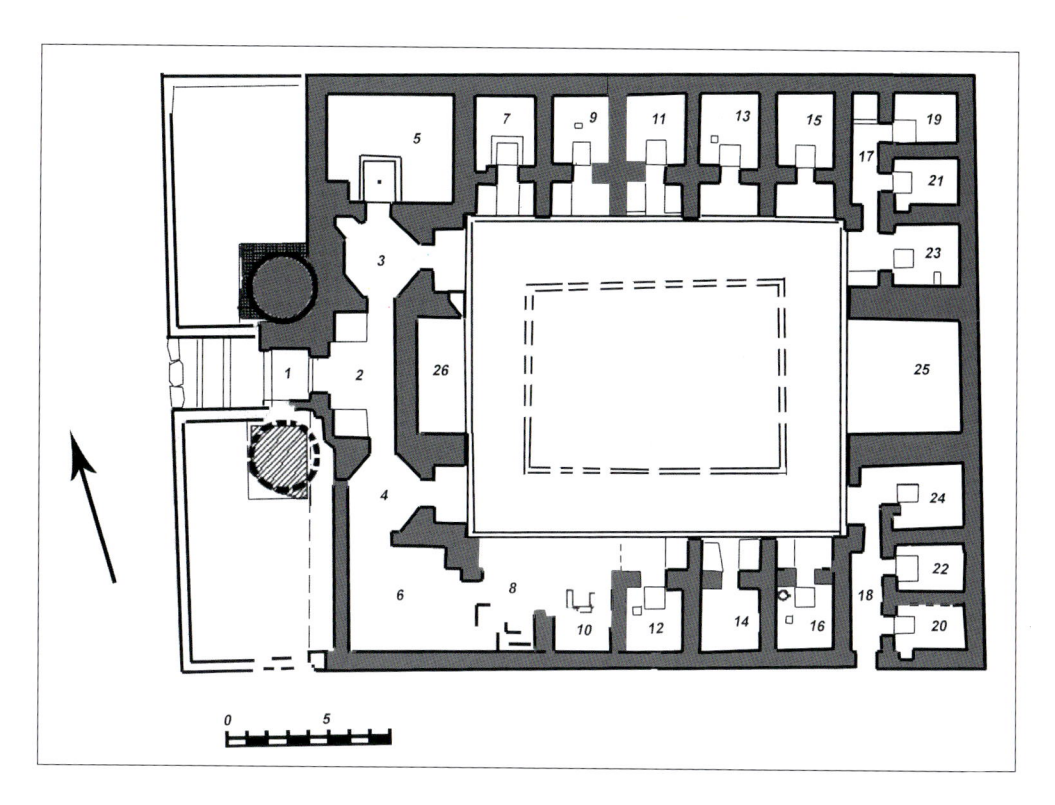

Plate VI-26
Plan of Sauran Medrese (according to Baipakov, Akymbek, 2008)

Plate VI-27
Fragments of glazed "*hanaka*" portal tiles

Plate VII-1
MS. Ayasofya 3034, ff.1b, 2a

Plate VII-2
MS. Ayasofya 3034, ff. 89 b, 90 a (correctly, ff. 90b, 91 a)

FEWUC Chairman's Salutation of the First Issue of the *International Journal of Eurasian Studies* by CFES CASS

Babis Ziogas

Since the first issue of the journal *Eurasian Studies* was published in the Chinese language in 1999 by the Center for Eurasian Studies (CFES) of the Institute of History of the Chinese Academy of Social Sciences (CASS), it has become an ideas exchange platform for new discoveries and breakthrough ideas of Chinese and international historians. For many years, highly original research work totally unknown to the international history community could not become available widely to non-Chinese speaking scholars and the general public. On the other hand researchers from China and other Eurasian countries did not have access to the international research in the Eurasian studies field.

Eurasia has been the location of the birth, formation, domination, contestation, and extinction of major civilizations, and the exchange of goods, ideas, and religions between them. It is the most fertile cultural soil on our planet. There is no major civilization that did not leave its mark here and did not interact with others, in either harmony or violence.

The trade, migration, and interaction between nations on the Eurasian steppes preludes today's globalization. Eurasian studies, as an indispensable component of world history studies, have consistently attracted increasing interest among historians all over the world over the centuries. Each nation at different historic moments sees the 'Other' through the prism of its dominant ideology. It is only science that makes possible the dialogue of international researchers. CFES CASS has developed a leading team of researchers of the highest qualification and productivity, and their scientific work output continues the tradition of Confucius, Zhang Qian, and Sima Qian.

The Foundation for East-West Understanding and Cooperation (FEWUC) aims at assisting the scientific material understanding of the civilizations of East and West through such studies of the region's history, culture and economy. FEWUC's ambition is to contribute to the development of the social sciences of history and economics, sponsoring and managing original research projects, fostering and spreading original ideas, and creating platforms for dialogue.

The Foundation, as exclusive sponsor, supports the publication of the *International Journal of Eurasian Studies* (works of internationally recognized history researchers), as well as the sister publications of *Eurasian Studies* (works by Chinese researchers) and *Monograph Series on Eurasian Cultural and Historical Studies* (major works previously unpublished in English) so as to augment and encourage researchers and readers from different language backgrounds in a global dialogue.

The successful publication of *International Journal of Eurasian Studies* would have been impossible without the diligent work of its two editors Prof. Yu Taishan and Prof. Li Jinxiu from CFES CASS. It was their inspiration that brought together so many distinguished researchers covering so many interesting topics in the most representative and harmonious caveat of methodologies and new ideas. We would also like to extend our gratitude to Dr. Bruce Doar and all the authors and translators.

Scientific dialogue is the only means to develop harmonious international cooperation among the diverse cultures of the Eurasian continent that will not only advance the subject of Eurasian Studies but will also impact on the resolution of political, societal and religious conflicts.

前　言

編　者

　　內陸歐亞學從誕生之日起便是一門國際化的學問，不僅有多國學者參與研究，作爲內陸歐亞歷史文化載體的文獻也涉及多種語言，許多國家在歷史上和現實中與內陸歐亞更有著政治的、經濟的、文化的深刻淵源。因此，加強各國學者之間的溝通與互動尤爲重要。

　　有鑒於此，本刊於 20 世紀末創辦之時，就有意將它辦成一個國際論壇，學刊章程中曾明確規定：來稿語言爲英、日、德、法、俄者，"可以原文發表"。由於一些具體原因，在一段時間內，這一規定有名無實。

　　隨著幾次有關內陸歐亞的國際學術討論會的召開，出現了外國學者在中國刊物發表論文的需求。在第 6 期以降各期《歐亞學刊》中，非漢語論文的篇幅明顯增多正是這種趨勢的反映。

　　爲了回應全球化的形勢下，內陸歐亞學發展對學刊提出的新要求，真正體現創刊的初衷，在得到東西理解合作基金會的支持後，我們終於下決心改版。新版《歐亞學刊》（國際版）中，英語論文將佔 50% 以上，其餘爲漢、日、德、法、俄語論文。

　　在《歐亞學刊》改版的的同時，我們開始編輯《絲瓷之路：古代中外關係史研究》，其中特闢 "內陸歐亞" 专欄。也就是說，漢語內陸歐亞學論文的篇幅將不會減少。

　　東西理解合作基金會的宗旨是在理解的基礎上合作，通過合作加深理解。讓我們和國際內陸歐亞學界的同行一起利用這個平臺來實踐這個宗旨吧！

2010 年 2 月

CONTENTS

Babis Ziogas (Greece)

FEWUC Chairman's Salutation of the First Issue of the *International Journal of Eurasian Studies* by CFES CASS ·· i

编者 (**Editors**, China)

前言 (Foreword) ·· iii

Alexey A. Kovalev (Russia)

The Great Migration of the Chemurchek People from France to the Altai in the Early 3rd Millennium BCE ·· 001

Katheryn M. Linduff and Sandra Olsen (USA)

Between Eurasia and China: Saddles Excavated in Xinjiang at Zaghunluq and Subeshi ··············· 059

E. V. Perevodchikova (Russia)

On the Contacts between the Scythian Animal Style of the Eurasian Steppe and Chinese Art ··········· 076

Bartłomiej Szymon Szmoniewski (Poland)

Between West and East: Anthropomorphic and Zoomorphic Representations in the Forest-Steppe Belt and Steppe Zone of Eastern Europe ·· 088

Matteo Compareti (Italy)

Recent Investigations on Sasanian Painting ·· 108

Sergey S. Minyaev (Russia)

Xiongnu Royal Tomb Complex in the Tsaraam Valley 153

HAYASHI Toshio (Japan)

On the Origin of Turkic Stone Statues 181

Erbulat A. Smagulov (Kazakhstan)

Summary of Archeological Studies of the Site of Medieval Sauran in 2004-2009 199

Leslie Wallace (USA)

The Ends of the Earth: The Xiongnu Empire and Eastern Han Representations of
　the Afterlife from Shaanxi and Shanxi 232

余太山 **(YU Taishan**, China)

吐火羅問題 (The Tocharian Question) 259

楊軍 **(YANG Jun**, China)

烏桓山與鮮卑山新考 (New Research on the Wuhuan and Xianbei Mountains) 286

Stephanos Kordoses (Greece)

Byzantine-Turkic Relations and the Wider Eurasian Alliances during the Perso-Byzantine Wars 296

張緒山 **(ZHANG Xushan**, China)

漢籍所見拜占庭帝國地理、歷史與傳說 (Knowledge of the Geography, History and Legends
　of the Byzantine Empire Presented in Chinese Sources) 313

Naran Bilik (China)

The "Han" in the Three Mirrors of History, Foreigners and Minorities: An Indexical-
　Embodiment Interpretation 335

Shamsiddin S. Kamoliddin (Uzbekistan)

On the Origins of the Place-name Buxārā 348

李錦繡 **(LI Jinxiu**, China)

《西域圖記》考 (A Study on *Xiyu Tuji* [*Illustrated Record of the Western Regions*]) 359

A. Melek Özyetgin (Turkey)

Criminal Law Practices among Turfan Uigurs according to Civil Documents ································ 375

青格力 (Qinggeli, China)

蒙元時期蒙古文書中的"威懾語"("*Sürdegülülge üge*" ["threatening words"] in Ancient Documents of the Mongol Empire and the Yuan Dynasty) ································ 398

赤坂恒明 (AKASAKA Tsuneaki, Japan)

『集史』第一巻「モンゴル史」校訂におけるアラビア語版写本 Ayasofya 3034 の価値 (On the Significance of MS. Ayasofya 3034 for the Textual Criticism of "History of the Mongols" in *Jami' al-Tawarikh*) ································ 421

李花子 (LI Huazi, China)

朝鮮時代的長白山踏査記與《白山圖》(Changbai Mountain in the Light of Notes by Korean Explorers and *Painting of the White Mountain* of the Joseon [Chosŏn] Era) ········ 441

DING Yizhuang (China)

Official Genealogies and PRIVATE Genealogies of the Eight Banners in the Qing Dynasty ········ 457

The Great Migration of the Chemurchek People from France to the Altai in the Early 3rd Millennium BCE

Alexey A. Kovalev

Field research at Early Bronze Age sites in Dzungaria and the Mongolian Altai started in the first half of the 1960s (fig.1). Chinese archaeologist Li Zheng was the first to reflect different types of burial constructions in the Ertix basin and to connect neighboring stone statues with them. His field report was first published in 1962.[1] After that, ten rectangular enclosures with stone receptacles and statues were excavated by Yi Manbai in the Ke'ermuqi 克爾木齊 (correctly Qiemuerqieke 切木爾切克, Chemurchek) River basin in Altay county in 1963.[2] (fig.2) In the 1990s Wang Bo and Wang Linshan [3] investigated barrows of this type and mentioned stone statues as well. In most cases Chinese Altai "Ke'ermuqi" burial constructions [4] were rectangular stone enclosures orientated, as a rule, along their longer sides in a west-east direction, and in rare cases-north-south. At the middle of their eastern (or southern) side a stone statue or stone pillar is usually erected. Inside each stone enclosure, along its long side, there is a line of stone receptacles made of large upright stone slabs, each receptacle containing several burials (fig.11: 1).

As a result of the exploration, Wang Bo undertook an attempt to classify and to date the burial constructions as well as different kinds of stone sculptures.[5] Wang Bo believed the majority of sculptures to be synchronous with burials in stone receptacles and dated them back to the Bronze Age. However many scholars supposed that all statues in the southwest foothills of the Altay belong to the Turkic period,[6] at best partly to the Early Iron Age.[7] In Russian literary sources "sculptures from Kermutsi", known due to a publication in 1962, were dated to the Turkic period.[8] Yu.S.Khudiakov attributed these statues to the same period and insisted on this opinion until most recently.[9]

Mu Shunying and Wang Mingzhe proposed to date the material of the most ancient burials at the Ke'ermuqi burial site to 1200-700 BCE on the basis of their opinion that this material possesses similar features to that of "Karasuk" culture.[10] Wang Bo was the first to distinguish a new and unique "Qiemuerqieke" culture.[11] By this denomination he included all monuments and casual finds of the Bronze Age in North Dzungaria, irrespective of the obvious multinational origins of this material.

Chen Ge and Wang Bo, in the articles cited, compared "Chemurchek" vessels in toto to pottery of the "Afanasievo" and "Karasuk" cultures, the data on which they took from the very old monograph by S. V. Kiselev. In their monograph of 1996 Wang Bo and Wang Linshan compared a censer from the M24 enclosure and round-bottomed vessels from the M16 enclosure (the "Ke'ermuqi cemetery") (fig.2: 8) with censers and vessels of Afanasievo culture.[12] Yu.A.Zadneprovsky, V.I.A.Semenov, and V.I.Molodin in collaboration with S.V.Alkin also included the most ancient Chemurchek burials within the range of Afanasievo monuments,[13] which means that they dated these burials to the second half of the 4th millennium BCE as the latest possible period.

Of course, the materials from "Ke'ermuqi" differ greatly from those of Afanasievo culture, and cannot be attributed to it. Earthenware vessels, which look like they belong to Afanasievo culture and which have been found in "Ke'ermuqi" complexes, can only point to some cultural connections with the Afanasievo tribes which lived to the north. For western scholars, I demonstrated this in my article published in 2000,[14] but unfortunately they still consider Ke'ermuqi to be a Afanasievo burial site, despite the fact that already in 1998 A.V.Varenov had showed that such an approach was mistaken.[15] A.V.Varenov analyzed in detail the different points of view of Chinese and Russian scholars on the question of the dating and cultural attribution of the Chemurchek monuments, and laid the ground for distinguishing a unique culture. However, he came to the wrong conclusion in dating the "great stone receptacles from Ke'ermuqi" to the 13th-8th or even to the 10th-8th centuries BCE, despite the fact that he ascribed the censer from enclosure M24 to Afanasievo culture.

In 1998, during the exploration of the Chemurchek River basin, I found remains of stone burial constructions, which were formerly excavated by Yi Manbai, and established the unity of stone enclosure 2 excavated by Yi Manbai with a stone statue at Kayinarl 喀依納爾 2:2 (fig.30: 6), which was published by Wang Linshan and Wang Bo in 1996.[16] This fact confirmed my conclusion about the synchronism of most of the stone sculptures from the Ertix region with the main burials in the stone receptacles at the Chemurchek ("Ke'ermuqi") burial site, dating them to the period from the second half of the 3rd millennium to the first half of the 2nd millennium BCE, in accordance with the analogies in burial goods.[17] In my article published in Germany in 2000,[18] I proposed that a separate culture of the Early Bronze Age which had its origin in Western Europe existed in Dzungaria. I also attributed Eastern Kazakhstan and Altay petroglyphs and other images of bulls with "two legs" and S-shaped horns and the stone vessel from Uglovo, Altay region (Russia), as belonging to Chemurchek culture,[19] as well as the statue from Inya village (Russian Republic of Altay).[20] That provided an opportunity to define the area of the spread of the Chemurchek population.

In 2002 Lin Meicun also proclaimed the earliest burials from "Ke'ermuqi" to be synchronous with Afanasievo culture, basing himself on the analogies in Russian materials (according to the very poor illustrations published in western countries).[21] However, Shui Tao, on the basis of S.V.Kiselev's very poor and old pictures of Karasuk and Okunevo (named Karasuk) vessels, dated the "Ke'ermuqi" stone receptacles to the period of the second half of the 2nd millennium BCE.[22]

Recently we learned that new vessels typical of Afanasievo culture (a censer and one egg-shaped vessel) were found in a newly discovered Chinese Chemurchek stone receptacle.[23] The most recently published paper of Lin Yun [24] included a detailed review of the opinions of Chinese scholars concerning the dating of "Ke'ermuqi" monuments. Lin Yun also came to the well-founded conclusion that Chemurchek culture was contemporary with Afanasievo culture, but Lin Yun erroneously dated Afanasievo and Chemurchek cultures to 2200-1900 BCE on the basis of the obsolete dating of Afanasievo (C-14 dates without calibration, the ideas of Soviet specialists of the 1950s about the dating of Afanasievo typical vessels, etc.). Today we date Afanasievo culture to no later than from the middle of the 3rd millennium BCE, according in particular to calibrated dates of radiocarbon analysis.[25] Prof. Lin Yun is perfectly right that Chemurchek culture was the earliest culture of the Bronze Age in China, but he was unfortunately unaware that I came to this conclusion ten years ago, published papers devoted to this topic in Russia and Germany,[26] and made reports for the International Symposium on the Problems of North China Archaeology organized by the Institute of Archaeology, CASS, in September 2004 in Beijing (see: Kovalev A., "Qiemuerqieke Culture: The Most Ancient Culture of the Bronze Age in China, Its Origins in Western Europe and the Cultural Influence on the Neighboring Cultures of Kazakhstan, Russia and Mongolia").

No radiocarbon analysis of materials from the Chinese "Ke'ermuqi" stone receptacles has been carried out up to now. In October 2008 some bone material was gathered from two modern robber pits within the Chemurchek rectangular enclosures. These enclosures were elongated west-eastwards and stone statues were erected along their eastern sides, and the robbers made pits inside the stone receptacles. These monuments are situated on the southeastern outskirts of the Kayinarl settlement (Qiemuerqieke, Altay county).

Radiocarbon analysis of this material was carried out in the laboratory of Uppsala University. It yielded a date Ua-37018 (3305 ± 95 BP; with probability of 95.4% that is 1830-1400 CalBC) for mound 1 (47° 48.911′ North and 87° 51.477′ East) (secondary burial), and second date Ua-37019 (4020 ± 55 BP; with probability of 95.4% that is 2900-2300 CalBC) for mound 2 (47° 48.888′ North and 87° 51.539′ East) (main burial). Thus the data from radiocarbon analysis supports the opinion that we can date the appearance of the "Ke'ermuqi" type stone enclosures with stone receptacles or boxes in Dzungaria to not later than from the middle of the 3rd millennium BCE.

In 1998-2000 the International Central-Asian Archaeological Expedition was organized by A. Kovalev and St. Petersburg State University in cooperation with the Institute of Archaeology of the National Academy of Science of Kazakhstan and with Russian Altai State University. The expedition undertook excavations of 12 rectangular stone enclosures of the Early Bronze Age in the Alkabek River basin (Eastern Kazakh region) (burial places Akhtuma, Aina-Bulak I, II, Kopa, Bulgartaboty) near the Chinese border (3-5 kilometers west of Habahe 哈巴河 county military farm 兵團農場 in Xinjiang (N° 185) (fig.3). Barrows excavated in the Alkabek River basin consisted of rectangular enclosures made of stone slabs; an "entrance" marked with huge slabs is placed in the middle of the eastern side of the enclosure (fig.6). A dry stone corridor (passage) made of small flat slabs leads to the burial pit. The dry masonry walls of these corridors surround the burial pit. In all barrows, without exception, burial pits are situated 2-5 meters eastwards from the center to the "entrances". At the burial site called Kopa 1, a stone stele that had been worked to resemble a human figure was erected by the eastern side of the enclosure.

The excavated burials contained pottery (fig.3: 3) which has analogies with the burial goods of the Elunino culture of Altai dating back to 2300-1800 BCE.[27]

Radiocarbon dates obtained from the investigated mounds (13 dates were obtained) are characterized by great variability (including cases of difference within the data from one and the same burial). However, if the most divergent dates from either end of the range are excluded (SOAN 4855 (4850±50 BP), SOAN 4856 (4995±35 BP) from one end, and SOAN 4375 (2735 ±85 BP), SOAN 5344 (2800±75 BP) from the other, the remaining dates fit into the period from the middle of the 3rd millennium BCE to the middle of the 2nd millennium BCE. Most of these dates (6 of them) were obtained from bone material found in the burial pit of the mound 3 of the Aina-Bulak I burial site. A combined date (R_Combine) obtained for the bones belongs to the period between the 19th and 18th centuries BCE (Tab. 1). It is most likely that this tomb was

Table 1. R_Combine ^{14}C date of the barrow Aina-Bulak 1-3.

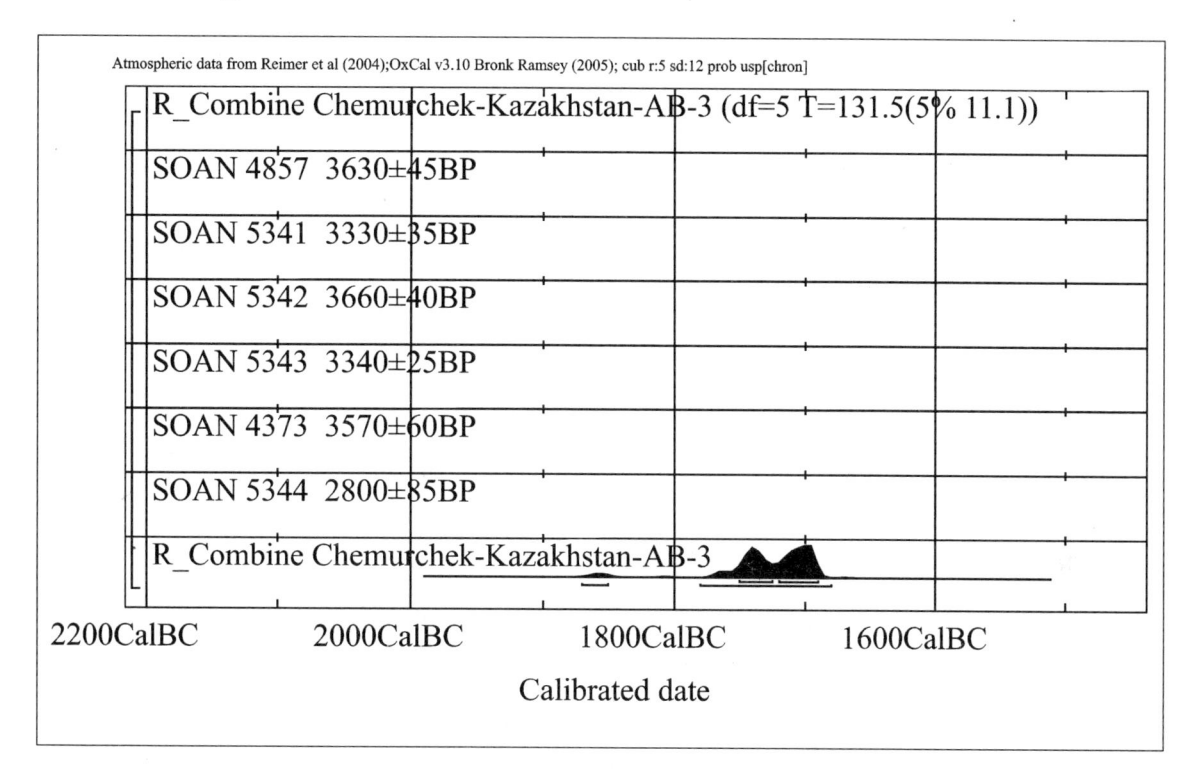

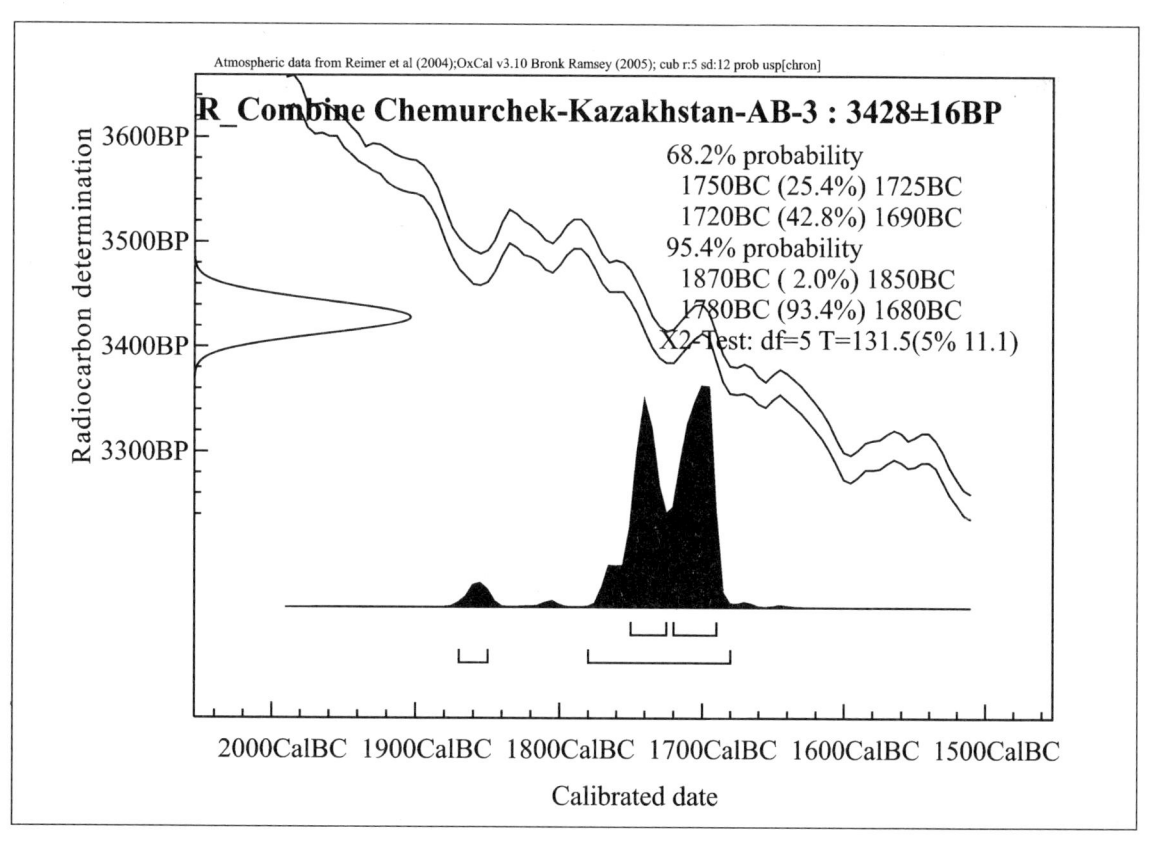

R_Combine Chemurchek-Kazakhstan-AB-3 (df=5 T=131.5(5% 11.1))

SOAN 4857	3630±45BP
SOAN 5341	3330±35BP
SOAN 5342	3660±40BP
SOAN 5343	3340±25BP
SOAN 4373	3570±60BP
SOAN 5344	2800±85BP

R_Combine Chemurchek-Kazakhstan-AB-3 : 3428±16BP

68.2% probability
1750BC (25.4%) 1725BC
1720BC (42.8%) 1690BC
95.4% probability
1870BC (2.0%) 1850BC
1780BC (93.4%) 1680BC
X2 Test: df=5 T=131.5(5% 11.1)

not the earliest of all the excavated burials, because the date we have for the neighboring similar mound 1 of the Aina-Bulag I burial locus is 3920±40 (SOAN 4156), and fits in the period from 2570 to 2280 CalBC with a probability of 94.5% (all calibrated dates adduced in this paper were obtained using a program Ox Cal v. 3.0 and are given with a probability of 94.5 %). (This radiocarbon analysis was conducted in the laboratory of the Institute of Geology of the Siberian Branch of the Russian Academy of Sciences).

So we can conclude that the above mentioned monuments appeared on the north-western border of Xinjiang in the second half of the 3rd millennium BCE.

In 2002 D. Erdenebaatar first discovered the Chemurchek culture burial site on Mongolian territory in Yagshiin Khodoo (Bulgan, Hovd Aimag). After this our International Central-Asiatic Archaeological Expedition (on this occasion in collaboration with the Institute of History of the Mongolian Academy of Sciences and Ulaanbaatar University) excavated six barrows of Chemurchek culture near the center of Bulgan Sum of Khovd Aimag (burial sites Yagshiin Khodoo, Kheviin Am, Buural Kharyn Ar) (fig.4), as well as four rectangular burial enclosures in Ulanhus Sum of Bayan-Ulgii Aimag (Kulala-Ula (Khul-Uul), barrow 1, Kurgak-Govi (Khuurai Gov'), barrow 2, Kumdi-Govi (Khundii Gov'), Kara-Tumsik (Khar Khoshuu) (fig.5).[28]

Barrows excavated by our expedition in Bayan-Ulgii looked like rectangular stone enclosures, orientated along their longer sides in a west-east direction (Kulala-Ula-north-south), which included burial pits (fig.7). Stone pillars (stelae) were erected by the eastern side of two of four abovementioned mounds: the stele near the barrow of Kulala-Ula was found by the southern side of the mound and had been worked to resemble a human forso (fig.4: 3). Near the barrow of Kara-Tumsik one of these stelae colored with red ochre (ruddle) was found inserted upright into the ground inside the enclosure by the eastern side of the tomb (fig.32: 1).

Some bone tools which were found in these barrows (fig.4: 5) are similar to tools of Elunino culture (2300-1800 BCE),[29] while pottery (fig.4: 13) and stone balls (fig.4: 10,11) look like findings which belong to Okunevo culture (2200-1700 BCE).[30]

The barrow Kurgak-Govi 2 had been coupled with the barrow Kurgak-Govi 1 of Afanasievo culture at a separate burial place. Charcoal from the earliest (ritual) pits of the previously mentioned Chemurchek barrow Kurgak-Govi 2 were dated from the same period (ca. 2800-2600 BCE) with charcoals used as filling of the burial pit of barrow 1 belonging to Afanasievo culture; ^{14}C dates of charcoal from earliest pits of the nearest Chemurchek barrows Kulala Ula 1, Kumdi-Govi, and Kara-Tumsik also belonged to the same period (Table 2).[31]

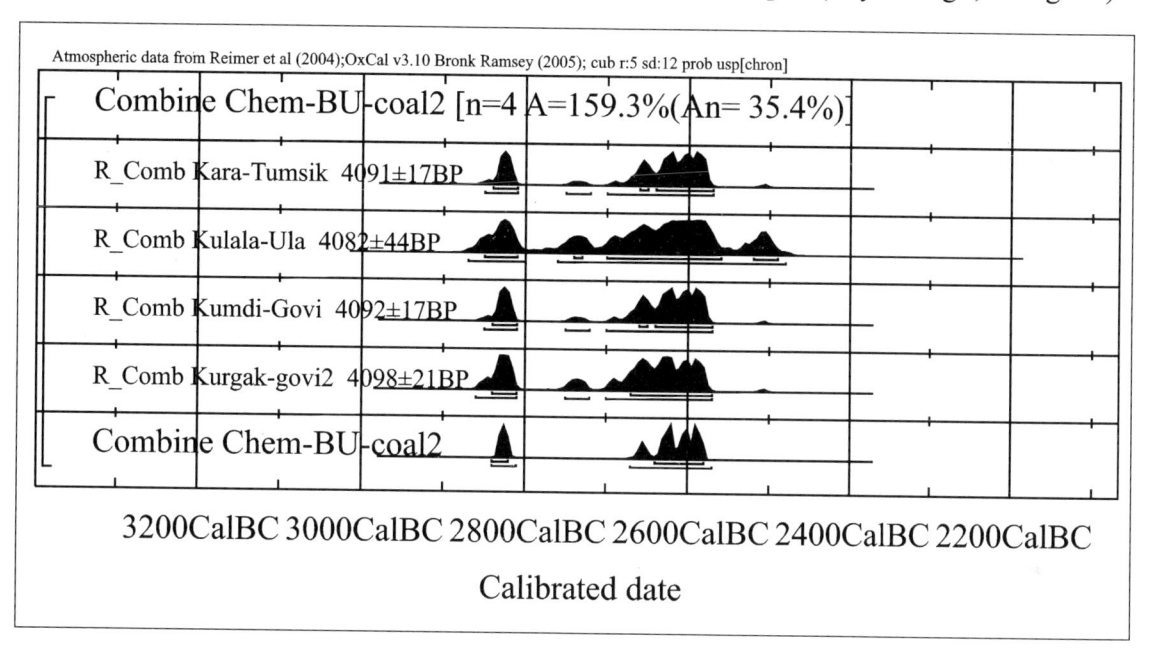

Table 2. R_Combine ^{14}C dates from Chemurchek earliest pits (Bayan-Ulgii, Mongolia).

```
Atmospheric data from Reimer et al (2004);OxCal v3.10 Bronk Ramsey (2005); cub r:5 sd:12 prob usp[chron]
```

Combine Chem-BU-coal2 [n=4 A=159.3%(An= 35.4%)]

R_Comb Kara-Tumsik 4091±17BP

R_Comb Kulala-Ula 4082±44BP

R_Comb Kumdi-Govi 4092±17BP

R_Comb Kurgak-govi2 4098±21BP

Combine Chem-BU-coal2

3200CalBC 3000CalBC 2800CalBC 2600CalBC 2400CalBC 2200CalBC

Calibrated date

Secondary Chemurchek burials from these barrows date back to 2500-2200 calBC judging from the four ^{14}C dates. It may indicate that in the earliest period of existence of Chemurchek culture, its population in the Altai region could coexist with the population of Afanasievo culture. A pillar erected by the eastern side of the aforementioned Afanasievo culture Barrow 1, as well as findings of bone arrowheads similar to arrowheads from the Kulala-Ula 1 and Kara-Tumsik barrows (fig.4: 7, 9), also confirm this supposition.

The burial places of Bulgan look like huge stone receptacles, oriented east-west and constructed of massive stone slabs which are situated on the ancient surface or inserted into the soil, and used as a crypt for many burials (up to 10 persons) (fig.5). Stone containers were reinforced from the outside (not covered!) by surrounding stone or soil cairns which overlapped one another and were supplied with "façades" of light boulders (figs. 8-10).

We discovered that the Yagshiin Khodoo 1, 3, Kheviin Am 1, and Buural Kharyn Ar mounds consisted of three such cairns ("façades"), all other mounds of two. Chemurchek barrows in the Bujant River valley are of the same construction, namely the mound described by V.V.Volkov near "the third brigade of Tolbo Sum" and barrows Ulaan Khudag I-12 and Ulaan Khudag II-3, investigated by the Bujant Russian-Mongol Archaeological Expedition. The first of the latter included three cairns/façades and the second two cairns/façades.[32]

Near the eastern side of the barrow Yagshiin Khodoo 3 was erected a typical Chemurchek statue [33] of a man wearing a helmet, with his face turned to the south, with an uncovered chest, and holding a "crook" and a bow in his hands (fig.30: 4). On the eastern side of the barrow Kheviin-Am 1 was discovered a ritual portal-shaped "entrance" that had been made of thin vertical stone slabs and pavements made of boulders (fig.10). The walls of the Bulgan stone receptacles were decorated in ancient times using a red paint (fig.33: 1-3). Similar burial stone boxes, with stone statues erected near them, were discovered in the basin of the Ertix 額爾齊斯河 River. I observed such sites in the Chemurchek River basin in Altai county,[34] and a barrow of similar construction near Samute 薩木特 in Tangbaleyuzi village, Qinghe county 青河縣唐巴勒玉孜 associated with a stone statue of the Chemurchek type.[35] Moreover, a similar stone box with two surrounding stone cairns was discovered by S.Grushin and excavated by S.Grushin and A.Kovalev in 2006 in the Tretiakovo district of Altai Region (Russia), near the Kazakhstan border.

Stone boxes from Bulgan and Hovd sum yielded lead and copper ornaments (fig.5: 4-7) and a pottery vessel (fig.5: 11) which are similar to artifacts belonging to Elunino culture (2300-1800 BCE).[36]

In general we managed to obtain 18 radiocarbon dates for stone boxes of the "Bulgan" type.[37] Despite the fact that a mixed bone material was often taken for the radiocarbon analysis, and this bone material corresponded with the whole period of a sepulcher using dates from different stone boxes appeared rather close. Most dates belonged to the last quarter of the 3rd millennium BCE. The earliest combined (R_Combine) data obtained for sepulchers of the "Bulgan" type is the date from Yagshiin Khodoo-3 mound (2470-2150 CalBC, Table 3), a stone statue was found very near this mound.

Thus burial monuments showing a number of specific features which distinguish them from all the other known monuments of the Early Bronze Age of Eastern Europe and Asia, suddenly appeared in the foothills of Mongol Altai from Zaisan Lake to the Bulgan River not later than in the middle of the 3rd millennium BCE.[38] All specific features are not represented in the complex in every mound, but they are spread over separate regions, resulting in the origin of peculiar types of burial constructions. The independent, but simultaneous, appearance of several original innovations of burial construction in one and the same region appears quite impossible. We can suppose that firstly there was one source of all these innovations, but later tribes of a single culture spread over the Altai and preserved separate and different combinations of features of the burial rite traditions. But the question remains: Where are all the specific features of Chemurchek mounds represented as a whole complex? It emerges that this situation is found in western and southern France. Besides the analogies in the construction of burial mounds, we find here analogies in the form and

Table 3. R_Combine ¹⁴C date of Yagshiin Khodoo burial mound.

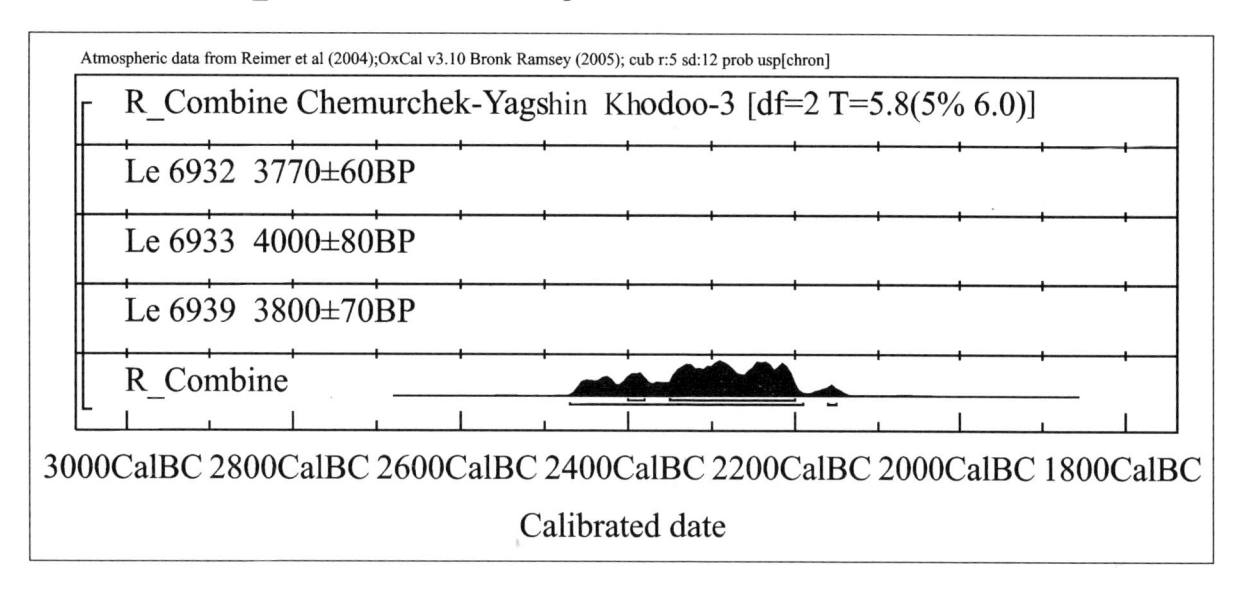

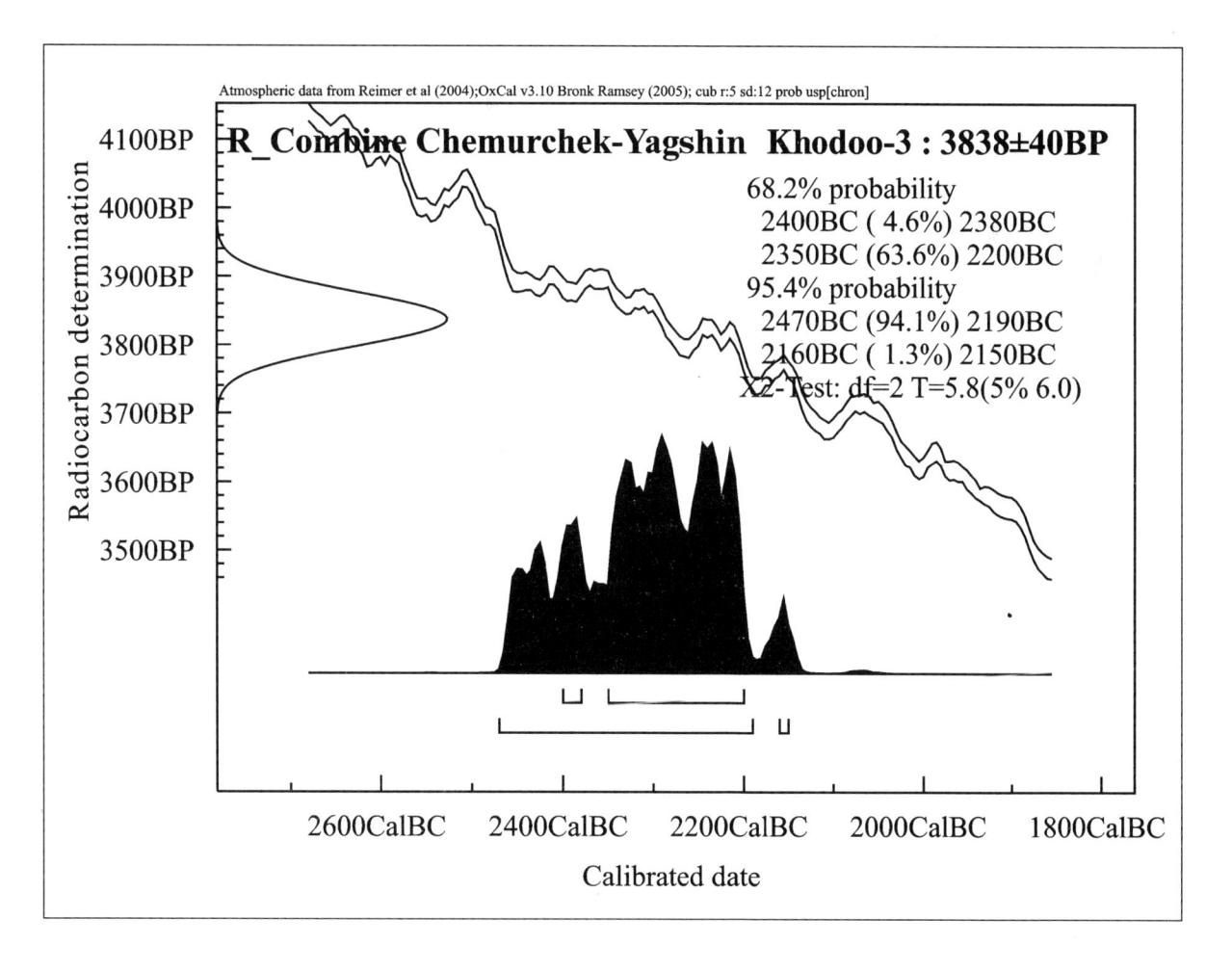

Atmospheric data from Reimer et al (2004);OxCal v3.10 Bronk Ramsey (2005); cub r:5 sd:12 prob usp[chron]

R_Combine Chemurchek-Yagshin Khodoo-3 [df=2 T=5.8(5% 6.0)]

Le 6932 3770±60BP

Le 6933 4000±80BP

Le 6939 3800±70BP

R_Combine

3000CalBC 2800CalBC 2600CalBC 2400CalBC 2200CalBC 2000CalBC 1800CalBC

Calibrated date

Atmospheric data from Reimer et al (2004);OxCal v3.10 Bronk Ramsey (2005); cub r:5 sd:12 prob usp[chron]

R_Combine Chemurchek-Yagshin Khodoo-3 : 3838±40BP

68.2% probability
  2400BC (4.6%) 2380BC
  2350BC (63.6%) 2200BC
95.4% probability
  2470BC (94.1%) 2190BC
  2160BC (1.3%) 2150BC
X2-Test: df=2 T=5.8(5% 6.0)

ornamentation of vessels, and in the decoration of stone sculptures. All the analogies from Western Europe date from the period preceding the appearance of Chemurchek monuments in the Altai. Nothing like those shapes of burial construction and pottery has been ever found among the monuments of the 3rd millennium BCE on the territory between France and Altai. This is why we suppose that some part of the population of south-western Europe migrated to the Altai at the beginning of the 3rd millennium BCE.

Anthropological data on the Chemurchek people are also indicative of their western origin. Unfortunately, no one intact skull has been found in Chemurchek burials in Kazakhstan. However, specialists of the Institute of Genetics of the Russian Academy of Sciences carried out a DNA-analysis of those findings and proved that the considered remnants of two male persons from barrow Aina-Bulak 1-3 belonged to 'Europeans' by the mother's line (mitochondrial DNA).[39] Chemurchek mounds we excavated in Mongolia yielded skulls of brachycephalic europoid type, according to a conclusion of the Department of Anthropology of the National University of Mongolia. Those people differed strictly from the people of Afanasievo culture, who were tall and dolichocephalic as usual. Of course, we cannot be firmly convinced of the place of origin of Chemurchek people judging from the anthropological data only. But these data together with their burial rites and data on vessel forms lend credence to the idea of West European origins. There are multitudes of archaeological cultures known from the territory lying between France and China, which inhabited this broad territory before the appearance of the Chemurchek people in Inner Asia (that is before the middle of the 3rd millennium BCE). Those cultures were the Afanasievo culture of Altai, "eneolithic" cultures of Kazakhstan, "eneolithic" cultures of Western Siberia (Bolshemysskaya kultura, etc.), Repino, later classical Yamnaya, and early Catacombnaya cultures which had spread westwards, and the entire Eurasian steppe was occupied by these. But burial constructions of those cultures had nothing in common with that of Chemurchek culture, and also the types of Chemurchek vessels appear unique for the region. Excluding vessels of Afanasievo and Elunino origin (see above), the Chemurchek pottery and stone vessels are specific forms without any decoration or with a decoration of deeply scratched lines with triangular scallops. All cultures of the Eurasian steppes of that period had absolutely different pottery.

The elongated proportions of the Chemurchek enclosures of the "Bayan-Ulgii" and "Ke'ermuqi" types (fig.11: 1-3) can be traced back to ritual rectangular or trapeziform enclosures, the so-called "*tertres tumulaires*", which had been constructed in 5th-4th millennium BCE in western and south-western France (fig.11: 4-7). There are no signs of burial within such constructions, however signs of fire, pottery, charcoal, and burnt bones are usually found, and occasionally pits filled with stones and soil mixed with charcoal, stone pavements (pavings), and enclosures [40] (Briard, 1992; Patton, 1993: 48-56; L'Helgouac'h, 1998: 330-336; Le Roux, 1995: 45-47; Joussaume, Laporte, 2006: 322-330). Moreover, on the examples of the mounds of Kumdi-Govi and Kurgak-Govi 2 our expedition established the fact that the rectangular enclosures in Bayan-Ulgii had been first used for ritual purposes: a pit had been dug in the center of the enclosuer, filled with soil mixed with charcoal, and after it a burial was arranged in the contents of this pit, and only then was the space within the enclosure filled with stones.

As already mentioned, cairns which enveloped a central stone chamber at its perimeter and partially overlapped each other to form a kind of a "stepped pyramid" (fig.8-10) appeared to be a unique feature of mounds which were investigated by our expedition in Bulgan Sum of Khovd Aimag. This pyramid was not built bottom-up, but from the center to the outside! These cairns might consist of stones or of soil covered with a stone layer. The mounds of Yagshiin Khodoo 1, 3, Kheviin Am 1, and Buural Kharyn Ar in particular consisted of three such cairns ("façades"); all other mounds of two. The mounds of this type which I examined in China were of the same construction, as well as the barrows Ulaan Khudag I-12 and Ulaan Khudag II-3, investigated by the Bujant Russian-Mongol Archaeological Expedition. The first of the latter included three cairns, and the second, two cairns (see above).

The place of origin of this tradition one should search for within the region of the Atlantic coast of France (i.e., Basse-Normandie, Bretagne, Pays-de-Loire, Poitou-Charentes), and the most southern sites which possess this constructive feature were found in the region of Midi-Pyrenees and Languedoc-Rousillon. Only here monuments of an earlier period were discovered, which included overlapping perimetral cairns in their construction. The number of these cairns could reach ten. Jean L'Helgouac'h who should be acknowledged as a patriarch of Breton archaeology compared this system of "façades" with onion skin.[41] Such "façades" overlapping each other like onion skin were revealed in the construction of the majority of passage graves (*les tombes à couloir*) of western France, with cairns remaining undamaged [42] (fig.12-16). Cairn façades of such mounds are made of stone slabs laid flat one over the other, using "dry masonry". These monuments originated at the beginning of the 5th millennium BCE, and were built up to the middle of the 4th millennium BCE; burial activities within these monuments continued up to the end of the 4th millennium BCE; and at the end of 4th millennium BCE all passage graves were stopped up and abandoned.[43]

In most cases monuments of the later period—so-called gallery graves ("*allées couvertes*") and "dolmens" which belonged to even later times (about the last third of the 4th-mid-3rd millennium BCE),[44] lost the "multiplicity" of "façades", which were reduced to one cairn along the perimeter of a "gallery" or of a burial chamber. However, among them there were monuments with perimetral cairns, which formed overlapping "façades"—those were the earliest "gallery graves", and also the dolmens of southern France. All of them are attributed to the last third of the 4th millennium BCE and to the beginning of the 3rd millennium BCE.

Thus these are the last monuments with the above-mentioned significant peculiarity, which existed during the time period close to the time of the appearance of the Chemurchek tribes in Altai. The perimetral cairns of the earliest "gallery graves", which are not high and are faced with inclined or upright stone slabs, not with a dry stone façade, very closely resemble the "Bulgan" type of Chemurchek mounds. Judging from published drawings, there were two such cairns in the construction of the barrows Liscuis I, II (Côte-d-Armor, Bretagne) (fig.17: 4-5). Both cairns were not higher than one meter, made of soil and small stones, and faced with inclined stone slabs. Cairns around a gallery grave of Lisquis II and a V-shaped chamber of an earlier mound of Lisquis I were erected in the same way, all these mounds being of ovoid shape.[45] Data of radiocarbon analysis on these monuments were presented in a paper by J.Muller: Liscuis II: Gif-3994 4450±110 BP (3500-2850 CalBC), Gif-3585 4170±110 BP (3050-2450 CalBC); Lisquis III: Gif 4076 4200±110 BP (3100-2450 CalBC), Gif 4075 3680±110 BP (2500-1750 CalBC); Lisquis I: Gif 3099 5140±110 BP (4250-3700 CalBC).[46]

A passage grave of the site Ti-ar-Boudiged in Brennilis, Finistere showed a similar construction: here an inner cairn of stone was traced around a chamber, overlapped by a second perimetral cairn made of soil. This latter was propped up with upright slabs (fig.17: 2-3).[47] Radiocarbon data obtained from burnt bones from this mound is as follows: Gif-8730 = 4570±70 BP, that is 3520-3020 calBC. Perimetral cairns with dry stone façades were a part of the construction of the Bilgroix gallery grave in the department of Morbihan in Britanny, for which there are three radiocarbon dates of charcoal, connected with the period of the monument functioning point on the end of the 3rd millennium BCE: LQG-568=4320±140 BP (3400-2550 CalBC), Ly-5706=4280±45 BP (3030-2700 CalBC), Gif-9406=4400±60 BPG (3340-2900 CalBC).[48] The most southern gallery grave with perimetral cairns (having traditional façades) is the dolmen de Saint-Eugéne in the Aude (Roussillon) (fig.17: 1), which dates from the period around 3000 BCE [49] (Guilaine, 1998: 52-53, 57, 142; Guilaine, 2006: fig.1; Sauzade, 2008: 345-346).

Some dolmens possess an outer stone platform with a "façade" made with dry masonry or of upright slabs, which is surrounded by another perimetral stone cairn (figs.18,19). Such are the *"dolmens à vestibule"* or *"dolmen angevin"* du Quercy with a short portal of standing slabs,[50] for example the dolmen du Pech from Saint-Antonin-Noble-Val (Tarn-i-Garonne),[51] dolmen de la Devèze-Sud in Marcilhac-sur-Célè (Lot);[52] dolmen 2 de Foumarène-Nord in Montricoux, dolmen 3 de la Ferme du Frau from Cazals (Tarn-i-Garonne), dolmen du Rouzet in Larroque (Tarn), and dolmen du Verdier in Carjac (Lot).[53] The origin of this architectural peculiarity was traced by J. Lecornec to the traditions of building passage graves, monuments of this type dating back to the edge of 4th-3rd millennia BCE.[54] Chemurchek barrows of the Bulgan type preserved the remains of portals of standing stones: the imitation of this portal was excavated at the eastern side of Kheviin Am 1 barrow and a thin upright stone slab was excavated between the barrow and sculpture in the Yagshiin Khodoo 3 barrow (see fig.10). The closest analogy of the "Bulgan" type of the Chemurchek mounds is dolmen de l'Ubac near Goult (Vaucluse), which belongs to the same period. This dolmen was investigated in 2000; its construction was reinforced from the outside with a soil perimetral cairn, the cairn was faced with stone slabs, and one more cairn was made along the perimeter of the first one, also faced with stone slabs.[55]

Burial enclosures from Kazakhstan consist of a passage with dry stone walls surrounding a burial chamber, which is usually situated asymmetrically within the enclosure. Such passages with dry stone walls were earlier built only in the burial monuments of the Atlantic cost of western Europe, in the above-mentioned passage graves. Here these passages appear to be the most distinctive feature of mounds from the beginning of the 5th millennium BCE to the mid-4th millennium BCE (see all the publications devoted to passage graves from the corresponding references above).

In the 4th millennium BCE upright slabs were used with increasing frequency as an additional bearing in erecting of passages. During the Late Neolithic period gallery graves were completely built of upright stone slabs, and in the latest dolmens, such as the "angevin" type or "Quercy dolmens", small portals were made of upright slabs.[56]

However one unique region appears where the dry masonry is a sign of megalithic monuments of the Later Neolithic. In 1953 J.Arnal distinguished a specific group of monuments in the south of France, and characterized them as "prehistoric chamber tombs with dry-stone side-walls". These monuments are spread not only through Eastern Languedoc and the basin of the Lower Rhône, but also eastwards up to the Italian border, in the departments of Hérault, Gard, Ardèche, Buches-du-Rone, Vaucluse, and Alpes-Maritimes (fig.15).[57] The distinctive feature of these monuments is the use of dry masonry in building passages which continue towards a dolmen, and sometimes in erecting the chamber itself. There are cases when a chamber is almost united with a passage into a single whole, which appears to be the closest analogy to the "Kazakhstan" type of Chemurchek barrows. The investigation of the burial inventory of the monuments of this type in Languedoc showed that the time of their building goes back to the period from last third of the 4th millennium BCE to the beginning of the 3rd millennium BCE, that is "before the origins of Fontbouisse culture".[58]

The excavations of the Chemurchek barrows yielded some examples of pottery and stone vessels, as well as some stone vessels found by chance and represented in museums in Xinjiang. As already mentioned, some pottery which we found in the Chemurchek burials of Kazakhstan and Mongolia closely resembles typical pottery of Elunino culture. Elunino was a major culture, whose population occupied steppes to the northwest of the Altai mountains in the approximate period of 2300-1800 BCE.[59] Today tens of large settlements of this culture have been discovered, and on their territory the remains of metallurgical activities have been traced. The settlements themselves occupied rather large territories. The Elunino people were occupied mainly with stock-breeding. The anthropology of the population was mixed, with europoid and mongoloid types presented, mithochondrial DNA showing mongoloid features. Today we consider typical pottery of Elunino culture to be flat-bottom vessels flared upwards, covered with stamps of various types. It is possible that this pottery tradition was of local origin, because similar vessels are known from Neolithic monuments of North Kazakhstan. That is why the findings of pottery of the Elunino type in the northern part of the area of Chemurchek culture can be considered a result of cultural contacts between the Chemurchek and Elunino populations. The same explanation can be given for the similarity of types of lead and tin-bronze adornments as well as the appearance of typical Elunino bone tools (so called scutchers) in Chemurchek burials.[60] We can also suppose, that the europoid component of Elunino culture was directly connected with the penetration of the Chemurchek population from southern areas.

However the majority of earthenware and stone vessels which were found in Xinjiang and in the southern Mongolian Altai differ strongly from those of contemporary and former traditions by shape and ornament. Earthenware and stone vessels are characterized by the same types of forms and decorations, which is why we discuss them together. This unique tradition is characterized by spheroid, ellipsoid, "bomb", and flat bottom pot shapes of vessels, slightly narrowing to the mouth and base; vessels do not have any emphasized neck or flared mouth, the mouths of all vessels being slightly contracted (figs.21, 27). The most usual type of decoration looks like a horizontal line with triangular scallops stretched under a vessel's rim. Pottery of such shapes, almost without decoration, is characteristic of the Later and Final Neolithic in the west and south of France and also in Spain. In Brittany such vessels are attributed to a so-called Conguel type (figs. 24-25).[61] In the Poitou region these shapes are found within the context of Peu-Richard and Artenac cultures [62] (fig.26), and southwards this type of pottery is characteristic of the Ferrieres culture and its surrounding,[63] the pottery of the Ferrieres type including spheroid, as well as "bomb" and "sack" shapes (figs. 22-23, 28-29). The decoration of stretched horizontals and multiplied triangular scallops appears to be a particular sign of the pottery of this culture. Among pottery of the northern territories a similar ornamentation is also present, but rarely. A pottery of spheroid shape with contracted mouth and stretched horizontals is most typical of the Later Neolithic of Spanish Galicia and of the Atlantic cost of the Iberian peninsula as a whole.[64] It is worth mentioning that the Ferrieres pottery was spread over almost the same territory as the "dolmens du Quercy" and the above-mentioned chambers with dry stone side-walls. This pottery was found mainly in grottoes, during excavations of settlements, but is usually dated from the same time as the burial constructions mentioned above, that is from the end of the 4th to the beginning of the 3rd millennium BCE.[65]

Stone statues chiseled by Chemurchek people are an absolutely peculiar phenomenon in the territory of Asian steppes in the 3rd millennium BCE (fig.30). When my abovementioned paper was published in Germany in 1999, about 35 prehistoric statues were known from Northern Xinjiang. To date two more sculptures were discovered near Chemurchek mounds in Mongolian territory near the town of Bulgan, and I have also learned of about 30 new unpublished statues during my survey of different sites in Chinese Altai. Some of them were found near rectangular Chemurchek barrows.

If there are any doubts about the attribution of these sculptures to Chemurchek culture, my investigations with Wang Bo can dispel these. Firstly, many of the statues were found established in the vicinity of Chemurchek burials, containing early inventory, and with no doubt they belong to these burials. Secondly, the differences between Chemurchek sculptures and Turkic statues are essential. No local sources of this tradition were found. If we consider the statues of the Black Sea region which date from the nearest period of time prior to the existence of Chemurchek culture, we have determined that their style differs greatly from Chemurchek style, but the most similar statues can be found much further westwards in France.

As I have already mentioned, the specific features of Chemurchek statues are the following: the flattened face is marked by protruding contours and a straight relief nose is usually connected with it. The eyes are marked by protruding circles or disks. A girdle or a necklace sometimes consisting of several rows is modeled on the neck. Judging from indicated pectoral muscles, the figures are portrayed in the nude. In one case shoulder-blades were depicted as two protruding contours, which nearly met in the center of the back. Statue-menhirs of the Black Sea region are distinguished by shoulder-blades modeled as triangles;

they do not show a protruding contour around faces, and the eyes are marked by grooves.[66] They also possess peculiarities which are not signs of Chemurchek statues.

Some statue-menhirs from southern France are characterized by the protruding contour of the perimeter of a face, connected with a straight nose, with the eyes shown by protruding circles or disks, the shoulder-blades marked by two curls, and one or several girdles decorating the neck [67] (fig.31: 1-4, 8, 10). A shepherd's crook with a hooked upper end is usually depicted on the statues of southern France [68] (fig.31: 1-2), of the Black Sea region, and on Chemurchek sculptures. Some Chemurchek stelae are decorated with a bow. The same pictures of bows we can see on the sculptures of the Later Neolithic of the Midi-Pyrenees and Sion (Switzerland)[69] (fig.31: 5-7). It should be mentioned that images of bows and arrows are typical of earlier megalithic burial chambers of Britanny (Runesto, Île Longue, Le Déhus, Gavrinis, Barnenez).[70] On some Chemurchek statues a girdle is supplemented with hanging triangles, and similar adornments we can see on statues in Switzerland, Northern Italy, Spain [71] (fig.31: 5, 7, 9) which belong to the period of the Final Neolithic and the beginning of the Bronze Age; however we can suppose that some of them date from the beginning of the 3rd millennium BCE.

Chemurchek statues display a mouth depicted with its angles turned down, and the European statues of 4th-3rd millennium BCE do not show a marked mouth. The closest analogy of this tradition can be found in much earlier statues from the settlement of Lepenski Vir in Croatia, which date back to the 5th millennium BCE. My opinion is that this tradition influenced the origin and development of sculpturing traditions of the Late Neolithic of Europe, but the transitional forms have not yet been found.

According to several of these features, namely the protruding contour of the face, the girdle with triangular scallops, and a bow and crook in the hand, statues of the "Sion-Aosta" type in Alpes, groupe 2, 3 of Gard in Pyrenees and some findings from Catalonia [72] (fig.31: 1-7, 9) appear to be most similar to Chemurchek statues. But the Chemurchek tradition could have originated from the junction of these different types.

Many groups of French statues are connected with burial constructions. In the early passage graves of Brittany anthropomorphic stelae were erected by the entrance inside a grave (Guennoc III).[73] The East Languedoc stelae of Gard type 2 (fig.31: 1-2) are found in the corridors of burial grottoes, particularly in a grotto of Meunier where the entrance of a burial construction was framed with two stelae.[74] Also excavations of a megalithic burial place dated to 2900-2700 BCE in Sion (Valais, Switzerland) brought evidence that stone statues (fig.31: 5-7) were primarily erected by entrances to the dolmen portals [75] (Harrison, Heydt, 2007). It is most possible to date statues of Sion-Aosta type (very similar to Chemurchek) and Languedoc statues with protruding contours of faces and crooks to the early 3rd millennium BCE, very close to the beginning of Chemurchek culture in Altai.

In southern France we also can find analogies of the cases when stelae were erected near Chemurchek burial constructions instead of statues. Particularly in the Kara-tumsik mound (fig.7) a trapezoid stele had been dug in, its wide part upwards, and many similar "steles-haches" of trapezoid shape were found in southern France in the vicinity of burials of the Later Neolithic. These sites are situated in the departments of Vaucluse, Lot, and Herault [76] (fig.32). At the Château-Blanc burial site (Ventabren, Bouches-du-Rhône) mentioned above, stelae were dug in with the narrow end downwards at the western side of the cairns of mounds Nos. 1 and 2. These burial mounds date from the Late Neolithic (*c.* 3400-2900 BCE).[77]

In Chemurchek burials we discovered drawings made with red ochre looking like rows of triangular scallops (fig.33: 1-3), which can be compared with ochre drawings and gravures in the megaliths of Spain [78] (fig.33: 6-11). In the neolithic burials of Germany there are also pictures of rows of triangles and other drawings which resemble those of Chemurchek culture, for example a picture from Golitzsch [79] (fig.33: 4-5) can be compared with a drawing from the Yagshiin Khodoo 3 mound.

CONCLUSION

Thus in this paper we attempt to present elements of Chemurchek culture which have no other analogies except those in the Neolithic of France: in the mounds' construction these were overlapping perimetral cairns, burial corridors with dry stone side-walls, the specific style of stone statues, and the peculiar shapes of vessels. Evidently the fact that all these elements of culture had been transferred over 6,500 kilometers to the Mongolian Altai can only be explained by migration.

The results of the presented research can throw light on the problem of the origins of the Tokharians because the Tokharian-speaking people moved from the West to the heart of Asia in this period (according to glotto-chronological data) and the Tokharian language belongs precisely to the western Indo-European languages. If it was a migration of Proto-Tokharians we have possibilities of recognizing territories of inhabitancy of other Old Western Indo-European dialects: the Proto-Tokharian language had the closest connections with Proto-Germanic and Proto-Italian.[80] These dialects should have been spread in the vicinity of the territory of the Proto-Tokharians, as we established here-namely in the vicinity of southern France.

CAPTIONS AND REFERENCES FOR ILLUSTRATIONS

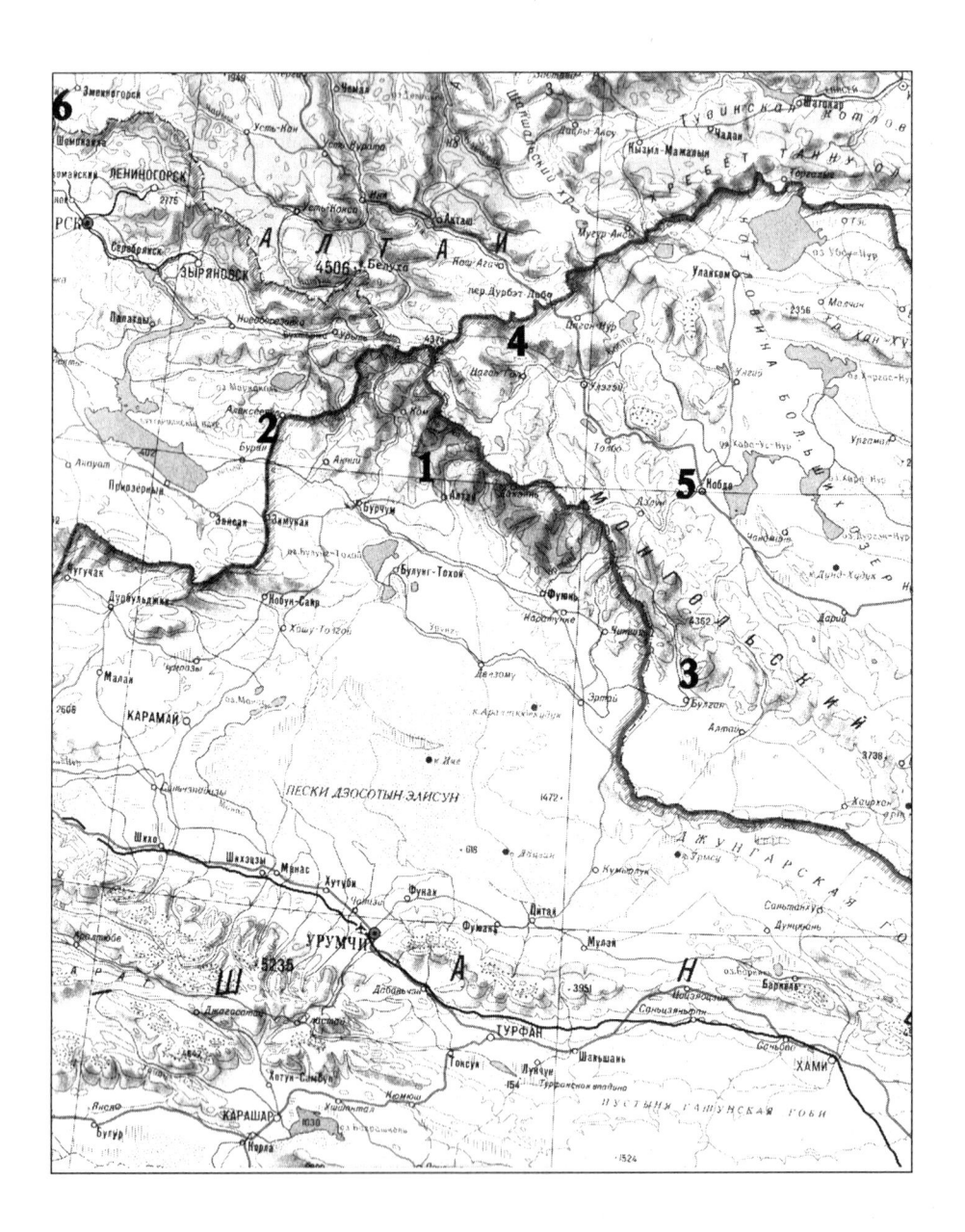

Fig.1. Map of excavated barrows of Chemurchek culture: 1, "Ke'ermuqi" burial place (Chemurchek township, Altai county, Xinjiang); 2, Aina-Bulak, Kopa, Bulgartaboty, Akhtuma cemeteries (Kurchum district, East-Kazakhstan region, Kazakhstan); 3, Yagshiin Khodoo, Kheviin Am, Buural Kharyn Am burial places (Bulgan Sum, Khovd Aimag, Mongolia); 4, Kulala Ula, Kurgak Govi 2, Kumdi Govi, Kara Tumsik barrows (Ulankhus Sum, Bayan-Ulgii Aimag, Mongolia); 5, Ulaan hudag I, II, Shar Sum burial places (Khovd Sum, Khovd Aimag, Mongolia); Ust'-Kamenka II burial place (Tretyakovo district, Altai region, Russia)

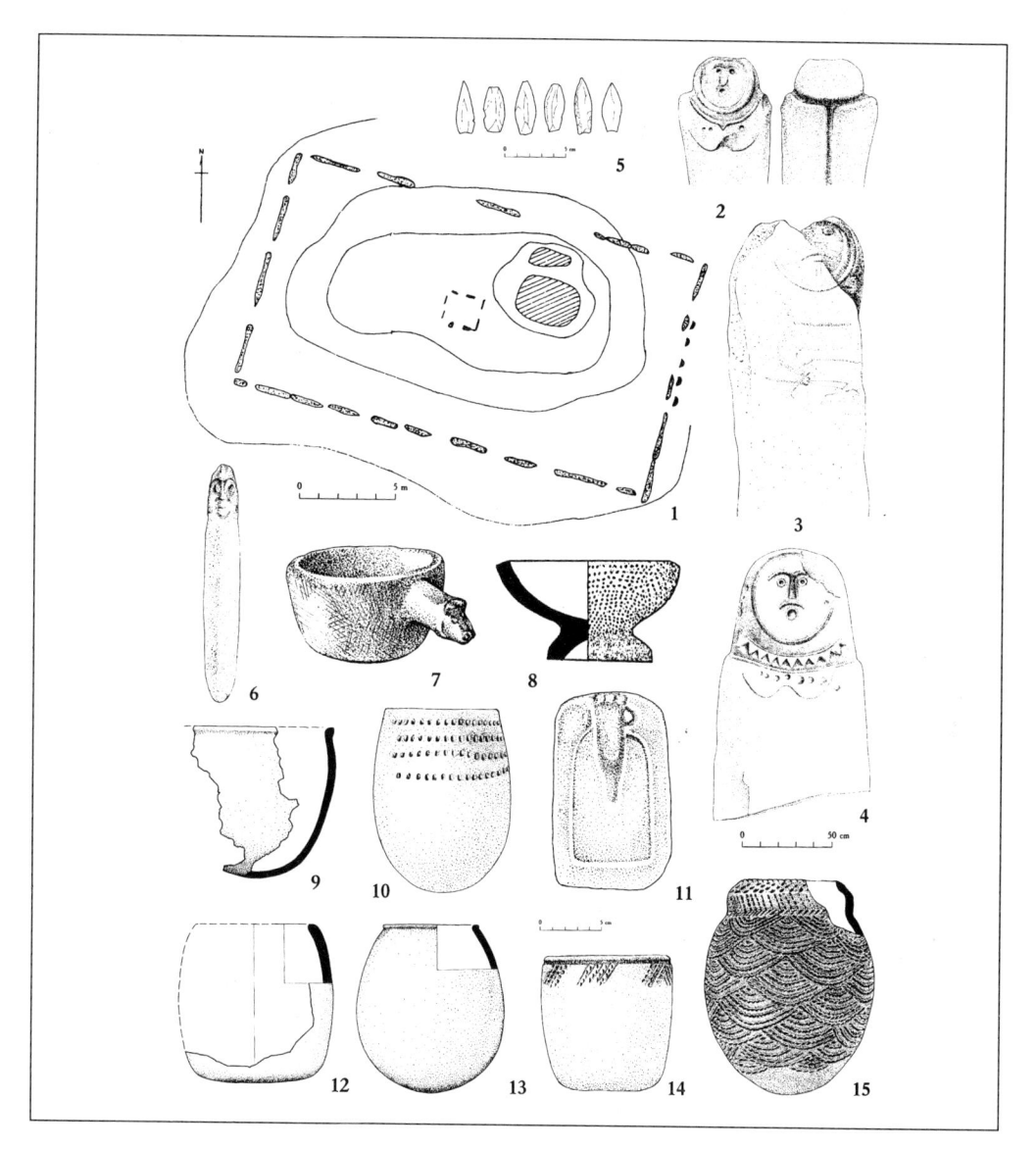

Fig.2. Chemurchek burials from Chemurchek river basin (Altai county, Xinjiang): 1, plan of Kayinarl 1 barrow (with stone sculptures Ke'ermuqi 6-9 by numbering of Li Zheng) (by Wang Bo, 1996). Others by Kovalev 2000: 2, stone sculpture Kayinarl 2 N2 after numbering of Wang Linshan and Wang Bo (after numbering of Li Zheng: Ke'ermuqi 2); 3, stone sculpture N3 from Kayinarl 1 barrow after numbering of Wang Linshan and Wang Bo (stone sculpture Ke'ermuqi 8 after numbering of Li Zheng); 4, stone sculpture Kayinarl 2 N2 (after numbering of Wang Linshan and Wang Bo), erected 3m east from east wall of stone fence of barrow Ke'ermuqi M2 excavated by Yi Manbai in 1963; 5, stone arrowheads from stone boxes m1 and m2 of barrow Ke'ermuqi M7; 6, small stone sclpture from separate stone box (may be like "Bulgan" barrows) Ke'ermuqi M21; 7, stone vessel with sculpture of ox head from Ke'ermuqi M16 Barrow; 8, pottery censer belonging to Afanasievo culture from stone box of Ke'ermuqi M24 barrow; pottery vessel, found by A.Kovalev near robbed stone box M2 of Ke'ermuqi M17 barrow; 10, potteries from cairn of Ke'ermuqi M16 barrow; 11, stone mould from complex of metalworking tools found in Ke'ermuqi M17; 12, pottery vessel from stone box in Ke'ermuqi M2 barrow; 13, stone vessel from stone box m2 of Ke'ermuqi M7 barrow; 14, pottery vessel from stone box m1 of Ke'ermuqi M7 barrow; and 15, potteries from cairn of Ke'ermuqi M16 barrow

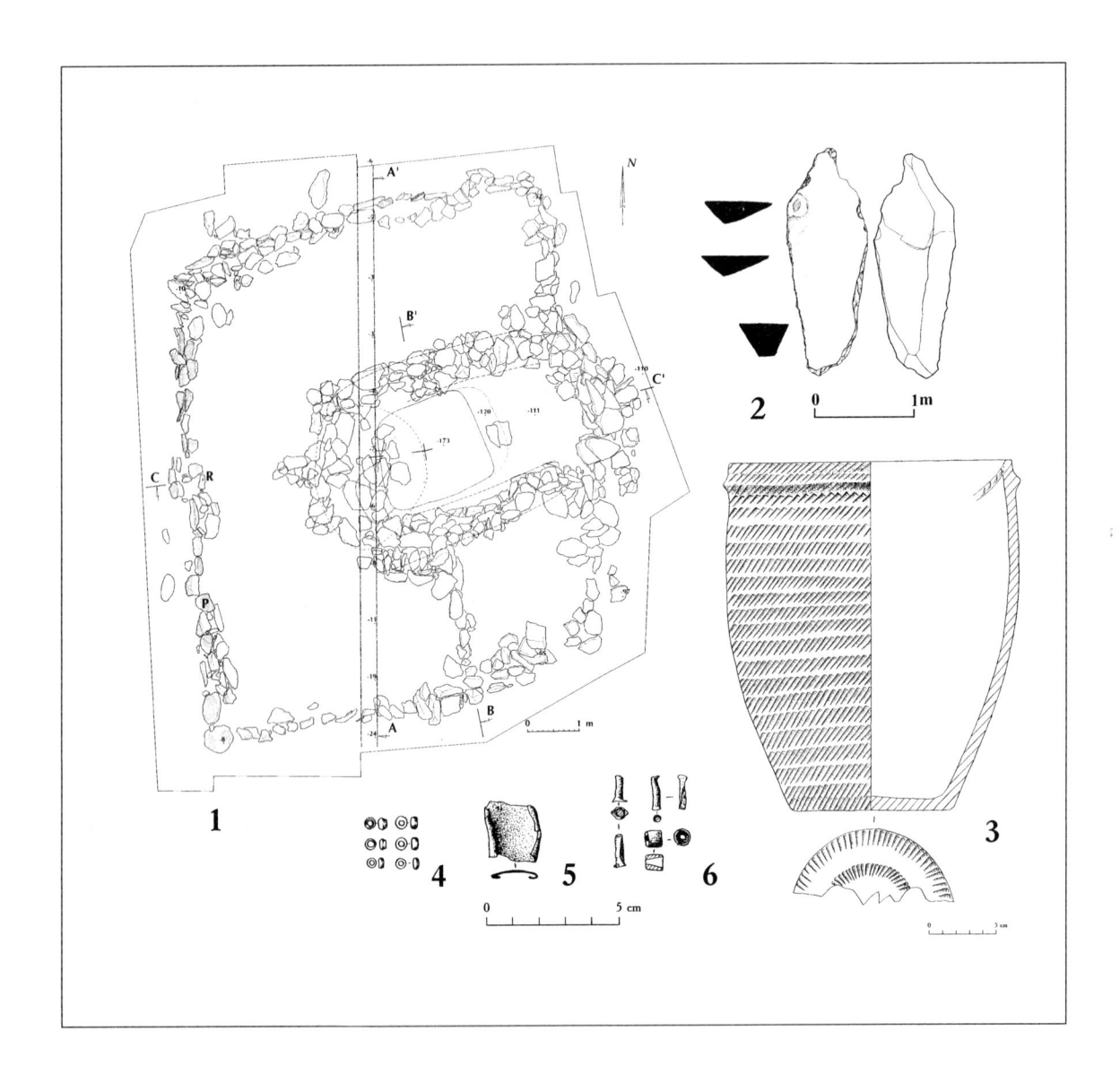

Fig.3. Eastern Kazakhstan Chemurchek barrows: 1, plan of Akhtuma barrow; 2, stone stele erected 10 m from eastern side of stone fence of Kopa 2 barrow; 3, pottery vessel from burial pit of Bulgartaboty 1 barrow (reconstruction); 4, small argillithic beads from burial pit of Bulgartaboty 2 barrow; 5, part of bronze bracelet from burial pit of Bulgartaboty 2 barrow; 6, bronze tubes and stone bead from Kopa 2 barrow

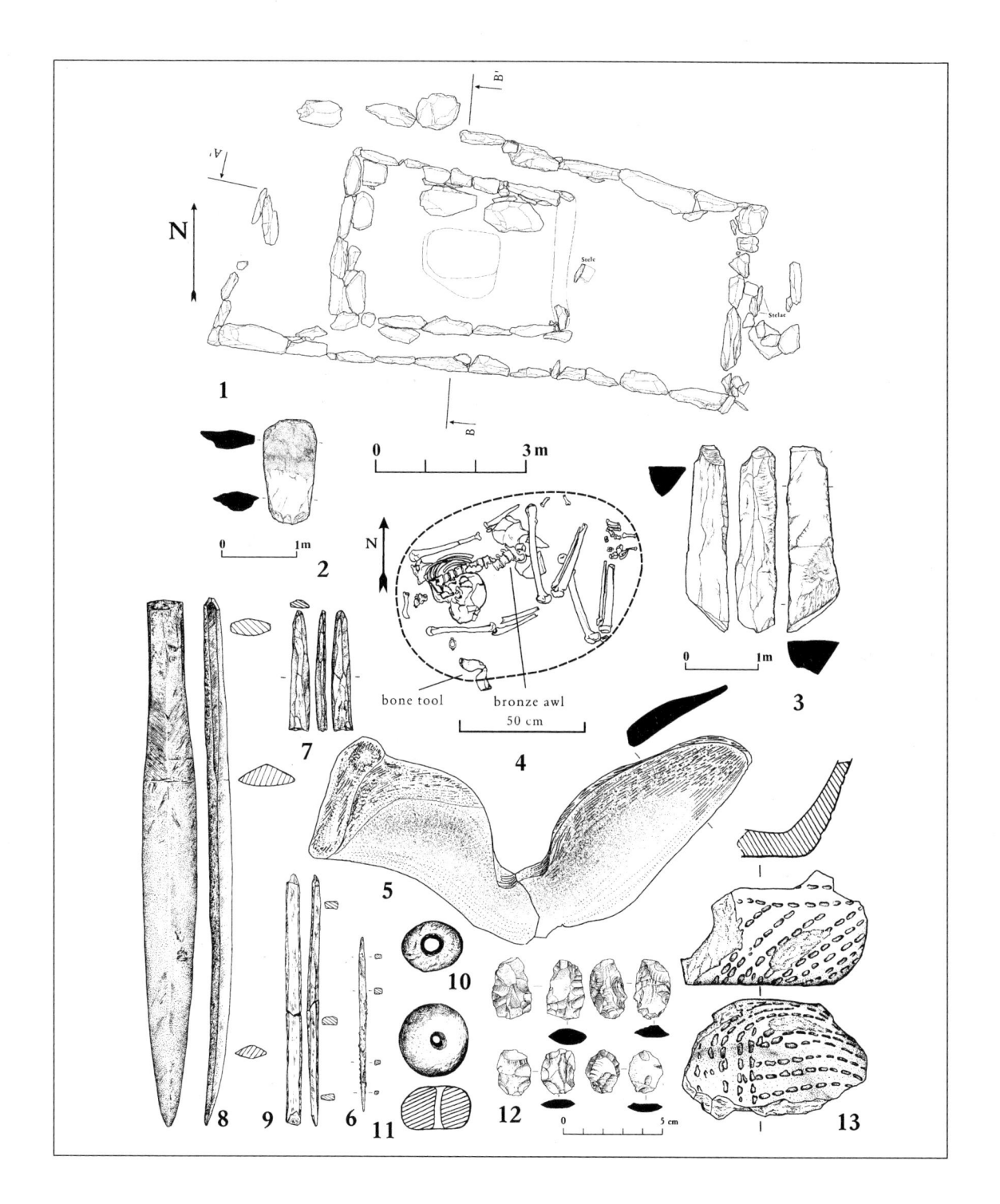

Fig.4. Chemurchek barrows of Bayan-Ulgii Aimag, Mongolia: 1, plan of Kara Tumsik barrow; 2, stone stele with okhra painting from Kara Tumsik barrow; 3, stone stele erected 2m to south from southern side of stone fence of Kulala Ula barrow; 4, plan of secondary burial 2 in Kumdi Govi barrow; 5 and 6, bone tool and bronze awl from the secondary burial 2 in Kumdi Govi barrow; 7, 8, and 10, part of bone arrowhead (7), bone dagger (8), and stone ball (9) from burial pit of Kulala Ula barrow; 9, bone arrowhead from burial pit of Kara Tumsik barrow; 11, stone ball from earliest pit of Kumdi Govi barrow; 12, stone tools from secondary burial 1 in Kurgak Govi 2 barrow; 13, part of pottery vessel from burial pit of Kara Tumsik barrow

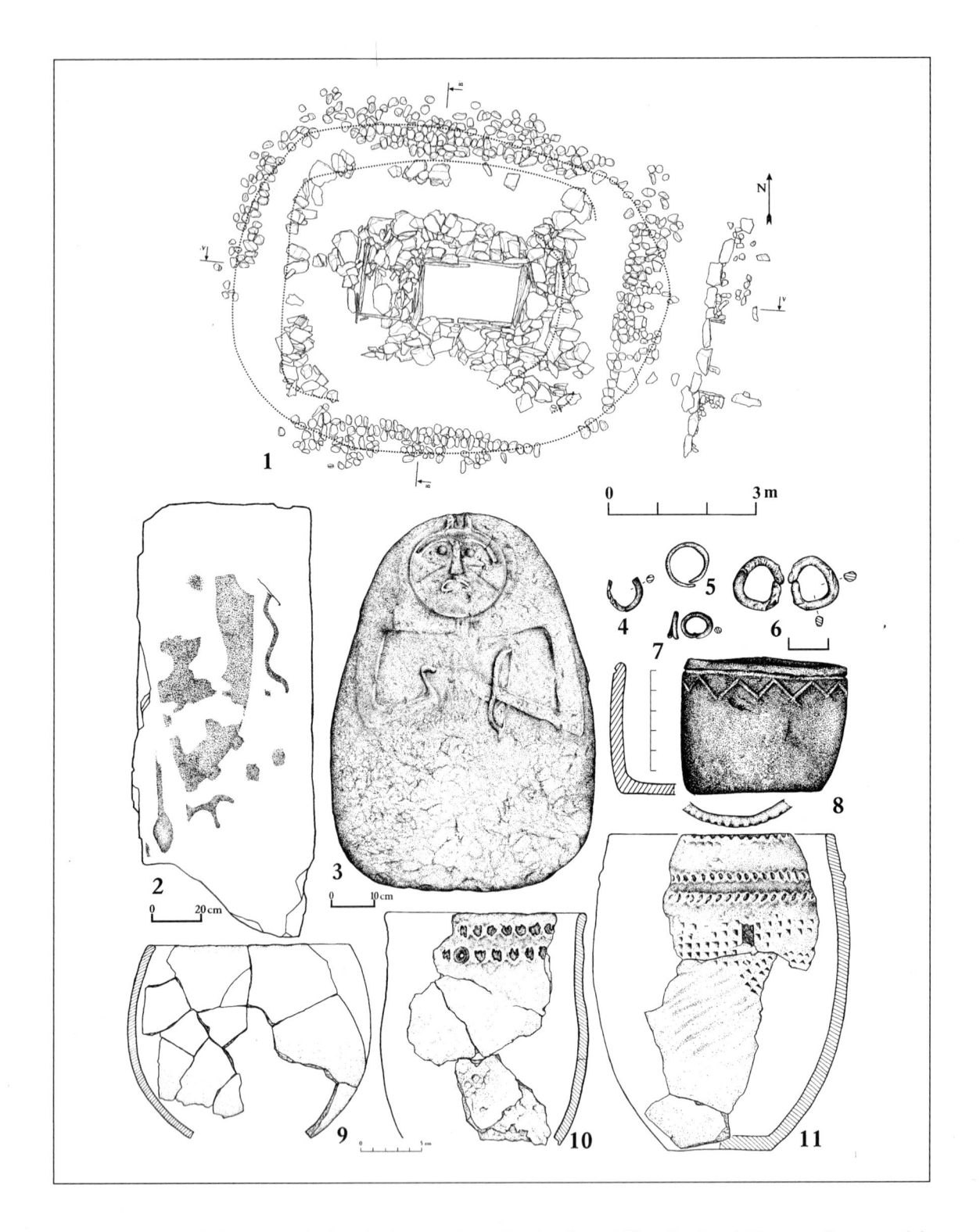

Fig.5. Chemurchek barrows of Khovd Aimag, Mongolia: 1, plan of Kheviin Am 1 Barrow; 2, stone slab with okhra painting from stone box of Yagshiin Khodoo 3 barrow; 3, stone sculpture erected to the east of Yagshiin Khodoo 3 barrow; 4, 5, and 7, lead and bronze (7) earrings from stone box of Yagshiin Khodoo 1 barrow; 6, lead earring from stone box of Yagshiin Khodoo 3 barrow; 8, stone vessel from stone box of Buural Kharyn Ar barrow; 9-11, pottery vessels from stone boxes of Yagshiin Khodoo 1 (9, 10) and Yagshiin Khodoo 3 (11) barrows

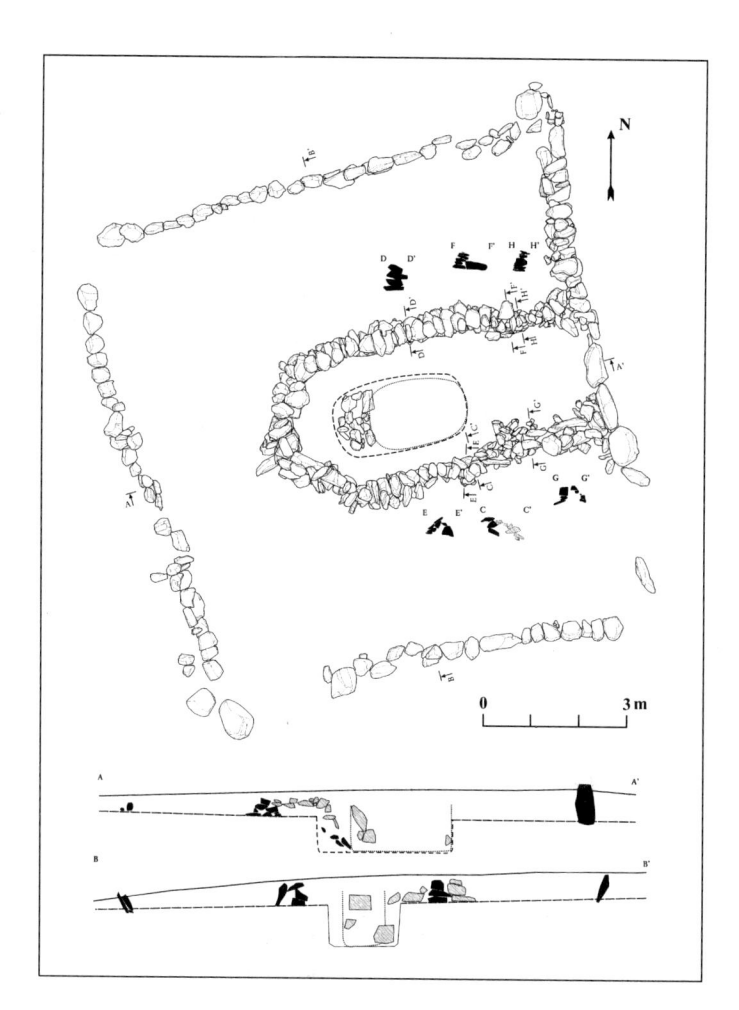

Fig.6. Chemurchek Aina Bulak I barrow 3 (Kurchum district, East Kazakhstan region, Kazakhstan)

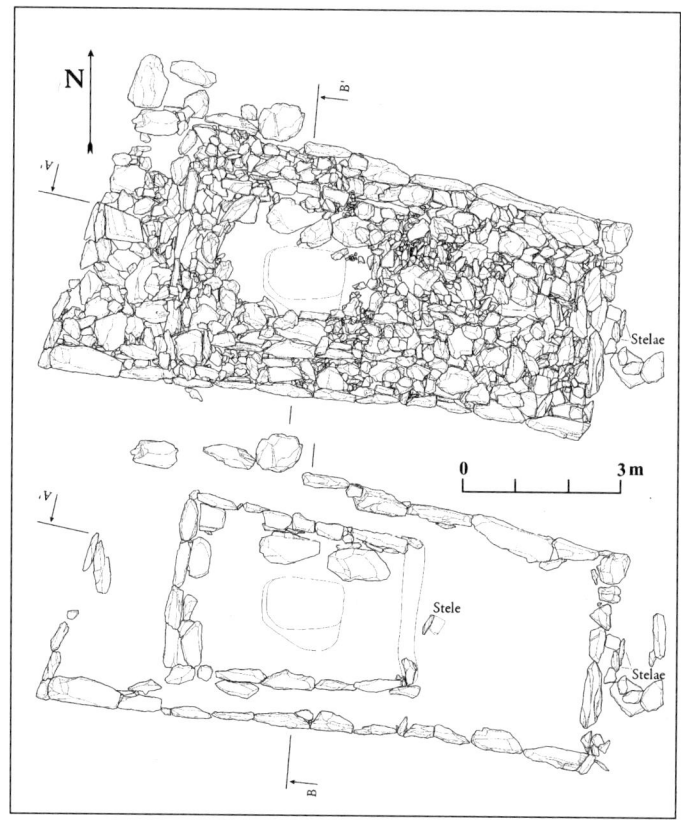

Fig.7. Chemurchek Kara Tumsik (Khar Khoshuu) barrow (Ulaanhus Sum, Bayan-Ulgii Aimag, Mongolia)

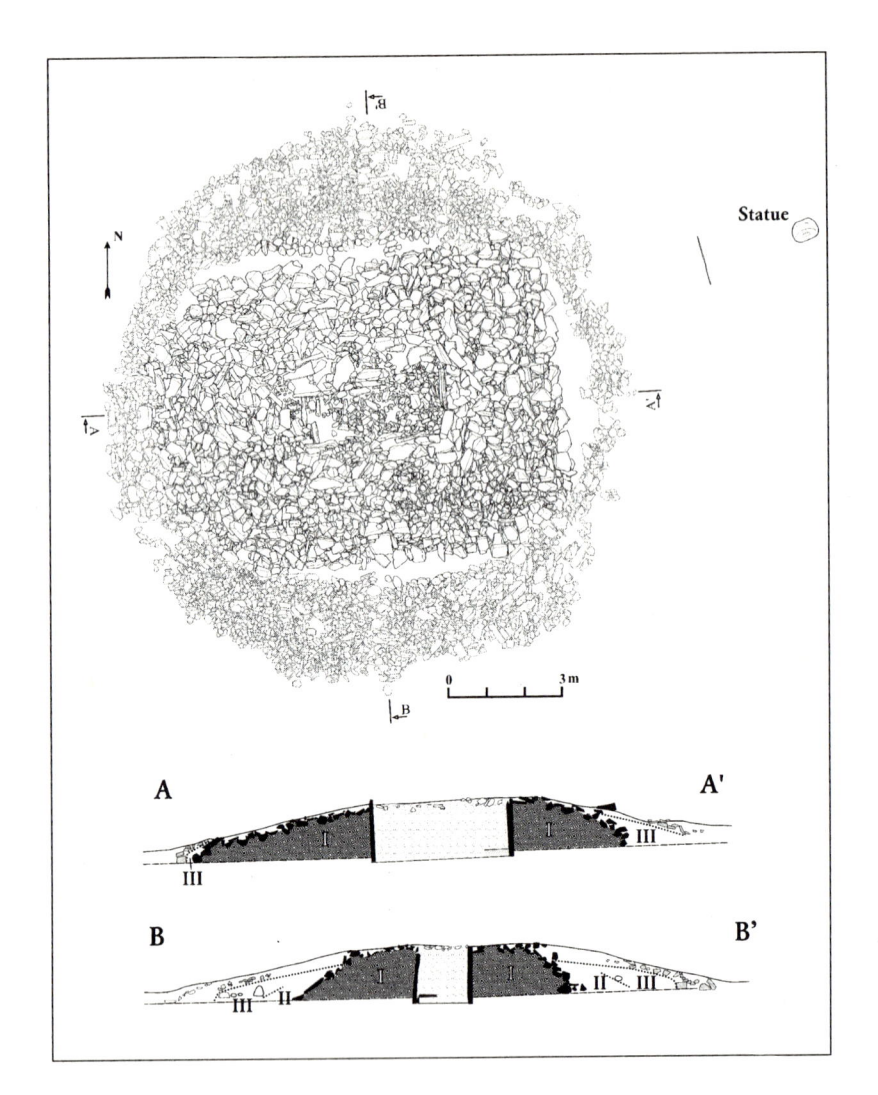

Fig.8. Chemurchek Yagshiin Khodoo barrow (Bulgan Sum, Khovd Aimag, Mongolia). I, II, III-overlapping perimetral cairns

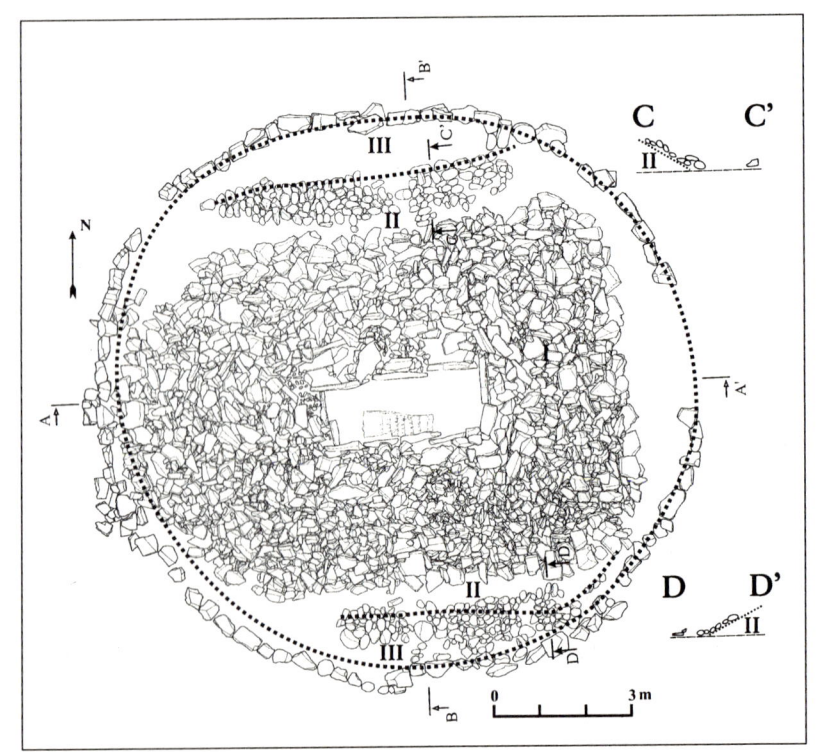

Fig.9. Chemurchek Yagshiin Khodoo barrow (Bulgan Sum, Khovd Aimag, Mongolia). After the destruction of cairn III and cleaning of cairn II. I, II, III-overlapping perimetral cairns

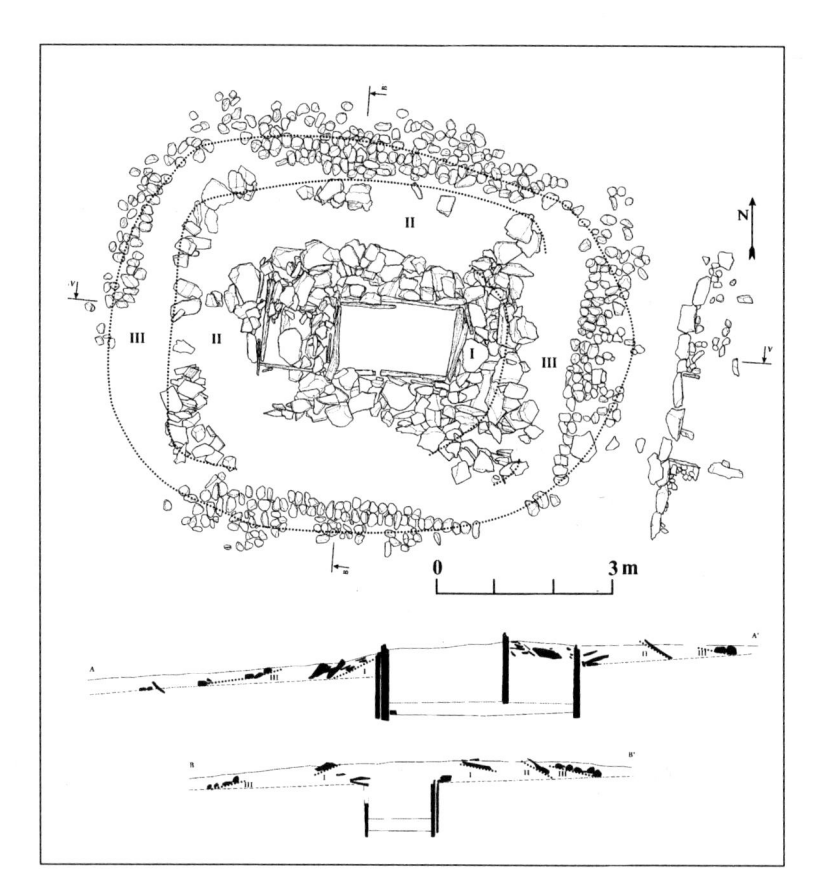

Fig.10. Chemurchek Kheviin Am barrow (Bulgan Sum, Khovd Aimag, Mongolia). After destruction of cairn III and cleaning of cairn II. I, II, III-overlapping perimetral cairns

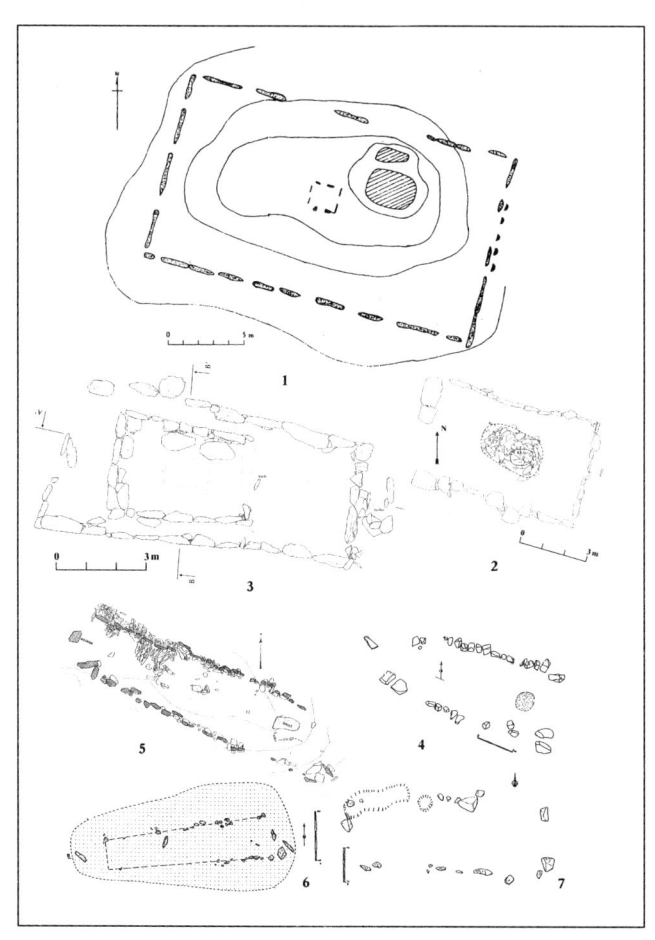

Fig.11. Chemurchek rectangular funerary fences: 1, Kayinarl 1 with statues "Ke'ermuqi 6-9" by Li Zheng (Qiemuerqieke township, Altai county, Xinjiang)[81]; 2, Kumdi Govi (Bayan-Ulgii, Mongolia); 3, Kara-Tumsik (Bayan-Ulgii, Mongolia). "Tertres tumulaires" of Western France[82]: 4, Notre Dame de Lorette (Le Quillo, dep. Côtes-d'Armor); 5, La Croix Saint-Pierre (Saint-Just, dep. Ille-et-Vilaine); 6, La Croix Madame (Saint-Just, dep. Ille-et-Vilaine); 7, La Gaudinais (Langon, dep. Gironde)

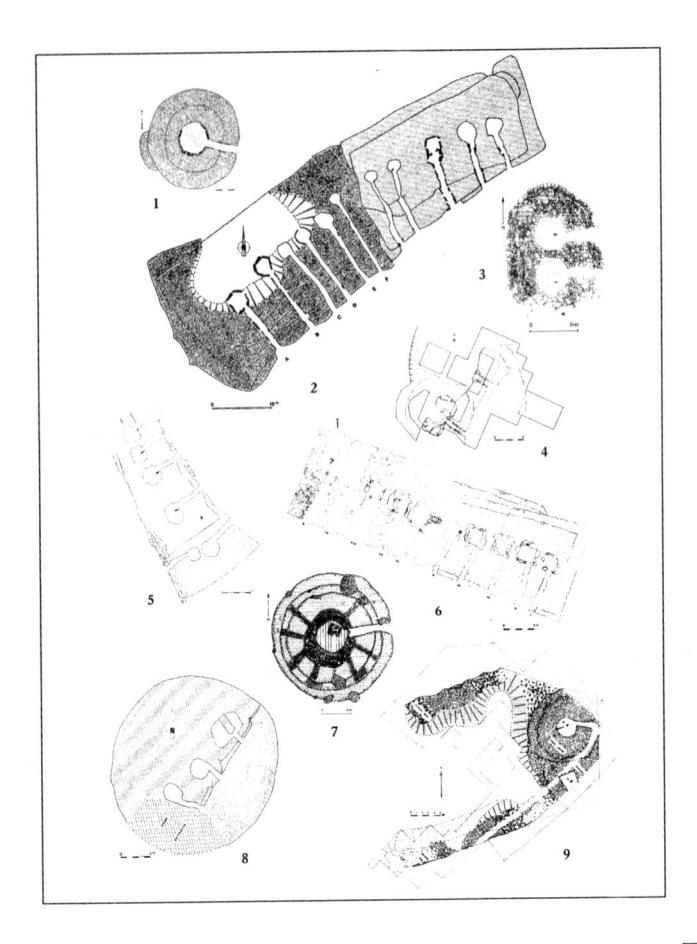

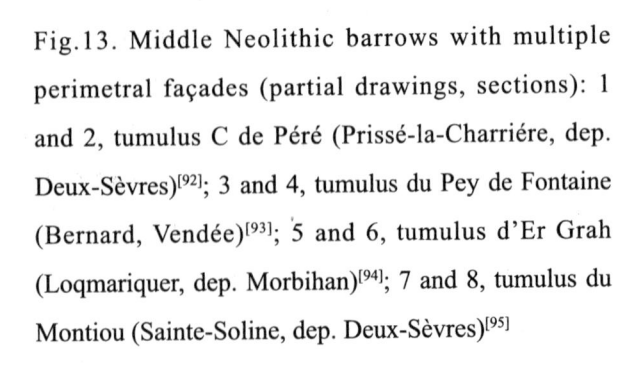

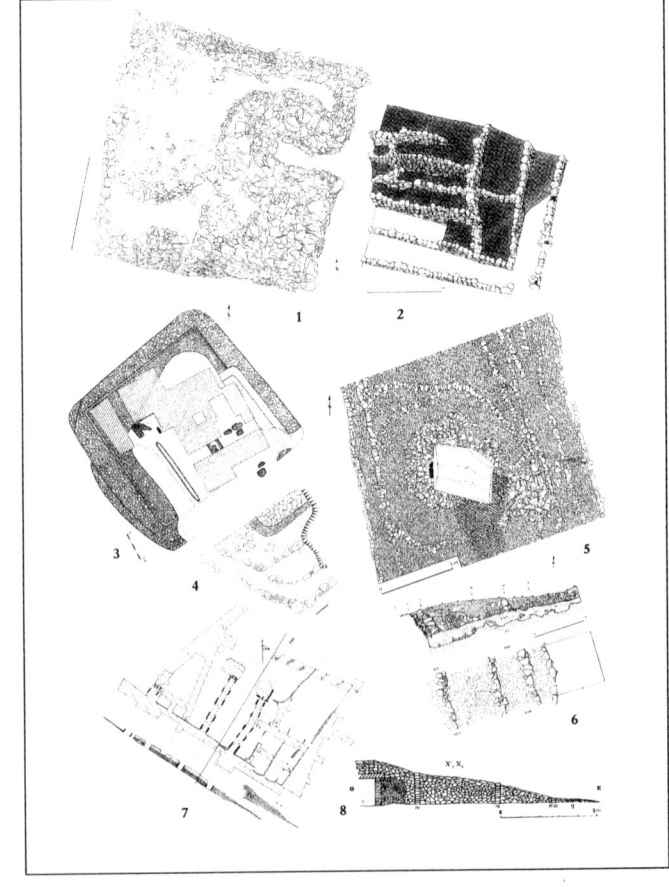

Fig.12. Middle Neolithic period barrows with multiple perimetral façades (second half of 5th millennium BCE): 1, tumulus "Ciste des Cous" (Bazoges-en-Pareds, dep. Vendée)[83]; 2, cairn de Barnenez (Plouézoch, dep. Finistère)[84]; 3, dolmen A of la Bruyére de Hamel (Condé-sur-Ifs, dep. Calvados)[85]; 4, cairn de Ty-Floc'h (Saint-Thois, dep. Finistère)[86]; 5, cairn 3 of Guennoc (Plouguerneau, dep. Finistère)[87]; 6, tumulus du Planti (Availles-sur-Chizé, dep. Deux-Sèvres)[88]; 7, Ernes (dep. Condé-sur-Ifs)[89]; 8, cairn de Île Carn (Ploudalmézeau, dep. Finistère)[90]; 9, cairn de la Butte à Lucerne (Vierville, dep. Manche)[91]

Fig.13. Middle Neolithic barrows with multiple perimetral façades (partial drawings, sections): 1 and 2, tumulus C de Péré (Prissé-la-Charriére, dep. Deux-Sèvres)[92]; 3 and 4, tumulus du Pey de Fontaine (Bernard, Vendée)[93]; 5 and 6, tumulus d'Er Grah (Loqmariquer, dep. Morbihan)[94]; 7 and 8, tumulus du Montiou (Sainte-Soline, dep. Deux-Sèvres)[95]

Fig.14. Middle Neolithic period barrows with multiple perimetral façades (second half of 5th-first half of 4th millennium BCE) from Poitou: 1, tumulus F0-F1[96]-F2[97] of Bougon (dep. Deux-Sèvres) (detail); 2, dolmen "La Grosse Pierre" (St.-Radegonde, dep. Charente-Maritime)[98]; 3, tumulus B of Boixe (dep. Charente)[99]; 4-6, tumuli A, B, and C of Champ-Châlon (Benon, dep. Charente-Maritime)[100]

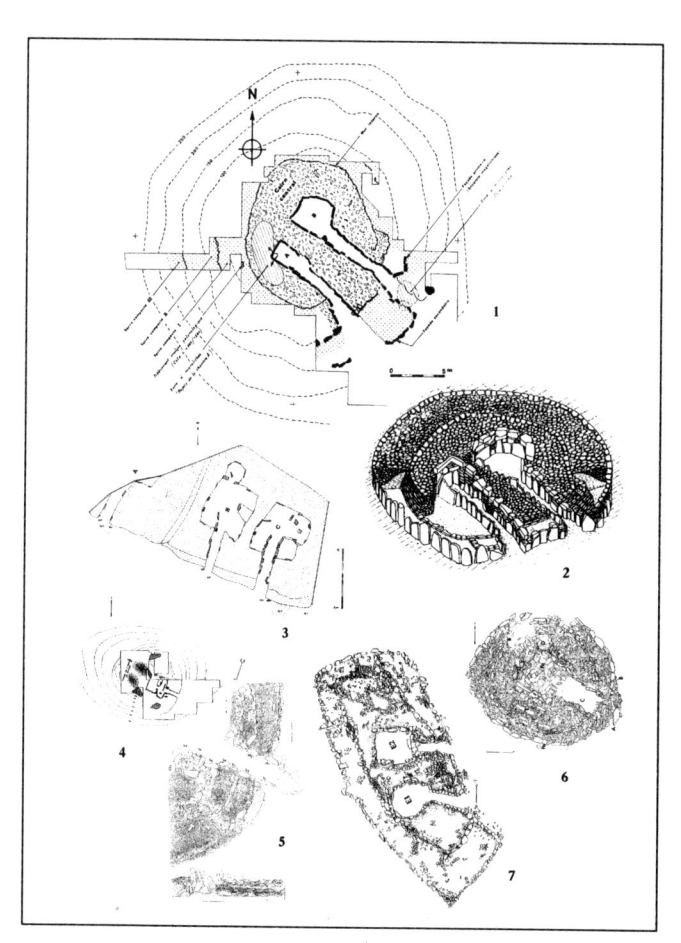

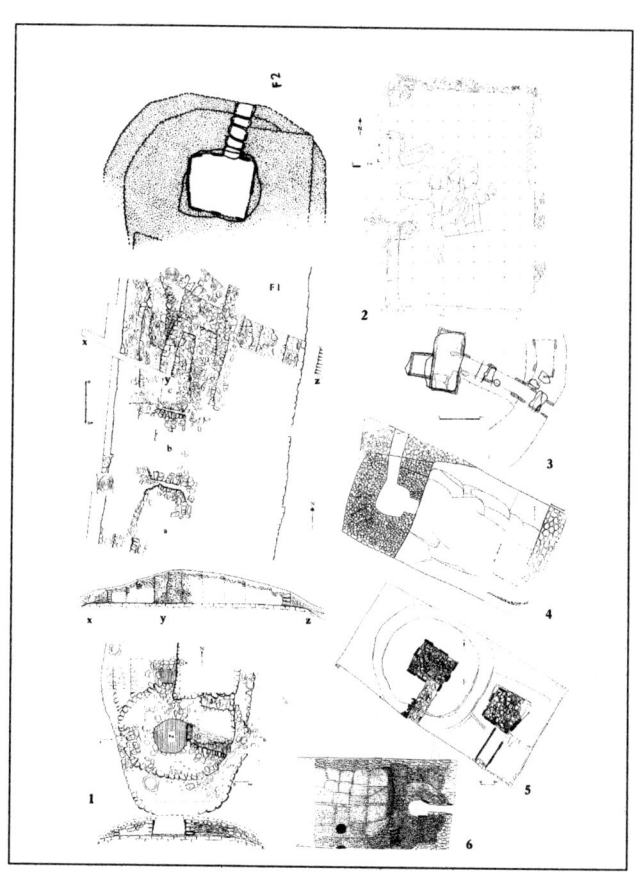

Fig.15. Middle Neolithic period barrows with multiple perimetral façades (4th millennium BCE): 1 and 2, tumulus of Dissignac (Saint-Nazaire, dep. Loire-Atlantique)[101]; 3, cairn of Kerleven (Forêt-Fouesnant, dep. Finistère)[102]; 4 and 5, dolmen of Château-Bû (Saint-Just, dep. Ille-et-Vilaine)[103]; 6, dolmen of Saint-Croix-del-Pierre (Saint-Just, dep. Ille-et-Vilaine)[104]; 7, tumulus E of Bougon (dep. Deux-Sèvres)[105]

Fig.16. Middle Neolithic period barrows with multiple perimetral façades (4th millennium BCE): 1 and 2, cairn of Mousseaux (Pornic, dep. Loire-Atlantique)[106]; 3 and 4, dolmen of Cruguellic (Plœmeur, dep. Morbihan)[107]; 5 and 6, dolmen of Josseliere (or du Pissot) (Clion-sur-Mer, dep. Loire-Atlantique)[108]; 7 and 8, cairn 1 of "Min goh Ru" nearby Larcuste (Colpo, dep. Morbihan)[109]

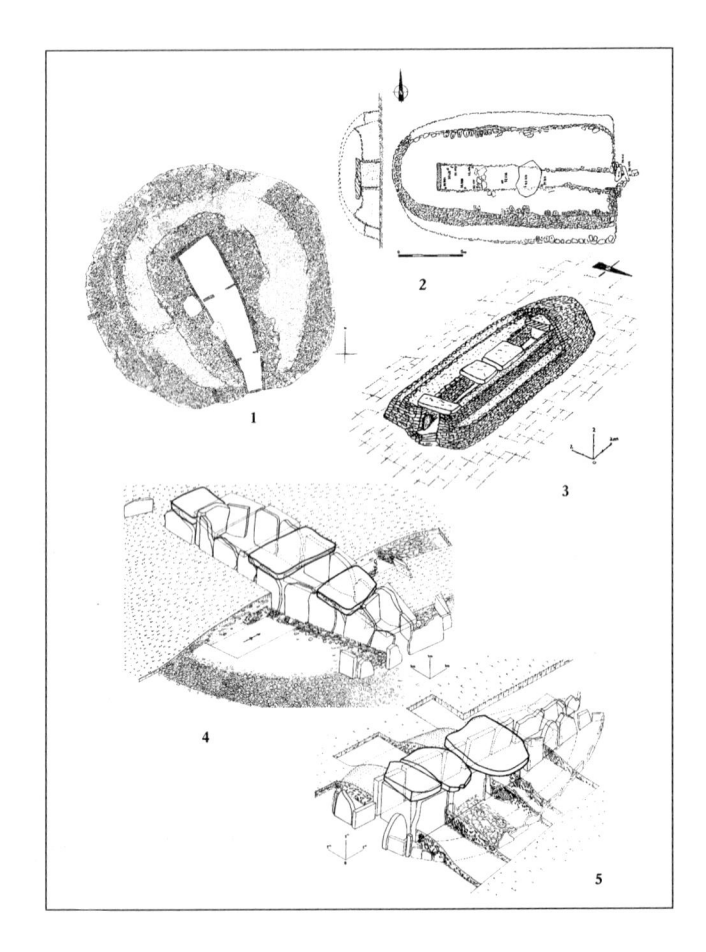

Fig.17. Late Neolithic period gallery graves with multiple perimetral façades (end of 4th millennium BCE): 1, dolmen of Saint-Eugène (Laure-Minervois, dep. Aude)[110]; 2 and 3, gallery grave of Bilgroix (Arzon, dep. Morbihan)[111]; 4, gallery grave Liscuis III (Laniscat, dep. Côtes-d'Armor)[112]; 5, gallery grave (in "V") Liscuis I (Laniscat, dep. Côtes-d'Armor)[113]

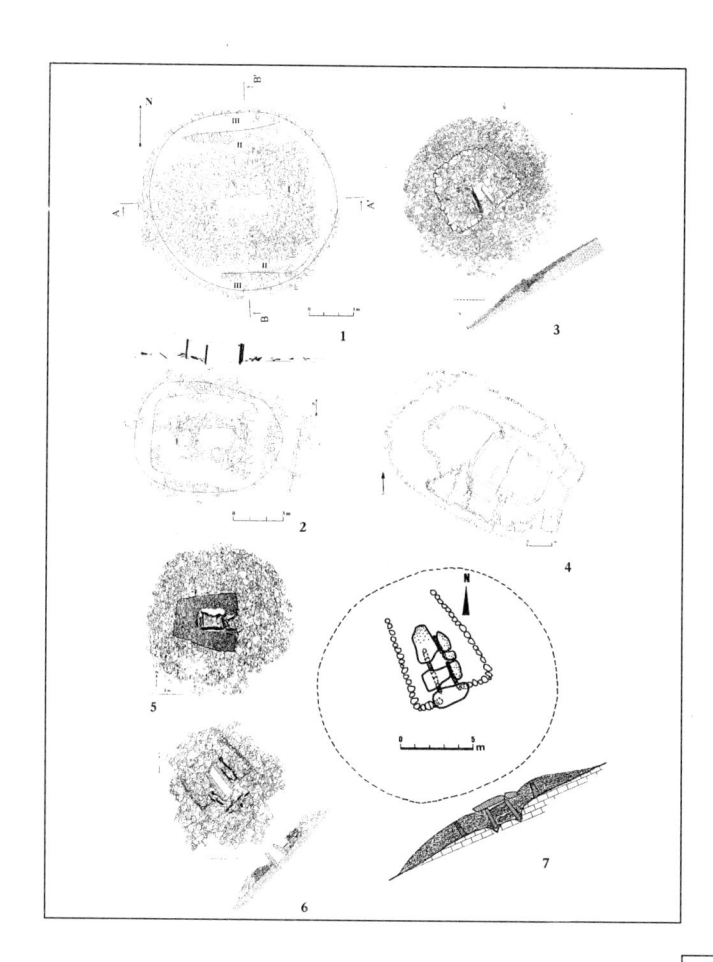

Fig.18. Chemurchek barrows and dolmens of "angevin" type of south-western France (early 3rd millennium BCE): 1, Yagshiin Khodoo 3 Chemurchek barrow; 2, Kheviin Am 1 Chemurchek barrow; 3, dolmen 2 of Foumarène-Nord (Montricoux, dep. Tarn-et-Garonne)[114]; 4, dolmen E 134 of Taize (Deux Sèvres)[115]; 5, dolmen 3 de la Ferme du Frau (Cazals, dep. Tarn-et-Garonne)[116]; 6, dolmen of Devèze-Sud (Marcilhac-sur-Célè, dep. Lot)[117]; 7, dolmen of Verdier (Cariac, dep. Lot)[118]

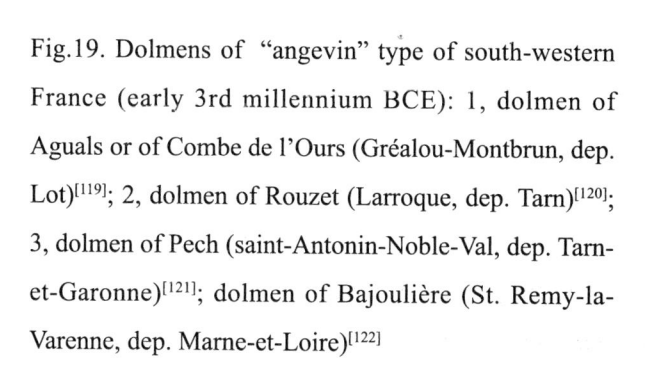

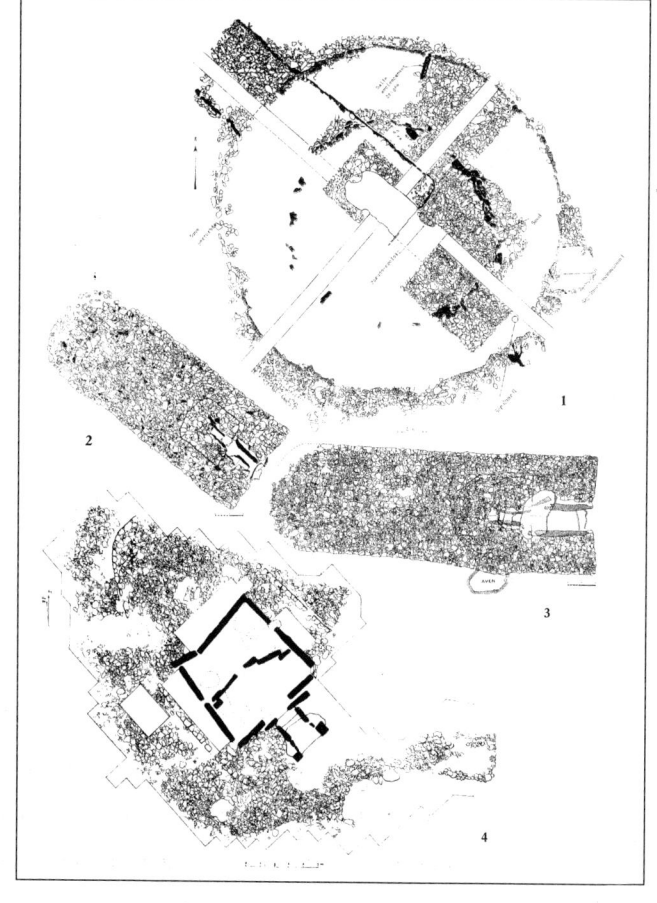

Fig.19. Dolmens of "angevin" type of south-western France (early 3rd millennium BCE): 1, dolmen of Aguals or of Combe de l'Ours (Gréalou-Montbrun, dep. Lot)[119]; 2, dolmen of Rouzet (Larroque, dep. Tarn)[120]; 3, dolmen of Pech (saint-Antonin-Noble-Val, dep. Tarn-et-Garonne)[121]; dolmen of Bajoulière (St. Remy-la-Varenne, dep. Marne-et-Loire)[122]

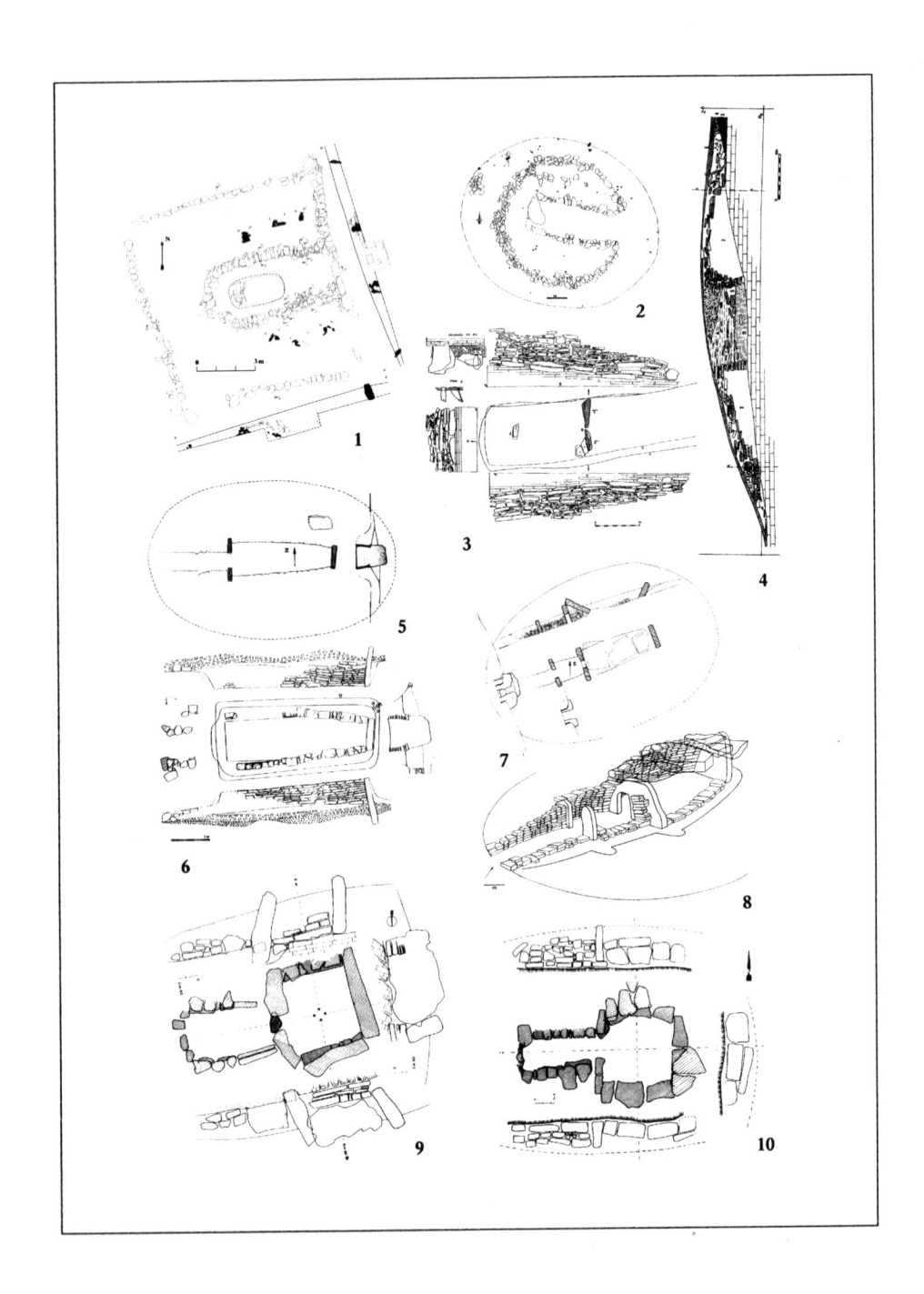

Fig.20. Chemurchek barrow and "chamber tombs with dry-stone side-walls" of southern France: 1, barrow 3 of Aina-Bulak I Chemurchek cemetery; 2-4, Dolmen de Souillac (dep. Lot)[123]; 5-6, dolmen de Coutinargues (Fonteville, dep. Buches-du-Rhône)[124]; 7-8, dolmen du Pouget (dep. Hérault)[125]; 9, dolmen de Peygros (Mons, dep. Var)[126]; 10, dolmen du Caillassoux (Saint-Vallier-de-Thiey, dep. Alpes-Maritimes)[127]

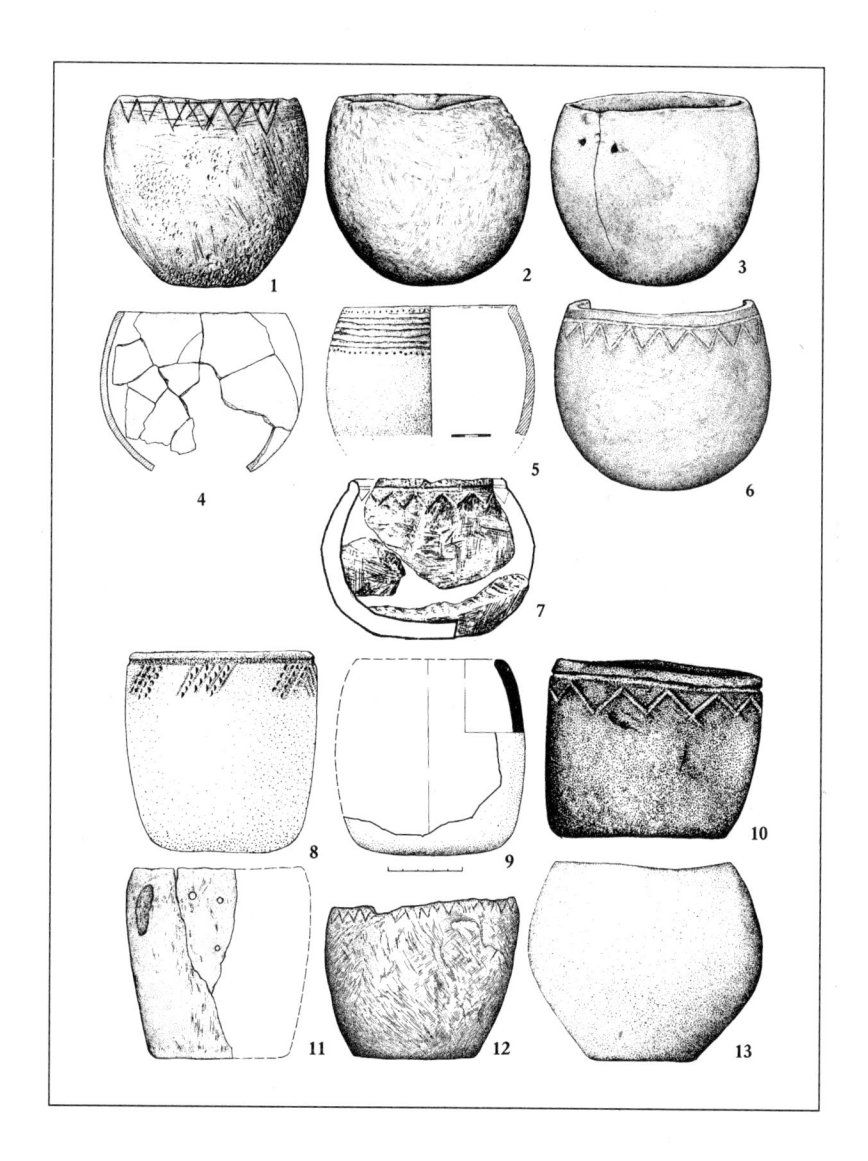

Fig.21. Chemurchek stone (1-3, 7, 10-12) and earthware (4-6, 8, 9, 13) vessels: 1, Shar Sum I, barrow 1 (Khovd Sum, Khovd Aimag, Mongolia)[128]; 2, Mulei County Museum (Xinjiang) (courtesy of Shui Tao); 3, "Ke'ermuqi" (Qiemuerqieke) cemetery, barrow M2, stone box 1[129]; 4, Yagshiin Khodoo barrow 1 (Bulgan Sum, Khovd Aimag, Mongolia); 5, Ulaan Khudag II, barrow 3 (Khovd Sum, Khovd Aimag)[130]; 6, Kuxicun (Aweitan township, Altay Shi, Xinjiang)[131]; 7, Ulaan Khudag I, barrow 12 (Khovd Sum, Khovd Aimag, Mongolia)[132]; 8, "Ke'ermuqi" (Qiemuerqieke) cemetery, barrow M7, stone box 1[133]; 9, "Ke'ermuqi" (Qiemuerqieke) cemetery, barrow M2, stone box 1 (Museum of the Institute of Archaeology and Cultural Heritage of Xinjiang, drawing by A.Kovalev); 10, Bural Kharyn Ar (Bulgan Sum, Khovd Aimag, Mongolia); 11, Yagshiin Khodoo barrow 2 (Bulgan Sum, Khovd Aimag, Mongolia); 12, Kheviin Am barrow 1 (Bulgan Sum, Khovd Aimag, Mongolia); 13, Khalzan-uzuur II barrow 4 (Khovd Sum, Khovd Aimag, Mongolia) (courtesy of A.A.Tishkin, D. Erdenebaatar)

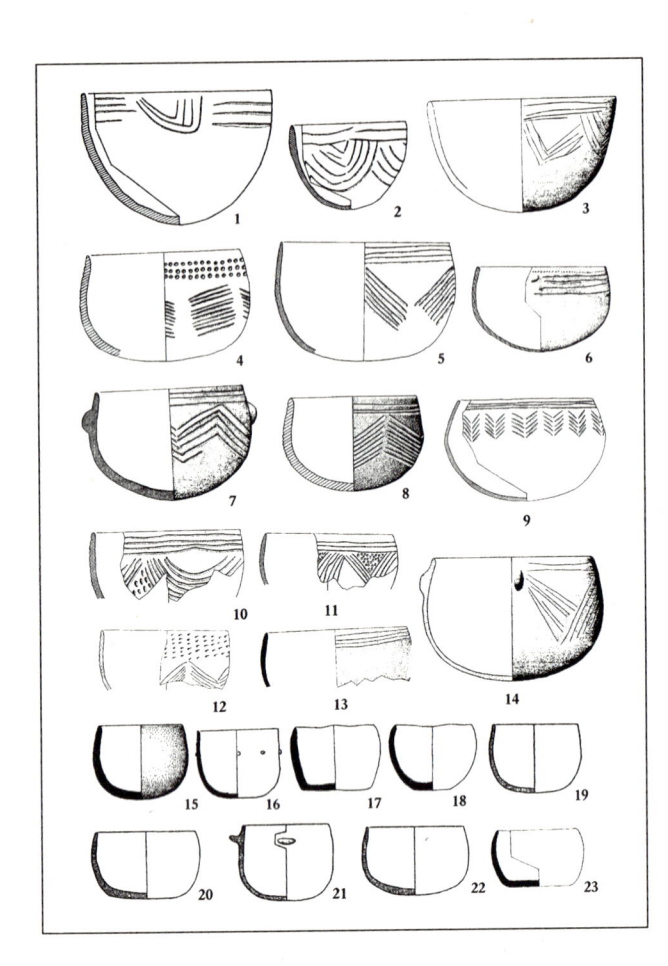

Fig.22. Pottery of Ferrieres culture: 15, hypogee of Crottes (Roaix, Vaucluse)[134]; 17, 18, and 23, grotte du Pins (Blandas, dep. Gard)[135]. Others by X. Gutherz[136]

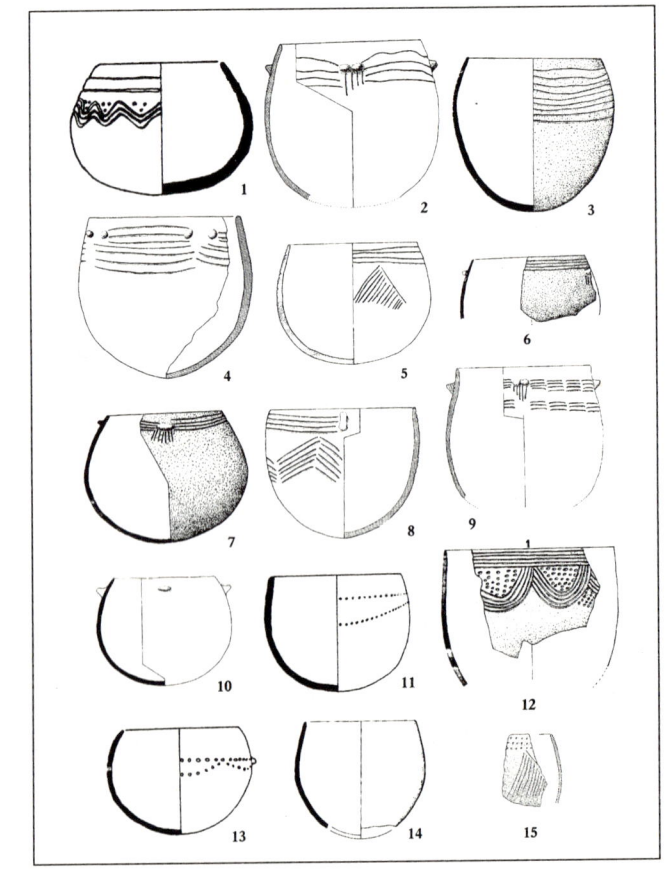

Fig.23. Pottery of Ferrieres culture: 10, grotte du Pins (Blandas, dep. Gard)[137]; 14, site de la Roquette (Tresques, dep. Gard)[138]. Others by X. Gutherz[139]

Fig.24. Late Neolithic pottery of Brittany: 1 and 5, cairn de Ty-Floc'h (Saint-Thois, dep. Finistère)[140]; 2-4, cairn de Île Carn (dep. Finistère)[141]; 10 and 18, gallery grave de Bilgroix (Arzon, dep. Morbihan)[142]. Others by R. Polles[143]: 6, Champ-Grosset (Qessoy); 7 and 17, dolmen de Conguel (Quiberon); 8 and 9, La Ville-Drun (Plestan); 11, Cercado (Carnac); 12-13, Er-Yoh (Houat); 14, Butten-er-Hah (Groix); 15, dolmen south of Mané-Meur (Quiberon); 16, Le Rocher (Le Bono); 19, Port-Blanc (Saint-Pierre-Quiberon)

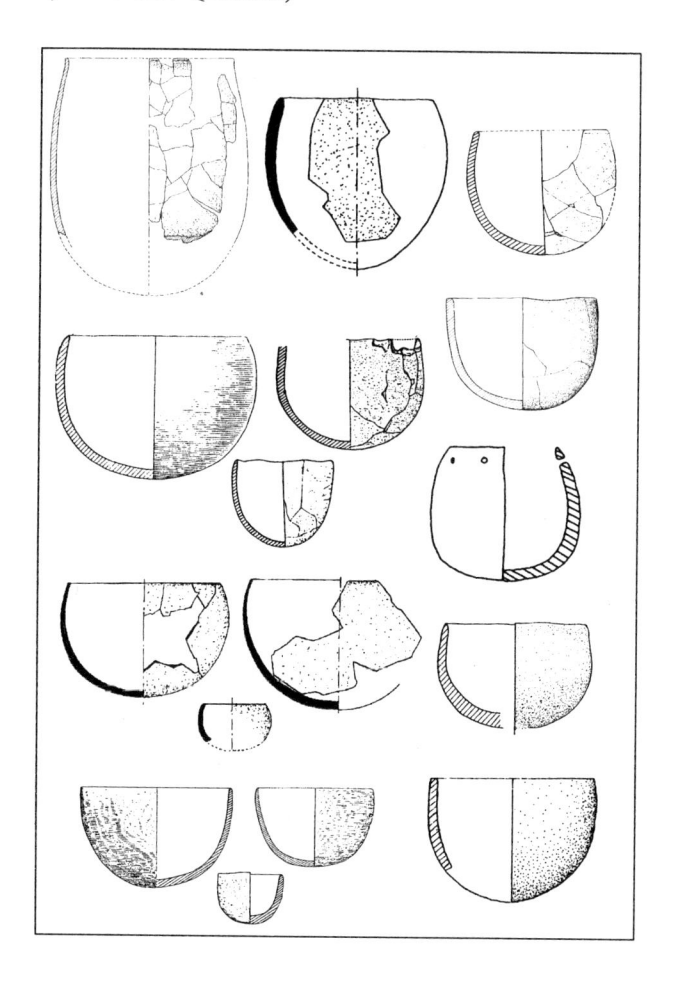

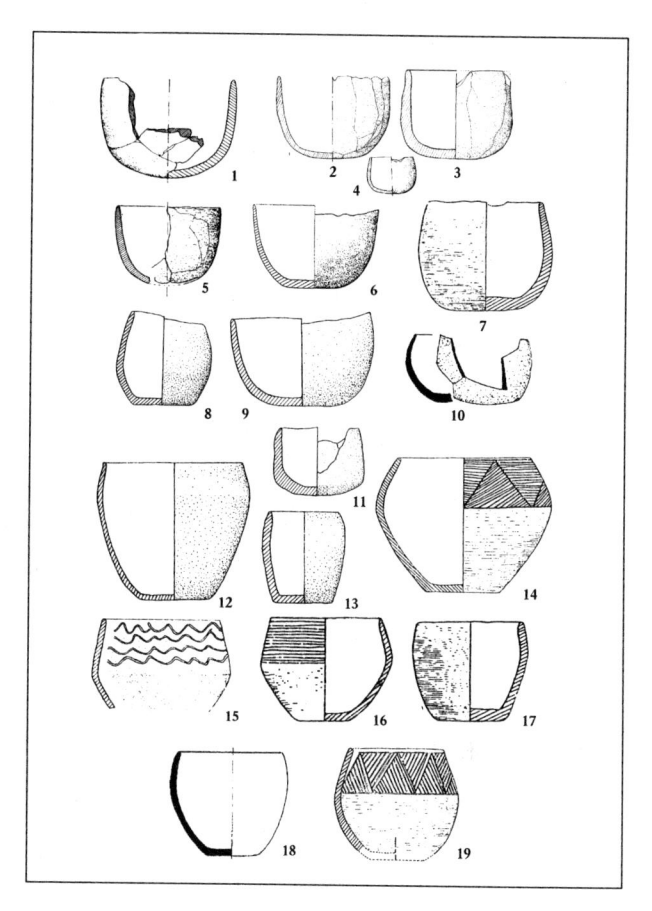

Fig.25. Late Neolithic pottery of Brittany: 1, cairn 1 of "Min goh Ru" near Larcuste (Colpo, dep. Morbihan)[144]; 2, dolmen of cairn 2 of Petit-Mont (Arzon, dep. Morbihan)[145]; 3, cairn of Kerleven (Forêt-Fouesnant, dep. Finistère)[146]; 7, cairn de Barnenez (Plouézoch, dep. Finistère)[147]; 8, Men-ar-Romped (Lannon, Côtes-d'Armor)[148]; 9-11, gallery grave of Bilgroix (Arzon, dep. Morbihan)[149]. Others by R. Polles[150]: 4-6, Qrec'h-quillé (Saint-Quay-Perros); 12, Bilgroez (Arzon, dep. Morbihan); 13-15, dolmen de Conguel (Quiberon); 16, Er-Yoh (Houat)

— 033 —

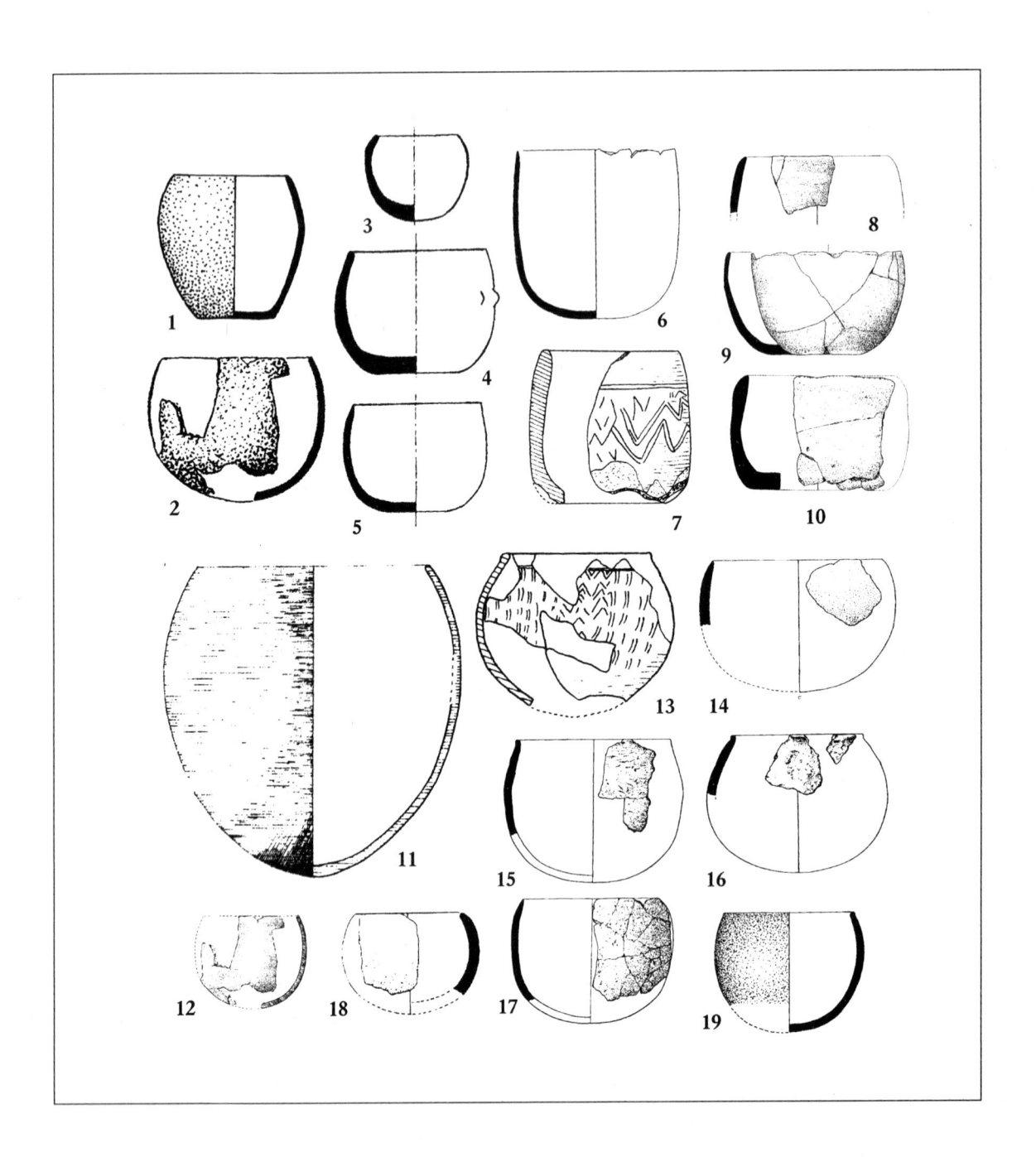

Fig.26. Middle and Late Neolithic pottery from Poitou: 1, dolmen E 136 de Monpalais (Taize, dep. Deux Sèvres)[151]; 2, grotte del Bellefonds (Vienne)[152]; 3-5, dolmens of Chenon (dep. Charente) (3, 4-dolmen A1, 5-dolmen A6)[153]; 6, Fontrèal (Castelnau-d'Estrétefonds, dep. Haute-Garonne)[154]; 7, Peu-Richard (Thénac (dep. Charente-Maritime)[155]; 8-10, Saintonge (Charente)[156]; 11-12, Abri de Bellefonds[157]; 13, Chaillot à la Jard (dep. Charente-Maritime)[158]; 14, tumulus du Pey de Fontaine (Bernard, dep. Vendée)[159]; 15-17, Roquefort (Charente-Maritime)[160]; 18, Le Camp des Prises (Mâchekoul)[161]; 19, tumulus "Ciste des Cous" (Bazoges-en-Pareds, dep. Vendée)[162]

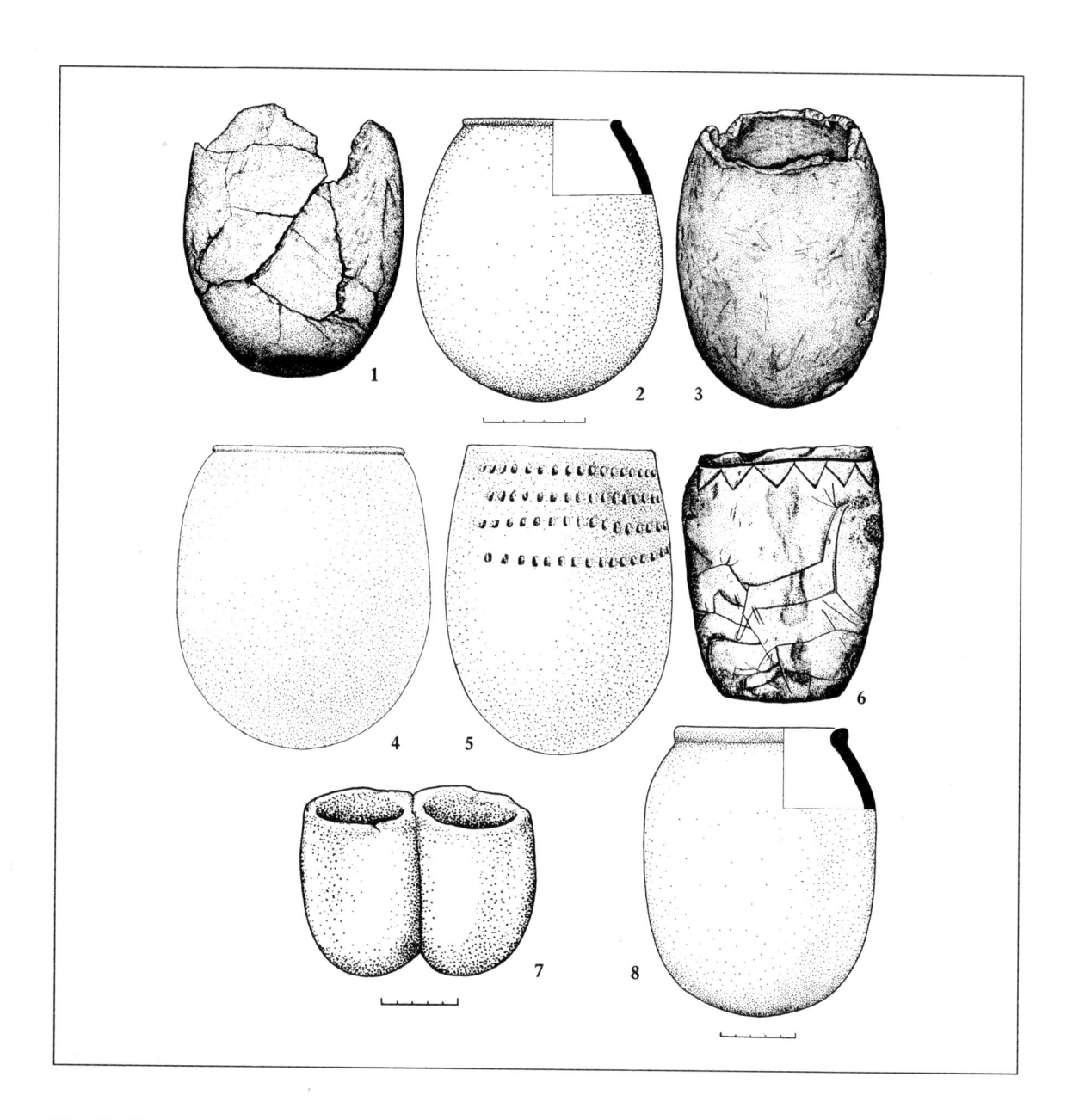

Fig.27. Chemurchek stone (2-4, 6-8) and earthware (1, 5) vessels: 1, Ulaan Khudag I, barrow 12 (Khovd Sum, Khovd Aimag, Mongolia)[163]; 2, "Ke'ermuqi" (Qiemuerqieke) cemetery, barrow M7, stone box 2 (Museum of the Institute of Archaeology and Cultural Heritage of Xinjiang, drawing by A.Kovalev); 3, Hanasi County Museum (Xinjiang) (courtesy of Shui Tao); 4-5, "Ke'ermuqi" (Qiemuerqieke) cemetery, barrow M16 (4 after [164], 5, Museum of the Institute of Archaeology and Cultural Heritage of Xinjiang, drawing by A.Kovalev); 6, Laptev Log (Uglovo district, Altai region, Russia)[165]; 7, "Ke'ermuqi" (Qiemuerqieke) cemetery, barrow M3, stone box[166]; 8, "Ke'ermuqi" (Qiemuerqieke) cemetery, barrow M8, stone box[167]

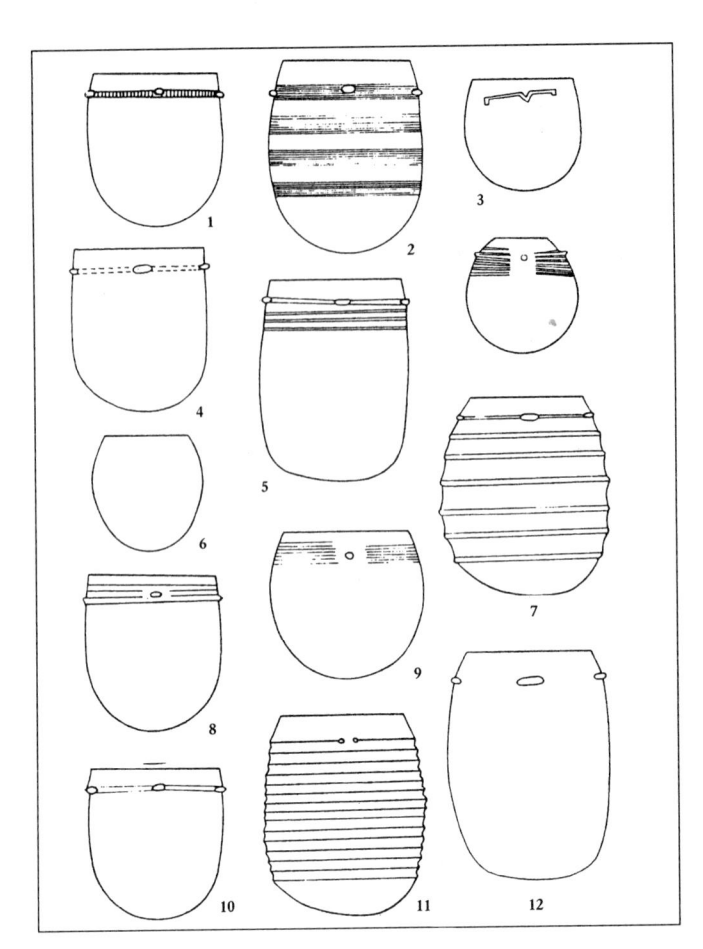

Fig.28. Pottery of Ferrieres culture from Ardeché valley (Gard)[168]

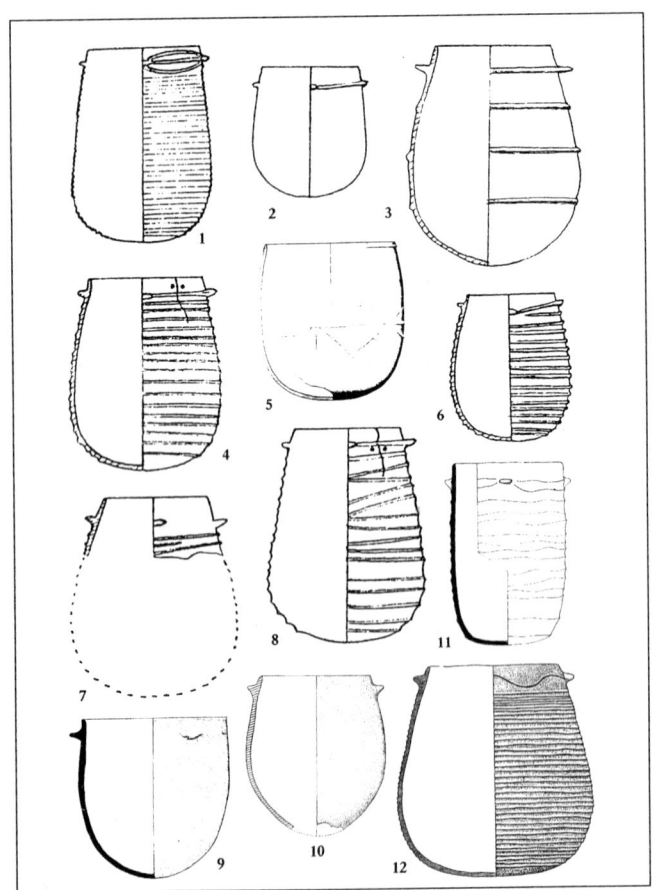

Fig.29. Pottery of Ferrieres culture[169]

— 036 —

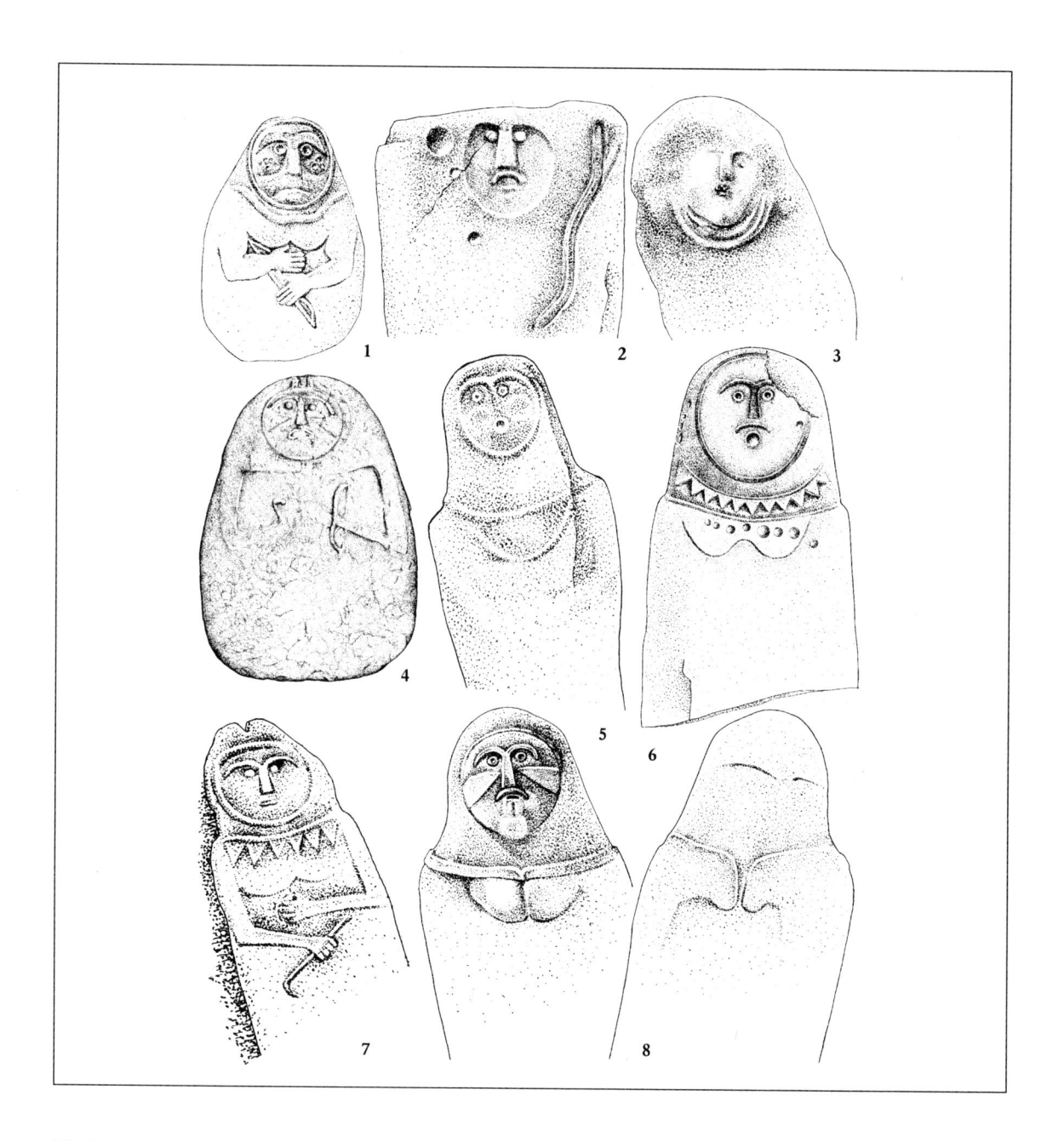

Fig.30. Stone statues of Chemurchek culture: 1, Kekeshemulaokemuqi 2 (nearby barrow of "Bulgan type" with stone box) (Qiemuerqieke township, Altai county, Xinjiang)[170]; 2-3, Kanatas (by the eastern side of square stone fence with cairn inside) (Qiemuerqieke township, Altai county, Xinjiang)[171]; 4, Yagshiin Khodoo barrow 3 (Bulgan Sum, Khovd Aimag, Mongolia); 5, Kekeshemulaokemuqi 1(Qiemuerqieke township, Altai county, Xinjiang)[172]; 6, Kayinarl 2 No 2 (by the eastern side of barrow M2 "Ke'ermuqi" (Qiemuerqieke) cemetery) (Qiemuerqieke township, Altai county, Xinjiang)[173]; 7, Wuqiubulak (Burjin county, Xinjiang)[174]; 8, Kayinarl 1 (Ke'ermuqi 6 by Li Zheng) (by the eastern side of rectangular stone fence enclosing cairn) (Qiemuerqieke township, Altai county, Xinjiang)[175]

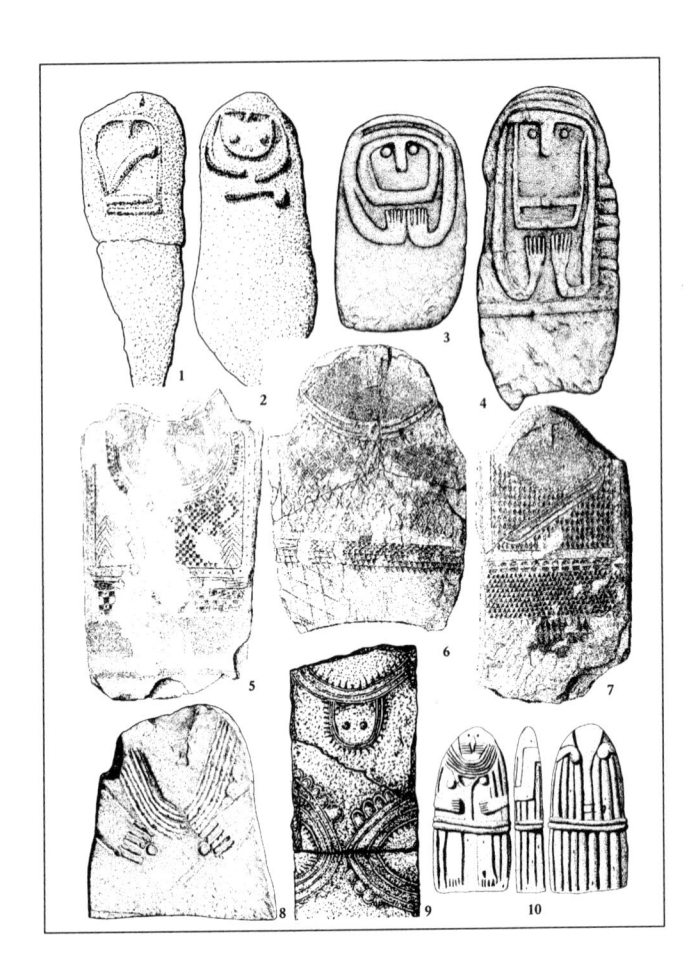

Fig.31. West European stone statues (early 3rd millennium BCE): 1, Aven Meunier I (dep. Gard)[176]; 2, Collorgues I (dep. Gard)[177]; 3, dep. Gard[178]; 4, Maison-Aube (Montagnac, dep. Gard)[179]; 5-7, Petit-Chasseur (Sion, Valais, Switzerland)[180]; 8, Craïs (Brousse-le Château, dep. Aveyron)[181]; 9, stele de Passanant (Tarragona)[182]; 10, "la Dame de Saint-Sernin" (Saint-Sernin-sur-Rance, dep. Aveyron)[183]

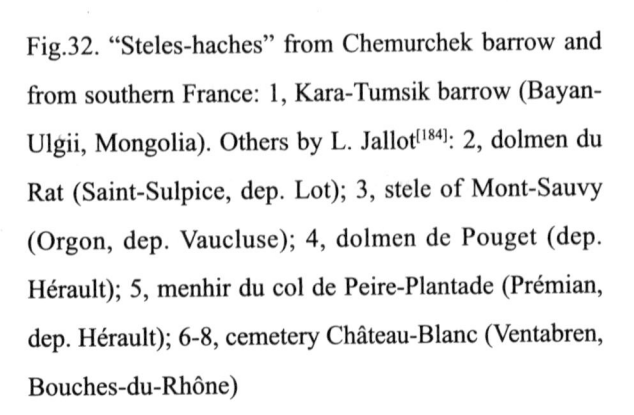

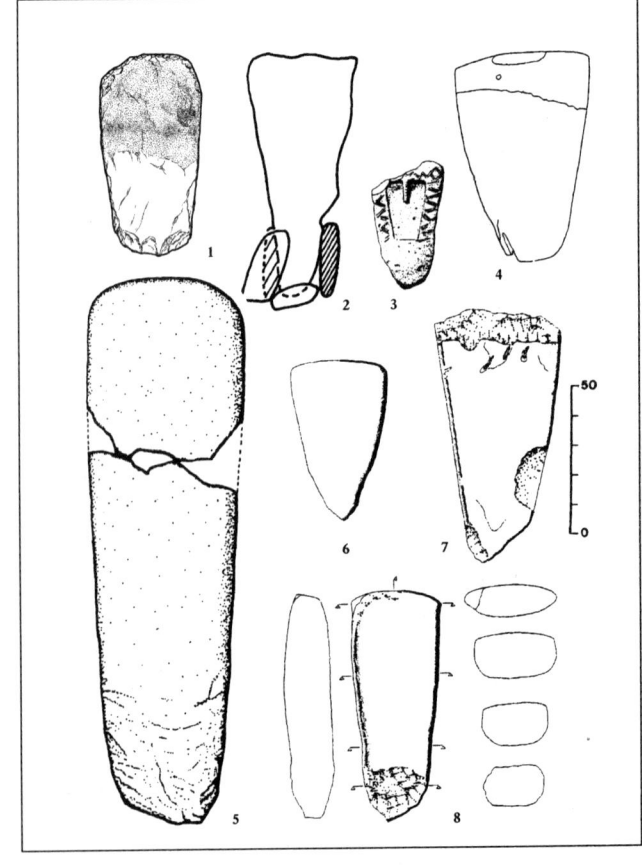

Fig.32. "Steles-haches" from Chemurchek barrow and from southern France: 1, Kara-Tumsik barrow (Bayan-Ulgii, Mongolia). Others by L. Jallot[184]: 2, dolmen du Rat (Saint-Sulpice, dep. Lot); 3, stele of Mont-Sauvy (Orgon, dep. Vaucluse); 4, dolmen de Pouget (dep. Hérault); 5, menhir du col de Peire-Plantade (Prémian, dep. Hérault); 6-8, cemetery Château-Blanc (Ventabren, Bouches-du-Rhône)

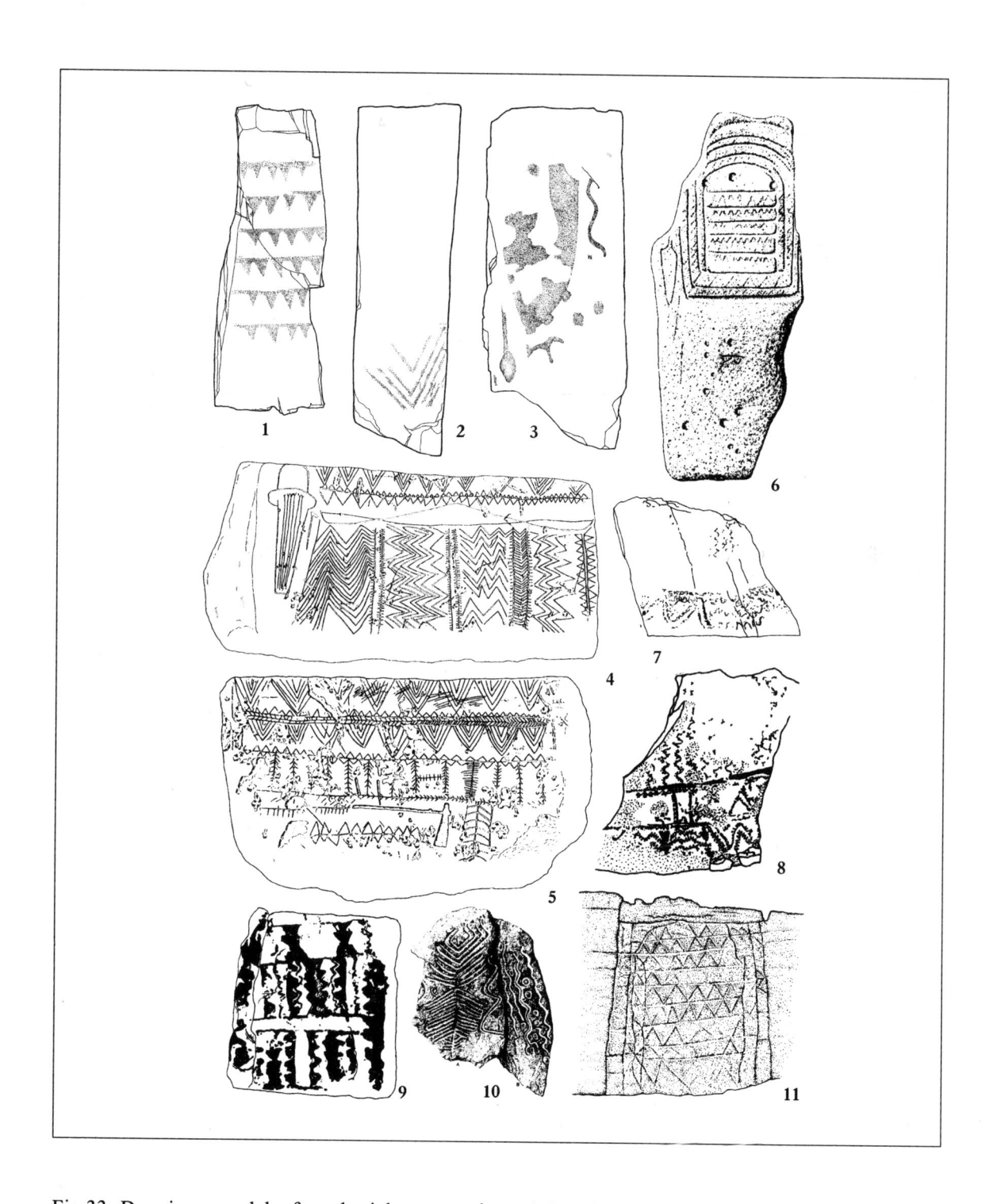

Fig.33. Drawings on slabs from burial constructions: 1-3, ochre drawings on slab stones from burial chamber of Yagshiin Khodoo barrow 3 (Khovd Aimag, Mongolia); 4-5, Göhlitzsch (Leuna, Landkreis Merseburg-Querfurt, Germany)[185]; 6, stele of Sejos (Cantabria, Spain)[186]; 7-8, Galicia, Spain[187]; 9, Pedralta or Cota (Concelho Viseu, distr. Viseu, Spain)[188]; 10, Serém de Cima (Concelho Sever do Vouga, distr. Aveiro, Spain)[189]; 11, stele of Garabandal (Cantabria, Spain)[190]

Notes

[1] Li Zheng 李證, "Altay diqu shiren mu diaocha jianbao" 阿勒泰地區石人墓調查簡報, *Wenwu* 文物, 1962:7-8, pp.103-108.

[2] Xinjiang Shehui Kexueyuan Kaogu Yanjiusuo 新疆社會科學院考古研究所, "Xinjiang Ke'ermuqi gumu fajue jianbao" 新疆克爾木齊古墓發掘簡報, *Wenwu*《文物》, 1981:1, pp.23-32.

[3] Wang Linshan 王林山 and Wang Bo 王博, *Zhongguo Aletai Caoyuan Wenwu* 中國阿勒泰草原文物 (Shenzhen: 1996).

[4] Xinjiang Shehui Kexueyuan Kaogu Yanjiusuo 新疆社會科學院考古研究所, "Xinjiang Ke'ermuqi gumu fajue jianbao" 新疆克爾木齊古墓發掘簡報, *Wenwu*《文物》, 1981:1, pp.23-32.

[5] Wang Bo 王博 and Qi Xiaoshan 祁小山, *Sichouzhilu Caoyuan Shiren Yanjiu*《絲綢之路草原石人研究》(Urumqi: 1996), pp.153-215.

[6] Debaine-Francfort C., "Archéologie du Xinjiang des origines aux Han: IIeme partie", *Paléorient*, 1989, v. 15/1, 183-213: 197-198.

[7] Chen Ge 陳戈, "Xinjiang kaogu yuangu wenhua chulun" 新疆考古遠古文化初論, *Zhongya Xuekan*《中亞學刊》, 1995, vol. 4, pp.6-72: 38.

[8] Литвинский Б.А., "Могильники Или-Казахского автономного округа. Каменные изваяния", *Восточный Туркестан в древности и раннем средневековье. Хозяйство, материальная культура* (Москва:1995), *Глава 4. Погребальные памятники*, pp.297-302: 299-300.

[9] Худяков Ю.С., «Древнетюркские изваяния из Восточного Туркестана», *Древние культуры Центральной Азии и Санкт-Петербург. Материалы всероссийской научной конференции, посвященной 70-летию со дня рождения Александра Даниловича Грача. Декабрь 1998 года* (Санкт-Петербург: 1998), 215-219: 218; Худяков Ю.С., Комиссаров С.А., «*Кочевая цивилизация Восточного Туркестана*» (Новосибирск: 2002), 92-96.

[10] Xinjiang Shehui Kexueyuan Kaogu Wenwu Yanjiusuo 新疆社會科學院考古文物研究所, *Xinjiang Gudai Minzu Wenwu*《新疆古代民族文物》(Urumqi: 1985): 4.

[11] Wang Bo 王博, "Qiemuerqieke wenhua chutan: Kaogu wenwu yanjiu" 切木爾切克文化初探：考古文物研究, *Xibei Daxue Kaogu Zhuanye Chengli Sishi Zhounian Wenji, 1956-1996*《西北大學考古專業成立四十周年文集（1956-1996）》(Xi'an: 1996), pp.274-285.

[12] Wang Linshan 王林山 and Wang Bo 王博, *Zhongguo Aletai Caoyuan Wenwu*《中國阿勒泰草原文物》(Shenzhen: 1996), p.89.

[13] Заднепровский Ю.А. "Культурные связи населения эпохи бронзы и раннего железа Южной Сибири и Синьцзяна", *Проблемы культурогенеза и культурное наследие. Часть II. Археология и изучение культурных процессов и явлений* (Санкт-Петербург: 1993): 99; Семенов Вл.А., «Древнейшая

миграция индоевропейцев на Восток (К столетию открытия тохарских рукописей)», *Петербургский археологический вестник*, Вып. 8 (Санкт-Петербург: 1993), 25-30: 26; Молодин В.И., Алкин С.В., «Могильник Гумугоу (Синьцзян) в контексте афанасьевской проблемы»б *Гуманитарные исследования: итоги последних лет. Сборник тезисов научной конференции к 35-летию гуманитарного факультета НГУ.* (Новосибирск: 1997), 35-39: 38.

[14] Kovalev A., "Die ältesten Stelen am Ertix. Das Kulturphänomen Xemirxek.", *Eurasia Antiqua* 5, 1999 (Berlin: 2000), 135-178.

[15] Варенов А.В., "Южносибирские культуры эпохи ранней и поздней бронзы в Восточном Туркестане", *Гуманитарные науки в Сибири*, 1998, №3, 60-72 (*Серия: Археология и этнография*).

[16] Kovalev A., "Die ältesten Stelen am Ertix. Das Kulturphänomen Xemirxek.", *Eurasia Antiqua* 5, 1999 (Berlin: 2000), 135-178: 140-141.

[17] Kovalev A., "Die ältesten Stelen am Ertix. Das Kulturphänomen Xemirxek.", *Eurasia Antiqua* 5, 1999 (Berlin: 2000), 135-178: 160.

[18] Kovalev A., "Die ältesten Stelen am Ertix. Das Kulturphänomen Xemirxek.", *Eurasia Antiqua* 5, 1999 (Berlin: 2000), 135-178:150, 152, 157, 167.

[19] Кирюшин Ю.Ф., Симонов Е.Н., "Каменный сосуд из Угловского района", *Сохранение и изучение культурного наследия Алтайского края. Материалы научно-практической конференции. Выпуск VIII* (Барнаул: 1997), 167-171. Кирюшин Ю.Ф., *Энеолит и ранняя бронза юга Западной Сибири (*Барнаул: 2002): 58-59.

[20] Кубарев В.Д., *Древние изваяния Алтая. Оленные камни.* (Новосибирск: 1979): 8-10; Кубарев В.Д., *Древние росписи Каракола* (Новосибирск: 1988): 88-90.

[21] Lin Meicun 林梅村, "Tuhuoluoren de qiyuan yu qiantu" 吐火羅人的起源與遷徙, *Xinjiang Wenwu*《新疆文物》, 2002: 3-4, pp.69-82.

[22] Shui Tao 水濤, "Xinjiang qingtong shidai zhu wenhua de bijiao yanjiu: Fulun zaoqi zhong-xi wenhua jiaoliu de lishi jincheng" 新疆青銅時代諸文化的比較研究——附論早期中西文化交流的歷史進程, in Shui Tao, *Zhongguo Xibei Diqu Qingtong Shidai Kaogu Lunji*《中國西北地方青銅時代考古論集》, 水濤著 (Beijing: Science Press 科學出版社, 2001), pp.6-47.

[23] Zhang Yuzhong 張玉忠, "Burjin faxian de caihui shiguan mu" 布林津發現的彩繪石棺墓, *Xinjiang Wenwu* 新疆文物, 2005:1, pp.124-125.

[24] Lin Yun 林沄, "Guanyu Xinjiang beibu Qiermuqieke leixing yicun de jige wenti: Cong Burjin xian chutu de taoqi shuoqi" 關於新疆北部切爾木切克類型遺存的幾個問題——從布林津縣出土的陶器說起, *Qingzhu He Bingdi Xiansheng Jiushi Huachen Lunwenji* Editorial Committee《慶祝何炳棣先生九十華誕論文集》編輯委員會 ed., *Qingzhu He Bingdi Xiansheng Jiushi Huachen Lunwenji*《慶祝何炳棣先生九十華誕論文集》(Xi'an: Sanqin Chubanshe 三秦出版社, 2008), pp.717-733.

[25] Svyatko S.V., Mallory J.P., Murphy E.M., Polyakov A.V., Reimer P.J., Schulting R.J., "New radiocarbon dates and a review of the chronology of prehistoric populations from the Minusinsk Basin, Southern Siberia, Russia", *Radiocarbon*, Vol.51, No.1, 2009, pp.243-273: Fig.7.

[26] Kovalev A., "Die ältesten Stelen am Ertix. Das Kulturphänomen Xemirxek", *Eurasia Antiqua* 5, 1999 (Berlin: 2000), pp.135-178; Ковалев А.А., "Чемурческий культурный феномен: его происхождение и роль в формировании культур эпохи ранней бронзы Алтая и Центральной Азии", *Западная и Южная Сибирь в древности. Сборник научных трудов, посвященный 60-летию со дня рождения Юрия Федоровича Кирюшина* (Барнаул: 2005), 178-184; Ковалев А.А., "Чемурческий культурный феномен (статья 1999 года)", *«А.В.». Сборник научных трудов в честь 60-летия А.В. Виноградова* (Санкт-Петербург: 2007), 25-76.

[27] Кирюшин Ю.Ф., *Энеолит и ранняя бронза юга Западной Сибири* (Барнаул: 2002); Кирюшин Ю.Ф., Грушин С.П., Тишкин А.А., *Погребальный обряд населения эпохи ранней бронзы Верхнего Приобья (по материалам грунтового могильника Телеутский Взвоз I)* (Барнаул: 2003); Кирюшин Ю.Ф., Малолетко А.М., Тишкин А.А., *Березовая Лука-поселение эпохи бронзы в Алейской степи. Т 1* (Барнаул: 2005); Кирюшин Ю.Ф., Грушин С.П., Папин Д.В., "Проблемы радиоуглеродного датирования археологических памятников бронзового века Алтая", *Теория и практика археологических исследований: сборник научных трудов / отв. ред. А.А. Тишкин* (Барнаул : Изд-во Алт. ун-та, 2007), Вып. 3, 84-88.

[28] A.A.Kovalev 科瓦列夫, Д. Erdenebaatar 額爾德涅巴特爾, "Menggu qingtong shidai wenhua de xin faxian" 蒙古青銅時代文化的新發現, *Bianjiang Kaogu Yanjiu*《邊疆考古研究》, vol.8, 2009.

[29] Кирюшин Ю.Ф., Малолетко А. М., Тишкин А.А. *Березовая Лука-поселение эпохи бронзы в Алейской степи. Т 1* (Барнаул: 2005), 195-199.

[30] Семенов Вл. А., "Окуневские памятники Тувы и Минусинской котловины (сравнительная характеристика и хронология)", *Окуневский сборник. Культура. Искусство. Антропология* (Санкт-Петербург: 1997), 152-160: 157-158; Лазаретов И.П., "Окуневские могильники в долине реки Уйбат", *Окуневский сборник. Культура. Искусство. Антропология* (Санкт-Петербург: 1997), 19-64: 31-36; Леонтьев С. Н. "К вопросу о керамической традиции окуневской культуры Среднего Енисея", *Окуневский сборник 2. Культура и ее окружение* (Санкт-Петербург: 2006), 260-272.

[31] Ковалев А.А., Эрдэнэбаатар Д., Зайцева Г.И., Бурова Н.Д., "Радиоуглеродное датирование курганов Монгольского Алтая, исследованных Международной Центральноазиатской археологической экспедицией, и его значение для хронологического и типологического упорядочения памятников бронзового века Центральной Азии", *Древние и средневековые кочевники Центральной Азии* (Барнаул: 2008), 172-186: 173; A. A.Kovalev 科瓦列夫, Д. Erdenebaatar 額爾德涅巴特爾, "Menggu qingtong shidai wenhua de xin faxian" 蒙古青銅時代文化的新發現, *Bianjiang Kaogu Yanjiu*《邊疆考古研究》, vol.8,

2009, tables 1, 2.

[32] Тишкин А.А., Грушин С.П., Мунхбаяр Ч., "Археологическое изучение объектов эпохи бронзы в урочище Улаан худаг (Ховдский аймак Монголии)", *Теория и практика археологических исследований,* Выпуск 4, 2008, 85-92: фото 17, 18.

[33] See Wang Bo 王博 and Qi Xiaoshan 祁小山, *Sichouzhilu Caoyuan Shiren Yanjiu* 絲綢之路草原石人研究 (Urumqi: 1996): stone figures (*shiren* 石人) Eanos.1-7, 14, 16-18, 20, 22, 23, 26-28, 30, 31, 34, 38, 41-46, 49, 50; Kovalev A., "Die ältesten Stelen am Ertix. Das Kulturphänomen Xemirxek", *Eurasia Antiqua* 5, 1999 (Berlin: 2000), 135-178: Tab. 3-8.

[34] Wang Linshan 王林山 and Wang Bo 王博, *Zhongguo Aletai Caoyuan Wenwu* 中國阿勒泰草原文物 (Shenzhen: 1996), p.47, figs.100, 101; Kovalev A., "Die ältesten Stelen am Ertix. Das Kulturphänomen Xemirxek ", *Eurasia Antiqua* 5, 1999 (Berlin: 2000), 135-178.: 145.

[35] The statue from Samute barrow was published in Wang Linshan 王林山 and Wang Bo 王博, *Zhongguo Aletai Caoyuan Wenwu* 《中國阿勒泰草原文物》(Shenzhen: 1996), p.37, fig.65; 王博, 祁小山, 絲綢之路草原石人研究 (烏魯木齊 : 1996): 石人 no. 161-Ea-6, 163 頁 .

[36] Кирюшин Ю.Ф., Тишкин А.А., "Находки свинца при исследованиях памятников эпохи ранней бронзы и свидетельства их производства в предгорно-равнинной части Алтайского края", *300 лет горно-геологической службе России. История горнорудного дела, геологическое строение и полезные ископаемые Алтая* (Барнаул: 2000), 8-12.

[37] Ковалев А.А., Эрдэнэбаатар Д., Зайцева Г.И., Бурова Н.Д., "Радиоуглеродное датирование курганов Монгольского Алтая, исследованных Международной Центральноазиатской археологической экспедицией, и его значение для хронологического и типологического упорядочения памятников бронзового века Центральной Азии", *Древние и средневековые кочевники Центральной Азии* (Барнаул: 2008), 172-186: 173; A. A.Kovalev 科瓦列夫, Д. Erdenebaatar 額爾德涅巴特爾, "Menggu qingtong shidai wenhua de xin faxian" 蒙古青銅時代文化的新發現, *Bianjiang Kaogu Yanjiu*《邊疆考古研究》, vol.8, 2009, table 3.

[38] Ковалев А.А., "Чемурчекский культурный феномен: его происхождение и роль в формировании культур эпохи ранней бронзы Алтая и Центральной Азии", *Западная и Южная Сибирь в древности. Сборник научных трудов, посвященный 60-летию со дня рождения Юрия Федоровича Кирюшина* (Барнаул : Изд-во Алт. гос. ун-та. 2005), 178-184: 179-180; Ковалев А.А. "Чемурчекский феномен как продукт эволюции мегалитов Атлантического побережья Франции (по материалам радиоуглеродного датирования мегалитических гробниц Западной Европы и памятников чемурчекской культуры)", *Роль естественно-научных методов в археологических исследованиях. Сборник научных трудов* (Барнаул: Изд-во Алт. ГУ, 2009), 130-140.

[39] Куликов Е.Е., Кирюшин Ю.Ф., Серегин Ю.А., Тишкин А.А., Полтараус А.Б., "Результаты палеогенетических исследований (по материалам погребений младенцев на памятнике Березовая

Лука)", *Кирюшин Ю.Ф., Малолетко А.М., Тишкин А.А. Березовая Лука-поселение эпохи бронзы в Алейской степи. Т 1*(Барнаул: 2005), 216-224: 222.

[40] Briard J., "Les tertres tumulaires néolithiques de Bretagne interieure", *Actes du 17e Colloque Interrégional sur le Néolithique, Vannes, 1990* (Rennes: 1992), 55-62 (Revue archéologique de l'Ouest, Supplément no.5); Patton M., *Statements in Stone: Monuments and Society in Neolithic Brittany* (London-New York: 1993), pp.48-56; L'Helgoulac'h J., "Les groupes humaines du Ve au IIIe millénaire", *Préhistoire de la Bretagne* (Rennes: Éditions Ouest-France, 1998), 231-427: 330-336; Le Roux Ch.-T., *Les mégalithes et les tumulus de Saint-Just* (Paris: 1995), 45-47 ; Joussaume R., Laporte L., "Monuments funéraires néolitiques dans l'ouest de la France", *Origine et développement du mégalithisme de l'ouest de l'Europe. Actes du colloque international, 26-30 octobre 2002, Bougon (France) / Joussaume R., Laporte L., Scarre C.-dir. 2 vols.* (Niort: 2006), 319-343: 322-330.

[41] L'Helgouac'h J., "The megalithic culture of Western France: Continuity and change in extraordinary architecture", *Studien zur Megalithik-Forschungsstand und ethnoarchäologische Perspektiven / Beinhauer K.W., Cooney G., Gucjsch Ch.E., Kus S. (Hrsg.) (Beiträge zur Ur-und Frügeschichte Mitteleuropas 21)* (Mannheim-Weissbach: 1999), 133-141.

[42] Le Roux Ch.-T., L'Helgouac'h J., "Le cairn mégalithique avec sépultures à chambres comparatimenteés", *Annales de Bretagne*, T. LXXIV, 1967, Num. 1, 7-52; L'Helgouac'h J., "Le tumulus de Dissignac à Saint-Nazaire (Loire-Atlantique) et les problèmes du contact entre le phénomene mégalithique et les sociétés à industrie microlithique", *Acculturation and Continuity in Atlantic Europe mainly during the Neolithic period and the Bronze Age: Papers presented at the IV Atlantic Colloquium, Ghent 1975 / Edited by S. J. De Laet (Dissertationes archaeologicae gandenses. Vol. XVI)* (Brugge: De Tempel, 1976), 142-149; L'Helgouac'h J., Lecornec J., "Le site mégalithique "Min goh Ru" prés de Larcuste à Colpo (Morbihan)", *Bulletin de la Société préhistorique française*, T. 73, 1976, 370-397; Le Roux Ch.-T., Lecerf Y., "Le dolmen de Cruguellic en Plœmeur et les sépultures transeptées armoricaines", *L'Architecture mégalithique: Colloque du 150e anniversaire de la Société Polymathique du Morbihan* (Vannes: 1977), 143-160; Joussaume R., "Le dolmen à couloir dit "la Ciste des Cous" à Bazoges-en-Pareds (Vendée)", *Bulletin de la Société préhistorique française*, T. 75, 1978, No 11-12, 579-596; Germond G., Joussaume R., Bizard M., "Le Tumulus du Montiou à Sainte-Soline (Deux-Sévres): Premières campagnes de fouilles (Premier bilan)", *Bulletin de la Société Historique et Scientifique des Deux-Sévres*, T. XI, No 2-3, 1978, 129-188; Le Roux Ch.-T., Lecerf Y., "Le cairn de Ty-Floc'h à saint-Thois (fouilles de 1978-1979)", *Bulletin de la Société archéologique du Finistére*, Vol. 108, 1980, 27-49; L'Helgouac'h J., Poulain H., "Le cairn des Mousseaux à Pornic et les tombes mégalithiques transeptées de l'estuaire de la Loire", *Revue archéologique de l'Ouest*, 1984, № 1, 15-32; Le Roux Ch.-T., *Les mégalithes et les tumulus de Saint-Just*. (Paris: 1995): 38-47; L'Helgouac'h J., Le Roux Ch.-T., "Morphologie et chronologie des grandes architectures de l'Ouest de la France d'après les travaux récents",

Le Néolithique de la France. Hommage à Gérard Bailloud. / Demoule J.-P., Guillaine G.-dir. (Paris: 1986), 181-191; L'Helgouac'h J., Le Gouestre D., Poulain H., "Le monument mégalithique transepté de la Josseliere (ou du Pissot) au Clion-sur-Mer (Loire-Atlantique)", *Revue archéologique de l'Ouest,* Vol. 6, 1989, 31-50; Dron J.-L., San Juan G., "Ernes-Condé-sur-Ifs (Calvados): habitat puis nécropole au Néolithique moyen. Présentation liminaire", *Actes du 17e Colloque Interrégional sur le Néolithique, Vannes, 1990 (Revue archéologique de l'Ouest, Supplément no 5)* (Rennes: 1992), 31-42.; 36, fig.8; Lecornec J., *Le Petit Mont (Arzon-Morbihan) (Documents Archéologiques de l'Ouest)* (Arzon: 1994); Le Roux Ch.-T., *Les mégalithes et les tumulus de Saint-Just* (Paris: 1995): 38-47; Bouin F., Joussaume R., "Le tumulus du Planti à Availles-sur-Chizé (Deux-Sèvres)", *Le Néolithique du Centre-Ouest de la France: Actes du XXIe colloque inter-régional sur le Néolithique, Poitiers, 14-16 octobre 1994* (Chavigny: 1998), 169-182; Gomez de Soto J., "La nécropole de la Boixe à Vervant, Maine-de-Boixe, Celettes (Charente). Nouvelles recherches sur le monument C", *Le Néolithique du Centre-Ouest de la France. Actes du XXIe colloque inter-régional sur le Néolithique, Poitiers, 14-16 octobre 1994* (Chavigny: 1998), 183-191; Chancerel A., Kinnes I., "Du bois dans l'Architecture: le tumulus de la commune Sèche à Colombiers-sur-Seulles", *Au bout du couloir: les mégalithes en Normandie et dans les îles Anglo-Normandes* (Weris: 1998), 45-47; L'Helgouac'h J. "Les groupes humaines du Ve au IIIe millénaire", *Préhistoire de la Bretagne* (Rennes: Éditions Ouest-France, 1998), 231-427: 242-269, 311-330; Joussaume R., "Le tumulus du Pey de Fontaine au Bernard (Vendée)", *Gallia Préhistoire*, T. 41, 1999, 167-222; Mohen J.-P., Scarre Ch., *Les Tumulus de Bougon. Complexe mégalithique du Ve au IIIe millénaire* (Paris: Éditions Errance, 2002) : 25-65; Joussaume R., "Du réaménagement des monuments funéraires néolithiques dans le Center-Ouest de la France", *Sens dessus dessous. La recheche du sens en Préhistoire* (Amiens: 2003), 157-171; Joussaume R., *Les tumulus de Champ-Châlon à Benon (Charente-Maritime) et les chambres funéraires à couloir du Poitou et des Charentes. (Groupe Vendéen d'études préhistoriques. No 42).* (La Roche sur Yon: 2006); Le Roux Ch.-T., Gaumé É., Lecerf Y., Tinévez J.-Y., *Monuments mégalithiques à Loqmariaquer (Morbihan). Le long tumulus d'Er Grah dans son environnement. / Le Roix Ch.-T.-dir. (XXXVIII-e supplément à" Gallia Préhistoire")* (Paris: CNRS Editions, 2006); Joussaume R., Laporte L., "Monuments funéraires néolitiques dans l'ouest de la France", *Origine et développement du mégalithisme de l'ouest de l'Europe. Actes du colloque international, 26-30 octobre 2002, Bougon (France) / Joussaume R., Laporte L., Scarre C.-dir. 2 vol.* (Niort: 2006), 319-343: 330-338.

[43] Patton M., *Statements in Stone. Monuments and Society in Neolithic Brittany* (London-New York: 1993), 167-170.

[44] Müller J., "Die absolutchronologische Datierung der europäischen Megalithik", *Tradition und Innovation: Prähistorische Archäologie als historische Wissenschaft. Festschrift für Christian Strahm / Fritsch B., Maute M., Matuschik I., Müller J., Wolf C. (Hrsg.). (Internationale Archäologie-Studia honoraria 3)* (Rahden/Westf.: 1997), 63-105: 74,78, Abb. 11; Müller J. "Zur Entstehung der europäischen Megalithik",

Studien zur Megalithik-Forschungsstand und ethnoarchäologische Perspektiven / Beinhauer K.W., Cooney G., Gucjsch Ch.E., Kus S. (Hrsg.) (Beiträge zur Ur-und Frügeschichte Mitteleuropas 21) (Mannheim-Weissbach: 1999), 51-81: 58-59.

[45] Le Roux Ch.-T. "Circoncription de Bretagne", *Gallia Préhistoire*, T.18, 1975, 511-539: 514-518; Le Roux Ch.-T. "Circoncription de Bretagne", *Gallia Préhistoire*, T.20, 1977, 407-432: 411-415.

[46] Müller J., "Die absolutchronologische Datierung der europäischen Megalithik", *Tradition und Innovation: Prähistorische Archäologie als historische Wissenschaft. Festschrift für Christian Strahm / Fritsch B., Maute M., Matuschik I., Müller J., Wolf C. (Hrsg.) (Internationale Archäologie-Studia honoraria 3)* (Rahden/Westf: 1997), 63-105: 84, 95.

[47] Le Goffic M., "Le dolmen de Ti-ar-Boudiged en Brennilis", *Bulletin de la Société archéologique du Finistère*, T. CXXIII, 1994, 131-162: 138-147, figs. 4-7.

[48] Lecornec J., "L'allée couverte de Bilgroix, Arzon, Morbihan", *Bulletin menzuel de la Société Polymathique du Morbihan*, T.122, 1996, 15-64.

[49] Guilaine J., *Au temps des dolmens. Mégalithes et vie quotidienne en France méditerranéenne il y a 5000 ans* (Toulouse: Éditions Privat, 1998), 52-53, 57, 142 ; Guilaine J., "Le phénomène dolménique en Méditerranée Nord-Occidentale", *Origine et développement du mégalithisme de l'ouest de l'Europe. Actes du colloque international, 26-30 octobre 2002, Bougon (France) / Joussaume R., Laporte L., Scarre C.-dir. 2 vol.* (Niort: 2006), 253-282: fig.1; Sauzade G., "L'architecture des tombes dans le Sud", *Archéologie de la France. Le Néolithique / Coord. sc. Tarrête J., Le Roux Ch.-T.* (Paris: Picard-Ministère de la culture et de la communication, 2008), 336-351: 345-346.

[50] Clottes J., "Le mègalithisme en Quercy", *L'Architecture mégalithique. Colloque du 150e anniversaire de la Société Polymathique du Morbihan* (Vannes: 1977), 7-70.

[51] Guilaine J., *Au temps des dolmens. Mégalithes et vie quotidienne en France méditerranéenne il y a 5000 ans* (Toulouse: Éditions Privat, 1998): 46-47.

[52] Lagasquie J.-P., Barreau D., Rocher A., "Le dolmen de la Devèze-Sud à Marcilhac-sur-Célè (Lot): Approche méthodologique et resultats de la fouille", *Bulletin de la Société préhistorique française*, T. 93, 1996, No. 3, 425-433.

[53] *Mégalithisme et Société. Table ronde S.N.R.S. des Sables d'Olonne (Vendée). 2-4 Novembre 1987 / R.Joussaume-dir.* (La Roche Sur Yon: 1990): 113-124.

[54] *Mégalithisme et Société. Table ronde S.N.R.S. des Sables d'Olonne (Vendée). 2-4 Novembre 1987 / R.Joussaume-dir.* (La Roche Sur Yon: 1990): 113-124; Sauzade G., "L'architecture des tombes dans le Sud", *Archéologie de la France: Le Néolithique / Coord. sc. Tarrête J., Le Roux Ch.-T.* (Paris: Picard-Ministère de la culture et de la communication, 2008), 336-351: 342-343.

[55] Sauzade G., Buisson-Catil J., Bizot B., "Le Dolmen de l'Ubac à Goult (Vaucluse) et son environnement immédiat", *Temps et espaces culturels. Actualité de la recherche. Actes des Quatrièmes Rencontres Méridionales*

de Préhistoire Récente, Nîmes, 28-29 octobre 2000 / Gascó J., Gutherz X., De Labriffe P.-A.-dir. (Mémoire d'Archéologie Méditerranéenne, n° 15, Lattes) (Nîmes : 2003), 335-346 ;.Sauzade G., "L'architecture des tombes dans le Sud", *Archéologie de la France: Le Néolithique / Coord. sc. Tarrête J., Le Roux Ch.-T.* (Paris: Picard-Ministère de la culture et de la communication, 2008), 336-351.

[56] L'Helgouac'h J., Le Roux Ch.-T., "Morphologie et chronologie des grandes architectures de l'Ouest de la France d'après les travaux récents", *Le Néolithique de la France. Hommage à Gérard Bailloud. / Demoule J.-P., Guillaine G.-dir.* (Paris: 1986), 181-191; Le Roux Ch.-T., "Réflexions autour d'une chrono-typologie du mégalithisme Armoricain des V-e et IV-e millénaires avant J.-C.", *Mégalithismes de l'Atlantique à l'Ethiopie / Guilain G.-dir.* (Paris: Editions Errance, 1999), 41-56; Joussaume R., Laporte L., "Monuments funéraires néolitiques dans l'ouest de la France", *Origine et développement du mégalithisme de l'ouest de l'Europe. Actes du colloque international, 26-30 octobre 2002, Bougon (France) / Joussaume R., Laporte L., Scarre C.-dir. 2 vol.* (Niort: 2006), 319-343: 330-338; Guilaine J., "Le phénomène dolménique en Méditerranée Nord-Occidentale", *Origine et développement du mégalithisme de l'ouest de l'Europe. Actes du colloque international, 26-30 octobre 2002, Bougon (France) / Joussaume R., Laporte L., Scarre C.-dir. 2 vol.* (Niort: 2006), 253-282: figs.1,2.

[57] Guilaine J., *Au temps des dolmens. Mégalithes et vie quotidienne en France méditerranéenne il y a 5000 ans* (Toulouse: Éditions Privat, 1998), 34-41; Guilaine J., "Le phénomène dolménique en Méditerranée Nord-Occidentale", *Origine et développement du mégalithisme de l'ouest de l'Europe. Actes du colloque international, 26-30 octobre 2002, Bougon (France) / Joussaume R., Laporte L., Scarre C.-dir. 2 vol.* (Niort: 2006), 253-282: 263-266, figs.1,2; Bordreuil M., Bordreuil M.-Ch., Jallot L., "Dolmens à murs latéraux en pierre sèche en Languedoc Oriental (France), étude préliminaire", *Origine et développement du mégalithisme de l'ouest de l'Europe. Actes du colloque international, 26-30 octobre 2002, Bougon (France) / Joussaume R., Laporte L., Scarre C.-dir. 2 vol.* (Niort: 2006): 283-291.

[58] Bordreuil M., Bordreuil M.-Ch., Jallot L., "Dolmens à murs latéraux en pierre sèche en Languedoc Oriental (France), étude préliminaire", *Origine et développement du mégalithisme de l'ouest de l'Europe. Actes du colloque international, 26-30 octobre 2002, Bougon (France) / Joussaume R., Laporte L., Scarre C.-dir. 2 vol.* (Niort: 2006): 283-291: 288-291.

[59] Кирюшин Ю.Ф. *Энеолит и ранняя бронза юга Западной Сибири* (Барнаул: 2002); Кирюшин Ю.Ф., Грушин С.П., Тишкин А.А., *Погребальный обряд населения эпохи ранней бронзы Верхнего Приобья (по материалам грунтового могильника Телеутский Взвоз I)* (Барнаул: 2003); Кирюшин Ю.Ф., Малолетко А.М., Тишкин А.А., *Березовая Лука-поселение эпохи бронзы в Алейской степи. Т 1* (Барнаул: 2005); Кирюшин Ю.Ф., Грушин С.П., Папин Д.В., "Проблемы радиоуглеродного датирования археологических памятников бронзового века Алтая", *Теория и практика археологических исследований: сборник научных трудов / отв. ред. А.А. Тишкин. Выпуск 3.* (Барнаул : Изд-во Алт. ун-та,

2007), 84-88.

[60] A.A.Kovalev 科瓦列夫, Д. Erdenebaatar 額爾德涅巴特爾, "Menggu qingtong shidai wenhua de xin faxian" 蒙古青銅時代文化的新發現, *Bianjiang Kaogu Yanjiu*《邊疆考古研究》, vol.8, 2009.

[61] Polles R. *Contribution a l'etude de la ceramique du néollithique final de la Bretagne. Memoire de Maîtrise du second cycle. Universite de Paris I. Vol. I-II.* (Paris: 1983).

[62] Joussaume R., Pautreau J.-P., *La Préhistoire du Poitou. Poitou-Vendée-Aunis des Origines à la conquête romaine* (Rennes: Editions Ouest-France, 1990); Laporte L., "Quelques reflections sur le Néolithique final du Centre-Ouest de la France", *Revue archéologie de l'Ouest*, No 13, 1996, 51-74.

[63] Gutherz X., *Les cultures du néolithique recent et final en Languedoc oriental. Universite de Provence (Aix-Marseille I). These de doctorat de 3e cycle (sciences prehistioriques). Vol. 1-2.* (Marseille: 1984); Georjon C., Forest V., "Le site de la Roquette à Tresques (Gard) et le Néolithique final du bassin Rhodanien", *Gallia Préhistorie*, V. 41, 1999, 253-297; D'Anna A., "Le Néolithique final en Provence", *Chronologies néolithiques: De 6000 à 2000 avant notre ère dans le Bassin rhodanien. Actes du Colloque d'Ambérieu-en-Bugey, 19 et 20 septembre 1992 (XIe Recontre sur le Néolithique de la région Rhône-Alpes) / Voruz J.-L.-dir. (Documents du Département d'Anthropologie de l'Université de Genève, no 20)* (Ambérieu-en Bugey: 1995), 265-286.

[64] Bosch i Lloret À., Tarrús i Galter J., *La cova sepulcral del neolític de l'Avellaner (Cogolls, Les Planes d'Hostoles. La Garrotxa)* (Girona: 1990); Márques C. C., Leisner G., Leisner V., *Los sepulcros megaliticos de Huelva. Excavationes arqueolgicas del plan nacional 1946. (Ministerio de educacion nacional. Comisaria general de excavationes arqueológicas. Informes y memorias. No 26)* (Madrid: 1952); Prieto Martínez P., "La cerámica neolítica en Galicia. Estudio de síntesis desde la perspectiva de la Arqueologiá del Paisaje", *Actas del III Congreso del Neolítico de la Península Ibérica / Arias Cabal P., Ontañón Peredo R., García-Moncó Piñeiro C.-ed.* (Santander: Servicio de Publicaciones, Universidad de Cantabria: 2005), 337-348.

[65] Gutherz X., Jallot L., "Le Néolithique final du Languedoc Méditerranéen", *Chronologies néolithiques, De 6000 à 2000 avant notre ère dans le Bassin rhodanien. Actes du Colloque d'Ambérieu-en-Bugey, 19 et 20 septembre 1992 (XIe Recontre sur le Néolithique de la région Rhône-Alpes) / Voruz J.-L.-dir. (Documents du Département d'Anthropologie de l'Université de Genève, no 20)* (Ambérieu-en Bugey: 1995), 231-263. (Documents du Département d'Anthropologie de l'Université de Genève, no 20).

[66] Telegin D.Ya., Mallory J.P., *The Anthropomorphic Stelae of the Ukraine: The Early Iconography of the Indo-Europeans* (Washington: 1994).

[67] D'Anna A., *Les statues-menhirs et stèles athropomorphes du midi Mèditerranien* (Paris: Editions du CNRS: 1977); D'Anna A., "Les statues-menhirs en Europe à la fin du Néolitique et au début de l'Âge de Bronze", *Statues-menhirs des énigmes de pierre venues du fond des âges / sous la direction d'Annie Philippon* (Rodez: Éditions du Rouergue, 2002), 150-177; D'Anna A., Gutherz X., Jallot L., "L'art mégalithique

dans le midi de la France: les steles anthropomorphes et les statues-menhirs néolitiques", *Actes du 2ème Colloque International sur l'Art Mégalithique, Nantes, 1995. (Revue Archéologique de l'Ouest, Supplément No. 8)* (Rennes: 1996), 179-193; Jallot L., "Enquête typologique et chronologique sur les menhirs anthropomorphes: études de cas dans le Sud de la France, l'Ouest, l'Arc alpin et la Bourgogne", *Actes du 2ème colloque international sur la statuaire mégalithique, Saint-Pons-de-Thomières du 10 au 14 septembre 1997. (Archéologie en Languedoc. Revue de la Fédération archéologique de l'Herault. No 22.)* (Montpellier: 1998), 317-350; Pedrotti A., "Gli elementi d'abbigliamento e d'ornamento nelle statue stele dell'arco alpino", *Actes du 2ème colloque international sur la statuaire mégalithique, Saint-Pons-de-Thomières du 10 au 14 septembre 1997 (Archéologie en Languedoc: Revue de la Fédération archéologique de l'Herault. No 22.)* (Montpellier: 1998), 299-315.

[68] Bordreuil M., Bordreuil M.-Ch., "Recherches sur les statues-menhirs porteuses de "haches", *Actes du 2ème colloque international sur la statuaire mégalithique, Saint-Pons-de-Thomières du 10 au 14 septembre 1997. (Archéologie en Languedoc. Revue de la Fédération archéologique de l'Herault. No 22.)* (Montpellier: 1998), 265-272.

[69] D'Anna A., *Les statues-menhirs et stèles athropomorphes du midi Mèditerranien* (Paris: Editions du CNRS, 1977).

[70] Boujot C., Cassen S., Defaix J., "La pierre décorée du caveau et les gravures régionales nouvellement découvertes", *Éléments d'architecture. Exploration d'un tertre funéraire à Lannec er Gadouer (Erdeven, Morbihan)/ Constructions et reconstructions dans le Néolothique morbihannais. Prpositions pour une lecture symbolique / Cassen S., Boujot C., Vaquero J.-dir.* (Chauvigny: Editions chauvinoises, Mémoire 19, 2000), 279-298.

[71] Pedrotti A., "Gli elementi d'abbigliamento e d'ornamento nelle statue stele dell'arco alpino", *Actes du 2ème colloque international sur la statuaire mégalithique, Saint-Pons-de-Thomières du 10 au 14 septembre 1997. (Archéologie en Languedoc. Revue de la Fédération archéologique de l'Herault. No 22.)* (Montpellier: 1998), 299-315; Cura-Morera M., Castells J., "Evolution et typologie des mégalithes de Catalogne", *L'Architecture mégalithique. Colloque du 150e anniversaire de la Société Polymathique du Morbihan.* (Vannes: 1977), 71-97.

[72] Pedrotti A., "Gli elementi d'abbigliamento e d'ornamento nelle statue stele dell'arco alpino", *Actes du 2ème colloque international sur la statuaire mégalithique, Saint-Pons-de-Thomières du 10 au 14 septembre 1997. (Archéologie en Languedoc. Revue de la Fédération archéologique de l'Herault. No 22.)* (Montpellier: 1998), 299-315; D'Anna A., Gutherz X., Jallot L., "L'art mégalithique dans le midi de la France: les steles anthropomorphes et les statues-menhirs néolitiques", *Actes du 2ème Colloque International sur l'Art Mégalithique, Nantes, 1995. (Revue Archéologique de l'Ouest, Supplément No. 8)* (Rennes: 1996), 179-193; Cura-Morera M., Castells J., "Evolution et typologie des mégalithes de Catalogne", *L'Architecture mégalithique. Colloque du 150e anniversaire de la Société Polymathique du Morbihan* (Vannes: 1977), 71-97.

[73] Le Roux Ch.-T., "Du menhir à la statue dans le mégalithisme armoricain", *Actes du 2ème colloque international sur la statuaire mégalithique, Saint-Pons-de-Thomières du 10 au 14 septembre 1997. (Archéologie en Languedoc. Revue de la Fédération archéologique de l'Herault. No 22.)* (Montpellier: 1998), 217-235.: 219-220.

[74] Montjardin R., "Menhirs et statues-menhirs en Ardèche", *Actes du 2ème colloque international sur la statuaire mégalithique, Saint-Pons-de-Thomières du 10 au 14 septembre 1997. (Archéologie en Languedoc. Revue de la Fédération archéologique de l'Herault. No 22.)* (Montpellier: 1998), 197-205; Colomer A., *Les grottes sépulcrales artificielles en Languedoc oriental. (Archives d'Ecologie Préhistorique Toulouse, no4)* (Toulouse: 1979): 33-35, 84-87.

[75] Harrison R., Heydt V., "The Transformation of Europe in the Third Millennium BC: the example of "Le Petit-Chasseur I + III" (Sion, Valais, Switzerland)", *Prähistorische Zeitschrift*, 2007, B. 82, H. 2, 129-214.

[76] Jallot L., "Enquête typologique et chronologique sur les menhirs anthropomorphes: études de cas dans le Sud de la France, l'Ouest, l'Arc alpin et la Bourgogne", *Actes du 2ème colloque international sur la statuaire mégalithique, Saint-Pons-de-Thomières du 10 au 14 septembre 1997. (Archéologie en Languedoc. Revue de la Fédération archéologique de l'Herault. No 22.)* (Montpellier: 1998), 317-350: 326-328, fig.2.

[77] Hasler A., "Les stèles de la nécropole tumulaire néolithique de Château-Blanc (Ventabren, Bouches-du-Rhône)", *Actes du 2ème colloque international sur la statuaire mégalithique, Saint-Pons-de-Thomières du 10 au 14 septembre 1997. (Archéologie en Languedoc. Revue de la Fédération archéologique de l'Herault. No 22.)* (Montpellier: 1998), 105-112.

[78] Cura-Morera M., Castells J., "Evolution et typologie des mégalithes de Catalogne", *L'Architecture mégalithique. Colloque du 150e anniversaire de la Société Polymathique du Morbihan* (Vannes: 1977), 71-97; Rodríguez Cazal A.A., *O Megalitísmo: A primeira arquitectura monumental de Galicia. (Bibliotheca de Divulgación: 4. Serie Galicia)*(Santiago de Compostela: Universidade, Servicio de Publicacións e Intercambio Científico, 1990); Leisner V., *Die Megalithgräber der Iberischen Halbinsel. Der Westen. 4. Lieferung. (Madrider Vorschungen. Band 1)* (Berlin: 1998).

[79] Müller D. W., "Ornamente, Symbole, Bilder-zum megalithischen Totenbrauchtum in Mitteldeutschland", *Actes du 2ème Colloque International sur l'Art Mégalithique, Nantes, 1995. (Revue Archéologique de l'Ouest, Supplément No. 8)* (Rennes: 1996), 179-193; Müller D. W., "Petroglyphen aus mittelneolitischen Gräbern von Sachsen-Anhalt", *Studien zur Megalithik-Forschungsstand und ethnoarchäologische Perspektiven / Beinhauer K.W., Cooney G., Gucjsch Ch.E., Kus S. (Hrsg.). (Beiträge zur Ur-und Frügeschichte Mitteleuropas 21)* (Mannheim-Weissbach: 1999), 199-214.

[80] Adams D.Q., "The Position of Tocharian among the Other Indo-European Languages", *Journal of the American Oriental Society*, Vol.104, 1984, pp.395-402.

[81] Wang Bo 王博, "Qiemuerqieke wenhua chutan: Kaogu wenwu yanjiu" 切木爾切克文化初探, 考古文物研

究, *Xibei Daxue Kaogu Zhuanye Chengli Sishi Zhounian Wenji, 1956-1996*《西北大學考古專業成立四十周年文集（1956-1996）》(Xi'an: 1996), pp.274-285, ill.1.

[82] Le Roux Ch.-T., *Les mégalithes et les tumulus de Saint-Just, Ille-et-Vilaine. Évolution et acculturations d'un ensemble funéraire (5000 à 1500 ans avant notre ère)* (Paris: Éd. du C.T.H.S., 1995): figs.26, 29.

[83] Joussaume R., "Le dolmen à couloir dit "la Ciste des Cous" à Bazoges-en-Pareds (Vendée)", *Bulletin de la Société préhistorique française*, T. 75 (1978), No. 11-12, 579-596: fig.3.

[84] L'Helgouac'h J., "Les groupes humaines du Ve au IIIe millénaire", *Préhistoire de la Bretagne* (Rennes: Éditions Ouest-France, 1998), 231-427: 244.

[85] Dron J.-L., San Juan G., "Ernes-Condé-sur-Ifs (Calvados): habitat puis nécropole au Néolithique moyen. Présentation liminaire.", *Actes du 17e Colloque Interrégional sur le Néolithique, Vannes, 1990* (Rennes, 1992), 31-42. (Revue archéologique de l'Ouest, Supplément no 5): fig.9.

[86] Le Roux Ch.-T., Lecerf Y., "Le cairn de Ty-Floc'h à Saint-Thois (fouilles de 1978-1979)", *Bulletin de la Société archéologique du Finistére*, T. 108 (1980), 27-49: fig.3.

[87] Giot P.-R. *Barnenez. Carn. Guennoc.* Vol. I-II (Rennes. 1987).

[88] Bouin F., Joussaume R., "Le tumulus du Planti à Availles-sur-Chizé (Deux-Sèvres)", *Le Néolithique du Centre-Ouest de la France. Actes du XXIe colloque inter-régional sur le Néolithique, Poitiers, 14-16 octobre 1994.* (Chavigny, 1998), 169-182: fig.2.

[89] Dron J.-L., San Juan G., "Ernes-Condé-sur-Ifs (Calvados): habitat puis nécropole au Néolithique moyen. Présentation liminaire", *Actes du 17e Colloque Interrégional sur le Néolithique, Vannes, 1990. (Revue archéologique de l'Ouest, Supplément no 5)* (Rennes, 1992), 31-42: fig.8.

[90] Giot P.-R., *Barnenez. Carn. Guennoc.* Vol. I-II. (Rennes, 1987).

[91] *Mégalithisme et Société. Table ronde S.N.R.S. des Sables d'Olonne (Vendée). 2-4 Novembre 1987,* R.Joussaume-dir. (La Roche Sur Yon, 1990): fig.44.

[92] Laporte L., Joussaume R., Scarre Ch., "Le tumulus C de Péré à Prissé-la-Charriére (Deux-Sèvres)", *Gallia Préhistoire*, T. 44 (2002), 167-214: figs.7, 27.

[93] Joussaume R., "Le tumulus du Pey de Fontaine au Bernard (Vendée)", *Gallia Préhistoire*, T. 41(1999), 167-222: figs.10,14.

[94] Le Roux Ch.-T., Gaumé É., Lecerf Y., Tinévez J.-Y., *Monuments mégalithiques à Loqmariaquer (Morbihan). Le long tumulus d'Er Grah dans son environnement. (XXXVIII-e supplément à " Gallia Préhistoire")*, Le Roux Ch.-T.-dir. (Paris: CNRS Editions, 2006): figs.47, 50.

[95] Germond G., Joussaume R., Bizard M., "Le Tumulus du Montiou à Sainte-Soline (Deux-Sèvres). Premières campagnes de fouilles. Premier bilan.", *Bulletin de la Société Historique et Scientifique des Deux-Sèvres*, T. XI(1978), No. 2-3, 129-188: figs.21, 23.

[96] Mohen J.-P., Scarre Ch., *Les Tumulus de Bougon. Complexe mégalithique du Ve au IIIe millénaire.*(Paris:

Éditions Errance, 2002): figs.39, 49.

[97] *Mégalithisme et Société. Table ronde S.N.R.S. des Sables d'Olonne (Vendée). 2-4 Novembre 1987* R.Joussaume-dir. (La Roche Sur Yon: 1990): fig.22.

[98] Gachina J., "Le dolmen de "La Grosse Pierre" à Ste-Radegonde (Charente-Maritime)", *Le Néolithique du Centre-West de la France. Actes du XXIe colloque inter-régional sur le Néolithique, Poitiers, 14-16 octobre 1994.* (Chavigny: 1998), 193-202.

[99] *Mégalithisme et Société. Table ronde S.N.R.S. des Sables d'Olonne (Vendée). 2-4 Novembre 1987,* R.Joussaume-dir. (La Roche Sur Yon: 1990): fig.29.

[100] Bouin F., "Les tumulus néolithiques de la foret de Benon", *Groupe Vendéen d'études préhistoriques*, No 27, 1992, 21-36: 36.

[101] L'Helgouac'h J., "Le tumulus de Dissignac à Saint-Nazaire (Loire-Atlantique) et les problèmes du contact entre le phénomene mégalithique et les sociétés à industrie microlithique", *Acculturation and Continuity in Atlantic Europe mainly during the Neolithic period and the Bronze Age. Papers presented at the IV Atlantic Colloquium, Ghent 1975, Edited by S. J. De Laet (Dissertationes archaeologicae gandenses. Vol. XVI)* (Brugge: De Tempel, 1976), 142-149: fig.2; L'Helgouac'h J. "Les groupes humaines du Ve au IIIe millénaire", *Préhistoire de la Bretagne* (Rennes: Éditions Ouest-France. 1998), 231-427.

[102] Le Roux Ch.-T., L'Helgouac'h J., "Le cairn mégalithique avec sépultures à chambres comparatimenteés de Kerleven, commune de la Forêt-Fouesnant (Finistère)", *Annales de Bretagne*, T. LXXIV (1967), Num. 1, 7-52.

[103] Le Roux Ch.-T., *Les mégalithes et les tumulus de Saint-Just, Ille-et-Vilaine. Évolution et acculturations d'un ensemble funéraire (5000 à 1500 ans avant notre ère)* (Paris: Éd. du C.T.H.S., 1995): figs.12, 17.

[104] Le Roux Ch.-T., *Les mégalithes et les tumulus de Saint-Just, Ille-et-Vilaine. Évolution et acculturations d'un ensemble funéraire (5000 à 1500 ans avant notre ère)* (Paris: Éd. du C.T.H.S., 1995): fig.37.

[105] Mohen J.-P., Scarre Ch. *Les Tumulus de Bougon. Complexe mégalithique du Ve au IIIe millénaire* (Paris: Éditions Errance, 2002): fig.58.

[106] L'Helgouac'h J., Poulain H., "Le cairn des Mousseaux à Pornic et les tombes mégalithiques transeptées de l'estuaire de la Loire", *Revue archéologique de l'Ouest*, № 1, 1984, 15-32: figs.3, 8.

[107] Le Roux Ch.-T., Lecerf Y., "Le dolmen de Cruguellic en Plœmeur et les sépultures transeptées armoricaines", *L'Architecture mégalithique. Colloque du 150e anniversaire de la Société Polymathique du Morbihan.* (Vannes. 1977), 143-160: fig.1. Le Roux Ch.-T. "Circoncription de Bretagne" , *Gallia Préhistoire*. T. 20. 1977, pp.407-432: fig.34.

[108] L'Helgouac'h J., Le Gouestre D., Poulain H., "Le monument mégalithique transepté de la Josseliere (ou du Pissot) au Clion-sur-Mer (Loire-Atlantique)", *Revue archéologique de l'Ouest*, T. 6 (1989), 31-50.

[109] L'Helgouac'h J., Lecornec J.. "Le site mégalithique 'Min goh Ru' prés de Larcuste à Colpo (Morbihan)", *Bulletin de la Société préhistorique française*, T. 73 (1976), 370-397: fig.4; L'Helgouac'h J. "Les groupes

humaines du Ve au IIIe millénaire", *Préhistoire de la Bretagne* (Rennes: Éditions Ouest-France, 1998), 231-427: 264.

[110] Guilaine J., *Au temps des dolmens. Mégalithes et vie quotidienne en France méditerranéenne il y a 5000 ans* (Toulouse: Éditions Privat, 1998).

[111] Lecornec J., "L'allée couverte de Bilgroix, Arzon, Morbihan", *Bulletin menzuel de la Société Polymathique du Morbihan*, T. 122 (1996), 15-64: figs.5, 28.

[112] Le Roux Ch.-T., "Circonscription de Bretagne", *Gallia Préhistoire*, T. 20 (1977), 407-432: fig.14.

[113] Le Roux Ch.-T., "Circonscription de Bretagne", *Gallia Préhistoire*, T. 18(1975), 511-539: fig.4.

[114] *Mégalithisme et Société. Table ronde S.N.R.S. des Sables d'Olonne (Vendée). 2-4 Novembre 1987, R.Joussaume-dir.* (La Roche Sur Yon: 1990): fig.54.

[115] Gutherz X., "Le mégalithisme en Poitou-Charente. Aquis, recherches, protection et mise en valeur", *La France des dolmens et des sépultures collectives (4500-200 avant J.-C.), Soulier Ph., Masset, Cl.-dir.*(Paris: Editions Errance, 1995), 281-290: fig.3.

[116] *Mégalithisme et Société. Table ronde S.N.R.S. des Sables d'Olonne (Vendée). 2-4 Novembre 1987, R.Joussaume-dir.* (La Roche Sur Yon: 1990): fig.58.

[117] Lagasquie J.-P., Barreau D., Rocher A., "Le dolmen de la Devèze-Sud à Marcilhac-sur-Célè (Lot). Approche méthodologique et resultats de la fouille", *Bulletin de la Société préhistorique française*, T. 93 (1996), No. 3, 425-433: fig.1.

[118] *Mégalithisme et Société. Table ronde S.N.R.S. des Sables d'Olonne (Vendée). 2-4 Novembre 1987, R.Joussaume-dir.* La Roche Sur Yon. 1990: fig.64.

[119] Lagasquie J.-P., Barreau D., Rocher A., "Le Dolmen des Aguals ou de la Combe de l'Ours, communes de Gréalou-Montbrun (Lot, France)", *Origine et développement du mégalithisme de l'ouest de l'Europe. Actes du colloque international, 26-30 octobre 2002, Bougon (France), Joussaume R., Laporte L., Scarre C.-dir. 2 vol.* (Niort: 2006), 293-303: 295.

[120] *Mégalithisme et Société. Table ronde S.N.R.S. des Sables d'Olonne (Vendée). 2-4 Novembre 1987, R.Joussaume-dir.* (La Roche Sur Yon: 1990): fig.55.

[121] Guilaine J., *Au temps des dolmens. Mégalithes et vie quotidienne en France méditerranéenne il y a 5000 ans* (Toulouse: Éditions Privat, 1998): 47.

[122] Gruet M., Passini B., "La Bajoulière en St. Remy-la-Varenne (Marne-et-Loire). Foulle et restauration d'un grand "Dolmen Angevin", *Revue archéologique de l'Ouest*, T. 3(1986), 29-46: fig.4.

[123] Girault J.P., *Le Dolmen de Souillac à murs de pierres sèches (Lot)* (Cabrerets: 1986): figs.5, 9, 17.

[124] Guilaine J., *Au temps des dolmens. Mégalithes et vie quotidienne en France méditerranéenne il y a 5000 ans* (Toulouse: Éditions Privat, 1998): 39; Beyneix A. *Traditions funéraires néolithiques en France Méridionale (6000-2200 avant J.-C.)* (Paris: Éditions Errance, 2003).

[125] Guilaine J. *Au temps des dolmens. Mégalithes et vie quotidienne en France méditerranéenne il y a 5000 ans.* (Toulouse: Éditions Privat, 1998): 40; *Mégalithisme et Société. Table ronde S.N.R.S. des Sables d'Olonne (Vendée). 2-4 Novembre 1987 , R.Joussaume-dir.* (La Roche Sur Yon: 1990): fig.68.

[126] *Mégalithisme et Société. Table ronde S.N.R.S. des Sables d'Olonne (Vendée). 2-4 Novembre 1987 / R.Joussaume-dir.* (La Roche Sur Yon: 1990): fig.69.

[127] Sauzade G., "Les sépultures collectives Provençales", *La France des dolmens et des sépultures collectives (4500-200 avant J.-C.), Soulier Ph., Masset, Cl.-dir.* (Paris: Editions Errrance, 1995), 292-328: fig.6.

[128] Кирюшин Ю.Ф., Тишкин А.А., Грушин С.П., Эрдэнэбаатар Д., Мунхбаяр Ч., «Археологические исследования в Монголии и на Алтае», *Проблемы археологии, этнографии, антропологии Сибири и сопредельных территорий. Том XV. Материалы итоговой сессии Института археологии и этнографии СО РАН 2009 года* (Новосибирск: 2009), 287-290: рис. 1.

[129] Xinjiang Shehui Kexueyuan Kaogu Yanjiusuo 新疆社會科學院考古研究所, "Xinjiang Ke'ermuqi gumu fajue jianbao" 新疆克爾木齊古墓發掘簡報, *Wenwu* 文物, 1981:1, 23-32: fig.3.

[130] Тишкин А.А., Грушин С.П., Мунхбаяр Ч., "Археологическое изучение объектов эпохи бронзы в урочище Улаан худаг (Ховдский аймак Монголии)", *Теория и практика археологических исследований*, Выпуск 4 (2008), 85-92: рис. 3.

[131] Wang Linshan 王林山 and Wang Bo 王博, *Zhongguo Aletai Caoyuan Wenwu* 中國阿勒泰草原文物 (Shenzhen: 1996), p.20 (fig.17).

[132] Тишкин А.А., Грушин С.П., Мунхбаяр Ч., "Археологическое изучение объектов эпохи бронзы в урочище Улаан худаг (Ховдский аймак Монголии)", *Теория и практика археологических исследований*, Выпуск 4 (2008), 85-92: рис. 2.

[133] Xinjiang Shehui Kexueyuan Kaogu Wenwu Yanjiusuo 新疆社會科學院考古文物研究所, *Xinjiang Gudai Minzu Wenwu* 新疆古代民族文物 (Urumqi: 1985).

[134] Beyneix A., *Traditions funéraires néolithiques en France Méridionale (6000-2200 avant J.-C.)* (Paris: Éditions Errance, 2003): 152.

[135] Roudil J.-L., Vincent P., "La grotte du Pins (Blandas, Gard)", *Bulletin de la Société archéologique du Finistére*. T. 69 (1972), Etudes et Travaux, fascicule 2, 570-584: fig.12.

[136] Gutherz X., *Les cultures du néolithique recent et final en Languedoc oriental. Universite de Provence (Aix-Marseille I). These de doctorat de 3e cycle (sciences prehistioriques). Vol. 1-2.* (Marseilles, 1984).

[137] Roudil J.-L., Vincent P., "La grotte du Pins (Blandas, Gard)", *Bulletin de la Société archéologique du Finistére*, T. 69 (1972), Etudes et Travaux, fascicule 2, 570-584: fig.5.

[138] Georjon C., Forest V., "Le site de la Roquette à Tresques (Gard) et le Néolithique final du bassin Rhodanien", *Gallia Préhistorie*, T. 41 (1999), 253-297: fig.17.

[139] Gutherz X., *Les cultures du néolithique recent et final en Languedoc oriental. Universite de Provence (Aix-

Marseille I). These de doctorat de 3e cycle (sciences prehistioriques). Vol. 1-2. (Marseilles, 1984).

[140] Le Roux Ch.-T., Lecerf Y., "Le cairn de Ty-Floc'h à Saint-Thois (fouilles de 1978-1979)", *Bulletin de la Société archéologique du Finistére*, T. 108(1980), 27-49: fig.6.

[141] Giot P.-R., *Barnenez. Carn. Guennoc.T. I-II.* (Rennes, 1987).

[142] Lecornec J., "L'allée couverte de Bilgroix, Arzon, Morbihan", *Bulletin menzuel de la Société Polymathique du Morbihan*, T. 122 (1996), 15-64: figs.10, 12.

[143] Polles R., *Contribution a l'etude de la ceramique du néollithique final de la Bretagne. Memoire de Maîtrise du second cycle. Universite de Paris I. Vol. I-II.* (Paris, 1983).

[144] L'Helgouac'h J., Lecornec J., "Le site mégalithique "Min goh Ru" prés de Larcuste à Colpo (Morbihan)", *Bulletin de la Société préhistorique française*, T. 73 (1976), 370-397: fig.13.

[145] Lecornec J., *Le Petit Mont (Arzon-Morbihan). (Documents Archéologiques de l'Ouest)* (Arzon: 1994): fig.27.

[146] Le Roux Ch.-T., L'Helgouac'h J., "Le cairn mégalithique avec sépultures à chambres comparatimenteés de Kerleven, commune de la Forêt-Fouesnant (Finistère)", *Annales de Bretagne*, T. LXXIV (1967), Num. 1, 7-52.

[147] Giot P.-R., *Barnenez. Carn. Guennoc. Vol. I-II.* (Rennes: 1987).

[148] Marchat A., *Etude d'un recensement de mégalithes dans l'arrondisment de Lannon (Côtes-du Nord). Universite de Paris I. Memoire de maitrise.* (Paris: 1989).

[149] Lecornec J., "L'allée couverte de Bilgroix, Arzon, Morbihan", *Bulletin menzuel de la Société Polymathique du Morbihan*, T. 122 (1996), 15-64: figs.13, 16.

[150] Polles R., *Contribution a l'etude de la ceramique du néollithique final de la Bretagne. Memoire de Maîtrise du second cycle. Universite de Paris I. T. I-II.* (Paris: 1983).

[151] Joussaume R., Pautreau J.-P., *La Préhistoire du Poitou. Poitou-Vendée-Aunis des Origines à la conquête romaine* (Rennes: Editions Ouest-France, 1990): 327.

[152] Joussaume R., Pautreau J.-P., *La Préhistoire du Poitou. Poitou-Vendée-Aunis des Origines à la conquête romaine* (Rennes: Editions Ouest-France, 1990).

[153] Gauron E., Massaud J., *La nécropole de Chenon. Etude d'un ensemble dolménique charentais (XVIIIe supplément d' Gallia préhistoire')* (Paris: Éditions du CNRS, 1983): fig.45.

[154] Ponts F., Chalard P., Salgues T., Jarry M., Bevilacqua R., Montécinos A., Bruxelles L., "Le site néolitique de Fontréal. Un exemple d'occupation en zone humide dans la vallée der la Garonne (Castelnau-d'Estrétefonds-Haute-Garonne)", *Bulletin de Préhistoire du Sud-Ouest*, No 11 (2004), F. 2, 173-215.

[155] Burnez C., "L'origine et developpement du Néolithique dans le centre-ouest de la France", *Die Anfänge des Neolthiqums vom Orient bis Nordeuropa. Teil VI. Frankreich* (Köln: Böhlau Verlag, 1971), 166-177: pl.109.

[156] Fischer F., Bradfer I., Lanreau C., Semelier P., Burnez C., Brauyguier S., Leroyer Ch., "Extension de la civilisation des Matignons en Saintonge (Charente) et vallée de la Dronne (Dordogne)", *Bulletin de*

Préhistoire du Sud-Ouest, No 14 (2007), F. 1, 57-148: nos.1, 2, 9.

[157] Patte É., "Quelques sépultures du Poitou, du Mésolithique au Bronze moyen", *Gallia Préhistoire*, T. XIV (1971), F. 1, 141-244: fig.14.

[158] Burnez C., "L'origine et developpement du Néolithique dans le centre-ouest de la France", *Die Anfänge des Neolthiqums vom Orient bis Nordeuropa. Teil VI. Frankreich* (Köln: Böhlau Verlag, 1971), 166-177: pl.109.

[159] Joussaume R., "Le tumulus du Pey de Fontaine au Bernard (Vendée)", *Gallia Préhistoire*, T. 41 (1999), 167-222: fig.29.

[160] Roussot-Laroque J., "Le groupe de Roquefort dans son contexte Atlantique", *Revue archéologique de l'Ouest. Supplément no 1.* (Rennes: 1986), 167-188.

[161] Polles R. *Contribution a l'etude de la ceramique du néollithique final de la Bretagne. Memoire de Maîtrise du second cycle. Universite de Paris I. T. I-II* (Paris: 1983): fig.36.

[162] Joussaume R. "Le dolmen à couloir dit "la Ciste des Cous" à Bazoges-en-Pareds (Vendée)", *Bulletin de la Société préhistorique française*, T. 75(1978), No. 11-12, 579-596: fig.8.

[163] Тишкин А.А., Грушин С.П., Мунхбаяр Ч., "Археологическое изучение объектов эпохи бронзы в урочище Улаан худаг (Ховдский аймак Монголии)", *Теория и практика археологических исследований*, Выпуск 4 (2008), 85-92: рис. 3.

[164] Xinjiang Shehui Kexueyuan Kaogu Wenwu Yanjiusuo 新疆社會科學院考古文物研究所, *Xinjiang Gudai Minzu Wenwu* 新疆古代民族文物 (Urumqi: 1985).

[165] Кирюшин Ю.Ф., Симонов Е.Н., "Каменный сосуд из Угловского района", *Сохранение и изучение культурного наследия Алтайского края. Материалы научно-практической конференции. Выпуск VIII* (Барнаул: 1997), 167-171.

[166] Xinjiang Shehui Kexueyuan Kaogu Wenwu Yanjiusuo 新疆社會科學院考古文物研究所, *Xinjiang Gudai Minzu Wenwu* 新疆古代民族文物 (Urumqi: 1985).

[167] Xinjiang Shehui Kexueyuan Kaogu Yanjiusuo 新疆社會科學院考古研究所, "Xinjiang Ke'ermuqi gumu fajue jianbao" 新疆克爾木齊古墓發掘簡報, *Wenwu* 文物, 1981:1, pp.23-32, fig.3.

[168] Gutherz X., *Les cultures du néolithique recent et final en Languedoc oriental. Universite de Provence (Aix-Marseille I). These de doctorat de 3e cycle (sciences prehistioriques). T. 1-2.* (Marselle: 1984).

[169] Gutherz X., *Les cultures du néolithique recent et final en Languedoc oriental. Universite de Provence (Aix-Marseille I). These de doctorat de 3e cycle (sciences prehistioriques). T. 1-2.* (Marseilles: 1984).

[170] Wang Linshan 王林山 and Wang Bo 王博, *Zhongguo Aletai Caoyuan Wenwu* 中國阿勒泰草原文物 (Shenzhen: 1996), p.35 (fig.60).

[171] Kovalev A., "Die ältesten Stelen am Ertix. Das Kulturphänomen Xemirxek.", *Eurasia Antiqua* 5, 1999 (Berlin: 2000), 135-178: Abb. 6.

[172] Kovalev A., "Die ältesten Stelen am Ertix. Das Kulturphänomen Xemirxek.", *Eurasia Antiqua* 5, 1999

(Berlin: 2000), 135-178: Abb. 6.

[173] Kovalev A., "Die ältesten Stelen am Ertix. Das Kulturphänomen Xemirxek.", *Eurasia Antiqua* 5, 1999 (Berlin: 2000), 135-178: 140, Abb. 4.

[174] Wang Linshan 王林山 and Wang Bo 王博, *Zhongguo Aletai Caoyuan Wenwu* 中國阿勒泰草原文物 (Shenzhen: 1996), p.37 (fig.66).

[175] Kovalev A., "Die ältesten Stelen am Ertix. Das Kulturphänomen Xemirxek", *Eurasia Antiqua* 5, 1999 (Berlin: 2000), 135-178: 140, Abb. 3.

[176] D'Anna A., *Les statues-menhirs et stèles athropomorphes du midi Mèditerranien* (Paris: Editions du CNRS, 1977): fig.27.

[177] D'Anna A., *Les statues-menhirs et stèles athropomorphes du midi Mèditerranien*. (Paris: Editions du CNRS, 1977): fig.26.

[178] D'Anna A., Gutherz X., Jalot L., "L'art mégalithique dans le midi de la France: les steles anthropomorphes et les statues-menhirs néolitiques", *Actes du 2ème Colloque International sur l'Art Mégalithique, Nantes, 1995. (Revue Archéologique de l'Ouest, Supplément No. 8)*(Rennes: 1996), 179-193: fig.4.

[179] D'Anna A., "Les statues-menhirs en Europe à la fin du Néolitique et au début de l'Âge de Bronze", *Statues-menhirs des énigmes de pierre venues du fond des âges, sous la direction d'Annie Philippon* (Rodez: Éditions du Rouergue, 2002), 150-177: 168.

[180] Gallay A., "Les Stéles anthropomorphes du site mégalithique du Petit-Chasseur à Sion (Valais, Suisse)", *Statue-stele e massi incisi nell'Europa dell'eta del rame (Notice Archeologiche Bergomensi)*, 3 (Bergamo: Civico Museo Archeologico, 1995), 167-194.

[181] Serres J.-P., "Les statues-menhirs du groupe rouergat", *Statues-menhirs des énigmes de pierre venues du fond des âges, sous la direction d'Annie Philippon*. (Rodez: Éditions du Rouergue, 2002), 54-91: 69.

[182] Cura-Morera M., Castells J., "Evolution et typologie des mégalithes de Catalogne", *L'Architecture mégalithique. Colloque du 150e anniversaire de la Société Polymathique du Morbihan* (Vannes, 1977), 71-97: fig.9.

[183] D'Anna A., *Les statues-menhirs et stèles athropomorphes du midi Mèditerranien* (Paris: Editions du CNRS, 1977): fig.14.

[184] Jallot L., "Enquête typologique et chronologique sur les menhirs anthropomorphes: études de cas dans le Sud de la France, l'Ouest, l'Arc alpin et la Bourgogne", *Actes du 2ème colloque international sur la statuaire mégalithique, Saint-Pons-de-Thomières du 10 au 14 septembre 1997. (Archéologie en Languedoc. Revue de la Fédération archéologique de l'Herault. No 2.)* (Montpellier: 1998), 317-350: 326-328, fig.2.

[185] Müller D. W., "Ornamente, Symbole, Bilder-zum megalithischen Totenbrauchtum in Mitteldeutschland", *Actes du 2ème Colloque International sur l'Art Mégalithique, Nantes, 1995. (Revue Archéologique de l'Ouest, Supplément No. 8)* (Rennes: 1996), 179-193: figs.2, 5.

[186] Bueno Ramirez P., De Balbín Behrmann R., "Novedades en la estatuaria antropomorfa megalítica española", *Actes du 2ème colloque international sur la statuaire mégalithique, Saint-Pons-de-Thomières du 10 au 14 septembre 1997(Archéologie en Languedoc. Revue de la Fédération archéologique de l'Herault. No 22.)* (Montpellier: 1998), 43-60.: fig.7.

[187] Rodríguez Cazal A.A., *O Megalitísmo: A primeira arquitectura monumental de Galicia* (Bibliotheca de Divulgación: 4. Serie Galicia) (Santiago de Compostela: Universidade. Servicio de Publicacións e Intercambio Científico, 1990): 129.

[188] Leisner V., *Die Megalithgräber der Iberischen Halbinsel: Der Westen. 4. Lieferung* (Madrider Vorschungen. Band 1) (Berlin: 1998), table17.

[189] Leisner V., *Die Megalithgräber der Iberischen Halbinsel: Der Westen. 4. Lieferung* (Madrider Vorschungen. Band 1) (Berlin: 1998).

[190] Bueno Ramirez P., De Balbín Behrmann R., "Novedades en la estatuaria antropomorfa megalítica española", *Actes du 2ème colloque international sur la statuaire mégalithique, Saint-Pons-de-Thomières du 10 au 14 septembre 1997. (Archéologie en Languedoc. Revue de la Fédération archéologique de l'Herault. No 22.)* (Montpellier: 1998), 43-60: fig.8.

BETWEEN EURASIA AND CHINA: SADDLES EXCAVATED IN XINJIANG AT ZAGHUNLUQ AND SUBESHI

Katheryn M. Linduff and Sandra Olsen

Introduction

Sometime between six and four thousand years ago, human beings discovered that by riding on horseback they could travel at greater speeds and for longer distances than they could on foot. This discovery transformed the course of human history, enabling more efficient exploration and incursions into remote lands. Without such transport, and the ability to move goods, weapons and food, conquerors such as Alexander the Great (356-323 BCE) could never have made their conquests of Asia nor could the Xiongnu have successfully developed and held their empires together. It is assumed by many that the saddle was developed when chariot warfare was replaced by cavalry to conquer new territories, and probably first by the nomadic peoples of Eurasia. However, material evidence suggests that there was a delay of several centuries before the saddle had widespread usage in cavalry warfare and many armies, including the Assyrians, Persians, and Greeks, were highly successful without it. When and where the saddle was first devised has been debated for a long time, but recent information from excavations in western China may offer new insight into the issue.

The Problem: Horseback Riding

The earliest depictions of horse riding date back to Sumerian times in Ur (Ur III period), *circa* 2300 BCE. Several clay tablets exhibit a man riding a horse or other equid (donkey or perhaps donkey-onager) bareback or with a simple girth strap to hold onto (Owen 1991,

Moorey 1970). There is also a remarkable gold headband from the burial of a woman at Ur that depicts a number of animals, including a man mounted on an ungulate, possibly an equid (Hansen 1998).

Around 1,000 BCE is thought to be the approximate time when horseback riding became ubiquitous. Before that there is limited evidence for riding in the form of wall paintings and models from Egypt and western Asia, but in these urbanized centers, where draught animals were economically more important, riding was an activity primarily reserved for grooms, scouts, and messengers, rather than royalty or cavalry. Examples of riding come from Egyptian temple walls that document riders called "scouts", dating to the Eighteenth Dynasty, or about 1580 BCE (Schulman 1957:263). One possible exceptional example of a high status individual riding a horse is pictured in the tomb of Pharaoh Horemheb, from the 14th century BCE (Chevenix-Trench 1970:13, Pl. I-4.1). In the image from the tomb of Horemheb (1332-1306 BCE), the rider is seated well back on the animal's haunches, in a fashion still used by donkey riders (Pl. I-1). Other scattered references of riding include mention of Babylonians riding horses in the reign of Nebuchadnezzar I, around 1200 BCE (Jankovich 1971).

The art of horsemanship provided extreme mobility and speed for the military as an effective instrument of war on many kinds of terrain (Beattie 1981:15). The Assyrians began using mounted fighters in the ninth century BCE (Chevenix-Trench 1970:16), as the first authentic reference to Assyrian cavalry dates from 890 BCE. The Assyrian kings, Assur-Nasir-Pal (884-59 BCE) and Shalmaneser III (859-24 BCE) employed mounted troops (Chevenix-Trench 1970:16). In a scene of the Assyrian cavalry of Tiglath-Pileser III, dating from the eighth century BCE, the rider was seated well forward, without a saddle, but with reins attached to a neck collar. The mounted figure is in a warlike posture carrying a spear (Jankovich 1971:43), and despite sporadic early depictions of riding in the Near East, it is the peoples of the Eurasian steppe who are most often credited with the earliest fabrication of the saddle.

The arts of the early nomads of the first millennium BCE in the Eurasian steppe are characterized by representations of many animals, although the horse is relatively rare. It is only in the late 5th or 4th century BCE that representations of horses with riders occur.[1] In the Black Sea region, "Greco-Scythian" objects, such as the distinctive comb from Solokha, the Chertomlyk vase, and other vessels, jewelry and ornaments illustrate horses and riders in some detail. The horse and rider also appear at approximately the same time in regions to the east. Horses and riders are depicted on a locally made felt hanging and the 'foreign-made' pile carpet [2] from Kurgan V at Pazyryk (Pl. I-2), as well as in a hunt scene on a cup from

Kurgan 1 at the same site, and the bone sculpture from Kurgan 3 from Filippovka (Aruz *et al* 2001: 170-171, Pl. 111). These examples show horses with saddles, and confirm their use no later than the 4th century BCE (Griaznov 1969: Pl. 134).

The Eurasian Saddle: Excavated Examples

We know that the lifestyles of the nomadic cultures varied and that they evolved from earlier Bronze Age cultures in which vehicles such as battle-chariots existed. Riding was probably first developed to accommodate pastoralism and migrations of complex herds and human groups prior to the second millennium BCE. Assigning a beginning point is difficult because of the lack of preservation of rawhide tack, but the large scale production of thongs and some osteological and dental modifications on horses from the Copper Age Botai culture (Olsen 2001, Outram *et al* 2009), in northern Kazakhstan, suggest that an early date of 3300 BCE for riding is feasible.

The earliest definitive tack that can be documented in Eurasia occurred in the Early Bronze Age (Bokovenko 2000:304-5), circa 1800 BCE, where antler cheek pieces with blunt spikes or burrs on their inner surface emerged. The design of this type of cheek piece, which is also found in the Near East, resembles those on a modern "run-out" bit, and indicates that they were most probably used on draught animals (Littauer 1969).

The initial stage of the Scythian culture, documented at Arzhan between the 9th and 7th centuries BCE, is characterized by the mass production of the basic elements of the bridle. Many types of cheek-pieces (at least 11) have been identified and they are generally made of bronze. By the end of the 7th century BCE, the new Pazyryk style cheek-pieces have a wide distribution from Mongolia to Hungary. These new cheekpieces did not include studs so common on cheek-pieces used to guide driven horses, but rather smooth inner surfaces which could be used on horses under saddle where riders depended on their legs for directional guidance. Thus an efficient bridle for riding was developed, as was the saddle, and documented at Pazyryk in the later 5th or 4th century BCE (Bokovenko 2000).

The initial construction of the saddle is often attributed to the pastoral peoples of Eurasia, perhaps largely because of the spectacular examples of saddles with attached girths and probably a treed frame found at Pazyryk in 1929. The saddles preserved and excavated in kurgans I, II, III, IV, V and VI, are fully evolved and are evidently a widespread Scythian type (Rudenko 1970:129) (Pl. I-2). All the saddles have pairs of leather straps secured to the edge of the cushions, front and back, an upper girth-strap, breast-and crupper-straps. The saddles consisted of two cushions formed from strips of leather stitched together with sinew thread, and on some a wooden spacer is included (kurgans III-VI). The cushions were filled with deer hair or occasionally with sedge grasses. These saddles raised the rider's weight off the spine of the horse and distributed it to the horse's flanks directly behind the withers. This not only made riding more stable, but also saved the horse from injury to the vulnerable bony projections of the thoracic vertebrae caused by the rider's body pounding on the horse's back. Saddle covers were of the same shape as the cushions and were cut from soft, thin black or white felt, dyed red or blue. They were attached to the cushions at front and back, and sometimes at the ends, with wooden arch bows. The saddles in barrows III-VI have large bows, sometimes trimmed with leather or covered with red lacquered wooden pommels. The sweat-cloths were of the same shape as the saddle, cut from white, soft and thick felt (Rudenko 1970:131-132). These assemblages offered additional comfort to the rider as well as the opportunity for a spectacular display as they were often highly adorned with wooden, woolen, and/or felt attachments.

Other frozen tombs excavated nearby in the Altai, in the Ukok plateau at Ak-Alakha, and at Berel in eastern Kazakhstan confirm a contemporary regional mortuary practice and artifact style. Like Pazyryk, these tombs included saddles as part of horse sacrifice and display of status. For instance, beginning in 1997 an international team began to excavate Tomb 11 at Berel. Several features of the tomb suggested to the excavators that it had belonged to an important member of the local leadership (Francfort 1999:49-57). The owner's high status was indicated by the size of the kurgan (63m in diameter) and the tomb chamber (2×4m), the fine construction of the tomb chamber (pine and larch board framework with a ceiling of birch bark sheets, felt, and a layer of twigs), as well as the presence of large gilded wooden ibex horns (70cm) attached to two of thirteen of the sacrificed horses.

Berel's Tomb 11 contained two remarkably preserved bodies of a young man and an older woman, as well as plentiful funerary goods and well-preserved architecture. Perhaps of the greatest interest for our purposes, it included the ceremonially adorned bodies of thirteen sacrificed horses (Samashev 2000:41). The animals were laid out in two layers, seven on the bottom and six on the top. The horses were outfitted in bits, bridle pendants, gilded wooden garlands, red fabric saddle blankets and saddles (Pl. I-3). The saddle covers were decorated with multicolored felt appliqués and embroidered with designs from the Scytho-Siberian animal tradition. The animal imagery on the horse regalia includes feline predators, griffins, sheep, ibexes, deer and elk, as well as plant motifs. All were made of carved wood covered with gold or tin leaf. Saddles were cinched to all horses and were constructed of leather pouches, stuffed with wool or grass (Francfort 1999:48). The horse farthest to the east wore large imitation ibex horns carved of wood, wrapped in red leather, and gilded along the scalloped border. The ibex horns may have had a symbolic value as the mark of a supreme leader, which is still noted in the region today according to Samashev (2006:43). The bronze dagger with a gold foil-wrapped hilt hung from the saddle pad suggests a military connection for the horses, even though short swords are typically weapons of an infantry! Here, as Henri-Paul Francfort says, "a new chapter has (sic) opened in the history of equitation…" (Francfort 1999:61).

The cemetery at Ak-Alakha, on the Ukok Plateau in the southern Altai close to the Ak-Alakha River (left bank), is about 70-80 km east of Berel. Between 1990 and 1995 N. Polos'mak excavated a group of frozen kurgans of the Pazyryk type and period, dating from the 4th to the 3rd centuries BCE. A horse in full regalia—a saddle, saddle blanket, and long skirts that would have hung before and behind the rider's leg (Polos'mak, n.d.) (Pl. I-4)—was excavated intact.

In his report, Francfort proposed that the peoples buried at Berel and Ak-Alakha must have belonged to the same cultural group (1999:63). He argued that the nomadic peoples of the Altai, now documented in burials at several sites, were not isolated, but took part in vast trading movements that in the 4th century went from Achaemenid Persia to China (Francfort 1999:62). He further speculated that these discoveries expose the regional synthesis of arts that include inspiration from Pazyryk and other areas of the Altai. In addition, Frankfurt reminds us that the arts of these nomads supplement and synthesize elements from older local sources, as well as Chinese art and that of the Achaemenids after Darius. The figures of elk and other animals, for example, document older traditions from Bronze-Age Siberia; the images of horned lions, leonine griffins, and sphinxes seem to come out of decorative programs at palaces at Susa and Persepolis; and felines may have been inspired by eastern Zhou bronzes of China (Francfort 1999:62). He suggests that it may have been the gold in the mountains that was sought by peoples beyond Siberia and that sparked trade and exchange.

Certainly the analogies in type and style of funerary imagery and practice have long suggested these links and have initiated speculation about how and why these connections might have been made. However, only recently has archaeology supplied actual examples that show linkages further to the east, especially in present-day western China, in the Xinjiang Uighur Autonomous Region (Chen and Hiebert 1995; Linduff 2000; Mei 2000). Both tomb types and their contents, including saddles, suggest concretely that this area and its pastoral peoples had participated in exchange with eastern Eurasia as well as dynastic

China. There is some question, however, about which direction the arrows of transmission point, and about the nature of the exchange—either as the result of an economic drive or of a search for procurement of exotica.

The Examples from Xinjiang

Three sites in present-day central southern and northern Xinjiang have yielded saddles that are comparable to those from Pazyryk (Pl. I-2). These finds confirm the easternmost and earliest use of the saddle, from as early as the 8th century BCE at Zaghunluq (MXUAR 2003:89-136; He 1999:70-93; Mallory and Mair 1999:153-4). In addition, a second find at Subeshi, near Turfan, dating from about 280 BCE (Lu 2001: 94-113; Mallory and Mair 1999:25, 215), and another at Sampula, near Khotan, dating from the first part of the second century to first centuries BCE, offer evidence of its continued use in the region.

The cemetery at Zaghunluq lies on the border of the Taklamakan Desert beyond the oasis in Chärchän (Qiemo) City, in Xinjiang, and was in use from about 1000 BCE to about the fifth century CE (fig. 1).[3] The only textual notice of Chärchän is from the *History of the Han* and suggests that in the third century BCE it was a small state in the 'Western Regions' that included 230 households, 1610 people, and 320 qualified soldiers (*Hanshu Xiyu Zhuan*). By then, it was an outpost of the Han military, from the Chinese point of view.

The cultural remains of the graveyard at Zaghunluq can be divided into three phases dating to between the 10th century BCE and the 5th century CE. The one grave of the first phase is a rectangular earth shaft tomb typical of the region in the late Neolithic. Funerary goods include polychrome pottery and wooden articles dated to about 1000 BCE. Ninety tombs have been excavated from the second phase, from which the saddle comes, and date from between the 8th and the 1st century BCE. There the graves were all rectangular shaft tombs with or without a wooden framed chamber—a feature shared with the Altai graves. Sixty-nine of the tombs yielded intact remains of the occupants, preserved well in the very dry and saline conditions of the area. Several of the corpses were either tattooed or had painted designs on their faces and arms.

Dressed in tunics and pants, many wore hats and foot wrappings, and were buried with wooden combs and tools, including spindles and whorls. Objects made of wood and clay were the largest number of grave goods, although stone, iron, copper items were also found. Animal sacrifices were made in some tombs, and included sheep horns, heads, and scapulae;

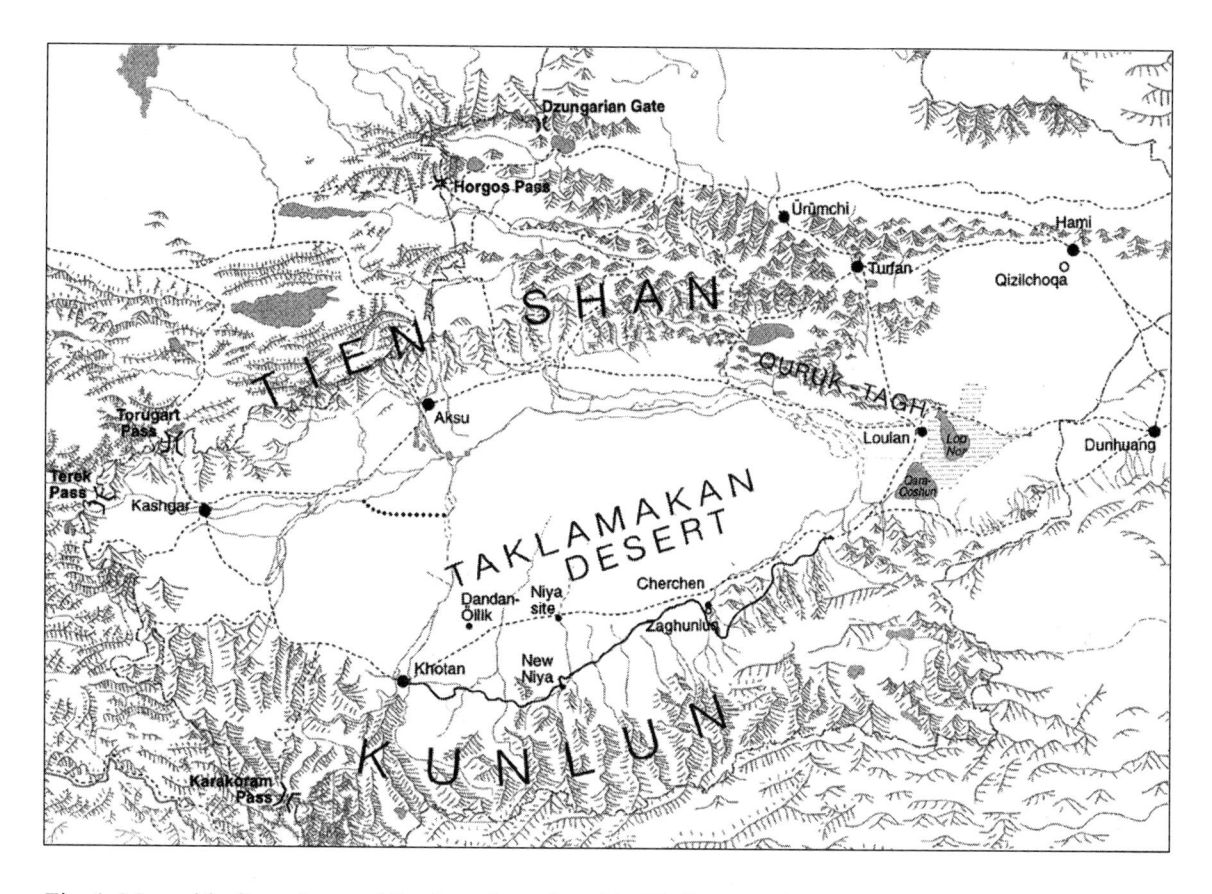

Fig. 1. Map with sites where saddles have been found in Xinjiang, PRC

horse heads, teeth, and jaws, but no whole animal sacrifices. The custom of placing food in the grave was popular and included both mutton as well as products made from flour (Pl. I-5). The deceased were buried singly, with two to five individuals, or collectively in secondary burials of 10 to 20 individuals. Most were placed in a flexed supine position, and the rest are in a prone position with a local variation in which the knees were flexed upward and held in place by a wooden support.

The third phase dates from the first to the sixth centuries CE and is characterized by catacomb tombs, a new type for this region. Lacquer and silk of Chinese dynastic types, as well as imported glass and bone beads have been found in these tombs. Phase three was dated based on its grey wheel-thrown pottery, found throughout Xinjiang and further east into dynastic China in the first throughout the fifth centuries CE.

Of primary interest here are tombs from Phase Two. Four C14 samples were made from this Phase and provide dates ranging from c. 860 to 350 BCE [M1 (792+60 BCE); M4 (388+59 BCE); M14 (761+61 BCE); and M24 (896+61 BCE)] (MXUAR 2003:132).[4] Imported silks of Chinese metropolitan types and black-slipped pottery typical of southern margins of the Taklamakan Desert were found in the tombs from the entire period. From this Phase, two particular tombs concern us: M14 (with a carbon date of 761+61 BCE) and M2 with comparable grave goods to M14 and presumably of a similar date in the mid-eighth century BCE.

Tomb M14 is in the southwestern sector of the cemetery. The pit was filled with fine, yellowish, sandy earth, mixed with fragments of woolen textiles and reed grasses. The tomb was two-tiered with platforms around a chamber with sloping sides and a wooden chamber shell, similar to those described at Berel. With traces of construction materials preserved in this tomb, the structure of the wooden shells was reconstructed by the excavator. They consisted of reed and grass bundles wrapped with woolen textiles and bound with woolen twine that created a thatched top (about 15cm. thick); under that was a layer of tamarisk branches set directly on the rafters. The size of M14 at the top was 7 (E-W) by 5.6 meters (N-S); the chamber was 5 (N-S) by 3.6 (E-W) meters and 1.4 meters deep.

M14 was a joint burial of 19 occupants; all intact bodies were placed in a flexed supine position. Among the 19, 15 were adults, four were male and 11 female; the genders of two were unclear; and two were infants. Burial furniture included ten woolen blankets and two woolen chin pads. Grave goods were set around the occupants: one pottery bowl, one single-lugged ceramic pot, two whetstones, one wooden bow, one wooden reed (for weaving), two wooden vertical harps of Eurasian type, one wooden bow case part, two wooden combs, two wooden waist plaques, one wooden long-toothed comb, five wooden spindle wheels, three wooden canes, one wooden single-handled bowl, one wooden single-handled pot, one wooden cassette, one lacquered wooden stick, a stone bead, six glass beads, one bronze ring and some carved wooden objects and woolen bags and hats (Wang 1999: MXUAR 2003).

The tomb shares many features with those described at Berel: a two-level tomb chamber faced with wooden and reed or grass wall and roof covers; a preference of carved wooden artifacts; woolen carpets and woven fabrics; attire including woven wool tunics, pants, and long cloaks as well as leather and felt boots; and two vertical wooden harps. None of these features is typical of dynastic Chinese burials of the interior, but all are analogous or show cultural affinities to eastern Eurasia in terms of their artifacts, burial traditions, and pastoral lifeway. In addition, the pottery is a local black-slipped type. Perhaps the most striking discovery relating to pastoral cultures is the unique pair of hobbles for horses made of wood and woolen rope discovered in M14 (fig. 2). Still favored among mobile peoples

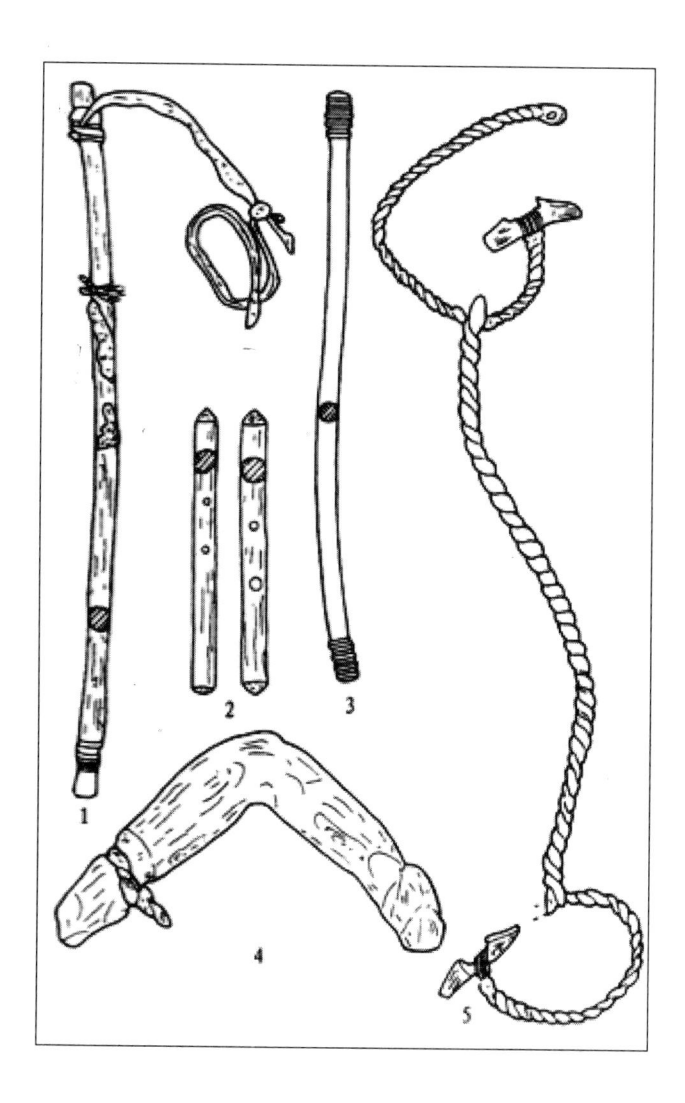

Fig. 2. Hobbles, line drawing, from Zaghunluq, Xinjiang, PRC, Tomb 2, wood and twine (After: *KGXB* 2003/1:105. fig. 7)

of the steppelands of Kazakhstan and other areas, they provide a portable, relatively secure controlling device that immobilizes the animal without necessitating the construction of a pen or corral, except for breeding. The people of Zaghunluq were therefore, keeping and training horses, as well as probably herding animals as part of their year-round activities. In addition, they were weaving cloth from wool probably collected from their own flocks. Preserved in these tombs are the tools and products of an agro-pastoral community (bread) whose identity at death included references to that lifestyle.

The chamber of Tomb M2 at Zaghunluq held four individuals as well as grave goods that included a round-based clay jar; a sacrificed horse, buffalo and an ass (?); wooden combs; a milking pail; knitting needles; arrows and a variety of woolen textiles--the typical equipment of hunter/pastoralists. The well-preserved bodies of the two adults, a male and a female, wore woven woolen cloaks and leather boots. Their faces were painted with yellow and red designs. The construction of the tomb was similar to M14 consisting of a large opening at the top tapering to the tomb chamber that was covered with a reed and tamarisk matting, but five distinctive layers, as opposed to two at M14, were determined. The most remarkable find in this previously entered tomb, was in the first layer. There, placed on a one meter long and 0.75 meter wide rectangular white felt blanket, were leather covered saddle cushions filled with sheep fleece (Pl. I-6). Constructed in precisely the same fashion as those from Pazyryk, this was the first of its kind discovered this far east. Under it was a brown robe of coarse wool thread of a twill weave of local manufacture.

The dating of this tomb as reported by Ahmat Rashid gives a calibrated C14 date of about 950 BCE (Laboratory of the Institute for Cultural Relics, Conservation Science of the Chinese National Bureau of Cultural Relics: 2840+80 years BP, calibrated to 2960+115 years BP; 1999:74; Rashid and He 2001). However, this date is not given by the excavator Wang Bo in his report published in 2003. Based on the comparability of M2 to M14 in contents and shape, M2 may be dated to about 761+61 BCE. Whatever its true date, it is much earlier than Pazyryk, Berel and Ak-Alakha. The excavator is very careful to draw parallels among artifact types from Zaghunluq and those produced in the interior of dynastic China, and to point out analogies to materials from eastern Kazakhstan and the Altai, as well as to point out continuity with local traditions, especially in the ceramics.

These tombs contain artifacts that were used in hunter/pastoral lifeways, are absent of weapons, and show no signs of violence. Could it be that this context documents an early use of the saddle for domestic purposes including herding and travel? Anyone who has ridden any distance on a horse or herded for any length of time, knows that comfort is greatly aided by an even gaited, strong and healthy horse; a good saddle; and well-muscled legs on the rider! This region in Xinjiang is far from other population concentrations on the edge of a formidable desert—if they were in contact with other areas, they traversed across long distances. The distance from the site of Zaghunluq northeast to Turfan as the crow flies is, for instance, over 1000 km (633 miles) and from Zaghunluq west to Khotan over rider! This region in Xinjiang is far from other population concentrations on the edge of a formidable desert—if they were in contact with other areas, they traversed across long distances. The distance from the site of Zaghunluq northeast to Turfan as the crow flies is, for instance, over 1000 km (633 miles) and from Zaghunluq west to Khotan over 400 km (269 miles) (fig. 1)! Probably herders then as they are now, burial goods recovered show that these peoples had developed skills in weaving, and probably felting industries. Perhaps

Zaghunluq was located at a camp on a trade route—similar to that suggested by Francfort for Berel and the gold trade network. At Berel the elite were clearly consumers of gold for purposes of display on locally produced artifacts, although gold was surely not available to all in their community. In the case of the residents of Zaghunluq, if they were producing woven woolen fabrics for trade as well as for local consumption, they would have needed to move herds and/or goods.

A second, but much later site in Xinjiang, has also yielded a saddle (fig. 1). Called Subeshi after the Uighur word meaning "origin of water", it is located in a village north of the Tarim Basin, outside of Turfan (in Pichuan, Shanshan County). The burial and habitation site were constructed on an old oasis that had water from the upper reaches of the Tuyuk Gorge (Lu 2001). Both three-roomed dwellings and the graveyard at Subeshi, excavated between 1980 and 1992, document a long-term camp or a year-round settlement. Lü Enguo, the excavator, reported radiocarbon dates that range from c. 490 + 85 BCE (M?) to 280 + 80 BCE (M15, C III), but does not always identify from which tomb or house site materials come (Lü 2001). The discussion must generalize from that, therefore, until more precise information is available.

Thirteen undisturbed tombs of two types have been opened: shaft tombs, and shaft tombs with a side chamber, or catacomb tombs.[5] The tombs, he reports, from throughout the period have wood-covered chambers. Wooden and pottery bowls are all of the same shape and size, often with spiral designs. Most containers held foodstuffs that include sheep-goat heads, ribs, and legs—mutton appears on most funerary platters. Some of the pottery contains grains (millet), noodles, cubes of meat, meat congee, rice, etc. The unearthed bows and arrows are among the best-preserved materials and are contained separately in leather bags holding the bow and three to four arrows with iron or horn or what might have been antler tips. Leather bags also contain medicines, cosmetics, and other small personal items.

A most remarkable find is in the tomb (M134) of a male—a complete horse saddle with crupper, and bridle (Pl. I-7). Found lying next to the corpse, the saddle is made of two pieces of soft leather sewn together symmetrically—with a cantle and pommel formed at the ends of the leather pouches. The saddle pouches are filled with white deer fur and are quilted by stitching through each from inside to out. Both the front and back are decorated with bone ornaments; leather strips; and a very wide pair of girths, one of leather and the other of wool. Bone buttons and iron hooks were added to the saddle for convenience in carrying items. The bridle is made of leather and is similar to those still used in the area today. There is a leather buckle for hanging an ornamental tassel. The cheek pieces are made of *toghraq* (wild poplar found in the Tarim Basin) and the bit is of iron with two rings. There were no stirrups.

This also appears to be a working saddle, perhaps on display at the funeral as a signifier of the special status of the deceased, or perhaps of his occupation. The position of the deceased would not appear to be based on military prowess, as no equipment in the tomb indicates that activity. The tombs excavated at the site are part of a community cemetery, and this is the only saddle found there to date to our knowledge. This suggests restricted use and/or special significance for burial and perhaps for life.

Discussion and Conclusion

These finds in Xinjiang are remarkable and extend the geographic extent of traditions that are commonly associated with the Eurasian steppe. They document a life style that continued in this region for a very long time, even after there was direct contact with the dynastic Chinese from the interior. If the radiocarbon dates can be verified, the range of dates for the saddles from the 8th to the 4th centuries BCE and later could document repeated contact with areas both to their east and west, while remaining largely isolated since artifacts and products document contact with both Eurasia and dynastic China.

From the 5th to the 3rd centuries BCE Chinese society underwent significant change. Warfare among the regional city-state system was perpetual and increasingly fierce, and many technical and tactical inventions took place. For example, the official adoption of mounted warfare by the Chinese is traditionally dated to 307 BCE when King Wu Ling of the Zhao State decreed that Zhao soldiers should wear nomadic dress and ride astride in battle in an effort to improve their military effectiveness in interstate warfare (So and Bunker 1995:29). The whole of the society, including for the first time the peasants, was organized at the time to meet the needs of war, and major innovations in social organization resulted. War itself was theorized and integrated into an all-inclusive cosmological system (Yates 1999:9). From this time on in the fourth century BCE there is no question that the Chinese as well as the peoples of the eastern Eurasian steppe used cavalry, including saddles. This is well documented at Pazyryk and in newly excavated clay figures of horses and riders from Xianyang (XCWKY 1996) (Pl. I-8).

The regions to the west of dynastic China, in Xinjiang, during the period from the

8th to the 4th century BCE, remained largely self-sufficient, while probably engaged in trade. The sites from both periods discussed today show no signs of territorial expansion around Xinjiang, either by stretching outward toward their neighbors or by intrusion from outside. The material culture and customs recorded in burials document a local investment in technological innovation, material culture, and burial customs that borrow and/or import from others, while remaining locally integrated throughout many centuries. These would seem to have been communities of peoples of like customs, subsistence patterns and economies—ones that used the horse for transport and for herding. If so, this early example of a saddle from Zaghunluq may simply have been used for moving herds or for travel associated with trade. In this scenario, the saddle would have had quite a peaceful duty and beginning!

BIBLIOGRAPHY OF WORKS CITED

Aruz, Joan, Ann Farkas, Andrei Alekseev, and Elena Korolkova (eds.)
    2001   *The Golden Deer of Eurasia: Scythian and Sarmatian Treasures from the Russian Steppes*, NY and New Haven: The Metropolitan Museum of Art, Yale University Press.

Beattie, Russel H.
    1981   *Saddles*, Norman: Oklahoma University Press.

Bokovenko, Nikolai
    2000   "The origins of horse riding and the development of ancient Central Asian nomadic riding harnesses", in Davis-Kimball, Eileen M. Murphy, Ludmila Koryakova, Leonid T. Yablonsky, (eds.), *Kurgans, Ritual Sties, and Settlements: Eurasian and Iron Age*, Cambridge: BAR International Series 890.

Chang, Claudia (ed.), and Katherine S. Guroff (assoc. Ee.)
    2006   *Of Gold and Grass: Nomads of Kazakhstan*, Foundation for Arts and Education.

Chen, Kwang-tzuu and Frederick T. Hiebert
    1995   "Late prehistory of Xinjiang in relation to its neighbors", *Journal of World Prehistory*, 9:2:243-300.

Chevenix-Trench, Charles
    1970   *A History of Horsemanship*, Garden City, NY: Doubleday & C.

Clutton-Brock, Juliet
    1992   *Horse Power: A History of the Horse and the Donkey in Human Societies,* London: Thames and

Hudson.

Francfort, Henri-Paul

1999 "The frozen mausoleum of the Scythian prince", *Ligabue Magazine* 35, pp.42-63.

Goodrich, Chauncy

1984 "Riding astride and the saddle in ancient China", *Harvard Journal of Asiatic Studies*, vol. 44, no. 2, pp.279-306.

Griaznov, Mikhail P.

1969 *The Ancient Civilization of Southern Siberia*, trans. by James Hogarth, New York: Cowles Book Company.

Jankovich, Miklos

1971 *They Rode into Europe*, London: George Harrap and Company.

Lerner, Judith

1991 "Some so-called Achaemenid objects from Pazyryk", *Source,* vol. X, no. 4, pp.8-15.

Linduff, Katheryn M., Rubin Han and Shuyuan Sun

2000 *The Beginnings of Metallurgy in China*, Lampeter: Mellen Press.

Lü Enguo 呂恩國

2001 "Subeisi gushi" 蘇貝希古屍 (The mummies of Subeshi), in Wang Binghua 王炳華 ed., *Xinjiang Gushi: Gudai Xinjiang Jumin ji qi Wenhua* 《新疆古屍: 古代新疆居民及其文化》(The Ancient Corpses of Xinjiang: The Inhabitants of Ancient Xinjiang and their Culture), Ürümchi 烏魯木齊: Xinjiang Renmin Chubanshe 新疆人民出版社, pp.94-113.

Mallory, J. P. and Victor Mair

2000 *The Tarim Mummies: Ancient China and the Mystery of the Earliest Peoples from the West*, London: Thames and Hudson.

Mei Jianjun

2000 *Copper and Bronze Metallurgy in Late Prehistoric Xinjiang: Its Cultural Context and Relationship with Neighboring Regions,* London: BAR International Series 865.

Moorey, P.R.S.

1970 "Pictorial evidence for the history of horse-riding in Iraq before the Kassite period", *Iraq* vol. 32, no. 1, pp.36-50.

MXUAR =Museum of Xinjiang Uyghur Autonomous Region, CPAM of Bayinggolin Mongolian Autonomous Prefecture, and CPAM of Chärchän County 新疆維吾爾自治區博物館，巴州文管所，且末縣文管所.

2003 "Xinjiang Chärchän Zaghunluk yihao mu fajue baogao" 新疆且末扎滾魯克一號墓地發掘報告 (Excavation of tomb no. 1 at Zaghunluk, Chärchän, Xinjiang", *Kaogu Xuebao* 《考古學報》, no.1, pp.89-136.

Olsen, Sandra

    2001   "The importance of thong-smoothers at Botai, Kazakhstan", A. Choyke and L. Bartosiewicz eds., *Crafting Bone: Skeletal Technologies through Time and Space*, pp. 197-206. BAR International Series 937. Oxford: Archaeopress.

    2006   "Early horse domestication: Weighing the evidence", S.L. Olsen, S. Grant, A.M. Choyke and L. Bartosiewicz eds., *Horses and Humans: The Evolution of Human-Equine Relationships*. Oxford: BAR, International Series 1560: 81-113.

Outram, A., N. Stear, R. Bendrey, S. Olsen, A. Kasparov, V. Zaibert, N. Thorpe, and R. Evershed

    2009   "The earliest horse harnessing and milking", *Science* 323, pp.1332-1335.

Owen, David I.

    1991   "The first equestrian: An Ur III glyptic scene", *Acta Sumerologica* 13:259-273.

Polos'mak, N.V.

    2001   "Vsadniki Ukoka", Infolio-press.

Rashid, Ahmat 阿合實提·熱西提 and He Dexiu 何德修

    2002   "*Zhahongluke gushi*" 扎洪魯克古屍 (The mummies of Zaghunluq), in Wang Binghua 王炳華 ed., *Xinjiang Gushi: Gudai Xinjiang Jumin ji qi Wenhua* 《新疆古屍: 古代新疆居民及其文化》 (The Ancient Corpses of Xinjiang: The Inhabitants of Ancient Xinjiang and Their Culture), Ürümchi 烏魯木齊: Xinjiang Renmin Chubanshe 新疆人民出版社, pp.70-93.

Reimer, Paula J.

    1999   "A new twist in the radiocarbon tale", *Science*, 21 December, vol. 294, pp. 2529-2535, 2494-2495.

Rudenko, Sergei I.

    1970   *Frozen Tombs of Siberia: The Pazyryk Burials of Iron Age Horsemen,* Berkeley and Los Angeles: University of California Press.

Rubinson, Karen S.

    2006   "'Animal style' art and the image of the horse and rider Ērān ud Anērān", in Compareti, Matteo, Paola Raffetta, and Gianroberto Scaria eds., *Studies Presented to Boris Il'ič Maršak on the Occasion of His 70th Birthday*, Venezia: Libreria Editrice Cafoscarina, pp.533-542.

Samashev, Zainolla S.

    2006   "Culture of the nomadic elite of Kazakhstan's Altai region (Based on materials from the Berel necropolis), in Claudia Chang (ed.) and Katherine S. Guroff (assoc. ed.), *Of Gold and Grass: Nomads of Kazakhstan*, Foundation for Arts and Education, pp.35-44.

Schulman, A. R.

    1957   "Egyptian representation of horseman riding in the New Kingdom", *Journal of Near Eastern Studies*, vol. 16.

Schomberg, Reginald C. F.

    1930   "The climatic conditions of the Tarim Basin", *The Geographical Journal* 75 (4): 313-320.

So, Jenny F. and Emma C. Bunker

    1995   *Traders and Raiders on China's Northern Frontier*, Arthur M. Sackler Gallery, Smithsonian Institution and the University of Washington Press.

Wang Binghua 王炳華 ed.

    2000   *Xinjiang Gushi: Gudai Xinjiang Jumin ji qi Wenhua*《新疆古屍: 古代新疆居民及其文化》(The Ancient Corpses of Xinjiang: The Inhabitants of Ancient Xinjiang and Their Culture), Ürümchi: 烏魯木齊 Xinjiang Renmin Chubanshe 新疆人民出版社.

XCWKY=Xianyang City Wenwu Kaogu Yanjiusuo 咸陽市文物考古研究所

    1996   "Brief report on the excavation of the Qin tomb at the Xianyang Petroleum Steel Pipe and Cable Plant" 咸陽石油鋼管鋼繩廠秦墓清理簡報, *Kaogu yu Wenwu*《考古文物》, no. 5.

Yates, Robin

    1999   "Early China", in *War and Society in the Ancient and Medieval Worlds*, Kurt A. Raaflaub and Nathan S. Rosenstein (eds.), Center for Hellenic Studies, Cambridge, MA: Harvard University Press, pp. 7-45.

NOTES

[1] This topic is discussed by Karen S. Rubinson (2006) where she suggests that these images appear when they do only after the populations have moved to a more semi-nomadic lifestyle.

[2] The carpet from kurgan no. 5, which displays horses with riders, is not likely a nomadic product (Lerner 1991:12).

[3] All information on the graves at Zaghunluq comes from the excavation report, MXUAR: 2003:89-136, unless otherwise noted.

[4] There is difficulty with certifying all C-14 dates at this time. See Paula J. Reimer, "A New Twist in the Radiocarbon Tale, *Science*, 21 December, vol. 294, pp. 2529-2535, 2494-2495.

[5] The information reported on the excavation of Subeshi comes from Lü 2001:94-113.

ACKNOWLEDGEMENTS: Sophie Legrand (University of Paris), Wang Bo (Institute of Archaeology, Xinjiang), Leslie Wallace and Han Jiayao (University of Pittsburgh), prepared and/or sent images of excavated materials directly to us. Margaret McGill (University of Pittsburgh, FFA Library) diligently searched for texts that no ordinary human being could find! Thanks to them all. A version of this paper was given first at the Turfan Conference in 2008 and in 2010 at Hofstra University.

On the Contacts between the Scythian Animal Style of the Eurasian Steppe and Chinese Art

E.V. Perevodchikova

I. Introduction

The Scythian 'Animal Style' is one of the main characteristics of the great cultural community of early nomads of the Eurasian steppe, and its origins are a riddle that has not yet been solved. The 'Animal Style' came into existence quite abruptly in the first half of the 1st millennium BCE, although the exact date of this event is not yet established: some researchers believe it was in the 8th century BCE, while others place it in the 7th century BCE. This early nomadic community was variously designated the Scythian world, the Scytho-Siberian world, or the Scytho-Siberian historical-cultural unity, named for the nomadic inhabitants of the steppe on the northern coast of the Black Sea described and made famous in Herodotus' *Histories*. Concerning this community, the name "Scythian" is quite conventional and is used for the whole nomadic community, but we should be aware that the nomadic peoples of the eastern steppe territories were not just ethnic Scythians. We should similarly regard the Scythian Animal Style as referring to the art of all the early nomadic peoples of the Eurasian steppe, not only that of the Scythians.

The question of the origins of the Scythian Animal Style is part of the question of the origins of the early nomads in general, as the two events are intertwined. The problem is that the style has no roots in the antiquities of the previous steppe cultures, nor does it have roots in the antiquities of the surrounding territories. The most reasonable explanation of this situation is the polycentric origins of the Animal Style, which formed as a result of the citation of animal images in the traditions of the surrounding civilizations.[1] This explanation coincides with the idea of the polycentric origins of the early nomadic community.[2]

The main characteristics of Scythian art were described by the famous Russian historian and archaeologist M.I. Rostovtzeff.[3] According to the rules of this art, the main features of animals should be accentuated. Accentuation in the Scythian Animal Style was achieved in different ways. One was exaggeration of the main features of the animal. In Scythian art we usually see animals with very big eyes, ears, mouths, paws, or horns; birds feature large beaks, sometimes spiraliform. These parts of the animals could also be transformed into other images; the claws of beasts or the antlers of deer could be transformed into the beaks of birds of prey. The shoulders of various animals could similarly be transformed into bird heads, and so on.

The Animal Style was not used to depict all animals, but only some types: beasts of prey (felines and others), animals with hooves (deer, ibexes, goats, sheep), and birds (usually birds of prey). These animals were depicted in definite postures, of which the repertory was as strict as the repertory of the types of animals. Each kind of animal could only be depicted in its own postures: only beasts of prey could be presented in circular arrangements or be depicted with legs bent at right angles, only animals with hooves could shown in a recumbent position, and so on. Being strictly connected with the types of animals, their postures may be also regarded as their signs-just like the accentuated features of the animals.

There were also features common to animals of different types: usually their surface was modeled in planes joining at an angle. This relief modeling usually accentuated the shoulders and thighs of the animal, as well as its details. The manner of depicting the eyes of animals was also common to all animal types.

There are thus groups of characteristics of images in the Scythian Animal Style. Some characteristics are common to the images of all types of animals (surface relief, accentuation of shoulder and thigh, depiction of eyes). Other groups are common to some groups of animals (birds, beasts of prey, animals with hooves) — the depiction of ears, nostrils, legs and paws, and the specific positions for different groups of animals. There are also characteristics—a particular type of horn—specifically for each kind of animal with hooves.

The very idea of accentuation of the main parts of the animal renders the image of the animal somewhat conceptual, the characteristics of images being various kinds of signs. Thus the groups of characteristics more or less common to some groups of animals may be regarded as a system of signs relevant or irrelevant to the groups of animals. This system reflected the zoological classification of Scythian world.[4]

This sketch of the main principles of Scythian art is necessary in understanding this art as a logically organized system of signs and rules, which lived throughout the entire history of the Animal Style, in spite of all the formal changes in its masterpieces. As in any other traditional art, the rules of the Scythian Animal Style were predicated on the possibility of variation in following them. In contact with surrounding artistic traditions, this system could borrow features and place them according to its own rules. These theses are important for our main subject.

II. The Features of Chinese Art in the Scythian Animal Style of some Eastern Steppe Territories

After achieving an initial commonality throughout the entire territory of the steppe (with only small local differences) by about the 5th century BCE, the Animal Style then began to break down into several local variants. The specific features of the local variants partly derived from the art of surrounding territories as a result of contacts between the steppe nomads and their neighbors. From these contacts the Scythian animal style borrowed features of surrounding traditions. In this way the art of the Pontic steppes acquired features of Greek and Thracian art, the Animal Style of the Northern Caucasus region acquired features of Graeco-Persian art and Caucasian art, and so on.

In the masterpieces of the Animal Style in some eastern parts of the Eurasian steppe we can see the features of Chinese art. They may be traced in the antiquities of Altai, southern Kazakhstan, Xinjiang, and some nearby territories of Centtral Asia.

The famous barrows of Altai are unique because of the frozen tombs in them. The frozen soil in the burials conserved all organic materials, and so we have a number of items in wood, leather, wool, and other materials. Many are masterpieces of the Animal Style. The first archaeologist who examined this phenomenon was the famous Russian orientalist, ethnologist and archaeologist V.V. Radlov who excavated Berel and Katanda barrows in 1865.[5] Later, in the 1920s Soviet archaeologists M.P. Griaznov [6] and S.I. Rudenko began the excavations of the famous Pazyryk barrows. In the 1940s and 1950s S.I. Rudenko excavated Pazyryk, Tuekta and Bashadar barrows.[7] On the cusp of the 20th and 21st centuries N.V. Polos'mak excavated barrows with frozen tombs on the Ukok plateau.[8] Many specimens of ancient art were yielded through the excavation of the Berel barrows by Z. Samashev (the Kazakhstan expedition).[9]

M.P. Griaznov mentioned the Chinese character of one of the ornamental motifs (dating it to the Han epoch) and was thus the first scholar to note the Chinese influence in the Altai antiquities.[10]

However, the first systematic argumentation of the thesis of the Chinese impact on the Altai barrows was presented by S.V. Kiselev. On the basis of the items of Chinese import from the barrows of Altai he dated these barrows to the Han era. He also described some ornaments from Pazyryk as Chinese, found resemblances in the visages of animals to *taotie* masks, and attributed some figures of birds as Chinese 'phoenixes' of the Han period. Synchronizing the Pazyryk barrows with the Sarmatian epoch, he considered the resemblance of the Altai and Scythian antiquities of Eastern Europe and some features of Achaemenid art to be the result of archaization in the style of Altai art.[11]

S.I. Rudenko dated the Altai barrows to the 5th-4th centuries BCE on the basis of parallels between Altai items and Achaemenid art. Convinced that connections with China could not be dated before the Han epoch, he denied all Kiselev's theses concerning Chinese parallels in the art of Altai.[12]

The dating of these barrows by Rudenko was believed to be true until most recently, as were his conclusions regarding the Achaemenid parallels. The Chinese parallels were forgotten along with Kiselev's dating.

But, could Kiselev have possibly been correct regarding the Chinese features of the art of the Altai barrows? Do they not exist though dated to another time? Dating them to the 5th-4th centuries BCE synchronizes them with the Late Zhou, the Warring States period of Chinese history. Of course, at that time China was not yet a vast empire with extensive international links, but let us try to find some features of the Chinese Art in the antiquities from the Altai barrows of the 5th-4th centuries BCE; they should be dated to the Warring States period, coeval to the Achaemenid period in Iran.

We can see some dragon-like images (fig. 1: 1) with curved horns and open mouths which resemble Chinese examples.

There is a series of images of beast heads *en face* (feline-according to the definition by Rudenko),[13] which are quite similar to the *taotie* mask motifs in Chinese art found in the Pazyryk barrows (fig. 1: 3-6) They have some characteristics of *taotie* images. We can see curled horns (fig. 1: 4, 5), sometimes transformed into ears with curls (fig. 1: 3, 6). This transformation looks quite logical because circular horns of *taotie* resemble large exaggerated ears in the Scythian tradition and may have been understood by the Altai people as ears (there are also examples of *taotie* depictions with horns transformed into ears in Chinese art of the Zhou era).[14] Other characteristics of *taotie*-the absence of the lower jaw and the specific form of the eyes-confirm the impression of similarity. In one case (fig. 1: 2) it is difficult to know whether we are looking at a *taotie* or a horned Achaemenid griffin.

Fig. 1. Specimens of the Animal Style of Altai with features of Chinese art (after S. I. Rudenko's works): 1, Torque, reconstruction, Pazyryk (Rudenko, 1953, fig. 79); 2, Bridle pendant, Pazyryk (Rudenko, 1960, fig 159a); 3, Bridle ornament, Tuekta (Rudenko, 1960, fig. 144ф); 4-6, Bridle ornaments, Pazyryk (Rudenko, 1960, fig. 144о, д, ц); 7, Bridle ornament, Katanda (Rudenko, 1960, fig. 150и)

These features may also be seen in the art of areas neighboring the Altai regions. We can mention the golden plaques resembling Chinese *taotie* masks found in the Issyk barrow in southern Kazakhstan, [15] and similar plaques from Kyrgyzstan [16] and from eastern Turkestan.[17] The images of dragon-like creatures with horns were found in southern Siberia, and since the 18th century they have been part of the so-called Siberian collection of Peter I.[18]

T. Frish found one specifically Chinese composition in the art of Altai: the beast rolled around its head *en face* [19](the heads of Scythian rolled beasts are usually depicted in profile and never placed in the center of composition) fig. 1, 7.

Another characteristic of the Animal Style of the Altai barrows suggestive of Chinese art is the plentiful number of various curls covering almost the whole figure of an animal, but accentuating its main parts: the ears, nostrils, paws, shoulders, and thighs. Something of this can be seen in ancient Chinese art from the Shang-Yin period and throughout the Zhou epoch.[20]

However, some of these features may also be seen in Achaemenid art. The horned griffins are one of the favorite fantastic creatures of this tradition and are called 'griffins of the Achaemenid type'.[21] Curls adorning nostrils and mouths are also usual in Iranian art (the so-called 'lotus form'), as are the ornamental figures on the shoulders of an animal. Even the handles of vessels in the form of a horned fantastic creature with its head turned backwards are mutual to both traditions.

M. I. Rostovtzeff saw these parallels in 1929, when both the early Chinese art and the Altai barrows were barely known, and he explained some common features of Scythian

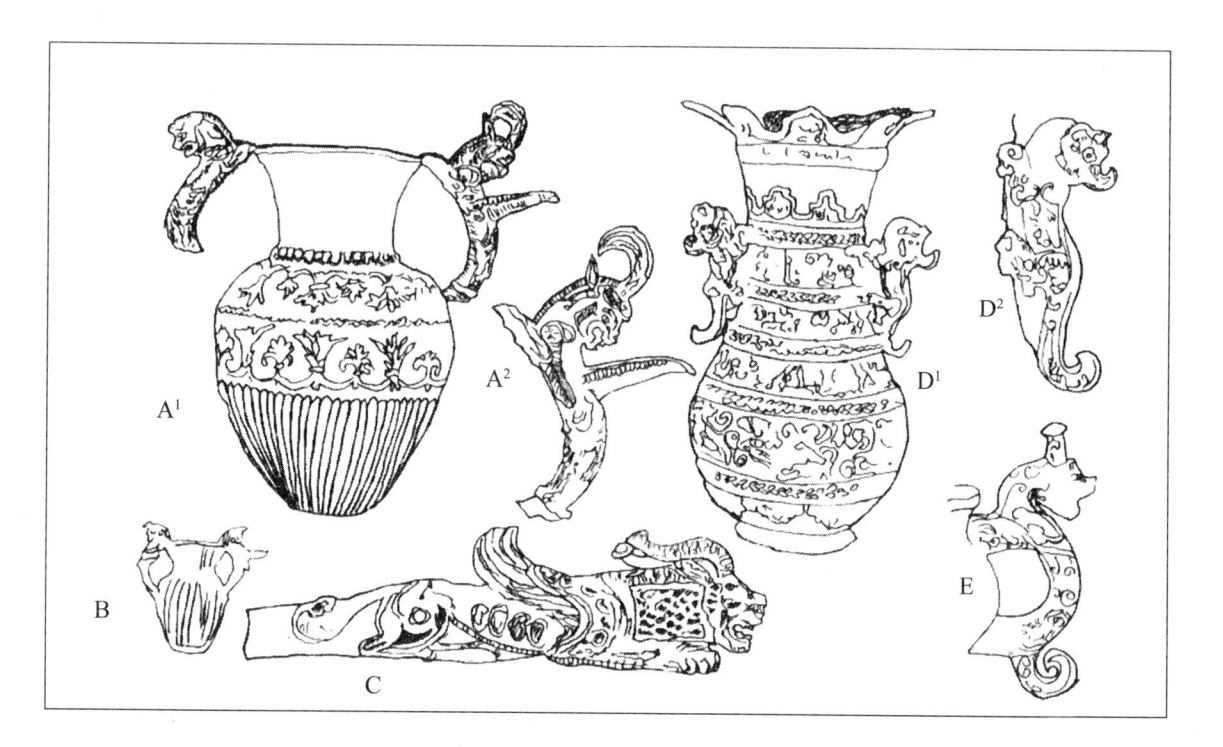

Fig. 2. Images of horned creatures in Persian and Chinese Art (after Minns, 1942, Pl. XV): A, Duvanli, Bulgaria; B, Persepolis, relief; C, Siberian collection of Peter I; D, Cull collection; E, Loo collection

and Chinese art in terms of the nomadic influence on Chinese culture in the Late Zhou era. Regarding the similarity of types of fantastic creatures of the Far and Near East, he raised the question of whether Chinese and Mesopotamian art derived from the same source.[22]

E.H. Minns saw these parallels in 1942 and demonstrated them through illustrations (fig. 2).[23] Since that time nothing changed: nobody has explained the parallels. Were they mere coincidence, the evidence of contacts between Iran and China in the pre-Han era, or the result of the mixture of the features of the two traditions in nomadic culture? Nobody knows, although early Chinese art is much better known now than in the time of Minns.[24]

III. The Animal Style and Chinese Craftsmen

Another episode of contacts between the Scythian Animal Style and Chinese art concerns the sphere of production of the works of art.

The excavations at the end of the 20th and beginning of the 21st century yielded information about the production of some masterpieces of the Animal Style in the eastern steppe territories.

The famous barrow Arzhan-2 in Tuva excavated by K.V. Chugunov, G. Parzinger, and A. Nagler revealed a series of works of art made in gold. Many are genuine masterpieces of ancient art. Although the works of art from Arzhan-2 stylistically belong to the Animal Style of the nomadic people and have no evident foreign features, the fine character of their technique raises the question of whether they were made by some foreign craftsmen.[25] Several items feature inlays of glass, and so nomadic craftsmen could not have made these. The production of glass in the 1st millennium BCE was known in the Near East and, since Zhou times, in China.[26]

Studying the gold dagger from Arzhan-2 (fig. 3), K. V. Chugunov noticed some Chinese parallels in the ornamental motifs in its decoration. These ornamental elements concern irrelevant parts of the decoration and so provide information about the "handwriting" of the craftsman.[27] This is the only note concerning Chinese stylistic parallels in the complex of Arzhan-2.

Other important work was done by R.S. Minasian. Being a specialist in ancient technologies of metalwork, he studied iron weapons with gold decoration and decided that it would have been too difficult to forge them. He subsequently examined iron daggers of the

Tagar culture of southern Siberia and noted they were cast, not forged, and so the same may be supposed concerning the Arzhan iron weapons decorated with gold. But casting iron in the Early Iron Age was known only in China, so these weapons could have been made by Chinese craftsmen for the nomads because of their purely nomadic forms and style.[28]

Therefore, we may suggest that there is a group of masterpieces in the Animal Style in Arzhan-2 barrow made by Chinese artisans. This hypothesis is possible because of technological research. As far as the style is concerned, we see almost nothing Chinese in it: it looks like a local modification of the Scythian Animal Style.

At the end of the 20th century the great barrow Filippovka 1 was excavated in Southern Ural region by A.H. Pshenichniuk. Although it had been plundered in ancient and modern times, its treasury with a quantity of gold items was not damaged.

Many works of art were found in the 1 Filippovka barrow.[29] Some of them were undoubtedly nomadic work: large carved wooden sculptures of deer, and some bone items. There were also precious vessels of Achaemenid production and other imported objects in the barrow.

Among other objects, we should specially note iron weapons decorated with gold and a series of gold ornaments on wooden vessels-all of them decorated in the Scythian Animal Style. The style of the Filippovka images of animals, though found in the Ural region, is quite eastern, with good Altai and Siberian analogies.[30]

Fig. 3. Iron dagger with gold ornamentation, Azhan-2 (after Chugunov, 2008, 99, fig. 1)

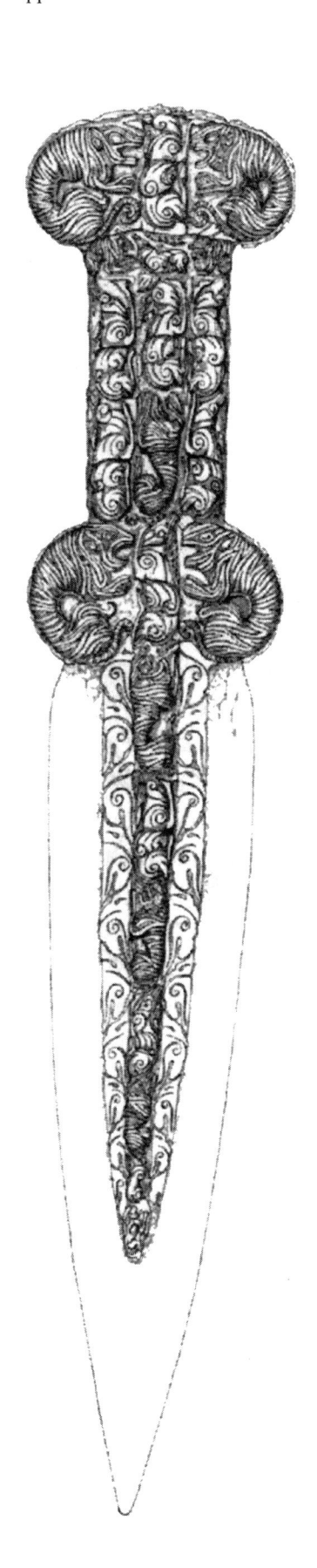

Wooden vessels are traditional artefacts of nomadic life and are often decorated with gold appliqué pieces. The study of the Filippovka applications revealed different techniques of production: these objects were either cast or carved from thin golden sheet. The ornaments may also have been either cast or engraved. As a result of correlation of characteristics of the applications, we can see that different groups of items should be interpreted as having been made in different workshops. Interestingly, some cast specimens were inlaid with glass, and so we must conclude that some of the gold appliqué pieces could not have been made by nomadic craftsmen, but only by foreign artisans.[31] Of course, we do not yet have direct evidence of the presence of Chinese craftsmen, but on the basis of the Altai stylistic parallels and glass inlays we cannot deny the possibility of their work in this situation. The presence of iron swords and daggers decorated with gold (though not studied technologically) makes this situation typologically similar to that at Arzhan-2.

IV. Conclusion

Comparing the above two cases we discern a paradoxical situation: artefacts bearing features of foreign tradition produced by local nomadic artisans, or artefacts bearing the style of nomadic art but produced by foreign craftsmen? To understand the reasons for this situation, we should compare these alternatives.

Carving wood and bone was traditional work in the nomadic cultures of Altai. Working in this tradition necessitated knowledge of rules which allow some variations, so that an artisan knowing the traditional rules could feel sufficiently free to change some features of the objects he was making. He could also appropriate new images from foreign traditions and translate them into the code of his native system. In interpreting these new foreign images he could make no mistakes in creating something new but traditionally proper. As a result we see beautiful works of art undoubtedly belonging to the Scythian Animal Style, but with some evident foreign features. This process may realize the thesis outlined in the Introduction regarding how a system borrows new features from the surrounding world and places them according to its own rules.

In the case of the Arzhan-2 and Filippovka barrows we see foreign craftsmen working for the nomadic aristocracy. The masters in this situation, the nomads, wanted to receive things aesthetically proper from the point of view of their own tradition, but the artisans could not be sufficiently free in this situation because the tradition was foreign to them. This situation is made more complicated for us because the works of Scythian art made by non-nomadic artisans had no features of any foreign artistic tradition. We know that Chinese craftsmen made iron weapons, but we can say nothing about other classes of object, although we know that glass production was known only in the Near East and China. Therefore, in this case our reconstruction of the situation is more hypothetical.

We should also note that masterpieces of foreign production, though not so free in variations, are nevertheless not simple copies-they look organically part of the Scythian Animal Style. The reason for this may be found in the very fact that a system of signs and rules served as the basis of the Animal Style (see Introduction). This system seems quite intelligible for different kinds of foreigners: for ancient foreign craftsmen, for modern researchers who can understand the rules of the system and, unfortunately, for modern craftsmen making fake items nowadays.

This short essay does not attempt a thorough description of all the phenomena remarked here, but this beautiful cross-cultural dialogue in the ancient history of the eastern part of the Eurasian steppe is a broad field awaiting further research.

Notes

[1] Е.В.Переводчикова, *Язык звериных образов. Очерки искусства евразийских степей скифской эпохи* (М., 1994), 63-86.

[2] М.П. Грязнов, «Об едином процессе развития скифо-сибирскиих культур», *Тезисы докладов Всесоюзной археологической конференции «проблемы скифо-сибирского культурно-исторического единства»* (Кемерово, 1979); И.В Яценко, Д.С Раевский, «Некоторые аспекты скифо-сарматской проблемы (обзорная статья)», *НАА* (М., 1980), no.5.

[3] M. Rostovtzeff, *The Animal Style in South Russia and China* (Princeton, 1929), 28-29.

[4] Е.В.Переводчикова. *Язык звериных образов*, 28-41.

[5] В.В.Радлов, *Из Сибири* (М., 1989), 445-451.

[6] М.П Грязнов," Раскопки на Алтае".*СГЭ*, (Л.,1940), вып. 1; М.П. Грязнов, *Первый Пазырыкский курган* (Л., 1950).

[7] С.И .Руденко, *Культура населения Горного Алтая в скифское время*. (М.-Л., 1953); С.И. Руденко, *Культура населения Центрального Алтая в скифское время*. (М.-Л., 1960).

[8] Н.В Полосьмак, *Всадники Укока* (Новосибирск, 2001).

[9] Z.Samašev, "Die Furstengräber von Berel", *Im Zeichen des goldenen Greifen* (München, 2007), 132-139.

[10] М.П.Грязнов, «Раскопки на Алтае», 18.

[11] С.В.Киселев, *Древняя история Южной Сибири (МИА, no.9)*, (М.-Л., 1949), 200-216.

[12] С.И. Руденко, *Культура населения Горного Алтая*, 345-360; С.И.Руденко, *Культура населения Центрального Алтая*, 162-172.

[13] С.И. Руденко, *Культура населения Центрального Алтая*, 281.

[14] W. Watson, *Style in the Arts of China* (New York, 1975), 38-42.

[15] К.А. Акишев, *Курган Иссык*. (М., 1978), 96-97, табл. 13, 14.

[16] К.А. Акишев *Курган Иссык*, 75-76, рис. 86, 87.

[17] Б.А. Литвинский, М.Н. Погребова, Д.С. Раевский, «К ранней истории саков Восточного Туркестана», *НАА* (М, 1985), no. 5, 72-73.

[18] С.И. Руденко, *Сибирская коллекция Петра I, САИ, Д3-9* (М.-Л., 1962) табл. XVI, XVII.

[19] T. Frisch, "Scythian art and some Chinese parallels", *Oriental Art* (London, 1949), vol. II, no.1, 63-64.

[20] For examples, see: O. Siren, *A History of Early Chinese Art*, vol. 1 (New York, 1971), pl. 10A, 46, 61; T. Frisch, *op. cit.*, 22, fig. 4; *The Jades from the Yin Sites at Anyang* 殷墟玉器 (Beijing, 1981), nos. 1, 2, 4, 6, 85-89, 92.

[21] G. Azarpay, "Some classical and Near Eastern motifs in the art of Pazyryk", *Artibus Asiae*, 1959, v. 2, no. 4, 334.

[22] M, Rostovtzeff, *op. cit.*, 70-74.

[23] E. H. Minns, *The Art of the Northern Nomads* (L., 1942), 25-35.

[24] Е.В.Переводчикова, *Язык звериных образов*, 135-138.

[25] К.В. Чугунов, Г Парцингер., А. Наглер, «Ювелирные изделия из кургана Аржан-2. Вопросы происхождения комплекса», *Ювелирное искусство и материальная культура. (Тезисы докладов)* (СПб., 2003), 129.

[26] J. Rawson, *Ancient China: Art and Archaeology* (London, 1980), 137.

[27] К.В. Чугунов, «Звериный стиль кургана Аржан-2: к постановке проблемы.», *Изобразительные памятники: стиль, эпоха, композиции. Материалы тематической научной конференции* (СПб, 2004), 275; К.В. Чугунов, «Кинжал-акинак из кургана Аржан-2», *СГЭ, 62* (СПб,2004), 74 ; К.В. Чугунов, «Некоторые особенности искусства кургана Аржан-2»,*Труды II (XVIII) Всероссийского археологического съезда в Суздале*, Том II (М., 2008), 98-101.

[28] Р.С. Минасян, «Сибирские железные кинжалы скифского времени»,*СГЭ, 62* (СПб., 2004), 68-71.

[29] *The Golden Deer of Eurasia: Scythian and Sarmatian Treasures from the Russian Steppes* (New York, 2000).

[30] Е.Ф. Королькова, *Звериный стиль Евразии. Искусство племен Нижнего Поволжья и Южного Приуралья в скифскую эпоху (VII-IV вв. до н.э.). Проблемы стиля и этнокультурной принадлежности*

(СПб., 2006), 41-51.

[31] Е.В.Переводчикова, «Золотые оковки сосудов из 1 Филипповского кургана: к постановке вопроса о месте производства», *Музейні читання. Матеріали наукової конференції «Ювелірне мистецтво- погляд крізь віки» 12-14 листопада 2007 р* (Київ, 2008), 67-69.

LIST OF ABBREVIATIONS

МИА: *Материалы и исследования по археологии СССР*
НАА: *Народы Азии и Африки*
САИ: *Археология СССР. Свод археологических источников*
СГЭ: *Сообщения Государственного Эрмитажа*

Between West and East: Anthropomorphic and Zoomorphic Representations in the Forest-Steppe Belt and Steppe Zone of Eastern Europe

Bartłomiej Szymon Szmoniewski

The representations of humans and animals (predators) in metal mounts from initial phases of the early Middle Ages in Eastern Europe are a specific cultural phenomenon (fig.1). They can be considered from various perspectives, which are interlinked and form a whole picture when taken together. The symbolic meaning of the representations is inseparably connected with the socio-economic background of the area where the objects have been found. While analyzing them, one has to consider the complex cultural and historical processes, whose influence is undeniable in the creation of some images, mostly the religious ones.

This article studies some issues posed by a complex analysis of metal figures (applications, belt elements, dies) of humans and animals. The main subject will be the reconstruction of their symbolic significance within the reconstructed meaning systems, as well their cultural affiliations, i.e., their ethnic attribution.

Anthropomorphic Shapes

Based on a stylistic analysis we can distinguish three varieties of human representations in this territory: a) Martynivka, b) Moshchenka, and c) Peregradnaia-Trebuieni.[1]

The Martynivka variety (fig. 2) includes four representations of mounts in human shape found in the hoard from Martynivka (near Cherkassy) in Ukraine, together with five mounts in the shape of animals (classified as the Martynivka variety of the animal representation), one from an unknown location in the region of Cherkassy,[2] and one from an unknown location in Southern Dobruja in Bulgaria.[3]

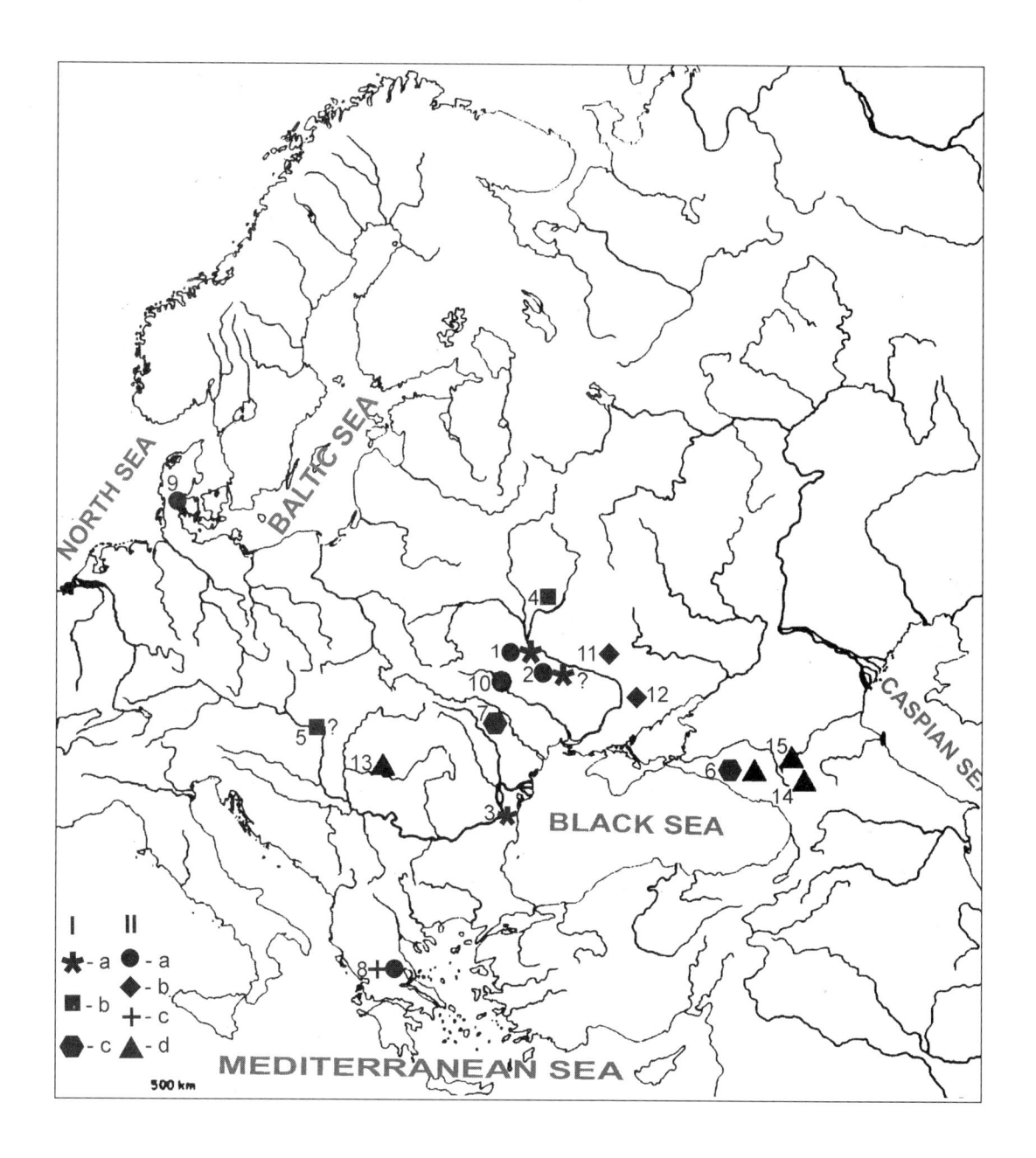

Fig. 1. Distribution of anthropo and zoomorphic mounts. I. Anthropomorphic shapes: a-Martynivka variety; b-Moshchenka variety; c-Peregradnaia-Trebujeni; II. Zoomorphic shapes: a-Martynivka variety; b-Mala Pereshchepino variety; c-Velestinon variety; d-Felnac-Kamunta variety. (1-Martynivka, Ukraine, 2-unknown place in Cherkassy region, Ukraine, 3-unknown place in Southern Dobruja, 4-Moshchenka, Ukraine, 5-unknown place in Carphatian Basin, 6-Peregradnaia, Karachaievo-Charkasia, Russia, 7-Trebujeni, Republic of Moldova, 8-Velestinon, Greece, 9-Nydam, Denmark, 10-Skibintsy, Mytkovska isle, Ukraine, 11-Mala Pereshchepino, Ukraine, 12-Voznesenka, Ukraine, 13-Felnac, Romania, 14-Kamunta, North Ossetia, Alania, Russia, 15-Kugul', Stavropol region, Russia)

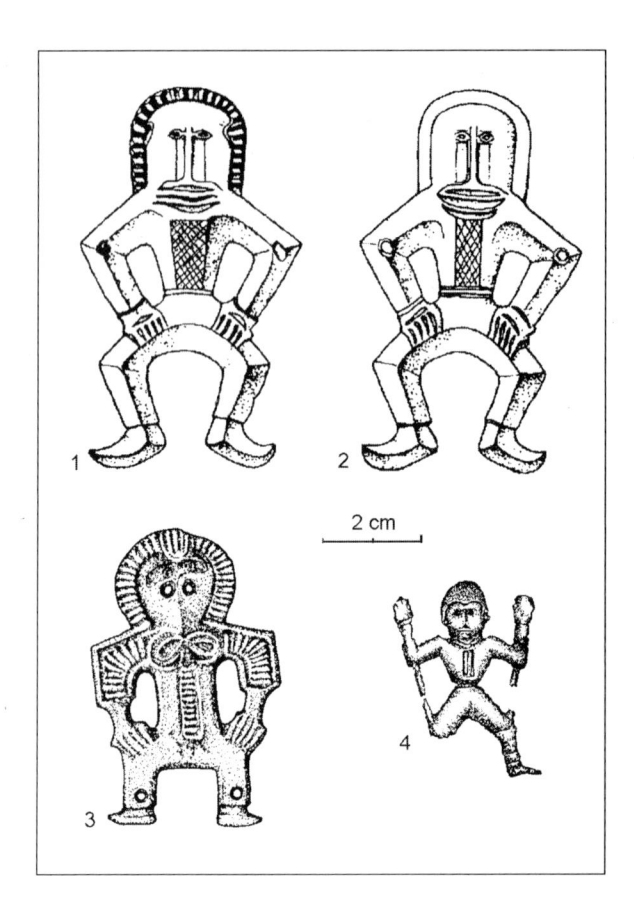

Fig. 2. Examples of the Marytnivka variety of human figural mounts: 1, 2-Martynivka, Ukraine; 3-unknown place in Cherkasy region, Ukraine; 4-unknown place in Southern Dobruja, Bulgaria. (1, 2 after Pekarskaja, Kidd 1994, 3-after Levada 2004, 4-after Jotov 1991)

The Martynivka human-shaped mounts have realistic representations of the body, in sharp contrast to the highly stylized and disproportionate head. The legs are slightly bent and spread outwards, with some kind of footwear on each foot. The hands are equally bent, resting on the hips. Thickened engravings at the wrists may designate bracelets. The much distorted cylindrical head has only an outlined mouth and nose, with delicately marked eyebrows and eye sockets. There are two types of headband representations, either a simple band, or one with radial decoration. Along the chest and down to the waist, there is a separate rectangle decorated with a series of diagonal, overlapping cuts.[4] Judging by the published illustration, the Martynivka human-shaped mounts seem to have been partially gilded (fig. 2: 1-2).

The body posture on the Cherkassy figurine is similar: bent arms with hands resting on the hips, but because of the schematic representation it is difficult to determine whether the position of the legs is the same. Moreover, the head is round with holes for eye sockets and with exaggerated eyebrows. However, similar to one of the Martynivka figurines, the headband is represented as radial engravings around the face. There is also a tongue-like protrusion with vertical grooves above the head (fig. 2: 3).

The bronze human representation from Southern Dobruja, based on a stylistic analysis, is close to the mounts described earlier. The differences are visible in the shape of the head and arrangement of the hand to the hip (fig. 2: 4).

The second is the Moshchenka variety (fig. 3: 1 and 2), which includes a die (?) and mount (?) from Moshchenka (Chernihiv region) in Ukraine [5] and two related items from unknown locations in the Carpathian Basin [6] and in the Lower Dnieper region of the Cataracts.[7] The body posture of the figurine from Moshchenka is characterized by bent arms and legs and the equally comparable, disproportionate representation of the head. The head is round with hair represented as radially distributed grooves (fig. 3: 1). Similarly, the figurine from the Carpathian Basin has grooves spreading radially from the forehead, as well as clearly marked eyes, nose, moustache, and mouth (fig. 3: 2). The second figurine from an unknown place in southern Ukraine has bent legs spreading outwards and the bent arms with

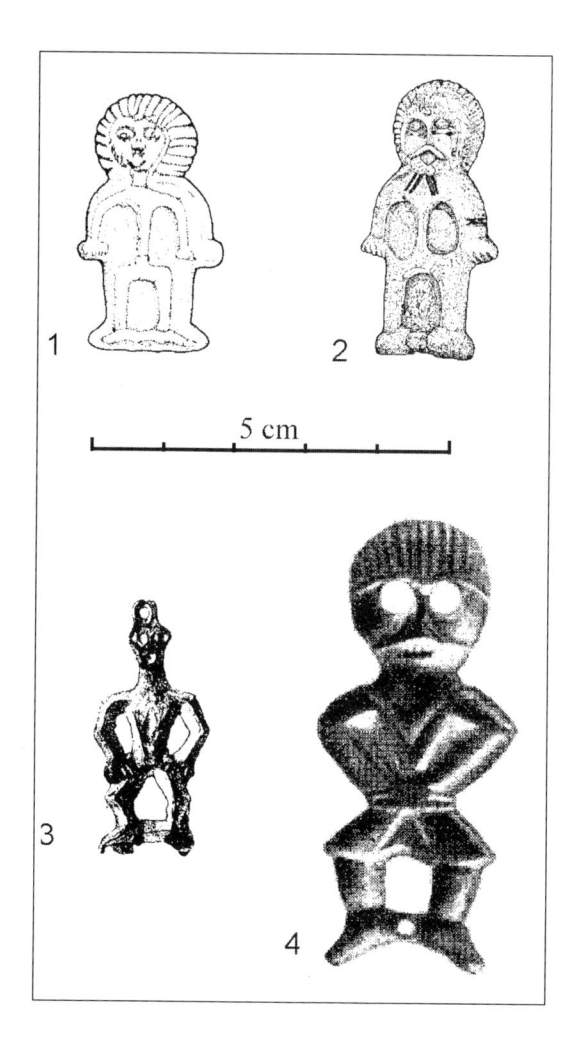

Fig. 3. Examples of the Moshchenka (1, 2) and Peregradnaja-Trebujeni (3, 4) variety of the human shaped mounts: 1-Moschenka, Ukraine, 2-unknown place in Carpathian Basin, 3-Trebujeni, Republic of Moldova; 4-Peregradnaia, Karachaievo-Charkasia, Russia. (1-after Gavritukhin 2004; 2-after Kiss 1984, 3-after Smirnov, Rafalovich 1965; 4-after Minaeva 1957)

hands on the hips.

I have also mentioned mounts analogical to the finds described above, which can be classified as the Peregradnia-Trebujeni variety (fig. 3: 3 and 4), including finds from Peregradnaia stanitsa (Karachayevo-Cherkesiia region, Caucasus, Russia) and Trebujeni (the Orhei district, Republic of Moldova).[8] The Pregradnaia mount was found together with an animal-shaped figurine of the Felnac-Komunta variety.[9] The representation of humans in the Peregradnaia mount is equally schematic, with body posture and head composition in clear parallel to the Martynivka mounts: bent legs spreading outwards, bent arms with hands resting on the waist, oval head with large eye sockets, and outlined nose and mouth. The hair is rendered by a number of vertical grooves above the forehead (fig. 3: 4). The pendant from Trebujeni is more schematic but the idea is analogical to those described above (fig. 3: 3).

Zoomorphic Shapes

Based on the analysis of the materials available, including ready-made objects such as metal applications, belt elements and dies to produce applications, we can perceive four stylistic varieties: a) Martynivka (Martynovka), b) Mala Pereshchepino, c) Velestínon, and d) Felnac.[10]

The Martynivka variety (fig. 4) includes mainly animal applications from treasure finds in Martynivka (near Cherkassy),[11] Ukraine; Cherkassy area,[12] Ukraine; Trubchëvsk (near Bryansk), Russia [13]; Pen'kovka settlement—Mytkovska isle near Skibintsy village (near Vinnytsya), Ukraine [14]; and the die from the Velestínon treasure (near Magnísia) in Thessaly, Greece.[15] The list also includes a zoomorphic application from Nydam, Jutland in Denmark.[16]

The most frequently mentioned stylistic variety is represented by the Martynivka treasure, after which it was named. The find consists of five zoomorphic and four anthropomorphic [17] representations which do not belong to one homogenous stylistic group. As Wojciech Szymański [18] has justly remarked, they could be divided into two types according to their physical properties. The first group includes slim-shaped images, seemingly caught in movement with open mouths and protruding tongues and fangs. The limbs end in a roughly marked claw (fig. 4: 1). The other group, according to the same scientist, contains specimens of massive proportions, less dynamic with slightly bent limbs ending in a kind of hoof. The mouth was gaping with peg-like teeth (fig. 4: 4).

Fig. 4. Examples of the Martynivka variety of animal shaped mounts: 1, 4-Martynivka, Ukraine, 2-unknown place in Cherkassy region, 3-Velestinon, Greece, 5-Nydam, Denmark, 6-Skibintsy, Mytkovska isle, Ukraine.(1, 4-after Pekarskaja, Kidd 1994, 2-after Levada 2004, 3-after Werner 1953, 5-after Rieck 1996, 6-after Khavliuk 1963)

The closest stylistic resemblance to the above mentioned applications, but of a dynamic variety, is visible in the representations from the treasure found in the Cherkassy area. At first sight they seem almost identical, but a closer analysis reveals differences. Firstly, their silhouettes are plumper, and the position of the legs is less dynamic. A different shape and ornamentation are characteristic of the shield which is interpreted as a mane. The greatest similarity is shown in the limbs which end with talons. Fanciful flowing tails, ending in a small shield are an interesting decorative element. The mouth is open with peg-like teeth resembling fangs (fig. 4: 2).

One of the 21 bronze dies found at Velestínon, Magnísia region in Thessaly in Greece shows a general stylistic similarity to the above mentioned variety. The artefact possesses—

like the applications described above—a shield of limbs joined together and ending with roughly marked claws. An arching back makes one think of an animal crouched before leaping. The mouth is differently shaped, on the outside limited by a vertical strip, while on the inside it is widening with a protruding tongue. The tail is short and raised (fig. 4: 3).

The next animal representation comes from the Penkovka settlement on Mytkovska isle near Skibintsy village in Ukraine. Apart from the general similarity shown in the shape of the body and the limbs, the other elements are different. There is a remarkable presentation of the head en face with precisely marked rears, eye sockets and a grooved mane (fig. 4: 6).

This plane with the mouth *en face* is a clear reference to the anthropomorphic representations of the Martynivka and Cherkassy treasures, in which the faces are presented in the same way. Under the mouth, in the center of the body there is a surface which could be a kind of shield but is devoid of any ornamentation.

Equally remarkable are three outlined applications from the Trubchëvsk treasure. The first possesses a characteristic ornamented shield, at the body decorated with three and at the mouth with two grooves. The slim body has one slight bent hind leg with grooves resembling claws. The mouth pattern resembles that of the Velestínon die, open-work, with fangs and an eye socket in the form of a hole. The next application also has a slim body and smooth surface with a marked hump, which may be the remnants of a shield. The mouth is open with a peg-like tooth (two joined teeth). The third artefact is only an outline devoid of any ornamentation, and its form is similar to the static group of animal figurines from Martynivka but of smaller size.

Finally, we have a lion application from the swamp site in Nydam in Denmark. The artefact was made by casting, partially gilded. It is an artistic representation of a predator with a short, oval head and open mouth with two sharp teeth and a convex eye. On the neck there is a surface ornamented with fish scale (overlapping, semicircular, engraved dents). On one side the decoration ends with a strip ornamented with alternately engraved incisions, separated in the middle by one groove decorated with a fishbone ornament. In the place where the upper part of the foreleg should begin there is a damaged ornament with three circular dents. The other preserved limb is characteristic of predators, with the claw specific for the majority of representations described here (fig. 4: 5).

The Mala Pereshchepino variety (fig. 5) includes finds from Mala Pereshchepino near Poltava in Ukraine[19] and from Voznesenka in southern Ukraine.[20] The lions from Pereshchepino are embossed in precious foil, the same way as predators from Voznesenka. They are in sitting positions and the first two have a marked crest on the surface in the shape

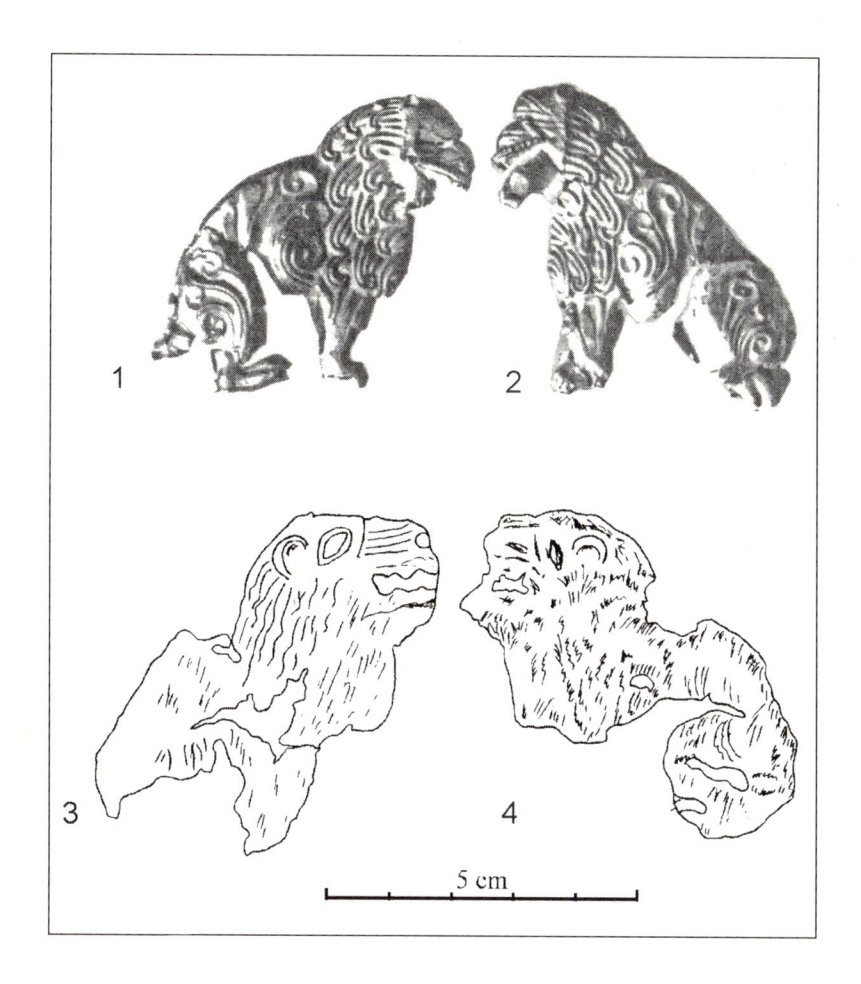

Fig. 5. Examples of the Mala Pereschepiono variety of the animal shaped appliqué: 1, 2-Mala Pereschepino, Ukraine, 3, 4-Voznesenka, Ukraine.(1-4 after Komar 2006, 1 and 2 without scale)

of locks (fig. 5:1 and 2). The lions from Voznesenka (fig. 5: 3 and 4) are partly damaged and more stylized then those from Pereshchepino. As I have mentioned about the presented embossed lions from Voznesenka, silver partly broken lion statuettes have been found.[21]

The other stylistic group, named the Velestínon variety (fig. 6: 1-7) for the purposes of this article, consists of zoomorphic representations from the find in Velestínon.[22] The find contains 21 dies made of bronze or copper alloys, eight of which are animal representations. One of the dies was recognised as belonging to the Martynivka variety. Within this variety two subtypes can be seen. The first is represented by three samples of predators, which because of their physical features can be identified as felines. Each of them is presented in different positions: two are static, with their heads in profile and *en face*; one is dynamic, with the head *en face*. The other subgroup containing four specimens can be interpreted as images of canines (wolves). Two of the representations are compositions made of a predator and a human figure, and a predator with a cub in its mouth. The remaining two highly stylized specimens show many stylistic features common to all predator representations.

Fig. 6. Examples of the Velestinion variety of animal representations: 1-7 Velestinion, Greece, (after Werner 1953)

The variety known as Felnac-Kamunta (fig. 7) is represented by five artefacts, three of which are dies used for producing applications. Two dies were found in the Felnac deposit, jud. Arad, Romania,[23] one comes from Kamunta, respublika North Ossetia in the Caucasus,[24] and, finally, two applications were found in the northern part of the Caucasus in Pregradnaja stanica, respublika Karachay-Cherkessia [25] and Kugul' kray Stavropol'.[26] This variety is stylistically the most homogenous. The three specimens mentioned first show a striking stylistic similarity. Two dies from Felnac depict predators probably from the canine family (wolves) in a dynamic stance, slim with straight forepaws and the hind legs slightly bent. The mouths are elongated, open, without the characteristic fangs. On the neck there is the characteristic surface with the ornament of vertical and diagonal grooves representing the animal's mane (fig. 7: 1 and 2). In the case of the Kamunta die, the general pattern is almost identical, the only difference being the mouth with changed proportions and so resembling

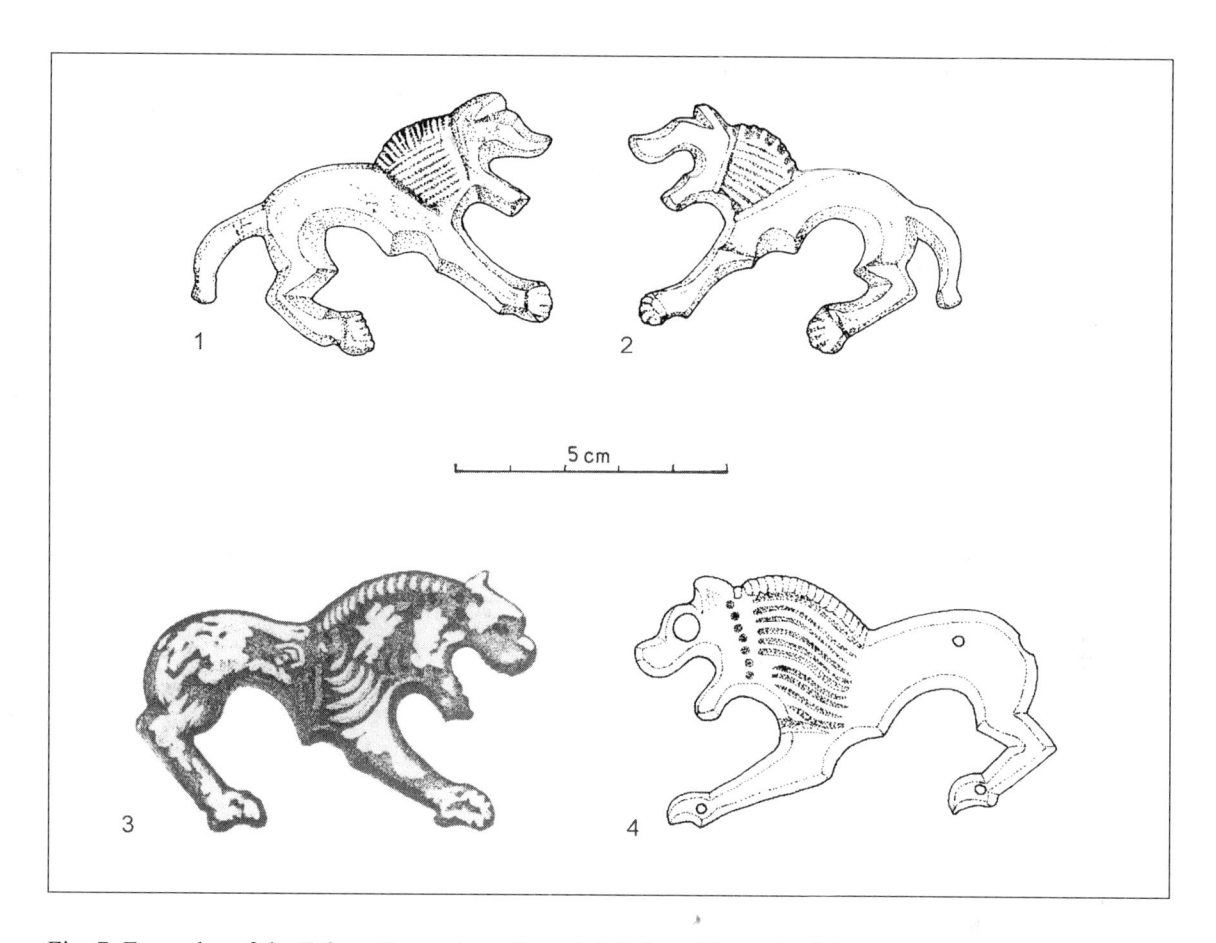

Fig. 7. Examples of the Felnac-Kamunta variety: 1, 2-Felnac, Romania, 3-Kamunta, North Ossetia, Alania, Russia, 4-Peregradnaja, Karachaievo-Cherkasia, Russia. (1, 2 after Garam 2001; 3-after Werner 1953, d-after Ambroz 1989)

more a lion's head (fig. 7: 3). The application from Pregradnaja has a similar form, with a surface where the body meets the mouth with a series of vertical and slightly curved cuts. The decoration ends towards the mouth with a series of circular dents. The mouth is wide open with a circular drilled-through eye socket (fig. 7:4). The last one, an application from cemetery Kugul', is broken.

Function and Symbolism

The interpretation of the symbolic meaning of the zoomorphic representations is a complex and difficult task. Therefore clarification of the role of symbols in old cultures seems indispensable here. Symbols and their meanings are specific to concrete cultural traditions.[27] They can be individual, made only to serve a concrete task, but the most important are those which have become known to everybody, making them the property of the whole culture. Creating symbols is a result of the need for conceptual organization and ordering of reality. The last element is extremely significant for creating various symbolic systems in various communities.[28] It is used mainly to present and define human attitudes towards the other world, the supernatural or the transcendental. It must be remembered, however, that our interpretation can be different from that of the maker of an object who gave symbolic meaning to the representations based on his knowledge of the surrounding world.[29]

Firstly, I would like to focus on the function of analyzed artefacts, their place and number in the ritual composition and then on symbolic meanings. In the literature there has been an ongoing discussion of the issue, limited mainly to the interpretation of these applications as elements of clothing (jacket),[30] harness,[31] saddle ornaments,[32] or decorative elements of a chest or other container serving a special purpose.[33]

The most interesting suggestion about the function of human-and animal-shaped metal mounts was put forward by Wojciech Szymański. He divided the analyzed objects from the Martynivka treasure into four group compositions consisting of one anthropomorphic and two zoomorphic images, pointing out the recurring numbers. The composition group was reconstructed as a pyramid pattern, at the base of which are two zoomorphic images (a lion, a hippopotamus) with their heads facing each other, representing light and darkness.[34] The pattern is completed by a human figurine, which is interpreted as the image of the tribal leader, the incarnation of god on earth [35] or, more likely, the sun-god sitting on the throne by symbolic extension.[36] A similar pattern can be used to reconstruct the composition of the set of applications from the Cherkassy area, although it has to be mentioned that only lions appear there. Therefore, another pyramid pattern is possible but with the lions facing outwards, which changes the symbolic meaning of the representation (Pl. II-1). As mentioned above, such a pattern represents the eastern and western horizons with the sun, symbolized by an anthropomorphic figure, traveling between them.

W. Szymański, in his plastic version of the composition of applications from Martynivka, has assumed that they could have been spaced individually on four surfaces, making a unified whole.[37] The surfaces could have been on the front and back part of a priest's or a shaman's robes (fig. 8). Therefore a few words must be added concerning the symbolic meaning of the shaman's robes, which is the reflection of the cosmos shown through a complicated pictorial and numerical system. According to A. Szyjewski, the shaman's robe differed from the attire of other members of the community, and was the shaman's attribute and distinguishing feature.[38]

The essential aspect is its division into four parts reflecting four supernatural powers and, again, the four points of the compass. It is worth noticing that it is divided into right and left sides and red and black colors, which are associated with the other and the netherworld as well as with the solar and lunar powers.[39] The applications in the above-mentioned composition may be elements of the attire of a high-ranking individual performing specific functions in the local community, including ritual ones.[40] The remaining individual finds of applications or belt elements could be parts of bigger sets no longer preserved. The possibility of using them as objects with magical and apotropaic properties has also to be considered.[41]

It is worthwhile having a closer look at some aspects of the religion of the Bulgarians here. The sun had immense significance, as well as the eastern horizon as the adoration of the rising sun; it is supposed that there also existed a cult of the moon. So, as I mentioned above, we would be dealing here with the light and the dark side. The central character here is the khagan, the messenger and representative of god, and consequently the great priest.[42] The symbolism of animal representations described briefly above focuses on adoration of the sun and the dark. So, according to the division, we would have the sun represented by a human figurine and two horizons or the sun and night.

In the case of the set of zoomorphic figurines we are discussing, there is no uniform interpretation in the literature on the subject. Most attention was paid to the Martynivka treasure. According to B. A. Rybakov, whose concept was generally accepted by Russian researchers, those artefacts were images of horses.[43] A different opinion was expressed by Joachim Werner,[44] who interpreted them as predators—lions. A few years ago it was suggested that the figurines should be divided into two types of images of lions and hippopotamuses; it was, however, unfounded.[45] It was W. Szymański [46] who discussed the anthropomorphic and zoomorphic representations most thoroughly. Based on a detailed analysis, I justify the division of the animal representations into two groups: a) the felines—lions, and b) the ungulates—hippopotamuses.

Selected dies from the Velestinon treasure are also interpreted as images of lions, a sea lion, a tiger, and other predators.[47] Interpreting one of the representations as a sea lion seems highly unlikely. In my opinion it is a stylized representation of a recumbent predator from a feline family, with an outstretched hind leg. Similar representations, differing only in the position of the head, are known from Lombard burial sites ex. in Castel Trosino in Italy.[48] Two more dies can be identified as stylized images of lions, while all the others seem more likely to represent predators from the canine family, which is suggested by their physical features. The same applies to the dies from Felnac and applications from Caucasus, which seem to resemble wolves. But the Kamunta die shows numerous features of predators from the feline family. The embossed appliqués from Mala Pereshchepiono and Voznesenka are interpreted as lions.[49]

Concluding the debate on the species of particular representations, I would like to devote a few lines to discussing their symbolism. The lion is the most frequently represented animal, since because of its strength it is ascribed both good and evil characteristics.[50] First of all, it symbolizes the sun, as killer-lions were sun-heroes. However, because of its dualism, it can be regarded both as *lumineux* and *obscur*. The composition consisting of two lions with their heads directed outwards is the symbol of the two opposite horizons—eastern and western and, hence, the daily journey of the sun in the sky.[51]

The hippopotamus is a symbol of great energy and brutality; it is associated with evil forces. Only in one case is it perceived as having positive meaning—when it is an image of a female—the symbol of fertility.[52]

The wolf symbolizes, on the one hand, night and night killing and, on the other, the sun which brings death with its rays and causes droughts. For Türk tribes the wolf symbolizes war. In this context, we should mention the dog, which, like the wolf, is a symbol of chthonic gods of darkness, death and the moon. It is also a symbol of fidelity, courage and wariness, the guardian of the netherworld.[53] The dog was a valuable animal god for Türk tribes.[54]

While discussing the basic symbolic meanings of zoomorphic representations, one should mention the horse, since a group of slim animals from Martynivka shows certain features of horse anatomy. The horse is a symbol of sunlight and moonlight, day and night. A set of two horses represents the morning and the evening star, which accompany the sun.[55] Like the dog, the horse was an important animal in the pantheon of Türk gods.[56]

Ethnic Attribution

The meaning attached to images of humans and animals goes back to antiquity, as illustrated in many media, such as mosaic, pottery painting, or metalwork.[57] Early medieval human-shaped clasps or pendants are known from several burial sites in northern Italy, the northern Black Sea coast, the Caucasus region, and the Volga-Ural area.[58] Animal-shaped mounts have been found in Dalmatia,[59] on the northern Black Sea coast, in Greece,[60] in northern

Italy, and in the northern Caucasus region.[61] Besides zoomorphic figurines, images of lions may be found in Byzantine [62] and Sasanian art.[63]

The anthropomorphic and zoomorphic metal mounts and dies occur most frequently in the forest-steppe belt and the steppe of present day Ukraine and the northern Caucasus (fig. 1).

Defining the ethnic attribution of the representations described here is rather complicated. The area of the forest-steppe zone occupied by the Penkovka settlement was, in the earlier phases of the middle ages, the area where various cultural influences converged and clashed. Therefore, it is an arduous task to define the ethnic component of this culture based on archaeological data. Some researchers tend to define the Penkovka culture as a polyethnic structure,[64] while others regard it as homogenous.[65] O. M. Prykhodniuk emphasizes strong bonds between the Penkovka people and Türk tribes.[66] The steppe zone was a central place in the migration of the nomads from Asia to the Mediterranean world [67] and a melting pot of nomadic tribes. [68]

Various tribes settled also in the areas of the northern Caucasus. In the mid-sixth century Kutrigur-Bulgarians had settlements in the steppes located to the west of the Don River, Onogur-Bulgarians had their dwellings on the Kuban, while the steppes stretching between the Don and the Kuban belonged to Utigur-Bulgarians.[69] The early history of the Bulgars is very interesting. According to Peter Boodberg [70] and Sanping Chen, the name Buluoji known from early sixth century Chinese sources can be identified as the Bulgars from the Volga and the Danube.

Present day Ossetia was inhabited by Iranian tribes, the Alans among others. After *ca.* 550 and until the end of the 580s or 590s, the lands of both groups were incorporated into the rising Türk Qaganate encompassing an enormous stretch of the Eurasian continent, from Korea to the Black Sea.[71] During the civil war of 581 to 593, the qaganate split into an eastern and a western "wing", the latter under the leadership of the Bulgar Dulo clan.[72] Under Kubrat, the emerging "Great Bulgaria" occupied the lands between the Ergeni Upland, the Volga and Don Rivers to the east; the Sea of Azov and the Dnieper River to the east; and the Kuban River to the south. The northern neighbors of Greater Bulgaria must have been the descendents of the Antes.[73] Kubrat himself may have been buried on the northern frontier of his polity, if the Mala Pereshchepyno assemblage is indeed his grave.[74] In any case, the assemblage contained luxuries of undoubtedly Byzantine origin.[75] After Kubrat's death in *ca.* 650, his polity disintegrated and Greater Bulgaria was occupied by the Khazars.[76] The Khazar Qaganate ruled for three centuries over the steppe lands of Eastern Europe, away from the developments taking place in Central Asia, within the Eastern Türk Qaganate.[77]

It seems that we should look for the origin of the idea of using anthropomorphic and zoomorphic images as decorative elements with deep symbolic meaning in four areas: a) the Byzantine Empire (Eastern Rome), b) Sassanid Empire, c) Northern Caucasus, and, d) Türk Qaganate.

The images of lions and hippopotamuses are clear evidence of contacts with Byzantium. Applications showing such exotic animals as lions, dolphins, or peacocks, eagerly used as saddle or shield ornaments by the Lombards, were produced in the lands of the eastern empire.[78] The Sassanid (Iranian) direction is also probable, where numerous representations of fighting scenes with lions, and anthropomorphic seated images are known. In the case of the northern Caucasus, despite close contacts with both the Byzantine and the Sassanid (Iranian) circles,[79] a native style was created with images of predators resembling canines. According to V. B. Kovalevskaia, the anthropo-zoomorphic and zoomorphic representations, e.g., the Martynivka ones, are talismans characteristic of the Iranian Alans' manufacture.[80] The statuettes of the lions also played an important role in the religious rituals of ancient Türks.[81] Presence of the animal statuettes was remarked by the Byzantine envoy Zemarchus during his embassy to Sizabul, the qagan of the Türks in 568 "in which there were gilded wooden pillars and a couch of beaten gold, which was supported by four golden peacocks. In front of this dwelling were drawn up over a wide area wagons containing many silver objects, dishes and bowls, and a large number of statues of animals also of silver and in no way inferior to those which we make, so wealthy is the ruler of the Türks".[82]

Neither is it possible, at the present stage of research, to answer the question asked by W. Szymański: with which ideological system can we associate the symbolic meanings and the function of zoomorphic and anthropomorphic images? I fully agree with the answer he gave, namely that 'he connected the trends of various origins, with a significant role of Iranian and Byzantine, relict Germanic, and maybe Türk motifs'.[83] However, I would pay greater attention to analyzing the motifs connected with the latter tribes.

NOTES

[1] B. Sz. Szmoniewski, "*Two Worlds, One Hoard: What Do Metal Finds from the Forest-Steppe Belt Speak about?*" in F. Curta ed., *The Other Europe in the Middle Ages. Avars, Bulgars, Khazars and Cumans*, Leiden-Boston 2008, pp. 263-296.

[2] M. Levada, *Pizdnyi rimskyi-rannyi vizantyis'kyi chasi* in: Platar. Kolektsyia predmetiv starovyni rodyn

Platonovikh ta Tarut. Katalog, Kiev 2004, p. 215, no. 24.

[3] V. Jotov, *Bronozova figura ot Uzhna Dobrudzha*, Vekove 1-2, 1991, pp. 21-23; S. Stanilov, *Khudozhestveniiat metal na B'lgarskoto Khanstvo na Dunav (7-9 vek)*, Sofia 2006, 231, fig. 2.

[4] For detailed pictures, see L. V. Pekarskaja, D. Kidd, *Der Silberschatz von Martynovka (Ukraine) aus dem 6. und 7. Jahrhundert*, Monographien zur Frühgeschichte und Mittelalterarchäologie, Falko Daim (ed.), (Innsbruck 1994), pp. 118, 119 with figs. 25 and 26.

[5] I. O. Gavritukhin, *Srednedneprovskie ingumtsi vtoroi poloviny V-VI v.* In Kul'turnye transformatsii i vzaimovliianiia v dneprovskom regione na uskhode rimskogo vremeni i v rannem srednevekov'e, eds. V. M. Goriunova, O. A. Shcheglova, St. Petersburg, 2004, 210, 218 fig. 3.2.

[6] A. Kiss, *Archäologische Angaben zur Geschichte der Stättel des Frühmittelalters,* Alba Regia 21, 1984, 198 fig. 20

[7] O. M. Prykhodniuk, *Pienkovskaia kul'tura*, Voronezh, 1998, 143 fig. 75.8.

[8] T. M. Minaeva, *Nakhodka bliz stanitsy Pregradnoj na r. Urupe*, in *Kratkie Soobschenia Instituta Istorii Materialnoi Kul'tury*, 68 1957, p. 133, fig. 52/1.; G. D. Smirnov and J. A. Rafalovich *Ranneslavianskie nakhodki VI-VII vv. iz Starogo Orkheia*, Izvestiia Akademii Nauk Moldavskoi SSR 12,1965, fig. 1.

[9] B. Sz. Szmoniewski, *Cultural Contacts in Central and Eastern Europe: What do Metal Beast Images Speak about?*. In *Ethnic Contacts and Cultural Exchanges North and West of the Black Sea from the Greek Colonization to the Ottoman Conquest*, ed. V. Cocojaru, Iasi, 2005, p. 429.

[10] B. Szmoniewski, *Cultural...*, pp. 426-429.

[11] L. V. Pekarskaja, D. Kidd, *Der Silberschatz von Martynovka (Ukraine) aus dem 6. und 7. Jahrhundert*, Monographien zur Frühgeschichte und Mittelalterarchäologie, Falko Daim (ed.), Innsbruck, 1994.

[12] M. Levada, *Pizdnyi...*, p. 215, no. 43, 44.

[13] O. M. Prykhodniuk, V. A. Padin, N. G. Tikhonov, *Trubachevskii klad antskogo vremenii*, in: I. Erdély, O. M. Prykhodniuk, *Materialy I tys. n.e. po arkheologii i sitorii Ukrainy i Vengrii*, Kiev 1996, pp. 79-102.

[14] P. I. Khavliuk, *Ranneslavianskie poseleniia Semenki i Samchintsy v srednem techenii Iuzhnogo Buga*, in *MIA* 108, 1963, p. 321, fig. 2.

[15] J. Werner, *Slawische Bronzefiguren aus Nordgriechenland*, Abhandlungen der Deutschen Akademie der Wissenschaften zu Berlin, Klasse für Gesellschaftswissenschaften, Jahrgang 1952, Nr. 2, Berlin 1953, pp. 3-8, pl. 1-6.

[16] F. Rieck, *Nydam-rige fund i farligt miljø*, Marinarkoeologisk Nyhedsbrev fra Roskilde, Roskilde 1996, pp. 5-6.

[17] According to B. A. Rybakov there should be 12 applications including 4 anthropomorphic and 8 zoomorphic, see B. A. Rybakov, *Drevnie rusy. K voprosu ob obrazovanii iadra drevnorusskoi narodnosti v svetle trudov I. V. Stalina* in *Sovetskaia Arkheologiia* 1953 (XVII), p. 88.

[18] W. Szymański, rewiev, L. V. Pekarskaja, D. Kidd, *Der Silberschatz von Martynovka (Ukraine) aus dem 6. und 7. Jahrhundert*, Monographien zur Frühgeschichte und Mittelalterarchäologie, Falko Daim (ed.),

Innsbruck 1994, in *Archeologia Polski* 41 (1996) 1-2, pp. 198-199; W. Szymański, *Wokół skarbu z Martynowki*, in H. Kóčka-Krenz, W. Łosiński (eds), *Kraje słowiańskie w wiekach średnich. Profanum i sacrum* Poznań 1998, p. 359.

[19] J. Werner, *Der Grabfund von Malaja Pereščepina und Kuvrat. Kagan der Bulgaren*, Bayerische Akademie der Wissenschaften Philosophish-Historische Klasse Abhandlungen, H. 91 München, 1984; A. V. Komar, Pereshchepinskii kompleks v kontekste osnovnykh problem istorii i kultury kochevnikov Vostochnoi Evropy VII-nach. VIII v, in: Stepi Evropy v epohu srednovekov'ia 5, 2006, p. 68, fig. 26:4, 5.

[20] A. V. Komar, *Pereshchepinskii* ..., pp. 68, 26: 4 and 5.

[21] A. V. Komar, *Pereshchepinskii* ..., p. 70, fig. 28: 3, 36: 25.

[22] J. Werner, Slawische..., see also D. Kidd, *The Velestinon (Thessaly) Hoard-A Footnote*, in Falko Daim (ed.), *Awarenforschungen*, Archaeologia Austriaca Monographien, vol. I (Vienna 1992), pp. 509-515.

[23] E. Garam, *Funde byzantinischer Herkunft in der Awarenzeit vom Ende des 6. bis zum Ende des 7. Jahrhunders*, Monumenta Avarorum Archaeologica (Budapest 2001), pl. 137.

[24] E. Chantre, *Recherches anthropologiques dans la Caucase, tome III*, (Paris-Lyon 1887), p. 94, pl. XIX/2, J. Werner, Slawische..., pl. 1/1-5, 2/1-8, 3/1-8, J. Werner, *Der Grabfund von Malaja Pereščepina und Kuvrat, Kagan der Bulgaren*, Bayerische Akademie der Wissenschaften Philosophish-Historische Klasse Abhandlungen, H. 91 München 1984, fn. 114.

[25] T. M. Minaeva, *Nakhodka bliz stanitsy Pregradnoj na r. Urupe*, in *Kratkie Soobschenia Instituta Istorii Materialnoi Kul'tury*, 68 1957, p. 133, fig. 52/2.

[26] A. K. Ambroz, *Khronologiia drevnostei severnogo Kavkaza V-VII vv.* (Moscow 1989), p. 80, fig. 24/14.

[27] C. Renfrew, P. Bahn, *Archaeology: Theory. Methods and Practice*, New York, 1996, p. 369.

[28] A. Szyjewski, *Etnologia religii*, Kraków 2001, pp. 76, 91.

[29] C. Renfrew, P. Bahn, Archaeology..., p. 375.

[30] W. Szymański, *Wokół*..., p. 362.

[31] L. V. Pekarskaja, D. Kidd, Der Silberschatz..., pp. 28, 31.

[32] Gy. László, *Études archéologiques sur l'histoire de la société des Avares*, in *Archaeologica Hungarica* 34 (1955), pp. 276-278, fig. 81-82; A. Kiss, *Archäologische Angaben zur Geschichte der Stättel des Frühmittelalters*, in *Alba Regia* 21 (1984), pp. 191, 197, fig. 16, 17.

[33] W. Szymański, *Wokół*..., pp. 362, 363.

[34] W. Szymański, *Wokół*..., p. 362.

[35] L. V. Pekarskaja, D. Kidd, Der Silberschatz..., pp. 28, 29.

[36] W. Szymański, *Wokół*...,p. 362.

[37] Szymański, *Wokół*...,p. 362.

[38] A. Szyjewski, *Etnologia*..., p. 369.

[39] A. Szyjewski, *Etnologia...*, p. 369.

[40] W. Szymański, *Wokół...*, , 1998, p. 363.

[41] J. Werner, *Der Grabfund...*, p. 114.

[42] E. Tryjarski, *Protobułgarzy*, in K. Dąbrowski, T. Najgrodzka-Majchrzyk, E. Tryjarski, *Hunowie Europejscy, Protobułgarzy, Chazarowie, Pieczyngowie*, Wrocław– Warszawa–Kraków–Gdańsk 1975, pp. 221, 222.

[43] B. A. Rybakov, *Drevnie...*, pp. 76, 87, 88, fig. 21.

[44] J. Werner, *Slawische...*, p. 5, and idem, *Slawische Bügelfibeln des 7. Jarhunderts*, in: G. Behrens, J. Werner, *Reinecke Festschtrift* (Mainz 1950), p. 169.

[45] O. M. Prikhodnjuk, A. M. Shovkopljas, S. Ja. Ol'govskaja, T. A. Struina, *Martynovskij klad*, in *Materialy po Arkheologii, Istorii i Etnografii Tavrii* 2, 1991, pp. 82, 88.

[46] W. Szymański, *review...*, 1996, pp. 198, 199.

[47] J. Werner, *Slawische...*, p. 4.

[48] H. Dannheimer, *Ostmediterrane Prunksättel des frühen Mittelalters*, in *Bayerische Vorgeschichtsblätter* 65 (2000), pl. 28.

[49] A. V. Komar, *Pereschepinskii...*, 69-70.

[50] L. Réau, *Iconographie de l'art Chrétien*, vol. I, Paris 1955, p. 92.

[51] A. de Vries, *Dictionary of Symbols and Imagery*, Amsterdam–London 1974, pp. 300, 301; J. Chevalier et Alain Gheerbrant, *Dictionnaire de symbols, Mythes, reves, coutumes, gestes, formes, figures, couleurs, nombres,* Paris 1982, p. 463.

[52] A. de Vries, *Dictionary...*, p. 253; J. Chevalier et Alain Gheerbrant, *Dictionnaire...*, p. 406.

[53] W. Kopaliński, *Słownik symboli* (Warszawa 1990), pp. 463-465.

[54] E. Tryjarski, *Protobułgarzy...*, p. 224.

[55] W. Kopaliński, *Słownik...*, p. 157.

[56] E. Tryjarski, *Protobułgarzy*, p. 223.

[57] D. Kidd, *The Velestinon...*, p. 511; Drandaki ΥΓΙΕΝΩΝ ΧΡΩ ΚΥΡΙ(Ε)* A late Roman brass bucket with a hunting scene,* ΜΟΥΣΕΙΟ ΜΠΕΝΑΚΗ 2 2002, pp. 37-53.

[58] O. v. Hessen, *Secondo contributo alla archeologia Longobarda in Toscana. Reperti isolati e di provenienzia incerta,* Accademia Toscana di Scienze e Lettere La Colombara, Studi XLI Firenze 1975, pp. 36 and 108, pl. 6/1, 2 and 3; H. Dannheimer, *Ostmediterrane...*, pl. 28, pl. 31/4; V. B. Kovalevskaia *Khronologija drevnostej severokavkazkikh Alan*, in V. Ch. Tmenov, *Alany. Istorija i kul'tura-Alantä: istori ämä kul'turä,* Vladikavkaz 1995, pp. 141-45; Gavritukhin, *Sredneprovske...*, p. 210.

[59] Z. Vinski, *Kasnoantički starosjedioci u salonitanskoj regiji prema arheološkoj ostavštini predslavenskog supstrata*, in *Vjesnik za Arheologiju i Historiju Dalmatinsku*, 69, 1967, pp. 16-21, pl. XI, XII, XIII/1-3.

[60] G. R. Davidson, *The minor objects*, Corinth XII, 1952, fig. 68/934.

[61] M. Kazanski, *Les plaques-boucles mediterraneennes des Ve-Vie siecles, Archeologie Medievale 24,* 1994, p. 190 fig. 17.2 and 3; Dannheimer, *op. cit.*, 2000, pls. 28 and 31.4.

[62] Ch. Diehl, *Manuel d'art byzantin*, vol. I, Paris 1925, fig. 130, 132, 134.

[63] D. Collon, *Ancient Near Eastern art*, London 1995, p. 206, fig. 172.

[64] W. Szymański, *Słowiańszczyzna wschodnia. Kultura Europy wczesnośredniowiecznej*, vol. I, Wrocław 1973, pp. 31-34; I. O. Gavritukhin, A. M. Oblomskij, *Gaponovskij klad i ego kul'turno-istoricheskij kontekst*, in *Ranneslavjanskij Mir* (Moscow) 3, 1996, pp. 121-124, 141-144.

[65] M. B. Ljubichev, *Pen'kivs'ka kul'tura: shche raz pro teritoriju ta etnichnu prinadlezhnost'*, in R. V. Terpilovskij, *Etnokul'turni protsesi v Pivdenno-Skhidniy Evropi v I tisjacholitti n.e.*, Kiev–L'vov 1999, pp. 123-131.

[66] O. M. Prikhodnjuk, *Voenno-politicheskiy sojuz antov i tjurskiy mir po dannymi istoricheskikh i arkheologicheskikh istochnikov*, in *Materialy po Arkheologiii Istorii i Etnografii Tavrii* 7, 2000, pp. 134-167.

[67] "The preaseance of the Early Türks analysed", D. Sinor, *Réflexions sur la présence Turco-Mongole dans le Monde Méditerranéen et Pontique a l'époque Pré-Ottomané*, Acta Orientalia Acadamiae Scientiarum Hung. XXXVI (1-3), 1982, 485-501.

[68] See e. g. P. B. Golden, The peoples of the south Russian steppes, in: *The Cambridge History of Early Inner Asia*, D. Sinor ed. Cambridge, 1990, pp. 256-270.

[69] E. Tryjarski, *Protobułgarzy...*, p. 164.

[70] P. Boodberg, *Two notes on the history of the Chinese frontier-II. The Bulgars of Mongolia*, Harvard Journal of Asiatic Studies 1, 1936, 291-307; S. Chen, Some remarks on the Chinese "Bulgar", *Acta Orientalia Acadamiae Scientiarum Hung.* 51, (1-2), 1998, pp. 69-83.

[71] E. Tryjarski, *Protobułgarzy...*, p. 172. For the Türks Qaganate, see L. Gumilev, *Dzieje dawnych Turków*, Warszawa, 1972, 56; B. Gafurow, *Dzieje i kultura ludów Azji Centralnej. Prehistoria, starożytność, średniowiecze*, Warszawa, 1978, 229; D. Sinor, The establishment and dissolution of the Türk empire, in: *The Cambridge History of Early Inner Asia*, Cambridge, 1990, 285-316; D. Sinor and S, G. Klyashtorny, The first Türk Empire (553-682), in: *History of Civilisation of Central Asia III. The Crossroads of Civilisations: AD 250 to 750*, eds. B. A. Litvinsky, Zhang Guang-da and R. Shabani Samghabadi, Paris, 1996, 327-347.

[72] E. Tryjarski, *Protobułgarzy...*, p. 172. For the civil war, see L. Gumilev, *Dzieje...*, 98-111; B. Gafurow, *Dzieje...*, pp. 229-30.

[73] D. Angelov, *Obrazuvane na bagarskata narodnost*, Sofia, 1971, 191-92; E. Tryjarski, *Protobułgarzy...*, p. 174.

[74] A. Róna-Tas, *Where was Khuvrat's Bulgharia ?*, Acta Orientalia Acadamiae Scientiarum Hung. 53 (1-2), 2000, pp. 1-22.

[75] J. Werner, *Der Grabfund...*; A. Avenarius, *Die byzantishe Kultur und die Slawen*, Vienna-Munich, 2000, pp.

22-23 and figs. 1-3.

[76] E. Tryjarski, *Protobułgarzy...*, p. 175; T. Nagrodzka-Majchrzyk, *Chazarowie*, in K. Dąbrowski, T. Najgrodzka-Majchrzyk, E. Tryjarski, *Hunowie Europejscy, Protobułgarzy, Chazarowie, Pieczyngowie*, Wrocław-Warszawa-Kraków-Gdańsk 1975, p. 397.

[77] L. Gumilev, *Dzieje...*, pp. 140-42.

[78] H. Dannheimer, *Ostmediterrane...*, pp. 193-205.

[79] A. Carile, *Political Interactions between Byzantium and Iran in the VIIth Century*, in Cs. Bálint (ed.), *Kontakte zwischen Iran, Byzanz und der Steppe im 6.-7. Jahrhundert, Varia Archaeologica Hungarica X*, Budapest–Napoli–Roma 2000, pp. 185-192; I. Ecsedy, *Contacts between Byzantium and Iran*, in Cs. Bálint (ed.), *Kontakte zwischen Iran, Byzanz und der Steppe im 6.-7. Jahrhundert, Varia Archaeologica Hungarica X*, Budapest-Napoli-Roma 2000, pp. 209-213.

[80] V. B. Kovalevskaia, *Khronologiia...*, pp. 143, 145.

[81] A. V. Komar, *Pereshchepinskii...*, pp. 68, 69.

[82] Menander the Guardsman, in R. C. Blockley, *The History of Meander the Guardsman*, Liverpool, 1985, p. 121.

[83] W. Szymański, *Wokół...*, p. 363.

RECENT INVESTIGATIONS ON SASANIAN PAINTING

Matteo Compareti

Painting still represents one of the aspects least investigated of Sasanian and, more generally, of pre-Islamic Persian art because of the extremely fragmentary state of the wall-paintings recovered in Iran. An up-to-date study on Sasanian painting was recently published by An De Waele when the previous version of this article was nearing completion.[1] Because of the great delay in its publication, it is now time for a revision of the previous version of the article in order to avoid repeating the results already advanced by De Waele and to consider new discoveries of the pictorial graffiti of the Sasanian period.

The Pre-Sasanian Period

Because of the undeniable admiration by Latin, Greek and Muslim authors, painting seems to have had a prominent position in the decoration of Sasanian buildings. Monumental painting in Persia existed during the Achaemenid period (539-330 BCE),[2] but the few extant fragments do not allow us to say much about it. Geometrical decorations embellished the architectonic elements at Pasargadae (dated to the reign of Cyrus II the Great, 559-530 BCE) and at Persepolis (period of Darius I, 522-486 BCE),[3] while the only specimens of human figures come from Susa, all recovered at the Shaur building (period of Artaxerxes II, 404-359/58 BCE). Their style does not appear so different from the Persepolis and Susa reliefs, with a preference for the reproduction of figures in profile.[4] The archaeological activity which has started in Iran in the last years allowed the discovery of a few new paintings dated to the Achaemenid period (most likely to the 6th-5th century BCE) at Dahan-e Gholaman

(Sistan). The paintings represent extremely stylized animals and hunting scenes.[5]

Paintings dated to the Seleucid period (*c.* 312-162 BCE) were found at Susa but they are not fully documented.[6] There is clear evidence for the Parthian domination in Persia under the Arsacid dynasty (*c.* 250 BCE-226 CE).[7] Specimens of Parthian painting and graffiti were recovered at Assur (1st-2nd century) and Hatra in Mesopotamia (today's northern Iraq),[8] and Lakh-mazar (Khorasan Province, Birjand, Kuch village) [9] while recently even at Nisa (Turkmenistan) — the first Arsacid capital — some remains have been found during excavations.[10] The paintings of Hatra are particularly interesting because they present many characteristics which are a prelude to Sasanian artistic production. Archaeological excavations suggest a late Parthian chronology for the paintings, executed just before the destruction of the city perpetrated by the Sasanians at the time of Shapur I (241-272): in fact some murals were unfinished possibly just for this reason.[11] The scenes are divided into bands separated by geometric or vegetal frames and represent hunters on horseback in the act of shooting arrows at their prey (fig. 1) or piercing them with a lance. What is surprising in these paintings is the treatment of the theme of the royal hunt. In fact it is reproduced exactly as it appears in many works of art of the following Sasanian period (especially metalwork), according to a sanctioned court typology.[12] The horses are always represented harnessed and in the position of the "flying gallop" — according to a well known scheme in Parthian art but one that probably originated in the art of the steppe [13] — while the hunters wear soft garments and sometimes headgear, with the bust depicted frontally but with the head in three-quarter view.[14] The paraphernalia reflects Sasanian customs of the early period, as does the presence of the quiver.[15] In the scene with the hunter wearing a turban and killing a boar with a lance, it is possible to observe the shape of a second dead animal in the lower part of the mural. According to a widely accepted theory, in Sasanian art the dead animal is the same one reproduced twice, alive on the right side of the composition confronting the knight (or fleeing from him)[16] and also lying under the horse's legs, alluding to the infallibility of the hunter, usually a royal character beloved by Ahura Mazda.[17]

In the so-called North Palace at Hatra other paintings were recovered during archaeological excavations. Such paintings are Hellenistic in style and in the subjects depicted (Aphrodite and Eros?), even if at least one hunting scene clearly denotes typical Iranian elements.[18] As it will be observed below, in Sasanian art there are many borrowings from Hellenistic art, as for example in the Bishapur mosaics.

Fig. 1. Hatra, Parthian mural painting of building A, west wall (Venco Ricciardi 1996: fig. 6)

The Sasanian Period

Hunting and battle scenes were the favorite themes in Sasanian painting. Ammianus Marcellinus, the Roman historian who participated in the attack of the Emperor Julian (360-363) against Ctesiphon, was a reliable witness of the events of that campaign. On the way to the Sasanian capital he observed a pavilion with paintings described as hunting and battle scenes.[19]

According to Byzantine sources, the Emperor Heraclius (610-641) would have seen during the plundering in the Sasanian domain in 628 "Khusrau's own image in the domed roof of the palace, as though enthroned in Heaven, and around it the Sun and the Moon and the Stars".[20] However, from the text it is not clear if this was a painted image or a statue.

The Islamic sources, though more numerous, do not say much about mural paintings in Persia dated to the Sasanian epoch. At the time of Mas'udi (10th century) there still existed a palace in the district of Istakhr, in the province of Fars, with remains of Sasanian paintings. Tabari (838/39-921/23) and Ta'alibi (11th century) refer to the paintings of the exploits of the Sasanian Emperor Bahram V Gor (421-439) in the palace of Khavarnaq, commissioned by the Lakhmid king Mundir (*c.* 430-473) of Hira.[21] The Lakhmids (or Nasrids) were an Arabic dynasty who ruled in what is today northeastern Saudi Arabia and southwestern Iraq, vassals of the Sasanians, at whose court Bahram V lived as an hostage according to an oriental custom.[22] Other Islamic sources celebrate the paintings or mosaics of Ctesiphon with their scenes of the capture of Antioch by Khosrow I Anushiravan (531-579) [23] and in the *Hudud al-'alam* (10th century) it is clearly written that the buildings of the Sasanian kings at Balkh were embellished with paintings.[24] According to Yaqut (1179-1229) — who was quoting Ibn al-Faqih — Khosrow II Parvez (590-628) was depicted in the paintings of the castle of Dukkan, near Kermanshah, triumphant over the Chinese Emperor, the Turk Qaghan, the Roman Emperor and the King of Sind.[25] The famous Persian author Nizami (*c.* 1141-1209) speaks about Sinnimar, the architect who built the Khavarnaq and who was helped by Shida, a skilful painter, architect, and astronomer active at the court of Bahram V Gor.[26] Nizami also celebrates Shapur who was the most famous painter at the time of Khosrow II.[27] A few hints concerning Sasanian paintings can be found in the *Shahnama* of Firdusi.[28]

The first specimen of a painting ascribable to the Sasanian period is a battle scene recovered at Dura Europos, executed in a crude technique, and dated to the time of the Persian occupation, between 253 and 256 (fig. 2).[29] A detailed study on this painting already exists so it will not be discussed here; however it is important to draw attention to its remarkable similarity to the roughly contemporary Ardashir I relief at Firuzabad (3rd century),[30] and to the fact that it is considered the work of Persian occupiers and not the result of "oriental influences".

At Dura Europos were also discovered graffiti dated to the Sasanian occupation period (fig. 3).[31] Other graffiti considered Sasanian appear (as already observed) at Hatra (fig. 4), possibly at the Bactrian site of Kara Tepe (southern Uzbekistan) (fig. 5),[32] Lakh-mazar (Khorasan)[33] (fig. 6) and Bandyan (fig. 7).[34] In such cases the main subjects also appear to be the human figure together with animals and hunting scenes. In one graffito at Bandyan in a hunting scene the (royal?) archer is depicted wearing a coat of mail and in the act of shooting an arrow in the direction of a horned animal which seems already dead. A second animal appears on the opposite side of the hunter in the same position as the first. It is not clear if this is a local version of the Iranian iconographic solution already observed in the paintings and in the graffiti at Hatra (figs. 1, 4). Other animals appear in the graffito at Bandyan and one ram (?) presents a brand on its thigh perhaps because this hunt happened in a royal *paradeisos*.

The most interesting graffiti are those at Persepolis most likely dated to the period

Fig. 2. Dura Europos, House of the Sasanian Battle Mural (Goldman, Little 1980: fig. 7)

immediately preceding the coronation of Ardashir I (224-241) as Emperor (fig. 8).[35] Here the figures are represented in profile, standing or equestrian, all bearded and wearing garments and paraphernalia unquestionably adopted by official Sasanian art such as the lattice decoration on the caftan and the circular ornament on the shoulders.[36] In two cases the king holds the beribboned ring, a symbol recurrent in Parthian and Sasanian art with a connection to the *xwarenah* or glory of Ahura Mazda (or another deity) bestowed on the Emperor or to the concept of the contract between a sovereign and a god.[37] Floating ribbons—one of the peculiarities of Sasanian art [38]—appear tied to the crown and the shoes of the royal figures and to the horses' legs as well. The harnesses of the horses present another element characteristic of the Sasanian period as do the so-called hanging tassels which adorn the animal mounted by the Persian Emperor.[39]

Among the works of art at Bishapur, in the province of Fars, there are the famous mosaics discovered by the French archaeologist Roman Ghirshman, who recognized their strong similarity to the contemporary Roman mosaics in the Syrian province.[40] Bishapur was founded by Shapur I around 260, possibly exploiting the numerous Roman slaves deported to Persia after the Sasanian victory over the Emperor Valerian (252-268) which happened not far from Edessa. It can be noted immediately that there is preference for figures depicted in a three-quarter view and in profile.[41] In the mosaic appears one of the main characteristics of Sasanian royal representations, the floating ribbons, here tied to the hair of a female harpist.

A large mosaic from Tell Khwaris (Iraq), formerly kept in the Archaeological Museum of Baghdad seems to be late Sasanian or early Islamic and it was argued that, possibly, it represents a Christian subject.[42] Unfortunately, few details had survived: it is possible only to recognize a stag in front of a tree and tulips on the ground, pairs of peacocks and other birds along the frame, and geometric design (Pl. III-1).

The recent discovery of important Sasanian mural paintings at Gor (Firuzabad, Fars) and the scant information about them made available by D. Huff caused a great sensation among students of pre-Islamic Iranian art: a new aspect of Sasanian history of art will probably start after their publication. At present they are only partially known through some indistinct images on the internet.[43]

In Persia proper, Sasanian paintings surviving in a not too fragmentary state of preservation are all dated to the 4th century. A fragmentary mural painting from Susa considered to be early Sasanian was recently proposed to be Parthian (Pl. III-2).[44] It is possible to state that the only human figure (and his horse) partially preserved at Susa, in the act of shooting an arrow, is reproduced larger than the hunter behind him, alluding to a certain importance of the archer which is emphasized by his precious garments embellished with lattice decoration. Although the painting is in a poor condition, it does not seem that the rear part of the horse was adorned with the hanging tassels characteristic of the Sasanian Emperor, so its identification as a generic royal character seems more appropriate. An element of the mural at Susa which is of great interest is the disc resembling a naïve reproduction of the sun painted in front of the smaller horse on the left of the composition. In fact it is extremely similar to at least one of the round decorations that appear together with the zigzag band in the painting at Dura Europos (fig. 2).[45] It is not

Fig. 3. Dura Europos, Sasanian (?) graffito (Goldman 1999: fig. 7)

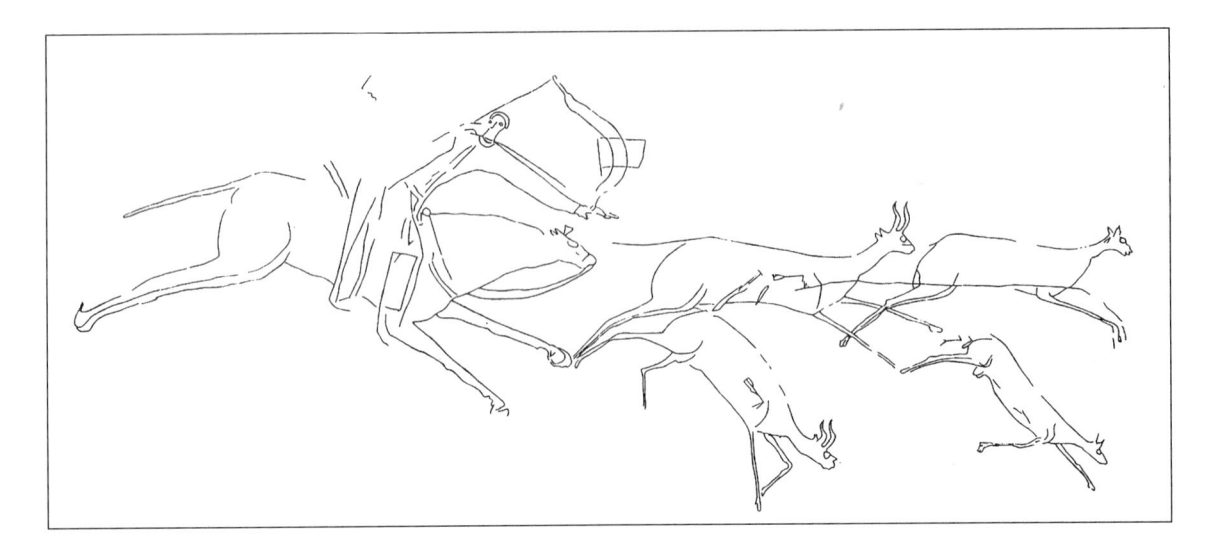

Fig. 4. Hatra, Parthian graffito (Venco Ricciardi, 1998: fig. 7)

clear if the element has a symbolic meaning (possibly even astronomical-astrological) but, while in the Dura Europos mural it could easily be a decoration, its presence at Susa raises some doubts. Nevertheless, if the fragment from Susa is really a sample of Parthian art, the presence of such elements in that painting proves once more that the Sasanians were deeply indebted to the Parthian artists for their own artistic production.

Rare fragments of mural paintings were recovered at Iwan-e Karkha (not far from Susa) in a very bad state of conservation.[46] In one fragment it is possible to see the final part of an object identified as a sheath and in another one a lattice decoration, possibly a section of the garments of a noble figure.

The last Sasanian paintings dated to the 4th century (attributed to the reign of Shapur II) were recovered at Hajyabad, in Eastern Fars.[47] The paintings are badly damaged, but the archaeologists reconstructed the general composition of the panels of a large battle scene, with frontal or three-quarter view human busts inscribed in roundels, separated by vegetal or geometrical decorations (Pl. III-3).[48] The paintings are executed according to the usual secco technique. While the rest of the battle scene is too fragmentary, one hypothesis for the disposition of the paintings with human busts has been proposed, even if the identification of the characters is not clear. M. Azarnoush—the excavator of the site—refused to identify the anthropomorphous figures as divine beings, preferring to discern, cautiously, the portraits of the lord of the manor house and other important members of the Sasanian family, among whom is Hormizd II Kushanshah (c. 302-309).[49] Such identification is not completely convincing because it is in contrast with the precepts of Sasanian art concerning frontal representations discussed above. The same chronology of the site of Hajyabad is based on the identification of some stucco busts with royal figures reproduced frontally as portraits of Shapur II.[50] In the description of one very well preserved stucco bust, the final part of the diadem of the crown is defined as "a leaf-like decorative pattern, now mostly broken". Because of its fragmentary state it is not possible to say much about this decoration. However, it less resembles part of a diadem than part of an element depicted behind the head of the bust, for example a halo with rays.[51]

For the following period, the only traces of Sasanian secco painting come from Tepe Hissar-Daaghan (5th-6th century) [52] and Ctesiphon (6th century).[53] The paintings from the two places are extremely damaged and it is possible to discern only a few details but it is clear that they represented human figures.

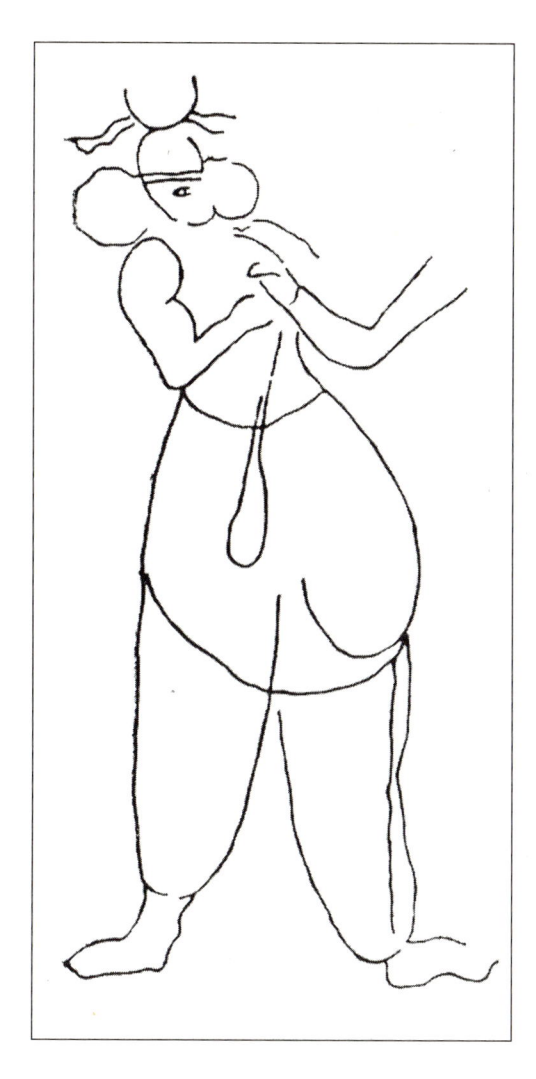

Fig. 5. Kara-tepe, drawing of a "Sasanian visitor" (Ставиский 1982: fig. 11)

Recently a new Sasanian site dated to the 5th-7th century was excavated at Mele Hayram, in southern Turkmenistan. The archaeologists who investigated the site are convinced that it is a fire temple and, on the southern and western wall of room IV, traces of mural paintings were found. Unfortunately a complete record of the pictorial decorations does not yet exist but, according to the excavation reports, the subjects of the paintings would have been geometrical and vegetal designs while the so-called pearl roundel motif appears.[54]

According to V. Lukonin and B. Marshak the vase found at Merv (Turkmenistan) during the excavation of a Buddhist site is actually a specimen of (late) Sasanian painting showing a complete cycle of the life of a person who could be identified, possibly, as its owner.[55] It is interesting to note that the theme of the cycle also includes a religious aspect which is definitely Zoroastrian in character.

Fig. 6. Lakh-mazar, Sasanian (?) graffito (Yamauchi, 1996: 6.3.4)

Even if the paintings reported in this list are very few and in many cases too fragmentary, some peculiarities of Sasanian pictorial art can be traced. Since the Persians were always depicted as being fond of hunting, the first thing to be noted is that the animals are normally represented in the act of the "flying gallop". In the representation of human figures the main characteristic of the face are the eyes, which are depicted as large and open wide, while the bodies are slim with the arms held tightly to the chest. The artists did not seem to search for naturalness in reproducing human subjects; in fact the figures are depicted with a measure of stiffness, evidently fixed by precise rules which can also be observed, for example, in Sasanian metalwork. This last consideration suggests the existence of a well established Sasanian pictorial school with a long tradition. In P. Harper's opinion, the particular treatment of drapery in a post-Sasanian silver-gilt plate kept in the Metropolitan Museum of Art, which was possibly produced in Tabaristan (Caspian region of Iran), might be dependent on a painting tradition not yet investigated by scholars. The suggestion would be supported

Fig. 7. Bandyan, Sasanian graffito (detail after Rahbar, 2004: fig. 8)

by the fact that such a style later influenced some Byzantine and Western paintings.[56] Stiffness confers solemnity to the scenes and allows a parallel with contemporary Byzantine art (especially mosaic and painting). Very interesting decorative elements borrowed from Sasanian art can be observed especially in Byzantine mosaics and paintings dated to the period between the 5th and 9th centuries.[57]

The characteristics enumerated above can be observed in a unique fragmentary wall painting recovered at Paykand and reconstructed by Russian archaeologists.[58] It is possible to recognize the figure of a kneeling bearded person with a bottle in his hands in front of the leg of a second figure with fur trousers (another peculiarity of Sasanian art observed for example in some metalwork) which is of larger dimensions and probably represents a divinity (fig. 9). The style of this mural painting is definitely extraneous to Sogdian canons as observed at Afrasyab, Varakhsha, Panjakant, and at the same site of Paykand. This fragment allows one to consider the existence of a second Sogdian school of painting earlier than the

Fig. 8. Persepolis, Sasanian graffito of north wall of the "harem" (Calmeyer 1976: fig. 3)

one usually identified at the sites just mentioned, which is definitively linked or even derives from Sasanian models probably because of its vicinity to the Persian Empire.[59]

It would be possible to insist on the secular character of Sasanian painting in agreement with Ammianus Marcellinus. However, hints regarding the enigmatic religiosity of the ruling class are constant in Sasanian art and scholars, such as Bivar, even consider some hunting scenes—represented especially on metalwork—as a reference to esoteric Mithraism.[60] Painted bowls with magic inscriptions were recovered at Mesopotamian sites dated to the

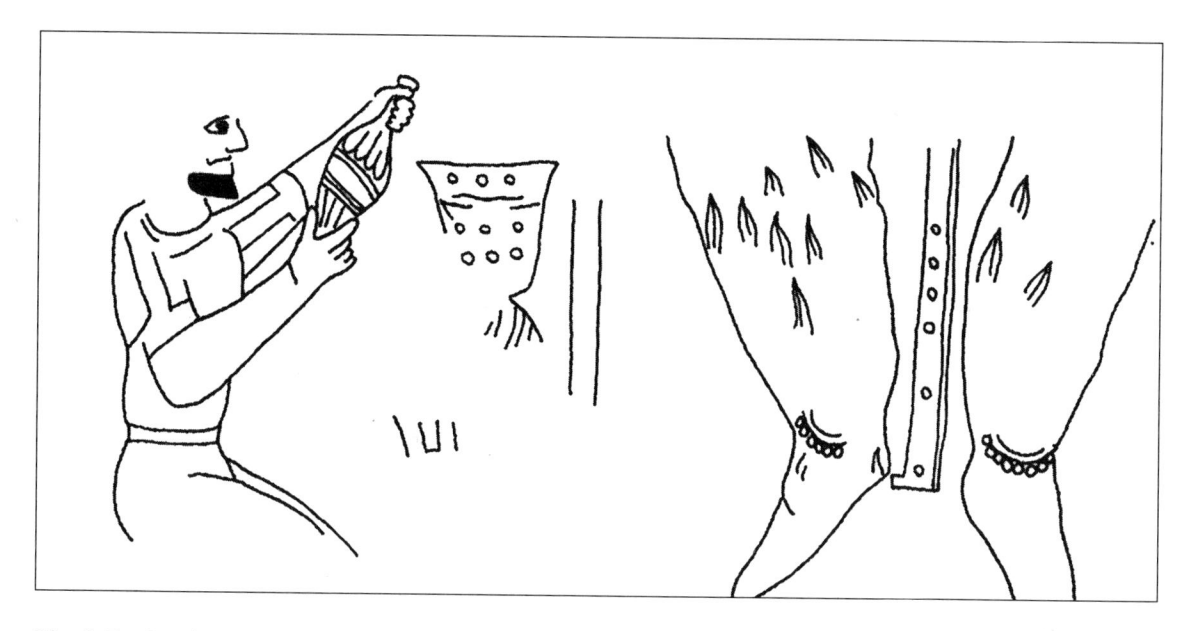

Fig. 9. Paykand, "western Sogdian" mural painting (reproduction after Семенов, 2001, p.35)

period between 600 and 650. They are an example of popular belief and had an apotropaic role represented by the figure of the demon bound with ropes.[61] Examples of secco paintings probably dated to the Sasanian period with religious scenes (apart from the busts of Hajyabad considered not to be divine) appear at Kuh-e Khoja,[62] Ghulbyan[63] (Faryab Province, northwestern Afghanistan) and Dokhtar-e Noshervan[64] (also in Afghanistan), localities quite far from the core of the Persian Empire, where elements belonging unquestionably (though not exclusively) to the Sasanian repertoire appear in local contexts executed according to the style characteristic of every Central Asiatic region of Iranian culture.[65] An important detail common to every mural painting cited above is the presence of a donor (or donors) in typical Iranian dress praying in front of the divinity. The donors wearing caftans and high boots can be observed almost everywhere in Central Asia and also in rare late Gandharan paintings.[66]

Finally, some remarks can be made about a supposed pre-Islamic tradition for illustrated manuscripts. In Sasanian art illustrated manuscripts should have occupied a prominent place but unfortunately no example of these celebrated volumes has been preserved. The Islamic sources reveal the existence of the portraits of the twenty-seven Sasanian sovereigns-each reproduced with his proper garments, crown and weapons-collected in a book observed by two Arabian authors around the 10th century. Mas'udi saw it in 915 at Istakhr, not far from Persepolis.[67] Around the middle of the 10th century Istakhri described a manuscript practically identical observed in southern Persia.[68] In D. Talbot Rice's opinion, the same Istakhri, while recording a not well identified monument, was talking about the paintings, now lost, that would have adorned the cave of Shapur I at Bishapur.[69] The book quoted by the two Arab authors probably served as a basis for the Mojmal al-Tawarikh, a text composed in Persian in 1126 by an anonymous writer with the description of the costumes of the Sasanian Emperors surviving unfortunately without images.[70] Most likely, the Sasanians promoted the translation of Greek and Indian works especially during the 5th-6th centuries. In particular, the Islamic sources relied on Pahlavi versions of the *Pancatantra* (possibly illustrated) and of an astrological text entitled *Tankalusha* embellished with illustrations copied from the original Greek.[71]

According to B. Marshak there is yet another piece of evidence about the Sasanian component in the art of the illustrated manuscript: this is a fragment of a Manichaean book recovered at Turfan by a German expedition in the beginning of the last century and now kept in Berlin. The style of this painting is clearly different to the other specimens of Manichaean miniatures recovered in Xinjiang because, according to the Russian scholar, its model was definitely a Sasanian illustrated manuscript which is now lost.[72]

Another aspect of Sasanian miniatures known through literary sources is represented by the Manichaean tradition of illustrated manuscripts. Mani himself is celebrated by Christian and Islamic authors as an exceptional painter, a fact that presupposes the diffusion of pictorial art in Persia during the early Sasanian period, even if no Manichaean manuscript has survived in Persia proper.[73] A unique fragment of an illustrated manuscript on paper cautiously dated to the 9th century has been defined as "the link of the pre-Islamic Iranian paintings with the Muslim world of Persian miniatures" (fig. 10).[74] The scene seems to depict a bearded man teaching two younger disciples under a tree. The spiraliform folders on the long tunics worn by the three figures remind one of the technique already observed depicting something similar on the garment of a figure on a piece of metalwork considered by Harper to come from Tabaristan. The miniature probably represents exactly what the American scholar had already conjectured.[75] Considering its chronology and its clear connection with Central Asian Manichaean illustrated manuscripts this fragment could hardly be considered a work produced in Persia; however it is still the only evidence which can provide an idea of pre-Islamic miniatures on Iranian soil.

Fig. 10. Fragment of an illustrated manuscript on paper, Central Asia (?) private collection (reproduction after Porter, 1997: fig. at p. 10)

The Post-Sasanian Period

Apart from illustrated manuscripts an important Sasanian component can be observed in Islamic mural painting, especially in the works of art of the Umayyads (661-750)—still influenced by Hellenistic-Byzantine elements—and the Abbasids (750-1258), which were more Iranized.[76]

One of the first examples of direct Sasanian influence on early Islamic art is provided by the mosaics in the Dome of the Rock at Jerusalem, c. 692.[77] Here spread wings—a typical symbol of Sasanian kingship—are depicted together with vegetal elements (Pl. III-4). The motif of the spread wings continued to be used as a favorite decorative element also in later monuments in the Holy Land as in the mosaics of the Church of the Nativity at Bethlehem.[78]

In the paintings at Qusayr 'Amra (Jordan, second quarter of the 8th century), the Sasanian Emperor is represented together with the other five "kings defeated by Islam" although not too realistically. Four of the kings can be recognized because of inscriptions in Greek and Arabic above their heads. The painter (or painters) had probably only some idea of Sasanian symbols of kingship as the spread wings on the crown of the Persian royal figure are reproduced too simply (fig. 11).[79] The main source of inspiration for such mural paintings seems to have been Hellenistic art and it is possible that Byzantine painters might have worked on them.[80] In any case, as already observed above, the only literary sources for this kind of representation can be found in the works of Muslim authors who were describing the kingdoms in relationship to Sasanian Iran.[81]

Not all scholars agree on the identification of the specific subjects as neighboring kings who were defeated by Islam; some prefer to regard them as the brothers of the Umayyad Caliph.[82] As noted above, Islamic literary sources about mural paintings of the time of Khosrow II mention explicitly that neighboring sovereigns were represented as subjects of the Sasanian king and an inscription at Qusayr 'Amra would identify one of the six kings as Roderick, the last Visigoth ruler of Spain who was defeated by the Umayyads in 711-712. If at least one king represents a historical character, then it is possible that the other five also were. Unfortunately, the other inscriptions do not help to identify exactly those royal characters

Fig. 11. Qusayr 'Amra, Umayyad mural painting (detail after Fontana, 2002: fig. 3b)

called Khosrow (i.e., "Sasanian Emperor"), Kaesar (Byzantine Emperor), and Negus (the sovereign of Abyssinia). It was noted that, if the Persian king at Qusayr 'Amra represents an historical figure, then consideration should also be given to Yazdigard III (632-651) or his son Peroz who lived in exile at the Chinese court of the Tang Emperor Gaozong (650-683).[83] A very interesting identification of the six figures at Qusayr 'Amra was proposed by M. Di Branco. Starting from the word "Muqawqis" written in kuphic style on the robe of the "Byzantine Emperor", he argued that the painting had at least two phases, during the second of which some names, such as Kaesar and most probably Roderick, were added. The presence of the Muqawqis (the patriarch of Alexandria) would point to the other figures being relevant persons depicted as ambassadors to the Prophet Muhammad; apart from the Muqawqis, they could include the Byzantine Emperor, the Sasanian Shahanshah, the Negus, the Ghassanid sovereign, and the Prince of Yamamah.[84]

An attempt to identify one of the foreign ambassadors in the Sogdian painting of the western wall at Afrasyab (ancient Samarkand) as Yazdigard III has been already proposed by M. Mode (fig. 12).[85] He based this identification on the comparison between that figure and the king in the reliefs of the boar hunt at Taq-e Bostan: in fact, they have similar faces and headgear (not a crown) and their garments are embellished with so-called *Simurgh* motifs although in the Sogdian inscriptions which can be observed in the same scene there is no mention at all of any Sasanian

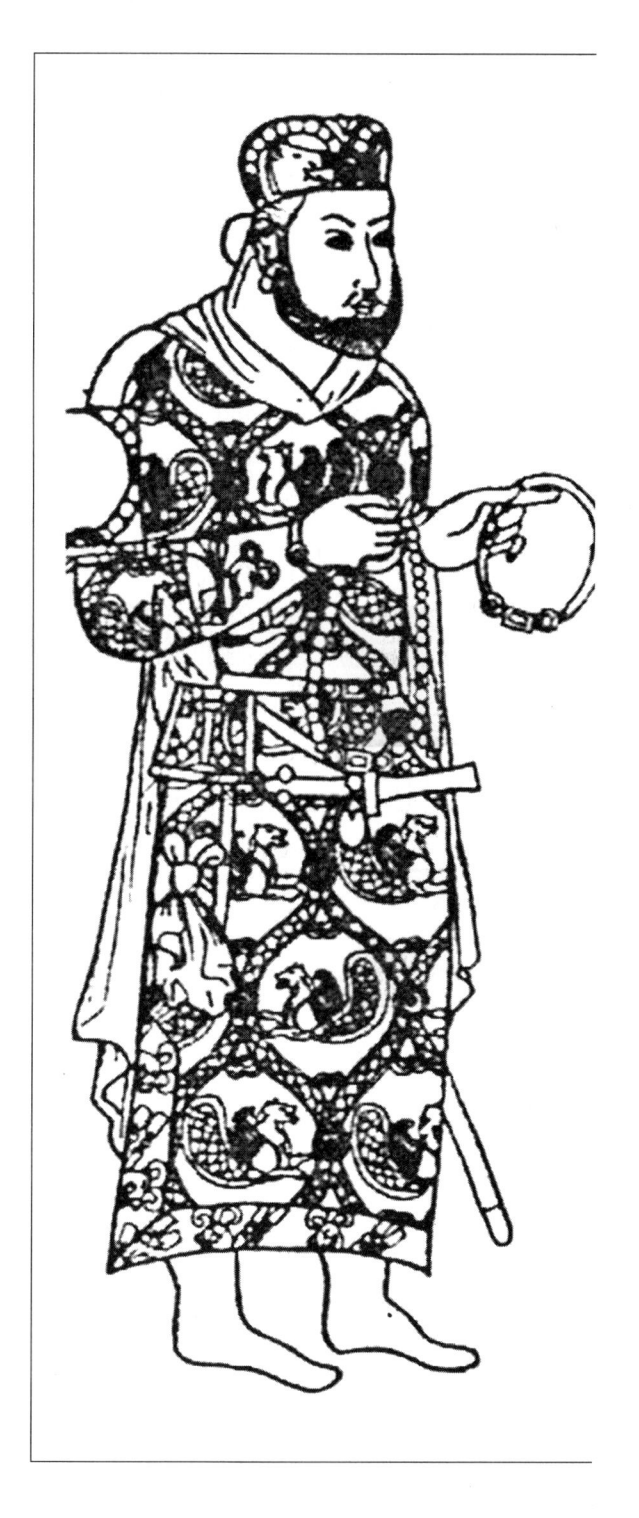

Fig. 12. Afrasyab, detail of the painting on the west wall of the so-called "Hall of the Ambassador (Альбаум 1975: fig. 4)

king. However it must be said that Taq-e Bostan has been attributed to Khosrow II (590-628) or Ardashir III (630) [86] but never before to Yazdigard III although it could be considered that a kind of common iconography existed for all the Sasanian sovereigns.

Recent studies also demonstrated that the Sogdians very clearly had in mind such a concept of royal exaltation as it can be observed in the paintings of the so-called "Hall of the Ambassadors" at Afrasyab, dated around 660. At Afrasyab almost every wall was dedicated to a different land: China was represented on the northern wall, India on the eastern one, while the western and southern walls were reserved for festivities celebrated in Samarkand, most likely to be identified as the local New Year (*Nawruz*). It is worth observing that the sovereigns in the painting are represented as larger than ordinary people and, so, it is not possible to explain why the figure identified by Mode as Yazdigard III is so small. Most likely, the Chinese and the Indians on the northern and eastern walls, respectively, are similarly celebrating their own festivities with a search for synchronization with the Samarkand *Nawruz*.[87] As F. Grenet has recently observed, the "Hall of the Ambassadors" cycle should be considered the work of professional astrologers.[88] The astrological-astronomical element at Qusayr 'Amra is represented by a zodiac cycle painted on a dome of the building and not by specific gestures or attitudes of those kings. It is very likely that at Qusayr 'Amra professional astrologers were also active, although it is impossible to connect the six kings with that zodiac since the two paintings appear on different walls.

Certainly, there are other elements at Afrasyab borrowed from late Sasanian art such as the so-called *Simurgh* on the garments of a foreign envoy considered above. Among the most debated late Sasanian symbols of kingship the so-called *Simurgh* is very representative. This is a winged creature with the face and the forelegs of a dog, paws of a lion and a long tail which resembles that of a peacock or a fish. Even if some students of Iranian culture have proposed identifying this monstrous creature with a manifestation of royal glory,[89] it is interesting to observe that the *Simurgh* was accepted and represented often in early Umayyad art and coinage.[90] Single representations of the *Simurgh* within circular frames (often pearled) were recovered at Qasr al Hayr al Gharbi (Syria, first half of the 8th century), at Qasr al Hallabat (Jordan, first half of the 8th century), and at Khirbat al-Mafjar (Palestine, second quarter of the 8th century) (fig. 13).[91]

At the same sites many other decorative elements and subjects clearly appear to have been borrowed from Sasanian art because they were highly esteemed by the Umayyad ruling class. In another painting which embellished the pavement at Qasr al Hayr al Gharbi, for example, the figure of the animal hunted by the archer is reproduced below his horse (fig.

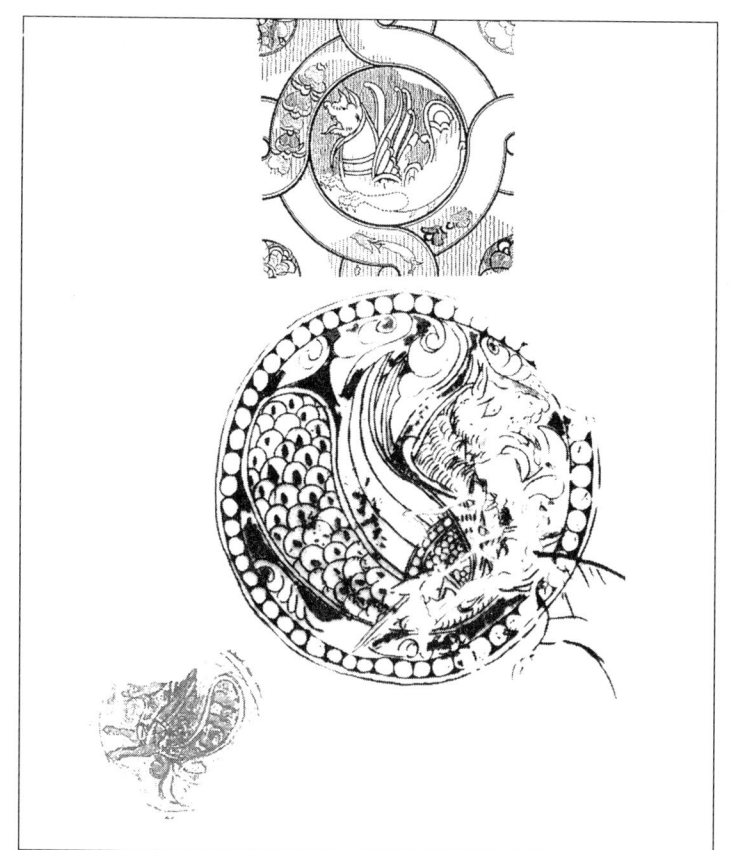

Fig. 13. Different kinds of Umayyad *Simurgh* from Qasr al Hayr al Gharbi, Qasr al Hallabat and Khirbat al-Mafjar (reproduction after Fontana, 2002: fig. 9c, 11c, tav. 4)

Fig. 14. Qasr al Hayr al Gharbi, Umayyad mural painting (detail after Fontana, 2002: pl. 8)

14) according to a very well known Sasanian formula. The same position of the archer riding the horse reminds one of many Sasanian silver dishes while the floating ribbons attached to his body are clearly rooted in Sasanian official art. Above the hunting scene there are two musicians under arches exactly as can be observed in Sasanian metalwork. The association of hunting and banqueting scenes is possibly an allusion to the funerary sphere although there are not many parallels in Sasanian art.[92] A second painting was found together with the one just observed, although its characteristics seem to be a mixture of Hellenistic and Iranian features. In fact, the pearl roundel containing the bust of a female figure is definitely borrowed from Persia but the subjects inside and outside the circular frame belong to the pagan traditions of the Hellenized east (fig. 15).

Fig. 15. Qasr al Hayr al Gharbi, Umayyad mural painting (detail after Fontana, 2002: pl. 9)

Other painted pearl roundels embellished the buildings of the Abbasid period at Samarra (Iraq, end of the 9th century)[93], and these accorded to a taste which is definitely Iranian (also Hellenistic) in derivation but close to Central Asian specimens. This observation appears very clearly in the representation of human faces and in the attitudes of the figures depicted in the act of hunting and dancing (fig. 16). Very similar elements survived in pictorial art (and not only) for many centuries after the fall of the Sasanians, and their effects were perceived even out of the sphere of Islamic dominion, as far as Norman Sicily in the decoration of the Cappella Palatina in Palermo and the Cefalù Cathedral (both dated around 1140),[94] and in a series of so-called *Simurgh* which can be observed in the Armenian Church of St. Grigor of Tigran Honenc' (1215), now in Eastern Turkey (Vilayet of Kars).[95]

The winged creature transporting a woman in the Cappella Palatina was a subject

Fig. 16. Samarra, Abbasid painting from the Ghawsaq palace (Otto Dorn, 1964: fig. 31)

known in Persian art and represented at least on one enigmatic Sasanian silver dish where the monster is a giant bird with big pointed ears. Most likely, the origin of the scene in the Sasanian metalwork can be traced back to Indian art,[96] although V. Lukonin had proposed identifying it as a representation of the equinox: the two naked figures in the lower part of the scene are holding a bow and an axe which are allegories for the sun and the moon, respectively, that is to say, day and night.[97] Its meaning should then be searched for within the sphere of Sasanian culture. As very recent investigations are attempting to demonstrate, it appears increasingly evident that the astrological element was highly esteemed by the Sasanians exactly as by all the other peoples in contact with them. It should therefore come as no surprise if old theories about Iranian culture which were originally considered not too convincing will be reevaluated in the future.

In Persia, the first paintings (both wall-paintings and ceramics) dated to the Islamic period were recovered at Nishapur, at that time the capital of the Samanid Emirate (875-1005).[98] Paintings dated to the Seljukid period (1037-1194) are known from central Persia and Anatolia,[99] again according to stylistic traditions deeply rooted in Central Asian art but with many elements borrowed from Sasanian Iran. The same observation can be advanced for western Central Asia as in the paintings at Lashkari Bazar (Afghanistan) dated to the 11th century (Ghaznavid period, 962-1186).[100] According to Islamic literary sources, numerous illustrated manuscripts existed in Persia during the Seljukid domination but they were mostly lost and the few specimens which have survived are just a minimal part of this and are also difficult to date.[101]

Islamic illustrated manuscripts belong to a different tradition although several details could be considered a borrowing from pre-Islamic period. Too many specimens are known to be considered here although at least two frontispieces recently reconsidered deserve particular attention. They are part of the Miscellany Collection H. 2125 of Topkapi Saray Museum (Istanbul) and share several elements with the paintings of the western and southern wall of the so-called "Hall of the Ambassadors" at Afrasyab. In fact, not only the representation of the parade and royal banquet in the two frontispieces remind us of the Sogdian paintings at Afrasyab but also the theme itself of an important festivity inherited by the Turkish and Mongol invaders directly from traditions rooted in Central Asian pre-Islamic culture.[102] The "Buddhist background" recognized in these two miniatures by E. Esin thirty years ago [103] actually denotes local features, most likely Sogdian or, in any case, strong Iranian peculiarities.

Conclusion

All the paintings dated to the post-Sasanian period just mentioned display Iranian elements borrowed from Sasanian and Central Asian artistic traditions readapted according to the taste of the different local artists. Sasanian features were very popular among Muslim painters who continued to reproduce subjects rooted in pre-Islamic Iranian culture. However, while the Central Asian (particularly Sogdian) component has been studied for a long period, covering a great amount of material, for the Sasanian period it is not yet possible to say very much. A new field of investigation is opened up by the study of the 7th century paintings at Afrasyab and especially the astronomical-astrological features of the scenes depicted there. Unfortunately, it is not yet possible to say how important the Sasanian borrowings were in those Sogdian paintings although the excavations of several bullae from the fortress Kafir Kala (not far from Samarkand), covering a long span of time, show in many cases iconographical formulae typical of Sasanian official art (together with Pahlavi inscriptions).[104] It is extremely difficult to determine a chronology for those bullae and, so, to know if such formulae had been borrowed from Sasanian art, arrived together with Persian immigrants who escaped the Arab advance, or even arrived with the Arabs who were great admirers of the very non-iconoclastic Sasanian culture.

In a few words, those students of Sasanian art whose interests focus on paintings are still obliged to rely mainly on post-Sasanian production, a fact destined to change if the renewed interest in modern Iran for pre-Islamic archaeology will allow the discovery of new instructive relics in line with the response during the excavations in Gor.

NOTES

[1] De Waele (2004). On Sasanian paintings see also: Луконин (1977: 210-21); Scarcia (2003: 105-07); Marshak (2002.a: 11-12).

[2] Traces of even earlier wall-paintings were discovered in the Province of Fars (District of Bayza) during the excavation of the site of Tell-e Malyan (*c.* 3200 BCE): Nickerson (1977: figs. 2, 6-8). Another pre-Achaemenid site with geometrical paintings dated before 6th century BCE is that of Baba Jan: Goff (1970: pl. III a-d). Four painted wooden beams embellished with scenes of Persians fighting nomads wearing pointed caps is now part of the Archäologische Staatssammlung, Munich: Summerer (2007). The origin of these painted panels is unknown but it was argued that, most likely, they could have been produced in Achaemenid Anatolia. On Greek sources about evidence of Achaemenid paintings see: Marshak (2002.a: 8).

[3] Nunn (1988: pl. 108-109). Also at Persepolis were recovered Achaemenian graffiti : Herzfeld (1941: pl. LXXII); Roos (1970).

[4] Perrot, Le Brun, Labrousse (1971: 40, fig. 19); Calmeyer (1985-87: 577); Nunn (1988: pl. 110); Boucharlat (1989: fig. 1); *ibid.* (1997a: 61, colour pls. XIV-XV); *ibid.* (1997b: 502, fig. 665). Some paintings on pottery and walls recovered in Anatolia are considered specimens linked to the Achaemenid expansion in the region: Boardman (2000: 200, figs. 5.84-85a,b).

[5] Sajjadi, Moghaddam (2004: fig. 9); Sajjadi (2007).

[6] Boucharlat (2002: 330). According to Bivar there is some evidence to support a chronology for a part of the paintings at Kuh-e Khoja (Sistan) to the Seleucid period: Bivar (2003). According to the Syriac version of the *Pseudo-Callisthene*, Alexander himself ordered an image of the goddess Nana to be painted in a temple in

Samarkand: Axunbabaev, Grenet (1990: 371); Grenet (2004: 1061).

[7] Iranian elements can be observed in the wall paintings (and graffiti) of Syrian cities such as Dura-Europos (1st-2nd century CE). See: Кошеленко (1966: 178-89, figs. at pp. 183, 185); Colledge (1979:148-49); Schlumberger (1970: 106-111, figs. at pp. 104-111); Ghirshman (1962: 47-50, figs. 59, 61, 63a-63c.); Downey (1994); Leriche (1996: 589-92); Millar (1998). For the graffiti at Dura-Europos, see: Goldman (1999). For Palmyra (2nd-3rd century CE), see: Giuliano (1963); Colledge (1976: 83-87, 221-34, pls. 114-18; 1987); Browning (1979: 25, 36-37). For Edessa (early 3rd century) see: Leroy (1957: 317, 324-25, 334, 342, pl. XXII; 1961: 161-67, fig. 1-2); Segal (1970: 9-16, 40, pls. 1-3, 16.b, 17.a, 43-44); Drijvers (1994: 409); Lieu (1997: 174). Iranian components linked to Parthian art appear also in northern regions far from Persia, as the funerary paintings at Pantikapaeum (today Kerch, in Crimea), dated cautiously to the 1st century: Maenchen-Helfen (1957-58: figs. 1-2); Blavatskij (1959: 932-34); Ghirshman (1962: 265, fig. 341); Античные государства Северново Причерноморья (1984: pls. CVII 2-3, CIX 1).

[8] Andrae (1933 reprint 1967: 111-14, fig. 46, pls. 61-62); *ibid.* (1938: fig. 78); Кошеленко (1966: 189, fig. at p. 183); Ghirshman (1962: fig. 60); Шлюмбержер (1985: 108, fig. 101); Downey (1985-87: 585); Neugebauer (1954: fig. 1); Venco Ricciardi (1992: fig. 13); Venco Ricciardi (1996); al-Salihi (1996). For the graffiti at Hatra, see: Al-Shams (1981); Venco Ricciardi (1998); Venco Ricciardi (2004). As discussed briefly below, the hunting scenes in the graffiti at Hatra already display a typical iconographic solution greatly appreciated in Sasanian art.

[9] Henning (1953); Mizbani, Salimi (2002: 2, 17). Other graffiti representing human heads in profile with Parthian inscriptions have been found at Kal-e Jangal, in Southern Khorasan but they have not been investigated sufficiently. See: communication through the Sasanika mail-list by Mehr Kian, archaeologist and director of Ayapir Cultural Heritage Base (Iran).

[10] Invernizzi (1992); *ibid.* (1998); Curtis (2000: 24); Pilipko (2000). From Mansur-Tepe (Turkmenistan) come paintings of a bearded face and a female face on fragments of vases dated to the 2nd-1st century BCE: Кошеленко (1977: fig. 76); Koshelenko, Lapshin, Novikov (1989: figs. 7-10); Gajbov, Košelenko, Novikov (1991: figs. 6-7). The same authors refer to murals that have now disappeared (*ibid.*: 88). For very recent Parthian fragmentary paintings from Qaleh Zahak (Iranian Azerbayjan), see: Qandgar, Esmaili, Rahmatpour (1383/2004: 202-203).

[11] Venco Ricciardi 1996: 164.

[12] On a discussion about the central or provincial Sasanian metalwork production, see: Harper, Meyers (1981). See also: de Francovich (1984: 96-97, figs. 131-33).

[13] Кошеленко (1966: fig. at p. 201); Ghirshman (1962: 264-66, fig. 119, 340-46); Lo Muzio (2003).

[14] It is correct to assert that Parthian art has a preference for the frontal representation of human figures-see for example: Schlumberger (1960: 262-64); Bianchi Bandinelli (1966: 323-24); Schlumberger (1966:

385-86); Ghirshman (1962: 1-12)-but this consideration cannot be applied in general because exceptions do exist. In fact, the archer in mother of pearl from Shami dated to the 2nd-1st century BCE and the archer in the relief of the Berlin Staatliche Museen dated to the 1st-3rd centuries-see: Ghirshman (1962: fig. 125.a, 340)-are both depicted in profile. Regarding Sasanian art, it is clear that there is a general preference for the reproduction of human figures in profile or in three-quarter view but frontal representations do exist even if rare. The Sasanian Emperor is reproduced frontally in some official representation when seated on the throne with his hands on the hilt of his sword: Schlumberger (1960: 290-91); *ibid.* (1966); Harper, Meyers (1981: 99-122). In Sasanian seals the frontal view is a privilege of divinities and heroes: Gyselen, Gignoux (2000: 301-2). The frontal representation of the king on Sasanian coins is not normal and the explanation of such an iconography on some specimens is still open to discussion: Gyselen (1993: 128); Gyselen, Gignoux (2000: 294). Possibly, Khosrow II adopted frontality on his coins as a result of Byzantine influence: *ibid.* (2000: 301-2). In Kushan coinage there is a similar resolution in the difference between the representation of the king (body frontal but with the face in profile) and the divinities such as the Buddha (always frontal): Rosenfield (1967: pls. I-XII, especially pl. V.88); Tanabe (1974).

[15] Overlaet (1993: 93).

[16] The different typologies of metalwork with hunting scenes are analyzed in detail in: Harper, Meyers (1981: 40-98).

[17] De Francovich (1984: 89-9). See also: Gignoux (1983: 117-8). Also in the *Megalopsychia* hunting mosaic at Antiochia (5th-6th centuries), where Sasanian influence is very clear, there is the scene of a hunter in the act of piercing a leopard, while a second animal lies on the ground: Lavin (1963: fig. 7).

[18] Al-Salihi (1996).

[19] Dimand (1972: 17-18); Goldman, Little (1980: 292); Marshak (2002.a: 11); Drijvers (2006).

[20] L'Orange (1953: 19-20).

[21] Arnold (1938-39 reprint 1967: 1811); Morgenstern (1938-39 reprint 1967): 1373, note 4; Peters (1977-1978: 104-5, note 79). According to M. Dimand (1972: 18), it was the same Emperor who ordered the realization of such paintings in his palace. The paintings discovered at Hira are defined as "Sasanian in character" by the excavator, see: Talbot Rice (1931: 280-82); *ibid.* (1934: 54-57).

[22] The episode calls to mind the habit of keeping Chinese hostages at the Kushan court. According to the records of the Chinese Buddhist traveller Xuanzang (*c.* 600-664), one of the buildings at Kapisha (Afghanistan) still "bore paintings of the hostages on the walls" at the time of his visit in 7th century: Rosenfield (1967: 37).

[23] Денике (1938: 20); Arnold (1965: 63); Dimand (1972: 18); Schippmann (1993: 136); Kröger (1993: 447).

[24] Minorsky (1970: 108).

[25] Луконин (1977: 210-19); Gray (1979: 315); Creswell (1979a: 408); Grube (1989: 201); Fontana (2002: 77).

For some information on the probable identification of this castle during the 1960s by the archaeologist Leo Trümpelmann: Fowden (2004: 285).

[26] Soucek (1972: 11-12); Bernardini (1992).

[27] Soucek (1972: 15-18).

[28] Fontana (2002: 85).

[29] Grenet (1988: 138-43); Leriche (1996: 592).

[30] Ghirshman (1962: figs. 163-64, 166-67); Goldman, Little (1980: 287). This point was stressed also by De Waele (2004: 349-50). Regarding the topos of the "individual duel" fought by a Sasanian general it would be interesting to remember as Bahram Chobin during the 6th century and Sambat Bagratuni at the beginning of the 7th century respectively decided the end of a battle (or of a war) against Central Asian people (most likely Turks) challenging the chief of their opponents in an individual duel. On individual duels in Panjakant mural paintings, see: Azarpay (1981: fig. 60).

[31] Goldman (1990: fig. 2); *ibid.* (1999: 42, fig. C.6). Nevertheless, strong Parthian stylistic formulae still exist in these drawings.

[32] Goldman (1999: 38); Ставиский (1982: 39, fig. 11). The site is Buddhist.

[33] Yamauchi (1996: 143-45, figs. 6.3.1-6.3.4); Mizbani, Salimi (2002). The lion from Lakh-mazar is depicted more realistically than the many representations of lion hunting on Sasanian metalwork or in the Sar Mashad rock relief: Harper, Meyers (1981: pls. 14, 25, 37); Trümpelmann (1975).

[34] Rahbar (2004: 12).

[35] Herzfeld (1941: 308, figs. 401-402); Calmeyer (1976: figs. 3-4); Ramjou (2004); Callieri (2006).

[36] On a study of the Sasanian garments mostly obtained from sculpture, metalwork and post-Sasanian textiles, see: Kawami (1992); Goldman (1993); Scerrato (1994a); Goldman (1997).

[37] Tanabe (1984: 34-35); Kawami (1987: 41 note 251); von Gall (1990); Vanden Berghe (1988); Kaim (2009). This ornament has important links with the textile decoration in official representation of the king: Jeroussalimskaja (1993: 116); Domyo (1997: 19).

[38] Kuwayama (1976: 396-402); Bromberg (1983: 256-261); *ibid.* (1990).

[39] The detail was first noted by Tanabe (1980); *ibid.* (1990: 53; 1998: 98). The hypothesis of the Japanese scholar is supported by the presence of the same elements in a unique silver plate decorated with an enthronement scene, unquestionably linked to Sasanian royal kingship (its provenance is obscure). The two hanging tassels are applied to the extremities of a crescent on the top of the throne of the central royal figure surrounded by his entourage: *Sasanian Silver* (1967: cat. 12). Six elements resembling the same tassels appear also in a frieze at Naqsh-e Rostam; they are attached to insignia supported by a page behind an equestrian royal character: Sarre (1922: pl. 83).

[40] Ghirshman (1962: 140-46). On the Roman-Dionysiac features of such mosaics, see von Gall (1971);

Keall (1990: 288); Balty (1993); Balty (2006). At the Louvre Museum (where some of those mosaics are displayed) it is reported that there were also decorative paintings (flowers) in the same hall in which the mosaics were recovered. Very fragmentary traces of mosaics with a Greek inscription were also discovered at Susa: Ghirshman (1952: 9-10, fig. 11). Floor mosaics existed also at Ctesiphon-see: Monneret de Villard (1966: 279); Kröger (1993: 447)-and in western Persia: Balty, Briquel-Chatonnet (2000, *non vidi*). On an interesting description of a mosaic depicting Khosrow I fighting Byzantines: Shahbazi (2001: 342).

[41] Ghirshman (1956); *ibid.* (1962: 180-86).

[42] Costa (1971); Hauser (2007: pl. 8). In some cases, buildings in Iraq considered to be late Sasanian have painted decorations: Finster (1976: 90-91).

[43] http://www.chn.ir/news/?section=2&id=29609 (I thank Touraj Daryaee for his kindness in directing me to this web page). See also: http://www.cais-soas.com/News/2006/February2006/19-02.htm. During a recent workshop on Sogdiana organized by Desmond Durkin-Meisterernst (28-29 November 2007, Berlin), Prof. Huff kindly informed me that the mural paintings present several people and one of them is bringing an animal like an offering (possibly dedicated to a divinity?). Although the ceramics found in the room of the paintings at Gor should be dated to the Islamic period, the paintings do not look Islamic at all and there are also some enigmatic architectonic elements which are difficult to identify and date.

[44] Ghirshman (1952: 11-12); *ibid.* (1962: 183, fig. 224); Boucharlat (1987: 358); Gasche (2002: 187); De Waele (2004: 354).

[45] Goldman, Little (1980: 285, fig. 2). Two similar elements also appear beside the head of the king in a silver plate of the Pushkin Museum (Tchedine, Russia) which is possibly post-Sasanian and was produced in the provinces external to Persian Empire: Harper, Mayers (1981: pl. 21).

[46] Ambrosetti (1961); Ghirshman (1962: 181); Gyselen, Gasche (1994: 34, pl. X); De Waele (2004: 355-58). For Ghirshman the paintings were executed according to the fresco technique.

[47] Azarnoush (1977: 172-73); *ibid.* (1994: 167-82, figs. 157-62, pls. XXVIII-XXXV); De Waele (2004: 358-65). During the excavations the archaeologists realized that there were other paintings. Such paintings remain still unexcavated today: Azarnoush (1994: 167).

[48] Parallels with a decorative pattern particularly exploited in Persia and in Central Asia were correctly identified by Azarnoush (1994: 174-75).

[49] The characters wear garments embellished with small roundels arranged in quite separate groups of three in the Sasanian fashion: Goldman (1993: figs. 22-28, 32).

[50] Azarnoush (1994: 102-5, 109-10, stuccoes catalogue nos. 17, 20, pl. VII); Catalogue Roma (2001: cat. 151). The busts are attributed to Shapur II because of the particular kind of crown considered by Azarnoush (1994: 181) characteristic for each Sasanian Emperor. Unfortunately, the validity of such a theory was criticized by several scholars: Harper, Meyers (1981: 65-66, 125, 138-39); Peck (1993: 413-15).

[51] Azarnoush (1994: 104). On early Islamic stuccoes from Chal Tarkhan-'Eshqabad the figures representing a royal character were reproduced frontally and featured a halo with rays: Sarre (1922: pl. at p. 152); Erdmann (1943 reprint 1969: pl. 37); Ghirshman (1962: fig. 229); Thompson (1974: fig. 2); *ibid.* (1974b: pls. II, figs. 1-2, XX.I). Bivar (1998: 106-8, pls. XIV.c, XV.b) cautiously recognized in the lost paintings of the 38-meter Buddha niche at Bamiyan the portraits of Shapur II and Bahram I Kushanshah, both represented-according to Sasanian artistic formulae-in three-quarter view and, curiously enough, with a halo behind the head. On other studies on these "royal figures", see: Tarzi (1977: 7, 11, pls. 9, 12); Tanabe (2004); Compareti (2008). This latter detail was studied extensively by K. Tanabe (1984: 42), in whose opinion "the disk-nimbus symbolizes the celestial world of the righteous dead or *fravashis* whom the Zoroastrians regarded as living eternally in the endless light of Ohrmuzd, *asar roshnin*". So the paintings at Bamiyan (and, consequently, also those at Hajyabad) should be considered subsequent to Shapur II's reign or contemporary but executed by artists not familiar with central Sasanian art, even if the royal portraits are in three-quarter view. The royal figures as the large representation of Surya-Mithra on his chariot at Bamiyan do not wear garments embellished with the typical decoration with pearl roundels (very diffused in Central Asia from the 6th century onwards), present in other paintings at Bamiyan: Tarzi (1977: pls.D 57 155, D 58 156, D 59 157, A 5).

[52] Schmidt (1937: 336-38, figs. 174-75); Ambrosetti (1966); Adle (1993); Dyson (1997); De Waele (2004: 365-68). The technique is not reported but it seems most likely to be the same as that at other Sasanian sites. The site could be post-Sasanian: Marshak (2002.a: 12).

[53] Schmidt (1934: 18); Morgenstern (1967: 1373); Reuther (1967: 532-33); Christensen (1971: 461); Kröger (1982: 88-89, pl. 29); *ibid.* (1993); Invernizzi (1997); Sims (2002: fig. 25); De Waele (2004: 368-70).

[54] Kaim (2002: 218).

[55] Луконин (1977: 219-21); Marshak (2002.a: 12). On a recent study of this vase: Manassero (2003). For a Sogdian attribution of that vase, see: Mode (2009).

[56] Harper (1972: 164).

[57] Among the most interesting mosaics there are the specimens from Antioch (5th-6th century), see: Wilber (1937); Lavin (1963: 199-204, figs. 2, 7); A. Grabar (1971: 685-86, pl. VI. 2, VII. 1); *ibid.* (1980: 106, figs. 113, 115); Ghirshman (1962: figs. 405-6). See also the beribboned birds from the church of St. Demetrius at Nikopolis and St. Vitale at Ravenna: Kitzinger (1951: fig. 19); Bromberg (1983: 258). For the paintings, mostly from Cappadocian churches, see: Thierry (1970: 470, figs. 7-8, 12, 23; 1976: fig. 39, scheme 10); A. Grabar (1971: pl. XV, fig. 2); Bromberg (1983: 258). For a very interesting hypothesis on a Byzantine derivation for the hunt of Bahram V Gor, see: Fontana (2000: 17-18, note 7).

[58] Семенов (2001: 35); Семенов, Адыов (2006: fig. 2).

[59] Compareti (2006.a: fig. 20).

[60] Bivar (1995). On hunting as one of the main occupations of the ruling class under the Sasanians, see:

Gignoux (1983). Religious representations appear intermingled with battle and hunting scenes also in the Bandyan stucco panels (5th century), which rendering is connected with pictorial art exactly as for the Taq-e Bostan friezes: Rahbar (1998: pls. III-X, figs. 5-10). On Taq-e Bostan and Sasanian pictorial art, see: Christensen (1971: 460-61); Morgenstern (1938-39 reprint 1967: 1373, the same author reports traces of pigment on the monument); Genito (1999: 382; 2001: 135); De Waele (2004: 371-72). In her study on Afrasyab paintings, Silvi Antonini (1989: 130) observes that the water scene in these Sogdian paintings "is reminiscent of the walls of the Great Grotto in Taq-e Bostan". Scarcia and Marshak agree on the uncertainty of the actual religion professed by the Sasanian sovereigns: Scarcia (2000: 190, note 70).

[61] Franco (1978-79: 234, fig. 2); Harper, Skjærvø, Gorelick, Gwinnett (1992: 45, figs. 2-3); Simpson (2000: 59, pl. 31).

[62] Herzfeld (1941: pls. CI-CIV); Ghirshman (1962: 41-45, figs. 55-58); Kawami (1987, figs. 16, 23, 26-27). Herzfeld and Ghirshman attributed a religious significance to many scenes while Kawami was more cautious. The Kuh-e Khoja paintings-even if mostly re-dated to the Sasanian period-display unique characteristics regarded as the unrepeatable result of the encounter of Hellenistic, Iranian-Central Asian and even Buddhist elements: Colledge (1979: 149-50); Schlumberger (1970: 56-59); Downey (1985-87: 582-83); Schlumberger (1986.a: 1046); Kawami (1987a: 25). In this last author's opinion there were three styles in the painting decoration at the site, viz. Buddhist, Hellenistic and Sasanian: Kawami (1987a: 25). At least one painted fragment is believed to belong to the Parthian period: Facenna (1981); Catalogue Roma (2001: cat. 140). On the chronology of the site, see: Kawami (1987a); *ibid.* (1987b: 153-54); Mousavi (1999); Ghanimati (2000:144-46). See also note 6 of the present article.

[63] Grenet, Lee, Pinder-Wilson (1980); Lee, Grenet (1998); Grenet (1999). The painting is dated to the 4th or early 5th century (Lee, Grenet 1998: 81). On new discoveries of possible pre-Islamic fragmentary paintings in Afghanistan, at the fortress of Chehel Burj, see: Lee (2006: 238-41).

[64] Klimburg-Salter (1993: fig. 2). On Dokhtar-e Noshervan painting and Sogdian art see: Mode (1992); Marshak (1995/96: 309-10, note 5).

[65] On pre-Islamic Central Asian painting, see the bibliography quoted by: Косолапов, Маршак (1999); Marshak (2002.a).

[66] Khan (2000); Kurita (2003: fig. 868); Khan, Mahmood-ul-Hasan (2004). The same scheme can be observed in some terracotta panels from the Kurita Collection which are considered to be 4th century Bactrian (and, most likely, non-Buddhist), see: Carter (1997). Donors do not appear in published Buddhist mural paintings from Tapa Sardar (Afghanistan): Silvi Antonini, Taddei (1981).

[67] Carra de Voux (1897: 150-51).

[68] Monneret de Villard (1923: 982); Arnold (1965: 63, 82); Dimand (1972: 18); Gray (1977: 14); Fontana (1997: 463); Fontana (1998: 34).

[69] Talbot Rice (1946).

[70] Mohl (1841: 258-68).

[71] Nallino (1922: 356-362); Борисов (1939). On the problems related to the Pahlavi versions of the *Pancatantra*: Raby (1987/88: 390-91); Raby (1991); De Blois (1991); Marshak (2002.a: 12).

[72] Marshak (2002.a: 12).

[73] Cumont (1913); Monneret de Villard (1923 translated in English and published in: *A Survey of Persian Art*, eds A. U. Pope and Ph. Ackerman, V, London, New York, 1938-39 reprint 1967: 1820-28); Arnold (1924: 14-23); Gray (1961: 15); Christensen (1971: 202-5); Piemontese (1995); Klimkeit (1998: 271-75); Sims (2002: 20-2). An Arabic source speaks of the violent persecution against the Manichaeans at the time of the Abbasid Caliph al-Muqtadir (908-932) when many precious books were publicly burnt and molten gold and silver cast from the fire, see: Gray (1961: 15). The unique specimens of Manichaean illustrated manuscripts and paintings were recovered at the beginning of the 20th century during the first European explorations in the Tarim Basin (Eastern Turkestan, nowadays Xinjiang Uyghur Autonomous Region, China), see: Cumont (1913); Monneret de Villard (1923); Von Le Coq (1973); Catalogue New York (1982: 174-82); Chao (1996); Klimkeit (1998: 275-82); Gulácsi (2001). On the existence of a Sogdian miniature school presumed from details in mural paintings from Panjakant, see: Marshak (1999: 133-34).

[74] Porter (1997: 10). The figure was also published by: Shishkina, Pavchinskaja (1992: 26). The language of the manuscript is Arabic.

[75] See note 56 of the present article.

[76] Ettinghausen (1962: 18, 20, 26, 29-30, 34-35, 42-43, 61, 63, 92, 147, 160-161, 170, 185); Arnold (1965: 62-65, 82); Monneret de Villard (1966: 278-86); Dimand (1972: 61-63); Gray (1979: 313-16); Grube (1989: 200); Bloom (1991); Grube (1994: 418); O. Grabar (1997: 808); Baer (1999); Fontana (2001); Fontana (2002: 17, 23, 37-38, 76); Sims (2002: 23-30). For a specific study on Sasanian elements in Islamic art treated more generally, see: Rosen-Ayalon (1984). On the Sogdian influence on Islamic painting, see: Azarpay (1981: 171-80); Raby (1987/88); O. Grabar (1997: 807). It is highly probable that an important pictorial tradition existed among the Arabs before Islam exactly as for other artistic expressions: Monneret de Villard (1966: 255, 257); King (2004). Specifically on pre-Islamic Arab paintings, there are the fragments from Palace B at Shabwa, Hadramawt (nowadays north-western Yemen), testifying to the presence of a pictorial tradition which intermingled Hellenistic and local elements in South Arabia, see: Audouin (1991: figs. 7-9). Other fragmentary paintings from present day Saudi Arabia were found at Qaryat al-Faw: Nicolle (2005: 14). The chronology of the paintings is still disputed but it could be fixed to within the span of the 3rd-5th centuries. On some traces of early Islamic pictorial decoration from Kufa (Iraq): Fontana (2002: 17-18, fig. 1).

[77] Ettinghausen (1962: figs. at pp. 18, 21, 23); Monneret de Villard (1966: 286-87); Gautier-van Berchem (1979: 278-81, 286-96); Ettinghausen Grabar (1987: fig. 7); O. Grabar (1989: 67-81, figs. 29-30); Talbot Rice (1991:

figs. 3-5).

[78] Hunt (2000: 253-55, fig. 9). According to a legend spread throughout the Christian world, during the invasion of Palestine by Khosrow II (614), the Persians spared the Church of the Nativity because they recognized in its mosaics the representation of the Magi Kings: Harvey, Lethaby, Dalton, Cruso, Headlan (1910: 19-20).

[79] The spread wings on the crown of the Sasanian Emperor at Qusayr 'Amra did not appear in the pictures of the painting but only in the reproductions by A. L. Mielich: Fontana (2002: fig. 3b). On the spread wings in Sasanian art, see: Compareti (2009.a). Sasanian representatives have also been reproduced in Chinese art, and they appear together with an inscription which identifies them. The representation of a "man from Persia" appears in a painting on silk dated to the 5th century but his garments and headgear are probably an invention of the artist: *ibid.* (2003: 202).

[80] O. Grabar (1954); Ettinghausen (1962: fig. at p. 31, appendix figs. 1-4); Arnold (1965: 57); Almagro, Caballero, Zozaya, Almagro (1975); Blazquez (1981); O. Grabar (1989: 63-67, figs. 25-26); Sourdel-Thomine, Spuler (1990: figs. 32-34, 36-37, pls. VI, VIII-X); Fontana (2002: 22-25); Fowden (2004). Creswell (1979a: 408) criticized the interpretation by O. Grabar.

[81] See note 25 of the present article.

[82] Blazquez (1981: 163-168).

[83] Almagro, Caballero, Zozaya, Almagro (1975: p. 57, pl. XVII.a).

[84] Di Branco ((2007).

[85] Mode (1993: 59-75). Mode's hypothesis was accepted uncritically by: Fowden (2004: 284).

[86] Tanabe (2006).

[87] Compareti, Cristoforetti (2005); Compareti (2006.b); *ibid.* (2006-2007); *ibid.* (2007); *ibid.* (2009.b). M. Mode did not accept such an identification and exposed his conclusion in a recent article: Mode (2006).

[88] Grenet (2006: 49).

[89] Bausani (1978); Marshak (2002.b: 37); Compareti (2006.c).

[90] Treadwell (2008: 377, fig. 8).

[91] Hamilton (1959: figs. 251-54); Ettinghausen (1962: fig. at pp. 35, 37, 39); *ibid.* (1972: 17-65); Schlumberger (1986b: 14-16, pls. 34-38, 40.b); Sourdel-Thomine, Spuler (1990: pls. XII-XIII); Fontana (2002: 27-34, tav. 4).

[92] Compareti (2007: 20).

[93] Herzfeld (1927); Ettinghausen (1962: appendix figs. 5-6); Otto-Dorn (1964: 98-114); Esin (1973/74: 71-88); Creswell (1979b: 242-43); Ettinghausen, Grabar (1987: fig. 107); Sourdel-Thomine, Spuler (1990: figs. 126, 128, pls. XXII-XXIII); Fontana (2002: 37-39).

[94] Monneret de Villard (1950); Ettinghausen (1962: figs. at pp. 45-46, 48-49); Scerrato (1985: 359-398); Gelfer-Jørgensen (1986); Grube (1994); Scerrato (1994b); D'Erme (1995).

[95] Cuneo (1988: 658-59); Donabédian, Thierry (1989: fig. 384); Schippmann (1993: fig. 132).

[96] Azarpay (1995).

[97] Луконин (1977: 95). See also: Marshak (1998: 88).

[98] Wilkinson (s. d. 1973); Grube (1980: 23, fig. 2); Wilkinson (1986); Fontana (2002: 77-83); Sims (2002: 24-40). During the present author's visit to the site of Paykand in autumn 2002 and 2003, some painted structure dated to the Samanid period had been excavated but unfortunately no particular decoration survived.

[99] Grube (1980: 24-25, fig. 3); Grube (1989: pls. 4, 6); Fontana (2002: 88-91, 105-7); Sims (2002: 26-40).

[100] Schlumberger (1952); *ibid.* (1978); Otto-Dorn (1964: colour pls. At pp. 139, 141); Fontana (2002: 84-86). On other Islamic paintings at Samarkand dated to the Qarakhanid period (12th-13th century), see: Karev (2003); *ibid.* (2005).

[101] Sims (2002: 32).

[102] Compareti (forthcoming).

[103] Esin (1977).

[104] Cazzoli, Cereti (2005).

BIBLIOGRAPHY

Ackerman, Ph. (1938-39 reprint 1967) Textiles Through the Sāsānian Period, in ed. U. A. Pope and Ph. Ackerman *A Survey of Persian Art* II (Text), 681-715. Teheran, London, New York, Tokyo.

Adle, C. (1993) Dāmgān. in *Encyclopaedia Iranica*, ed. E. Yarshater VI, 632-38. Costa Mesa (California).

Альбаум, Л. И. (1975) *Живопись Афрасиаба*. Ташкент.

Almagro, M., Caballero, L., Zozaya, J., Almagro, A. (1975) *Qusayr 'Amra. Residencia y baños omeyas en el desierto de Jordania*. Madrid.

Ambrosetti, G. (1961) Iwān-i Karkhah, in *Enciclopedia dell'Arte Antica Classica ed Orientale* IV, 282. Roma.

— (1966) Tepe Hissar, in *Enciclopedia dell'Arte Antica Classica ed Orientale* VII, 711-712. Roma.

Andrae, W. (1938) *Das Wiedererstandene Assur*. Leipzig.

Andrae, W., Lenzen, H. (1933 reprint Osnabrück 1967) *Die Partherstadt Assur*. Leipzig.

Античные государства Северново Причерноморья, (1984) Археология СССР. Москва.

Arnold, T. W. (1924) *Survivals of Sasanian and Manichaean Art in Persian Painting*. Oxford.

— (1938-39 reprint 1967), Painting and the Art of the Book. Book Painting. A. The Origins, in *A Survey of Persian Art from Prehistoric Times to the Present*, ed. A.U. Pope and Ph. Ackerman V, 1809-19. Teheran, London, New York, Tokyo.

— (1965) *Painting in Islam. A Study of the Place of Pictorial Art in Muslim Culture*. New York.

Audouin, R. (1991) Sculptures et peintures du château royal de Shabwa, *Syria* LXVIII, 165-81.

Axunbabaev, X., Grenet, F. (1990) Fouilles de la mission franco-soviétique à l'ancienne Samarkand (Afrasiab): première campagne, 1989. II Le chantier sous la mosquée cathédrale. *Comptes Rendus de l'Acedémie des Inscriptions et Belles Lettres* II, 370-80.

Azarnoush, M. (1983) Excavations at Hājīābād, 1977. First Preliminary Report. *Iranica Antiqua* XVIII, 159-76.

— (1994) *The Sasanian Manor House at Hājīābād, Iran*. Firenze.

Azarpay, G. (1981) *Sogdian Painting. The Pictorial Epic in Oriental Art*. Berkeley-Los Angeles-London.

— (1995) A Jataka Tale on a Sasanian Silver Plate. *Bulletin of the Asia Institute* 9, 99-125.

Baer, E. (1999) The Human Figure in Early Islamic Art: Some Preliminary Remarks. *Muqarnas* XVI, 32-41.

Balty, J. (1993) Les mosaïques, in B. Overlaet (a c.) *Splendeur des Sassanides. L'empire perse entre Rome et la Chine [224-642]*, 67-69. Bruxelles.

— (2006), Mosaïques romaines, mosaïques sassanides: jeux d'influences réciproques in eds. J. Wiesehöfer, Ph. Huyse, *Ērān ud Anērān. Studien zu den Beziehungen zwischen dem Sasanidenreich und der Mittelmeerwelt*, 29-44. München.

Balty, J., Briquel-Chatonnet, Fr. (2000) Nouvelles mosaïques inscrites d'Osrhoene. *Monuments Piot* 79, 31-72.

Bausani, A. (1978) Un auspicio armeno di capodanno in una notizia di Iranshahri (Nota ad Ajello), *Oriente Moderno*, 317-319.

Bernardini, M. (1992) Aspects litéraires et idéologiques des relations entre aristocratie et architecture à l'époque timouride, in ed. L. Golombek, M. Subtenly *Iran and Central Asia in the Fifteenth Century*, 36-43. Leiden, New York, Köln.

Bivar, A. D. H. (1995) The Royal Hunter and the Hunter God: Esoteric Mithraism Under the Sasanians?, in *Au Carrefour des religions*. Mélanges offerts à Ph. Gignoux, *Res Orientales* VII, 29-38. Bur-sur-Ivette.

— (1998) The Sasanian Princes at Bamiyan, in ed V. S. Curtis, R. Hillenbrand and J. M. Rogers *The Art and Archaeology of Ancient Persia. New Light on the Parthian and Sasanian Empires*, 103-10. London, New York.

— (2003) Cosmopolitan Deities and Hellenistic Traces at Kuh-e Khāja in Sistan, in: ed. C. G. Cereti, M. Maggi, E. Provasi, *Religious Themes and Texts of pre-Islamic Iran and Central Asia. Studies in Honour of Professor Gherardo Gnoli on the Occasion of His 65th Birthday*. 1-5. Wiesbaden.

Blavatskij, V. O. (1959) Crimea, in *Enciclopedia dell'Arte Antica Classica ed Orientale* II, 930-36. Roma.

Blazquez, J. M. (1981) Las pinturas helenisticas de Qusayr 'Amra (Jordania) y sus fuentes. *Archivo Español de Arqueologia*, 54/143-144, 157-202.

Bloom, J. (1991) Abbasidi, in *Enciclopedia dell'Arte Medievale* VIII, 5-10. Roma.

Boardman, J. (2000) *Persia and the West. An Archaeological Investigation in the Genesis of Achaemenid Art*.

London.

Борисов, А. Я. (1939) Об одном иллюстрированном астрологическом трактате сасанидского времени, in *III Международный конгресс по иранскому искусству и археолоии*, 31-33. Ленинград.

Boucharlat, R. (1987) Suse à l'époque sasanide. Une capitale prestigieuse devenue ville de province. *Mesopotamia* XXII, 357-66.

— (1989) Le palais d'Ataxerxes au bord du Chaour, *Dossiers/ histoire et archeologie* 138, 68-70.

— (1997.a) Susa Under Achaemenid Rule, in ed. J. Curtis *Mesopotamia and Iran in the Persian Period. Conquest and Imperialism 539-331 B.C.*, 54-67. London.

— (1997.b) Susa. Dagli Achemenidi ai Sasanidi, in *Enciclopedia dell'Arte Antica Classica ed Orientale*, Secondo supplemento 1971-1994 V, 501-3. Roma.

— (2002) Greece. vii. Greek Art and Architecture in Iran, in: *Encyclopaedia Iranica*. XI, 329-33. New York.

Bromberg, C. A. (1983) Sasanian Stucco Influence: Sorrento and East-West. *Orientalia Lovaniensia Periodica* 14, 247-67.

— (1990) Sasanian Royal Emblems in the Northern Caucasus, in ed. G. Gnoli, A. Panaino, *Proceedings of the First European Conference of Iranian Studies*. Part 1. *Old and Middle Iranian Studies*, 1-17. Rome.

Browning, I. (1979) *Palmyra*. London.

Callieri, P. (2006) At the Roots of Sasanian Royal Imagery: the Persepolis Graffiti, in *Ērān ud Anērān. Studies Presented to B. I. Maršak in Occasion of His 70th Birthday*, eds. M. Compareti, P. Raffetta, G. Scarcia: 129-148.

Calmeyer, P. (1976) Zur Genese altiranische Motive: IV. "Persönliche Krone" und Diadem; V. Synarchie. *Archaeologische Mitteilungen aus Iran* 9, 45-95.

— (1985-87) Art in Iran. iii. Achaemenian Art and Architecture, in ed. E. Yarshater, *Encyclopaedia Iranica*, II, 569-80. London.

Carra de Voux, B. (1897) *Maçoudi. Le livre de l'avertissement*. Paris.

Carter, L.M. (1997) Preliminary Notes on Four Painted Terracotta Panels, in eds. R. Hallchin, B. Hallchin, *South Asian Archaeology, 1995*, 573-588. Cambridge, New Delhi, Calcutta.

Catalogue New York (1982) *Along the Ancient Silk Routes. Central Asian Art from the West Berlin State Museums*. New York.

Catalogue Roma (2001) *Antica Persia. I tesori del Museo Nazionale di Tehran e la ricerca italiana in Iran*, ed. P. D'Amore, G. Di Flumeri, G. Lombardo, M. Jung, P. Piacentini, P. Torre. Roma.

Cazzoli, S., Cereti, G. C. (2005) Sealings from Kafir Kala: Preliminary Report. *Ancient Civilizations from Scythia to Siberia* 11, 1-2, 133-164.

Chao, Huashan (1996) New Evidence of Manichaeism in Asia: a Description of Some Recently Discovered Manichaean Temples in Turfan. *Monumenta Serica* 44, 267-315.

Christensen, A. (1971) *L'Iran sous les Sassanides*. Osnabrück.

Colledge, M.A.R. (1976) *The Art of Palmyra*. London.

— (1979) *L'impero dei Parti. Un grande popolo dell'antica Persia, dominatore delle terre tra Cina e Roma*. Roma.

— (1987) Parthian Cultural Elements at Roman Palmyra. *Mesopotamia* XXII, 19-28.

Compareti, M. (2003) The Last Sasanians in China. *Eurasian Studies* II, 2. 197-213

— (2006.a) Iconographical Notes on Some Recent Studies on Sasanian Religious Art (with an Additional Note on an Ilkhanid Monument by Rudy Favaro), *Annali di Ca' Foscari* XLV, 3, 163-200.

— (2006.b) A Lecture of the Royal Hunt at Afrasyab Based on Chinese Sources, in *Royal Nawrūz in Samarkand. Acts of the Conference Held in Venice on the Pre-Islamic Afrāsyāb Painting*, eds. M. Compareti, É. De La Vaissière. 173-184. Rome.

— (2006.c) The So-Called *Senmurv* in Iranian Art: A Reconsideration of an Old Theory, in *Loquentes linguis. Studi linguistici e orientali in onore di Fabrizio A. Pennacchietti (Linguistic and Oriental Studies in Honour of Fabrizio A. Pennacchietti)*, eds. Pier Giorgio Borbone, Alessandro Mengozzi, Mauro Tosco. 185-200. Wiesbaden.

— (2006-2007) Further Evidence for the Interpretation of the «Indian Scene» in the Pre-Islamic Paintings at Afrāsyāb (Samarkand). *The Silk Road* 4/2, 32-42.

— (2007) The Paintings Concerning Chinese Themes at Afrāsyāb, in *The Chinese Scene at Afrāsyāb and the Iranian Calendar*, eds. M. Compareti and S. Cristoforetti. 9-32. Venice.

— (2008) The Painting of the "Hunter King" at Kakrak: Royal Figure or Divine Being? *Annali di Ca' Foscari* XLVI, 4.

— (2009.a) Tra il Palatino a Limburgo: considerazioni su alcune stele armene di età pre-islamica. in: *Acculturazione e disadattamento*, ed. D. Guizzo, 7-27. Venezia.

— (2009.b) *Samarcanda centro del mondo. Proposte di lettura del ciclo pittorico di Afrasyab*. Venezia.

— (forthcoming) Coronation and Nawruz: A Note on the Reconstruction of the Missing King at Afrāsyāb (Old Samarkand). *International Conference on the Occasion of B. I. Marshak's 75th birthday*.

Compareti, M., Cristoforetti, S. (2005) Proposal for a New Interpretation of the Northern Wall of the «Hall of the Ambassadors» at Afrasyab, in *Central Asia from the Achaemenids to the Timurids: Archaeology, History, Ethnology, Culture. Materials of an International Scientific Conference Dedicated to the Centenary of Aleksandr Markovich Belenitsky*, ed. V. P. Nikonorov. 215-20. St. Petersburg.

Costa, P.M. (1971) The Mosaic from Tell Khwāris in the Iraq Museum. *Iraq* XXXIII, 1-2, 119-124.

Creswell, K.A.C. (1979.a) *Early Muslim Architecture*. I, Part II, Umayyads (A.D. 622-750). New York.

— (1979.b) *Early Muslim Architecture*. II, Early 'Abbāsids, Tūlūnids, and Samānids, A.D. 751-905. New York.

Cumont, M. (1913) Mâni et les origines de la miniature persane, *Revue archéologique* XXII, 82-86.

Cuneo, P. (1988) *Architettura armena*, 2 vols. Roma.

Curtis, V.S. (2000) Parthian Culture and Costume, in ed. J. Curtis *Mesopotamia and Iran in the Parthian and Sasanian Periods. Rejection and Revival c. 238 B.C.-A.D. 642*, 23-34. London.

D'Erme, G. M. (1995) Contesto architettonico e aspetti culturali dei dipinti del soffitto della Cappella palatina di Palermo. *Bollettino d'Arte* 92, 1-32.

De Blois, F. (1991) The *Pancatantra*: From India to the West-and Back. *Marg* XLIII, 1, 10-15.

De Francovich, G. (1984) Il concetto della regalità nell'arte sasanide e l'interpretazione di due opere d'arte bizantine del periodo della dinastia macedone: la cassetta eburnea di Troyes e la corona di Costantino IX Monomaco di Budapest, in ed. V. Pace, *Persia, Siria, Bisanzio e il Medioevo artistico europeo*, 79-138. Napoli.

De Waele, A. (2004) The Figurative Wall Painting of the Sasanian Period from Iran, Iraq and Syria. *Iranica Antiqua* XXXIX, 339-81.

Денике, Б. (1938) *Живопись Ирана*. Москва.

Di Branco, M. (2007) I sei principi di Qusayr 'Amrah fra Tardoantico, ellenismo e Islam. *Rendiconti dell' Accademia Nazionale dei Lincei* XVIII, 4, 597-620.

Dimand, M. (1972) *L'arte dell'Islam*. Firenze.

Domyo, M. (1997) Late Sassanian Textile Designs in the Reliefs at Tāq-i Bustān. *Bulletin du Liason du CIETA* 74, 18-27.

Donabédian, P., Thierry, J.-M. (1989) *Armenian Art*. New York.

Dorigo, W. (1971) *Late Roman Painting*. London.

Downey, S. B. (1985-87) Art in Iran. iv. Parthian, in ed. E. Yarshater *Encyclopaedia Iranica* II, 525-46. Costa Mesa (California).

— (1994) Dura-Europos, in *Enciclopedia dell'Arte Antica Classica ed Orientale*, Secondo supplemento 1971-1994 II, 401-3. Roma.

Drijvers, H.J.W. (1994) Edessa, in *Enciclopedia dell'Arte Antica Classica ed Orientale*, Secondo supplemento 1971-1994 II, 408-11. Roma.

— (2006) Ammianus Marcellinus' Image of Sasanian Society, in eds. J. Wiesehöfer, Ph. Huyse, *Ērān ud Anērān. Studien zu den Beziehungen zwischen dem Sasanidenreich und der Mittelmeerwelt*, 45-69. München.

Dyson Jr., R.H. (1997) Tepe Hissar, in *Enciclopedia dell'Arte Antica Classica ed Orientale*, Secondo supplemento 1971-1994 V, 662-63. Roma.

Erdmann, K. (1943 reprint 1969) *Die Kunst Irans zur Zeit der Sasaniden*. Mainz.

Esin, E. (1973/74) The Turk al-'ağam of Sāmarrā and the Paintings Attributable to Them in the Ğawsaq al Hāqānī. *Kunst des Orients* IX/1-2, 47-88.

— (1977) A Pair of Manuscripts from the Miscellany Collection of Topkapı. *Central Asiatic Journal* XXI/1,

13-35.

Ettinghausen, R. (1962) *La peinture arabe*. Genève.

— (1972) *From Byzantium to Sasanian Iran and the Islamic World*. Leiden.

Ettinghausen, R., Grabar O. (1987) *The Art and Architecture of Islam: 650-1250*. Harmondsworth.

Facenna, D. (1981) A New Fragment of Wall-painting from Ghāga Šahr (Kuh-I Khāğa -Sīstān, Iran). *East and West* 31,83-97.

Finster, B. (1976) Sasanidische und früislamische Ruinen im Iraq. *Baghdader Mitteilungen* 8.

Fontana, M. V. (1997) Miniatura. Islam, in *Enciclopedia dell'Arte Medievale* VIII, 452-62. Roma.

— (1998) *La miniatura islamica*. Roma.

— (2000) Ancora sulla caccia di Bahrām Gūr e Āzāda, in *Haft Qalam. Cento pagine in onore di Bianca Maria Alfieri da parte dei suoi allievi*, 15-37. Napoli.

— (2001) Arte Protoislamica, in *Antica Persia. I tesori del Museo Nazionale di Tehran e la ricerca italiana, in Iran*, 157-61. Roma.

— (2002) *La pittura islamica dalle origini alla fine del Trecento*. Roma.

Fowden, G. (2004) The Six Kings at Quṣayr 'Amra, in: *La Persia e Bisanzio*, 275-90. Roma.

Franco, F. (1978-1979) Five Aramaic Incantation Bowls from Tell Baruda (Choche). *Mesopotamia* XIII-XIV, 233-49.

Gajbov, V., Košelenko, G., Novikov, S. (1991) Nouveaux documents pour une histoire des religions dans le Turkménistan méridional à l'époque parthe et sassanide, in ed. P. Bernard, F. Grenet, *Histoire et cultes de l'Asie centrale Préislamique*, 85-94. Paris.

Gall (von), H. (1971) Die Mosaiken von Bishapur und ihre Beziehung zu den Triumphreliefs des Shapur I. *Archaeologische Mitteilungen aus Iran* 4, 193-205.

— (1990) The Figural Capitals at Taq-i Bostan and the Question of the so-called Investiture in Parthian and Sasanian Art. *Silk Road Art and Archaeology* 1, 99-122.

Gasche, H. (2002) Une residence parthe dans le quartier nord de la ville royale de Suse. *Akkadica*. 123, 2, 183-90.

Gautier-van Berchem, M. (1979) The Mosaics of the Dome of the Rock in Jerusalem, in K. A. C. Creswell, *Early Muslim Architecture*. I, *Part I, Umayyads (A.D. 622-750)*, 211-322. New York.

Gelfer-Jørgensen, M. (1986) *Medieval Islamic Symbolism and the Painting in the Cefalù Cathedral*. Leiden.

Genito, B. (1999) Sasanidi, in *Enciclopedia dell'Arte Medievale* X, 381-86. Roma.

Ghanimati, S. (2000) New Perspectives on the Chronological and Functional Orizons of Kuh-e Khwaja in Sistan. *Iran* XXXVIII, 137-50.

Ghirshman, R. (1952) Cinq campagnes de fouilles à Suse (1946-1951). *Revue d'Assyriologie et d'archéologie orientale* XLVI/1, 1-18.

— (1956) *Bishapur II. Les mosaïques sassanides*. Paris.

— (1962) *Are Persan. Partes et Sassanides*. Paris.

Gignoux, Ph. (1983) La chasse dans l'Iran sasanide, in ed.G. Gnoli *Orientalia Romana, Essays and Lectures* 5, *Iranian Studies*, 101-18. Roma.

Giuliano, A. (1963) Arte palmirena, in *Enciclopedia dell'Arte Antica Classica ed Orientale* V, 908-17. Roma.

Goff, C. (1970) Excavations at Bābā Jān, 1968: Third Preliminary Report. *Iran* 8, 141-56.

Goldman, B. (1990) Foreigners at DuraEuropos: Pictorial Graffiti and History. *Le Muséon* 103, 5-25.

— (1993) Later Pre-Islamic Riding Costume. *Iranica Antiqua* XXVIII, 201-46.

— (1997) Women's Robing in the Sasanian Era. *Iranica Antiqua* XXXII, 233-300.

— (1999) Pictorial Graffiti of Dura-Europos. *Parthica* 1, 19-105.

Goldman, B., Little, A. M. (1980) The Beginning of Sasanian Painting at Dura-Europos. *Iranica Antiqua* XV, 283-99.

Grabar, A. (1971) Le rayonnement de l'art sassanide dans le monde chrétien, in *La Persia nel Medioevo*, 377-707. Roma.

— (1980) *L'età d'oro di Giustiniano*. Milano.

Grabar, O. (1954) The Painting of the Six Kings at Qusayr 'Amra. *Ars Orientalis*, 1, 185-87.

— (1989) *Arte islamica. La formazione di una civiltà*. Milano.

— (1997) Omayyadi, in *Enciclopedia dell'Arte Medievale*, vol. VII, 802-12. Roma.

Gray, B. (1961) *La peinture persane*. Genève.

— (1979) The Tradition of the Wall Painting in Iran, in ed. R. Ettinghausen, E. Yarshater, *Highlights of Persian Art*, 313-29. Boulder (Colorado).

Grenet, F. (1988) Les Sassanides à Doura-Europos (253 ap. J.-C.). Réexamen du matériel épigraphique iranien du site, in ed. P. L. Gautier, B. Helly, J. P. Rey-Coquais, *Géographie historique au Proche-Orient*, 133-58. Paris.

— (1999) La peinture sassanide de Ghulbiyan, in *Empires perses. D'Alexandre aux Sassanides. Dossiers d'archeologie* 243, 66-67.

— (2004) Maracanda/Samarkand, une métropole pré-mongole. Sources écrites et archéologique. *Annales*, 5-6, 1043-67.

— (2006) What was the Afrasyab Painting About?, in eds. M. Compareti, É. De La Vaissière, Royal Nawrūz in Samarkand. Acts of the Conference held in Venice on the Pre-Islamic Afrāsyāb Painting, Suppl. n. 1, Rivista degli Studi Orientali, LXXVIII, 43-58. Roma.

Grenet, F., Lee, J., Pinder-Wilson, R. (1980) Les monuments anciens du Gorzivan (Afghanistan du Nord-Ouest). Studia iranica 9, 69-98.

Grube, E. J. (1980) *La pittura dell'Islam. Miniature persiane dal XII al XVI secolo*. Bologna.

— (1989) Painting, in ed. R.W. Ferrier, *The Arts of Persia*, 200-31. New Haven, London.

— (1994) La pittura islamica nella Sicilia normanna del XII secolo, in *La pittura in Italia. L'Altomedioevo*, 416-31. Milano.

Gulácsi, Z. (2001) *Corpus Fontium Manicheaorum. Series Archaeologica et Iconographica. I. Manichaean Art in Berlin Collections*. Turnhout.

Gyselen, R. (1993) Les monnaies, in *Splendeur des Sassanides. L'empire perse entre Rome et la Chine [224-642]*, 127-30. Bruxelles.

Gyselen, R., Gasche, H. (1994) Suse et Ivān-e Kerkha, capitale provinciale d'Ērān-xwarrah-Šāpūr. Note de géographie historique sassanide. *Studia Iranica* 23/1, 19-35.

Gyselen, R., Gignoux, Ph. (2000) Un dieu nimbé de flammes d'époque sassanide. *Iranica Antiqua* XXXVI, 291-314.

Hamilton, R. W. (1959) *Khirbat al Mafjar. An Arabian Mansion in the Jordan Valley*. Oxford.

Harper, P. O. (1972) An Eighth Century Silver Plate from Iran with a Mythological Scene, in ed. R. Ettinghausen, *Islamic Art in The Metropolitan Museum of Art*, 153-68. New York.

— (1992) Imagery and Tipology, in P.O. Harper, P.O. Skjærvø, L. Gorelick, A. J. Gwinnett, A Seal-Amulet of the Sasanian Era: Imagery and Typology, the Inscription, and Technical Comments, *Bulletin of the Iranian Institute*, n. s. 6, 43-49.

Harper, P. O., Meyers, P. (1981) *Silver Vessels of the Sasanian Period. Volume one: Royal Imagery, The Metropolitan Museum of Art*. New York.

Harvey, W., Lethaby, W. R., Dalton, D. M., Cruso, H. A. A., Headlam, A. C. (1910) *The Church of the Nativity at Bethlehem*. London.

Hauser, S.R. (2007) Christliche Archäologie im Sasanidenreich, in eds. A. Mustafa, J. Tubach, G.S. Vashalomidze, *Inkulturation des Christentums im Sasanidenreich*, 93-136. Wiesbaden.

Henning, W. B. (1953) A New Parthian Inscription. *Journal of the Royal Asiatic Society*, 132-6.

Herzfeld, E. (1927) *Die Ausgrabungen von Samarra*, III. *Die Malerein von Samarra*. Berlin.

— (1941) *Iran in the Ancient Near East*. London, New York.

Hunt, L.-A. (2000) Art and Colonialism: the Mosaics of the Church of Nativity in Bethlehem (1169) and the Problem of "Crusader Art", in *Byzantium, Eastern Christendom and Islam. Art at the Crossroads of the Medieval Mediterranean*. Vol. II. 224-60. London.

Jeroussalimskaja, A. (1993) Soieries sassanides, in *Splendeur des Sassanides. L'empire perse entre Rome et la Chine [224-642]*, 113-19. Bruxelles.

Invernizzi, A. (1992) Review of von Gall 1990. *Mesopotamia* XXVII, 251-257.

— (1995) Hatra, in *Enciclopedia dell'Arte Antica Classica ed Orientale*, Secondo supplemento 1971-1994 III, 33-37. Roma.

— (1996) Arte partica, in *Enciclopedia dell'Arte Antica, Classica ed Orientale*, Secondo supplemento 1971-1994 IV, 264-68. Roma.

— (1997) Veh-Ardašīr, in *Enciclopedia dell'Arte Antica Classica ed Orientale*, Secondo supplemento 1971-1994 V, 962-63. Roma.

— (1998) Parthian Nisa. New Lines of Research, *Historia 122. The Arsacid Empire: Sources and Documents*, 45-59. Stuttgart.

Kaim, B. (2002) Un temple du feu sassanide découverte à Mele Mairam, Turkménistan Méridional. *Studia Iranica* 31, 2, 215-30.

— (2009) Investiture or Mithra. Tpwards a New Interpretation of So Called Investiture Scenes in Parthian and Sasanian Art. *Iranica Antiqua* XLIV, 403-415.

Karev, Y. M. (2003) Un cycle de peintures murales d'époque qarākhānide (XIIe-XIIIe siècles) à la citadelle de Samarkand : le souverain et le peintre. *Comptes Rendus de l'Académie des Inscriptions & Belles-Lettres* IV, 1685-1731.

— (2005) Qarakhanid Wall Pintings in the Citadel of Samarqand : First Report and Preliminary Observations. *Muqarnas* XXII, 45-84.

Kawami, T. S. (1987.a) Kuh-e Khwaja, Iran, and Its Wall Paintings, the Records of Ernst Herzfeld. *Metropolitan Museum Journal* 22, 13-52.

— (1987.b) *Monumental Art of the Parthian Period in Iran*. Leiden.

— (1992) Archaeological Evidence for Textiles in Pre-Islamic Iran. *Iranian Studies* 25/1-2, 7-18.

Keall, E. J. (1990) Bīšāpūr, in ed. E. Yarshater, *Encyclopaedia Iranica* V, 287-89. Costa Mesa (California).

Khan, M. N. (2000) *Buddhist Paintings in Gandhara*. Peshawar.

Khan, M.A., Mahmood-ul-Hasan (2004) Discovery of Mural Paintings from Jinan Wali Dheri, Taxila Valley, *Journal of Asian Civilizations* 27, 14-27.

King, G. R. D. (2004) The Paintings of the Pre-Islamic Ka'ba. *Muqarnas* XXI, 219-29.

Kitzinger, E. (1951) Studies on Late Antique and Early Byzantine Floor Mosaics. *Dumbarton Oaks Papers* 6, 81-122.

Klimburg-Salter, D. (1993) Dokhtar-i Noshirwan (Nigar) Reconsidered. *Muqarnas* X, 355-68.

Klimkeit, H.-J. (1998) On the Nature of Manichaean Art, in ed. M. Hauser, H.-J. Klimkeit, *Studies in Manichaean Literature and Art*, 270-90. Leiden, Boston, Köln.

Косолапов, А. И., Маршак Б. И. (1999) *Стенная живопис Средней Азии и Центральной Азии*. Санкт Петербург.

Кошеленко, Г.А. (1966) *Культура Парфии*. Москва.

— (1977) *Родина Парфиян*. Москва.

Kröger, J. (1982) *Sasanidischer Stuckdekor. Ein Beitrag zum Reliefdekor aus Stuck in sasanidischer und frühislamischer Zeit nach den Ausgrabungen von 1928/9 und 1931/2 in der sasanidischen Metropole Ktesiphon (Iraq) und unter besonderer Berücksichtigung der Stuckfunde vom Taht-i Sulaimān (Iran), aus Nizāmābād (Iran) sowie zahlreicher anderer Fundorte.* Mainz am Rhein.

— (1993) Ctesiphon, in ed. E.Yarshater *Encyclopaedia Iranica* VI, 446-48. Costa Mesa (California).

Kurita, I. (2003) *A Revised and Enlarged Edition of Gandhāran Art II. The World of the Buddha.* Tokyo.

Kuwayama, Sh. (1976) The Turki Šāhis and Relevant Brahmanical Sculptures in Afghanistan. *East and West* 26/3-4, 375-407.

L'Orange, H. P. (1953) *Studies on the Iconography of Cosmic Kingship in the Ancient World.* Oslo.

Lavin, I. (1963) The Hunting Mosaics of Antioch and Their Sources. A Study of Compositional Principles in the Development of Early Mediaeval Style. *Dumbarton Oaks Papers* 17, 179-286.

Lee, J. L. (2006) Monuments of Bamiyan Province, Afghanistan. *Iran* XLIV, 229-52.

Lee, J. L.,Grenet, F. (1998) New Light on the Sasanid Painting at Ghulbiyan, Faryab Province, Afghanistan. *South Asian Studies* 14, 75-85.

Le Coq (von), A. (1973) *Die buddhistische Spätantike in Mittelasien. II. Die manichäischen Miniaturen.* Graz.

Leriche, P. (1996) Dura Europos, in ed. E. Yarshater *Encyclopaedia Iranica* VII, 589-93. Costa Mesa (California).

Leroy, J. (1957) Mosaïques funéraires d'Édesse. *Syria* XXIV, 306-42.

— (1961) Nouvelles découvertes archéologiques relatives a Édesse. *Syria* XXXVIII, 159-69.

Lieu, S. (1997) Edessa, in ed. E. Yarshater *Encyclopaedia Iranica* VIII,174-175. Costa Mesa (California).

Lo Muzio, C. (2003) Una scena di caccia dalla necropoli di Kopeny (Minusinsk), in ed. M. V. Fontana and B. Genito *Studi in Onore di Umberto Scerrato per il suo settantacinquesimo compleanno.* Vol. II, Napoli: 519-538.

Луконин, В. Г. (1977) *Искусство древнего Ирана.* Москва.

Manassero, N., (2003) Il vaso dipinto di Merv. *Parthica* 5, 131-52.

Marshak, B. I. (1995/96) On the Iconography of Ossuaries from Biya-Naiman. *Silk Road Art and Archaeology* 4, 299-321.

— (1998) The Decoration of Some Late Sasanian Silver Vessels and Its Subject-Matter, in ed. V. S. Curtis, R. Hillenbrand and J. M. Rogers *The Art and Archaeology of Ancient Persia. New Light on the Parthian and Sasanian Empires*,84-92. London, New York.

— (1999) L'art sogdien (IVe au IXe) siècle, in ed. P. Chuvin, *Les arts de l'Asie Centrale*, 114-63. Paris.

— (2002.a) Pre-Islamic Painting of the Iranian Peoples and Its Sources in Sculpture and the Decorative Arts, in: E. Sims. *Peerless Images. Persian Painting and Its Sources.* New Haven, London.

— (2002.b) *Legends, Tales, and Fables in the Art of Sogdiana.* New York.

Millar, F. (1998) Dura-Europos Under Parthian Rule, *Historia 122. The Arsacid Empire: Sources and Documents*, 473-92. Stuttgart.

Minorsky, V. (1970) *Hudūd al-'Ālam" The Regions of the World". A Persian Geography 372 A.H.-982 A.D.*

London.

Mizbani, N., Salimi, S. (2002) *Birjand*. Tehran.

Mode, M. (1992) The Great God of Dokhtar-e Noshirwān (Nigār). *East and West* 42, 473-83.

— (1993) *Sogdien und die Herrscher der Welt. Türken, Sasaniden und Chinesen in Historiengemälden des 7. Jahrhunderts n.Chr. aus Alt-Samarqand*. Frankfurt am Main, Berlin, Bern, New York, Paris, Wien.

— (2006) Reading the Afrasiab Murals: Some Comments on Reconstructions and Details, in eds. M. Compareti, É. De La Vaissière, *Royal Nawrūz in Samarkand. Acts of the Conference held in Venice on the Pre-Islamic Afrāsyāb Painting*, Suppl. n. 1, *Rivista degli Studi Orientali*, LXXVIII, 107-28. Roma.

— (2009) Sogdiana.vi. Sogdian Art, in *Encyclopaedia Iranica (online version: www.iranica.com web-page accessed October 21 2009)* ed. E. Yarshater.

Mohl, J. (1841) Extraits du Modjmel al-Tewarikh relatifs à l'histoire de la Perse (Suite). *Journal Asiatique* XI, ser. 3, 258-301.

Monneret de Villard, U. (1923) Arte manichea. *Reale Istituto Lombardo di Scienze e Lettere* serie II, LVI/I-V, 971-84.

— (1950) *Le pitture del soffitto della Cappella Palatina di Palermo*. Roma.

— (1966) *Introduzione allo studio dell'archeologia islamica*. Venezia-Roma.

Morgenstern, L. (1938-39 reprint 1967) Mural Painting, in ed. A. U. Pope and Ph. Ackerman, *A Survey of Persian Art* V, 1365-90. Teheran, London, New York, Tokyo.

Mousavi, M. (1999) Kuh-e Khadjeh, un complexe religieux de l'est iranien, in *Empires perses. D'Alexandre aux Sassanides. Dossiers d'archeologie* 243, 81-84.

Nallino, C. A. (1922) Tracce di opere greche giunte agli Arabi per trafila pehlevica, in ed. T. W. Arnold and R. A. Nicholson, *A Volume of Oriental Studies Presented to E. G. Browne on his 60th Birthday*, 345-63. Cambridge.

Neugebauer, O. (1954) On the Hatra Zodiac. *Sumer* X/1, 1954, p. 91.

Nickerson, J. W. (1977) Malyan Wall Paintings. *Expedition* 19/3, 2-6.

Nicolle, D. (2005) *Atlas histórico del mundo islámico*. Madrid.

Nunn, A. (1988) *Die Wandmalerei und der glasierte Wandschmuck in Alten Orient*. Leiden, New York, København, Köln.

Otto-Dorn, K. (1964) *Islam*. Milano.

Overlaet, B. (1993) Organisation militaire et armement, in *Splendeur des Sassanides. L'empire perse entre Rome et la Chine [224-642]*, 89-94. Bruxelles.

Peck, E. H. (1993) Crown. ii. From the Seleucids to the Islamic Conquest, in ed. E. Yarshater, *Encyclopaedia Iranica* VI, 408-18. Costa Mesa (California).

Perrot, J., Le Brun, A., Labrousse, A. (1971) Recherches archéologiques à Suse et en Susiane en 1969 et en 1970.

Syria X, 21-51.

Peters, F. E. (1977-1978) Byzantium and the Arabs of Syria. *Les annales archèologiques arabes syriennes*, XXVII-XXVIII, 97-113.

Piemontese, A. M. (1995) Dottrina e arte di Mani secondo lo scrittore persiano'Oufi, con una glossa sul libro "Gemello", in ed. P.G. Domini, C. Lo Jacono, L. Santa Maria, *Un ricordo che non si spegne. Scritti dei docenti dell'Istituto Universitario Orientale in memoria di Alessandro Bausani*, 287-307. Napoli.

Pilipko, V. N. (2000) On the Wall-Paintings from the Tower-Building of Old Nisa. *Parthica* 2, 69-86.

Porter, Y. (1997) Des origines à l'âge d'or des XVe-XVIe siècles. *Dossiers de l'art. Peinture persane* 36, 8-19.

J. Qandgar, H. Esmaili, M. Rahmatpour (1383/2004) Kavoshaye-e bastanshenakhti-ye Qal'eh Azdahak, Hastrud, in M. Azarnoush ed. *Proceedings of the International Symposium on Iranian Archaeology: Northwestern Region, Iranian Center for Archaeological Research,* 193-228. Tehran .

Raby, J. (1987/88) Between Sogdia and the Mamluks: A Note on the Earliest Illustrations to Kalīla wa Dimna. *Oriental Art* n. s. XXXIII/4, 381-98.

— (1991) The Early Illustrations to *Kalilah wa Dimnah*". *Marg* XLIII, 1, 16-31.

Rahbar, M. (1998) Découverte d'un monument d'époque sassanide à Bandian, Dargaz (Nord Khorassan). Fouilles 1994 et 1995. *Studia Iranica* 27, 2, 213-50.

— (2004) Le monument sassanide de Bandiān, Dargaz: un temple du feu d'après les dernieres découvertes 1996-98. *Studia Iranica* 33, 1, 7-30.

Razmjou, Sh. (2004) Ernst Herzfeld and the Study of Graffiti at Persepolis, in ed. A. C. Gunter, S. K. Hauser, *Ernst Herzfeld and the Development of Near Eastern Studies, 1900-1950*, 315-41. Leiden.

Reuther, O. (1938-39 reprint 1967) Sasanian Architecture. *A.* History, in ed. U. A. Pope and Ph. Ackerman, *A Survey of Persian Art* II (Text), 493-578. Teheran, London, New York, Tokyo.

Roos, P. (1970) An Achaemenid Sketch Slab and the Ornaments of the Royal Dress at Persepolis. *East and West* n. s. 20/1-2, 51-59.

Rosen-Ayalon, M. (1984) Themes of Sasanian Origin in Islamic Art. *Jerusalem Studies in Arabic and Islam* 4, 69-80.

Sajjadi, S. M. S. (2007) Wall painting from Dahaneh-ye Gholaman (Sistan). *Ancient Civilizations from Scythia to Siberia* 13, 1-2, 129-154.

Sajjadi, S. M. S., F. S. Moghaddam (2004) Peintures et gravures murales découvertes à Dahan-e Gholāmān, Sistān. *Studia Iranica* 33, 2, 285-96.

al-Salihi, W. (1996) Mural Paintings from the North Palace at Hatra. *Mesopotamia* 31, 197-202.

Sarre, F. (1922) *Die Kunst des alten Persien*. Berlin.

Sasanian Silver. Late Antique and Early Mediaeval Arts of Luxury From Iran (1967). Ann Arbor.

Scarcia, G. (2000) Cosroe Secondo, San Sergio e il Sade. *Studi sull'Oriente Cristiano* 4, 171-227.

— (2003) La Persia dagli Achemenidi ai Sasanidi (550 a.C.-650 d.C.), in: G. Curatola, G. Scarcia. *Iran. L'arte persiana*, 9-125. Milano.

Scerrato, U. (1985) Arte islamica in Italia, in: F. Gabrieli, U. Scerrato, *Gli Arabi in Italia*, 271-571. Milano.

— (1994.a) Stoffe Sasanidi, in ed. M. T. Lucidi, *La seta e la sua via*, 75-82. Roma.

— (1994.b) Arte normanna e archeologia islamica in Sicilia, in ed. M. D'Onofrio, *I Normanni, popolo d'Europa 1030-1200*, 339-49. Venezia.

Schippmann, K. (1993) L'influence de la culture sassanide, in *Splendeur des Sassanides. L'empire perse entre Rome et la Chine [224-642]*, 131-41. Bruxelles.

Schlumberger, D. (1952) Le palais ghaznévide de Lashkari Bazar. *Syria* XXIX, 251-70.

— (1960) Descendants non-méditerranéens de l'art grec. *Syria* XXXVII, 253-319.

— (1978) *Lashkari Bazar. Une résidence royale ghaznévide et ghoride. 1 A. L'architecture*, D.A.F.A., XVIII, (planches). Paris.

— (1966) La représentation frontale dans l'art des Sassanides, in *La Persia ed il mondo greco-romano*, 383-93. Roma.

— (1970) *L'Orient hellénisé. L'art grec et ses héritiers dans l'Asie non méditerranéenne*. Paris.

— (1986.a) Parthian Art, in ed. E. Yarshater, *The Cambridge History of Iran*, 3 (2), *The Seleucid, Parthian and Sasanian Periods*, 1027-54. Cambridge, London, New York, New Rochelle, Melbourne, Sydney.

— (1986.b) *Qasr el-Heir el Gharbi*. Paris.

Schmidt, E. F. (1937) *Excavations at Tepe Hissar Damghan*. Philadelphia.

— (1934) L'expédition de Ctésiphon en 1931-1932. *Syria* XV, 1-23.

Segal, J.B. (1970) *Edessa, the Blessed City*. 1970.

Семенов, Г. Л. (2001) Новые данные о раскопках в Пайкенде. *Из истории кульурного наследия Бухары*. 27-37. Бухара.

Семенов, Г. Л., Адыов Ш. Т. (2006) Арсенал на цитадели Пайкенда, in eds. C. Silvi Antonimi, JD. K. Mirzaakhmedov, *Ancient and Medieval Culture of the Bukhara Oasis*. 36-43. Samarkand-Rome.

Shahbazi, A. Sh. (2001) Painting, in: ed. A. Sh. Shahbazi, *The Splendour of Iran. Vol. I. Ancient Times*. London, 342-47.

al-Shams, M. A. (1981) Arabic Drawings from Hatra. *Sumer* XXXVII/1-2, 146-58 (in Arabic with an English summary).

Shishkina, G. V., Pavchinskaja, L. V. (1992) D'Afrasiab à Samarcande, in: *Terres secretes de Samarcande. Ceramiques du VIIIe au XIIIe siècle*, 11-27. Paris.

Sims, E. (2002) *Peerless Images. Persian Painting and Its Sources*. New Haven, London.

Silvi Antonini, C. (1989) The Paintings in the Palace of Afrasiab (Samarkand). *Rivista degli Studi Orientali*, LXIII/1-3, 109-44.

Silvi Antonini, C., Taddei, M. (1981) Wall Paintings from Tapa Sardār, Ghazni, in ed. H. Härtel, *South Asian Archaeology, 1979*, 429-438. Berlin.

Simpson, St. J. (2000) Mesopotamia in the Sasanian Period: Settlement Patterns, Arts and Crafts, in ed. J. Curtis, *Mesopotamia and Iran in the Parthian and Sasanian Periods. Rejection and Revival c. 238 BCE-AD 642*, Proceedings of a Seminar in Memory of Vladimir G. Lukonin, 57-66. London.

Soucek, P.S. (1972) Nizāmī on Painters and Painting, in ed. R. Ettinghausen, *Islamic Art in the Metropolitan Museum of Art*, 9-21. New York.

Sourdel-Thomine, J., Spuler, B. (1990) *Die Kunst des Islam*, Frankfurt am Main. Berlin.

Средняя Азия и Дальний Восток в эпоху средневековья (1999) Археология СССР. Москва.

Ставиский, Б.Я. (1982) *Основные итоги изученя Кара-Тепе. Кара-Тепе V. Будиские памятники Кара-Тепе в Старом Термезе*. Москва.

Summerer, L. (2007) Picturing Persian Victory: The Painted Battle Scene on the Munich Wood. *Ancient Civilizations from Scythia to Siberia* 13, 1-2, 3-30.

Talbot Rice, D. (1932) The Oxford Expedition at Hira, 1931. *Antiquity* VI, 276-91.

— (1934) The Oxford Expedition at Hira. *Ars Islamica* 1/1, 51-73.

— (1946) The Cave of Shapur and Sasanian Painting. *Bulletin of the Iranian Institute* 6, 30-34.

— (1991) *Islamic Art*. London.

Tanabe, K. (1974) Kanishka I's Coins with the Buddha Image on the Reverse and Some References to the Art of Gandhara. *Orient* X, 31-56.

— (1980) An Essay on a "Tassel" Represented in the Armour-Clad Equestrian Image of the Larger Grotto, Taq-i Bustan. *Oriento*, XXIII 1, 65-82 (in Japanese with an English Summary).

— (1984) A Study of the Sasanian Disk-Nimbus: Farewell to its Xvarnah-Theory. *Bulletin of the Ancient Orient Museum* VI, 29-50.

— (1990) Positive Examples of Sasanian Influence on Gandharan Art, in ed. C. Bautze-Picron, *Makaranda. Essays in Honour of J. C. Harle*, 51-62. Delhi.

— (2004) Foundations for Dating Anew the 38meter Buddha Image at Bâmiyân, *Silk Road Art and Archaeology* 10, 177-223.

— (2006) The Identification of the King of Kings in the Upper Register of the Larger Grotte, Taq-i Bustan: Ardashir III Restated, in eds. M. Compareti, P. Raffetta, G. Scarcia, *Ērān ud Anērān. Studies Presented to Boris I. Maršak on the Occasion of His 70th Birthday*, 583-601. Venezia.

Tarzi, Z. (1977) *L'architecture et le décor rupestre des grottes de Bāmyān*, 2 vols. Paris.

Thierry, N. (1970) Les peintures murales de six églises du Haut Moyen Âge en Cappadoce, *Comptes Rendus de l'Académie des Inscriptions et Belles-Lettres*, 444-80.

Thompson, D. (1974) *Stucco From Chal Tarkhan-Eshqabad Near Rayy*. Warminster.

Treadwell, L. (2008) The Copper Coinage of Umayyad Iran, *The Numismatic Chronicle* 168, 331-381.

Trümpelmann, L. (1975) *Das Sasanidische Felsrelief von Sar Mashad*. Berlin.

Vanden Berghe, L. (1988) Les scènes d'investiture sur les reliefs rupestres de l'Irān ancien: évolution et signification, in eds. G. Gnoli, L. Lanciotti, *Orientalia Iosephi Tucci Memoriae Dicata. Vol. II*, 1511-1531. Roma.

Venco Ricciardi, R. (1992) Archaeological Research at Hatra Preliminary Report on the 1989 Season. *Mesopotamia* XXVII, 189-98.

— (1996) Wall Paintings from Building A at Hatra. *Iranica Antiqua* XXXVI, 147-65.

— (1998) Pictorial Graffiti in the City of Hatra, in: ed. E. Dąbrowa, *Ancient Iran and the Mediterranean World. International Conference in Honour of Professor Józef Wolski. Electrum* 2, 187-205. Kraków.

— (2004) Immagini graffite dall'edificio A di Hatra. *Parthica* 6, 203-25.

Wilber, D. N. (1937) Iranian Motifs in Syrian Art. *Bulletin of the American Institute for Iranian Art and Archaeology* 5, 22-26.

Wilkinson, C. K. s. d. [1973] *Nishapur: Pottery of the Early Islamic Period*. New York.

— (1986) *Nishapur. Some Early Islamic Buildings and Their Decoration*. New York.

Yamauchi, K. (1996) New Discoveries of Iranian Archaeology (1). *Bulletin of the Ancient Orient Museum* XVII, 123-49.

XIONGNU ROYAL TOMB COMPLEX IN THE TSARAAM VALLEY

Sergey S. Minyaev

The Xiongnu, otherwise known as the Asiatic Huns, created a powerful alliance of cattle-breeding tribes in the late third to early second century BCE and then dominated the eastern part of Central Asia for four centuries. Systematic studies of Xiongnu archaeological sites have been carried out for more than a century. At present, materials of considerable value in the characterization of settlement complexes (the Ivolga fortress, the Dureny settlement) and cemeteries of various types (the cemeteries of Ivolga, Derestuj, etc.) have been obtained (Davydova, 1995; Davydova, 1996; Davydova, Minyaev, 2003; Davydova, Minyaev, 2008; Minyaev, 1998). However, elite barrows, which usually contain important information about social structure, material culture, and the art of a particular society, are neither well-known nor systematically investigated using archaeological techniques. Meanwhile, such burials (traditionally called "royal") usually contain valuable information for characterization both of the material and spiritual culture of a community and of its social structure.

In 1996 the Trans-Baikal Archaeological Expedition of the Institute for the History of Material Culture, Russian Academy of Sciences, St. Petersburg, initiated a survey of the Tsaraam valley, situated 1.5 km to the south of Naushki village (Buriat Republic, Russian Federation) (fig. 1). Archaeological work at the Tsaraam cemetery began in the nineteenth century with the discovery of the site in June 1896 by the pioneer of Xiongnu archaeology, Iu. D. Tal'ko-Gryntsevich. He recorded "more than 20 barrows, dispersed in a forest" in the Tsaraam location. In June 1903, Tal'ko-Gryntsevich and Ia. S. Smolev excavated five of the burials. All of them had been robbed, and only a few artifacts were found (Tal'ko-Gryntsevich 1999: 117-118). Tal'ko-Gryntsevich drew a schematic map with an approximate location of the burial site; however, over time the cemetery was forgotten. In September 1996 the cemetery was rediscovered by the Trans-Baikal Expedition, which made an accurate map marking the location of all barrows. The survey showed that in the valley were concentrated the largest burial structures of the Xiongnu now known in Russia, and these are among the largest anywhere. In 1997, the expedition began to excavate the cemetery and chose to focus on the large and central Burial Complex No. 7. The Russian Humanities Foundation, the Institute of History of Material Culture, the Russian Academy of Sciences, and the US National Geographic Society provided financial support for this project. Excavations during the field seasons of 1997-2005 investigated surface and internal constructions of Barrow No. 7 and the ten adjacent sacrificial burials. Chinese silk items, a Chinese chariot, lacquered artifacts, textiles, felt, jade, gold, silver, bronze and iron objects, funeral dolls and an "animal cemetery" were found. As a result of the excavation we now have extremely important new data about the society and culture of the Xiongnu confederation.

Site Description

The Tsaraam valley is situated 30 km to the west of the town of Kiakhta (Kiakhta district of the Buriat Republic, Russian Federation; fig.1), not far from the Russian-Mongolian border (E. 106° 08' 61.3", N. 50° 21' 22.8"; 650-670 masl). The length of the Tsaraam valley from north to south is 1.5 km, and its width approximately 700m east to west. Low mountains with pine forest border the eastern section of the valley while the western section opens on the Selenga River valley. Mixed conifer and deciduous trees cover the lower slopes of the valley while the central portion is open with plowed fields and grassland vegetation. Agriculture has been carried on in the valley since the nineteenth century, and in more recent times mechanized plowing has been used to prepare fields on a fairly large scale. As a result of these activities, many of the stone surface features marking burial areas have been destroyed.

Almost all barrows of the Tsaraam cemetery are situated in the central part of the valley. The total known burial area measures approximately 600m north-south and 400m east-west. The largest barrow of the cemetery is located in the northern part of the valley, and 300m to the southwest a line of seven additional large barrows stretches from the northeast to southwest. The large barrows have similar surface construction, which includes a low square mound with a round depression in the center. Around several of the large barrows are located smaller barrows, which, according to both the historical sources and recent archaeological evidence, are likely to have been sacrificial interments. The combination of a central large barrow ringed by several smaller barrows can be considered a single mortuary complex (fig.2).

Judging from their external and internal structural similarity to other Xiongnu sites such as Noin Ula or the Elm valley, the Tsaraam tomb complexes presumably date to the Xiongnu period. The Tsaraam group also features large burials and is therefore thought to be related to the highest social strata of the Xiongnu confederation.

Surface and Internal Structures of the Central Barrow

Barrow No. 7 is not only the largest Xiongnu barrow in Russia but also one of the largest known at present anywhere. The surface construction of the central barrow consists of a quadrangle-shaped platform surfaced with clay. It measures approximately 29 × 28m with a height of approximately 1.5m above the present surface. The entrance chamber is 20m long and extends to the south of the central platform. The walls of the platform are sided with stone slabs marking the perimeter of the walls. Several stone stelae were discovered, some of which were intact and others of which had fallen away from the platform.

A single longitudinal and seven perpendicular partitions divided the upper section of the burial pit into nine distinct compartments (fig.3). Each partition was constructed from wooden logs stacked one upon another, sometimes having a thickness of two to three logs. Four covers of the burial chamber were excavated under the partitions. The uppermost cover of the burial chamber consisted of stone plates and wood; under the logs was a reed stratum. The second cover of the burial chamber was situated in 1.5-1.7m below the upper one and covered the entire area of the burial pit. This second cover consisted of large stone plates, stacked in close proximity to each other. There was also a thin stratum of reeds 0.7m below the second cover. In both the upper and second covers, there was some difference between the eastern and western parts. The eastern part of the second cover consisted of large plates and boulders approximately 100 × 70cm in area and with a thickness of 40-50cm. The stone plates of the western half of the cover were of smaller size, approximately 40 × 50cm and with a thickness of only 10-15cm. At each corner of the burial pit on the level of the second cover there were small-sized stones lying on top of the large ones. The third cover was 11m below the modern surface. This third cover consisted of large stone plates; under the stones there was a stratum of pebble, charcoal, birch cortex, and small-sized stones. Bones of domesticated animals were found along the northern edge of the third cover, among them skulls of horses, cows, sheep, and goats which were placed in line with each other. Near the skulls were tail and leg bones. The fourth cover, located one meter below the third one, consisted of large stone plates, birch cortex, a stratum of pebbles mixed with small-sized stones, and a stratum of charcoal. This fourth cover was situated directly on the roof of the burial chamber.

Intraburial Construction (Pls. IV-4~6)

The burial chamber itself consisted of three chambers: an external framework, an internal framework, and the coffin. The external chamber consisted of seven rows of squared beams; the overall height of the chamber was *ca.* 170-180cm. The longitudinal and transverse beams were connected by means of interlocking joints of tongue-and-groove construction cut through the entire width of each beam. There were no additional reinforcing connectors between the beams.

The ceiling of the chamber consisted of boards 20-35cm wide laid in an east-west direction. The boards were placed flush with one another, without any connectors holding them together or attaching them to the upper beams of the chamber. The ends of the ceiling boards rested on the upper beams of the frame, and in the middle on three transverse beams laid equidistant from one another in a north-south direction. The ceiling beams rested on the upper beams of the chamber (which had notches cut in them to secure the beams) and on columns located along the interior of the northern and southern walls of the chamber. In the northern section of the burial structure along the external wall of the external chamber were three columns, and another three columns were parallel to the first along the northern wall of the internal frame. Along the southern wall of the chamber were another three analogous columns. Thus, each of the three ceiling beams of the external chamber had five points of support: two on the northern and southern upper beams of the chamber (where the ends of the beams were fitted into special notches), two on the columns on the northern side, and one more on the southern columns. The external chamber rested on a floor of beams laid in an east-west direction. The internal frame consisted of five rows of squared beams each measuring 20 × 20cm. The construction of the rows of the frame was analogous to the construction of the rows of the external chamber. As in the case of the external chamber, the frame had a covering of transverse boards and a floor similarly constructed of transverse boards. The coffin inside the frame had been destroyed to a considerable degree by the robbery from the southern end and by the subsequent collapse of the chamber. One may suppose that its floor and roof consisted of two boards laid lengthwise; the side walls of the coffin were made of wide boards, one on each wall.

The Inventory of Barrow No. 7

Objects Found Inside the Burial Pit: The Chinese Mirror

Fragments of a Chinese bronze mirror (Pl. IV-1) were found under the logs at the second level of the longitudinal partition in the center of the burial pit, 218cm below the surface. The ten fragments of the mirror were in the following positions: six lay one above the other and the remaining four alongside them. Taken together they do not form a complete mirror (its center is only partially preserved), although they suffice to reconstruct its size and decoration. The diameter is 13cm; around its edge is a rim 2.1cm wide and 3cm thick. The characteristic elements of the decoration make it possible to identify a wide range of analogies and reconstruct the entire decorative scheme.

Apart from the smooth rim, on the reverse surface of a mirror of that type are several concentric ornamental bands. Directly adjoining the rim is a narrow (3mm) band with a comb-tooth pattern, inside of which is the main ornamental band with images which were separated from the center of the mirror also by a narrow band with a comb-tooth pattern. A smooth protruding band 3mm wide separated the outer bands from the center, where there was a pierced knob for hanging the mirror. Narrow protruding lines divided into four sectors the area around the knob and the inner smooth band. In each sector in turn were three round knobs or nipples, the central one of which was connected with the protruding smooth band by three short lines.

The main ornamental band situated between the two narrow bands with the comb-tooth pattern was divided into four sectors by means of small rounded projecting knobs. The area between the knobs was covered by virtually identical compositions, the center of which was a large scroll in the shape of a comma. It is possible that initially this was the depiction of the body of an animal which with time had been transformed into a geometric composition. Above and below this scroll were figures of birds, or, more rarely, other animals.

Mirrors of this type are not uncommon. They are known in museum collections; some examples of such mirrors have been found in archaeological excavations both of the Han Dynasty itself and in Xiongnu excavations of that same period on the territory of Mongolia and Russia. (See, e.g., Tal'koGryntsevich 1999, p. 50, fig. 3; Chou 2000, p. 39, fig. 20, Cheng and Han 2002, fig. 25:1,2 and fig. 26:1,2; Wenwu 1977, fig. 27:2.) According to the standard classification (Zhongguo tongjing 1997, p. 247) they belong to the group of mirrors "with four nipples and four S-shaped figures" (or dragons). The given group is dated normally between the 1st century BCE and 1st century CE.

An important characteristic of the mirrors from Xiongnu sites is their fragmentary state. Unlike those in Han burials the mirrors in most Xiongnu burials are found either in separate fragments or in several pieces of a mirror that had been intentionally broken. Evidence of the intentional breaking of mirrors is seen, for example, in the mirror discovered in a residence in the fortress of Bayan-Under, where it was unearthed along with the iron knife used to break it (Huns 2005, p. 46, fig. 63).

It is very likely that the Tsaraam mirror, initially intact, had likewise been intentionally broken. Traces of scale clearly visible on its surface indicate that the mirror had been broken by heating it to a high temperature and then abruptly cooling it, possibly in cold water. After that, some of the fragments were removed and the rest placed under the beams of the longitudinal partition. Removed as a result of this process were the central knob of the mirror, the three nipples dividing the main ornamental zone into parts, and two segments with ornament in the form of the central "comma" and adjoining birds. The depiction of a bird above the "comma" in the third section has also been damaged. In essence then, the only remaining complete segment is the fourth one. We note in particular that although the third and fourth segments had been broken into several parts during the ritual, these parts were not removed but placed in the grave pit along with other fragments. At the same time, a small fragment of the mirror with the dividing knob between the third and fourth segments was removed along with two other fragments with nipples. The fragment with a nipple which was placed in the grave pit had first been subjected to strong secondary heating, as a result of which the knob had melted. The melting of the nipple was a result specifically of that second heating of a separate fragment, since otherwise the adjoining more delicate parts of the mirror would also have melted.

Thus one can hypothesize that during the burial ceremony a special ritual was performed over the mirror, a ritual which was possibly the norm for the burial practices of the Xiongnu. The ritual involved subjecting the mirror to mechanical or heat treatment and breaking it into several fragments. One or several of such fragments accompanied the dead, while other parts of the mirror were removed and possibly preserved by the family or relatives of the deceased in order subsequently to accompany other burials and serve as a kind of sign of recognition upon meeting in the other world. The burial of some parts of the mirror in the grave pit and the removal of others (of analogous design) suggests that such mirrors and the ritual actions performed over them served as a kind of connecting link between the world of the living and the world of the dead, symbolizing in both worlds the unity of the collective which the deceased had left behind.

Objects Found Inside the Burial Pit: The Chinese Chariot

A Chinese chariot was found in the center of the barrow at a depth of 10.5-11m (Miniaev, Sakharovskaia, 2007). To its north, at the wall of the pit about a meter from the incline of the fifth step at a depth of 10m were the skull, two neck vertebrae, and the metapodials of a horse. The arrangement of the chariot's parts suggests that its body had been placed beneath the third cover when the pit was being filled, while the canopy and wheels were found above the stones of the third cover in the center of the barrow and thus must have been located above the level of that ceiling (fig. 4). Probably the chariot had been set onto the stones of the fourth cover where it was buried by the filling of the pit as well as by the gravel, pebbles, charcoal, and slabs of the third ceiling (the canopy and the wheels of the chariot having remained above the latter; fig. 5). When the fill of the pit sank, the parts of the chariot were displaced: in the process, the movement of stone slabs, gravel, and pebbles—acting like millstones—inflicted serious damage. Some time later, the chariot was further disturbed by robber passages: the northern passage damaged part of the harness and frame, while the southern one crossed the presumed location of the seat, in the process demolishing a considerable part of the canopy. Altogether, the parts of the chariot were very poorly preserved: the wooden parts and organic material of the canopy had decayed almost completely, while the bronze and iron fastenings of the harness had been severely oxidized and lost their original structure. Here is a description of the preserved parts of the chariot [fig. 5].

The remains of the canopy were in the center of the pit 4m from its northern edge above the stones of the third cover. The canopy consisted of a wooden frame, over which some organic material had been stretched. The base of the frame was composed of thin wooden strips about 4cm wide set crosswise, to which were attached a number of thick arched twigs. The base included as well thinner twigs 1-1.5cm in diameter, arrayed radially from the center of the frame. The organic cover of the frame was duo fold, its upper layer consisting of a dark organic material (leather or felt), below which there was a thin layer of cloth. This canopy covering was fixed to the strips and twigs of the frame with thin, iron L-shaped nails.

The inside of the canopy was coated with red lacquer, which preserved traces of geometric ornament rendered in white, brown, and dark-red paints (Pl. IV-2). A robber trench had destroyed the southern part of the canopy.

The front yoke-pole of the chariot was found on the layer of pebbles and charcoal under the stones of the third cover of the pit, 2.5m north of the canopy. Its western edge had been completely destroyed during the collapse of the third cover. The preserved length of the pole was 2.5m; its diameter was 18-20cm. A bronze ferrule 10cm long and 7cm in diameter was attached to the eastern tip of the pole. The ferrule had completely oxidized and been crushed by the pressure of the fill. Probably a similar ferrule had been attached to the western, destroyed end of the pole. Five pairs of square mortises measuring 3×1.5cm for attaching parts of the harness were discernible. They began 12cm from the eastern tip of the yoke-pole and ran along its entire length at intervals of 40-45cm (the mortises in each pair were spaced 4cm apart). Near the mortises were fragments of bronze, probably traces of arc-shaped harness "rings" or guides which had been set into the mortises.

Remains of yoke-heads were uncovered at the western and eastern sides of the yoke-pole, as well as in its center. These consisted of boards 4cm thick, 8cm wide, and with the preserved length of 25-30cm. The position of the western yoke-head in situ suggests that the heads were attached to the yoke-pole by means of special incisions. The lower parts of the yoke-heads were not preserved. In the upper part of the western and central yoke-heads there was a cylindrical projection on which a bronze ferrule had been placed. On the eastern head, this projection had been broken off in antiquity but its traces were discernible in the upper part of the head. The entire surface of the yoke-pole and yoke-heads was coated with black lacquer, over which a geometrical pattern was drawn in white and red paint. Stylistically, fragments of this pattern are similar to that on the inside of the canopy of the chariot.

The two wooden shafts of the chariot were beneath the front yoke-pole lying parallel to each other in a N-S direction and 60cm apart. They were very poorly preserved: their southern parts had been cut off by the robber trench; the preserved length was 95-100cm. Traces of lacquer and a pattern rendered in red and white paints were visible on the surface of the shafts. Near the eastern shaft at a distance of 10cm from it was a line of iron oval plates with holes on the shorter sides. Probably these had once been sewn onto the leather straps of the harness or the reins. Below this line of plates, 30cm to the east, was an iron ring 6.5cm in diameter.

The remains of the wooden wheels were located 1m south of the shafts, on the stones of the third ceiling. The lower part of the western wheel was in the layer of pebbles and gravel underlying that ceiling. The wheels were spaced 2m from one another, each consisting of a felloe, spokes and, possibly, a central disc into which the ends of the spokes had been inserted and in the center of which the iron hub of the axle had been placed. The wheels were considerably damaged by the pressure of the filling of the pit and ceilings. The wheels were 120cm in diameter and had 22 spokes whose thickness was 3-4cm. Remains of a number of iron shackles were traceable around the felloe of the western wheel. Tiny fragments of red and white paint were preserved on the felloe and spokes. The felloe and the adjoining parts of the spokes were painted red to a length of 10-12cm, whereas the rest of the spokes was painted white. Practically nothing of the central parts of the wheels survives; nevertheless traces of red paint detected there suggest that the central disc of the wheel into which the spokes had been inserted was painted red.

Small iron hubs with two projections were uncovered directly outside of the wheels in the pebble layer which underlay the third ceiling. There were traces of wood on the outer side of the hubs. Large iron hubs with three projections on the outside of each were found under the wheels in the pebble layer of the third ceiling. These also bore traces of wood on the outer side, whereas in the center of the large and small hubs no traces of wood have been detected. The iron nails with which the hubs were fixed to the wooden cores of the wheels were preserved on the outer side of the larger hubs.

The rear yoke-pole: This is an arbitrary designation for this part of the chariot, since its real purpose still is not clear. A number of facts suggest, however, that it is not the axle of the chariot, viz.:

—the difference between the diameter of the pole and the inner diameter of the large iron hubs into which the axle must have been inserted;

—the separate position of the bronze axle-caps (as described below), which were usually put onto the ends of the axle and whose diameter differs from that of the rear pole (which furthermore had its own bronze caps).

In its shape and dimensions (7cm in diameter and about 3m long) the "rear yoke-pole" resembled the front pole. The largest part of the pole had been cut off by the northern robber trench; only its eastern and western ends were preserved. Bronze caps 5.5cm in diameter and 7cm long were placed on the tips of the pole. On the surface of the caps was a small cylindrical flange. Two arc-shaped iron fastenings were driven into the yoke-pole 3-4cm from these caps. Possibly some elements of the harness (straps or ropes) once passed through these fastenings. The surface of the rear yoke-pole showed traces of lacquer and a pattern rendered in white paint.

Wooden elbow-rests of the seat: After the wheels had been removed, directly below them were found remains of some pinewood blocks which possibly were once the elbow-rests of the seat. These consisted of boards 3-4cm thick, decayed and compressed by the powerful pressure of the filling of the pit. The elbow-rests presumably measured 25-50cm. A painted geometrical design could be made out on their lacquered surface.

The body of the chariot: After the wheels had been cleared and removed, remains of a trellised frame of the chariot and bronze axle-terminals were uncovered in the space between the wheels and the remains of the chariot shafts. The remains of the frame consisted of several wooden laths, 2-3cm. thick, from which the trellised part of the body had been constructed. The laths were attached to each other with iron nails where they crossed. The northern and southern parts of the trellised frame of the chariot, as well as, perhaps, the entire seat had been destroyed by the robber trenches. North of the trellised frame, under its wooden laths, were two cylindrical bronze axle-caps at whose bases were circular flanges (Pl. IV-3). The axle-caps were 10cm long and 12cm in diameter in their base and 5cm in diameter on the top. In the lower part of the caps there were rectangular holes measuring 3×1.5cm for insertion of the pins. In their upper part they had L-shaped projections probably to fix the straps of the harness. The iron pins, found lying between the caps, were 10cm long with a rectangular section and a ring or eye on one end.

The absence of the wheel axle and the unusual position of the pair of axle-caps (beneath the trellised body) suggest that the chariot had been placed in the tomb in a disassembled and possibly incomplete state. It is also noteworthy that the presence of three yoke-heads implies the use of three horses in the team. However, as mentioned above, only the skull, two cervical vertebra, and metapodials of a single horse were discovered. This horse was evidently laid in the tomb according to the principle of "a part instead of the whole".

The construction of this chariot and its decorations have very close parallels among Chinese chariots of the Han period. The most comprehensive study of these chariots distinguishes a number features very similar to those of the chariot from Tsaraam (Wang, 1997). Like the Han examples, the Tsaraam chariot has a canopy consisting of a wooden framework covered by some organic material, four wooden posts supporting the canopy, a trellised seat, and wooden "elbow-rests". The body of the chariot and the painting of the wheels are remarkably closely paralleled in a recently restored chariot from the burial of the famous Han general Huo Qubing who fought against the Xiongnu (Cooke 2000). The use of two yoke-shafts on the Tsaraam chariot suggests it was originally intended for a team of three horses, whereas the single central shaft typical of the Han chariots implies an even number of horses on the team.

Written sources often attest that chariots were among the gifts offered by the Han court to the first-rank Xiongnu nobility. Thus in 51 BCE Shanyu Huhanye received along with other gifts a "chariot with a seat" (Taskin 1968-1973, vol. 2, p. 35). Subsequently, as mentioned in *Han Shu*, on more than one occasion the *shanyu* was given presents similar to those he received the first time (*ibid.*, pp. 36, 37, 51). During the epoch of Wang Mang (9-24 CE), who intended to divide the Xiongnu into separate nomadic bands and to set his own chief at the head of each, one of the Xiongnu deserters, the Right Liyuwang Xian was awarded the title of Xiao Shanyu and, among other presents, given a "chariot with a seat and a chariot with a drum" (*ibid.*, p. 57). In 50 CE the *shanyu* of the southern Xiongnu, Bee (the grandson of Huhanye ruling under the same name as his grandfather) was granted "a carriage with a seat and an umbrella of feathers and a team of four richly harnessed horses" (*ibid.*, p. 72). In 143 CE the southern *shanyu* Hulanzhuo in the throne hall of the imperial palace was granted along with other gifts "a chariot with a black top harnessed to a team of four horses, a chariot with a drum, and a chariot with a seat"; the *shanyu*'s wives were granted "two carriages decorated with gold and brocade and draught horses" (*ibid.*, p. 94).

It is thus quite possible that the chariot found in Tsaraam was also a gift from the Han court to one of the representatives of the Xiongnu elite. However, judging by the evidence from *Han Shu* we might connect the chariot with a different event. In Wang Mang's reign, the above-mentioned Xiao Shanyu's son, Deng, who was then at the imperial court as a hostage, was executed because of his father's desertion to the northern Xiongnu and his brother's frequent raids on the borderlands. At the demand of the Xiongnu the corpses of Deng and some other noblemen executed together with him were returned to their homeland for burial. The bodies were "laid into chariots" for transport (*ibid*, p. 62). We may not rule out that later these chariots were buried in the tombs together with other funerary offerings.

It should be emphasized that in any case the records of chariots either as gifts or in connection with funerary ceremonies concern only the first-rank Xiongnu nobility, i.e. *shanyus*, their wives, or sons. This fact is a further confirmation of the probability that Barrow No. 7 at Tsaraam is a burial of a representative of the Xiongnu elite, possibly a *shanyu*. Parts of chariots were found also in the Xiongnu royal tombs at Noin-Ula, but unfortunately the archaeological record from that site is insufficiently precise to permit reconstructing their details.

Objects Found in the Burial Chamber

Most of the burial goods were located in the corridors between the walls of the chamber, the frame, and the coffin.

The western external corridor

Several sets of harness (iron bits, cheek-pieces, and harness buckles) and two burial dolls were found there. Iron hooks, found in the walls of the external chamber suggest that originally the bridle arrays had hung on such hooks and ended up on the floor of the chamber only after its deformation.

The doll found in the center of the western corridor (the northern of the two, to which we have given the provisional designation "Doll No.1") was formed in the following fashion (fig. 6, Pl. IV-7). The head of the doll was made of a human skull, which, judging by the baby teeth, was that of a 2-4-year-old child. On the skull of the doll were six braids of black stiff hair, which probably had been attached to the skull using some kind of glue. Along with the braids on the skull were two round beads made of gold foil and inlaid with turquoise. Two more braids were in front and in back of the skull and two braids in the waist region along with iron plaques. Wooden sticks covered with red lacquer formed the extremities of the doll.

Under the birch bark containers was a birch bark circle, on which was found a fragment of a Chinese bronze mirror. On one of the birch bark containers were unique drawings, showing the Xiongnu camp with carts and yurts placed on carriers and the profile of a person in a helmet — possibly a copy of a depiction on some coin (Pl. IV-8).

In front of and behind the skull of the doll were several iron buckles, a bit, cheek-pieces, and fragments of iron objects. Probably they were not connected to the inventory of the doll but originally had hung on the wall of the chamber and also ended up on the floor after its deformation.

The other doll found in the western corridor, given the provisional designation "Doll No. 2" was formed in an analogous fashion (fig. 7). It lay one meter to the south of Doll No.1. The core of Doll No. 2 was also a human skull, which had completely disintegrated. Only small baby teeth were preserved, on the basis of which it was determined that the skull might have belonged to a child only a few months old. In the vicinity of the skull was a short braid of stiff black hair. The modeling of the upper extremities could not be determined. The lower extremities were made of thin iron plates, placed in a wooden sheath and covered with red lacquer.

In the vicinity of the neck of Doll No. 2 was a necklace of glass, turquoise, fluorite, and large crystal beads. In the vicinity of the waist of the doll were two corroded iron plates measuring 20 × 11cm lying on the leather strap of a belt, which was preserved only in fragments and in places had been covered with red lacquer. A loop of beads, consisting of now almost completely scattered glass beads, had been suspended from the belt. There were some heart-shaped fluorite and amber beads as well. Below the waist of Doll No. 2 under the bottom beam of the outer chamber were remains of a crushed wooden lacquered vessel with geometric ornament. Inside the vessel were fragments of a bronze mirror, a piece of mica, two wooden combs, and a collection of iron needles in a wooden holster. On the exterior of the vessel was a Chinese inscription, which Prof. Michele Pirazzoli-t'Serstevens has analyzed (Pirazzoli-t'Serstevens, 2007).

The eastern external corridor

The finds in this corridor were practically the same as those in the western one. Here there were also sets of bridles (consisting of iron bits, cheek-pieces, and buckles) and burial dolls. The burial doll which lay in the center of the eastern corridor to the south of the pieces of harness and which was given the provisional designation "Doll No. 3" was formed in the same way as the dolls in the western corridor (fig. 8). The skull of the doll had practically completely disintegrated. In the vicinity of the skull lay several braids of stiff black hair, on the ends of which were little turquoise, glass, and amber beads. Lacquered wooden sticks formed the extremities. Near the neck on both right and left in the vicinity of the skull were remains of two round pendants of wood covered with lacquer which possibly had been formed from the walls of wooden lacquered cups.

At the waist of the doll were also two wide corroded iron buckles measuring 19×12cm. Behind the head of the doll were remains of a wooden object (possibly a box), on which was a small birch bark container and a large fragment of a Chinese mirror.

The fourth doll apparently had been removed by the robbers; only its feet remained.

The western internal corridor

In the western internal corridor there were practically no artifacts, only two bronze coffin handles were found near the southwestern and southeastern corners of the coffin.

The eastern internal corridor

The finds in this corridor were confined to its southern part (Pl. IV-10), since robbers had destroyed the northern part. These finds included sets of harnesses — iron bits, cheek-plates, silver chest medallions for horses (phalars) with images of mountain goats (fig. 9), bronze harness-plates, bronze plaques with depictions of a running goat (fig. 10); arrowheads, a lacquered wooden staff, a braid, a lacquered wooden cup, and a lacquered wooden quiver with iron arrowheads.

The northern external corridor

The entrance of a looter had destroyed this corridor, but fragments of ceramics, animal bones and lacquered wooden objects were found here.

The southern external corridor

Nothing was found here, but in that corridor, attached to the interior wall of the external chamber, were remains of a woolen carpet which had been destroyed by the shifting of the beams of the chamber.

The southern internal corridor

A flat iron ring and two iron fasteners were found here.

The finds inside of the coffin

The northern section of the coffin had been destroyed by robbers, but jade plaques of armor, a jade diadem (Pl. IV-12) and a skull of goat has covered in silver foil were found here. In the preserved southern section of the coffin were the remains of a covering of some organic material (felt or compressed fur), two iron buckles covered in gold foil and depicting a satyr (Pl. IV-13), and two gold fastenings. Next to the remains of a ritual sword were three gold objects decorated with turquoise inlay. Two of them may be finials; the third, with the image of a mountain goat is a small flask (Pl. IV-11).

Sacrificial burials of complex No. 7

Sacrificial burials of Barrow 7 were found ranged in two lines, 5 graves in each on the western and eastern sides of Barrow 7, and they undoubtedly formed a single burial complex with the latter (complex no. 7; fig.2).

The eastern group of sacrificial burials (fig. 11)

In the eastern group 5 sacrificial burials have been found, located 3-4m from each other and 25m from the eastern wall of Barrow 7. The northernmost burial 10 of the group was 25m to the east from the north-eastern corner of the over-grave structure of Barrow 7, the southernmost burial 11 was 21m to the east of the south-eastern corner of the central barrow. Thus the line of these burials was directed north-south, deviating only slightly to the west in its southern part. In fig. 11 on can see typical burials for the eastern and western lines.

The western group of sacrificial burials

Before the excavations, to the west of Barrow 7, in the underbrush of bushes and low elm trees, it was possible to trace remains of barrows on the modern surface. They represented a depression 1.2 m deep, enclosed by a low earthen bank, and outcrops of large stone slabs and smaller boulders on the surface of the ploughed field. As with the eastern group, during excavation of the entire area of the western group one found 5 burials ranged in a line, 3-4 m from each other and 25 m from the western wall of Barrow 7. Burial no. 12—the northernmost of the group—was situated 24m to the west of the NW corner of the over-grave structure of Barrow 7; the southernmost burial no. 16 was 28 m to the south-west of the SW corner of Barrow 7. The line of these burials, in general, was directed north-south, the graves in the middle of it being ranged strictly from north to south and the outermost ones (nos. 12 and 16) slightly deviating to the east in the southern part. It is possible that these burials also had over-grave structures, which were later disturbed and displaced during agricultural work.

The practice of human sacrifices in the burial tradition of the Xiongnu was recorded already by their contemporaries — ancient Chinese chroniclers. Sima Qian (145-87 BCE), who first compiled information about the Xiongnu in his *Shi Ji* (Records of the Historian), mentioned that "the most beloved servants and concubines followed the deceased into the grave, and the greatest number of such persons amounted to several thousand or hundreds". Pan Gu, author of *Han Shu* (History of the Han Dynasty), when redacting the text of *Shi Ji* replaced "several thousand or hundreds" in the above phrase for "several tens or one hundred" (Taskin, 1968: 136, comments 108). These divergences show that Han historians did not have at their disposal precise information about the number of humans offered in sacrifice during the burials of Xiongnu elite.

The first reliable information on such sacrifices was obtained from the Derestuy cemetery. During excavations of entire areas of this site it was discovered that the burials were arranged into complexes consisting of a central barrow surrounded by sacrificial burials, the number of the latter varying from one to three. The characteristic injuries on skeletons in sacrificial burials suggested with a high degree of probability a violent death of the interred (for details see: Миняев 1998: 41, 70).

The excavation of Complex no. 7 at Tsaraam essentially supplemented the data obtained from the Dyrestuy cemetery. Similarly to Dyrestuy, at Tsaraam characteristic injuries were also registered on skeletons. Thus in Barrow 6, the long extremities of the interred had not been disturbed by grave robbers, nevertheless bones of the feet and of the right hand were lacking, and bones of the left arm were lying in the inverse order: the ulna and the radius in the place of the humerus, and the latter in the place of the bones of the forearm. In Burial 15, the extreme phalanges of feet were absent, and an unnatural position of the wrists and left forearm suggests that the hands of the interred were bound. In addition, on most of the skeletons from Complex 7, one may observe unnatural deformations of certain bones which possibly indicate that the interred had some physical defects.

The number of sacrificial burials in Complex 7 amounts to 10; the planigraphy of the Tsaraam burials demonstrated that they formed two rows, comprising 5 burials in each, ranged almost symmetrically relative to the main barrow at its eastern and western sides.

As it is seen on the plan of the complex (fig. 2), the principles of arranging the burials in different groups, the sex and age composition of the interred are identical. Both in the western and eastern groups, only males were interred, a certain dependence between the position of a burial within the group and the age of the interred being clearly observable. The oldest (and almost all of the same age at 35 years) men were buried in the northernmost graves (Barrow 10 in the eastern group and Barrow 12 in the western). The age of the other dead consequently diminishes from north to south: the younger men and adolescents (aged 25-15 on average) were buried in the middle of each row, and in the southernmost graves (11 and 16) children of practically the same age (4-6 years old) were interred.

In both of the groups of burials of men and adolescents, *i.e.* in the four graves in the northern and central parts of each group, it is possible to trace a certain correlation between the position of the burial within the group, age of the interred, and the type of burial structures. The surface structures, as noted above, had been destroyed by ploughing, so that we may point only to a higher concentration of stones from disturbed embankments in the northern area of each group. The inner structures of the northern graves both in Barrow 10 (a coffin in a stone cist covered with several courses of slabs; an undercut in the northern wall of the pit; a charcoal make-up on the bottom of the pit) and in Barrow 12 (the coffin inside a timber frame placed into a stone cist and covered over with blocks of clay) in terms of their construction are the most complicated in each group. In burials at the center of each group, structures represented by wooden coffins inserted into stone cists are typical (fig.10), the construction of the coffins and cists being simpler than that of the northern burials. The simplest constructions have been found in the next to last burials (if one counts from north to south) of each row; in Grave 6 (the eastern group) and Grave 15 (the western group) such structures are represented only by coffins.

Differences depending on the position of a grave in the group may be observed also in the composition of the food laid out for the dead. Thus bones of several animals both of large and small horned cattle (for which a special catacomb in the northern wall of the pit was made) were found in Barrow 10 (the northernmost burial of the eastern group), while in Barrow 6 (next to the last in the eastern row) there were only bones of one sheep or goat (ribs and a tibia). One should add that in Barrow 10 a single horse skull was found.

All of the burials had been robbed. This fact makes the complete reconstruction of the composition and quantity of the grave goods impossible. We note, however, that weapons—bows (of which tips and central plates are usually preserved), iron and horn arrowheads and iron belt-plates—were found practically in all of the graves of men and adolescents. Numerous are also parts of horse harness—cheek-pieces made of horn in barrows 6, 11 and 15, and a horn saddle bow in Barrow 15.

Burials 11 and 16, the southernmost in each group, are an exception to the rule described above. Notwithstanding that the interred were children, the structures inside these graves were more complicated than those in the neighboring burials of an adolescent and a young man located to the north. In the eastern group, in grave 11 (child 4-6 years old), a wooden coffin was found in a stone cist covered with several courses of slabs, while a 16 year old adolescent in the neighboring grave 6 was buried only in a coffin. In the western group, the child in grave 16 (age-at-death 5 years) was buried in a wooden coffin placed in an imitation stone cist constructed of several large slabs, although in the neighboring grave 15, a man 25-30 years old was buried only in a coffin. The child burials have practically all been robbed, nevertheless the remains of the varnish coating of a wooden cup found in Barrow 16 (reminding us by the pattern of its decoration of the one found in Barrow 6 at the cemetery of Noin-Ula), a vessel and an iron belt plate from Barrow 11, similar to those found in other burials, suggest that the grave inventory in these child graves was not necessarily less, at least qualitatively, than the grave goods of adults.

The signs of violent death noted above lead to the conclusion that the described burials of armed men and adolescents, which surrounded the central Barrow 7, may be considered as the burials of "servants" mentioned in written documents (possibly the chief's "body-guards") killed during the funeral ceremony and "sacrificed" to their master in the other world. It seems that within such a social group of "servants" a number of ranks existed, and this fact was reflected in the revealed differences between the burial structures in different groups of sacrificial burials.

The status of the children buried in graves 11 and 16 thus far is not quite clear. They were buried together with the adult "servants" in the southernmost graves of the groups, completing logically the sex-and-age structure of each line of burials (the age-of-death decreasing from the northern graves to the southern). Possibly, these facts indicate that:

— by their origin these children belonged to the same social category of "servants" and were to inherit one of their ranks;

— the level of this inherited rank should potentially be higher in the other world than the actual lifetime status of the adolescent (eastern group) and young males (western group) interred in the neighborhood of these children;

— for these children therefore, in correspondence with their potential rank, more complex burial structures than for the older servants, interred close by, were constructed.

Thus, in terms of the number of burials, their planigraphy, the sexual composition of the interred, and the sets of grave goods, the sacrificial burials of Tsaraam significantly differ from similar burials at the Dyrestuy cemetery, where mostly women with various belt sets and adolescents were buried. One could suppose that these differences resulted from the differing status of the persons interred in the central barrows of the cemeteries. While at Dyrestuy, burial structures and funerary sets in central barrows suggest that the interred belonged to ordinary society, the central Barrow 7 at Tsaraam, judging by its size and the peculiarities of its construction, was a burial of some representative of the highest Xiongnu elite, or possibly even one of the chiefs (*shanyu*).

Of course, the suppositions proposed above must be verified during investigations of other burial complexes of elites using the method of excavation by entire areas. It also seems promising to employ palaeo-genetic analysis for defining the degree of kinship of the interred both in separate complexes and throughout the entire cemetery.

The Date of the Complex

I believe the central barrow and sacrificial burials to be a unique burial complex, put in place during one funerary ceremony, in one day or a maximum of several days (for detail see: Minyaev, 1998). The basis for determining the chronology of the complex is the inscription on the lacquered box found near Doll No. 2 (Pl. IV-11), fragments of four Chinese mirrors, and C-14 dates.

Prof. Michele Pirazzolit'Serstevens has made a reconstruction of the inscription:

[乘輿] [...] [...] [...] 年考工々賞造嗇夫臣康掾臣安主右丞臣 [...] 令臣 [...] 護工卒史臣尊省

She offers the following translation of this text:

[Fit for use by the emperor] made in the [?] year of the [? era] by the master artisan of the Kaogong imperial workshop Shang. Managed by the workshop overseer, your servant Kang, the lacquer bureau head, your servant An. Inspected by the Assistant Director of the Right your servant [?] , the Director your servant [?] and the Commandery Clerk for Workshop Inspection your servant Zun.

Based on the style and on the painted décor of the inscription, Michele Pirazzolit'Serstevens has concluded that the period between 8 BCE and 4 CE is a possible *terminus post quem* for the lacquer box from Tsaraam (Pirazzoli-t'Serstevens, 2007).

One can add that fragments of a lacquered cup with the same design as in Noin-Ula were found in the Tsaraam cemetery: in the northern corridor in the central Barrow No. 7 and in the Sacrificial Burial No. 16. It is very probable that the fragments can be dated from the same period as the Noyn-uul cemetery — not earlier than the end of the 1st century BCE

(Minyaev, Elikhina, 2009).

As Lai Guolong recently cautioned, dating on the basis of Chinese mirrors can be problematic, given the fact that too many examples in museum collections lack details about their provenance (Lai, 2006). With that caution in mind, I nonetheless feel that on the basis of modern classification (Zhongguo tongjing 1997) all four mirrors whose fragments were found in the central barrow in the burial pit and amid grave goods of the dolls can be dated between the end of the Western Han and early Eastern Han periods, that is not earlier than the 1st century BCE.

Eight C-14 dates were obtained in the laboratory of the Institute of the History of Material Culture [see table]:

Burial	Sample number	Original data, BP	1 sigma	2 sigma
Barrow No. 7 Logs of the fence in entry to the burial pit	Le-5930	2120±30	182-74 BCE	192-52BCE
Barrow No. 7 Charcoal between outside chamber and a wall of the burial pit	Le-7510	2130±20	200-35BCE	350-50 BCE
Barrow No. 7 The chariot	Le-7680	1925±40	50-130CE	40BCE-180 CE
Sacrificial Burial No. 12, the coffin	Le-5917	2050±25	56BCE-2CE	110BCE-14CE
Sacrificial Burial No. 13, the coffin	Le-5918	1945±25	24-116CE	18-122CE
Sacrificial Burial No. 14, the coffin	Le-5919	1900±25	82-130CE	70-210 CE
Sacrificial Burial No. 10, the coffin	Le-5920	2070±40	97-41BCE	153-3 BCE
Sacrificial Burial No. 15б, the coffin	Le-5921	1990±30	2-66CE	38BCE-66CE

While the dates fall within a broad range, calibration of values by the program OxCal suggests (with a probability 95.4 %) that the burials were made in approximately the period 30-120 CE.

In sum then, we know that the complex is no earlier than the end of the first century BCE and very likely is to be dated to the first half of the first century CE.

Conclusion

The scope of the finds so far at the Tsaraam complex is impressive, and suggests that continuing the excavations in the Tsaraam Valley will add substantially to our knowledge of the Xiongnu. Apart from the main tomb of Burial Complex No. 7, the sacrificial burials around it have yielded interesting information which we have discussed elsewhere (Minaev and Sakharovskaia 2002).

The facts explained above (the large size of Barrow no. 7, human sacrificial burials, the Chinese inscription with the phrase "fit for use by the emperor", parts of the chariot) are a further confirmation of the probability that Barrow no. 7 at Tsaraam is a burial of a representative of the Xiongnu elite, possibly one of the Xiongnu *shanyu* (chieftains).

The application of modern archaeological techniques to the excavation of Complex No. 7 in the Tsaraam Valley has yielded entirely new information about Xiongnu mortuary practice, the construction of such barrows, and Xiongnu social structure. New examples of Xiongnu art and material culture were discovered. Yet much needs to be done to complete the study.

Of course, full analysis of the results of such a large excavation remains to be carried out. Conservation of the finds is the first priority. The organic materials—such items as the birch bark containers, lacquer ware, and cloth—deteriorate rapidly; it is essential that the financial means be obtained for their proper preservation.

Study of the material must include DNA and morphological analysis of the skeletal remains and of faunal and botanical samples, and component analysis of ceramic and metal objects and organic materials such as the birch bark containers, lacquer ware, and textiles. The result should provide impressive new archaeological evidence concerning the organization, chronology, and regional interaction of the Xiongnu nomadic polity. This research will complement on-going projects in Kazakhstan, Mongolia, Inner Mongolia, and Xinjiang and will contribute to the developing theories on complex organization among nomadic groups.

LIST OF ILLUSTRATIONS (Copyright © Sergei S. Minyaev)

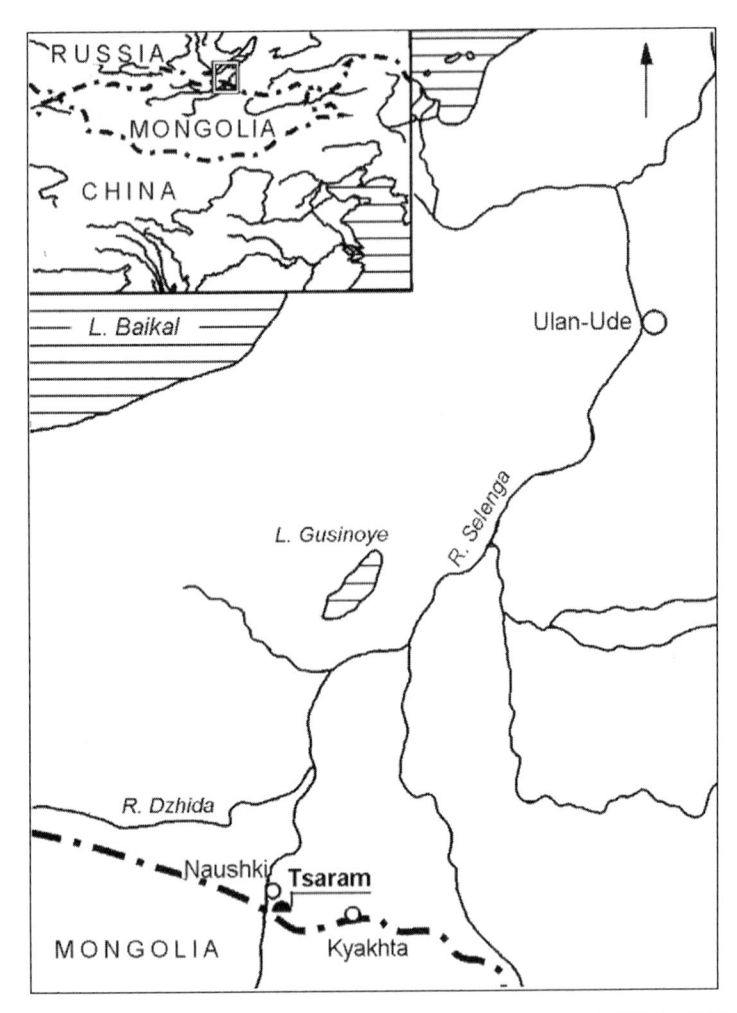

Fig. 1. Map showing location of the Tsaraam Valley

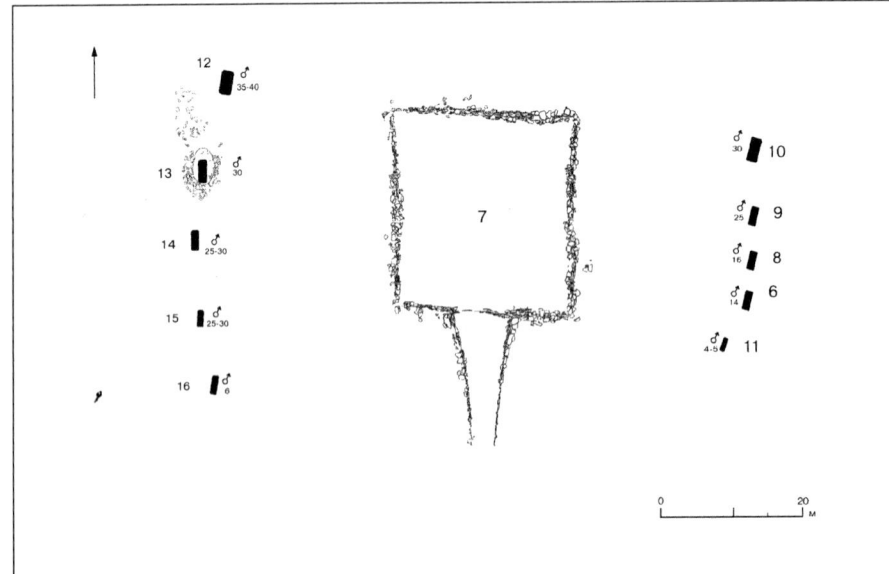

Fig. 2. Map of the complex no. 7

Fig. 3. Map of wooden construction in upper part of the burial pit

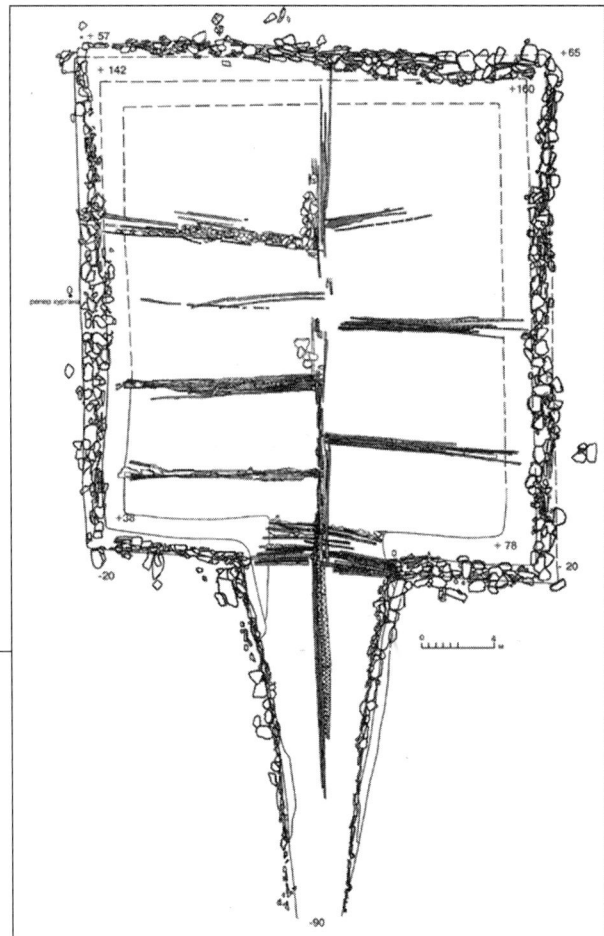

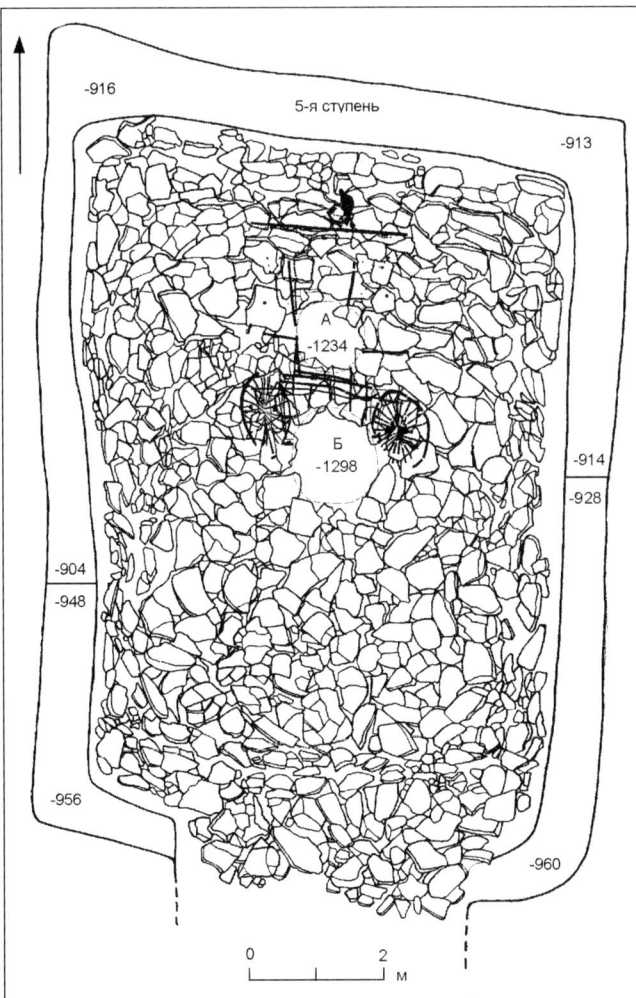

Fig. 4. Map of third cover with remains of the Chinese chariot

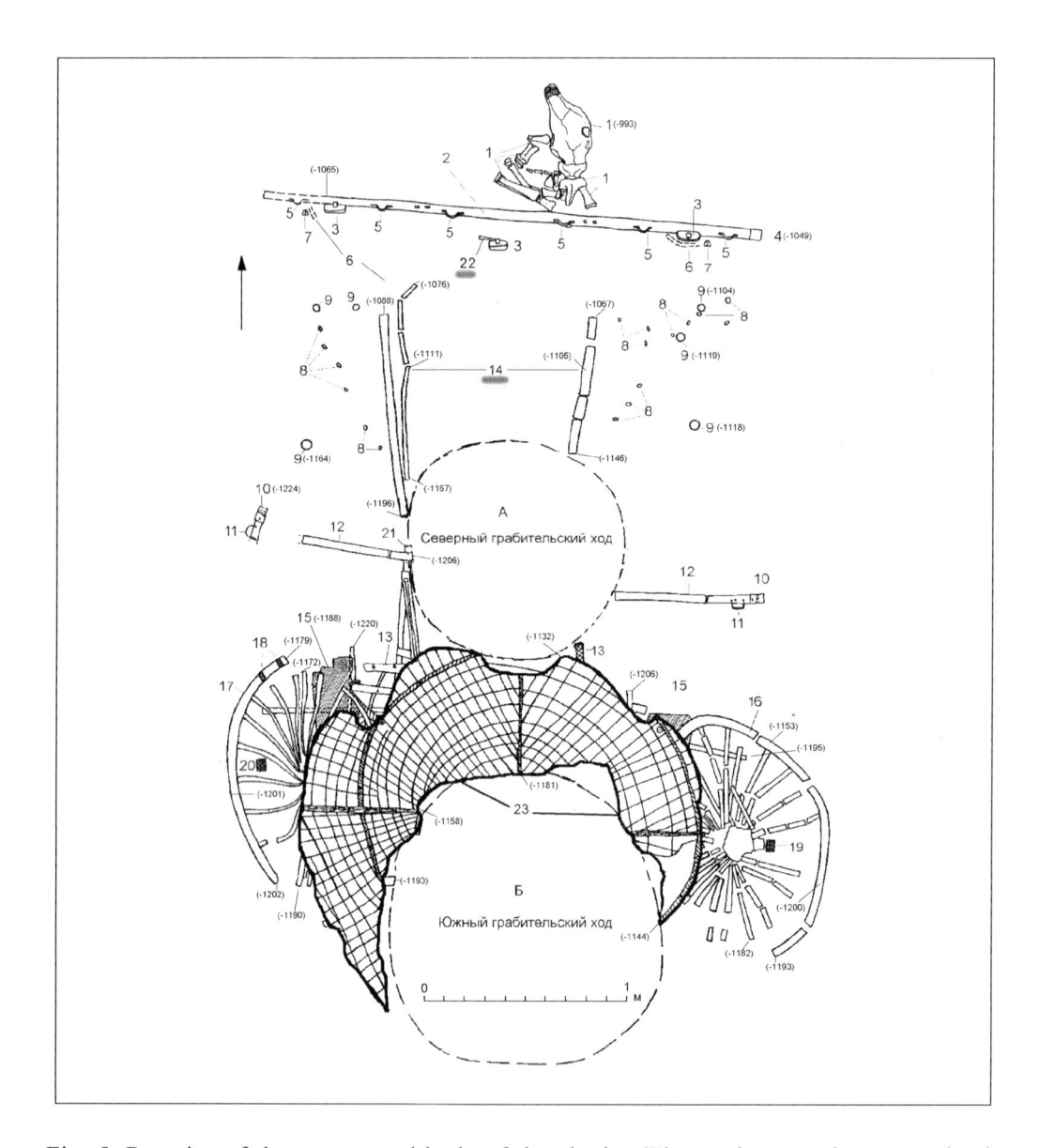

Fig. 5. Remains of the canopy and body of the chariot (Figures in parentheses are depth measurements. 1. Bones of a horse [skull and metapodials]. 2. Front yoke-pole. 3. Yoke-heads. 4. Bronze ferrule for front yoke-pole. 5. Bronze arc-shaped harness "rings." 6. Remains of thin round wooden poles. 7. Rectangular iron buckles. 8. Iron plates. 9. Iron rings. 10. Bronze ferrules for rear yoke-pole. 11. Iron rings. 12. Rear yoke-pole. 13. Remains of the lattice-work body of the chariot. 14. Shafts. 15. Elbow-rests for the seat. 16. Eastern wheel. 17. Western wheel. 18. Iron clamps. 19, 20. Small iron bushings. 21. Iron plate. 22. Bones of a lamb. 23. Canopy)

Fig. 6. Plan of the location of Doll No. 1 and nearby finds in the western corridor (*1*-iron fasteners with a transverse lug; *2*-iron belt ends; *3*-bronze mirror; *4*-birch bark barrel containers and a circle; *5*-shell hair-pins; *6*-lacquer wooden box or plate; *7*-fragment of an iron object; *8*-circular iron plates; *9*-iron holders; *10*-small wooden stick; *11*-jasper bead; *12*-lamella of red lacquer; *13*-leather straps; *14*-iron bits; *15*-iron cheek-piece of a horse harness; *16*- iron frame; *17*-plaits; *18*-fragment of a mandible; *19*-teeth; *20*-piece of mica; *21*-circular pendants of gold foil inlaid with turquoise; *22*-wooden lacquer sticks; *23*-iron plates; *24*-piece of leather; *25*-iron plate coated with red lacquer; *26*-iron rings; *27*-human cranium fragment in a plaster cast; *28*- iron screw with a ring-shaped top)

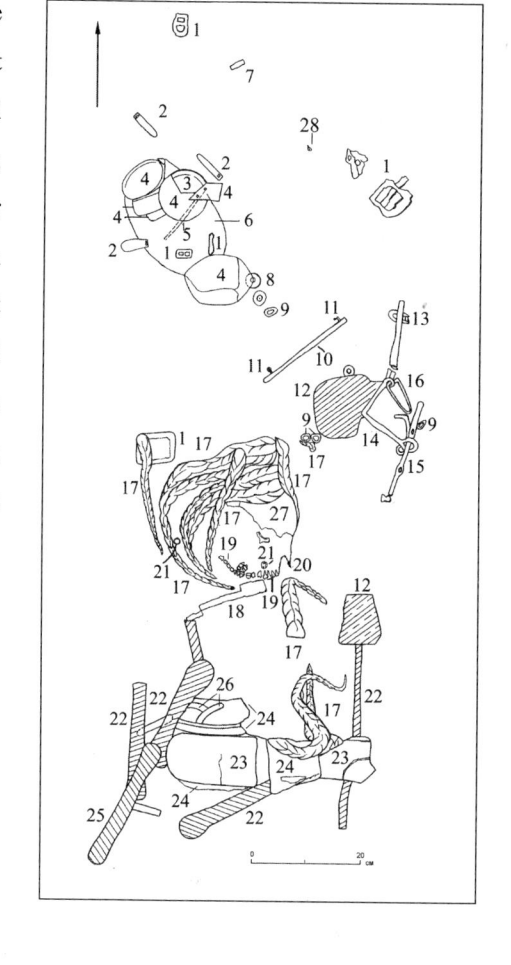

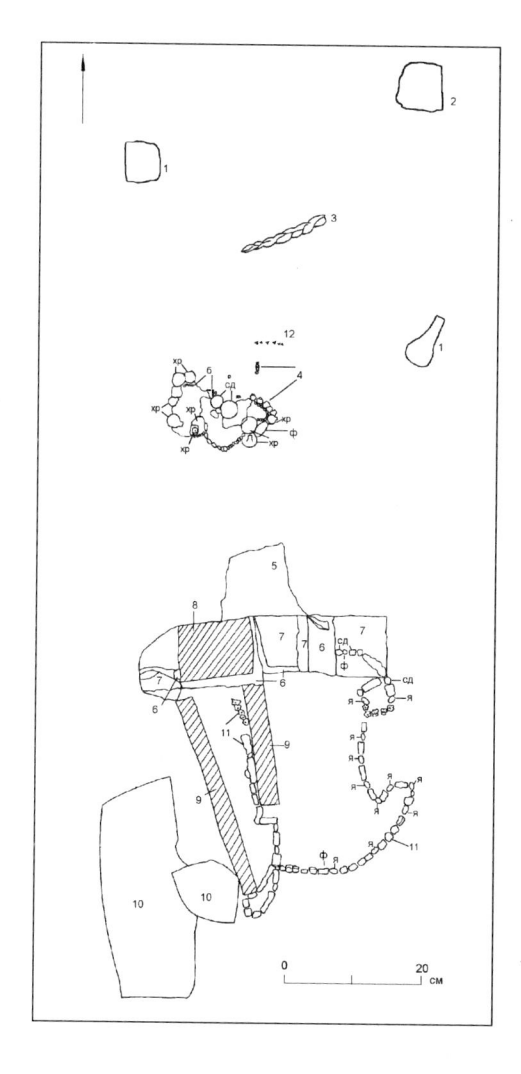

Fig. 7. Drawing of Doll No. 2 in situ in the western corridor (1. Iron objects. 2. Fragment of felt [?]. 3. Fragment of a braid. 4. A group of beads [a necklace?] [C—carnelian; T—turquoise; Cr—crystal; F— flourite; the rest-glass]. 5. Leather covered with red lacquer. 6. Leather. 7 Iron plates. 8. Wooden lacquered plate. 9. Iron plates, covered with red lacquer. 10. Fragments of a lacquered wooden container with an inscription. 11. String of beads [C—carnelian, F—fluorite, A—amber, the rest-glass]. 12. Human teeth)

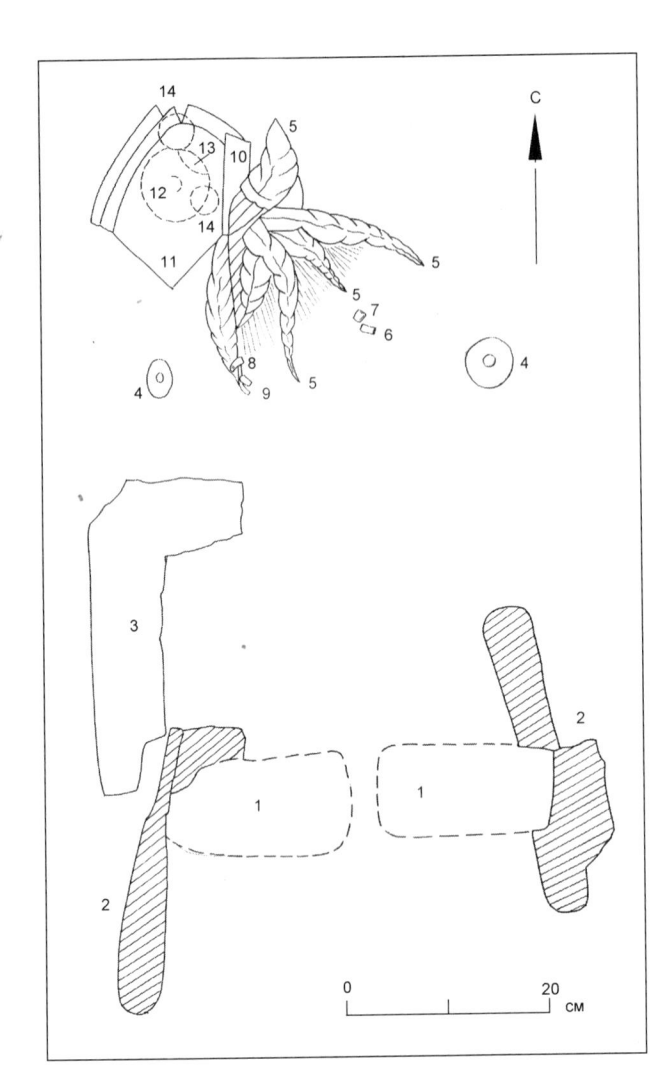

Fig. 8. Drawing of Doll No. 3 in situ in eastern corridor (1. Iron buckles. 2. Iron plate covered with red lacquer. 3. Fragments of red lacquer. 4. Wooden object covered with red lacquer. 5. Braids. 6. Fragment of clothes [?] [woolen cloth and organic material — either fur or felt]. 7. Pendants made from wall of a lacquered wooden cup. 8, 10. Turquoise beads. 9. Glass bead. 11. Amber bead. 12. Fragments of a bronze Chinese mirror. 13. Birch bark case for mirror. 14. Birch bark containers. 15. Fragments of a lacquered wooden cup. 16. Fragment of felt. 17. Hair. 18. Wooden comb. 19. Silk)

Fig. 9. Silver phalar decorating a horse harness

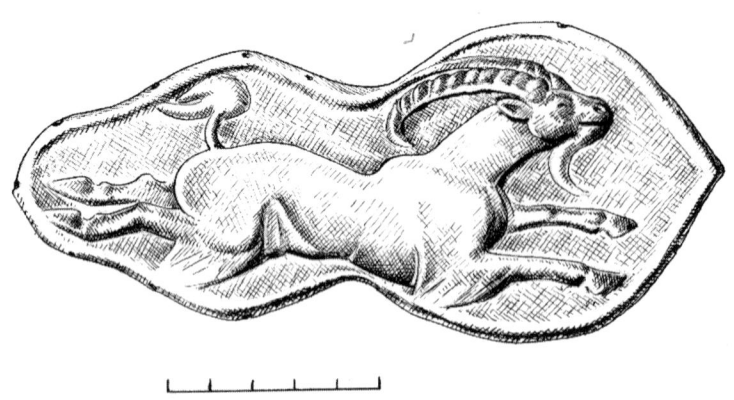

Fig. 10. Bronze plate with the figure of a jumping mountain goat

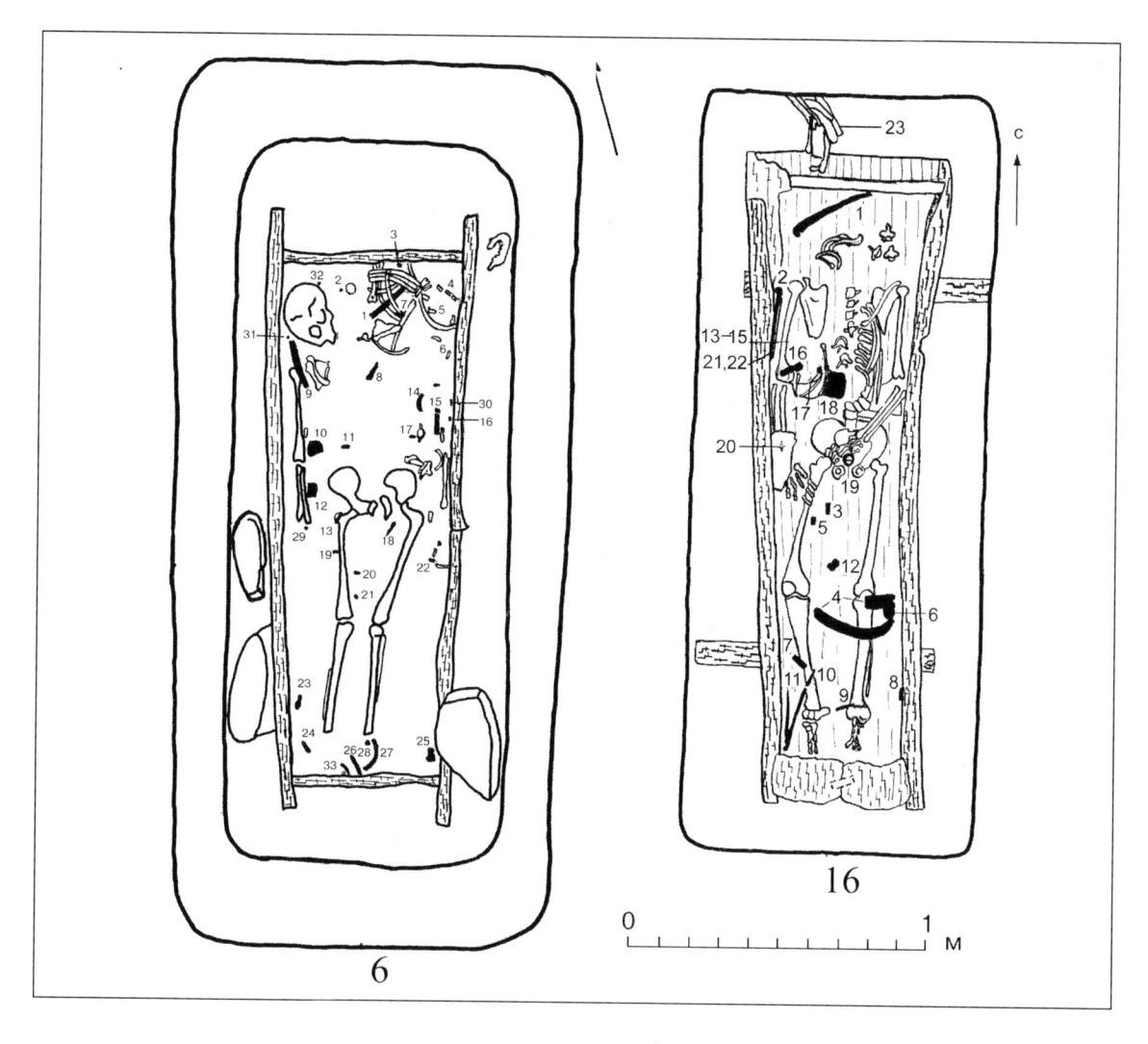

Fig.11. Sacrificial burials no. 6 and no. 16

ACKNOWLEDGEMENTS: The author is especially grateful to Dr. Maria Kolosova of the State Hermitage Museum for her classification of the wood samples, to Prof. Michele Pirazzoli t'Serstevens of The Sorbonne for her important observations regarding the Chinese inscription, and to Prof. Daniel Waugh for translation of the text from Russian.

REFERENCES

Chou Ju-hsi. *Circles of Reflection: The Carter Collection of Chinese Bronze Mirrors*. Cleveland: The Cleveland Museum of Art, 2000.

Cheng Linquan and Han Guohe. *Chang'an Han Jing* (Chang'an Han Mirrors). Xi'an: Shaanxi Renmin Chubanshe, 2002.

Cooke B. *Imperial China: The Art of the Horse in Chinese History*. Louisville, Kentucky: Harmony House, 2000.

Davydova A. *Ivolga fortress*. //*Archaeological sites of the Xiongnu*, vol. 1. St-Petersburg, 1995.

Davydova A. *Ivolga cemetery*. //*Archaeological sites of the Xiongnu*, vol. 2. St-Petersburg, 1995.

Davydova A., Minyaev S. *A complex of archaeological sites near Dureny settlement*. //*Archaeological sites of the Xiongnu*, vol. 5. St-Petersburg, 2003.

Davydova A., Minyaev S. *Xiongnu decorative bronzes*. //*Archaeological sites of the Xiongnu*, vol. 6. St-Petersburg, 2008.

Les Huns. Bruxelles: Europalia International, 2005.

Lai, Guolong. "The Date of the TLV Mirrors from the Xiongnu Tombs." *The Silk Road*, 4/1 (2006): 36-44.

Minyaev S. Dyrestuiskii mogil'nik (Derestui cemetery). *Arkheologicheskie pamiatniki siunnu*, vyp. 3. Saint-Petersburg, Evropeiskii dom, 1998.

Minyaev S., Elikhina J. On the chronology of Noen-uul barrows. *The Silk Road*, vol. 1, (2009).

Miniaev S., Sakharovskaia L. "Soprovoditel'nye zakhoroneniia 'tsarskogo' kompleksa No. 7 v mogol'nike Tsa ram." *Arkheologicheskie vesti* (St. Petersburg) 9 (2002): 86-118.

Miniaev S., Sakharovskaia L. "Investigation of a Xiongnu Royal Complex in the Tsaraam Valley." *The Silk Road* 4/1 (2006): 47-51.

Miniaev S., Sakharovskaia L. "Khan'skoe zerkalo iz mogil'nika Tsaram" (A Han Mirror from the Tsaraam Cemetery). *Zapiski Instituta istorii material'noi kul'tury* (St. Petersburg) 1 (2006): 77-82.

Miniaev S., Sakharovskaia L. "Khan'skaia kolesnitsa iz mogil'nika Tsaram" (A Han Chariot from the Tsaraam Cemetery). *Arkheologicheskie vesti* (St. Petersburg) 13 (2007): 130-140.

Pirazzoli-t'Serstevens M.A. Chinese inscription from a Xiongnu elite barrow in the Tsaraam cemetery. *The Silk Road*, 5/1, 2007, pp. 56-58.

Tal'ko-Gryntsevich Iul. Materialy k paleoetnologii Zabaikal'ia.(Materials on the Paleoethnography of the TransBaikal.). *Arkheologicheskie pamiatniki siunnu*, vyp. 4., St. Petersburg: Fond Aziatika, 1999).

V. S. Taskin, tr. and ed. *Materialy po istorii siunnu. (Po kitaiskim istochnikam)*, 2 vols. Moscow: Nauka, 1968-1973.

Wang Zhenduo. *Dong Han Che zhi Fuyuan Yanjiu* (Reconstruction and Study of the Eastern Han Chariot). Ed. and supplemented by Li Qiang. Beijing: Kexue Chubanshe, 1997.

Zhongguo Tongjing Tudian (Encyclopaedia of Chinese Mirrors). Comp. by Kong Xiangxing and Liu Yiman. Beijing:Wenwu Chubanshe, 1992 (reprinted 1997).

ON THE ORIGIN OF TURKIC STONE STATUES

HAYASHI Toshio

I. Introduction

In 545 CE, Wuwen Dai, the real power of the Western Wei, sent a Bukharan Sogdian as an envoy to the Turk-Tujue leader, Tumen, in response to his request to enter into diplomatic relations. Henceforth the friendly or hostile relations of the Tujue and the Chinese dynasties continued for two centuries, with little interruption.

Their mutual relations covered not only political and economic, but also cultural and customary, fields. It is well known that the fifth emperor of the Northern Qi sent a Chinese translator who rendered *Nirvana-sutra* from Chinese into Turkic [1] in c.574 [*BQS*: 267], and that Turkic costume, belt ornamentation and other elements, influenced the Chinese female fashion for male attire.

Some scholars consider that the stone statues at Zhaoling (the tumulus of Emperor Taizong; constructed in 636-649) and Qianling (the tumulus of Emperor Gaozong and Empress Wu; constructed in 684-706) also show the strong influences of Turkic burial customs [Cen 1958: 896; Cen 1982: 140; Ge 2002]. But others criticize this view [Chen G. 1980:189]. Did the Turkic stone statues influence Chinese stone statuary, or not? This problem is related to another question: when did the Turkic stone statues appear? If they had not existed during the First Tujue Qaghanate (552-630), then they could not have had an impact on the stone statues of Zhaoling.

I have surveyed archaeological sites in Mongolia for several seasons (in 1993, 1995-1997, 1999, 2003-2005)[2] and undertook a field trip to the Tang Emperors' tumuli in

2003. In this paper I will examine the date of the appearance of Turkic stone statues, as well as the interrelationship among Turkic, Chinese and Sogdian cultures, on the basis of my surveys and other scholars' studies.

II. Mausolea of the First Tujue Qaghanate

We know only one mausoleum which belongs undoubtedly to the First Tujue Qaghanate. This is the Bugut (Bugat) site on the western bank of Bayan Tsagaan River, Arhangaj ajmag, at a location of: N47°49′12.3″, E101°16′56.1″ (as surveyed on 2 September 2003). This site was excavated by Ts. Doržsren in 1956 and by V. E. Vojtov and S. G. Klyashtornyj in 1982. In 1997 our Japan-Mongol joint inscription expedition surveyed this site and took a rubbing of the stele with Sogdian and Brahmi inscriptions which was found here on a stone tortoise of red granite (Pl. V-1).[3] The length of the stone tortoise is 124cm, the width is 93cm at its lower part, and the height is 48cm [Moriyasu, Ochir 1999: Plate 1b]. The hole for the stele is about 36×17cm, but the depth is unknown, because the stele was tightly embedded in it with cement. The Sogdian inscription shows that it was built for the fourth Qaghan Tabo, Tatpar [4] (r.572-581) by the next Qaghan Niwar (or Išbara) (r.581-587).

On the upper part a pair of dragon heads is sculpted, but one of the heads is now lost. S. G. Klyashtornyj considered the dragons to be wolves and he found a baby's body under the wolf's belly [Kljaštornyj, Livšic 1972: 71]. But we were unable to find the baby's body (Pl. V-2).

The mausoleum is set on a rectangular platform (36 × 22m) enclosed by an inner ditch and an outer earthwork (59 × 30m) (Plate V-3) [Войтов 1996: 29]. The outer earthwork is truncated on its southeastern side, where "an entrance" might have been situated. On the northwestern part of a platform there is a square stone midden (7.5 × 7.5m), at the center of which is a hollow dug by robbers. S. G. Klyashtornyj hypothesized that under the stone heap there must be the remains of the cremation of a qaghan [Кляшторный 1984: 511]. In the center of the platform the postholes for a "shrine" were discovered by V. E. Vojtov. The "shrine" had a polygonal form with a "corridor" to the southeast [Войтов 1996: 105].[5]

We found a lot of fragments of roof tiles on the surface of the ground and in the section of a trench which had been dug by V. E. Vojtov (Plate V-4). Between the "shrine" and "entrance" lay stone pillars in a line along which they might have once stood. A row of standing stone pillars (some of them lying) extended outside of the earthwork to the southeast. V. E. Vojtov counted 258 stones extending 300 meters long outside the earthwork, but we counted only 276 (Plate V-5) [Войтов 1996: 29; Moriyasu, Hayashi 1999: 121].

According to "Account of the Northern Barbarians" in *Zhou Shu*:

> When the burial rites are over, they [the Tujue] erect stones to make a post on the grave. The number of stones corresponds to the number of [enemies] whom the dead man had killed during his lifetime. They hang the heads of sheep and horses on the post [*ZS*: 910].

The "Account of the Tujue" in *Sui Shu* adds that the number of stones sometimes amounted to a hundred or even a thousand [*SS*: 1864]. The old Turkic inscriptions or epitaphs (mostly of the 8th and 9th centuries) often mention *balbal*: "When my oldest son died of a disease, I erected General Qu (the slain general of the Khitan and Tatabi army) as a *balbal* [for him]" [Bilge Qaghan inscription, South 9; cf. Tekin 1968: 279]. Therefore it is confirmed that these stones should be called *balbal* stones.[6]

The same circumstances can be seen at the Tsetsüüh (Ider) site [7] on the eastern bank of Deed Tsetsüüh River, a tributary of Ider River, located at: N48°36′40.6″, E98°59′41.4″ (measured on 29 August 1999). This site was surveyed by S. G. Klyashtornyj and S. Haržaubai in 1976, and excavated by V. E. Vojtov and G. Menes in 1982 [Кляшторный 1984: 511-512; Войтов 1996: 22; Очир, Эрдэнэбаатар, 1999:88]. I visited this site in 1995 as a member of Japan-Mongol Historico-Ethnographical Expedition and again briefly in 1999 as a member of Japan-Mongol Archaeological Expedition.

I will illustrate the structure of this site, based on V. E. Vojtov's description and my own observation. The outer ditch is shallow and has a rectangular form, measuring about 70× 50m (Plate V-6). The inner earthwork is too low to distinguish from the inside platform. The earthwork was probably formed from the soil dug out from the ditch. The eastern earthwork has a break for an entrance, which opens to the east.

On the western part of the platform there is a very low stone heap (15m in diameter), on the center of which is a hollow opened up by robbers. S. G. Klyashtornyj suggested that under the stone heap there must be the remains of the cremation of a royal family, but this hypothesis could not be proved because the excavation was incomplete [Кляшторный1984: 511].

In the center there lies a stone tortoise (red granite) whose head was lost (Plate V-7). Its "head" faces the south, but it is unknown whether this situation is *in situ* or not. The length is 105cm, the width is 90cm in the lower part, and the height is 45cm. This is a basement for a stele but it is unfortunately now lost. In 1995 we heard from an elderly local that a stele had been there several decades before. A hole for the stele measures 40×23cm and its depth is 25cm. The size of the stone tortoise is almost the same as that of the Bugut tortoise but the size of the hole is slightly larger than that at Bugut.

In the excavated area was found a "bundle" of three logs, one of which was burnt to the base. V. E. Vojtov believed that these logs must have been columns for a roof of a "shrine" [Войтов 1996: 105]. The presence of a roof can be testified by the thousands of fragments of roof tiles which can be seen in sections of the middle layer, but the form of the "shrine" cannot be judged because of the narrow excavated area.

From the inside of the "shrine" *balbal*-stones line up to form a double file leading to the earthwork. From the outside of a ditch *balbal*-stones (210 pieces) line up in single file with a length of 308 m (Plate V-8) [Войтов 1996: 29].

The abovementioned structure of the Tsetsüüh site closely resembles that of the Bugut site in every element, and so V. E. Vojtov argued that the Tsetsüüh mausoleum was also built during the time of the First Tujue Qaghanate, although he did not specify who built it for whom [Войтов 1996: 28]. However, I have made a proposal concerning this question.

Our archaeological expedition discovered a fragment of a flat roof tile with several runic-form letters from among a pile of fragments which might have been gathered by the excavators of the former Soviet-Mongol expedition [8] (figs. 9, 10). The members of our expedition, A. Ochir and D. Erdenebaatar published a report about this tile [Очир, Эрдэнэбаатар1999].

I pointed out at the Congress in Ankara [9] that the Tsetsüüh mausoleum might have been dedicated to either the founder Bumin or to Niwar, after deciphering the short inscription on a tile fragment [Hayashi 2005a], and I now think that the founder Bumin is more appropriate and that the mausoleum might have been restored by the Third Qaghan Bilge of the Second Qaghanate period. I read a paper about these problems at the symposium held at Gorno-Altajsk in May 2009.[10] Regardless, this site also can be dated undoubtedly to the First Tujue Qaghanate.

Apart from these two sites, V. E. Vojtov listed two more sites which might have been mausolea of the First Tujue qaghans: "Gindin-bulak I" and "Sevžüül", because of the similarity of their structures [Войтов 1996: 27]. Concerning the latter,[11] he quoted only the short description by the Finnish expedition of 1909 [Halén 1982: 65], and he did not visit the site himself. In 2002 I searched for the site together with a Mongolian archaeologist, but the search proved fruitless.[12]

In 2003 I looked for the former and discovered it at the following location: N47°45′20.4″, E101°23′01.0″ (measured on 2 September 2003). However, the site is located on the eastern bank of Bayan Tsagaan River which is west from Gindin-bulak valley,[13] and I would like to designate it the Bayan-Tsagaan site.

A rectangular earthwork (measuring 57 × 41m by V. E. Vojtov, 56 × 35m by us) and a shallow inner ditch surround a platform in which there is a square construction made of plate stones, measuring 8 × 8m by V. E. Vojtov and 8.40 × 8.25m by us. From a square construction a row of *balbal*-stones extends to the east, to a distance beyond the earthwork of 732m, as measured by V. E. Vojtov, and of nearly 800m, according to our measurement. There could not have been a "shrine" at the site, because we were unable to discover any fragments of roof tiles. Nor did V. E. Vojtov find any post holes [Войтов 1996: 27]. There was also no stone statue.

I will sum up the original and foreign features of the mausolea belonging to the First Qaghanate:

1) The erected line of *balbal*-stones is of Turkic origin.[14]

2) A rectangular platform surrounded by a ditch and an earthwork is of unclear origin, but the orientation of an entrance (east or south-east) has a long tradition among the steppe nomads since the pre-Scythian period.

3) The stone construction on a platform is of unclear origin, but the "shrine" with roof tiles is of Chinese origin.

4) Setting a stele on a stone tortoise is of Chinese origin,[15] but the inscription is of western origin.

It is noteworthy that there were no stone statues at the Bugut, Tsetsüüh, and Bayan Tsagaan sites, although there were stone tortoises at the former two.

III. Did Turkic Stone Statues Exist during the First Qaghanate?[16]

Although there has been a controversy about the role of the Turkic stone statues, it is generally accepted that a Turkic stone statue commemorates the deceased [Шер 1966].

Hitherto many scholars have been convinced that the Turkic stone statues existed during the First Tujue Qaghanate,[17] on the basis of descriptions in *Zhou Shu* and *Sui Shu*. I will now examine these sources in detail. *Zhou Shu* describes the funeral customs of the Tujue as follows:

> When a man has died, the corpse is laid in his tent. Each of his children, grandchildren, male
> and female relatives kills a sheep and a horse and spreads them as offerings in front of the

tent. Then they ride on horseback and go around the tent seven times. Whenever they come to the entrance of the tent, they hurt their own faces with a sword and cry. Blood and tears flow copiously. They do so seven times and then stop. They choose a day, when they burn a horse and daily commodities of the dead with the corpse. They gather the remaining ashes and wait a time to bury them. When a man died in spring or summer, they wait till grass and trees become yellow and drop. When a man died in autumn or winter, they wait till flowers bloom and trees are in leaf. And then they make a hole and bury [the ashes]. On the burial day the relatives give offerings, ride on horseback, and hurt their own faces just like the first time ... [following passage cited previously] [ZS: 910].

The description in *Sui Shu* is quite similar but with small differences, as follows, concerning the grave:

[The relatives] erect timbers as grave-posts for the grave, in which they make a chamber. [On the walls of a chamber] the portrait and the battle scenes during his lifetime are painted [SS: 1864].[18]

Noting this difference, L. R. Kyzlasov argued that *Zhou Shu* describes a simple tomb for an ordinary nomad and that *Sui Shu* describes a painted chamber for a nobleman [Кызласов 1969: 39]. However we interpret "stones of enemies" we cannot find mention of "stone statues" in these two Chinese chronicles compiled in the 630s. We can only note mention of a painted portrait and battle scenes of the dead in *Sui Shu*. The descriptions in these chronicles cannot be considered as evidence for the existence of stone statues during the First Tujue Qaghanate.

Considering the lack of stone statues at the above-mentioned sites, Klyashtornyj and Vojtov concluded that human stone statues did not exist during the period of the First Tujue Qaghanate (552-630) [Кляшторный 1984: 512; Войтов 1986: 126; Войтов 1996: 107].

On the other hand, we have one piece of evidence for their existence during the First Qaghanate. Near the town of Zhaosu (Mongol-khülee), in the Ili district of Xinjiang, there stands a stone statue on a square platform surrounded by a deep ditch and an earthwork but without *balbal*-stones [Otsuka 1995:57]. On the lower part of this statue there can be deciphered a Sogdian inscription dated to the second half of the 6th century (Plate V-11). This deciphering and dating were proposed by the Japanese Iranologist, Yoshida Yutaka [Yoshida 1991: 76]. If his dating is correct then we must accept that a Turkic stone statue existed during the First Tujue period, at least in the western territory of the Tujue Qaghanate.

Otherwise the Sogdian inscription was first inscribed on the stele during the First Qaghanate and the stele was later remade into a stone statue during the Second Qaghanate.

After the collapse of the First Qaghanate in 630, the Xueyantuo led by Yinan Qaghan dominated the Mongolian plateau for a brief period. V. E. Vojtov argued that the Ungetu (or Unegt) site might have been the mausoleum of Yinan [Войтов 1987: 104-107]. This site is located on the northern bank of the Tuul (Tola) River: N47°33′12.3″, E105°50′59.3″ (measured on 26 September 2002). B. Ya. Vladimirtsov and G. I. Borovka partly excavated the site in 1925 and discovered rounded roof tiles with a lotus ornament (Plate V-12) [Боровка 1927: 77-78]. At the end of the 1970s V. E. Vojtov and D. Bayar excavated the western and eastern parts of a platform at the site.

The platform is surrounded by an inner ditch and an outer earthwork (60 × 40m) [Войтов 1996: 29]. In the western part of the platform there was a large sarcophagus of four plate stones on which a "shrine" with roof tiles might have stood, but neither a stone tortoise nor a stele was found. However, they did discover nearly 30 human stone statues and seated figures of a stone lion and a stone sheep at the site.[19] Outside the earthwork, 552 *balbal*-stones stood in a line extending to east-southeast for a distance of 2200m.

The representations of the Ungetu statues are unique. Their eyes and mouths are represented as round. The hands are placed on the chest and they hold neither vessels nor weapons (Plate V-13). D. Bayar first thought that the Ungetu statues were made by the Rouran, the predecessors of the Tujue, because of their "primitiveness" [Баяр 1978: 15-16]. But the grounds for his view are very weak, as he himself told me when he later revised his earlier view. It is certain that the thirty statues do not depict the qaghan. Such roughly made statues might have been a kind of *balbal*-stone [Войтов 1996: 86-87]. Roughly made statues with clasped hands in front of the chest can also be seen at the Köl Tegin mausoleum site (Plate V-14).

On the other hand, Vojtov asserted that the Ungetu mausoleum was dedicated to the qaghan of the Xueyantuo, Yinan, just after his death in 645. His main arguments are as follows: 1) two strata can be recognized at the site and the upper stratum seems to belong to the Second Tujue Qaghanate; and 2) *Xin Tang Shu* records that Yinan was domiciled north of the Tola (Tuul) River after the decline of the First Qaghanate [Войтов 1987: 104-107]. Although he himself told me that his theory is not too solid, I believe his view is worth reexamining.

It is noteworthy that the seated figures of a stone lion and a stone sheep and the roof tile-ends with lotus ornaments found at this site are clearly of Chinese origin.

IV. Stone Statues at Chinese Emperors' Tumuli

In China stone statues first appeared during the reign of Emperor Wudi (r. 141-87 BCE) of the Western Han in front of the tumulus of General Huo Qubing, but these became popular during the Eastern Han period (25-220 CE). However, most were of animals: lions, sheep, fantastic beasts, etc. On the contrary, life-sized human stone statues were very few (only two pairs are known), and they appeared at the end of the Eastern Han. These two pairs of statues might have been erected in front of local governors' tombs as guardians in Shandong province (Plate V-15) [Li 2004: 60-61].[20] Stone tortoise bases for steles also appeared at the end of the Eastern Han, as I mentioned in endnote 15.

During the Wei-Jin period (220-316) the rulers restrained themselves from constructing large-scale tumuli and erecting stone sculptures. The Eastern Jin Dynasty (317-410) which controlled the southern part of China continued this policy of restraint. During the Southern Dynasties (Song, Qi, Liang, Chen) a pair of stone *qilin*s (horned and winged lions) was erected in front of the rulers' tumuli, but the human stone statue was unknown [Paludan 1991; Hayashi 2006b].

In Northern China, the construction of royal tumuli revived during the reign of Emperor Xiaowen (r. 471-499) and his mother, Empress Dowager Wenming of the Northern Wei, who implemented a policy of Sinicization. To the south of the tumulus for the Empress Dowager were arranged a shrine, stone gates, a stele, and stone animals. According to Yang Kuan, the shrine was similar to the stone chamber celebrating Xianbei origins, but the other elements were introduced from Eastern Han Confucianism and Buddhism [Yang 1981: 71; 2003: 50]. Unfortunately all of the stone figures were lost, but it seems that there had been no human statue.

Human stone statues reappeared at the end of the Northern Wei. In 1991 a large stone statue without a head (height: 2.89 m) was found to the south of the mausoleum, Jingling, of Emperor Xuanwudi (Plate V-16) (r. 499-515). This statue holds a sword in its hands [Kitamura 2001: 172; Li 2004: 61].

In 1976 a similar stone statue of a figure holding a sword in its hands (3.14m in height), a head of a statue, and a sitting stone lion [21] were discovered just by the tumulus which has been confirmed to be Jingling of Emperor Xiaozhuang (buried in 531) [Huang 1978: 39; Paludan 1991: 83; Ren 1995: 159; Yang 1981: 112; 2003: 83, 85]. It is clear that these human statues played a role as imperial guardians [Yang 1981: 112-113; 2003: 85].

After the split into the Eastern and Western Wei Dynasties, stone animals and human statues were also erected beside the Yongling mausoleum of Emperor Wen of the Western Wei (buried in 551) [Ren 1995: 160]. But most of them have disappeared. In 1987 the tumulus of Gaocheng (buried in 549), the ruler of Eastern Wei, was excavated. On the south of the tumulus the excavators discovered a stone human statue, which must have once been one of a pair. There were, however, no human stone statues in front of the tumuli of emperors of the Northern Zhou (556-581) and Sui (581-618).

Ancient China thus had a tradition of erecting stone statues beside rulers' tumuli from the end of the Eastern Han. After a break of two or three centuries, this tradition was revived at the beginning of the 6th century in the Northern Wei Dynasty just before the birth of the Tujue First Qaghanate.

V. Zhaoling (Tumulus of Emperor Taizong) and the Shiveet-ulaan Site

The tumuli of the grandfather and father of the first Tang emperor, Li Yuan, were constructed in 618, just after the establishment of the Tang Dynasty, and the tumulus of Li Yuan himself was constructed in 635. These earliest tumuli of the Tang Dynasty were accompanied by stone animals and human statues [Chen 2001: 40; Liu 2003: 5]. According to Liu Xiangyang, a pair of stone human statues at the tumulus of the grandfather of Li Yuan represent military officers and are similar to statues at the Jingling mausoleum of Emperor Xiaozhuang of the Northern Wei [Liu 2003: 305].

The Zhaoling tumulus of the second emperor, Taizong, is a natural mountain, Jiuzongshan (1188 meters above sea level), but the mountain was largely remodeled.[22] The construction of Zhaoling was begun in 636 and completed in 649. On the southern slope the underground funerary palace and many tombs of princesses and retainers are arranged. In front of the funerary palace there must have been erected a pair of stone lions, which were later moved to a village south of the site.

On the northern slope, just beneath its summit, was constructed the mausoleum shrine, from which five steps continued downwards to the north (Plate V-17). On these steps stood the famous reliefs of the "Six Swift Horses" and fourteen stone statues of barbarian chiefs of the Tujue, Xueyantuo, Gaochang [Turfan], Tufan [Tibet], and other nations either subjugated by Tang or in peaceful relationships with Tang.

Fourteen statues were carved during the years 650-655. According to *Zizhi Tongjian*, when Taizong was buried in Zhaoling, some of the barbarian chiefs who were subjugated or had surrendered, wished to follow Taizong to the grave. However, the following emperor, Gaozong, dissuaded them from suicide. He ordered that the statues of the fourteen barbarian chiefs (some of whom had already died a few years before Taizong's death) be carved in stone, and that their names be carved on stones which were then lined up them inside the North Sima Gate [*Zizhi Tongjian* 199: 6269]. [23]

After the late-Qing period (in the 19th century) most were destroyed, but some of them and their stone bases were discovered during recent excavations by Chinese archaeologists. In October 2003 I visited the excavation site and could take photographs of the findings by virtue of the courtesy of the leader of the excavation team, Dr. Zhang Jianlin 張建林. I could verify that there were two statues with their hands in sleeves. Some statues featured typical Turkic hair styles (Plate V-18), which can be seen on many Turkic stone statues and on the paintings of Turkic delegates at Afrasiab (Samarkand).

In front of the tombs of princesses and retainers, most of whom died in the 640s-660s, there are arranged various stone monuments: pillars, steles on tortoises, tigers, sheep and guardians holding a sword.

There is a unique and interesting mausoleum of a Tujue royal family member (surely a qaghan), to be found at the Shiveet-ulaan site in Bulgan aimak, central North Mongolia. The location and the structure of this site are quite similar to Zhaoling but completely different from other Turkic royal mausolea. The mausoleum is located on the top of a hill, from which we have a fine view of the vast valley where the Hanüi River joins the Hünüi River, although other royal Turkic mausolea are located on the flat plain.

This site is surrounded by a stone rectangular enclosure (100 × 40m) with stone mounds at each corner and between the corners just like the ramparts of a castle (Plate V-19). In the western most elevated section lies a big stone mound (d: 35m) on which a hole was dug by robbers. At the eastern foot of a mound and on the lower eastern platform many human and animal statues stand and lie.

According to S. G. Klyashtornyj and V. E. Vojtov, in the hole there were many fragments of bricks and roof tiles which might have been parts of a shrine [Кляшторный 1978: 575; Войтов 1996: 30]. However, we could not find even a single brick or tile (I visited the site on three occasions-in 1996, 1997, and 2003). So I cannot say whether a building existed or not.

Human statues are all standing figures. At the mausolea sites for qaghans and royal family members of the Second Qaghanate, a cross-legged seated figure should have represented a commemorated deceased person. Consequently, standing figures could be interpreted as servants or guardians. It is not clear whether the statue of the deceased was not made or whether the statue has not yet been unearthed.

Most of the standing figures clasp their hands in front of their chests. Their hands are placed in their sleeves or they hold a cup. Some hold a baton or a sword. The triangular turndown collar is of Sogdian origin. Carved pochettes hang from the belts of the statues on the right side, and these objects would have been used by the living to hold fire-striking steels, flints, or talismans, in conformity to Turkic custom. These Sogdian and Turkic customs and styles were also popular in Tang China. We see servants with such foreign accoutrements in many mural paintings in Tang royal tombs.

Now all the heads of the statues have been lost. However, when G. J. Ramstedt visited here in 1912, he saw only one statue with a head [24] [Ramstedt *et al.* 1958: 82]. The statue wore a tall cap, and had large eyes, a big nose, and a heavy moustache (Plate V-20). Moriyasu Takao considers that the statue looks like a Sogdian [Moriyasu, Ochir 1999:141].

The stone animals are represented as seated figures (Plate V-21) except for one running lamb. At the left leg of one of the stone lions we can see a mountain goat or *tamga*, a signifier of the Ashina clan, the ruling family of the Tujue Qaghanate. Some statues might be possibly hidden under the stone mound. In 2003 we found a lion in a half-exposed situation, indicating that someone must have tried to dig it up.

Out of the eastern enclosure there is a stone base for a stele. The stele is now kept in a temple in the nearby town of Hairhan.[25] On the surface of the stele there are various roughly carved *tamga*s (Plate V-22). The opposite surface is uneven and, of course, bears neither sign nor letter. According to S. G. Klyashtornyj, the *tamga*s could number as many as seventy; this number coincides with the seventy persons who participated in the raising of Ilterish, Qutlugh Qaghan, the founder of the Second Tujue Qaghanate. He therefore believed this site, Shiveet-ulaan, to be the mausoleum for Qutlugh Qaghan (d. 692).

V. E. Vojtov agreed with this view and furthermore considered that this stele might have been one "common *balbal*" into which many *balbal*-stones were coordinated.[26]

According to our observation, the *tamga*s are carved roughly and scattered in a disorderly fashion, while the surface of the stele is polished smoothly. Therefore we cannot believe that this stele was made for carving *tamga*s. We believe that this stele might have been originally prepared for describing the achievements of the commemorated dead hero but it was not used for its primary purpose and the *tamga*s were subsequently carved on it secondarily [Moriyasu, Ochir 1999: 142].

On the other hand, V. D. Kubarev and D. Bayar believed that the Shiveet-ulaan site inherited the Ungetu site where only human standing figures exist, and they dated the site to the first half of the 8th century [Kubarev, Bayar 2002: 84].

V. E. Vojtov was of the view that the roughly-made human figures, clasping both hands in front of their chests, might have been erected as *balbal*-stones (Plate V-14). I agree with him, and so believe the Ungetu stone statues to be *balbal*-stones.

The Shiveet-ulaan statues were made more elaborately with concrete expression of costumes, belts, cups, pochettes, swords, and so on, while the Ungetu statues only show the face and hands. Therefore, the Shiveet-ulaan statues must have had another origin. I think that they were made under the influence of Zhaoling, and the location, the structure and the site might have been made for Ilterish Qaghan (d. 692) who lived under Tang rule.

VI. Concluding Remarks

Ancient China had a tradition of erecting stone animals and a pair of stone human statues as guardians in front of tombs beginning in the Eastern Han Dynasty. This tradition was broken for two or three centuries and revived at the end of the Northern Wei Dynasty. The Tang Dynasty clearly inherited that tradition from the Southern and Northern Dynasties but not from the Tujue (see Table at the end of this article).[27]

The royal family of the First Tujue Qaghanate of the eastern territory received a stele on a stone tortoise and tile-ends with lotus ornaments from China, and inscriptions and possibly funeral paintings from the Sogdians. But the custom of erecting *balbal*s was of local origin.

Only one statue, with a Sogdian inscription and found in Zhaosu (Ili district), may have dated to the First Qaghanate. If we accept this dating, we have to consider that a human statue appeared in the western territories of the Tujue earlier than in their eastern territories. Or the stele with the inscription of the First Qaghanate might have been re-made into a human statue during the Second Qaghanate.

After the collapse of the First Qaghanate, the qaghan family of the Xueyantuo might have erected roughly made human statues as *balbal*s and received animal statues from China, but this is not certain.

The royal family of the Second Qaghanate received human statues of servants and animal statues from China. They also fashioned a statue of the deceased hero, but this was a unique custom of the Tujue which did not come from China.

Thus, the Tujue-Turks of the eastern territories developed their own funerary customs, receiving Chinese and Sogdian cultural elements. And of course, the Chinese and Sogdians in turn received elements of Turkic culture. The Turkic, Chinese and Sogdian cultural complex was widely distributed in Northern China and Mongolia during the 6th-8th (or 9th) centuries.

NOTES

[1] It is not known what script was used to transcribe the Turkic language.

[2] During those seasons I surveyed not only the sites of the Turkic period but also earlier sites.

[3] The stele on the stone tortoise is now kept in the Museum of Arhangaj Ajmag. The Sogdian inscription on three sides of the stele is comparatively well preserved, while the Brahmi inscription on the reverse can scarcely be deciphered because it is worn away [Yoshida, Moriyasu 1999: 125].

[4] Hitherto this name has been transcribed as "Taspar" [Klyaštornyj, Livšic 1972: 74], but Yoshida Y. and Moriyasu T. propose that it be read "Tatpar" [Yoshida, Moriyasu 1999: 123], and they are followed in this by V. Rybatzki [Rybatzki 2000: 216].

[5] As a similar example, he cites the octagonal *yurt*-like "shrine" of Saryg-Bulun in Tuva which was built undoubtedly during the Second Tujue Qaghanate [Кызласов 1969: ris.7]. He therefore believes that the architectural tradition was long retained-from the First to the Second Tujue Qaghanate [Войтов 1996: 105].

[6] The word *balbal* has been used to indicate Turkic stone statues in academic and popular literature. However, *balbal* indicates a stone symbolizing a slain enemy, although some *balbal*s were roughly carved into human figures. So how did the Turks refer to a stone statue? S. G. Klyashtornyj proposed a theory that the word *bediz* might have been used to signify a stone statue [Кляшторный 1978: 244-248]. This word has a meaning of "decoration", but it is unclear whether it also has the meaning of "stone statue".

[7] V. E. Vojtov and S. G. Klyashtornyj call this site "Ider", but Ider is a name of a long river, along which there are many archaeological sites. This site is in fact located in the Valley of Deed Tsetsüüh River. Consequently the name "Tsetsüüh" which A. Ochir and D. Erdenebaatar adopted for the site is better [Очир, Эрдэнэбаатар: 1999].

[8] When I visited Moscow in 2004, I met Dr. Vojtov and asked him about this fragment, but he knew nothing about it.

[9] XIV. Türk Tarih Kongresi.

[10] The symposium was organized by Gorno-Altajsk State University and Frankfurt University under the leadership of Dr. M. Erdal.

[11] It is said that the site might have been located in present day Utgal-Tsaydam sum, Töv ajmag [Войтов 1996: 146].

[12] My friend Osawa Takashi told me that he recently discovered the Sevžüül site.

[13] The site is located 7.5km south-southeast from the Bugut site, although Vojtov describes it as being "10-12km east-northeast from the Bugut" [Войтов 1996: 146]. He must have confused this site with his "Bayan-Tsagan" [Войтов 1996: 148].

[14] Some of the Pazyryk kurgans are accompanied by a row of stones. I have also seen such an example in Northwest Mongolia. The custom of standing a row of stones by a kurgan may date back to the Scythian period.

[15] The practice of placing a stele on a stone tortoise first appeared at the end of the Eastern Han [Cao 1963: 66; Paludan 1991: 50-51; Hirase 1993: 4]. In the Tujue Qaghanate a stele on a stone tortoise was erected by a qaghan's mausoleum, although in China it was erected by the tomb of a subject or royal family member, except for the emperor. In the Uygur Qaghanate a stele on a stone tortoise had no relationship with a tomb or mausoleum, because the second qaghan, Gele, erected several such stelae.

[16] I have published an article and a book about various problems including the appearance and disappearance of the Turkic stone statues [Hayashi 2001; 2005b].

[17] For example, Yu. S. Khudyakov and Yu. A. Plotnikov propose that: (1) only rectangular stone enclosures appeared in the 4th-5th centuries; (2) stone statues with engraved faces were erected beside enclosures during the First Tujue Qaghanate; and (3) stone sculptures not only with faces but also with representations of dress and weapons continued from the Second Tujue Qaghanate until the end of the 10th century [Худяков, Плотников 1990: 124].

[18] Since the 1990s several Sogdian tombs have been discovered in the Central Plains, near China's ancient capitals. They are dated to the end of the Northern Dynasties and the Sui-Tang dynasties. It is noteworthy that various scenes from the lifetime of the deceased are depicted on the painted reliefs on stone panels of sarcophagus [MIHO 1997; Shaanxi-sheng 2003]. This funerary custom must have influenced the Tujue.

[19] Some of the statues had been kept in the Manjushri Open Museum near Zuun Mod, Töv ajmag, but recently they were returned to the Ungetu site.

[20] Several other stone statues of the same period are known in Sichuan province but these are not funerary [Paludan 1991: 46-49]. Also in Shandong province several stone statues (height: 1.1-1.5m) belonging to the Eastern Han and Wei-Jin periods have been found but their function is unknown [Li 2004: 62-64].

[21] This is the earliest example of a seated stone lion. All stone lions, including horned and winged versions, had previously been represented in the standing position.

[22] This was the first tumulus using a natural mountain. Most of the Tang emperors' tumuli were constructed by remodeling natural mountains.

[23] Liu Mau-tsai translated this passage into German: "innerhalb des nördlichen Aussentors des *Palastes*" [Liu 1958: 675] (itals. -Hayashi). Based on this translation, Ya. A. Sher misunderstood that those statues had been erected in the *palace*, not in front of a tomb. So he assumed that those statues had no relationship to

the Turkic stone statues which were erected in front of funerary sites [Шер 1966: 37].

[24] The photograph which was published in 1958 is reversed from right to left.

[25] Now the stele is used as a plate on which Lamaists pray with their bodies stretched out.

[26] *Balbal*-stones (ordinarily small or tall stones) must have represented enemies slain by the deceased warrior during his lifetime. Some of *balbal*-stones clearly depict human figures.

[27] Kitamura Takao also believes that the Tang statues of military officers inherited the tradition of the Northern Dynasties [Kitamura 2001: 172].

BIBLIOGRAPHY

Д. Баяр, 1978, "Tuulyn höndii deh türegiin ömnöh üeiin hün chuluuny tuhai" (On the stone statues of the pre-Turkic period along the Tuul River), *Studia Archaeologica* VII-10 (Улаанбаатар: 1978), 3-22.

Г. И. Боровка, "Археологическое обследование среднего течения р. Толы," in *Северная Монголия* II (Л.: 1927), 43-88.

BQS 《北齊書》 *Bei Qi Shu*, Beijing: Zhonghua Shuju, 1972.

Cao Dan 曹丹, "Lushan-xian Han Fan Min que qingli fuyuan" 蘆山縣漢樊敏闕清理復原 (The preliminary excavation and reconstruction of the tomb gate-tower of Fan Min of the Han in Lushan prefecture), *Wenwu* 《文物》, 1963-11, 65-66.

Cen Zhongmian 岑仲勉, *Tujue Jishi* 《突厥集史》 (Collection of Historical Sources on the Tujue), Beijing: Zhonghua Shuju, 1958.

Cen Zhongmian 岑仲勉, *Sui-Tang Shi* 《隋唐史》 (History of Sui and Tang), Beijing: Zhonghua Shuju, 1985.

Chen Anli 陳安利, *Tang Shiba Ling* 《唐十八陵》 (Eighteen Tumuli of the Tang Dynasty), Beijing: Zhonghua Qingnian Chubanshe, 2001.

Chen Guocan 陳國燦, "Tang Qianling shirenxiang jiqi xianming de yanjiu" 唐乾陵石人像及其銜名的研究 (A study on the Tang Dynasty Qianling stone statues and their names), *Wenwu Jikan* 《文物集刊》, 1980-2, 189-203.

Ge Chengyong 葛承雍, "Tang Zhaoling, Qianling fanren shixiang yu 'Tujuehua' wenti" 唐昭陵、乾陵蕃人石像與 "突厥化" 問題 (The stone statues of westerners at the Zhaoling and Qianling mausolea and the problem of Turkic features), *Ou-Ya Xuekan* 《歐亞學刊》, 2001-3, 150-162.

Harry Halén, *Memoria Saecularis Sakari Pälsi* (Helsinki: Suomalais-Ugrilainen Seura, 1982).

Hayashi Toshio 林俊雄, "Tokketsu no sekijin ni mirareru Sogudo no eikyou" 突厥の石人に見られるソグドの影響 (The Sogdian influences on Turkic stone statues), *Jinbun-Ronsyu (Soka University)* 《創價大學人文論集》, 1993-5, 27-44.

Hayashi Toshio 林俊雄, "Mongoria no sekijin" モンゴリアの石人 (Stone statues in Mongolia), *Bulletin of the*

National Museum of Ethnology (Osaka), 1996 21(1), 177-283.

Hayashi Toshio 林俊雄, "East-West exchanges as seen through the dissemination of the griffin motif", in Cs. Bálint, ed., *Kontakte zwischen Iran, Byzanz und der Steppe im 6.-7. Jahrhundert* (Budapest: Paulus-Publishing Verlag, 2000), 253-265.

Hayashi Toshio 林俊雄, "Several problems about the Turkic stone statues", *Yearbook of Turkic Studies* (Ankara, 2001), 221-240.

Hayashi Toshio 林俊雄, "Runic inscription on a roof tile found in Mongolia", in *XIV. Türk Tarih Kongresi III* (Ankara: Türk Tarih Kurumu, 2005a), 577-580, 4 figs.

Hayashi Toshio 林俊雄, *Yurasia no Sekijin* ユーラシアの石人 (Stone Statues in Eurasia) (Tokyo: Yuzankaku, 2005b).

Hayashi Toshio 林俊雄, "Sogdian influences seen on Turkic stone statues: Focusing on the fingers representations," in Matteo Compareti *et al.*, ed., *Eran ud Aneran: Studies Presented to Boris Il'ič Maršak on the Occasion of His 70th Birthday* (Venezia: Librairie Editrice Cafoscarina, 2006a), 245-259.

Hayashi Toshio 林俊雄, *Gurifin no Hishou* グリフィンの飛翔 (Flights of Griffins) (Tokyo: Yuzankaku, 2006b).

Hirase Takao 平勢隆郎, "Nihon kinsei no kifu-hi: Chuugoku oyobi Chousen hantou no rekidai kifu-hi to no hikaku wo tooshite" 日本近世の龜趺碑——中國および朝鮮半島の歷代龜趺碑との比較を通して (Tortoise-based stelae in the Edo period: In comparison with those from the Eastern Han Dynasty in China and from the Unified Silla Dynasty in Korea), *Toyo Bunka Kenkyuusho Kiyou*《東洋文化研究所紀要》, 1993 121, 1-85.

Huang Minglan 黃明蘭, "Luoyang Bei-Wei Jingling weizhi-de queding he Jingling weizhi-de tuice" 洛陽北魏景陵位置的確定和靜陵位置的推測 (Decision on the location of Jingling and conjecture on the location of Jingling of the Northern Wei in Luoyang), *Wenwu*《文物》, 1978-7, 36-39, 22.

Ю.С. Худяков, Ю. А. Плотников, "Древнетюркские каменные изваяния в южной части Убснурской котловины," in *Археологические, этнографические и антропологические исследования в Монголии* (Новосибирск, 1990), 111-125.

Kitamura Takasi 來村多加史, *Tou-dai Koutei-ryou no Kenkyuu*《唐代皇帝陵の研究》(Studies on the Tang Emperors' Tumuli) (Tokyo: Gakuseisha, 2001).

С. Г. Кляшторный, "Храм, изваяние и стела в древнетюркских текстах," in *Тюркологический сборник 1974* (М.: Наука, 1978), 238-255.

С. Г. Кляшторный, "Советско-Монгольская экспедиция," in *Археологические открытия 1982 года* (М.: Наука, 1984), 511-512.

S. G. Kljaštornyj, and Livšic, V. A., "The Sogdian inscription of Bugut revised", *Acta Orientalia Academiae Scientiarum Hungaricae*, 1972:26 (1), 69-102.

Л. Р. Кызласов, *История Тувы в средние века* (М.: Издательство Московского Университета, 1969).

Li Ling 李零, *Rushan yu Chusai*《入山與出塞》(Entering the Mountains and Crossing the Borders), Beijing:

Wenwu Chubanshe, 2004.

Liu Xiangyang 劉向陽, *Tangdai Diwang Lingmu* 唐代帝王陵墓 (Tumuli of the Emperors of Tang Dynasty), Xi'an: Sanqin Chubanshe, 2003.

MIHO MUSEUM, ed., *MIHO MUSEUM Minami-kan* MIHO MUSEUM 南館 (Catalogue of South Wing of MIHO MUSEUM) (Shiga: MIHO MSEUM, 1997).

Moriyasu Takao 森安孝夫, Hayashi Toshio, "Site of Bugut," in the following Report, p.121.

Moriyasu Takao, A. Ochir, ed., *Provisional Report of Researches on Historical Sites and Inscriptions in Mongolia from 1996 to 1998* (Osaka: The Society of Central Eurasian Studies, 1999).

А. Очир, Эрдэнэбаатар, Д., "Tsetsüühiin bichees" (Tsetsüüh inscription), *Studia Archaeologica*, 1999, XIX (10), 88-90.

Otsuka Noriyoshi 大塚紀宜, "Iwayuru Tokketsu no sekijin-bo ni tsuite" いわゆる突厥の石人墓について (On the so-called Tujue's stone statue tombs), in *Shiruku-roodo ni yotte musubareta, Chuugoku Shinkyou chiku to wagakuni Kyuushuu Chiku tono hikaku koukogaku-teki kenkyuu* 《シルクロードによって結ばれた、中國新疆地区と我が國九州地區との比較考古學的研究》 (A Comparative Archaeological Study of Xinjiang and Kyushu on the "Silk Road") (Fukuoka: Kyushu University, 1995).

A. Paludan, *The Chinese Spirit Road*, New Haven & London: Yale University Press, 1991.

Ren Changtai 任常泰, *Zhongguo Lingqin Shi*《中國陵寢史》 (History of Tumuli and Mausolea in China), Taipei: Wenjin Chubanshe, 1993.

V. Rybatzki, *Die Toñuquq-Inschrift*. Szeged: University of Szeged, 1997.

Shaanxi-sheng Kaogu Yanjiusuo 陝西省考古研究所, *Xi'an Bei-Zhou An Jia Mu*《西安北周安伽墓》 (The Tomb of An Jia of the Northern Zhou in Xi'an), Beijing: Wenwu Chubanshe, 2003.

Я. А. Шер, *Каменные изваяния Семиречья* (М.-Л.: Наука, 1966).

SS《隋書》*Sui Shu*, Beijing: Zhonghua Shuju, 1973.

T. Tekin, *A Grammar of Orkhon Turkic*, Bloomington: Indiana University, 1968.

В. Е. Войтов, "Археологические исследования В. Я. Владимирцова и новые открытия в Монголии," *Mongolica* (М.: Наука, 1986), 118-136.

В. Е. Войтов, "Каменные изваяния из Унгету," in *Центральная азия, новые памятники, письменности и искусства* (М., 1987), 92-109.

В. Е. Войтов, *Древнетюркский пантеон и модель мироздание* (М.: Государственный музей Востока, 1996).

Yang Kuan 楊寬, *Chuugoku Koutei-ryou no Kigen to Hensen*《中國皇帝陵の起源と變遷》 (On the Origin and Transition of Emperors' Tumuli of China), Tokyo: Gakuseisha, 1981.

Yang Kuan 楊寬, *Zhongguo Gudai Lingqin Zhidu Shi Yanjiu*《中國古代陵寢制度史研究》 (Studies on the History of Tumuli and Mausolea Systems in Ancient China) (translated and enlarged from Yang Kuan 1981), Shanghai: Shanghai Renmin Chubanshe, 2003.

Yoshida Yutaka 吉田豊, "Shinkyou Uyguru jichiku shishutu Sogudo-go shiryou" 新疆維吾爾自治區新出ソグド語資料 (Reports on the Sogdian texts newly discovered in Xinjiang), in *Studies on the Inner Asian Languages*, Kobe City University of Foreign Studies, 1990 VI, 57-83.

Yoshida Yutaka 吉田豊, Moriyasu Takao 森安孝夫, "Bugut inscription", in Moriyasu, Ochir, ed., *Provisional Report of Researches on Historical Sites and Inscriptions in Mongolia from 1996 to 1998*, Osaka: The Society of Central Eurasian Studies, 1999, 122-125.

ZS 周書 *Zhou Shu*, Beijing: Zhonghua Shuju, 1971.

Table: Stone Sculptures beside Tombs on the Eurasian Steppe and in China
[Key: **A**: animal; **B**: balbal; **BH**: balbal with human representation; **H**: human; **S**: stela; **ST**: stele on tortoise; **TL**: tile end with lotus ornament]

Year	West (North from Tianshan)	East (Mongolia, Altay)	China
100 BC			**A, H** (General Huo)
CE			**A**
100			**A, H** **ST** (till modern period)
200			No sculpture
300			(North)　(South) No sculpture
400			**TL** (till mediaeval) **A** (Xia)　**A** (Song) **A** (N. Wei)　**A** (Qi)
500	**H** (one example)	**B, ST, TL** (1st Tujue)	**H** (N. Wei)　**A** (Liang) **H** (W. Wei)　**A** (Chen) Sogdian sarcophagus
600	**H**?	**A, B, BH, TL** (Ungetu) **A, B?, H, S, TL?** (Shiveet-ulaan: Ilterish?)	**A, H, ST** (till modern), **TL** Earliest Tang tumuli Zhaoling (Taizong) Qianling (Gaozong & Wu)
700	**H**	**A, B, BH, H, ST, TL** (Hoshoo Tsaidam) No sculpture except **ST** (Uygur)	**A, H, ST, TL**
800	**H**	No sculpture except **ST** (Uygur)	**A, H, ST, TL**

Summary of Archeological Studies of the Site of Medieval Sauran in 2004 - 2009

Erbulat A. Smagulov

The city of Sauran was one of the most famous and important cities of medieval Kazakhstan situated on the Great Silk Road in the Syr-Darya river basin. Its past is preserved in the occupation layers of the Sauran Archaeological Complex (hereinafter referred to as SAC), comprising two major monuments-the site of the ancient city of Karatobe (mid-1st millennium CE-first half of 14th century CE) and the city of Sauran proper (14th-18th centuries). The monuments of the Sauran complex are situated administratively in the Turkestan district 40-50 km west of the city of Turkestan (Pl. VI-1) along the highway and railroad in the province of Southern Kazakhstan. Generally, in Central Asian historiography the area of the middle course of the Syr Darya river basin is characterized as a marginal zone in the development of Central Asian urban culture, as determined by specific local factors.

The cycle of recent preliminary archaeological studies has provided some answers to important questions of dating and location, historical topography and cultural peculiarities of the medieval city, and the results underscored the urgency and prospects of extensive studies with a view to laying the foundations for a museum at the site of the monuments, and made it possible to develop specific programs for subsequent archaeological study preserving the most representative structures (objects) for the purpose of founding an Architectural and Archaeological Open Air Museum.[1] Archaeological work on various scales and of different types has been carried out at structural elements of the Sauran Archaeological Complex during recent years, and the major task of this article is familiarizing readers with some of this work.

I. History of the Study of the Sauran Archaeological Complex

Almost one and a half centuries have passed since the scientific community, for historical reasons through Russian researchers and travelers, learnt of the site of the ancient city of Sauran, and so it makes sense to provide a brief summary of the major historical stages in its study.

As an archaeological monument, Sauran was mentioned in the papers of almost all distinguished Russian researchers in the historiography of this part of the world. Those publications were of course descriptive and educational in character. Fascinated by the picturesque nature and the mystery of these colossal ruins and the intuitive sense that this city was once of great importance for the history of the region, these researchers attempted to integrate what they observed with data supplied by medieval authors. The city was mentioned in P. I. Lerh's works, P. I. Pashino's itinerary, and A. P. Fedchenko's reports. These researchers all wrote about Sauran's surviving walls, and the ruins of the *medrese*.[2] The first excavations at the site of the ancient city were conducted by academician A. Gejns as early as 1866. But the level of development of Russian archeology at that time was still far from being able to solve or even articulate the problems which arose during excavation. A. Gejns had dug two pits about one meter deep and found pieces of broken earthen crockery and other "trash". "Not a single interesting artifact" captured his attention, so all findings remained intact.[3]

Scientific investigation of the Sauran ruins was initiated by the Southern Kazakhstan Archaeological Expedition (SKAE) in the late 1940s under the direction of Prof. A. N. Bernshtam, who developed a visual layout of the monument and dated the ancient city on the basis of the uncovered artifacts.[4] The location of the city immediately become one of the matters subject to dispute. If the location of the site of Sauran of the 13th-18th centuries was established, the pre-Mongol site of the city was not precisely located, since no strata were discovered with artifacts dating back to the period before the 13th century. It became clear that the city had been relocated at some time between the 13th and 14th centuries. This is a fairly common historical phenomenon for cities in general and for Central Asia in particular. The location of early Sauran [5] aroused all manner of speculation by authors writing about the historical geography of the region. Only more detailed historical study and topographic surveys made it possible to locate early Sauran in the area of the city of Karatobe adjacent to the later-dated Sauran and situated 3 km. south of it. Preliminary archaeological study of the city dated its upper occupation layer or the upper limit of the period of vigorous urban growth to the 12th-13th centuries.[6] It turned out that features of the upper occupation layer as well as the topography of the site of an ancient city are similar to those of the cities dated back to the 10th-12th centuries. Here topography clearly indicated a "Citadel", "Shakhristan", and "Rabat", all the fundamental structural elements of the medieval city [7] developed on foundations laid down in antiquity.

The 1970s and 1980s were marked by brisk archaeological studies carried out by Southern Kazakhstan Integrated Archaeological Expedition (SKIAE, under direction of K. A. Akishev) in Southern Kazakhstan, and Sauran once again attracted experts' attention. As a result of decoding aerial photos of the northwestern city neighborhood, traces of the *kariz* (the underground drainage galleries supplying ground water to the city) were registered. Ground observations followed, and a detailed paper was published, which related these traces to the *kariz* built with funding supplied by the local religious and financial potentate Mir-Arab [8] and mentioned by the medieval author Zeinatdine Wasifi. Fieldwork with a view to conducting an archaeological study of the Sauran *kariz* was carried out by SKIAE in 1986-88. Thus three lines of *kariz* were discovered and there was made an assumption that all three lines could make up the huge system mentioned by Wasifi with a source running around the medieval fortress of Mirtobe (Pl. VI-9).[9] But the excavation of some vertical wells only revealed an underground horizontal conduit at a depth of 7m.

Later study of the *kariz* systems in the vicinity of Sauran continued within the framework of the Turkestan Archaeological Expedition's (TAE headed by Smagulov E.A.) work program, which resulted in the acquisition of unique data.[10]

At the turn of the century TAE also surveyed stratigraphy of the ancient cities of Sauran and Karatobe.[11] An open test pit made in the Sauran urban core circled with fortifications revealed strata of the 13th-18th centuries and excavations carried out at Karatobe helped date its upper occupation layer, i.e. the upper limit of vigorous urban growth, back to the 12th-13th centuries. The stratigraphy and its relationship to the geological time scale turned out to be in succession which made it possible to conclude that the cultural stratification of these two sites represent history and culture of one and the same historical city of Sauran, and the burial grounds discovered under the initial construction horizon of the later-dated Sauran became the reason for advancing the hypothesis that the new city was built in the second half of the 13th-beginning of the 14th century at the site of an old city cemetery.[12] Thus, we can speak of the chronological and territorial succession of these two monuments that in its turn strengthens an argument in favor of the localization of the early or ancient city of Sauran at the site of the ancient city of Karatobe.

The reference by Makdisi in the 10th century to "the seven walls of Sauran" allegedly encircling the city,[13] provided an incorrect benchmark in searching for topographic realities. It must be admitted that this phrase is probably a mythological literary expression, an idiosyncratic cliché to emphasize the strength of the city's fortifications. It should be mentioned that the sacred number seven is also used in the description of the impregnable stronghold made of various metals and encircling Kangdiz, the legendary capital city of the Tur tribe, built by Siyavush in Kangh in the remote eastern reaches of Iranian territory.[14] Nevertheless, the detailed topographic survey of the city of Karatobe did reveal a unique layout of fortified city walls with salient angles purposefully built to strengthen its fortification properties. Such design features of fortified walls had not been seen previously in the fortifications of Medieval Kazakhstan.

Thus, we may assert that Sauran of the 4th (?)-13th centuries was located at the site of the ancient city of Karatobe and, not later than first half of the 14th century, was relocated to a new site under the same name.[15]

If previous archaeological studies of this monument were conducted intermittently, after 2004, when the site of an ancient city was entered in the state's "cultural heritage" program, the comprehensive study of this remarkable architectural and archaeological monument was systematized. The Institute of Archaeology named after A. H. Margulan selected the sites with the greatest potential for investigation and excavation with the express purpose of preserving and founding an Open Air Museum.[16] The excavation has now been completed of the ruins of the Cathedral Mosque of the 14th-15th centuries and the *medrese* [17] of the 16th century, as well as the investigation of the country mosque-*namazgoh* and suburban homesteads. Digging at the site of the main northern gateway and the site of the building situated opposite the mosque (Dig3) is coming to an end, as well as the excavation of the main street of the city running from the north front gateway to the square.[18]

As opposed to the site of late Sauran, the study of other monuments in the "Sauran Archaeological Complex" has not yet been entered in the "cultural heritage" state program and their detailed study is a matter for the future. As yet we have been fortunate to get private sponsors involved in the study of the ancient city of Karatobe-Antique Sauran.[19] Excavations at the sites yielded an abundance of artifacts which convincingly showed that Ṣauran in the 11th-13th centuries was one of the largest and most developed medieval cities in all respects and there is every indication that it was inferior to none in scale and importance, including even Otrar or other cities of Central Asia.[20] New materials discovered at Karatobe testify to an advanced urban lifestyle, and the highly developed trading activities and craftsmanship among the people living in Sauran.[21]

II. The Sauran Archaeological Complex

At a new stage of study we came to an understanding of the whole complex of diverse monuments concentrated in the Sauran micro-oasis of about 46km² in area. Systemic generalization of archaeological, historical, and topographical data led us to revise our understanding of an archaeological monument remaining at the site of Sauran, once the most famous medieval city of Kazakhstan. We now realized it occupied a vast space in the basin of the middle and lower reaches of the Tastaksay and Maidantal rivers with well preserved archaeological traces of various elements of urban architecture, which had been developing over the course of time. We now scientifically view the site of an ancient city as part of "an archaeological complex", with well preserved city monuments, a surviving necropolis, and residential suburbs with diverse elements of rural development or with traces of agricultural development. The uniqueness of Sauran is that all the fundamental elements of this archaeological complex are still in a satisfactory state of preservation and available for study. These elements (structures) are adjacent to each other, and often overlapping.[22]

In the literature on the subject from the time of its first archaeological survey, the city of Sauran has been regarded and described as a standalone city, oval in plan and encircled by fortified walls (Pls. VI-2, 3, 4).[23] The suburban zone with traces of mediaeval agricultural and irrigation layout planning is presumed to have been a vast farming district, the area of which has been variously and approximately estimated. Visual examination and aerial photography clearly revealed homesteads encircled by rectangular gardens and vineyards. Since P. Lerh, the city of Mirtobe located 6 km north [24] of Sauran has been described as having a relationship with the latter (Pl. VI-8). Researchers believe that this small fortification located close to the barrow (*sardoba*) [25] with a garden-park nearby was named after Mir-Arab, the nickname of the local sayyid Emir Abdallah, who according to Zeinatdine Wasifi was notable for building and presenting two unique life-giving *kariz* systems [26] to the city. At the end of the 1960s, as a result of decoding aerial photographs of the suburbs, the traces of the *kariz* supplying groundwater to the city [27] were discovered. The early history of Sauran is also related to the city of Karatobe, located 3km south of the late medieval fortress with cultural layers dating back to the period from the 1st century to the 13th century (Pl. VI-7).[28]

The history of the city of Sauran, given our present level of knowledge, is thus reasonably linked with a number of heterogeneous localized archaeological monuments of various degrees of complexity. Naturally each has its own distinct structure but together they form an ensemble (complex) tied by synchronous and diachronous structural links which characterize the phenomenon of a medieval city which is more amenable to study than if each monument were taken separately. Therefore, while analyzing and summarizing materials and observations, it is advisable to use the concept of "Sauran Archaeological Complex", which provides a better and more comprehensive understanding of the medieval urban culture of Kazakhstan.[29]

First we need to provide a brief description of the principal structural elements of the "Sauran Archaeological Complex".

1. The ancient city of Sauran

Decoding aerial photos of the ancient city together with the interpretation of topographic plans and visual observations makes it possible to describe Sauran of the 14th to 18th centuries as a typical late medieval city of Central Asia. Its city planning was developed in the post-Mongol period, when the new city was founded in the previously undeveloped area. The cities of that time were characterized by an encircled vast area forming the urban core (fortress, "*kala*") with a compact grid layout surrounded with an urban fringe with farmhouse planning at least as large in area. The urban core encircled by the wall was oval in plan inside the fortress, some sections of which have survived and rising in place 3 to 6-7 meters above the original ground (Pls. VI-2, 3, 4). This central part of the city (or "*kala*") extends 800m from northeast to southwest and 650m from northwest to southeast. The area of the "*kala*" towers 3-3,5m above the surrounding area. The wall of the city is built upon a stylobate 2-3m high. A detailed visual study of the surviving wall segments revealed that it had been built in at least two stages-the original wall (stage I) and its later refurbishment and renovation (stage II).

Initially the wall had castellated parapets still visible in parts of the walls of a later date (Pl. VI-4). Apparently, there was a shooting ground on top of the wall, which must have been very thick at the top (at least 2m) and even thicker at the bottom. The wall, which was initially vaulted and castellated and which featured regularly spaced notches, was made of plastered adobe brick. As a result of refurbishment and renovation, segments of the wall, which were completely destroyed, must have been re-erected while those which survived were covered with new armored walling. The top course of the new wall was elevated not less than 2-3m above the previous level. The wall was crowned with four round-shaped double-tiered towers protruding from its outer line.

There were two gateways leading to the city (Pl. VI-2). The front gateway is in the northeastern segment of the wall representing a strong fortified structure flanked with two double-tiered towers protruding outward. The gateway was made in the shape of a domed passage 20 meters long and paved with broad slabs. Outside the wall a deck, serving as a support for a wooden gangway over the wide (8-10m) moat, was attached to the area near the gateway. Segments of the wall near the gateway and towers all the way down to the bottom of the moat were covered with a layer of fired square-shaped bricks. The second gateway was made in the southeastern side of the city wall. Apparently there was also a third, emergency entrance made in the shape of an opening, 1.20m wide and 1.7m high, in the tower on the eastern side of the city wall.

Outside there was made a wide moat encircling the wall; today in some places it is 3m deep and 15-20m wide. An outcrop of rock from the moat was utilized to make a rampart 1-1.5m high and up to 5m wide.

The main street running from a small square near the northeastern front gateway divides the inner territory of the city into two identical zones lying to the northeast and southwest. At a distance of 150m from the southeastern edge of the fortress wall it abuts against the street running perpendicular and in a northwest-southeast direction. One of its sections leads to the southeastern gateway. Besides the two main streets, a number of small streets and cul-de-sacs, which make up the branching street network of the city of the 14th-18th centuries, have been traced in the topography of the city.

Some sections of the main street are 10m wide. The city street network can be clearly identified today in a depression between the elevated (up to 1-1.5m) residential areas or some monumental structures branching off the main street.

At a distance of 200m from the northern gateway, this main street runs into a big city square, 140×60m in size. At the point of intersection, its width reaches 18m. Barrows more than two meters high and covered with brick debris rise to the right and left of the street. Archaeological excavations revealed that to the left were the ruins of a *medrese* with the two minarets (prayer towers) mentioned by Wasifi and which survived down to the 19th century.[30] Opposite the medrese was another monumental structure with a doorway made in a shape of an arched *iwan* paved with cobblestones (Pl. VI-5). The excavation of this building has not yet been completed.

The square was rectangular with a long axis across the main street (Pls. VI-2, 20). Along the perimeter of the square were huge barrows, under which lay ruins of buildings made of square burnt bricks. Fragments of bricks found in large numbers on these barrows testify to this effect. Many of them were found on the northwestern and northeastern edges of the square.

Along the northwestern edge of the square was found the site of a square measuring approximately 30×35m in size. In 2001, the Turkestan Archaeological Expedition (TAE) carried out preliminary excavations at this site, which made it possible to suggest that it was the city's Jami Mosque,[31] and further excavations in 2004-2006 proved this idea to be true. We excavated the ruins of the mosque, which must have been Jami Mosque of Sauran of the 14th-15th centuries with a closed yard and *iwan* planning.[32]

City outskirts. Around the fortified walls of the city at a distance of about 500-1600m away were discovered ruins of farmsteads forming areas of various housing densities. Each farmstead included the house (preserved in various shapes of undulating land) and a plot of land encircled by a wall. The land was mainly used for melon or gourd orchards, gardens, vineyards, and grain crops. Plots of land and farmsteads are integrated into a uniform irrigation system comprising a head canal and small canals (*aryks*) branching from it. It is quite natural that the most densely populated area was the area along the bank of the streams and canals. The biggest houses measured 150×110m and 180×90m in size and occupied parcels of land ranging from 1.5 to 1.8 hectares. The medium-size farmsteads occupied an area of about 1 hectare, and the small farmsteads occupied less than 0.5 hectare. The majority of farmsteads were medium-sized. According to preliminary figures obtained by decoding aerial photographs, there were more than 900 farmsteads in the suburbs of Sauran. The most densely populated area was to the north, northwest and west of the city walls.

Unearthed artifacts (pottery, coins) made it possible to date the farmsteads in the vicinity of Sauran to the period between the 13th-14th and 15th-18th centuries. About 800m north of the city we excavated a dwelling of one farmstead which we dated to the 17th-18th century. (Pl. VI-6)

Necropolis. The late medieval necropolis of the city was located at a distance 200-300m east of the southeastern tower. Here, in rectangular shaped sites measuring $40-60 \times 40-80$m and surrounded with swollen clay walls one can distinguish small fences of the *torkulak* type enclosing subsiding graves, ruins of tombs, and sepulchral barrows. This necropolis is still worshipped by locals. Of the ruined tomb structures discovered at this site, the largest is believed to be the tomb of the saint Karakan-ata.[19] It is very likely that the legends of the locals echo the veneration of the saints, as well as possibly political figures, of medieval Sauran, in the vicinity of which they have been buried. The interweaving of actual events with myths and legends makes it difficult for us to form a clear picture of life in medieval Sauran.

Further detailed study of the topography of the ancient city will probably lead us to discover other important zones of the city. The delimitation, description, and study of the structural elements of the city are an indispensable part of the archaeological investigation of urban formations. In our case one of the tasks of paramount importance was defining the city's historical boundaries and providing an adequate description of the zone outside the walls of the fort.

2. The Ancient City of Karatobe: Ancient Sauran

The ancient city of Karatobe is the next significant large component of the Sauran Archaeological Complex. The historical profile of the city of Sauran based on original sources [33] cannot be complete without the written '*Nasabnama*' (History) of the *khodjas* of Southern Kazakhstan. Transmitted orally from generation to generation for many centuries, it was presumably first recorded in the 11th-12th century. This comparatively recently published source enables us to see the role the city of Sauran played in the penetration of Islam into the region in the first half of the 8th century. It mentioned that Sauran was formerly known as "Sulhan" and it was the site of fierce fighting between Muslims and infidels, whereupon a new city was built (which was probably the rebuilding of the former city). For example, the history describes how Muslims after fierce fighting defeated the army of Tubbat-dar, probably the local Christian (pagan?) governor, who escaped to Sauran: "Hadrat Shah 'Abd al-'Aziz-bab has become a martyr in this battle of Sairam. Thereafter Tubbat-dar, padishah of Sulhan, which the Turks now call Sauran, escaped...". Upon the seizure of Suzak, the Muslims approached Sauran from the northern foothills of the Karatau Mountains: "Thereafter Ishak-bab, having laid siege to the city of Sulhan and fighting several days and nights, killed forty thousand infidel Christians. Seven thousand Muslims became martyrs. Tubbat-dar, padishah, with two other padishahs of common origin was killed by the Christians. Afterwards Hadrat Ishak-baba converted the land of Turkestan [that is] Jassy, as well as Sujri, Karnak, Ikan, Temir-Kufkan, Bagistan, Yetti-kand, Altmysh, Otrar, Sygnak and other regions and places and all people settled in the land from sea to sea, which the Turk tribes call Tengiz, to become Mohammedans". It seems that the conquest of Sauran marked the subordination of the Southern Kazakhstan region to the Arab-Muslim armies and the mass conversion of the local urban population to Islam. However, the complete and final conversion to Islam took quite a long time: "Thereafter [after the conquest of Sauran/Sulhan, he (Hadrat Ishak-baba)] built three fortifications (walls) standing one around the other, encircling each other, and seven cathedral mosques; he conducted a war with infidel magicians for eighty years".[34]

In light of this information it becomes clear that the origins in Southern Kazakhstan folk legends of a number of "saintly martyrs" is related to such ancient cities as Sajram, Otrar, and Sauran, which used to be the heartland of the fight against Muslim expansion, and after the conquest were turned into outposts for the propagation of the new religion and culture. The history provided us with clues in our search for the similarities and the nature of some innovations in the medieval culture of the region. For example, the fortification technique ("cornered defensive installation") used in the layout of the external fortified walls encircling the ancient city of Karatobe (Ancient Sauran) could have been borrowed from the late Roman built-up fortifications of Byzantium.

Visual topographic surveys and the study of all available detailed aerial photographs of the city of Karatobe made it possible to present this site as a composite monument of urban culture. Its topographic survey showed that the three spaces encircled by walls were almost strictly concentrically inscribed within each other (Pl. VI-7).

The external walls circumscribed almost a perfect circle with a zigzag outline measuring 1900-2000m in diameter and 3km^2 in area. The walls had straight segments sometimes forming right angles here and there with other segments in the shape of an arc. They are poorly identified at the site but can be clearly decoded in the aerial photographs. We noticed that there seemed to be no regular fortification towers along the perimeter of this wall, but there were characteristic turnings of the wall at right angles which were not dictated by the topography. Apparently this is a specific built up technique used to construct fortifications which ensured that the flank defense of the most critical segments of the wall could be conducted from the upper gun slot gallery crowning the wall. As far back as antiquity walls crowned with meandering and castellated parapets were known in theory as "built-up fortification". According to expert opinion, this technique was also used in the construction of the southern wall of the city of Pendjikent in Central Asia.[35]

The area inside the wall was unevenly built up with high housing density, mainly in the west. A continuous housing development area occupied approximately a quarter of the inner area. The rest of the area most probably had no continuous development and could have been used for stationing a military camp consisting of light mobile structures. Judging by the serpentine riverbeds two small rivers flowed in the north of this area. The city proper with its continuous development was located between these two riverbeds. This site was initially square with a lateral length of each side of about 550m occupying an area of approximately 0.3km^2. The northwest corner of this area was at right angles. The other corners of this square site turned were cut and deformed due to recent leveling for fields and canals.

In the middle of this site the main barrow (ancient citadel) of the ancient city of irregular oval shape with its straight south wall towered 6-8m above the surrounding square area. The area of the ancient citadel was 340×280m. Right in the center of this barrow a swollen rectangular area measuring 130×115m can be clearly identified on the micro-topographical plan. The highest point of the whole city is registered on top of a solid barrow situated in the southeastern area of the site.

Today we can reconstruct three rows of concentric fortified walls (defense lines) in the city of Karatobe. The first (external) wall encircling an area of 3km² was about four kilometers long. The curved line of this wall attracted our attention. The inner almost square area of the city was encircled with a 2200m-long wall. A roughly 1000m-long wall encircled the oval shaped citadel situated in the center of the square.

As mentioned above, the upper limit of busy urban life in Karatobe is dated back to the 13th century.[36] This implies that the topography of the city described above characterizes the city of the 9th-10th centuries, i.e, in the Samanid and Karakhanid periods, a time of rapid growth of cities and sedentary culture in the region [37] on the whole, when urban life in Southern Kazakhstan reached its fullest flourishing.

The above-mentioned natural landscape features testify to the fact that the city was founded and initially built in accordance with strict city-building and architectural design. Its preliminary topographic and architectonic description (concentric zoning, fortification rationale, water situation, etc.) speak well for its high-level city-building art. Considering the fact that the old city has been slightly affected by the latest agricultural activity and its upper construction horizons of the 11th-13th centuries have not been overlaid with later-dated occupation layers, it must be admitted that this monument deserves long-term integrated investigation.

3. Mir-Tobe

A unique monument of country landscape gardening for medieval culture of Kazakhstan is the next component element of the Sauran Architectural Complex, which is Mirtobe. Usually this monument is described as a square fortification with a lateral length of approximately 70m and up to 5-6m high walls with some sort of land leveling and ruins of dwellings in its vicinity.[38] This area was described by the well-known author of the beginning of the 16th century Zeinetdine Wasifi [39] quoted on more than one occasion. It must be noted that the data given by him on the whole matches the district map material. Moreover, the interpretation of detailed aerial photographs made it possible to adjust and update them.[40] In addition to the square fortress of Mirtobe proper, we can clearly identify one more rectangle (Pl. VI-8) of similar dimensions to the east of it. Probably, here we have the strongly swollen ruins of the earlier fortifications that was not renovated under Mir-Arab who preferred to build a new one nearby.

As far as the *charbag* (garden-park) is concerned, it may either match the walled area around the fortress (at the first stage) or most likely was another layout design fenced about with straight walls. There are projections of regularly spaced towers along the southern wall. The area of the enclosure is approximately 300 × 800m. This layout design was actually built on the *kariz* lines and was somehow was connected with them, although it is not yet clear how. Inside the walls there was a pool as well as the ruins of some structure that must have been the utility rooms described by Wasifi. A line of another *kariz* is traced outside the wall. The area inside has a specific "comb" plan typical of vineyards and in the center there is a square shaped depression measuring 35 × 30m, which is assumed to be the ruins of a *sardoba*, a special domed underground facility mentioned by Wasifi for underground water collection and storage.

On the basis of the detailed survey of agricultural and irrigational works in the area of Mirtobe and north of Sauran it was established that the *kariz* of Sauran and Mirtobe structurally are not linked with each other and belong to different systems. They even use different underground water resources and consist of two *kariz* systems located in different zones.[41] According to Wasifi the source of the *kariz* built by Mir-Arab to supply water to the city of Sauran was located near Mirtobe but to date we have found no confirmation of this, nor any information regarding the dimensions of the "Mir-Arab *kariz*".[42]

4. Kariz

We were fortunate in acquiring new material using the "geological and archaeological" approach in our exploration, record keeping and documentation. The applied procedure made it possible to identify, document and map the traces of 235 *kariz* (actually there are many more) of various length in the area of medieval Sauran. If we assume that under the ring-type network clearly visible on the surface there are underground drainage galleries and measure these, then the total length of these exceeds 110km.

It is established that the medieval city of Sauran was located in the lower delta of three former mountain streams-Tastaksay, Aksay and Maidantal flowing from southern slopes of the Karatau Mountains towards Syr Darya River. They make three *talus* trains converging in the area of the antique cities of Karatobe and Sauran at the junction of their surface and underground waters. The Maidantal River has the largest surface and underground water flow, and its basin is a major water resource region. The flow of the Aksay River is not so high, but since it runs through central and low-lying country, it has middle and lower watercourses, fed by water at the junction of underground waters from two other streams. Except for the main canyon of the Tastaksay and Maidantal rivers and the lower reaches of the Aksay River, which have low but perennial flows, all other streams flow only in spring.

An exceptionally high concentration of *kariz* [43] traces has been discovered along these river beds. There is documentary evidence that the two Sauran *kariz* mentioned in the work of Wasifi were by no means unique and their structures have not yet been revealed. *Kariz* lines were built not only to supply water to the city, but also to irrigate the fields, and so they must have appeared here well before those built by Mir-Arab. In the arid environment of Central Asia, agriculture and large settlements could not have been satisfied only with mountain stream flows, which were fed mainly by floodwaters in spring. There was usually an acute water shortage in such hot-arid zones in summer. In order to meet this deficit and set up a reliable water base for agriculture, *kariz* were constructed using favorable local hydrological conditions and ensuring stable life-giving water for the crops and settlements (Pl. VI-10).

We have a long recorded and documented tradition of the utilization of underground water resources for the purposes of water supply to cities (Sauran, Turkestan) and the irrigation of the fields and gardens in the medieval period. The question arises of dating the *kariz* and studying their design and the origins of this technology in the region. In view of the importance of water resources in the local extremely arid environment we may consider the Sauran *kariz* water supply and irrigation system to be one of the most important elements of the archaeological complex. There is not enough information about *kariz* in Medieval Arab and Persian written sources, although in the description of any city of Central Asia or Khurasan water resources are usually mentioned. It is significant that in V.V. Bartol'd's fundamental review, only the *kariz* of Merv, Ferava, and Sauran are mentioned. [44] The ecological value of *kariz* water is now being recognized by contemporary hydro-ecologists,[45] and it is well known that *kariz* water is an object of veneration in the traditional culture of Central Asia. This water is treated as a "holy gift" sanctified by the rural nomadic and semi-nomadic people and the residents of the cities. For example, local residents of Samarkand until recently firmly believed in the miraculous medicinal properties of the Obirakhmat and Obimakhshat channel waters. These channels originate from underground spring waters (*karasu*).[46]

The *kariz* system, in addition to utilizing seasonal surface waters by means of "*togans*" and "*aryks*" clearly defined in the micro-topography of the area, ensured the operation of the vast agricultural zone situated in the basin of the above-mentioned rivers and in the vicinity of the city of Sauran. The traces of medieval agricultural and irrigation projects are clearly defined on the ground and are little impaired by recent activities. Their extent covers and integrates the above-mentioned component elements of the Sauran Archaeological Complex. On the whole this monument of the developed agricultural region of Sauran provides documentary information in support of the unique agricultural character of Central Asian cities.

III. Summary of the 2004-2009 archaeological investigations

1. Ancient City of Karatobe

In 2006 we started digging an area (Dig 2) of 15 × 15m in the SW section of the central barrow of Karatobe, which was supposed to be its citadel. The purpose was to excavate and study ruins of monumental citadel structures. However, the results failed to prove our assumptions. The stratigraphic data obtained and investigations made at Karatobe citadel (Dig 2) can be summarized as follows: Building structures of the upper construction horizon (UCH) were uncovered only on the southern and western sides of the barrow and, according to stratigraphy (1-2 layers) and outward appearance (walls, clay sofa, family hearth, and kitchen-midden), they represent fragments of a common residential unit towards the center, occupied by a layered trash dump. This construction horizon yielded a complex of original pottery of rough artistic execution characterized by echoes of "late Karakhanid" (Pl. VI-13). Only in the 5th layer was the top section of disintegrated walls of the second construction horizon (CH 2) was exposed. The base of the corner wall of some structure occurred in the middle of the 7th layer, i.e. the walls up to 1.2-1.4m high remained an integral part of this horizon. A stratified trash dump with fragments of glazed ceramics apparently of the "Karakhanid period" abutted on these walls. The third and the lowest construction horizon to date was marked in the 8th and 9th layers. As this dig showed in the highest central part of an ancient city there was a barrow made up of inclined ashy trash interlayers at least 4.5m thick accumulated for a long time (11th-13th centuries). This would mean that a permanent trash dump was located right in the center of the city! We wanted to find the reason for this, but to that end we had to significantly expand and deepen the area of digging.

We managed to study the stratigraphy of the upper occupation layers of the larger area (Dig 1) in the SE corner of the citadel (Pl. VI-12). The area of digging at the level of the UCH exceeded 2000m². Here we discovered compact planning of a residential community consisting of from one-to three-room houses. Some may be characterized as houses of well-to-do sections of the urban population. Of particular note, the house of one well-to-do local had an antechamber with built-in niches and inscription ornament on clay fillet decorating the ceiling. There were nine rooms in the house, each of them having a *tandoor* (mud stove) and built-in clay sofa (Pl. VI-12 rooms 25, 29). Room 14 was a semi-open antechamber with a sofa and passage to the left leading to the *mehmanhana* (living room 12) with a toilet facility (rooms 18,19) and a second passage to the right leading to a living space with two *tandoor* built at different times (room 25). A semi-open courtyard leads to the front (inner) lobby (room 20). Deep niches or closets were built into the walls, and to the right there was a wide sofa and flat stone column base in the center of the room. On top of the niches below the ceiling there was a ribbon cornice made of natural clay engraved with epigraphic ornament. This inner lobby leads to the main living space (room 29) with a П-shaped sofa, large *tandoor*, and fireplace in the corner. The other door in the lobby opened on an enfilade consisting of three rooms (rooms 28, 27, 21), the far room (room 21) obviously being a storeroom and the other two with wide sofas (rooms 28, 27) being bedrooms.

In all the other smaller houses the room with the *tandoor* (mud stove) made into a large clay sofa is considered to be the principal living space of the house. The interiors of the dwellings also include built-in fireplaces, granaries, central columns, etc. We found glazed pottery on a mass scale that we dated by direct analogy back to the 13th century; it was decorated with yellow, black, and dark-brown drawings against the background of green and yellow color enamel (Pl. VI-13). There was an abundance of ceramics with scratched ornament and green, acid-yellow, and manganese color spots and stains painted in the most diverse variations. Open vessels were predominantly made in the form of bowls with flat or disc-shaped concave bottoms with elbow bends at the top. The most frequent elements found in the décor were triangles in various versions and four-leafed rosettes with yellow-or green-color spots or a combination of scratched and spotty ornament, as well as segmentation and concentric bands filled with contrasting varicolored dots and stains. A special group of unglazed pottery was found consisting of jugs with figured painting on the external surface and made with brown-red or black engobe coating against light-colored background. The most widespread elements of its décor were spiral-shaped rosettes framed with dots, as well as S-like figures, bands of shaded triangles, and a combination of straight and wavy lines (Pl. VI-14).

The second construction horizon (CH2) has been investigated on a smaller area (about 300m^2), but it became clear that the layout of UCH, slightly modified, is similar to that of CH2. There are two types of glazed ceramics including those with three-color painting in brown, red and green against light-color background and the same painting under transparent water-white color enamel and those with scratched ornament on engobe coating under slightly colored enamel of light and dark green color. The elements of ornament are diverse and include spiral-shaped figures, leaves, flaky netting, and wavy and straight lines. Among the unglazed pottery we can single out a complex of ceramics covered with red dense engobe on a glossy surface and various ornaments made by combining stamped and incised, scratched, and pressed-in lines. This complex of ceramics is similar to that of 12th century Otrar, Chach, and Sogd. CH2 yielded a series of more than twenty copper and silver coins. According to P. Petrov, coins of Khorezmshah Mohammed ibn Tekesh are the most common identifiable coins. Therefore the upper limit of CH2 may be dated back to the first half of the 12th century.

CH2 overlays a stratum of desolation; a number of kitchen-middens, detritus pits, and ash disposal areas were found in the ruins of houses. So it appears that this site of urban development must have been abandoned at some time in the 11th century, possibly in the first half of the century. The habitable area in the city was reduced and former structures included detritus pits; their ruins were covered with kitchen midden, which yielded few items of ceramics of the 11th century.

Only a small area (20 × 15m) of the third construction horizon (CH3) has been excavated to date, and its ruins occur at the level of the 5th-7th layers. The rooms are of various plans, ranging from trapezoidal to rectangular and square. The direction of the walls, and the layout of rooms intended for various purposes in the dwelling houses of CH2 and CH3 have no successive relationship, as observed in the buildings of UCH and CH2. Characteristics of the building materials, as well as the construction process, changed. The main building material was rectangular adobe bricks of high quality. Mandatory elements of room decoration were sofas plastered with fine-dispersed clay and floor altars made of ceramic or clay situated in the center of the room (Pl. VI-15). Ceramics were represented by domestic ware of excellent quality painted in two colors (black and red) against a light background. Ornamental patterns were mostly plant motifs and epigraphic patterns in the form of horizontally elongated inscriptions under the serrated edge of the bowl. It is necessary to mention principal morphological characters of this complex. Vessels were mainly made in the form of semi-spherical and cone-shaped bowls with disc-shaped and slightly concave round bottoms. Unglazed pottery was represented by pots, jugs, kettles, and mugs. Similar pottery dating back to the second half of the 10th-beginning of the 11th centuries comes from Sogd and Chach.

Earlier dated construction horizons were discovered at a site measuring 260m² on the eastern edge of the barrow above the earlier citadel of the city. It is slightly inclined to the east. At its western edge R_1 point of -281 is fixed relative to the R_0 (trig point at the top of the barrow in the center of the city).

The UCH on the slope here is almost completely weathered and washed away. The second construction horizon (CH2) is in a better state of preservation. Ruins of its structures have been fixed at a depth of -350cm or 70cm from the original ground level. They are mostly represented by ruins of foundations made from quarry stones. The decayed wood that must have been used as waterproofing was above the foundations. Upon removing this construction horizon (CH2) we started excavating the rooms of the third construction horizon (Pl. VI-17). Diggings included the ruins of a room measuring 2.33 × 3.4m in area. The first level of the floor was marked at the depth of -446cm, the second at -462cm, with all levels relative to R_0.

While excavating structures of the CH2 we found some interesting artifacts, including amulets made in the shape of a pair of boots (one was whole, the other a fragment) (Pl. VI-18-1,2).[47] Diggings of the upper layer yielded a miniature chalcedony with a picture of a duck (Pl. VI-18-6) and an ornamented pendant made of turquoise (Pl. VI-18-5). In the underlying construction horizon (CH3 of the Karatobe general stratigraphy), we excavated room #1 which was square in plan and covered an area of 4.7×4.7m. Inside the room there were three wall sofas of various functions (Pl. VI-17). A rectangular shaped altar made of clay with an oval northern rim was discovered right in the center of the room. It was placed on the platform measuring 1.1×1.5m and elevated 20cm above the original floor level. An elevated rectangular area measuring 0.25×0.35m was found right in the center of the straight southern wall flange. A square platform (0.5×0.5m) 25cm high was 0.2m south of the altar edge. An unusual structure was found and investigated in the northeast corner of the room, right opposite the antechamber. It was a specially made rectangular-shaped compartment measuring 0.9× 1.2m. The extant wall, which rises to 1.1m is made of half-bricks (measuring 35×18-19×7-8cm). The compartment was choked up with trash that also filled the pit under the floor of the room. Fragments of ceramic vessels, bones, and a bronze seal ring (Pl. VI-18-4) were found in the trash at the top of the pit. This compartment must have been covered with a brick vault and on the western wall there was a specially made oval hole through which trash (ash, ceramics and bone debris) was thrown into the pit. Along the SE wall of the room there was a pedestal with a built-in round ceramic fireplace 0.6m in diameter.

The altar, the walls of the building, and the clay sofas were all coated with multi-layered plasterwork, with a total thickness of as much as 4-5cm. The excavation of the rooms revealed decorative elements (sofas, partitions, cornices, etc.) made with particular thoroughness.

Removing the coating material from the floor near the west wall of the altar revealed several fragments of unimpressive ceramics and two iron-clad plates of different sizes (Pl. VI-19-10, 11). It is also worth noting that a Turgesh coin was found in room 9 at the level of the floor of room 1 (Pl. VI-18-7).

If it turns out that this is the only room with sofas and fireplaces in the dwelling, then it must have been a living space with strongly pronounced religious attributes, or it was used as a special space for worship like a home chapel. While clearing the room we noticed that when it was abandoned the doorway at the end of the passage was walled up which is why it was subsequently preserved in an undamaged condition. Only when we have expanded and completed the excavation will we be able to retrace events at this site of residential development.

The wall of the underlying construction horizon (CH4) was found under room #1, the upper level of which (floor) was at a depth of-566 from the bench mark and the next was at a depth of-656cm. The top of an arched passage was traced in the south wall of the underlying construction horizon at a depth of-584cm, but these horizons have not been excavated yet.

Room #2 has an area of 4.5×5.25m. As yet we have retraced two stages related to the rearrangement of the interior of this room. There were clay sofas and a round altar in the center of the room. Therefore room #2 may be attributed to a group of premises for worship just like room #1 and must have been part of the same dwelling house, but was built only after room #1 was abandoned.

Room #1 has a multi-level floor. On the upper floor level was found a horseshoe-shaped ceramic altar (0.5×0.75m), 11cm-high walls of the altar were sunk into the floor, and in the center there was a round hole measuring 12cm in diameter and 9cm in depth. A *tandoor* (mud stove), 67cm in diameter, was built into the northern sofa opposite the altar; one *tandoor* was mounted inside the other, and the flue door (12cm high and 8cm wide) was at floor level.

The excavation of room #2 yielded a bronze belt buckle, a stone mould used to make jewelry, a knife handle made of bone, and an iron-clad plate (Pl. VI-19-3,9).

The second (first from the bottom) period of construction made room #2 habitable and is related to the 8th and 9th layers. The southern side of the room is almost square (4.35×4.45m) and its northern side is lengthened 85cm by the western wall segment. Sofas were made along the full length of the perimeter of the room except for the threshold. At a distance of 75cm from the northeast corner of the room was a *khum* (big vessel) without a bottom which would have been used as a drainage duct. A round clay altar was discovered in the center of the room; it was 85cm in diameter with a hole in the center measuring 12cm in diameter and 10cm deep. At a distance of only 10cm beneath this altar was another round altar 50cm in diameter with a hole in the center measuring 14-15cm in diameter and 8cm deep. Upon removing the remains of this altar underneath, we uncovered a hearth measuring 104×38cm. The remains of three clay on-floor hearth-altars, one under the other, were excavated in this room, as well as round ceramic altars-on the upper floor level.

In the northern part of the extended area (above room 4 and room 8, Pl. VI-17) we found the remains of the second construction horizon, the walls of which were made of *pahsa* (clay). We managed to trace in part two rooms, but failed to determine their area and elements of their interiors. At the depth of -376 we fixed the base of the *pahsa* (clay) walls of the rooms dated from CH2. A stratum of backfilling occurred below in the rooms dated from CH3. The layout of these rooms turned out to be completely different from those occurring in the overlying horizon. In the upper part of this backfilling we found fragments of polished black pottery engraved with a runic inscription (Pl. VI-20).[48]

Walls from 1.3m to 1.4m high survived in room #4 which dated from CH3. The room was square (4.65×4.65m). The doorway, approximately 0.9m wide, opened off the vestibule passage in the western wall of the room. Along the perimeter of the room there were clay sofas 0.95m wide; the one located near the southeastern corner had rounded off contours and was wider than the others, while the sofa against the western wall was narrow-only 0.77m with a *tandoor* (mud stove) built into it with an opening 0.3m in diameter and 0.5m high. Niches with edge moldings were built in the western, northern and southern walls. There is an interesting composition made of edge molding in the shape of doorway (?) with a decorated top in southern corner of the SW wall. At a small distance from the southeastern corner there are two columns, supporting a rectangular carved frieze (Pl. VI-21). The whole composition is made with artistic molding and later improved carving on natural clay which has then been coated with a layer of gypsum and clay mix. It is probably only a part of a greater composition decorating the center of this wall, but most of it together with the wall was later destroyed by a dust pit.

In the center of the room at a depth of -590cm from the benchmark there was a horseshoe-shaped altar, the walls of which were made of adobe brick to a height of 15cm. Below it was a square altar with rounded western side and a hole 18cm in diameter. The height of the altar was 10 to 15cm.

Excavation of room #4 exposed 8 levels of well-coated flooring, the total thickness of which was 25cm. Excavated in part were rooms #3, 8, 9, 6, and 7; these were service rooms bearing some relation to three other excavated rooms, apparently all of them forming three separate buildings when the area of digging is later extended, and each having a central living space used also as a space for worship. The ambiguous functional, confessional, ethnic and cultural purposes of such rooms [49] provide an interesting challenge to archaeology in Central Asia.

It is worth mentioning the variety of architectural techniques and décor of the rooms, which include polychrome painting on natural clay, alabaster molding and plastering, walls and other architectural surfaces painted red, as well as earthen strap molding and carving on natural clay, niches, friezes, etc. Rooms with similar altars in houses of the rich were also found in a number of other monuments of Southern Kazakhstan of the 8th-10th centuries, such as Altyntobe, Kujruktobe, Sidak, and Turkestan Kultobe. Here we were lucky enough for the first time to retrace detailed stratigraphy and to date the change from clay wall altars to ceramic altars. In the future, the area of digging (Dig1) must be extended westward and northward so it will be possible to excavate some households of CH3 and get an insight into the planning of houses, residential areas, and the development of the citadel in general. Stratigraphic features of this part of the citadel are determined by some monumental structure in the lower construction horizons that must have been used in any event up to the period of CH2. The preliminary spatiotemporal horizon of this site might be as follows: the upper construction horizon (UCH, practically non extant, save for some kitchen middens) may be dated back to the 12th-13th centuries; CH2: *pahsa* (clay) walls, room with ceramic altar, 10th-11th centuries; CH3: rooms #4, 2, 9, and 5 with multilevel floors, and repeated underlying monumental building planning, 8th-9th centuries.

Archaeological digging has yielded a large collection of various handicraft items, including ceramic, metal, glass tableware, craftsman's tools, various jewelry and adornments, belt accessories (Pl. VI-16), and items of household use, some produced locally and some obviously imported, brought along caravan routes of the Great Silk Road from handicraft centers of Maverranahr (Ma Wara un Nahr or Transoxiana), Khurasan, the Middle East, and China. These collections of artifacts provide detailed information on the culture and mode of life of the people of the major developed urban centers.[50]

The archaeological stratigraphy of Karatobe makes it possible to identify several stages in the development of techniques for manufacturing artifacts on a mass scale, and the evolution of their forms and artistic décor, especially of medieval ceramics from the mid-10th to the 13th centuries. We have also studied more closely the process of planning dwelling houses and residential urban districts, building technologies, etc.

Thus the archaeological studies getting underway in Karatobe provided prospects for the preservation of the site and the founding of an open-air museum revealing segments of the medieval city of Sauran so that visitors can see evidence of its spectacular flourishing, as well as providing an opportunity to investigate the early stages of urbanization in the region, as well as the ethnic and cultural history of the region. Segments of urban development have been prepared for the opening of a museum, including dwelling houses, public buildings, and fortifications, of the period from the 10th-13th centuries, together with sites of late medieval Sauran located nearby which visually demonstrate the process of development of urban culture in Southern Kazakhstan during the Middle Ages.

2. Central Square of the Ancient City of Sauran. Mosque

As mentioned above the remains of public buildings can be traced along the perimeter of the central city square. One such building situated on the western side of the square is presumed to be the former Cathedral Mosque of the city (Pls.VI-22, 23).

It has been established that the structure existed over two fundamental periods. In the second period it ceased to be used for its intended purpose and has been exposed to significant destruction when adapted to other purposes.[51] We found traces of temporary hearths and bonfires in the section supposed to be the *mihrab* of the Mosque.

Digging carried out at the site showed that the Mosque was constructed using traditional closed courtyard planning. All the rooms along the perimeter of the courtyard faced the central courtyard (*"sahn"*), which had an area of 15.3×17.8m. On the southwestern side of the courtyard was the principal part of the Mosque, the *mihrab* (*"zulla"*), the arched front portal of which faced the courtyard. The plan of this principal part of the complex had a five-aisled and double-column design with a covering arch (Pl. VI-23).[52] The width of the entrance niche is 6m. The arch rested upon massive pylons. The doorway 2.95m wide leads to a square (6×6m) hall in front of the *mihrab* niche. The area of the hall has been slightly extended by three niches 0.75m deep. The principal axis mounted *mihrab* was in one more niche measuring 0.75m in depth right in the center of the SW wall. Judging by the traces on the floor it was 1.5m wide and 1.2m deep. A hoard of copper coins wrapped in small cloth bundles each containing several coins was found in this hall under the square fired bricks. There was a total of 114 coins.[53] This was the only find of this type to date. Locals used to bring whatever alms (*"sadaka"*) to the mosque as small change wrapped in bundles, as copper coins were in greatest demand in everyday life. Bundles with coins were probably buried under the floor of the central hall of the mosque at a time when the disintegrating building had been abandoned, but was still visited by pilgrims as a sacred place of worship. Therefore this hoard of coins may date from the time of the mosque's destruction. In any event, the Sauran hoard of copper coins found in the mosque testifies to the fact that copper coins were used extensively by locals to support their economic and commercial activities and even penetrated the spiritual life of the city, which was feasible only from the end of the 16th to the beginning of the 17th centuries when the city was characterized by a high level of monetary relationships.

Unfortunately, the wall with the *mihrab*, as well as all the external walls of the structure, and some columns or pylons, on which an arched dome system rested, turned out to be completely without brick; there was not even brick flooring in some of the rooms. In a pile inside the central hall we found fragments of the base of the collapsed interior dome. The width of passages between the columns bearing the arched dome is 2.75cm; the width of each column is 1.15cm. It is obvious that the dome of the central *mihrab* hall was 6m in diameter and eight domes on its sides had a diameter of 3m.

The area of the *mihrab* ("*zulla*") along the line of the wall was approximately 31 × 12m and the area of the whole complex was 31×34m or a bit over 1000m^2. In its layout, the mosque is classified as a traditional closed courtyard type of the late Middle Ages. The isolated portal-dome double-column type *mihrab* is facing the courtyard, on three sides of which there was arch and domed one-column gallery. Sauran Mosque is an example of one of the versions of composite design. Similar Cathedral Mosques of larger dimensions are found nearby in Otrar (14th-15th centuries), Samarkand (Bibi-khanym, 167×109m, end of the 14th century), Tashkent (Jami Mosque, 91×36.5m, end of the 15th century) and in Bukhara (Kaljan Mosque, 126×81.4m, first quarter of the 16th century).

The wide front portal of the *mihrab*, the principal part of the mosque, faces the closed-type courtyard, at the center of which there is a principal axis mounted well with some capital structure above.[54] Next to it is a wide (16m) and deep (6m) *iwan* opening onto the courtyard (Pl. VI-23). The design features the symmetrical axis line of the *mihrab*, the entrance to the *mihrab* hall, and the well perpendicular to the axis of the front portal, which means that, facing the square, the southeast front wall slightly deviates from the axis of the rectangular courtyard, and that the front portal is asymmetrical to the whole structure.[55] Such an unusual layout of the complex was probably dictated by the location of the mosque. It was built on the north-western edge of a rectangular plaza and according to tradition the *mihrab* and one of the principal design axes must have been oriented south-westwards. The Sauran architects were thus challenged in much the same way as later Samarkand architects when perparing the design of the Tilla-kari Mosque in the Samarkand Registan. In both cases the front portal axis is perpendicular to the *mihrab*'s axis of symmetry.

Stepping over the threshold, the visitor finds himself in a small domed square room (3.5 ×3.5m). The wall opposite the front door was blind (or may have comprised a large decorative lattice); to the left and right of the front door there were archways probably leading to even smaller domed square rooms (2.6×2.6m) with exit doors opening onto the big courtyard and other premises of the complex. To the left there was the high arch of the front *iwan* leading to the *mihrab* of the Mosque; across the courtyard there were four arches of the west enfilade of domed rooms and to the right a wide *iwan* with flat roofing resting upon three columns.

From the fragments of surviving brickwork we were able to establish that the thickness of the external wall was 1.4m. The SE section of the front wall to the right of the front portal was made of 9-10 layers of brickwork, most of which have survived. It was an end wall segment of a large room (5.2×5.6m), which was used as a ceramic workshop for a long time during the second period after the Mosque ceased to be used for its intended purpose. Probably some parts of the Mosque had already been destroyed, and others adapted to workshops. At that time a large round double-deck kiln (diameter: 2.0m) for firing ceramic wares was built in the above-mentioned corner room.

The round tank (D1.9m) found in the courtyard close to the corner with the calcinating kiln and well structure can also be referred to the second period. The tank was buried in the ground at a depth of 50-65cm and encircled with clamp fired brickwork. A water drainage chute faced with brick ran all the way to the tank across the entire courtyard of the Mosque in a SW-NE direction skirting the walls of the well structure. This round tank was probably used to soak pot clay.

Digging at the site of the early Cathedral Mosque situated in the central square of Sauran is now completed. Although the Cathedral Mosque is classified as an architectural model of the Central Asian version of the "classical" hypostyle Mosque, there are few convincing arguments regarding the origin of this architectural style.[56] The state of preservation of the structural elements makes it possible to revive the architectural aspects of this interesting building (Pl. VI-24). Two exactly dated periods of its existence (as well as of the other public buildings of central square of Sauran) testify to some historic event which brought about a significant change in the medieval cities in the region. A similar phenomenon took place in the neighboring city of Otrar. Here the Mosque of the 14th-15th centuries was much bigger but of similar style, and it too was ruined and replaced by ordinary dwelling houses in the 16th century.[57]

Medrese. A massive rectangular barrow lay on the north-eastern side of the central square of Sauran, and we assumed that the ruins of a large structure made of fired brick lay concealed under the barrow. Archaeological digging at the site revealed an outstanding structure that could be identified as the *medrese*, which according to Wasifi was built at the end of the 15th-beginning of 16th century and the minarets of which remained intact until the second half of the 19th century.[58] The *medrese* was built in 1515 on the orders of Ubajdulla khan, governor of Bukhara. Sejid Shamsaddin Muhammad Kurty,[59] a friend of Wasifi, was appointed as chief priest. In his memoirs Wasifi described this *medrese* as having marvelous "swinging" minarets, one of which was ruined in 1867 and the other in 1878.[60]

The *medrese* was a rectangular (31.5×28m) courtyard complex. Protruding from the front arched portal were two minarets on either side along a northwestern orientation (Pl. VI-26). The diameter of each minaret base was 3.3m. At the bottom it was brick bonded with the front wall and portal, and only a half semicircle of it protruded from the front wall. The body of the minaret up to the roofing was probably solid and above it was hollow with a spiral staircase inside. One can get to the tower via the roof. The steps leading to the roof in the north wall of the north-east antechamber have survived.

Minarets were built on the rectangular shape footing (3.5×2.75m) 3m deep. The minaret footing was made of solid fired brick masonry (23-25×23-25×5-6cm) using clay mortar with a high level of ash impurities. To make the footing a pit was dug penetrating the underlying occupation layer. The bottom layer was made of masonry brick placed on edge by piling up 4-5 pieces in a staggered order. There was no bonding mortar used between the bricks, and they were only watered with a liquid mix of water and ash. Above were six layers of brick masonry placed flat-wise using lime mortar with a high content of ash. Above was another layer of bricks placed on edge in the order mentioned above and then another five layers of brick were placed horizontally, and this pattern was repeated all the way down the footing depth.

The edge of the 1m-high base of the *medrese* protruding from the front wall was decorated with a double row of fired brick fragments. The entrance staircase, 3.3m wide and 4.5m long, cut through the base leading up to the threshold of the arched *iwan*, which was 2.5m wide, and 2.25m deep (Pl. VI-25). The wide steps were covered with large (45×45×7cm) fired bricks. The threshold was paved with solid flat stones.

Above the front *iwan* there is an arch resting upon protruding pylons extended thanks to the closely coupled minarets. Once you enter the 1.9m-wide doorway you find yourself in an antechamber 5.8 × 2.9m in area. The front door is through a niche measuring 0.25-0.30m deep and 3.3m wide. There are wide clay sofas (1.3×1.7m) in the corners next to the entrance. The antechamber leads to two octagonal rooms, one on either side. The octagonal room to the left has an exit to the "*darshana*" (classrooms) and the courtyard. In the north wall we discovered the base of a staircase, most probably, leading to the minarets via the roof. The room to the right has passages leading to the courtyard and most likely to the mosque, which is unfortunately completely destroyed.

The rectangular courtyard (18×15m) was paved with bricks, which survive between two bands of *dandana* (band of bricks placed on end) 2m long. The bricks of the pavement in the center of the courtyard have been removed, with only a surviving segment. The first band of the *dandana* edges the courtyard along the pylon base line and the second is made at a distance of 2.5m and limiting the area to 11.7 × 8.5m. In the courtyard we found two principal axis-mounted *iwans* located opposite each other, both facing the courtyard. The area of the south-east *iwan* (540×540cm) is covered with a pointed dome (a fragment of which was found on the floor). The thickness of the weight-bearing walls was 155-156cm. The walls and massive supporting pylons were made of both adobe and fired bricks.

While digging in the rooms, it became clear that before their destruction they had been abandoned for some time when a thick drift band was formed, following which they were made habitable again. In front of each room there is an area with *tashnau* (drainage) buried in the floor. Wall niches were found in some rooms surviving in a more or less satisfactory state. The walls (back, side, front) in which niches were made must have been chosen arbitrarily. The floors in the rooms are covered with both whole and scrap fired bricks. At the time when the *medrese* functioned, they made the rooms more comfortable. Thus, for example, it was established that to heat the rooms they made stoves with chimney pipes in the corner of the room passing through the clay sofa and as a result the initial level of the sofas was slightly elevated. Chimney pipes (22cm in width) were made of fired bricks placed on the edge and the grooves formed were covered with whole bricks. Incense burners used to burn the herb "*adraspan*", the smoke of which considered to ward off evil spirits (actually disinfectant), were found in many of the cells. They were made of vertically placed fired bricks of 25× 25cm in dimension, buried 25cm deep in the floor. We may assume that all the rooms were covered with the domed roof since arch-shaped fragments of the dome and gypsum tiles trapezium-shaped in cross-section which were used to decorate the roof were found in a scrap heap. The walls were mainly plastered with gypsum mortar, except in some places faced with unglazed polished bricks. The portals were coated with decorative polychrome glaze.

Altogether 30 rooms of the complex in various states of preservation have been excavated, some of which were used as passages, antechambers, and *iwans*, but mainly as one-roomed cells or units called "*hudjra*" where the teachers and students of the *medrese* lived.

The fully excavated *medrese* constituted an architectural ensemble with one more fundamental building across the street made of fired brick with a portal once covered with polychrome glaze coating (Pl. VI-27). It was established that the base of the façade walls of this building ran for a distance of 18m that was the section width along the main street running from the north front gate to the central square of the city. There was one axis-mounted front portal, i.e. such structures forming an architectural and planning composition of the "*kosh/kos*" style when the front walls of the buildings face each other (Pl. VI-22).

Such planning was typical of medieval cities of the Muslim East.[61] Hence it appears that the general plan of this complex was that of a rectangular enclosure-courtyard type with a protruding front portal on the west façade facing the façade of the *medrese*.[62]

By 2009 we had excavated half of the assumed area of this architectural complex, but as yet have been unable to determine its functional purpose. If we proceed from the assumption that the architectural ensembles of Central Asian cities starting from the Timurid period "are characterized mostly by a complex of various religious and cultic buildings, including the mosques for everyday and Friday public worship; the *hanaka*, institutions for religious rites of Sufi community dervishes; the *medrese*, medieval institutions of higher education",[63] then the location of the *hanaka* in the central square of Sauran has not yet been identified. Therefore it is quite possible that this is that very building, situated opposite the *medrese* in a "*kosh/kos*" composition, just like in the Samarkand Muhammad-Sultan ensemble, where the *medrese* is opposite the *hanaka*; or like the original ensemble of the Timurid Registan,[64] where in the second half of the 15th century the grand portal of Ulugbek *medrese* was opposed to the splendid portal of the *hanaka* with a huge dome behind (as known today on the site of the *hanaka*, there is the later Shir-dor *medrese*). The north side of the square was occupied by a two-tiered caravan-sarai with a portal façade spaced into arched segments. According to experts, the outline of this portal façade was used in the construction of the Tilla-kari Mosque. Although digging continues at the "Sauran Registan" and is far from complete, we can confidently assert that we are lucky to be dealing with a magnificent example of an urban ensemble of religious (and secular?) architecture decorating the central square of the city. Apparently, this ensemble opens up a perspective on the monumental public buildings situated on both sides of the almost 200m long section of the central street (avenue) from the "Registan" to the inner square in front of the northern front gates of Sauran. This is also demonstrated by the topography of the ruins along the street fully paved with quarry tiles. Historians and architects call such an architectural ensemble a "longitudinal-axial",[65] along which housing had a perspective view of the city's enfilade of monumental buildings with richly decorated facades and arched portals facing each other. The principle of spatial architectural design of this most representative urban development was probably laid down during the historic period, when in the first quarter of the 14th century (or at the end of the 13th century) Sauran under Ordu's descendants temporarily became one of the capitals of Kok-Orda due to the relocation of the political center of the this Juchid's principality from the banks of the Irtysh river to the Syr Darya.[66] As far as we know at that time the city was relocated from the site of an ancient city of Karatobe to a new place, where now the walls of late Sauran rise. Most likely, this relocation of the city was related to a substantial restructuring of the state and political system as a result of the disintegration of the Mongol empire in the last quarter of the 13th century and the founding of new states in Eurasia. According to written sources of 1320, Sasy-Buka, the governor of Kok-Orda died and was buried in the city. His son Erzen built *medrese*, *hanaka* and mosques in Sauran and other cities of Southern Kazakhstan.[67] Sauran played the role of capital city for a long time being the residence of governors of various dynasties. In the 1480s the city was governed by Irenchi-sultan, son of Janibek, one of the first Kazakh khans.[68]

It is interesting to note that in the second quarter of the 15th century a number of Golden Horde cities, including the capital were relocated in the Volga region and in the whole North Caspian region. This was followed by what is known as the "problem of two capital cities". To explain this phenomenon, researchers have put forward a number of hypotheses ranging from internal and foreign policy to the environmental ecology. A comparatively recently published article casts doubt on these hypotheses save one, the explanation provided by changes in environmental ecology. According to V.V. Pachkalov,[69] new archaeological investigations and the analysis of accumulated numismatic collections indicate that there was a catastrophic transgression of the Caspian Sea in the second quarter of the 14th century and this played a major role in the relocation of a number of cities of the North Caspian region and in particular in the relocation of the capital city and the founding of Sarai al-Jedid ("New Sarai").

Of course, although such a solution refers to the cities of the Volga and Jaiik region,[70] this does not preclude this emergency and other factors in that historical period having an influence in other geographical zones of Eurasia, namely in the Aral region. As we all know the climate and ecology of the Caspian and Aral regions produce feed-back so we may speak of regression of the Aral Sea and its basin while transgression of the Caspian Sea occurs. L. N. Gumilev [71] describes this as the "concept of Eurasian humidification heterochrony", the phenomenon whereby the floor of the Aral Sea is exposed due to current regression. Significant shallowing of the Aral starting from the 14th century (or in the second half of the 13th century) may testify to the ongoing increasing aridity of the Syr Darya river basin, one of the principal rivers in the region. An extreme shortage of water could also be observed in large urban centers located in its basin, such as Sauran. Of late there has been convincing archaeological evidence of the fall in the level of water in the Aral Sea in the 16th century. Kazakhstan's archaeologists have recently discovered and investigated the ruins of settlements and necropolises dating to the 14th century [72] situated on the construction of branched *kariz* system which rely on deep seated ground water.[73] It must have been difficult if at all possible to supply the ancient city of Sauran (on the site of the ancient city of Karatobe) with enough *kariz* water for its needs. The environment of an area of 3-3.5km to the north, at the junction of water bearing detrital cones of three local small streams running down from the Karatau [74] mountains, must have been more favorable.

It is unlikely that there might be only one reason however convincing for the relocation of a large city to a new site. Probably, one more factor is related to the case with Sauran, which G.A. Fedorov-Davydov [75] discussed with regard to the Volga region cities. The aspiration of the local elites to become independent from the power of the Karakorum Great Khans may have also served as a sufficient supplementary motivation or rationale for implementing great town planning projects.

The implementation of such large-scale town planning was possible only in a capital city as an act of centrally organized political will, the onset of which was related to the fact of relocation and the laying down of new city foundations from scratch. The khans of a young state yielding to no other post-Mongol dynasty rulers could have carried out such active construction and implemented ambitious architectural projects. Naturally the authors of such architectural and town planning projects adhered to the overall development of city planning and architecture in Central Asia.

Notes

[1] Байпаков К.М., Смагулов Е.А. Средневековый город Сауран (Алматы: 2005).

[2] Гейнс А.К. Собрание литературных трудов. т.2 (СПб.: 1989), 225, 262-266.

[3] Топография Оренбургской губернии. Сочинение П.И. Рычкова. 1762 г. (Оренбург: 1887), 18-19; Лерх П. И. Археологическая поездка в Туркестанский край в 1867 г. (СПб.:., 1870), 14, 21, 31; Пашино П.И. Туркестанский край в 1866 г. Путевые заметки (СПб, 1868), 59-60; Федченко А.П. Путешествия в Туркестан (М.: 1950), 46.

[4] Бернштам А.Н. Проблемы древней истории и этногенеза Южного Казахстана.-Изв. АН КазССР, серия археолог. (67) 1950, №2, с. 82; Агеева Е.И., Пацевич Г.И. Из истории оседлых поселений и городов Южного Казахстана. ТИИАЭ, т. 5. 1958, с. 107-110.

[5] Агеева Е.И., Пацевич Г.И. Из истории оседлых поселений и городов..., с. 109-110; Байпаков К.М. Средневековая городская культура Южного Казахстана и Семиречья в VI-начале XIII в. Алма-Ата, 1986, с. 27.

[6] Байпаков К.М., Смагулов Е.А. Средневековый город Сауран, с.62-67.

[7] Свод памятников истории и культуры Казахстана. Южно-Казахстанская область, с.307; Байпаков К.М. Средневековые города Казахстана на Великом Шелковом пути. Алматы, 1998, с.65-70.

[8] Акишев К.А., Байпаков К.М. Кяризы Саурана//Вестник АН Каз.ССР, 4, 1973, с.76-78.

[9] Грошев В.А. Древняя ирригация Юга Казахстана. Алматы, 1996, с.184-186; Excavating vertical wells they failed to reach underground water-bearing horizons.

[10] Смагулов Е.А. Кяризы Туркестанского оазиса// Известия МОН РК, НАН РК, сер. общественных наук, №1, 2003, с.172-189; Deom J.M., Sala R. The 232 Karez of the Sauran region//Сохранение и использование объектов культурного и смешанного наследия современной Центральной Азии. Алматы, 2005, с.120-132.

[11] Смагулов Е., Туякбаев М., Ержигитова А. Краткие итоги исследований Туркестанской археологической экспедиции в 1999г.//Известия МОН РК, НАН РК, №1, 2000; Байпаков К.М., Смагулов Е.А. Средневековый город Сауран. Алматы, 2005, с. 74-77.

[12] Смагулов Е., Туякбаев М., Ержигитова А. Краткие итоги исследований Туркестанской археологической экспедиции в 1999г…

[13] МИИТ,т.1, с.185.

[14] Птицын Г.В. К вопросу о географии «Шах-наме»//ТОВЭ, т.IV, 1947, с.305-309; Кляшторный С.Г. История Центральной Азии и памятники рунического письма.СПб., 2003, с.213-216.

[15] Смагулов Е.А. Сауранский археолгический комплекс// Известия НАН РК, 1, 2007, с.126-134.

[16] Digs at the site of late Sauran were carried out under scientific direction of K.M.Baipakov, academician, and director of the Institute of Archaeology named after A. Margulan (Alma-Ata). Apart from the staff of the Institute, S. Akylbek (v.Shaulder), A.Erzhigitova (Shymkent), O.Lushpenko, N.Stolyarova (Tashkent), T.Krupa (Kharkov), A.Jumabayev (Bishkek), E.Zilivinskaya, and S.Yatsenko (Moscow) were all involved in the work carried out at the site of Sauran.

[17] It is established that this very *medrese* was described by Wasifi, an author of the 16th c.; and its one-of-a-kind swinging minarets were destroyed by the end of the 19th c. The unusual architecture of this structure attracted G.A.Pugachenkova's attention. (Пугаченкова Г.А. Сауранские башни// Труды САГУ, вып.LVII, Ташкент, 1954; Байпаков К.М., Акылбек С. Медресе средневекового Саурана//Археология степной Евразии. Алматы-Кемерово, 2008).

[18] Байпаков К., Смагулов Е.А., Ержигитова А., Туякбаев М. и др.// Исследования городищи средневекового Саурана // Мемлекеттік "Мәдени мұра" бағдарламасы бойынша 2005 жылғы Археологиялық зерттеулер жайлы есеп. Алматы, 2005, с.304-307; Смагулов Е.А. Архитектура Саурана// Промышленность Казахстана, 1, 2006., с.96-97.

[19] The 2006-2008 excavations have been sponsored by Social Fund "Olketanu" (Taraz) and we deeply appreciate the help rendered by its director E.Baimurzin.

[20] Смагулов Е.А., Столярова Н.П. Городище Каратобе-древний Сауран// Материалы международной научно-практической конференции «Древний Тараз и тюркская цивилизация». Тараз, 2007г., 22-24 октября. С.105-108; Смагулов Е.А. Средневековый Сауран: на перекрестке проблем и мнений// Материалы международной научной конференции «Роль степных городов в цивилизации номадов», посвященной 10-летнему юбилею г.Астана. 2 июля 2008г. Астана, 2008, С.190-197.

[21] Смагулов Е.А., Ержигитова А.А. Исследования Древнего Саурана//Известия НАН РК, сер.обществ. наук, №1, 2009. С.236-257.

[22] Смагулов Е.А. "Сауранский археологический комплекс...", 126-134.

[23] Лерх П. И. Археологическая поездка в Туркестанский край в 1867 г..., с.16-17; Свод памятников истории и культуры Казахстана. Южно-Казахстанская область. Алматы. 1994, с.308-310.

[24] Свод памятников истории и культуры Казахстана. Южно-Казахстанская область. Алматы. 1994, с.307.

[25] "Serdabe" according to P.Lerh. Underground water storage reservoir covered with a dome. (Лерх П. Археологическая поездка..., с.14). "Sardob" was a commonly used utility service and water supply facility in the cities of Central Asia, Khurasan, and the Middle East.

[26] Байпаков К.М., Смагулов Е.А. Средневековый город Сауран. Алматы, 2005, с. 74-77. Mir-i Arab or Abdallah al-Iamani al-Hadramauti, also known as the "builder" of medrese in Registan of Bukhara named after him-Mir-i Arab medrese (see about him: Бабаджанов Б. Мир-и Араб//Культура кочевников на рубеже веков (XIX-XX, XX-XXIвв): *Проблемы генезиса и трансформации. Мат. Международной конференции.* г.Алматы, 1995, с.88-102; Джураева Г.А. Мир-и Араб и политическая жизнь в Бухаре в XVIв//*Духовенство и политическая жизнь на ближнем и среднем Востоке в период феодализма.* (М., 1985, с.74-79).

[27] Акишев К.А., Байпаков К.М. "Кяризы Саурана...", 76-78.

[28] Свод памятников истории и культуры Казахстана. Южно-Казахстанская область, с.307; Байпаков К.М., Смагулов Е.А. Средневековый город Сауран..., с.62-65.

[29] Смагулов Е.А. "Сауранский археологический комплекс...", 126-134.

[30] Пугаченкова Г.А. Сауранские башни// Труды САГУ, вып.LVII, Ташкент, 1954.

[31] Смагулов Е.А. Город Сауран: перспективы исследования, консервации и музеефикации // Отан тарихы. №1-2, 2000, с. 100-109.

[32] Смагулов Е.А., Туякбаев М.К., Ержигитова А.А. Жума мечеть на Регистане Саурана//Отчет об археологических исследованиях по Государственной программе «Культурное наследие», Алматы, 2007, с.173-176.

[33] См.напр.: Байпаков К.М., Смагулов Е.А. Средневековый город Сауран. Алматы, 2005, с.60-62.

[34] Муминов А.К. Кокандская версия исламизации Туркестана//Подвижники ислама. Культ святых и суфизм в Средней Азии и на Кавказе. М., с.138-140.

[35] Беленицкий А.М., Бентович И.Б., Большаков О.Г. Средневековый город Средней Азии. Л., 1973, с.20;

Семенов Г.Л. Город и замок в раннесредневековом Согде//Культурные связи народов Средней Азии и Кавказа. Древность и средневековье. М., 1990, с.60.

[36] Смагулов Е.А., Ержигитова А.А. Продолжение исследования стратиграфии Древнего Саурана // Отчет об археологических исследованиях по Государственной программе «Культурное наследие» в 2008г. Алматы, 2009, с.204-210 .

[37] Беленицкий А.М., Бентович И.Б., Большаков О.Г. Средневековый город Средней Азии. Л., 1973, с.195.

[38] Свод памятников истории и культуры Казахстана. Южно-Казахстанская область.., с.307.

[39] Болдырев А.Н. Зайнатдин Васифи-таджикский писатель XVIв. М., 1957.

[40] In this article we used the aerial photographs and other materials of R. Sala and J.M. Deom. I take this opportunity of thanking R. Sala and J.M. Deom for their contribution to our joint work.

[41] Deom J.M., Sala R. The 232 Karez of the Sauran region//Сохранение и использование объектов культурного и смешанного наследия современной Центральной Азии. Алматы, 2005, с.120-132.

[42] Смагулов Е.А. Кяризы Туркестанского оазиса// Известия МОН РК, НАН РК, сер. общ-ых наук, №1, 2003, с.172-190; Байпаков К.М., Смагулов Е.А. Средневековый город Сауран..., с.73-80.

[43] For a description of the traces of the *kariz* found in the area, see the following papers: Акишев К.А., Байпаков К.М. Кяризы Саурана.., с.76-78; Смагулов Е.А. Кяризы Туркестанского оазиса..., с.172-190.

[44] Бартольд В.В. К истории орошения Туркестана//Сочинения, т.III, М., 1965, с.130, 138. 225.

[45] Турсунов А.А. От Арала до Лобнора. Гидроэкология бессточных бассейнов Центральной Азии. Алматы, 2002.

[46] Исамиддинов М.Х. Истоки городской культуры Самаркандского Согда. Ташент, 2002, с.16.

[47] These finds together with "boot" decorated with tree image (Pl. VI-17-3), earlier discovered in the same dig (CH2), extend the range of forms of popular amulets in the 10th- 12th centuries.

[48] This find was shown to I.L.Kyzlasov, who kindly agreed to give his expert opinion for which I would like to express my appreciation. In his comprehensive view, he noted in particular that "it is beyond any doubt that inscriptions discovered in Sauran do not belong to the famous Asian runic character set commonly called Orkhon-Yeniseian script. At the same time all these graphic signs are characteristic features of the so called Achiktash runic script of Central Asia. Probably we should withhold comment about this still mysterious cultural phenomenon. However, archaeological dating of the above mentioned epigraphic material suggests that it belonged to early Oguz or an even earlier substrate. The time and environment of the Achiktash runic script existence is yet to be determined. E.Smagulov's findings contribute to this purpose to a considerable degree and new archaeological discoveries in Sauran, hopefully, will facilitate it". As well as: "It is important that Achiktash runic script luckily found on the artifacts from Sauran belongs to the west branch of the runic script, the so-called Eurasian group of its own origin, independent of Orkhon-Yeniseian script by any standard". (Кызласов И.Л. Экспертное заключение о характере надписей на обломках глиняного сосуда, обнаруженных в 2008 г. на

городище Каратобе (Древний Сауран (Республика Казахстан)). Архив ТАЭ, с.1-2).

[49] Гуревич Л.В. "К интерпретации пенджикентских «капелл»", *Культурные связи народов Средней Азии и Кавказа. Древность и средневековье* (М.: 1990),.67-87; Филанович М.И. "К типологии святилищ огня Согда и Чача", *Городская культура Бактрии-Тохаристана и Согда* (Ташкент: 1987), 148-156.

[50] Some materials on certain artifacts found have been published: Смагулов Е.А., Ержигитова А.А. "Исследования Древнего Саурана..", 236-257.

[51] Байпаков К.М., Смагулов Е.А., Ержигитова А.А. и др. "Исследования городища средневекового Саурана..", 304-307.

[52] Смагулов Е. "Архитектура Саурана...", с.96-97.

[53] Бурнашева Р.З., Смагулов Е.А., Туякбаев М.К. Клады и монеты Туркестана (Алматы: 2006), 61-63.

[54] The well head has a diameter of 0,9m; the well is situated in the center of a rectangular structure measuring 4.4×4.95m in area.

[55] The base of the right pylon is all that remains of the front portal. Its width is 1.8m and it is 2.2m protruding from the face wall. The protruding portal ("*peshtak*") must have been 7.2m wide.

[56] См.например: Юсупова М.А. "К генезису и эволюции дворово-айванной композиции в архитектуре Средней Азии", *Культурное наследие Средней Азии (Ташкент, 2002), 284-290*; Шукуров Ш.М. *Образ Храма (М.: 2002), 46-53.*

[57] Акишев К.А., Байпаков К.М.. Ерзакович Л.Б. Отрар в XIII-XVвв. (Алма-Ата: 1987), 103-108.

[58] Байпаков К.М., Акылбек С. Ш. "Медресе средневекового Саурана...", с.76.

[59] Болдырев А.Н. Зайнаддин Васифи-таджикский писатель XVI в..., 160-161.

[60] Пугаченкова Г.А. "Сауранские башни...", с. 163.

[61] Гулямов Я.Г. "К вопросу о традиции архитектурных ансамблей в городах Средней Азии XVв", ИМКУ, вып.29 (Самарканд: 1998), 29-35.

[62] Акылбек С.Ш. "Медресе Саурана", *Материалы международной научной конференции «Роль степных городов в цивилизации номадов», посвященной 10-летнему юбилею г.Астана* (Астана: 2008), 321-329.

[63] Гулямов Я.Г. "К вопросу о традиции архитектурных ансамблей...", 29.

[64] Пугаченкова Г.А. Зодчество Центральной Азии. XVв. (Ташкент: 1976), 91-95.

[65] Пугаченкова Г.А. Зодчество Центральной Азии..., 96.

[66] Егоров В.Л. Историческая география Золотой Орды в XIII-XIVвв. (М.: 1985), 129.

[67] СМИЗО, т. 2 (М.-Л.: 1941), 129.

[68] Пищулина К.А. "Присырдарьинские города и их значение в истории казахских ханств", *Казахстан в XV-XVII вв. (Алма-Ата: 1969), 17-18.*

[69] Пачкалов А.В. "Трансгрессия Каспийского моря и история золотоордынских городов в Северном Прикаспии", *Восток-Запад: диалог культур и цивилизаций Евразии*, вып.8 (Казань: 2007), 171-180.

[70] Materials obtained as a result of the study of the newly discovered ancient site of the city of Jaiik situated on the right bank of the Ural river, strengthen argumentation of the hypothesis of relocation of the cities in the Caspian region due to the decisive role of ecological factors. While interpreting the reasons for the desolation of the city lying at the confluence of two rivers: the Ural and its tributary Chagan at the foot of Cretaceous hills, we refrained from giving an unambiguous answer to it, but we emphasized that in the one-layer monument only coins of the Uzbek khan were found. Moreover, the name of this site "Shakafni" (as marked on the map of Jenkinson) is presumably consonant with the name of the unexplored city of "Shakashin" built by the Nogai tribe on the Ural River in this place, where the Kindaly tributary flows into it. Only on this basis can we assume continuity through relocation of the city upstream. (see: Смагулов Е.А. "Проблемы исследования средневековых городов в Уральской области", *Известия МОН РК, НАН РК, сер. общественных наук*, №1 (2002), 91-102; Байпаков К.М., Смагулов Е.А., Ахатов Г.А. *Средневековое городище Жайык* (Алматы: 2005), 121-126).

[71] Гумилев Л.Н. Ритмы Евразии (М., 1993), 271-297.

[72] См.: Смагулов Е.А. "Находка и исследование мазара на дне Аральского моря", *Отан тарихы*, № 4 (2001), 77-82; Байпаков К.М. и др. "Археологические исследования на дне Арала", *Отчет об археологических исследования по Государственной программе «Культурное наследие» 2006 года* (Алматы: 2007), 120-122.

[73] Смагулов Е.А. "Кяризы Туркестанского оазиса..", 172-189.

[74] Deom J.M., Sala R. "The 232 Karez of the Sauran region..", 120-132.

[75] Федоров-Давыдов Г.А. Общественный строй Золотой Орды (М.: 1973), 80.

DEFINITIONS

ИИАЭ -	Institute of History, Archaeology and Ethnography
ИМКУ-	History of Material Culture of Uzbekistan
АН Каз.ССР-	Academy of Sciences of the Kazakh Soviet Socialist Republic
М.-	Moscow
МИИТ-	Materials and Studies on Turkmen History
МОН РК, НАН РК	Ministry of Education and Sciences of the Republic of Kazakhstan, National Academy of Sciences of the Republic of Kazakhstan
САГУ-	Central Asian State University
СМИЗО-	Golden Horde History Publication
СПб.-	City of St. Petersburg

THE ENDS OF THE EARTH: THE XIONGNU EMPIRE AND EASTERN HAN REPRESENTATIONS OF THE AFTERLIFE FROM SHAANXI AND SHANXI

Leslie Wallace

During the first and second centuries CE, Han settlers living near the present-day borders of Shaanxi, Shanxi, and Inner Mongolia built tombs with stone doorways that frequently depicted scenes of the hunt (figs. 1 and 2). The iconography of these hunting scenes, as well as their popularity, differs from Eastern Han tomb reliefs in other regions and focuses on the figure of the mounted archer who is often depicted turned backward in his saddle delivering the so-called "Parthian shot" (figs. 3 and 4). During the Eastern Han Dynasty (25-220 CE) the area in which these tombs were constructed was part of the Shang 上 and Xihe 西河 commanderies (jun 郡) and served as a safeguard against the encroachment of the expanding Xiongnu 匈奴 Empire. Previous scholarship has correctly associated hunting imagery in Shaanxi and Shanxi with the mixed culture and economy of the region, but has failed to take into account its significance in a mortuary setting. My research suggests that it was part of an iconographical program that focused on the depiction and facilitation of the passage of the deceased to the immortal paradise of the goddess Xiwangmu 西王母. Based on visual and textual sources, I argue that in these reliefs the dangerous borderlands between Heaven and Earth were equated with the world of the Xiongnu. In Han Dynasty texts, this world is described as a barren wilderness filled with various dangerous creatures, the most prominent being the Xiongnu themselves, who for much of the Han Dynasty remained the quintessential foe for the Han Chinese. Furthermore, I suggest that the prevalence of the mounted archer in these reliefs is based upon the Han conception of this figure as the ultimate warrior who was placed in these tombs to defeat in perpetuity the Xiongnu and the other denizens of the afterlife believed to thwart the deceased at every turn.

In order to understand the complex nature of such imagery, I will first establish the connection between the Xiongnu and representations of mounted archers. Then highlighting the martial nature of hunting imagery in Shaanxi and Shanxi, I will focus on the relationship between the figure of the mounted archer, traditional Chinese associations of hunting with warfare, and changing conceptions of the ideal warrior during the Han Dynasty. Following this, I turn to Han textual descriptions of the Xiongnu and the Northern Steppe demonstrating their affinities with the representations of the landscape and inhabitants of the borderlands between Heaven and Earth. Finally, I will look at depictions of foreigners in Eastern Han tombs to demonstrate how as political and cultural outsiders they were often represented as both benevolent and malignant denizens of the afterlife. I conclude that in hunting imagery in Eastern Han tombs from Shaanxi and Shanxi, the Xiongnu in death, as in life, were conceived of as ambiguous figures that were both friend and foe to the patrons of these images.

The Figure of the Mounted Archer

Hunting scenes from Shaanxi and Shanxi are dominated by the figure of the mounted archer who is represented individually, in groups or as part of chariot processions (figs. 3 and 4). In some scenes, mounted hunters may use other weapons such as spears or swords, although this is far less common. Unlike some of the mounted archers represented during the Western Han Dynasty (206 BCE-8 CE) that are depicted with a mixture of Han and non-Han attributes (fig. 5), most mounted archers in Shaanxi and Shanxi are clearly represented as Han Chinese. As I will show, however, these figures are still engaged in an activity that was strongly associated with the Xiongnu, known in Han texts as "*yingong zhi min*" 引弓之民 (lit., "the people who live by drawing the bow").[1]

The earliest appearance of the figure of the mounted archer in China is found on a third century BCE hunting scene decorating a Qin Dynasty (221-206 BCE) brick and a mural from the ruins of Palace No. 3 at the Qin capital of Xianyang 咸阳.[2] During the Western Han Dynasty the popularity of the mounted archer grew eclipsing scenes of chariot hunting, corded-arrow hunts, and archery contests that had been common throughout most of China during the Warring States period (475-221 BCE). Throughout the first and second centuries BCE it remained a popular motif and was represented on chariot ornaments, hill jars, lacquer ware, and tomb bricks (fig. 5).

The sudden appearance and popularity of the mounted archer has generated a number of theories regarding its origins all of which are based on the consensus that such imagery was not native to China. Esther Jacobson has argued most convincingly that it was adopted and adapted from Scytho-Siberian material culture. As she has shown, this motif from the beginning was associated with the nomadic lifestyle and material culture of those living to the north of central China.[3]

During the Warring States period contact with northern nomadic groups intensified as various states sought to push their borders northward. This contact resulted in a growing interest in foreign customs and material culture. During this time mounted archery and nomadic costume were first introduced by royal decree in the state of Zhao 赵 in 307 BCE in an attempt to conquer several neighboring non-Chinese and Chinese states.[4] Due to pressures from Chinese expansion and internal developments, these groups of people eventually joined forces and formed the Xiongnu Empire in the third century BCE. Contact and conflict intensified between the Xiongnu and Chinese with the founding of the Qin and Han Empires and the contemporaneous expansion of Xiongnu power.

Although during much of the Han Dynasty the Xiongnu were to remain the greatest real and perceived enemy of the Han Empire, historic records profess to the introduction and popularity of Xiongnu exotica that flowed into the Han Empire as gifts received from Xiongnu delegations and as commodities in what must have been extensive trading:[5]

夫中國一端之縵，得匈奴纍金之物……是以騾驢馲駝，銜尾入塞，驒騱騵馬，盡爲我畜，鼲貂狐貉，采旃文罽，充于内府……是則外國之物内流……

Thus a piece of silk can be exchanged with the Xiongnu for articles worth several pieces of gold…Mules, donkey and camels enter the frontier in unbroken lines; horses, dapples, and bays and prancing mounts, come into our possession. The furs of sables, marmots, foxes and badgers, colored rugs and decorated carpets fill the Imperial Treasury… foreign products keep flowing in…[6]

Within this context, the figure of the mounted archer was added to the iconographic vocabulary of the hunt in ancient China. Its popularity was due to a pervasive interest in foreign goods during the Western Han, Xiongnu military might, and firsthand encounters with the Xiongnu in full regalia on diplomatic missions to the Western Han capital of Chang'an.[7] This web of associations insured that it remained a popular motif decorating tomb goods throughout the Western Han Dynasty.

Although the figure of the mounted archer would continue to decorate hill jars during the Eastern Han, by the beginning of the first century CE, the popularity of such imagery had begun to wane. This was due to a number of factors that included the decline of the power of the court in dictating taste, the reemergence of regional art traditions, and the costly and often unsuccessful wars waged against the Xiongnu. It is not surprising that such factors led to the decline of the presence of the mounted archer in hunting imagery and the development of the regional hunting iconography at this time.

What is surprising is that that the mounted archer reappears as the most common element of hunting scenes in tombs in Shaanxi towards the end of the first century CE. As I will show, the return of the mounted archer in this region was not simply due to the geographical closeness of this area to the old Western Han capital, the work of provincial artists who were behind the times in tomb decoration, nor just a reflection of the mixed economy and culture of the region. Instead, as I will argue below, the prevalence of the mounted archer was the result of the tradition of the hunt as a form of military training in ancient China and the idea of the mounted archer as the warrior par excellence who could defeat the Xiongnu.

The Hunt, Warfare and Military Training

Although the prevalence of mounted archers in tomb reliefs from Shaanxi and Shanxi was connected to aspects of Xiongnu life in the Han mind, the popularity of hunting imagery in this region was also strongly associated with the use of the hunt as a form of military training and displays of martial prowess in ancient China. Although hunting may have been equated with warfare as early as the Shang Dynasty (c. 1500-1050 BCE), by the late Spring and Autumn period (770-475 BCE), hunting and warfare were inseparably linked in both linguistic usage and law. For example, *Zuo Zhuan* 左傳 (The Commentary of Zuo), records that as early as the seventh century BCE, the Grand Tutor of Jin 晉 was responsible for choosing both the sites of hunts that were used in military training and the commanders for the state's armies. Furthermore, whoever was in charge of the spring hunt in this state in the following year also became commander-in-chief of the army. Numerous other Eastern Zhou (770-256 BCE) texts record similar associations between hunting and warfare and in the *Shi Jing* 詩經 (Book of Songs), hunting and military prowess are eulogized in terms that are one and the same.[8]

This relationship between hunting and warfare continued during the Qin and Han dynasties. For example, in the "Liyi zhi" 禮儀志 (Treatise on ritual) in *Hou Han Shu* 后漢書 (History of the Later Han Dynasty), military exercises are recorded as part of the Quliu 貙

刘, a festival held during the autumn when the emperor hunted game that was offered to the ancestors at imperial tombs. At this time, *Hou Han Shu* records:

遣使者齎束帛以賜武官。武官肄兵，習戰陣之儀、斬牲之禮，名曰貙劉。兵、官皆肄孫、吳兵法六十四陣，名曰乘之。

Messengers are sent to give bundles of silk as presents to military officers, who drill the troops in military formations. The ceremony of slaughtering the sacrificial victims is known as the Quliu. The drilling by the troops in the sixty-four formations of the art of Sun and Wu is known as the *shengzhi*.[9]

The timing and performance of these activities during the Quliu festival seems to have followed seasonal associations advocated in several passages from the "Yue ling" 月令 (Monthly ordinances) of *Lüshi Chunqiu* 吕氏春秋 (Mr. Lü's Spring and Autumn Annals). This third century BCE compilation regulates hunting and military training to the declining months of the year that were viewed as a as a natural time of cold, death and decay.[10]

In *Zhou Li* 周禮 (*Rites of Zhou*), hunting was also part of the *Dayue* 大閱 ("Grand Review"), an elaborate military assessment which occurred in the eleventh month. This text seems to have provided the basis for the Grand Review described in Zhang Heng's 張衡 (78-139 CE) *Dongjing Fu* 東京賦 (Eastern Capital Rhapsody) that was held in the Western Park in the eleventh month. This review included complex military maneuvers and hunting. That smaller, but similar military inspections/exercises also occurred in the commanderies during the Han Dynasty is supported by several inscriptions on wooden strips excavated from Juyan 居延 (Edsen-gol), a military settlement during the Han Dynasty. Although these inscriptions do not specifically mention hunting, they do record archery competitions that were held during the autumn, a season as we have seen that was traditionally associated with hunting and the military.[11]

That similar reviews took place in Shang and Xihe commanderies is uncertain, but hunting imagery in these reliefs is strongly grounded in the tradition that associated hunting with military reviews and martial prowess. Based on inscriptions found in these tombs, we know that some of their occupants had served in life as officers in the Han army. Even the people who commissioned these tombs who were private individuals may have had direct contact with both the Han military apparatus along the Northern Frontier and/or Xiongnu warriors on a regular basis. As soldiers and civilians living in militarized settlements it is likely that the hunt was part of their daily lives and was not simply practiced for subsistence, but for military training and recreation as well.

It is possible that a whole complex of recreational hunting based on military training related to the subjugation of colonized peoples and the exploitation of natural resources lay behind the scenes of the hunt that decorate these tombs. Sadly our resources are too limited to explore such a possibility and its implications for hunting imagery in Shaanxi and Shanxi. But, as several scholars have noted, the basic interpretation of these reliefs as being related to the actual military training of the patrons of these images is beyond doubt. The significance of such imagery in tombs, however, is not simply an uncomplicated reflection of the exploits of the deceased as these scholars have suggested.[12] Instead in what follows, I will argue that in Shaanxi and Shanxi hunting imagery and its traditional relationship with warfare and military training helped to define a regional conception of the afterlife that was based on the complex relationship between the patrons of these images and their foreign neighbors.

The Xiongnu and Western Han Representations of Martial Valor

This complicated relationship and its effect on the conception of the afterlife in Shaanxi and Shanxi was based upon general Han beliefs that the Xiongnu were animal-like barbarians who lived in a barren wasteland. During the Han Dynasty, the figure of the mounted archer became the defining image of the Xiongnu in Han textual sources. Before examining texts that describe the Xiongnu as bestial and their homeland as inhospitable, I will argue that the popularity of the mounted archer in this region was based on the idea of the figure as the ultimate warrior who could defeat the Xiongnu cavalry. I also suggest that imagery from Shaanxi and Shanxi was dependent upon changes in the concept of the ideal warrior during the Western Han. These changes were the result of developments in the Han army and military tactics brought about by the initial superiority of mobile Xiongnu mounted warriors.

Although a fascination with many aspects of Xiongnu culture is attested to in visual and textual sources during the Western Han, the Xiongnu were contemporaneously viewed as hostile barbarians who threatened the Chinese way of life. The introduction to *Shi Ji* 史記 (Records of the Grand Historian) 110, "Xiongnu liezhuan" 匈奴列傳 (Account of the Xiongnu), summarizes the many ways in which the Xiongnu were believed to be different from the Chinese:

逐水草遷徙，毋城郭常處耕田之業，然亦各有分地。毋文書，以言語爲約束。兒能騎羊，引弓射鳥鼠；少長則射狐兔：用爲食。士力能毋弓，盡爲甲騎。其俗，寬則隨畜，因射獵禽獸爲生業，急則人習戰攻以侵伐，其天性也。

> They move about in search of water and pasture and have no walled cities or fixed dwellings, nor do they engage in any kind of agriculture. They have no writing, and even promises and agreements are only verbal. The little boys start out by learning to ride sheep and shoot birds with a bow and arrow, and when they get a little older they shoot foxes and hares, which are used for food. Thus all young men are able to use a bow and act as armed cavalry in time of war. It is their custom to herd their flocks in times of peace and make their living by hunting, but in times of crisis they go off on plundering and marauding expeditions. This seems to be their inborn nature.[13]

Throughout the *Shi Ji* and other Han sources, the Xiongnu are frequently presented as an antithetical "other" living a semi-nomadic lifestyle, not having writing, not honoring the aged, etc. All of these differences, however, are most commonly summarized in their epithet as "the people who live by drawing the bow" compared to the Han who "wear caps and girdles" (*guan-dai* 冠帶).

I suggest that the initial popularity of the motif of the mounted archer during the Western Han Dynasty was prompted by similar associations and was based on the fact that the Xiongnu through their skill as mounted archers were able to build an empire that threatened and rivaled the Han. Although the use of mounted cavalry had been introduced in the Chinese army during the Warring States period, the Qin and early Han armies were mainly composed of foot soldiers. The first ill-fated campaign against the Xiongnu in 201 BCE proved the superiority of the Xiongnu mounted warriors over the Chinese infantry. Economic instability during the early years of the Han Dynasty prevented immediate large-scale horse breeding and the expansion of the Han cavalry. But by the reign of Jingdi 景帝 (156-141 BCE), thirty-six grazing grounds where horses were broken and trained were created in the north and west to combat the superiority of the Xiongnu mounted cavalry.[14]

By the end of the second century BCE, the use of the chariot in battle, so frequently eulogized in *Shi Jing*, had given way to an army heavily comprised of mounted cavalry. Although this process had begun much earlier with the introduction of infantry and the development of massive armies through the extension of military service during the Eastern Zhou, it was the inability of the Han to deal with Xiongnu mounted warriors that signaled the final death knell for the war chariot in ancient China.[15] Han battle tactics were also adopted from the Xiongnu, with both sides often engaging in maneuvers that consisted of small parties mostly made up of horsemen. These parties would rapidly raid enemy territory in order to displace the enemy, seize cattle and horses, and bring about surrender.[16]

The threat of the Xiongnu and the adoption of new military tactics also meant that the model warrior of the Han Dynasty could no longer be the idealized generals and kings found in the *Shi Jing* who are valorized through descriptions of their war chariots and their skillful movements across the field.[17] Instead we find that two of the most famous generals of the Western Han Dynasty, Huo Qubing 霍去病 (140-117 BCE) and Li Guang 李廣 (d. 119 BCE) are described in their biographies as being skilled at riding and shooting. Although we are told in *Shi Ji* that archery was passed down in Li's family for ages, the archery for which both Li Guang and Huo Qubing were known was not the kind practiced in the ritualized and anesthetized archery contests described in *Shi Jing*, *Zhou Li* and *Li Ji* 禮記 (Book of Rites). Instead these generals are described as mobile riders who through their unconventional military tactics (ultimately derived from the Xiongnu) proved successful when other generals failed. Regarding Huo Qubing's first military foray, *Shi Ji* records that the general broke away from the main army with eight hundred men in search of grain and ultimately killed or captured a large number of Xiongnu riders.[18] It was such tactics, along with their skill as mounted archers that caused these generals to be respected and feared by both the Han and the Xiongnu.

By the time the figure of the mounted archer reappears in the tombs in Shaanxi in the first century, the power of the Xiongnu and the type of generals and army that could defeat them must have been firmly entrenched in the Han mind. Due to the immediate presence of their mounted enemy, military training in Shang and Xihe commanderies must have focused on developing the same skills that had made Huo Qubing and Li Guang famous. As such, the mounted archers in these tombs were not simply associated with the foreign lifestyles of the Xiongnu, but were also seen as the necessary means whereby the enemy could be engaged and defeated.

Xiongnu Lands as the Ends of the Earth/Wilderness

In this region, Han associations of the mounted archer with the Xiongnu were expanded in a regional conception of the afterlife that blended elements of Han mortuary belief with positive and negative conceptions of the Xiongnu. I suggest that the mounted archers in tombs from Shaanxi and Shanxi were dispatched in order to combat the various dangers that confronted the deceased on their journey to paradise. The possibility of an amalgamation of the perilous borderlands between Heaven and Earth and the world of the Xiongnu is corroborated by a number of Han texts that describe the Xiongnu lands as a northern wilderness located at the ends of the earth. In the second poem from *Hujia Shibai Pai* 胡笳十八拍 (Eighteen Songs on a Nomad Flute), Cai Wenji 蔡文姬 (b.177) who was taken prisoner by the Xiongnu in 195, laments:

> I was taken on horseback to the ends of the earth;
> Tiring of life, I sought death, but death would not come.
> The barbarians stink so. How can they be considered human?
> Their pleasures and angers are like the jackal and the wolf-how unbearable.
> We traveled to the end of the Tianshan, enduring all the frost and sleet;
> The customs are rude, the land is desolate-we are near the nomads' territories.
> An overcast sky stretches beyond ten thousand miles. Not a single bird is in sight.
> The cold sands are boundless; one can no longer tell the south from the north.[19]

Although grounded in her own experience as a hostage in the North, Cai Wenji's description is based on stereotypes that are first expressed in "Account of the Xiongnu (*Shi Ji*, fasc. 110), in which the Xiongnu domains are described as "swamps and saline wastes" 澤鹵, "north [where it is] cold and bitter (and) there is no water and pasture" 北寒苦無水草之地, and the "land [where the] cold and the killing frosts come early" 匈奴處北地, 寒, 殺氣早降.[20]

Such bleak descriptions of the lands where the Xiongnu lived resonate with Han and pre-Han conceptions of the afterlife. Poems from *Chu Ci* 楚辭 (*Songs of the South*), Han Dynasty tomb-quelling texts (*zhenmuwen* 鎮墓文), and an inscription from a tomb in Suide 綏德, Shaanxi, all reveal a conviction that upon death the deceased would find himself in a dangerous region between Heaven and Earth surrounded by ferocious animals, demons and monsters.[21] The sacred geography of *Shanhai Jing* 山海經 (*Classic of the Mountains and Seas*) supports these descriptions of the borderlands between Heaven and Earth describing countless oddities, uninhabitable lands, and malignant spirits that travelers would encounter as they move through the Middle Kingdom and the lands beyond.

Based on these texts, I suggest that in tombs from Shaanxi and Shanxi, the prevalence of the mounted archer and other motifs associated with Xiongnu life drew a parallel between the barren wastelands of the beyond and what was believed to be the desolate topography of the Xiongnu domain. That in the Han mind the Xiongnu were believed to live in a territory very close to the ends of the earth is further supported by comments made by Wang Chong 王充 (27-*c*.100 CE) in *Lunheng* 論衡 (*Critical Essays*), who remarked: "The north of the

Xiongnu is the border-land of the earth" 匈奴之北，地之邊陲 .[22] That the domains of the Xiongnu became associated with the wilderness of the afterlife may also be supported by the traditional Chinese belief in the North as the land of the dead.

Such correspondences may have also been motivated by fear of the very real possibility of being taken hostage to the Xiongnu lands, never to return. The story of the faithful official Su Wu 蘇武 (140-60 BCE) in *Han Shu* 漢書 (History of the Han Dynasty) provides the quintessential account of the loyal Han official exiled in a barbarian land. During his nineteen year sojourn in the north, *Han Shu* records that Su Wu was forced to live on the desolate shores of Lake Baikal and eat the seeds of grass stored in the burrows of field mice.[23] *Shi Ji* and *Han Shu* also record that other less loyal officials surrendered, were rewarded by the Xiongnu leader and took up the Xiongnu life. But we do not know the fate of many of the other soldiers and Chinese who settled this region and either surrendered to the Xiongnu in battle or were captured during raids. Although some of them may have fared well, for those living in Shang and Xihe commanderies, there must have been a constant fear of being captured during a Xiongnu uprising or raid and forced to live among the "barbarians" beyond the Great Wall.

I suggest that these fears had a direct impact on the conception of the afterlife in tombs in Shaanxi and Shanxi. In hunting imagery from this region the fears of the patrons of these images of living (and dying) in exile as well as the perceived inhospitable nature of the Xiongnu domains were subsumed into the horrors of the wilderness that confronted the deceased upon death. The coalescence of these two fears was, however, not simply the unwelcoming topography and climate of the Northern Steppe, but was also based upon Han conceptions of the inhabitants of this region.

The Xiongnu as Non-Human and Foreigners in Han Tombs

Visual representations of foreigners during the Han Dynasty provide another point of comparison that supports a connection between the Northern Steppe and the borderlands that confronted the deceased upon death. These images, corroborated by textual descriptions of the Xiongnu and other foreigners as animals or animal-like, suggest that the northern nomads could have joined the denizens of the afterlife in tombs from this region. Although there are not many depictions of foreigners in Shaanxi and Shanxi, the few representations that do exist can, with the help of other Han visual and textual records, be used to establish the multivalent purposes of and complicated attitudes toward foreigners depicted in tombs from Shaanxi and Shanxi.

Based on Han and pre-Han visual and textual records, we know that the fantastic creatures that inhabited the regions between Heaven and Earth were conceived of as animal-animal and man-animal hybrids. In Shaanxi, immortals (*xian* 仙) are often depicted in reliefs as avian hybrids, their conglomerate form suggesting their power of metamorphosis and incessant travels to and from paradise. However, these immortals were one of the few categories of beings who occupied the realms between Heaven and Earth and who were believed to be benign creatures. Instead, most of the denizens of these realms are depicted as evil and capricious spirits that seek to harm the deceased or the traveler at any turn. I suggest that the Xiongnu, like other foreigners, through their virtue of living geographically and culturally on the periphery of Chinese civilization were considered part of this other world. Whether they were perceived as benevolent or malignant creatures in Shaanxi and Shanxi was complicated by Han conceptions of foreigners whose marginality could be seen as both a positive and negative attribute.

In Eastern Han Dynasty tomb reliefs, foreigners are often depicted as man-animal hybrids and/or represented alongside immortals and other auspicious creatures. In a relief from Linyi 臨沂, Shandong, a foreigner is illustrated with a pair of immortals and has a pointed cap, exaggerated nose, and facial hair. The lower half of his body, subsumed in swirling clouds is more like that of a merman than a human (fig. 6). Similar figures with pointed caps, scales or fine hair are also depicted on the stone columns of the front chamber of a tomb in Yinan 沂南, Shandong (fig. 7). These figures suggest that foreigners, like immortals, were often seen as being half-man and half-animal. Since foreigners existed on the fringe of the Chinese world, they, like immortals, were also viewed as spiritually empowered figures that could assist the deceased in his journey to paradise.[24]

Similar conceptions may lie behind the representation of three figures that appear in a hunting scene depicted on a door lintel excavated at Dangjiagou 党家溝, Mizhi 米脂, Shaanxi, that shows two mounted archers and one archer on foot (fig. 8a). The mounted archer on the left is depicted with a bear-like face while his companion on the right is represented with rounded animal-like ears atop his head, although this could also be a headdress (fig. 8b, c). The third figure appears to be completely human, but with his long tunic, baggy pants, broad face and strange hair/headdress may very well represent a Xiongnu warrior (fig. 8d). His clothing and headgear are unlike the other hunters in the region (fig. 9) and the figure has more in common with the foreigners depicted in scenes of human-animal combat in Shaanxi (fig. 10). That the figures in the hunting scene from Dangjiagou represented the Xiongnu, or at the very least foreigners, is also supported by the fact that the tunic worn by the bear-headed figure has buttons on the left side, a recurring characteristic of foreigners in Han texts.[25]

The physical characteristics and dress of these figures as well as the dragon that is ridden by the figure on the right supports the otherworldly nature of this scene. I suggest that these three figures represent foreigners, possibly Xiongnu, who like the Chinese archers in the region, are represented battling the demons and dangerous animals that attempt to block the soul of the deceased during its journey. This interpretation and the successfulness of their endeavor is supported by the two winged figures in the pavilion in the center of the composition that probably represent the deceased.[26]

This relief as well as those which depict foreigners engaged in human-animal combat (fig. 10) imply that in Shaanxi and Shanxi, foreigners, because of their marginality and their close ties to the animal world, were believed to be appropriate figures to battle the malignant spirits (represented by animals) that inhabited the borderlands between Heaven and Earth. Such powers were based on the general belief that foreigners, because they were in closer contact with or were part of the animal world, were expert hunters, animal tamers and herders.[27]

The belief that foreigners were closer to or actually animals, however, had a much darker side in Han texts. In regards to the Xiongnu, this view is expressed by Han Anguo 韓安國 (d. 127 BCE) in *Shi Ji*:

今匈奴負戎馬之足，懷禽獸之心，遷徙鳥舉，難得而制也。得其地不足以爲廣，有其眾不足以爲強，自上古不屬爲人。

The Xiongnu move on the feet of swift war horses, and in their breasts beat the hearts of beasts. They shift from place to place as fast as a flock of birds, so that it is difficult to corner them and bring them under control. Though we win possession of their land, it would be no great addition to the empire, and though we ruled their hosts of warriors, they would do little to strengthen our power. From the most ancient times the Xiongnu have never been regarded as a part of humanity.[28]

This as well as other passages show that the Han Chinese considered the Xiongnu to be part of the animal rather than the human world and to be both an aberration and a threat to the existing order. Such attributes would have made them fitting companions to the ferocious hybrid creatures that inhabited the borderlands of the afterlife.

That the Xiongnu could have also joined these less felicitous creatures in tomb reliefs from Shaanxi and Shanxi is corroborated by Han reliefs that depict scenes of battle between barbarian and Han forces, variously designated now as 胡漢交爭圖 *Hu Han jiaozheng tu* or 胡漢戰爭圖 *Hu Han zhanzheng tu*. A few of these reliefs, such as the stone over the entrance to the tomb at Yinan, depict a battle between barbarian and Han forces that takes place over a bridge (fig. 11, "Battle at the Bridge"). The battle illustrated on the west wall of the Xiaotangshan 小堂山 shrine, however, shows a more common representation of this imagery and depicts a host of barbarians emerging from mountains to engage Han forces (fig. 12). The barbarians emerging from the mountains in these reliefs were possibly intended to represent the Xiongnu, as the major boundary and the site of many battles between Han and Xiongnu forces were the Yin Mountains 陰山 in Inner Mongolia.[29]

Xin Lixiang 信立祥, Lydia Thompson and Xing Yitian 邢義田 have argued that the barbarians depicted in some of these battle scenes represent attempts to block the travels of the deceased. Xin has argued that scenes of the Battle at the Bridge are symbolic of the battle between the forces of light and darkness and that the barbarians in these scenes are depicted as guardians of the netherworld. According to Xin, their defeat by Han warriors enabled the deceased to travel back and forth between the world of the dead and the ancestral shrine to receive sacrifices from his descendents. Lydia Thompson has argued that the barbarians illustrated in the Battle at the Bridge scene at Yinan represent demons that prevent the passage of the deceased to paradise; the Han soldiers in these scenes act as guardians and protectors of the dead. In a similar vein, Xing Yitian has argued that some battle scenes between barbarian and Han forces from Shandong illustrate the deceased being escorted by various gods to Mount Kunlun 昆侖山 or Mount Tai 泰山. He also argues that the barbarians in these scenes represent the obstacles that faced the deceased in their journey to the immortal world.[30]

Although not common in Shaanxi and Shanxi, a battle scene between barbarian and Han forces decorates the western wall of the front chamber of a tomb excavated at Baijiashan 百家山, Suide 綏德, Shaanxi (fig. 13a). In this relief, soldiers can be seen approaching a hilly area on which is perched several figures with drawn bows. In the foray, one figure has been decapitated and his headless body lies on the ground. This scene includes a number of elements that are shared with Sino-barbarian battle scenes from Shandong and Jiangsu. These include its association with a hunting scene, the decapitated figure in the middle of the foray and the barbarians either fleeing or coming from the mountains.

A major difference between this scene and depictions of other Sino-barbarian battles, however, is that the forces attacking the figures in the mountains wear two kinds of headgear and may represent different groups of people. This fact has led Xing Yitian to argue that, since these figures include foreign soldiers, this scene should not be identified as a Sino-barbarian battle scene. Although I agree that the depicted Han forces wear both Han and non-Han costumes and headgear, I would argue, based on the inclusion of the above listed elements that it shares with other Sino-barbarian battle scenes, that it is a regional variant of this category. The rationale for the inclusion of troops wearing foreign headgear in this scene is offered by Xing when discussing a "captive offering scene" that decorates a tomb relief also excavated from Suide, Shaanxi. This scene also includes an ambiguous mixture of hairstyles and dress. Here he suggests that the unique headgear of some of these figures might have been worn by Han officials who had absorbed habits of their foreign neighbors while also noting that the soldiers who occupied posts along the frontier were often not Han Chinese.[31]

Such reasoning probably also lies behind the ambiguity of the figures depicted in the battle scene from Suide. That the barbarian figures in this scene, like some of their counterparts in other regions, represented the obstacles that the deceased would face on his journey to paradise is suggested by other elements within the composition. To the right of the battle scene are a number of humans and animals including several figures playing a game, two foreigners on a camel, grazing horses, several other figures performing unidentifiable actions, and a pair of humans and a pair of deer copulating (fig. 13b). In general, the grazing animals, copulating figures, and the foreigners may suggest fecundity and, therefore, rebirth.[32] On the other side of the battle is a hunting scene with animals fleeing through the mountains. A boar, deer, fox, birds, and a dragon race toward the far left where several deer are depicted calmly eating the bark or leaves from trees (fig. 13c).

Although some parts of this composition may have been randomly combined with others, a number of elements suggest that the barbarians depicted in the hills, like some figures in scenes from Shandong, represent demons or malignant spirits who are attempting to block the passage of the deceased. The foreigners in a hilly landscape, figures copulating, the dragon and the placid animals depicted on the far left also create an atmosphere which suggests that the scenery and the actions taking place are not of this world. This interpretation is corroborated by the imagery depicted on the four vertical slabs that support this horizontal relief. These scenes depict immortals climbing on swirling tendrils that are an amalgamation of clouds and the fungus of immortality, as well as two large towers on which climbing figures suggest an alternate route to paradise (fig. 14).

I argue that this scene at Suide, like the hunting imagery in Shaanxi and Shanxi and some battle scenes unearthed in other regions, depicted and facilitated the passage of the deceased to paradise. The dangers that faced the deceased in this composition are represented by the foreigners lurking in the mountain who are facing defeat by Han cavalry. The role of such imagery is further implied by a number of elements in the composition that appear in reliefs that depict scenes of the hunt and immortals frolicking with animals in this region. These include the hunting scene itself and the docile animals on the far left of the composition that can be compared to the felicitous animals that frolic with immortals among mountainous clouds in other tombs. The figures copulating on the right are also similar to mating animals that appear among the cloudscapes frequented by immortals and animals in another relief from Suide.[33]

The representation of foreigners in hunting scenes and in this battle scene suggest a mixture of attitudes and feelings toward non-Han Chinese who could either thwart or aid the deceased on his journey to paradise, much as the living Xiongnu could either frustrate or help the Chinese living in the region.[34] Unfortunately it is difficult based on the representation of these figures to firmly identify them as Xiongnu by their physical characteristics, clothing and headgear due to the stereotyping of foreigners in Han visual culture. But it seems logical that such figures would have represented the foreigners with whom the patrons of these images had the most contact, regardless of the authenticity of their depiction.

The question that remains unanswered, however, is whether these foreigners were more frequently represented as auspicious or as ominous figures among the borderlands between Heaven and Earth. The reliefs themselves do not strongly suggest either alternative; individual interpretations of such imagery may have varied. It appears that non-Han Chinese were infrequently represented in tombs from Shaanxi and Shanxi with a somewhat balanced mixture of appreciation and apprehension. This ambiguous relationship is also visually realized in the hunting imagery in this region that frequently depicts Chinese as mounted archers, performing an activity adopted from the Xiongnu to combat their military power, in order to pass through the cold and barren regions of the afterlife. Such imagery, as I have argued, suggests the complex nature of associations between the Xiongnu, their domains, northern nomadic life, and representations of the afterlife in Shaanxi and Shanxi.

Conclusion

In this paper I have examined the figure of the mounted archer which dominates scenes of the hunt in Eastern Han tomb reliefs from Shaanxi and Shanxi. Rather than seeing these scenes simply as reflections of the unique political and social environment of this region, I have argued that their depictions were based upon a vision of the afterlife that equated the world of the Xiongnu with the uninviting borderlands between Heaven and Earth. The fulcrum of such imagery was the figure of the mounted archer who through his adoption of Xiongnu military and hunting tactics was able to defeat the animals, malignant spirits, and the Xiongnu themselves to insure the safe passage of the deceased to paradise.

The ambiguous nature of the mounted archer who assumes elements of the lifestyle of his enemies in order to defeat them is also present in the few reliefs that depict foreigners in this region. Sometimes, these figures are shown in hunting scenes where they are illustrated as aiding the soul of the deceased in its journey to paradise. In other scenes in Shaanxi and Shanxi, however, foreigners represent the malignant spirits that confronted the dead. Both sets of imagery, as well as the figure of the mounted archer expressed the complex nature of the relationship of Chinese settlers to their foreign neighbors who were conceived of as friend and foe to both the living and the dead. Such ambiguity was based on the mixed cultural and unstable political climate of the region that allowed the patron's fears of Xiongnu rebellion, possible exile and the Xiongnu themselves to be subsumed within their fears of the afterlife.

NOTES

[1] As opposed to the Chinese, who "wear caps and girdles" 冠帶. See: *Shi Ji* (*Records of the Grand Historian*) 《史記》, fasc. 110, "Xiongnu liezhuan" 匈奴列傳 (Account of the Xiongnu).

[2] For the brick, see: Li Jian, ed., *Eternal China: Splendors from the First Dynasties*, Dayton, Ohio: Dayton Art Institute, 1998, p. 98; for the palace mural, see Shaanxi-sheng Kaogu Yanjiusuoed., 陝西省考古研究所, *Qin Du Xianyang Kaogu Baogao* 《秦都咸陽考古報告》 (The Archaeological Report of the Qin Capital of Xianyang), Beijing: Kexue Chubanshe 科學出版社, 2004, fig. 12.1.

[3] Esther Jacobson, "Mountains and nomads: A reconsideration of the origins of Chinese landscape representation", *Bulletin of the Museum of Far Eastern Antiquities* 57 (1985), pp.133-179. Berthold Laufer has argued for similar origins of this imagery in *Chinese Pottery of the Han Dynasty*, 2nd edition, Rutland, Vermont and Tokyo: C. E. Tuttle Co., 1962, pp.212-222. Alexander Soper and Michael Sullivan have both claimed that the figure of the mounted archer and later Sassanid (226-651 CE) hunting scenes were descended from "lost" Achaemenian (550-330 BCE) hunting scenes. Such scenes still await discovery. See: Alexander Soper, "Early Chinese landscape painting", *Art Bulletin*, 23:2 (June 1941), p.147; "On the origin of landscape representation in Chinese art", *Archives of the Chinese Art Society of America*, 7 (1953),

pp.54-65; Michael Sullivan, *The Birth of Landscape Painting in China*, Berkeley: University of California Press, 1962, pp.43-46.

[4] *Shi Ji*, fasc. 43, "Zhao shijia" 趙世家 (The ruling house of Zhao). See: Sima Qian 司馬遷, *Shi Ji* 史記, Beijing: Zhonghua Shuju 中華書局, 1959 (1973 printing), p.1806.

[5] The first large-scale government market system between the Xiongnu and Chinese was established by Han Wendi 漢文帝 (r. 180-157 BCE), although private trade between the two parties had probably existed on the border for some time. See: Yü Ying-shih, "Han foreign relations", in Denis Twitchett and Michael Loewe eds., *The Cambridge History of China, Vol. I: The Ch'in and Han Empires, 221 B.C.—A.D. 220*, Cambridge: Cambridge University Press, 1986, p.388.

[6] Huan Kuan 桓寬, *Yan Tie Lun* 《鹽鐵論》, Shanghai: Shanghai Renmin Chubanshe 上海人民出版社, 1974, p.5. Translation based on Esson M. Gale, tr., *Discourses on Salt and Iron*, Leyden: E.J. Brill, Ltd., 1931, pp.14-15.

[7] Esther Jacobson, pp. 144-145.

[8] Mark Edward Lewis, *Sanctioned Violence in Early China*, Albany, NY: State University of New York Press, 1990, pp. 18, 35; *Zuo Zhuan*, Lord Wen, year 6. Yang Bojun 楊伯峻, *Chunqiu Zuo Zhuan* 《春秋左傳》, Beijing: Zhonghua Shuju 中華書局, 1981, pp. 544-545, 552-553.

[9] See: *Hou Han Shu*, fasc. 15, "Liyi zhi" (Treatise on ritual). Fan Ye 范曄, *Hou Han Shu* 《后漢書》 (History of the Latter Han Dynasty), Beijing: Zhonghua Shuju 中華書局: Xinhua Shudian 新華書店, 1965 (1973 printing), p. 3122. Translation based on Derk Bodde, *Festivals in Classical China: New Year and Other Annual Observances during the Han Dynasty, 206 B.C.-A.D. 220*, Princeton, NJ: Princeton University Press, 1975, p.328.

[10] Derk Bodde, p.330. These particular passages are found in entries for the 9th and 10th months. Chen Qiyou 陳奇猷, *Lüshi Chunqiu Xin Jiaoshi* 《呂氏春秋新校釋》, Shanghai: Shanghai Guji Chubanshe 上海古籍出版社, 2002, pp. 474, 523. For translation, see: John Knoblock and Jeffrey Riegel, tr., *The Annals of Lü Buwei*, Stanford: Stanford University Press, 2000, pp. 208, 225-226.

[11] In *Zhou Li* hunting and military exercises are not confined to the seasons of autumn and winter, but also take place in the middle month of each season. Derk Bodde, pp. 330, 351, 356-357.

[12] See: Li Lin 李林, Kang Lanying 康蘭英 and Zhao Liguang 趙力光, *Shaanbei Handai Huaxiang Shi* 《陝北漢代畫像石》 (Han Dynasty Tomb Reliefs from Northern Shaanxi), Xi'an: Shaanxi Renmin Chubanshe 陝西人民出版社, 1995, pp. 3-4; Kang Lanying 康蘭英, "Huaxiang shi suo fanying de Shang jun shoulie huodong" 畫像石所反映的上郡狩獵活動 (Hunting activities in the Shang commandery as reflected in tomb reliefs), *Wenbo* 《文博》, 1986(3), pp. 48-52; Lü Jing 呂靜, "Shaanbei Han huaxiang shi tanlun" 陝北漢畫像石探論 (An exploration and discussion of Han Dynasty tomb reliefs from Shaanbei), *Wenbo* 《文博》, 2004(4), pp. 24-29; Xin Lixiang 信立祥 and Jiang Yingju 蔣英炬, "Shaanxi, Shanxi Han huaxiangshi zongshu" 陝西, 山西, 漢代畫像石綜述 (A summary of Han Dynasty tomb reliefs from Shaanxi and Shanxi), in *Zhongguo Huaxiang Shi Quanji* 中國畫像石全集 (Collected Chinese Tomb Reliefs), vol. 5, Jinan 濟南: Shandong Meishu Chubanshe 山東美術出版社,

2000, p.11; Shaanxi-sheng Kaogu Yanjiusuo 陝西省考古研究所 and Yulin-shi Wenwu Guanli Weiyuanhui 榆林市文物管理委員會 eds., *Shenmu Dabaodang: Handai Chengzhi yu Muzang Kaogu Baogao*《神木大保當：漢代城址與墓葬考古報告》(Shenmu-Dabaodang: An Archeological Report of the Remains of a Han Dynasty City and Tombs), Beijing: Kexue Chubanshe 科學出版社, 2001, p.119.

[13] See: *Shi Ji*, fasc. 110, "Xiongnu liezhuan" (Account of the Xiongnu), Sima Qian, op. cit., p. 2879; for translation, see: Burton Watson tr., Sima Qian, *Records of the Grand Historian: Han Dynasty II*, Hong Kong and New York: The Research Centre for Translation and the Chinese University of Hong Kong and Columbia University Press, 1993, p. 129.

[14] Michèle Pirazzoli-t'Serstevens, *The Han Dynasty*, translated by Janet Seligman, New York: Rizzoli, 1982, pp. 30, 90. Chang Chun-shu also presents a discussion of Han Wudi's campaigns against the Xiongnu and the importance of horses and mounted cavalry. See: Chang Chun-shu, "Military aspect of Han Wu-ti's campaigns", *Harvard Journal of Asiatic Studies*, 26 (1966), pp. 148-173.

[15] Mark Edward Lewis, *Sanctioned Violence in Early China*, pp. 54-61.

[16] Michèle Pirazzoli-t'Serstevens, p.90.

[17] For examples see Ode no. 198, "Xiao rong" 小戎 (Small war chariot), *Qin feng*《秦風》(Odes of Qin) and no. 177, "Liu yue" 六月 (The sixth month), *The Minor Odes*《小雅》, "Tong Gong zhi shi" 彤弓之什 (Decade of Tong Gong). See: Arthur Waley, tr., *The Book of Songs*, Joseph Allen ed., New York: Grove Press, 1996, pp. 100-101, 150-151.

[18] See: *Shi Ji*, fasc. 109, "Li Guang liezhuan" 李廣列傳 (Biography of Li Guang). and *Shi Ji*, fasc. 111, "Wei Jiangjun Piaoqi liezhuan" 衛將軍驃騎列傳 (Biography of General Wei Qing and the Swift Cavalry General Huo Qubing). See: Sima Qian, *op. cit.*, pp. 2867-2878, 2928. For translation, see Sima Qian, *Records of the Grand Historian: Han Dynasty*, pp. 117-128, 169.

[19] Robert A. Rorex and Wen Fong, "Eighteen songs of a nomad flute, poem 2", *Eighteen Songs of a Nomad Flute: The Story of Lady Wen-chi: A Fourteenth-century Hand-scroll in the Metropolitan Museum of Art*, New York: Metropolitan Museum of Art; distributed by New York Graphic Society Greenwich, Connecticut, 1974.

[20] *Shi Ji*, fasc. 110, "Account of the Xiongnu". See: Sima Qian, op. cit., pp. 2896, 2903, 2912. For translation, see Sima Qian, *Records of the Grand Historian: Han Dynasty* II, pp. 141, 146, 155.

[21] For the inscription, see: Kang Lanying 康蘭英 and Wang Zhian 王志安, "Shaanxi Suide xian Sishilipu huaxiangshi mu diaocha jianbao" 陝西綏德縣四十里鋪畫像石墓調查簡報 (A brief report on a tomb Excavated at Sishilipu, Suide, Shaanxi), *Kaogu yu Wenwu*《考古與文物》, 2002(3), p.23.

[22] Wang Chong, *Lunheng*, 11:2, "Shuo ri" 説日 (Speaking of the sun). See: Wang Chong, *Lunheng* (Critical Discourses), Shanghai: Shanghai Renmin Chubanshe 上海人民出版社, 1974, p. 171. For translation, see: Alfred Forke tr., *Lun-Heng: Miscellaneous Essays of Wang Ch'ung*, vol. 1, 2nd edition, New York: Paragon Book Gallery, 1962, p. 263.

[23] See: *Han Shu*, fasc. 54, "Li Guang Su Jian zhuan" 李廣蘇建傳 (The biographies of Li Guang and Su Jian), in Ban Gu 班固, *Han Shu*《漢書》(History of the Han Dynasty), Beijing: Zhonghua Shuju 中华书局, 1968, pp. 2450-2470. For translation, see: Burton Watson tr., *Courtier and Commoner in Ancient China, Selections from the History of the Former Han by Pan Ku*, New York and London: Columbia University Press, 1974, pp. 34-45.

[24] Ref: Zheng Yan, "Barbarian images in Han period art", *Orientations*, vol. 29, no. 6 (June 1998), pp. 50-53.

[25] For a survey of the ways in which foreigners are depicted in Han Dynasty visual and textual sources, and of the differences between the two records and the difficulty of equating any figures with specific foreign peoples, see: Xing Yitian 邢義田, "Gudai Zhongguo ji Ou Ya wenxian tuxiang yu kaogu ziliao zhong de 'Hu ren' waimao" 古代中國及歐亞文獻, 圖像與考古資料中的'胡人'外貌 (The appearance of 'Hu barbarians' as seen in ancient Chinese and non-Chinese literary, pictorial and archaeological sources), *Meishu Shi Yanjiu Jikan*《美術史研究集刊》, 9 (2000), pp. 15-99.

[26] These figures could also represent Xiwangmu 西王母 and Dongwanggong 東王公. However, this goddess and god, respectively, are also represented, in their chicken and cow-headed forms, on the stones that flank either side of the tomb door.

[27] Roel Sterckx, *The Animal and the Daemon in Early China*, Albany, NY: State University of New York Press, 2002, pp. 108, 159-161.

[28] See: *Shi Ji*, fasc. 108, "Han Changru liezhuan" 韓長孺列傳 (The biography of Han Changru), Sima Qian, p. 2861; Burton Watson tr., *Records of the Grand Historian: Han Dynasty* II, p.112.

[29] See: Xing Yitian, "Handai huaxiang Hu Han zhanzheng tu de goucheng, leixing yu yiyi" 漢代畫像胡漢戰爭圖的構成類型與意義 (Composition, types, and significance of the scenes of Sino-barbarian battles in the pictorial art of Han China), *Meishu Shi Yanjiu Jikan*《美術史研究集刊》, 19 (2005), pp. 90-91.

[30] Xin Lixiang 信立祥, *Handai Huaxiangshi Zonghe Yanjiu*《漢代畫像石綜合研究》(Research on Han Dynasty Tomb Reliefs), Beijing: Wenwu Chubanshe 文物出版社, 2000, pp. 328-334; Lydia Thompson, "The Yinan Tomb: Narrative and Ritual in Pictorial Art of the Eastern Han" (25-220 C.E.)", PhD Dissertation, New York University, 1998, pp. 323-361; cited in Zheng Yan, *op. cit.*, p. 59. See: Xing Yitian, "Handai huaxiang Hu Han zhanzheng tu de goucheng, leixing yu yiyi", p.98.

[31] Xing Yitian, "Handai huaxiang Hu Han zhanzheng tu de goucheng, leixing yu yiyi", pp. 70, 80-83.

[32] Images of foreigners were worshipped in some regions as fertility gods during the Han Dynasty. See: Zheng Yan, op. cit., p.56.

[33] Copulating animals appear twice in the tomb of the Grand Administrator of Liaodong (Liaodong Taishou 遼東太守), Huangjiata 黃家塔 tomb no. 7, Suide, Shaanxi. See: Li Guilong 李貴龍 and Wang Jianqin 王建勤, *Suide Handai Huaxiangshi*《綏德漢代畫像石》(Han Dynasty Tomb Reliefs from Shaanxi), Xi'an: Shaanxi Renmin Meishu Chubanshe 陝西人民美術出版社, 2001, figs. 13 and 14.

[34] The few other representations of foreigners in this region support this interpretive dichotomy. A lintel from

Shenmu depicts a foreign elephant-tamer and a mounted archer with a *tianma* (heavenly horse) within a swirling cloudscape, see *Zhongguo Huaxiangshi Quanji*, vol. 5, fig. 223. A horizontal relief from Suide shows a procession with several foreigners traveling through mountains and contains an embedded hunting scene; a mounted archer is depicted in front of the mountain as in the scene that depicts the battle between barbarian and Han forces. These foreigners were probably intended to protect the deceased on his journey. See: Li Guilong and Wang Jianqin, *op. cit.*, fig. 65. Similar foreign figures, one with a camel, are depicted in Lishi, Shanxi. See: Li Lin, Kang Lanying and Zhao Liguang, *op. cit.*, figs. 653 and 654. Similar imagery can also be seen on a relief from Yulin, Shaanxi; see: *Zhongguo Huaxiangshi Quanji*, vol. 5, fig. 24. Another scene from Suide depicts a barbarian king presented with gifts and prisoners of war, a scene that also appears in some barbarian and Han battle scenes in Shandong and Jiangsu; see: Li Guilong and Wang Jianqin, *op. cit.*, fig. 69. Another relief from tomb no. 4, Mizhi, Shaanxi, depicts foreign warriors, but is damaged; see: Li Lin, Kang Lanying and Zhao Liguang, *op. cit.*, fig. 65.

FIGURES

The following abbreviations are used throughout the List of Figures in identifying frequently cited sources.

SB

Li Lin 李林, Kang Lanying 康蘭英 and Zhao Liguang 趙力光, *Shanbei Handai Huaxiangshi* 《陝北漢代畫像石》 (Han Dynasty Tomb Reliefs from Northern Shaanxi), Xi'an: Shaanxi Renmin Chubanshe 陝西人民出版社, 1995.

SD

Li Guilong 李貴龍 and Wang Jianqin 王建勤, *Suide Handai Huaxiangshi* 《綏德漢代畫像石》 (Han Dynasty Tomb Reliefs from Shaanxi), Xi'an: Shaanxi Renmin Meishu Chubanshe 陝西人民美術出版社, 2001.

SM

Shaanxi-sheng Kaogu Yanjiusuo 陝西省考古研究所 and Yulin-shi Wenwu Guanli Weiyuanhui 榆林市文物管理委員會 eds., *Shenmu Dabaodang: Handai Chengzhi yu Muzang Kaogu Baogao* 《神木大保當：漢代城址與墓葬考古報告》 (Shenmu-Dabaodang: An Archeological Report of the Remains of a Han Dynasty City and Tombs), Beijing: Kexue Chubanshe 科學出出版社, 2001.

ZG

Zhongguo Huaxiangshi Quanji 《中國畫像石全集》 (Collected Chinese Tomb Reliefs), vols. 1-8, Jinan 濟南: Shandong Meishu Chubanshe 山東美術出版社, 2000.

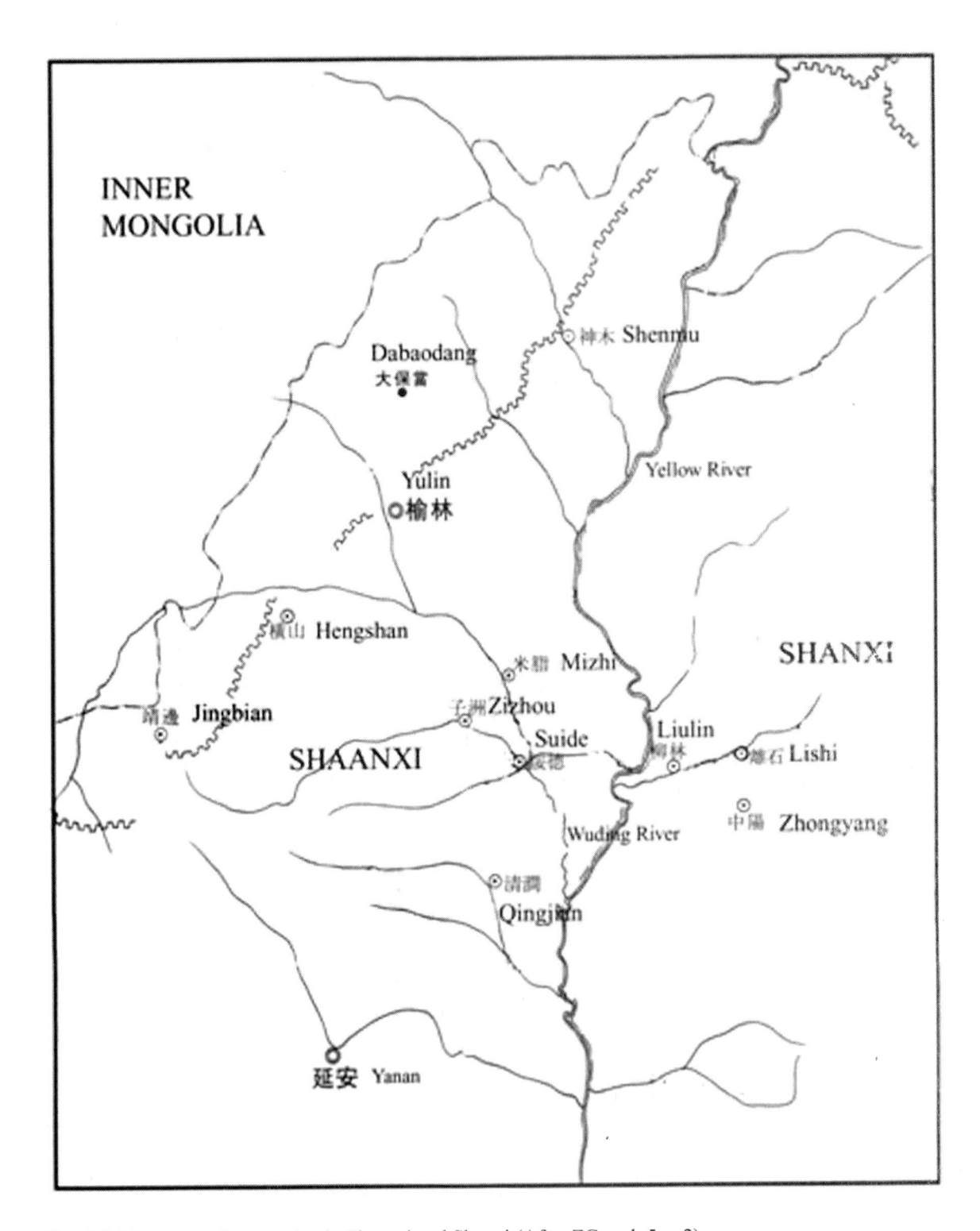

Fig. 1: Major areas of excavation in Shaanxi and Shanxi (After ZG, vol. 5, p.2)

Fig. 2: The carved stone doorway of Dabaodang 大保当 Tomb M2, Shenmu 神木, Shaanxi, Eastern Han Dynasty (After SM, plate 2.4)

Fig. 3: Mounted archers, Mizhi 米脂, Shaanxi, Eastern Han Dynasty (After SB p. 35, fig. 117)

Fig. 4: Chariot procession with mounted archers, Suide 綏德, Shaanxi, Eastern Han Dynasty (photograph by author)

— 253 —

Fig. 5: Line drawing showing a mounted archer depicted on an inlaid bronze chariot ornament, Sanpanshan 三盤山, Hebei, Western Han Dynasty (After Zheng Luanming 鄭灤明, "Dingzhou Sanpanshan cuo jin yin tong chesan dingxian shi neirong fenxi" 定州三盤山錯金銀銅, 車傘鋌紋飾內容分析 [An analysis of the decoration of an incised chariot ornament from Sanpanshan, Dingzhou], *Wenwu chunqiu* 文物春秋, 2000 [3], fig. 2)

Fig. 6: Foreigner depicted on a tomb relief excavated in Linyi 臨沂, Shandong, Eastern Han Dynasty (After ZG, vol. 3, fig. 69)

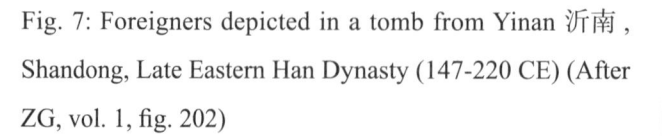

Fig. 7: Foreigners depicted in a tomb from Yinan 沂南, Shandong, Late Eastern Han Dynasty (147-220 CE) (After ZG, vol. 1, fig. 202)

Fig. 8a: Door lintel showing hybrid archers, Dangjiagou 党家溝, Mizhi, Shaanxi. Eastern Han Dynasty (After SB, p.25)

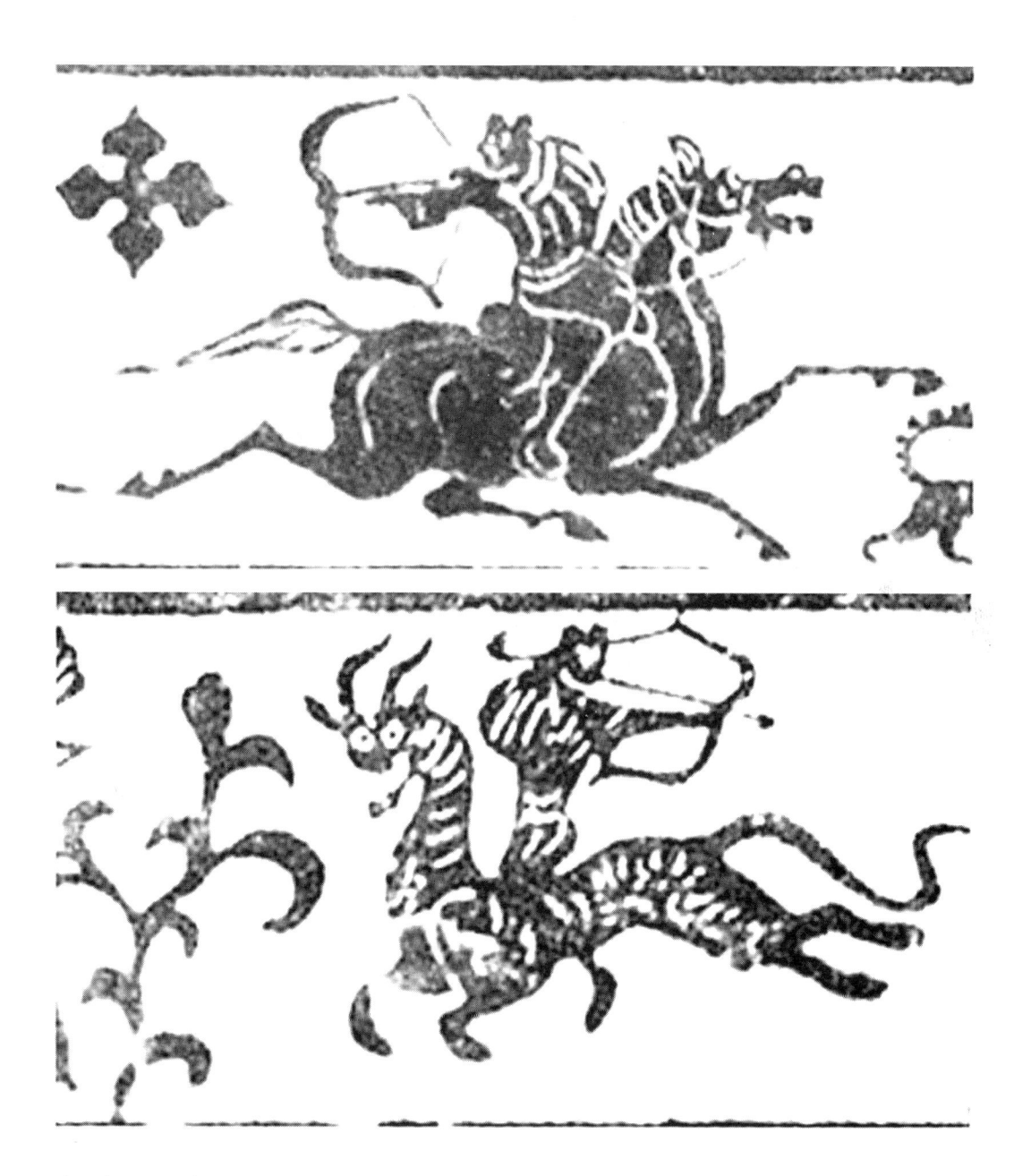

Fig. 8b,c: Details showing hybrid archers on a horse and a dragon, Dangjiagou, Mizhi, Shaanxi, Eastern Han Dynasty (After SB, p.25)

Fig. 8d: Detail showing a possible Xiongnu archer, Dangjiagou, Mizhi, Shaanxi, Eastern Han Dynasty (After SB, p.25)

Fig. 9: Detail of a lintel showing hunters on foot, Tomb of Tian Fang 田魴, Sishipu 四十鋪, Suide, Shaanxi, 92 CE (After SD, fig. 3)

Fig. 10: Scene of human-animal combat, Tomb of the Grand Administrator of Liaodong (Liaodong taishou 遼東太守), Huangjiata 黃家塔 tomb no. 7, Suide, Shaanxi, 90 CE (After SD, fig. 13)

Fig. 11: Detail of a battle over the bridge scene showing the barbarian forces; lintel over the doorway of the tomb at Yi'nan, Shandong, Late Eastern Han Dynasty, 147-220 CE (After ZG, vol. 1, fig. 179)

Fig. 12: Battle between Han and barbarian forces; detail of the west wall of the Xiaotangshan 孝堂山 Shrine, Shandong, Eastern Han Dynasty, 76-88 CE (After ZG, vol. 1, fig. 43)

Fig. 13a: Battle between Han and barbarian forces; detail of the west wall of a tomb excavated in Baijiashan 百家山, Suide, Shaanxi, Eastern Han Dynasty (After SD, fig. 29)

Fig. 13b: Detail of the scene to the right of the battle scene on the west wall of a tomb excavated in Baijiashan, Suide, Shaanxi, Eastern Han Dynasty (After SD, fig. 29)

Fig. 13c: Detail of the scene to the left of the battle scene on the west wall of a tomb excavated in Baijiashan, Suide, Shaanxi, Eastern Han Dynasty (After SD, fig. 29)

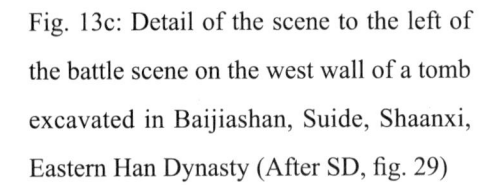

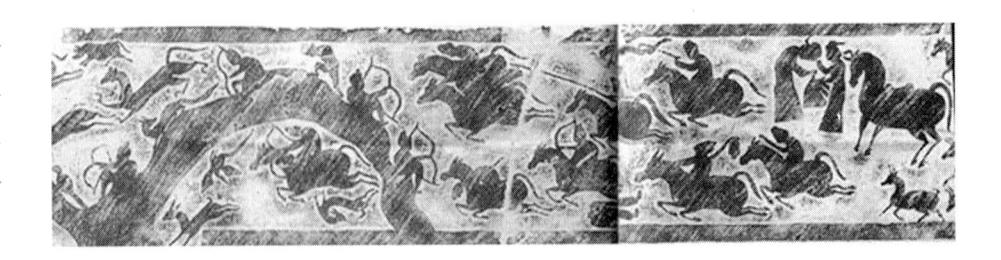

Fig. 14: Reliefs supporting the stone depicting the battle between Han and barbarian forces; west wall of a tomb excavated in Baijiashan, Suide, Shaanxi, Eastern Han Dynasty (After SD fig. 29)

吐火羅問題

余太山

吐火羅語文書的發現和對吐火羅語以及有關歷史地理問題的研究，既是比較歷史語言學界的大事，也是中亞學界的大事。蓋自十九世紀末到二十世紀初，在我國西北地區出土的古文書殘卷中，有若干以當時未知語言寫成，其一即"Toγrï語"，定名之前一度被稱爲"第一種語言"。[1] 定名的依據是回鶻文《彌勒會見記》（Maitreyasamitinātaka）的一則題記。該題記稱此記乃自 Toγrï 語文本譯爲突厥語（Türk）者，而 Toγrï 語文本乃由聖月（Aryač(a)ntrï）自印度語（Äntkäk）編譯而成。既然"第一種語言"的《彌勒會見記》有若干寫本的原編譯者正是聖月，可見這"第一種語言"應即 Toγrï 語。[2]

大部分殘存的 Toγrï 語資料是譯自梵語等的佛教文獻，年代在公元 500—800 年間。經研究，Toγrï 語屬印歐語系，且有 A 和 B 兩種方言，兩者的基本詞彙和語法結構相同或相似。A 方言被回鶻人稱爲 Toγrï 語，其本名則爲 Ārśi 語。[3] Ārśi 即"焉耆"（Ārgi）之突厥語譯。[4] B 方言則被回鶻人稱爲 Küsän 語。Küsän 即"龜茲"（Kučā, Kuči）之突厥語譯。[5] A 種方言主要流行於焉耆及高昌一帶，而 B 種方言則集中在龜茲，亦見於焉耆等地。

若干語言特徵表明（如：數詞 100 在 A 和 B 兩種方言中分別作 känt 和 kante，等於拉丁語的 centum），Toγrï 語屬於 centum 語組。[6] 其發祥地當在歐洲，與凱爾特語及其以東的日耳曼語、希臘語、波羅的語等有較密切的關係。[7] 這似乎表明操 Toγrï 語之族群在非常早的時代就脫離了印歐語系共同體，在經過長途跋涉後，有一部份東向進入了中國境內。

Toγrï 語的情況果如前述，就不僅給語言學家，也給歷史學家提出了一系列需要解釋的問題。

其一，不管操 Toγrï 語的族群起源於何處，既然它很早就來到中國，應在中國史籍中留下印蹟。換言之，他們究竟是以什麼名稱出現在中國史籍中的？

其二，果如多數學者所指，原始印歐語系部落起源於西方[8]，則操 Toγrï 語的族群是何時、大致沿著什麼路線東遷到達中國及其西北地區的？

其三，"Toγrï"一名究竟何指？按之對音，無妨視爲"Θογαρ, Θαγουρ-, Τοχαρ-, Tuχār,

Təχwār, Tukhār-"，亦即漢語"吐火羅"之對音。果然，操這種語言的族群和 Sacae（塞種）是什麼關係？蓋據 Strabo，Tochari 係 Sacae 部落之一。

其四，"Toγrï" 果即 Tochari，何故同時代 Tokharestan 以及其他 Tochari 人活動地區居民的語言並不操 Toγrï 語？尤其是被稱爲"吐火羅斯坦"（《大唐西域記》卷一所謂"覩貨邏國故地"）地區的居民的主要語言可能是伊朗語[9]，無疑不同於 Toγrï 語。[10] 玄奘的時期去出土 Toγrï 語文書的年代不遠，如果玄奘所記阿耆尼國和屈支國居民的語言分別是 Toγrï 語 A 和 B 兩種方言，則玄奘所記"覩貨邏國"的語言又該如何解釋？

其五，A 方言已有本名，回鶻人何故還稱之爲"Toγrï 語"？

其六，既然 B 方言被回鶻人稱爲 Küsän 語，且有譯自 Küsän 語之 Toγrï 語文獻，如《十業道譬喻鬘》（Daśakarmapathāvadānamālā）等，[11] 足見兩種方言有較大的區別，然則操 A、B 兩種方言之族群又是什麼關係？

以上六個問題中，最重要的是第一個問題，回答這個問題，中國學者責無旁貸。本文是我有關上述諸問題的一些思考，以第一個問題爲核心。

引起我們注意的是 Toγrï 語有多種方言。這應該是操這種語言之族群的分化導致的，因而操 Toγrï 語的族群可能以若干不同的名稱出現，不僅不同方言的族群可能有不同的名稱，操同一種方言的人亦可分屬不同的集團，從而具有不同的名稱。換言之，Toγrï 語族群應該具有若干漢語名稱，而能夠同時滿足以下三個條件者應予優先考慮：

一、其名稱應能與 Toγrï、Küsän 或 Ārśi 勘同。
二、其人登上中國歷史舞臺的時間足夠早，能與印歐語族的出現相銜接。
三、其語言和體貌特徵爲印歐人種的可能性不能排除。

在先秦典籍中，大致符合以上條件的有大夏、月氏和允姓之戎三者。以下依次敘說這三者的有關情況。

——— [12]

1. "大夏"最早見於《左傳》。《左傳·昭元年傳》載："遷實沈于大夏"。《左傳·定四年傳》載："命以《唐誥》而封於夏虛，啓以夏政，疆以戎索"。此大夏或夏虛既可能在翼城也可能在虞鄉、平陽或太原。

又，《呂氏春秋·本味篇》稱美"大夏之鹽"，鹽指解池之鹽，此大夏當在安邑。《戰國策·秦策四》稱："魏伐邯鄲，因退爲逢澤之遇，乘夏車，稱夏王，朝爲天子，天下皆從"。魏都安邑所在本爲夏虛即大夏之虛。

又，《史記·秦始皇本紀》等有"禹鑿龍門，通大夏"之語，此大夏在鄂，近龍門。《世本》

稱唐叔虞"居鄂",亦因其地有大夏之虛。

又,《史記·吳太伯世家》:"封周章弟虞仲於周之北故夏虛"。此夏虛在大陽。

以上文獻所見大夏或夏虛應即卜辭所見土方。"土方"之"土"[tha]不妨視爲"大夏"[dat-hea]之"大","土[方]"是"大夏"的省稱。兩者地望相同,均在殷之西北,亦即晉南。卜辭有"唐"或"唐土"亦即大夏。"唐"[dang]、"土"乃同名異譯。武丁曾封築大邑於唐土以鎮壓土方。

《詩·商頌》稱"禹敷下土方",《楚辭·天問》稱"禹之力獻功,降省下土方",知禹曾治理土方。而相傳禹都陽城、平陽、安邑、晉陽。如前述,平陽、安邑、晉陽均可能有大夏之虛。

要之,晉南亦即翼城(今翼城)、虞鄉(今永濟)、平陽(今臨汾西)、太原、安邑(今夏縣)、鄂(今臨汾西鄉寧縣)、大陽(今平陸)均有大夏之虛或夏虛,亦即大夏人的遺蹟。

2. 晉南的大夏人後遷至臨夏乃至河西。

《管子·小匡篇》載齊桓公西征"拘泰夏,西服流沙西虞"。同書"封禪篇"亦稱:桓公"西伐大夏,涉流沙"。這兩則記載中的"大夏"("泰夏")應在河西。

又,《穆天子傳》(卷四)稱穆天子西征曾經由"西夏氏"之地。"西夏"即大夏,其地亦在河西。稱爲"西夏",因大夏之故地更在其東。《穆天子傳》成書年代當早於前三世紀,所描述的時代至遲爲春秋,故所載"西夏"或即齊桓公所征討的大夏。此外,《呂氏春秋·古樂篇》等亦載往赴昆侖(今阿爾泰山)需經由大夏。

又,《山海經·北山經》所載敦薨之山和敦薨之水乃指今祁連山和黨河。"敦薨"與"大夏"得視爲同名異譯,上述山水皆因大夏人而得名。可知直至河西走廊西端均曾有大夏人活動。漢代"敦煌"[tuən-huang]郡應得名於"敦薨"[tuən-xuəng],亦即得名於"大夏"。

不僅河西曾見大夏活動,更東南的臨夏地區亦有其遺蹟。《漢書·地理志下》載隴西郡有縣名"大夏"。《水經注·河水二》則載:洮水"左會大夏川水……又東北逕大夏縣古城南"。

除遷往河西外,似乎還有一枝大夏人自晉南遷往晉北或河套以北。《史記·秦始皇本紀》載始皇帝二十八年(前219年)所作"琅邪臺銘"稱:"六合之內,皇帝之土。西涉流沙,南盡北戶,東有東海,北過大夏,人跡所至,無不臣者"。其中的地名"大夏"或者便是這支北遷大夏人的遺蹟。

托勒密《地理志》[13]所載Thaguri人、Thaguri山和Thogara城(VI,6)均應位於河西地區,業已由對藏語、和闐語有關文書的研究得以證實。Thaguri、Thogara均得視爲"大夏"的對譯。這可以視作旁證。[14]

3. 晉南的大夏可溯源於陶唐氏,即以堯部落爲宗主包括有唐氏在內的部落聯合體。

相傳"堯伐有唐"(《鶡冠子·世兵》)後,被封於晉南唐土,故稱"唐侯",而在繼嚳即位後,號陶唐氏,是因爲堯或其後裔曾有遷徙之舉,所居之地因而亦得名爲"唐";或譯稱爲"陶"、爲"唐","陶唐氏"一號由此而生。

有唐氏本爲一古國,地在夏虛。唐人之得名於大夏,正如商人之得名於商丘。可見就名稱

— 261 —

而言，"唐"即"大夏"。"陶"[du]、"唐"[dang]均"大夏"之略譯。

堯伐有唐氏後，其胤繁衍遷徙，晉南諸地遂有夏虛即大夏之虛。當然，其中若干也可能是堯所伐有唐氏之遺蹟。至於鄂地之大夏，很可能便是《逸周書·史記解》所見"西夏"。因被堯所伐，有唐氏有一枝西遷至今鄉寧一帶，後被其東鄰所并；翼城既在大夏之西，故稱"西夏"。《逸周書·王會解》有所謂"北唐戎"，或在太原晉陽。陶唐氏或有唐氏有一枝北上到達這一帶也未可知。

陶唐氏衰亡後，夏后氏命彭姓之豕韋氏鎮守其地。夏孔甲封陶唐氏之後劉累代豕韋氏守唐土，豕韋氏於殷末徙國於唐。周成王滅唐，遷之於杜。

劉累及其後裔，除服事夏商周者外，有一部分先後踏上了北遷、西徙之路。不妨認爲早在舜繼位之初，這種遷徙的序幕已經揭開。

西遷者已如前述，北遷者可能就是《逸周書·王會解》所載貢"茲白牛"的大夏，亦即同篇所附"伊尹朝獻篇"與"月氏"同列於"正北"的"大夏"。其地當在晉北或河套以北。"琅邪臺銘"所見"大夏"或者也是其遺蹟。

4. 中國史籍所載，除晉南、河西等地之大夏外，還有西域的大夏。據《史記·大宛列傳》等記載可以考知，西域之大夏國位於媯水（今阿姆河）之南，其人"土著"，約前130年，被西遷的大月氏人征服。

被大月氏征服的大夏國，一說應卽希臘巴克特里亞（Graeco-Bactria）王國。[15] 今案：此說未安。《史記·大宛列傳》載，大夏國"無大君長"，"兵弱，畏戰"。這與已知希臘巴克特里亞的情況不符，且"大夏"非Bactria之對譯。[16]

另外，希臘巴克特里亞王國亡於前140年左右，也就是說當大月氏西遷阿姆河流域時，該王國已滅亡了十年左右。因此，大月氏征服的大夏國不可能是希臘巴克特里亞王國。

據斯特拉波《地理志》[17]（XI, 8）的記載可以考知，滅亡希臘巴克特里亞王國的應爲自錫爾河北岸南下的Sacae（塞種）諸部：Asii、Gasiani、Tochari和Sacarauli。因此，大夏應即Sacae四部之一的Tochari。"大夏"[dat-hea]可以視爲Tochari的確切對譯。由於進入阿姆河流域，原來遊牧的Tochari人開始了農耕生活。

《史記·大宛列傳》"無大君長"云云，也許正反映了進入巴克特里亞的塞種各部互不統屬的局面。至於塞種諸部治下的巴克特里亞被稱爲"大夏"，則可能是因爲當時Tochari人是諸部名義上的宗主；否則，便是其人佔壓倒多數的緣故。

有學者在指大夏爲希臘巴克特里亞王國的同時，指Tochari人爲大月氏，試圖使斯特拉波關於塞種四部從希臘人手中奪取巴克特里亞的記載與《史記·大宛列傳》關於大月氏滅亡大夏的記載相一致。[18] 其實，斯特拉波所載Tochari是塞種，塞種和月氏在中國史籍中有明確區分，而且"月氏"與Tochari對音也不相符。由此可見大月氏不可能是滅亡希臘巴克特里亞王國的Tochari。滅亡大夏國的大月氏不見載於西史，猶如希臘巴克特里亞王國不見載於漢史，都是很正常的。

應該指出，Tochari 中國史籍稱之爲"吐火羅"或"吐呼羅"等。而首次將大夏和吐火羅聯繫起來的是《新唐書·西域傳下》："吐火羅，或曰土豁羅，曰覩貨邏，元魏謂吐呼羅者。居蔥嶺西，烏滸河之南，古大夏地。……大月氏爲烏孫所奪，西過大宛，擊大夏臣之。治藍氏城。大夏即吐火羅也"。此處所述"吐火羅"即大夏無疑就是《史記·大宛列傳》所載大夏，而顯然有別於大月氏。[19]

阿姆河流域的大夏人來自伊犁河、楚河流域：據斯特拉波《地理志》的記載可以考知，自錫爾河北岸南下、滅亡希臘巴克特里亞的 Asii、Tochari 等四部塞種來自伊犁河、楚河流域（《漢書·西域傳》所謂"塞地"）。塞種佔領這一地區的時間不能確知，但最早可能在前六世紀二十年代，亦即阿喀美尼朝波斯大流士一世即位（前 521 年）之前。

大月氏被匈奴擊敗、西遷至伊犁河、楚河流域時，將該處的塞種逐走。於是一部分塞種南下帕米爾，另一部分則退縮至錫爾河北岸。很可能由於繼續受到來自東方強鄰的壓力，包括若干 Tochari 人在内的部分塞種終於在前 140 年左右南渡錫爾河，經索格底亞那，侵入希臘人統治下的巴克特里亞，佔領了主要位於阿姆河南岸的後來被稱爲吐火羅斯坦的地區，《史記·大宛列傳》所見大夏國於是成立。

可能在部分塞種南下巴克特里亞的同時，另有一枝以 Tochari 人爲主的塞種進入費爾幹納盆地，建立了《史記·大宛列傳》所見大宛國。"大宛"[dat-iuan] 亦得視爲 Tochari 之異譯。[20] 南下帕米爾的塞種中，有一部分進入西北次大陸，另有一部分則可能東向進入塔里木盆地諸綠洲，後者之中亦有吐火羅人。《漢書·西域傳》所見西域南北道若干國名和地名，例如："渠勒"[gia-lek]、"桃槐"[do-huəi]、"渠犁"[gia-lyei]、"單桓"[duat-huan]、"兌虚"[duat-khia]、"丹渠"[tan-gia]，均得視爲 Tochari 之異譯。

5. 西域大夏遷自晉南還有以下一些旁證。

其一，西域大夏國的信息是張騫首次西使獲得的。張騫這次西使的目的地本是伊犁河、楚河流域的大月氏國。由於大月氏西遷，張騫跟蹤而至阿姆河流域，纔得知有大夏國。張騫在大夏地逗留了一年多，對當地的風土人情定有較充分的瞭解。因此，他採用"大夏"這一古稱命名一個由 Tochari 人建立的、當時業已臣服大月氏的國家，顯然不會僅僅出於爲 Tochari 找一確切音譯的考慮。他稱呼大夏國所臨阿姆河（該河時名 Vakhshu 即 Wakshu）爲"媯水"，考慮到晉南有一條媯水顯然是一個重要因素。《史記·五帝本紀》"索隱"引皇甫謐曰："媯水在河東虞鄉縣歷山西"。虞鄉，如前所述，相傳有夏虛即大夏之虛。張騫採用"大夏"這一名稱時，顯然想到了晉南乃至虞鄉的大夏。

其二，張騫首次西使旨在聯合月氏共同抵抗匈奴，雖因形勢變化，這一目的未能實現，然張騫此行往返一十三年，備歷艱辛，終於使西域諸國與西漢開始了雙向的交往，即史遷所謂"鑿空"。但是，《史記·建元以來侯者年表》在敘及張騫出使西域的功績時，提到的僅僅是"使絕域大夏"，隻字未及同時出使大月氏、大宛、康居之事。足見時人評價張騫西使是如何偏重大夏的發現！《漢書·敘傳下》竟用"博望杖節，收功大夏"八字總結張騫的一生，也就不足爲怪了。

又據《史記·西南夷列傳》，張騫歸國，"因盛言大夏在漢西南，慕中國，患匈奴隔其道，誠通蜀，身毒國道便近，有利無害"。從此，西漢開始大規模經營西南夷，並自元鼎三年（前114年）至元封二年（前109年）先後設置了牂柯、越巂、沈黎、汶山、武都、益州等郡；據同書"大宛列傳"，置郡的目的主要在於"欲地接以前通大夏"，而武帝確曾遣使十餘輩，企圖"出此初郡抵大夏"，終因昆明阻撓而未果。武帝不顧當時客觀條件，大事西南夷，正是張騫"盛言"的結果，可見張騫有關大夏的報告必有能深深打動武帝的地方。

嗣後，據《史記·大宛列傳》，"天子數問騫大夏之屬"。騫乃說武帝通使烏孫，其辭曰："既連烏孫，自其西大夏之屬皆可招來而爲外臣"。天子果以爲然，命騫使烏孫。據同傳，"騫因分遣副使使大宛、康居、大月氏、大夏、安息、身毒、于寘、扜罙及諸旁國"。張騫卒"後歲餘，騫所遣使通大夏之屬者皆頗與其人俱來，於是西北國始通於漢矣"。由此可知，張騫使烏孫雖有聯結烏孫抵抗匈奴的目的在，但歸根結蒂還是爲了招徠大夏，而大夏使者隨騫副使俱來，簡直被視作西北國通於漢的標識。

太初年間，李廣利征大宛，初戰不利，敗歸敦煌，公卿、議者皆願罷擊宛軍，獨武帝不以爲然。其原因，據《史記·大宛列傳》，乃在於武帝擔心，"宛小國而不能下，則大夏之屬輕漢，而宛善馬絕不來，烏孫、侖頭易苦漢使矣，爲外國笑"，"乃案言伐宛尤不便者鄧光等"，不惜"天下騷動"，再起大兵伐宛。在此，武帝首先考慮的仍然是大夏。

西漢君臣如此念茲在茲的大夏國，不過是一個早已臣服於大月氏的、兵弱畏戰的遠國。當時該國的中心完全處在大月氏王的控制之下，僅東部山區有五個互不統屬的翎侯。雖據《漢書·西域傳》，這五個翎侯有一定的自主權，能"共禀漢使者"，但以此爲外臣，意義畢竟不大。到底大夏的吸引力從何而來？目前看來祇有一個答案：張騫和武帝相信西域的大夏遷自晉南，乃陶唐氏之裔冑。蓋張騫身臨其境，沐浴陶唐氏之遺風，歸報於國，使好大喜功的武帝不勝嚮往之情。僅僅由於史遷謹慎，視張騫之見聞爲類似《山海經》之奇談，不敢言之，纔湮沒無聞至今。

其三，《史記·大宛列傳》稱："自大宛以西至安息，國雖頗異言，然大同俗，相知言。其人皆深眼，多鬚頿，善市賈，爭分銖"。所謂"自大宛以西至安息"，當然包括大夏國在內，蓋同傳又稱："大夏在大宛西南二千餘里"。張騫首次西使已取道大宛，親臨大夏地。嗣後，據同傳，"西北外國使更來更去"。《漢書·西域傳》且載大夏五翎侯曾"共禀漢使者"。可知漢人對西域大夏的情況是比較熟悉的，對西域大夏人體貌特徵的概括亦即"深眼、多鬚頿"沒有理由懷疑。

另一方面，據《史記·高祖本紀》載："高祖爲人，隆準而龍顏、美須髯"。而《漢書·高帝紀》贊曰引《春秋》晉史蔡墨有言："陶唐氏既衰，其後有劉累，學擾龍，事孔甲，范氏其後也"，並肯定高祖爲劉累之後。果然，"隆準而龍顏、美須髯"與"深眼、多鬚頿"如出一轍，恐非巧合。質言之，劉邦與西域大夏人體貌特徵的一致，正說明西域之大夏即吐火羅人的前身主要是以堯部落爲宗主、可能包括有唐氏在內的部落聯合體。這似乎也有助於理解武帝對西域大夏國的特殊興趣。

其四，《尚書·堯典》："乃命羲和，欽若昊天，厤象日月星辰"。羲和是陶唐氏的重要職官。而據《漢書·西域傳》，西域的大夏國有職官曰"翖侯"[xiəp-ho]，與"羲和"[xia-huai]讀音近似；翖侯源自羲和也未可知。

6. 總而言之，大夏可溯源於陶唐氏，其故地在晉南。其枝裔後來逐步遷離晉南，一部份北徙至河套以北，一部份西徙至臨夏和河西。最早在公元前七世紀二十年代，河西的部份大夏人西遷至伊犁河、楚河流域，與先後抵達該處的 Asii、Gasiani 和 Sacarauli 等部落結成聯盟，並西向伸張其勢力至錫爾河北岸。

約公元前 177/176 年，大月氏首次西遷，佔領伊犁河、楚河流域，包括大夏人在內的塞人遭驅逐，部份退縮至錫爾河北岸；部份南下帕米爾，或越興都庫什山南下，或東進塔里木盆地、佔有南北道包括焉耆和龜茲在內的一些綠洲。

公元前 140 年左右，在錫爾河北的塞人南下，其中一枝進入費爾幹納，一枝進入巴克特里亞，後者滅亡了希臘巴克特里亞王國。他們各自建立的政權（可能均以大夏人爲主），中國史籍分別稱之爲大宛國和大夏國。約十年後，大夏國被再次西徙的大月氏人滅亡。

二 [21]

1. "月氏"[njiuk-tjie]，也寫作"禺知"[ngio-tie]等。《穆天子傳》卷一："甲午，天子西征，乃絕隃之關隥。己亥至於焉居、禺知之平"。"焉居、禺知之平"或在今河套東北。

《逸周書·王會篇》附"伊尹朝獻篇"列"月氏"於"正北"。是篇係戰國時所作，所載以駒騄貢周之"月氏"可能是春秋時期的月氏，其居地當在黃河以西。

《管子·輕重乙》稱："玉出於禺氏之旁山，此皆距周七千八百餘里。其涂遠，其至阨"。"國畜"諸篇所載略同。"輕重甲"且說："懷而不見於抱、挾而不見於掖、而辟千金者，白璧也，然後八千里之禺氏可得而朝也。簪珥而辟千金者珍琳琅玕也。然後八千里之崑崙之虛可得而朝也"。"禺氏"之"旁山"產玉，此山卽"崑崙之虛"；是虛和月氏去周都距離大致相等。或因月氏一度壟斷玉石貿易，故所產之玉稱"禺氏之玉"。此處"崑崙"應指阿爾泰山，故在《管子》所描述的時代，月氏人已西向伸張其勢力至阿爾泰山東麓。"禺氏"[ngio-tjie]亦卽"月氏"。

又，《史記·大宛列傳》稱："始月氏居敦煌、祁連間"。"敦煌"應指"敦薨之山"卽今祁連山，"祁連"應指今天山。可知月氏故地東起今祁連山以北，西抵今天山、阿爾泰山東麓。結合以上有關先秦典籍所見月氏人活動範圍的描述，以及《史記·匈奴列傳》關於冒頓單于"西擊走月氏，南幷樓煩、白羊河南王"以後、匈奴"右方王將居西方，直上郡以西，接月氏、氏羌"的記載，可知月氏人的勢力曾一度東向伸展至河套內外。

2. 月氏（禺知）可能是有虞氏之一枝，遷自晉地。晉地之有虞氏則遷自魯地。

據《墨子》，"舜耕歷山，陶河瀕，漁雷澤，堯得之服澤之陽"。歷山、河濱、雷澤之地望，歷來注家的說法可大別爲兩類：一類置諸魯，另一類置諸晉。這可能是因爲"歷山"等地名既見於魯或齊、又見於晉。對此，合理的解釋應該是："歷山"等原係有虞氏在齊魯時居地之名稱，隨著舜，有虞氏最著名的部酋，自齊魯西遷，晉地也就出現了相同的名稱。"服澤之陽"，在蒲州，則不妨視作西遷有虞氏與陶唐氏接觸的最初地點。

據《尚書·堯典》，可知舜自魯西遷晉南後曾居於媯水之汭。媯水之汭因成爲舜所部有虞氏居地而得名"虞地"。

《孟子》稱舜爲"東夷之人"，《史記》稱舜爲"冀州之人"。結合兩者，可見舜率所部有虞氏自魯遷晉，終於從"東夷之人"變成了"冀州之人"。

3. 有虞氏乃顓頊部落自蜀遷魯之一枝。

《國語·魯語》稱："有虞氏禘黃帝而祖顓頊"。這表明有虞氏之起源至少可以追溯到顓頊。據《大戴禮記·帝繫》，可知顓頊之故地在若水（今四川雅礱江）流域。又據《國語·楚語下》等，顓頊族（更可能是其中之一枝）因佐少皞（少昊）自若水遷至窮桑。窮桑（亦作"空桑"），地在魯北。

顓頊以"高陽"爲"有天下號"，"高陽"[ko-jiang]應即"窮桑"[giuəm-sang]、"空桑"[khong-sang]之異譯。而有虞氏之"虞"[ngiua]亦不妨視作"高陽"或"空桑"之略譯（見疑、溪疑旁紐），有虞氏正是顓頊族東遷空桑的一枝即高陽氏之後。換言之，"有虞"與"高陽"實係同名異譯，乃東遷顓頊族之專稱。"空桑"或"窮桑"乃至"高陽"或"虞氏"等的原意均與日出有關。

東遷顓頊部族事實上的始祖很可能是《國語·鄭語》中與夏禹、商契、周棄並舉的虞幕，亦即顓頊之子窮蟬。"窮蟬"[giuəm-zjian]，亦得視爲"窮桑"之異譯。顓頊國號"高陽"、其子幕一名"窮蟬"，均因顓頊部落繼少昊之後居於窮桑之故。

要之，顓頊之一枝自若水東遷窮桑，始佐少昊，後取而代之，遂得號"高陽氏"即"有虞氏"。"有虞氏"或"高陽氏"最初可能得名於魯北之空桑山，但"空桑"一旦成了一個地緣政治集團的稱號，一般情況下會隨著這集團之人的遷徙而遷往各地。舜率所部有虞氏自魯西遷至晉南媯水之汭，將"空桑"一名也搬到了晉地；媯水之汭於是得名"虞地"。後來封於"虞地"的太伯之後亦因而得名爲"虞公"。

4. 舜亡後，部分有虞氏已經開始離開晉地。其中一枝有虞氏則經北地、安定等地西向進入河西。

大約在前七世紀二十年代末，河西的有虞氏即《管子·小匡》所謂"西虞"復西遷至伊犁河、楚河流域，同時或先後遷去的還有一部分大夏人和允姓之戎。蓋據《史記·秦本紀》載：穆公"三十七年（前623年）秦用由余謀伐戎王，益國十二，開地千里，遂霸西戎"。有虞氏等放棄河西，西遷伊犂河、楚河流域或在此時。

5. 西遷伊犂河、楚河流域的有虞氏等部在該處組成的部落聯合體被希羅多德《歷史》[22]（I，201；IV，13，16）稱爲 Issedones；其中，有虞氏可能就是斯特拉波《地理志》（XI，8）所載 Gasiani 人，允姓之戎和大夏分別爲 Asii 和 Tochari。至遲在六世紀二十年代末，Issedones 西向擴張至錫爾河北岸，逐走了原居該處的 Massagetae 人，從此與波斯人發生關係，被阿喀美尼朝波斯大流士一世（Darius I，前 521—前 486 年）的貝希斯登（Behistun）銘文稱爲 Sakā，Sakā 亦卽中國史籍所見 "塞種"。

由於大月氏人的西徙，塞種卽包括有虞氏在內的四部組成的部落聯合體放棄伊犂河、楚河流域，除一部分退縮至錫爾河北岸外，餘衆南下葱嶺，散處帕米爾各地。約公元前 140 年左右，塞種諸部紛紛離開錫爾河北岸，其中一枝渡過阿姆河，侵入並滅亡了希臘巴克特里亞王國，形成了中國史籍所謂 "大夏國"。約十年之後，這個主要由塞種四部構建的 "大夏國" 被來自伊犂河、楚河流域的大月氏人征服。

散處帕米爾地區的部份有虞氏後來還東向進入塔里木盆地諸綠洲，建立了一些城郭小國。《漢書·西域傳》所載西域國名和地名，例如：高昌 [ko-thjiang]、姑師 [ka(kia)-shei]、車師 [kia-shei]、危（佹）須 [khiai-sio]、龜茲 [khiuə-tziə]、休循 [xiu-ziuən] 等，地名有車延 [kia-jian]、居延 [kia-jian]、貴山 [giuət-shean] 等，均得與 "空桑"、"窮桑"、"高陽"、"虞氏"、"鳩茲" 等視爲同名異譯。"高昌"、"龜茲" 更與 "高陽"、"鳩茲" 前後、東西相映成趣。當然，以上國名或地名中有一些也可能是有虞氏在前七世紀末西向遷徙時留下的遺蹟。

6. 可能在一枝有虞氏西遷的同時，另一枝有虞氏北遷雁門。後者西向伸張其勢力抵達阿爾泰山東端，一度稱霸天山南北，壟斷了當時的東西貿易。直至公元前 177/前 176 年被北亞新興的遊牧部落匈奴擊敗，其大部纔被迫西徙伊犂河、楚河流域，逐走了原居該處的塞種。史稱這部分有虞氏卽月氏人爲 "大月氏"，而將留在原地的小部分人稱爲 "小月氏"。約公元前 130 年，伊犂河、楚河流域的大月氏人又被匈奴支持的烏孫人擊敗，放棄伊犂河、楚河流域，西徙至阿姆河流域，滅亡了當地的大夏國，定居下來。

大月氏領有大夏地後，直接統治 Bactra 及其周圍地區，而通過所謂 "五翖侯" 控制東部山區。"五翖侯" 均係原大夏國人，是大月氏人扶植的傀儡。

後來推翻大月氏，開創貴霜王朝的原貴霜翖侯丘就卻，應爲公元前 140 年左右入侵巴克特里亞的塞種諸部之一 Gasiani 之後裔，如前所述，Gasiani 卽公元前七世紀末以前西遷之有虞氏。"貴霜" [giuət-shiang]，亦得視爲 "空桑"、"禺知"、"月氏" 等的異譯。因此，中亞史上盛極一時的貴霜帝國，可以說也是西徙有虞氏建立的。

7. 以下是指月氏之先爲有虞氏的若干說明：

其一，名稱相同："禺知"、"禺氏" 等和 "月氏" 顯係同名異譯，與 "高陽"、"窮桑"、"空桑" 亦係同名異譯，而有虞氏之 "虞" 亦不妨視作 "高陽" 或 "空桑" 之略譯。《山海經·大荒北經》："逮之于禺谷"，郭注："禺淵……今作虞"。此 "禺"、"虞" 互通之例。

其二，有虞氏與月氏及其前身禺知的遷徙在時間和地域上可相銜接，可作出連貫的敘述。

其三，據《史記·大宛列傳》，張騫於公元前129年訪問大月氏歸國後向武帝報告稱：大月氏"都嬀水北爲王庭"。"嬀水"即今阿姆河。張騫稱阿姆河爲"嬀水"，顯係實錄。蓋如前述，舜所部有虞氏的發祥地正是晉地嬀水之汭。而如果相信《史記·五帝本紀》"正義"的說法：舜父"瞽叟姓嬀"，則舜自魯西遷後，所居"嬀汭"即"嬀水之汭"其實得名於父姓。由此可見，遠赴中亞的有虞氏即大月氏人之王庭所臨河水被張騫稱爲"嬀水"決非偶然。張騫命名時考慮的不僅僅是大夏與嬀水的關係，更重要的因素也許是有虞氏與嬀水的淵源。

其四，據《史記·大宛列傳》記載，月氏或大月氏是遊牧部落。但沒有明確的資料表明有虞氏是遊牧部落，似乎不能將有虞氏與月氏或大月氏勘同。其實不然。祇要條件具備，生活和生產方式是可以改變的。有虞氏在故地時即便是土著，一旦踏上西遷之路，特別是到達伊犁河、楚河流域的大草原後，轉變爲遊牧人不是不可想像的；而一旦到達阿姆河流域，特別在進入巴克特里亞的農耕區後，相對安定的生活環境，又使他們逐步放棄遊牧、趨向定居。再說，史載舜率有虞氏耕、漁、陶，乃至成聚、邑、都，豈不說明在舜之前沒有聚、邑、都的有虞氏，正是一個遊牧部落，至少存在過遊牧的生活方式。更何況，沒有理由認爲舜以後便完全不存在遊牧的有虞氏部落，也就是說北遷、西徙者正是有虞氏中一直以遊牧爲生者的可能性也不能排除。

8.總而言之，大月氏之前身月氏（禺知）之先爲有虞氏之一枝。其人自蜀遷魯，復自魯徙晉，後逐步遷離晉地。一枝經北地、安定等進入河西。大約在公元前七世紀二十年代末，這一枝復西遷至伊犁河、楚河流域，同時或先後遷去的還有部分大夏人和允姓之戎等。其人在該處組成的部落聯合體被希羅多德稱爲Issedones。Issedones後西向擴張至錫爾河北岸，並被波斯人稱爲Sakā。由於大月氏人的西徙，包括有虞氏在內的部份塞種放棄伊犁河、楚河流域，除一部分退縮至錫爾河北岸外，餘衆南下葱嶺，散處帕米爾各地，並東進塔里木盆地，佔有包括龜茲、焉耆在內的一些南北道綠洲。

另一枝有虞氏則北遷雁門。至遲在公元前三世紀二十年代，這一枝有虞氏已西向伸張其勢力抵達阿爾泰山東端，一度壟斷了東西貿易。直至公元前177/176年被匈奴擊敗，其大部纔被迫西徙伊犁河、楚河流域，逐走了原居該處的塞人。史稱這部分人爲"大月氏"，而將留在原地的老弱稱爲"小月氏"。約公元前130年，大月氏人又被烏孫擊敗，放棄伊犁河、楚河流域，西徙至阿姆河流域，滅亡了由約十年前進入該地的塞人所建"大夏國"。

三 [23]

1.允姓之戎始見於《左傳》。其人原居瓜州，其內徙陰地者，被稱爲陰戎。允姓在瓜州之居地名陸渾，內徙允姓又被稱爲陸渾戎，而陰地亦有地得名陸渾。陰地屬九州，故陸渾戎亦九州戎之一枝。

瓜州很可能在涇水上游,今平涼至固原一帶。"瓜州"[koa-tjie] 可以視作"月氏"或"禺知"之異譯。允姓原居地得名"瓜州"可能是該地曾被月氏征服的結果。

居於秦、晉西北即涇水上游的允姓受秦人迫逐,除一部分附秦並在後來被晉惠公徙往伊川外,可能有一部分遷往瓜州之西。

2.《廣弘明集・辨惑篇》載梁荀濟"論佛教表"引《漢書・西域傳》之文有曰:"塞種本允姓之戎,世居燉煌,爲月氏迫逐,遂往葱嶺南奔。"[24] 荀氏在此將允姓與塞種聯繫在一起。儘管荀氏所引《漢書》之文不見今本,因而也許僅僅是他個人的一種推測。但允姓屬於塞種的客觀可能性是存在的。

所謂"塞種"應即波斯人所謂 Sakā,其前身便是希羅多德所謂 Issedones。遲至前七世紀末,Issedones 已經出現在伊犁河、楚河流域、亦即《漢書・西域傳》所謂"塞地"。Issedones 後西向擴張至錫爾河北岸,從此被波斯人稱爲 Sakā。Sakā 原是波斯人對錫爾河北岸遊牧部落的泛稱。

塞種主要由 Asii、Gasiani、Tochari、Sacarauli 四部組成。Isse[dones] 實即四部中的 Asii("don"似爲表示場所的後綴,亦見於後世 Osset 語中)。在希羅多德描述的時代,伊犁河、楚河流域很可能已是四部的居地,故 Issedones 實際上成了一個部落聯合體的名稱。這個聯合體被稱爲 Issedones,也許是 Asii 人佔有統治地位的緣故。

前述秦穆公開疆拓土的舉動,很可能引起諸戎的西遷。允姓也許便在這時離開瓜州及其以西,西走塞地。這與希羅多德所載 Issedones 在伊犁河、楚河流域出現的時間正相符合。

據《漢書・西域傳》,伊犁河、楚河流域有地名"惡師"[a-shei],不妨視作 Issedones 之異譯,亦允姓據有塞地之證。"允姓"[jiuən-sieng] 不妨爲 Isse[dones] 或 Asii 的對譯。

3. 允姓(Asii)自瓜州逐步西遷至"塞地" 尚有軌蹟可尋:

在晉惠公十三年(前 638 年)即允姓、姜戎氏內徙的前後,已可能有一部分允姓遷至後來的金城郡境內,《漢書・地理志下》所載"允吾"、"允街"等地名即其遺蹟。此外,據《後漢書・西羌傳》,金城郡境內有"大允谷"。"大允谷"或因允姓所居而得名。

又據《漢書・霍去病傳》,張掖郡境內有"焉支山"(同書"匈奴傳上"作"焉耆山")。"焉支(耆)"[ian-tjie(tjiei)] 得視作"允姓"或 Asii 的異譯,允姓西遷經過此山時或曾留下部衆。

《左傳・昭九年傳》杜注稱瓜州即敦煌,固然非是。但杜氏似乎不至於僅僅因爲敦煌產好瓜便遽斷古瓜州在敦煌。杜氏曾親至河西,很可能發現敦煌一帶有允姓活動的蛛絲馬蹟,遂指該處爲古瓜州。這說明允姓西遷時曾經過該地並一度逗留。

《漢書・張騫傳》稱:烏孫"本與大月氏俱在祁連、燉煌間"。此處"祁連"指今天山,而"燉煌"即"敦煌"指今祁連山。在傳文描述的年代,具體而言爲公元前 177/176 年以前,烏孫的居地在今祁連山與天山之間。"烏孫"[a-siuən] 既得視爲"允姓"或 Asii 的異譯,不妨認爲烏孫是前七世紀末遷往伊犁河、楚河流域的允姓留在祁連山和天山之間的餘衆。

4. 公元前 177/176 年大月氏被匈奴冒頓單于擊破、放棄故地西遷。大月氏的進攻，使塞種（實卽 Asii、Gasiani、Tochari 等四族組成的部落聯合體）放棄了"塞地"，一部分塞種西向退縮至錫爾河北岸，其中一些 Asii 人更西走至鹹海、裏海以北，形成《史記·大宛列傳》所載"奄蔡"[iam-tsat]，亦卽西史所謂 Aorsi。另一些 Asii 人與其他三部一起侵入希臘巴克特里亞王國。一部分塞種還自"塞地"南下帕米爾，其中一些進入西北次大陸，另一些東向進入塔里木盆地，沿西域南北道建立了若干綠洲小國。《漢書·西域傳》所載城郭諸國名稱有"溫宿"[uen-siuet]、"烏壘"[a-liuei]、"焉耆"、"烏秅"[a-deai]、"伊循"[iei-ziuən] 等均可視作"允姓"或 Asii 的異譯，說明這些綠洲最早的開拓者可能是允姓卽 Asii 人。

值得注意的是："焉耆"，在佉盧文書中作 Argi，中古波斯語作 Ark；Argi、Ark 以及其王治之名"員渠"[hiuən-gia] 與"允格"的關係頗爲明顯；如果再考慮到焉耆王家姓"龍"[liong] 無妨視爲"陸渾"[liuk-huən] 的縮譯，其淵源便更清楚了。

5. 允姓是允格之後（"允姓"與"允格"[jiuən-keak] 得視爲同名異譯（[k] 齶化爲 [s]），允格乃金天氏卽少昊之裔。黃帝之子有二青陽，姬姓青陽與己姓青陽。前者卽玄囂，後者卽少昊。姬姓青陽降居泜水，降居若水者爲昌意。在昌意降居之前若水流域已有允姓國。這說明少昊之據有若水當先於昌意，若水應爲少昊可以追溯的最早故地。相傳少昊之子允格居郯、有子郯姓，郯之得名顯然是因爲少昊曾居若水之故。

據《漢書·西域傳》烏孫國王治"赤谷城"。《釋名·釋采帛》（卷四）："赤，赫也，太陽之色也"。又，《東觀漢記·顯宗孝明皇帝》（卷二）："建武四年五月甲申，皇子陽生，豐下銳上，顏赤色，有似於堯，上以赤色，名之曰陽"。由此可知，赤谷者，陽谷也。而《太平御覽》卷三引《尸子》："少昊金天氏邑於窮桑，日五色，互照窮桑"。《尚書·堯典》："分命羲仲，宅嵎夷，曰暘谷"。"僞孔傳"曰："東表之地稱嵎夷；暘，明也，日出於谷而天下明，故稱暘谷。暘谷、嵎夷一也。羲仲，居治東方之官"。"窮桑"、"嵎夷"[ngio-jiei] 得視爲同名異譯，知少昊金天氏所邑窮桑卽暘谷，亦卽陽谷。

又，《史記·大宛列傳》載烏孫始祖傳說曰："烏孫王號昆莫，昆莫之父，匈奴西邊小國也。匈奴攻殺其父，而昆莫生弃於野。烏嗛肉蜚其上，狼往乳之"。知烏孫的始祖與烏有關。"烏孫"一名或由來於這一傳說："烏孫"者，"烏之子孫"也。而"烏嗛肉蜚其上"云云，明此烏乃取食之鳥。

而《左傳·昭十七年傳》載少皞氏以鳥名官，知金天氏之始祖傳說與鳥類有關。其中司啓之"青鳥"卽倉庚又稱三足烏，爲西王母取食之神鳥。王充《論衡·說日篇》："日中有三足烏"。《淮南子·精神訓》："日中有踆烏"。高注："踆，猶蹲也。謂三足烏"。《太平御覽》卷三引《春秋元命包》曰："陽數起於一，成於二，故日中有三足烏"。烏孫王治名"赤谷"，表明烏孫人崇拜太陽。知三足烏與太陽崇拜有關。

由此可見，烏孫與金天氏兩者的始祖傳說存在某種內在聯繫。"烏孫"者，青鳥卽三足烏之子孫也。

最後，《山海經·大荒南經》"有羲和之國"。郭注引《啓筮》曰："有夫羲和之子，出於暘谷"。羲和之子所出"暘谷"既爲赤谷，知烏孫官號"翖侯"，得視爲"羲和"之異譯。

6. 總而言之，允姓之戎原居瓜州（涇水上游），因受秦人迫逐，徙於瓜州之西。至遲在前七世紀末，因秦穆公開疆拓土，其大部遂與一些大夏、禺知人一起抵達伊犁河、楚河流域，組成部落聯盟，其中允姓可能扮演了宗主的角色，因而該聯盟被希羅多德稱爲Issedones，後因擴張至錫爾河北岸，被波斯人稱爲Sakā。西遷過程中留在祁連山與天山之間的餘種，後來發展爲烏孫，進一步西走至鹹海、裏海以北者則爲奄蔡。

由於大月氏人的西遷，Issedones放棄伊犁河、楚河流域，除一部份退縮至錫爾河北岸外，其餘南下帕米爾，或進入西北次大陸，或東進塔里木盆地、進入焉耆等南北道綠洲。

允姓是允格之後，允格爲少昊之裔。有虞氏之祖顓頊降生於若水，蓋顓頊之父昌意據有若水，該水原爲少昊之居地。昌意據有若水之前已有允姓國，該國應爲少昊所建。而顓頊後來又東遷魯地輔佐少昊。凡此皆可見允姓與有虞氏關係之密切。兩者也許是同部別出的關係。"允姓"與"虞氏"、"烏孫"與"月氏"、Asii與Gasiani、"焉耆"與"龜茲"等等儘管代表不同的政治、部落實體，其名稱同出一源。

四

關於操Toγrï語之族群的起源，學者們提出了不少假說，其中似以中近東起源說最具合理性。說者以爲这一族群之前身應即楔形文字資料中常見的Guti人（結尾的i是名稱的一部份，加上Akkad語的格尾音就成爲Gutium等形式）。Guti人來自波斯西部山地。他們擊敗了巴比倫統治者納拉姆辛（Narâm-Sin），主宰整個巴比倫達百年之久，時在公元前2100年左右。楔形文字資料中另有名Tukriš（此名末尾的咝音可能是當地語音的格尾音，詞幹實爲Tukri）之部落，其居地從東面和東南面與Guti人居地鄰接。按之年代，Guti與Tukri要早於小亞的赫梯人。這兩者一起於前三千紀末離開波斯西部，經長途跋涉到達中國，部份定居，其餘繼續遊牧，遊牧者即後來見諸中國史籍之"月氏"。"月氏"與Guti乃同名異譯。"吐火羅"一名則來源於Tukri。[25]

上說的基礎是印歐人起源與中近東，由於較充分地消化了有關吐火羅語的研究成果而深受關注。[26]

以下試圖說明此說和以上有關大夏、月氏（禺知）的考證有著內在的一致性。

1. 名稱：說者以爲Guti和Tukri是兩個兄弟部族，在遙遠的過去共同從波斯出發，後來逐步融合成了一個新的整體。因此，既可用這一個、又可用另一個名稱稱呼他們。今案：既然Guti和Tukri可以分別和"月氏"和"大夏"勘同，則似乎可以認爲早在他們離開波斯之前，操Toγrï語之族群已經分化成兩個部落。或者說這一時期Toγrï語業已形成兩種方言。

說者以爲在中國史籍中操 Toγrī 語之族群是以"月氏"的名稱出現的，其人爲匈奴所逐西遷後纔以"Tochari"這一名稱爲各種語言的史料所著錄。具體而言：月氏西遷阿姆河流域後，"印度人、波斯人、粟特人、希臘人——人人都用這個新的名稱稱呼月氏，巴克特里亞本身也被叫做吐火羅斯坦（Toχāristān）即'吐火羅人之地'。似乎這個民族途中改變了名稱，而把月氏之名留在中國一邊，到了巴克特里亞就稱吐火羅人了"。其實不然，Toχāristān 在漢文史籍中也有對應的名稱："大夏"。如前所述，月氏西遷，征服大夏之後，纔立足阿姆河流域，月氏顯然有別於大夏。質言之，Guti 和 Tukri 在東遷後早已分道揚鑣。

2. 時間：禹的年代一般認爲在公元前 2100 年左右（學界暫以公元前 2070 年作爲夏代的始年），有虞氏、陶唐氏和顓頊的年代應該更在此前。說者據西史推定的 Guti 與 Tukri 人在巴比倫失敗的時間爲公元前三千紀末，認爲兩者從此離開波斯西部踏上東來征途。但我們不妨設想其人的東遷可能略早於此。換言之，不能排除他們在遷入波斯西部之前已有部份踏上東遷征途。果然，Guti 與 Tukri 的東來和陶唐氏和有虞氏的出現正相銜接。

3. 遷徙路線：Guti 和 Tukri（至少其中的一部份）在東遷的途中，首先到達今中國四川地區，這便是傳說中有虞氏始祖顓頊之由來。

三星堆高度發展的青銅文明，與中近東文明有某種聯繫是十分明顯的。至少從青銅雕像、神樹、權杖和和金面罩等若干因素構成的文化叢分析，巴蜀與西亞近東文明的交往最遲在公元前十四、五世紀已經存在了。[27] 其中，特別值得注意的是青銅神樹，應即若木。[28] 而相傳顓頊之故地在若水（今四川雅礱江）流域。[29] 如所周知，若木之所在爲若水。

儘管不能說三星堆的主人便是東來的操 Toγrī 語之族群，但至少說明巴蜀地區和中近東在遠古交往的可能性是完全存在的。

4. 陶唐氏和有虞氏，亦即東遷的 Guti 和 Tukri 兩者之間關係至爲密切。

其一，《國語·魯語上》：有虞氏"郊堯而宗舜"。《左傳·文十八年傳》則稱："舜臣堯……是以堯崩而天下如一，同心戴舜，以爲天子"。知有虞氏舜繼堯即位，兩者一脈相承。

而據《墨子》、《國語》等，堯、舜、禹、湯、文、武稱爲四代聖王。既然禹、湯、文、武無疑屬於夏、商、周三代，則堯、舜應同屬虞代。這是因爲儘管堯所出青陽一系與顓頊所出昌意一系一度是各自獨立發展的，但在後來有了聯繫。蓋據《史記·五帝本紀》："帝顓頊生子曰窮蟬。顓頊崩，而玄囂之孫高辛立，是爲帝嚳"。這裏所說由帝嚳繼承的"顓頊"祇能是前述東遷窮桑的一枝。玄囂之孫雖取代昌意之後，但"有天下號"，亦即以某一血緣關係集團爲核心發展起來的地緣政治集團的符號未變。蓋"高辛"[ko-sien] 與"高陽"一樣，亦得視爲"空桑"、"窮桑"或"嵎夷"之異譯。

既然"窮桑"、"高陽"、"高辛"是同名異譯，不無理由認爲帝嚳的繼承人堯也繼承了相同的國號。蓋"堯"[ngyə] 與"虞"[ngiua] 音近，與"高陽"、"高辛"等也不妨視作同名異譯，很可能一度也是"有天下之號"。堯繼承的既是少昊、顓頊的"天下"，與其說堯爲虞帝，不如說舜號"有虞氏"乃本堯之故號。堯作爲少昊窮桑氏、顓頊高陽氏和帝嚳高辛氏的繼承人自然也是虞帝。舜率所部有虞氏自魯遷晉在堯部落西遷之後，舜應即所謂"造唐"的羣臣之一。

其二，《管子》、《國語》均有齊桓公西征，拘秦（大）夏、服西虞（吳）的記載，時在前七世紀六十年代末至五十年代末。拘大夏與服西虞一前一後，似乎也表明了兩者在當地唇齒相依的關係。

其三，公元前140年左右，大批塞人渡錫爾河南下，一枝進入Ferghāna（費爾幹納），一枝進入Bactria（巴克特里亞）。後者滅亡了希臘巴克特里亞王國。他們各自建立的政權，《史記·大宛列傳》分別稱之爲大宛國和大夏國。值得注意的是大宛國，其國名是Tochari的對譯，其都城之名"貴山"，則是Gasiani的對譯；而"大夏"國內有"貴霜"（Gasiani）人。Guti和Tukri兩者後身之間的密切關係同樣可說明兩者本身之間的關係。

儘管有一部份東遷的Guti和Tukri分道揚鑣，終於出現了《史記》所載西遷大月氏征服大夏的事件，但這不能據以否定兩者的淵源。

5. 語言：指月氏、大夏爲東遷Guti、Tukri的基本證據應該是語言學資料。遺憾的是，至少目前，由於以下三個原因，不可能獲得這方面的證據。

其一，月氏、大夏，在中國典籍中有關記載非常貧乏。其前身有唐氏（陶唐氏）和有虞氏的事蹟更具傳說色彩，可供研究的語言學資料自然更爲稀少，真偽難辨。尤其重要的是，有關記載沒有出自月氏或大夏本族之手者，這增加了利用的困難。

其二，無論大夏還是月氏，在遷徙和發展過程中，不可能保持純粹的血統，勢必出現種類糅雜的情況。尤其是月氏，後來日益強大，役使許多異種部落，這些異種部落都可能自稱或被稱爲月氏。月氏實際上成了一個部落聯合體的名稱。類似的情況恐怕對於大夏也不可避免。僅阿姆河流域的大夏人數多達百萬，不能不認爲其種類早已不純。這也使得今日對其語言的探索障礙重重。

其三，Guti和Tukri人在長途遷徙過程中，勢必和操各種語言的族羣接觸，自己的原始語言的語法和詞彙不免受到形形色色外族語言的影響。由於異族通婚的存在，這種現象將更加嚴重，部份Guti和Tukri人甚至可能放棄自己的母語，改用其他語言。也就是說，同血統的部落可以操不同的語言。

正因爲如此，我們既不可能發現肯定月氏、大夏曾操 Toγrï 語的絕對根據，也不可能發現確鑿的反證。因此，我們祇能後退一步，採取一個近似的標準：尋找與月氏、大夏等有關的語彙，看看這些語彙能否用Toγrï語詮釋。經過學者的努力，這樣的語彙，儘管寥寥無幾，據說已有發現：

首先是月氏、大夏等數者所共有、可以用Toγrï語詮釋的語彙。這樣的語彙似乎祇有一個：翖侯（A *yapoy*, B *ype*）。

《漢書·西域傳》明載"大夏有五翖侯"。《尚書·堯典》載陶唐氏的重要職官有"羲和"。"翖侯"[xiəp-ho]，與"羲和"[xia-huai]讀音近似，應同出一源。

雖然沒有月氏有翖侯的直接記載，但大夏五翖侯役屬月氏，表明月氏認可"翖侯"這一稱號。且五翎侯之一爲貴霜翎侯，貴霜應即進入阿姆河流域的 Gasiani 人，其人與月氏同根同源。

另據《史記·大宛列傳》，烏孫也有翎侯。如前所述，烏孫與操 Toγrï 語之族群不無淵源。

而據《漢書·陳湯傳》，康居亦有翎侯號。康居人應該說一種 Sakā 語，其人有翎侯號可能在它作爲 Sakā 部落時受 Tochari 或 Gasiani 影響所致。

其次，分別與月氏、大夏等有關的語彙。如與月氏有關的"若苴"（A *ñäkci*, B *ñäkc(i)ye*）（見《史記·建元以來侯者年表》）、"祁連"（A *klyom*, B *klyomo*）（見《史記·大宛列傳》）[30]；與烏孫有關的"靡"（A *wäl*, B *walo*）（見《史記·大宛列傳》）等。[31] 而與焉耆有關的"爵離"（《後漢書·班勇傳》）、與龜茲有關的"雀離"（《水經注》卷二）、"昭怙釐"（《大唐西域記》卷一）等，均被視爲 Toχrï 語 *cakir* 之音譯。[32] 這些語彙果如說者所言，可以 Toγrï 語詮釋之，則亦可加強月氏、大夏數者曾操 Toγrï 語的證據。

其三，月氏等在中國北方活動時代漢語中出現的可以用 Toγrï 語詮釋的語彙。例如："狗"[*kooʔ, kəu]（A *ku*）、"䫉"[*maŋs, mǐan-]（A *mañ*）等。[33] 如果禺知、大夏等皆係操 Toγrï 語之族群，則應該是上古漢語中 Toγrï 語彙的主要來源。

既然如此，Toχrï 語 B 方言稱爲 Küsän 語的原因就不難說明了：Toχrï 語 B 方言本來是 Guti 的語言。而龜茲人亦 Guti 後裔之一枝。由於今天不是完全清楚的原因，龜茲人在較長時期內保留了其原始語言。

至於在阿姆河流域以及其他 Guti 和 Tukri 人及其後裔遷徙過程中可能停留的地區沒有發現 Toχrï 語文獻，而且有證據表明在這些地區的有些可指爲 Guti 和 Tukri 人後裔者所操並非 Toχrï 語，顯然是因爲其人放棄了自己的語言、轉而使用土著語言的緣故。

五

以下敘述允姓和操 Toχrï 語之族群的關係，重點在說明爲什麼 Toχrï 語 A 方言的本名爲 Ārśi 語。

1. 允姓（Asii）與大夏（Tochari）的關係。

河西地區既有允姓的、也有大夏的遺蹟。但是沒有證據表明兩者在河西地區有過接觸。已知遲至公元前七世紀五十年代末，河西已有大夏人。而允姓離開它在瓜州的故地恐怕最早也要到公元前七世紀三十年代初，到達河西或在二十年代末。

大夏離開河西，可能是受允姓等西遷引起的連鎖反應的影響。在伊犁河、楚河流域，大夏很可能被隨後到達的允姓征服，成爲後來被稱爲"塞種"的部落聯合體的組份之一。之所以認爲大夏在伊犁河、楚河流域曾被允姓征服，不僅是因爲中國史籍認爲塞種便是允姓，而且因爲希羅多德記載公元前七世紀末活躍在後來被稱爲"塞地"即伊犁河、楚河流域的部落時也祇提到 Isse[dones] 即允姓，而大夏又無疑曾與允姓同時活動於伊犁河、楚河流域的緣故。

苟濟引《漢書·西域傳》之文稱允姓之戎"世居燉煌"，固然可能是因爲誤以爲古瓜州位於當時的敦煌，其實遷入"塞地"的允姓來自涇水上游。但是如果考慮到"燉煌"得自"敦薨"，乃 Tochari 之異譯，似乎從允姓"世居敦煌"這一傳說中，可以窺見允姓和大夏的悠久聯繫。

約公元前 140 年，允姓與大夏一起南渡錫爾河，侵入希臘巴克特里亞王國。Trogus Prologues 稱佔領巴克特里亞的 Asiani（Asii）爲"Tochri 的王族"（XLII），[34] 則表明允姓佔支配地位的形勢至此並未變化。但是，公元前 129 年到達阿姆河流域的張騫卻祗知有大夏，不知有允姓，這很可能是因爲大月氏來犯時，作爲宗主，允姓首當其衝，受創深重，終於銷聲匿蹟。大夏由於人數衆多，其名反而顯彰。

離開"塞地"南下帕米爾，後來又進入塔里木盆地周邊諸綠洲的 Asii 和 Tochari 人也有保持著聯繫的。一個最好的例子便是焉耆國。該國國名"焉耆"、王治名"員渠"均係 Asii 人的遺蹟，而周遭山水名"敦薨"乃 Tochari 人的遺蹟。恐怕在焉耆國中允姓仍爲大夏（Tochari）人的宗主。

以上所述，都是大夏役屬允姓，下面似乎是一個例外。《漢書·西域傳》載有婼羌，其種遍佈西域南道，其中一枝，卽傳文所說辟在陽關西南的"婼羌國"，"其國王號去胡來王"。"去胡來"早已有人指出，應爲"吐火羅"之異譯，[35] 而"婼羌"可以認爲是允姓與羌人的混血種，蓋允格封鄐，有子鄐姓，允姓可溯源於允格之子。"婼"、"鄐"可通，"婼羌"實卽"鄐羌"。如前所述，臨夏既有允姓、又有大夏的遺址，該地復爲羌人出沒之處，由此沿祁連山南麓往西可達西域。陽關西南有以大夏人爲宗主的婼羌部落，或非偶然。

2. 允姓和月氏的關係。

其一，允姓之祖少昊曾據有若水。有虞氏之祖顓頊降生於若水，後復東遷魯北窮桑輔佐少昊。由此可見允姓與有虞氏（月氏前身）關係之密切。

其二，《穆天子傳》載穆天子西征，途經"焉居、禺知之平"。"焉居"[ian-kia] 得視爲"允姓"之異譯，見允姓與禺知關係之密切。

其三，允姓與禺知一起西遷伊犁河、楚河流域，成爲希羅多德所載 Issedones 之組份，以後又一起西赴錫爾河北岸，並從該處入侵巴克特里亞。

其四，烏孫和月氏同處河西及其以西地區，在匈奴強盛並驅逐月氏之前，兩者相安無事可知。這和允姓和禺知的歷史淵源是一致的。

其五，龜茲，其名與"禺知"、"月氏"同源，然《一切經音義》稱："或曰烏孫（Asii），或曰烏壘（Asii）"。此處雖用了"烏孫"一名，但未必是由於該地有烏孫人，而很可能是有允姓人的緣故。當時人但聞其音，不察其實，不恰當地用了"烏孫"這個已有特定內涵的譯稱。

其六，莎車（Sacarauli），《魏書·西域傳》稱之爲"渠莎"（Gasiani），《大唐西域記》卷十二稱之爲"烏鎩"（Asii），也說明了同樣的問題。

昌意降居之前據有若水的允姓國、自若水東遷窮桑的少昊族、作爲少昊族後裔的允姓之戎、以及後者西遷成爲塞種一部、且最終散處西域各地之 Asii 等雖然同出一源，但由於彼此際遇不同，可能在語言、習俗甚至體貌特徵上存在一定的差異。但是從允姓和有虞氏、大夏的特殊關係來看，他們應有共同的起源。

據此或可推論，允姓及其枝裔本屬操 Toχrï 語之族群。而允姓在許多場合都是 Tochari 之王族，這可以很好說明爲什麼 Toχrï 語 B 方言的本名是"Ārśi"。

最後，應予說明的是：既然少昊氏之號"窮桑"與"允姓"爲同名異譯，月氏前身有虞氏之祖顓頊之號"高陽"（即少昊之故號"窮桑"）與"虞氏"或"月氏"亦爲同名異譯，則"月氏"一名與"允姓"也是同名異譯。因此，河西乃至西域各地與"月氏"、"允姓"等類似的族名、國名、地名究竟得自月氏還是允姓頗難區分。不僅如此，西方史籍所載 Sakās 諸部中的 Gasiani 與 Asii（Asiani）固然可以使之分別對應於月氏與允姓，但也不妨倒過來指 Gasiani 爲允姓，指 Asii（Asiani）爲月氏。有關問題的徹底解決，祇能以俟來日了。

六

以下是若干補充：

1. Toχrï 語除了上述 A 和 B 兩種方言外，一說樓蘭–鄯善的土著語言即"犍陀羅語"（Gāndhārī）有很多 Toχrï 語因素，如缺少濁塞音（voiced stops）、送氣輔音（aspirated consonants）和擦音（spirants），這與 Toχrï 語是一致的。換言之，樓蘭—鄯善國的居民操一種與 A 和 B 兩種方言有些不同的 Toχrï 語，亦即可以認爲 Toχrï 語存在第三種方言。[36]

果然，Toχrï 語文獻在塔里木盆地出現的時間便大大提前了。問題在於：樓蘭—鄯善國的居民與上述操 A、B 兩種方言之族群又是什麼關係？

如所周知，"樓蘭"乃佉盧文書所見 Kroraimna（Krorayina）一名之漢譯。樓蘭國後來被漢人更名爲"鄯善"，其用意顯然在於使樓蘭國從此背匈奴向漢，改惡從善。但是，"鄯善"顯然祇能是一個音義兼顧的譯稱。換言之，"鄯善"一名本質上是一個樓蘭人能夠接受的名稱的漢語音譯，漢人不過是利用漢字字義賦予"向善"之意而已。"鄯善"之原名應爲 Kroraimna 人顯貴氏族或王族之名號。

據《漢書·西域傳》，鄯善國之西有精絕國，精絕國之南有戎盧國。"精絕"[dzieng-dziuat] 得視爲"鄯善"之異譯，"戎盧"[njiuəm-la] 得視爲"樓蘭"之異譯。這說明 Kroraimna 人曾進入精絕、戎盧兩地。

又，《後漢書·西域傳》載疏勒國有楨中城，應即《魏略·西戎傳》所見位於西域南道之楨中國。"楨中"[tieng-tiuəm]，與"鄯善"、"精絕"等亦得視爲同名異譯，似乎可以說明該處亦有 Kroraimna 人活動之蹤蹟。

又《大唐西域記》卷一二載有曷勞落迦城，位於瞿薩旦那"國北"、媲摩城之西。"曷勞落迦"[hat-lô-lak-keai]，與"樓蘭"（Kroraimna）顯然也是同名異譯。

Kroraimna人不僅進入南道，而且進入北道。證據如下：

《漢書·西域傳》載王莽始建國二年，西域都護但欽駐守"埒婁城"。埒婁城地望不詳，但無疑在龜茲國中。"埒婁"[liat-lo]得視爲"樓蘭"之異譯。同傳所載龜茲國附近小國之名"輪臺"[liuən-də]（《史記·大宛列傳》作"侖頭"[liuən-do]）亦得視爲"樓蘭"之異譯。

而《隋書·音樂志下》（卷一五）載龜茲樂部"歌曲有善善摩尼"。《悟空入竺記》稱："安西境內有前踐山、前踐寺"。[37] 所謂"安西"即安西都護府，治龜茲國都城，"前踐寺"即今庫車附近森姆塞姆（Simsim）千佛洞。"善善"[zjian-zjian]或"前踐"[dzian-dzian]與"鄯善"[zjian-zjian]均得視爲同名異譯。

"埒婁"、"輪臺"與"前踐"或"善善"等名稱同見於龜茲及其附近，表明曾有一枝Kroraimna人來到龜茲地區。

Kroraimna人與斯特拉波《地理志》（XI, 8）所載滅亡希臘巴克特里亞王國的Sacae四部之一Sacarauli同源。Sacarauli無妨視作Sakā [K]rauli之訛。Krauli又無妨視作Krorai[m]na之略。質言之Kroraimna便是Sakā Krorai[m]na之訛略。[38]

樓蘭—鄯善人果真是Sacarauli人，則不難解釋何以犍陀羅語有很多Toγrï語因素。

樓蘭—鄯善的Sacarauli人很可能是和塞種其他三部Tochari、Gasiani和Asii一起進入西域南道的，時間應在公元前177/176年塞種被大月氏逐出塞地、南下葱嶺之後。此前，Sacarauli和塞種其他三部曾長期共處於伊犁河、楚河流域，彼此有密切接觸可知。不管Sacarauli人的原始語言是什麼（很可能是一種東伊朗語），受到Toγrï語的影響不可避免。而獨處樓蘭—鄯善一地的Sacarauli人的語言終於在貴霜王國的影響下，發展成獨具特色的、以婆羅謎文爲載體的、有Toγrï語因素的犍陀羅語不是不可想像的。

2. 一說回鶻文題識中的twγry與粟特語《國名表》（nāfnāmak）中指稱吐火羅人的名稱 'tγw'r'k 對音不盡相符，此 twγry 大約相當於粟特文《九姓回鶻可汗碑》（Karabalgasun Inscription）[39]、《突厥文摩尼教文書》題識[40]和中古波斯語摩尼教頌歌[41]中的"四Twγry"（ctβ'r twγr'k），包括別失八里（Bišbalïq）、高昌（Qočo）等地。[42]

今案：此說未免執著。"四Twγry"果然指別失八里等地，則很可能是因爲在《九姓回鶻可汗碑》等描述的時代，上述諸地均爲吐火羅人所據有。至於twγry與粟特語《國名表》中指稱吐火羅的名稱 'tγw'r'k 對音不盡相符，則既可能是由於迻譯者不明究竟造成的，更可能是迻譯者有意爲之，以區別同名的不同的政治或地理實體。這兩種情況屢見於中國古代典籍所載西域國名、族名，粟特文書也許並不例外。

何況"四Twγry"僅僅是焉耆一地的名稱，並不是用來指稱上述諸地的。[43]

3. 1980年蘇聯 Л. Ю. Тугушева 刊佈《回鶻文譯本〈玄奘傳〉第五卷殘卷》，共十六葉，對應於漢文《大慈恩寺三藏法師傳》卷五末至卷終，計二百七十言。[44] 這是玄奘回國路程中從塔什庫爾幹到長安的一段歷程，所述及的三十多個地名大部分在今新疆地區。最值得注意的是，回鶻語譯文以 Toγrï 對譯玄奘所記之"覩貨邏故國"。一說此"覩貨邏故國"究竟何指未有定論。應是月氏自敦煌向西南發展，過婼羌以西時所建，故回鶻語之 Toγrï 實指月氏族云。[45]

今案：《大唐西域記》卷十二載：自尼壤城東"行四百餘里，有覩貨邏故國"。"覩貨邏"一名亦見同書卷一：

> 出鐵門至覩貨邏國（舊曰"吐火羅"，訛也）故地，南北千餘里，東西三千餘里，東阨蔥嶺（Pamir），西接波剌斯（Persia），南大雪山（Hindukush），北據鐵門（Shahr-i Sabz 南 90 公里），縛芻大河（Amu Daria），中境西流。

所謂覩貨邏國故地，無疑即西史所謂 Tokharestan，故《大慈恩寺三藏法師傳》卷五的"覩貨羅"應指 Tukhāra。

《新唐書‧西域傳》載于闐之東大砂磧名"圖倫磧"，"圖倫"[da-liuən] 亦得視爲 Tochari 之對譯。由此可知 Tochari 人亦曾居於于闐和且末之間。如前所述，Tochari 進入西域南北道，很可能在塞種被大月氏逐出伊犁河、楚河流域之後。

回鶻人將玄奘的"覩貨邏故國"譯作 Toγrï，說明 Toγrï 正是 Tukhāra（Tochari）的回鶻語譯，別無其他。當然，這並不表明在《玄奘傳》迻譯成回鶻語時，尼壤城之東的覩貨邏故國流行 Toγrï 語。

4.《西天路竟》（敦煌文書 S.383）有曰："又西行一日至高昌國，又西行一千里至月氏國，又西行一千里至龜茲國。"[46] 此處"月氏"當指"焉耆"無疑。[47]

何以宋初之人稱焉耆爲"月氏"？過去多以爲誤抄所致。其實，至少還有以下幾種可能性：

一、"月氏"和"焉耆"，音近，易誤。

二、"焉耆"得名於塞種四部之一的 Asii，但其餘各部（包括 Tochari 和 Gasiani 在內）也可能同時或先後入據該綠洲。蓋如前述，焉耆周遭山水均以"敦薨"爲名，知其地有 Tochari 人。竟稱"焉耆"爲"月氏"，則可能在《西天路竟》描述的時代，"月氏"則 Gasiani 人一度顯示了他們的存在。

三、焉耆與月氏之前身有密切的親緣關係，焉耆一地的 Asii 人中可能含有 Gasiani 人，祇要其地實際上被後者控制，焉耆一地也就被稱爲"月氏"了。

《路竟》撰寫於宋初，去焉耆立國已遠，什麼情況都可能發生，難以揣度。

5. 鳩摩羅什（344—413 年）所譯《大智度論》卷二十五有"兜呿羅（小月氏）"一語。[48] 按之鳩摩羅什的年代，此處所謂"小月氏"很可能指領有吐火羅斯坦的寄多羅貴霜人。

"兜呿羅"無疑指吐火羅斯坦，主要位於今阿姆河南岸。公元五世紀，或者說鳩摩羅什在世的年代，據有該地的是寄多羅貴霜人。由於種種原因，貴霜一直被稱爲"大月氏"，寄多羅人既以貴霜自居，則被鳩摩羅什稱爲"月氏"毫不奇怪，著一"小"字，可能是爲了區別於此前的"大月氏"，亦即一統興都庫什山南北的大貴霜國。

應該指出的是，寄多羅貴霜在《魏書‧西域傳》中是被稱爲"大月氏國"的：

大月氏國，都盧監氏城，在弗敵沙西，去代一萬四千五百里。北與蠕蠕接，數爲所侵，遂西徙都薄羅城，去弗敵沙二千一百里。其王寄多羅勇武，遂興師越大山，南侵北天竺，自乾陁羅以北五國盡役屬之。

《魏書·西域傳》所描述的寄多羅貴霜之勢力範圍包括興都庫什山南北，和公元二世紀極盛時期的大貴霜國差可比擬。寄多羅貴霜既爲大貴霜國之繼承者，故《魏書》稱之爲"大月氏國"。但寄多羅王"興師越大山，南侵北天竺，自乾陁羅以北五國盡役屬之"云云，鳩摩羅什已不及見。他僅知寄多羅貴霜人"都盧監氏城"而已，故以"小月氏"稱之。

《魏書·西域傳》另有"小月氏國"：

小月氏國，都富樓沙城。其王本大月氏王寄多羅子也。寄多羅爲匈奴所逐，西徙後令其子守此城，因號小月氏焉。在波路西南，去代一萬六千六百里。先居西平、張掖之間，被服頗與羌同。其俗以金銀錢爲貨。隨畜牧移徙，亦類匈奴。

這裏的"小月氏"應指寄多羅王爲"匈奴"即嚈噠人逐出吐火羅斯坦西徙後、盤踞富樓沙（Puruṣapura，即今白沙瓦）的寄多羅貴霜殘餘勢力，這情形在《魏書》編者看來頗類似《漢書·西域傳》所載大月氏爲匈奴所逐遠去，"其餘小衆不能去者，保南山羌，號小月氏"，因而稱之爲"小月氏國"。[49] 嚈噠勢力進入吐火羅斯坦，當在437年之後，故鳩摩羅什所謂"小月氏"與《魏書·西域傳》的小月氏無涉。

注释

[1] E. Leumann, "Über eine von den unbekannten Literaturspachen Mittelasiens". *Mémoire de l'Académie Impériale des Sciences de St.-Pétersbourg* VIIIᵉ série, IV~8 (1900), pp. 1-28. 參看耿世民"古代維吾爾語佛教原始劇本《彌勒會見記》（哈密寫本）研究"，載《新疆文史論集》，中央民族大學出版社，2001年，第170-194頁, esp. 174-175。

[2] F. W. K. Müller, "Beitrag zur genaueren Bestimmung der unbekannten Sprachen Mittelasiens", *Sitzungsberichte der Preussischen Akademie der Wissenschaften, Phil.-hist. Klasse*, Berlin, 1907, pp. 958-960.

[3] E. Sieg, "Ein einheimischer Name für Toχrï." *Sitzungsberichte der Preussischen Akademie der Wissenschaften, Phil.-hist. Klasse*, Berlin, 1918, pp. 560-565.

[4] 王靜如《重論ārśi、ārgi與焉夷、焉耆》，載《王靜如民族研究文集》，民族出版社，1998年，第153-162頁。論述這一問題以此文最中肯綮。另請參看黃盛璋《試論所謂"吐火羅語"及其有關的歷史地理和民族問題》，載《中外交通與交流史研究》，安徽教育出版社，2002年，第195-241頁，esp. 216-221。

[5] F. W. K. Müller, "Toχrï und Kuišan (Küšän)", *Sitzungsberichte der Preussischen Akademie der*

Wissenschaften, Phil.-hist. Klasse, Berlin, 1918, 566-586. F. W. K. Müller und A. von Gabain, "Uigurica IV", *Sitzungsberichte der Preussischen Akademie der Wissenschaften, Phil.-hist. Klasse*, Berlin, 1931, pp. 675-727. 羽田亨《吐魯番出土回鶻文摩尼教徒祈願文の斷簡》，載《羽田博士史學論文集·下卷（言語宗教篇）》，京都，1958 年，第 325-347 頁。

[6] E. Sieg und W. Siegling, "Tocharisch, die Sprache der Indoskythen", *Sitzungsberichte der Preussischen Akademie der Wissenschaften, Phil.-hist. Klasse*, Berlin, 1908, pp. 915-932.

[7] 有關 Toγrï 語在語言學上地位的論著很多，例如：Douglas Q. Adams, "The Position of Tocharian among the other Indo-European Languages", *Journal of the American Oriental Society* 103 (1984), pp. 395-402，等等。

[8] 關於原始印歐語系部落以及吐火羅人的起源有許多討論，參見徐文堪《揭開吐火羅人起源之謎》，載《吐火羅起源研究》，昆侖出版社，2005 年，第 49-103 頁。

[9]《大唐西域記》卷一："阿耆尼國（Angi）……文字取則印度，微有增損"。"屈支國（Kucha）……文字取則印度，粗有改變"。又記"覩貨邏國（Tokhāra）……語言去就，稍異諸國；字源二十五言，轉而相生，用之備物。書以橫讀，自左向右，文記漸多，逾廣窣利"。

[10] W. B. Henning, "The Bactrian Inscription", *Bulletin of the School of Oriental & African Studies* 23 (1960), pp. 47-55.

[11] 注 5 所引 F. W. K. Müller und A.von Gabain 文。1958 年，W. Winter 和 A. V. Gabain 發表了一件 Toγrï 語 B 與回鶻語合璧的摩尼教頌文（編號：U 103 T III D 260, 19; 260, 30）。在這件文書裏，明確用 Küsän 一詞指稱 Toγrï 語 B。見 A. von Gabain with W. Winter, *Türkische Turfantexte IX. Abhandlungen der Deutschen Akademie der Wissenschaften zu Berlin, Klasse für Sprachen, Literatur und Kunst*, 15. Jahrgang 1956 (published 1958), Nr. 2. 有關研究見 Вяч. Вс. Иванов, "К Определению Названия «Тохарского В» Языка", *Проблемы Востоковедения*, 1959/5, pp. 188-190. 另請參看耿世民《哈密本回鶻文〈十業道譬喻鬘〉初探》，載《維吾爾古代文獻研究》，中央民族大學出版社，2003 年，第 300-311 頁。

[12] 關於大夏及其前身陶唐氏的詳細考證，見余太山《古族新考》，中華書局，2001 年，第 1-2 頁。

[13] E. L. Stevensen, tr. & ed., *Geography of Claudius Ptolemy*, New York, 1932.

[14] 參看余太山《托勒密〈地理志〉所見絲綢之路的記載》，載《早期丝绸之路文獻研究》，上海人民出版社，2009 年，第 145-164 頁。

[15] 例如：A. V. Gutschmid, *Geschichte Irans and seiner Nachbarlander von Alexander dem Grossen bis zum Untergang des Arsaiden* 32, Tübingen, 1888. W. W. Tarn, *The Greek in Bactria and India*, London: Cambridge, 1951, pp. 283-287.

[16] A. K. Narain, *The Indo-Greeks*, Oxford, 1957, p. 181.

[17] *The Geography of Strabo*, with an English Translation by H. L. Jones, London, 1916.

[18] 持此說者，最早似乎爲 F. F. von Richthofen, *China, Ergebnisse eigener Reisen und darauf gegründeter Studien* I, Berlin, 1877, p. 439；注 15 所引 W. W. Tarn 書，pp. 283-287，也有類似觀點。

[19] 王靜如《論吐火羅及吐火羅語》，載《王靜如民族研究文集》，民族出版社，1998 年，第 89-152 頁。[原載《中德學志》第 5 卷第 1、2 期合刊，1942 年。]

[20] 有證據表明，大宛人亦操 Toγrï 語。See E. G. Pulleyblank, "Chinese and Indo-Europeans", *Journal of the Royal Asiatic Society* 1966, pp. 9-39.

[21] 關於大月氏及其前身有虞氏的詳細考證，見注 12 所引余太山書，第 29-52 頁。

[22] D. Grene (tr.), Herodotus, *The History*, The University of Chicago Press, Chicago & London, 1987.

[23] 關於允姓的詳細考證，見注 12 所引余太山書，第 53-76 頁。

[24] 載《廣弘明集》卷七，載《大正新修大藏經》第 52 冊，No. 2103: 0129a21。

[25] W. B. Henning, "The First Indo-Europeans in History", G. Ulmen (ed.), *Society and History Essays in Honor of Karl August Wittfogel*, The Hague, Paris, New York, 1978, pp. 215-230.

[26] Т. В. Гамкрелидзе & Вяч. Вс. Иванов, "Первые индоевропейцы в истории: предки тохар в древней Азии", *Вестник древней истории* (1989/1), pp. 14-39. 漢譯文爲"歷史上最初的印歐人：吐火羅人在古代中東的祖先"，載徐文堪注 8 所引書，第 397-437 頁。此文繼承和發展了 Henning 說。

[27] 段渝《古代巴蜀與南亞和近東的經濟文化交流》，載《社會科學研究》1993 年第 3 期，第 48-55, 73 頁。

[28] 徐朝龍《中國古代"神樹傳說"的源流》，載西江清高主編《扶桑與若木——日本學者對三星堆文明的新認識》，巴蜀書社，2002 年，第 205-228 頁。

[29] 參看李學勤《三星堆與蜀古史傳說》，載《走出疑古時代》，遼寧大學出版社，1994 年，第 204-214 頁。又，《玉海》卷一百三引"若水"作"弱水"，錄以備考。

[30] 林梅村《祁連與昆侖》，載《漢唐西域與中國文明》，文物出版社，1998 年，第 64-69 頁。

[31] 注 20 所引 E. G. Pulleyblank 文；E. G. Pulleyblank, "The Consonantal System of Old Chinese", *Asia Major* 9 (1962), pp. 246-248. W. Samolin, "Ethnographic Aspects of the Archaeology of the Tarim Basin", *Central Asiatic Journal* 4 (1958), pp. 45-67; 以及 Henning 注 25 所引文。

[32] 伯希和《吐火羅語與庫車語》，載馮承鈞譯《吐火羅語考》，第 111-133 頁；P. Boodberg, "Two Notes on the History of the Chinese Frontier", *Harvard Journal of Asialic Sturdies* 1 (1936), pp. 283-307, esp. 290-291; E. G. Pulleyblank, "An Interpretation of the Vowel Systems of Old Chinese and Written Burmese", *Asia Major* 10 (1963), pp. 200-221, esp. 206-207.

[33] 周及徐《漢語印歐語詞彙比較》，四川民族出版社，2002 年，第 190, 364-365 頁。Cf. E. G. Pulleyblank, "Why Tocharians?" *The Journal of Indo-European Studies* 23 (1995), pp. 415-430.

[34] 引自注 15 所引 W.W. Tarn 書，p. 286; A. K. Narain, *The Indo-Greeks*, Oxford, 1962, p. 162.

[35] 見黃文弼《重論古代大夏之位置與移徙》，載《黃文弼歷史考古論集》，文物出版社，1989年，第81-84頁。

[36] T. Burrow, "Tokharian Elements in the Kharoṣṭhī Documents from Chinese Turkestan", *Journal of the Royal Asiatic Society* 1935, pp. 667-675; H. W. Bailey, "Ttaugara", *Bulletin of the School of Oriental & African Studies* 8 (1937), pp. 883-921.

[37]《大正新修大藏經》第 51 冊，No. 2089: 0980c19。

[38] 以上關於鄯善國名義、鄯善人來源的考證詳見余太山《樓蘭、鄯善、精絕等的名義——說玄奘自于闐東歸路線》，載《兩漢魏晉南北朝正史西域傳研究》，中華書局，2003 年，第 477-485 頁。

[39] O. Hansen, "Zur soghdischen Inschrift auf dem dreisprachigen Denkmal von Karabalgasun", *Journal de la Société Finno-Ougrienne* 44 (1930), pp. 3-39, esp. 20.

[40] A. von Le Coq, "Türkische Maniehaica aus Chotscho I", *Phil.-hist. Khasse. 1911. Anhang. Abh. VI.* Vorgelegt von Hrn. Müller in der Sitzung der phil.-hist. Klasse am 19. Oktober 1911, Zum Druck verordnet am gleichen Tage, ausgegeben am 25, April 1912. pp. 393-451, esp. 417.

[41] F. W. K. Müller, "Handschriften-Reste in Estrangelo-Schrift aus Turfan, Chinesisch-Turkestan I", *Sitzungsberichte der Preussischen Akademie der Wissenschaften, Phil.-hist. Klasse*, Berlin, 1904, pp. 348-352, esp. 351.

[42] W. B. Henning, "Argi and the Tokharians", *Bulletin of the School of Oriental Studies* 9 (1938), pp. 545-571.

[43] 黃盛璋注 4 所引文，esp. 209-216。

[44] Л. Ю. Тугушева, *Фрагменты Уйгурской версии Биографии Сюань-изана*, Москва, 1980.

[45] 黃盛璋《回鶻譯本〈玄奘傳〉殘卷五玄奘回程之地望與對音研究》，注 4 所引書，第 24-287 頁。

[46] 見《英藏敦煌文獻（漢文佛經以外部份）》第 1 卷，四川人民出版社，1990 年，第 170 頁。

[47] 黃盛璋《敦煌寫本西天路竟歷史地理研究》，注 4 所引書，第 88-110 頁。

[48]《大正新脩大藏經》第 25 冊, No. 1509: 0243a09。

[49] 余太山《嚈噠史研究》，齊魯書社，1986 年，第 66-75 頁。

THE TOCHARIAN QUESTION

YU Taishan

This paper attempts to track the activities of the ethnic group which spoke the Toγrï language in China. The author believes that the Toγrï had various dialects. This must have been caused by abruptions of the ethnic groups who spoke this language. Thus it is possible that the ethnic groups who spoke this language appeared under various names. Not only did the ethnic groups who spoke different dialects possibly have different names, but the people who spoke the same dialect also had possibly different names. In other words, the ethnic groups who spoke Toγrï should have various Chinese names and should satisfy the following three conditions at the same time in order to take precedence over all others: (a) the names can be identified with Toγrï, Küsän or Ārśi; (b) the time when these tribal people emerged in the Chinese historical arena is early enough to connect with the appearance of the Indo-European language family; and (c) the possibility that they were Indo-European people in linguistic and physical characteristics cannot be discarded.

There are three tribes, the Daxia, Yuezhi, and Rong of the Surname Yun, who appear in pre-Qin books and records and who roughly accord with the above three requirements. The author then successively provides information about these three:

[1] Generally speaking, the Daxia can be traced back to the Taotang. Their homeland was located in the south of Jin. Later, their descendants slowly moved away from the south of Jin. One group of them moved north to the north of Hetao, and the other moved west to the regions of Linxia and Hexi. Possibly as early as the second decade of the sixth century BCE, elements of the Daxia people in the Hexi region moved to the valleys of the Rivers Ili and Chu, and composed a tribal confederacy with the Asii, Gasiani, Sacarauli, and others who successively arrived in the area, and so expanded their power as far as the northern bank of the Sry Darya.

[2] Around BCE 177/176, the Da Yuezhi occupied the valleys of the Rivers Ili and Chu during their first migration to the Western Regions, and the Sai tribes, including some of the Tochari people, were driven out. One group of them withdrew to the northern bank of the Syr Darya, another group moved south to the Pamirs. The latter crossed over the Hindukush or traveled eastwards into the Tarim Basin, and there occupied oases, including Yanqi and Qiuci, on the Southern and Northern Routes.

Around 177/176 B.C., the Sai tribes were forced to give up the valleys of the Ili and Chu Rivers because of western migration of the Da Yuezhi. Some of them moved south and separated in the Pamir Regions, then moved east and entered the oases of the Tarim Basin. About ten years later the state of Daxia was destroyed by the Da Yuezhi people who once more migrated west.

The ancestors of the Yuezhi (Yuzhi), the precursors of the Da Yuezhi, were a branch of the Youyu people. They moved from Shu to Lu, and then to Jin. They later began to move away from the land of Jin. A branch of them, passing Beidi and Anding, entered the region of Hexi. This branch moved west to the valleys of the Rivers Ili and Chu by the end of the second decade of the seventh century BCE. Some of the Daxia people and the Rong of the Surname Yun also moved there. The tribal association composed of the aforementioned Youyu people and the others there was described as "the Issedones" by Herodotus. The Issedones had expanded westwards as far as the right bank of the Syr Darya. After that, they were called "Sakās" by the Persians. A group of the Saka people, including the Youyu people, gave up the valleys of the Rivers Ili and Chu's; some fell back to the north bank of the Syr Darya, and the others moved south, split and separated in the Pamir Regions, and entered the

Tarim Basin to the east, and occupied oases, including Yanqi and Qiuci, on the Southern and Northern Routes because the Da Yuezhi moved westwards.

Another branch of the Youyu people moved north to Yanmen. By the second decade of the third century BCE at the latest, this branch of the Youyu people moved westwards and expanded their power west as far as the eastern end of the Altai Mountains, and monopolized East-West trade for a time. A large number of them were not forced to move west to the valleys of the Rivers Ili and Chu, displacing the Sai tribes who dwelt there, until they were defeated by the Xiongnu in 177/176 BCE. This group of the Yuezhi was known as the "Da Yuezhi" (the Great Yuezhi). The others who left their former lands were known as the the "Xiao Yuezhi" (Little Yuezhi). Around 130 BCE, the Da Yuezhi were defeated by the Wusun. They abandoned the valleys of the Rivers Ili and Chu, and moved west to the valley of the Amu Darya and overthrew the state of Daxia that had been founded by the Sakā people who had entered there approximately ten years previously.

[3] The Rong of the Surname Yun originally lived in Guazhou (in the upper reaches of the Jing River). They moved to the west of Guazhou, because they were forcibly driven away by Qin. A large group of them, together with some Daxia and Yuzhi people, arrived in the valleys of the Rivers Ili and Chu and formed a tribal confederacy towards the end of the seventh century BCE at the latest, because Duke Mu of Qin opened up these territories. Of them, the Rong of the Surname Yun probably played the role of suzerains, and so this confederacy was called the "Issedones" by Herodotus. They had expanded westwards as far as the northern bank of the Syr Darya, and were called the Sakā by the Persians. Those who were left behind between the Qilian and Tianshan Mountains developed into the Wusun tribe when they moved west, and those who moved further west to the north of the Aral and Caspian Seas were the Yancai.

The Issedones gave up the valleys of the Rivers Ili and Chu because the Da Yuezhi moved westwards. Some fell back to the north bank of the Syr Darya. The others moved south to the Pamir Region, one group entered the northwest of the Indian subcontinent, and another group went eastwards, probably entering the oases, including Yanqi, of the Tarim Basin.

The Rong of the Surname Yun were the descendants of Yunge, and Yunge was the descendant of Shaohao. Zhuanxu, ancestor of the Youyu people, was born in the valley of the Ruo River, because Changyi, the father of Zhuanxu dwelt in the valley of the Ruo, which was originally the settlement of Shaohao. There had been a state of the Surname Yun in the valley of the Ruo River before Changyi arrived and settled there. That state would have been established by Shaohao. Zhuanxu subsequently moved east to Lu to assist Shaohao. These sources explain the view that the people designated the Rong of the Surname Yun were closely related to the Youyu people. It is possible that originally both belonged to the same tribe, but they were later located in different locations due to their movement in separate groups. The names "Yunxing" and "Yushi", "Wusun" and "Yueshi", "Asii" and "Gasiani", "Yanqi" and "Qiuci", and so on, all derive from the same origin, even though they represented respectively different political or tribal entities.

[4] The ethnic group which spoke the Toγrï language came from the Near and Middle East. The precursor of the ethnic group must have been the Guti and Tukri who as seen in some documents in cuneiform script together left the west of Persia before the end of the third millennium BCE. They arrived in China after covering a great deal of ground, and first arrived in what is today the Sichuan region. The time that the Guti and Tukri moved east can just linked with the time when the Taotang and Youyu appeared. The Guti and Tukri can be identified with the Yuezhi and Daxia, respectively. The relations between Taotang and Youyu, i.e., the Guti and Tukri who moved east, were very close. There is evidence to show that some words concerning the Yuezhi and Daxia can be explained through the use of the Toχrï language.

[5] Toχrï B was originally the Guti's language, and the Qiuci people were a branch of the Guti. This is the causation that Toχrï B was called the Küsän language. Moreover, the Rong of the Surname Yun 允 and their branches belong to the ethnic group which spoke the Toγrï language. The Rong of the Surname Yun were the ruling clan of the Tochari on many occasions. This might explain why the autonym of Toχrï B is "Ārśi".

烏桓山與鮮卑山新考

楊軍

發源于烏桓山和鮮卑山的烏桓、鮮卑二族，在中國歷史上發揮過重要作用，但學界對兩山所在地卻眾說紛紜，目前在學界占主流的觀點也不無問題。本文試在梳理前人對此問題的研究的基礎上，談談個人的不同認識，以就正于史界先達諸君。

一

漢魏以下史籍皆沒有對烏桓山具體位置的記載，最早為我們提供烏桓山相對準確位置信息的是元修《遼史》。《遼史》卷三七《地理志》烏州條："本烏丸之地，東胡之種也。遼北大王撥剌占為牧[地]，建城，後官收，隸興聖宮。有遼河、夜河、烏丸川、烏丸山。"認為烏桓山在遼上京道所屬烏州境內，這成為清代學者研究烏桓山所在地的最主要依據。

最早討論烏桓山所在地的是清初地理學家顧祖禹（1631—1692），在其所著《讀史方輿紀要》中提到："赤山，在泰寧衛境。《烏桓傳》：在遼東郡西北數千里。後漢建武十六年，匈奴、鮮卑、赤山烏桓連兵入塞。永平初，遼東太守祭肜使鮮卑大都護偏何討赤山烏桓，大破之，即此。"[1] 顧祖禹認為烏桓山就是烏桓"死者魂靈歸乎赤山"[2]的赤山，這種觀點至今仍是學界通說，但他顯然是將作為烏桓發源地的赤山與烏桓南遷後居住地內的赤山混為一談了。顧祖禹認為："廢烏州在臨潢東南"[3]，"臨潢城在朵顏衛北"[4]。參考顧祖禹對兀良哈三衛地理位置的理解，"自廣寧前屯歷喜峰邊宣府者皆屬朵顏，自錦義度潢河至白雲山皆屬泰寧，自黃泥窪以東至開原皆屬福餘"，[5] 可見，顧祖禹認為遼烏州在今內蒙古自治區阿魯科爾沁旗境內，但我們並不清楚其依據是什麼。

受顧祖禹影響，乾隆時的幾部官書都認為烏桓山在今阿魯科爾沁旗境內。如，成書於乾隆三十二年（1767）的《御批歷代通鑒輯覽》認為："《遼史·地理志》烏州有烏丸山，今阿祿科爾沁西北有烏（聯）[聊]山，或曰即烏丸山。"[6] 成書於乾隆四十九年（1784）的乾隆《大清一統志》認為："阿祿科爾沁西北有烏聊山，或曰即烏桓山"，[7] "烏遼山在旗西北一百四十里，即烏丸山。"[8] 但我們需要注意到兩書"或曰即烏丸山"這種表述方式，顯然，將烏桓山定位于阿魯科爾沁旗是作者的推測，並沒有確實的證據。因此，成書於乾隆五十四年（1789）的《盛京通志》不采此說，認為："《遼史·地理志》烏州有烏丸山，永州有高澱山，饒州有青山、大福山、松山。按：烏州、永州、饒州俱當在今邊境，然諸山皆無考。"[9] 將烏丸山歸為"無考"之列，是比較慎重的作法。

成書於乾隆四十六年（1781）的《熱河志》認為："赤山當在今承德府本境，及灤平、豐寧二縣境內，而諸處俱無之，建昌縣境有赤山及大赤山，但其方位不合，難以傅會。"[10] 由此看來，乾隆時學者探討烏桓山所在地的主要方法是，在其可能的地域範圍內尋找與之發音接近的山名，這種研究方法顯然是有問題的。

但此後，張穆《蒙古遊牧記》肯定了前人的推測，認為阿魯科爾沁旗西北"百四十里有烏遼山，即烏丸山"。[11] 丁謙支持此說，並進一步論證：

> 烏桓因山得名。烏桓者，烏蘭之轉音也。蒙古語紅曰烏蘭，故《傳》中又稱為赤山。考《遊牧記》，阿嚕科爾沁旗北至烏蘭峰，與烏珠穆秦旗接界，又云：西北有烏遼山，即烏丸山，知烏桓、烏蘭、烏遼、烏丸，名雖小異，實即一山。此山高大，為內興安嶺南行正幹，所以部人東走時得據山以自保，用是尊之為神，故有人死靈歸是山之語。[12]

由於張穆、丁謙在邊疆史地研究方面所取得的成就，此說受到此後多數學者的支持，正如有的學者所說："張穆精於蒙古地理，其說雖不知何所據而云，但確屬允當。"[13] 此後，烏桓山即赤山，即今阿魯科爾沁旗的烏遼山，漸成為學界通說。還應該指出的是，受此說影響的學者往往將遼烏州的治所確定在今吉林省雙遼縣西北，認為烏州轄境相當於今內蒙古科爾沁左翼中旗和吉林雙遼縣地。[14] 按正常研究思路，本應該是通過遼烏州所在地來確定烏桓山所在地，現在卻正相反，是通過烏桓山所在地以定遼烏州所在地了。

清末曹廷傑率先提出依烏桓水確定烏桓山所在地的新研究思路，在其所著《東三省輿地圖說》一書中指出：洮兒河有二源，"南源曰歸喇里河，古名完水，發源烏珠穆沁右翼旗東之瑚蘇圖山，東北流數百里，會陀喇河入嫩江。《寰宇記》'完水在烏洛侯國西南，其水東北流，合于難水，《蕃中記》云：完水即烏桓水'是也。查烏桓本據今西遼河兩岸及歸喇里河西南地方，歸喇里河出其境內，故稱烏桓水，又稱完水"[15]。認為古之完水即烏桓水，亦即《遼史·地理志》烏州所載"烏丸川"，為洮兒河南源歸喇里河（今名歸流河或交流河），烏桓山當在歸喇里河流域。受此說影響的學者將遼烏州治所定在今內蒙古自治區興安盟突泉縣雙城子古城址。[16]

丁謙認為，《遼史·地理志》所載烏州境內的遼河、夜河、烏丸川三條河，"遼河即錫喇木倫河，夜河即哈喜爾河，烏丸川即烏爾渾河，（烏爾渾亦烏丸轉音）而烏丸山居於三水之間。凡此皆烏桓部地在今阿嚕科爾沁之明徵"[17]。研究思路類似曹廷傑，但卻維持顧祖禹至張穆的

— 287 —

舊說。事實上，丁謙此處的思考有一些混亂，正如陳漢章《遼史索隱》所說："丁氏既以哈喜爾河為上京臨潢府之按出河，不得又為此州之夜河。"但陳漢章認為，"夜河當為阿魯科爾沁旗西北二百三十里之尹劄漢河，即音劄哈河"，[18] 也是從維持舊說出發。

建國後，支持張穆說的學者以林幹為代表。林幹認為，東胡原活動區在今內蒙古東部老哈河上游東南至遼寧大、小凌河流域，被匈奴擊破後，烏桓一支便就近逃至老哈河以北的西喇木倫河流域，又渡河轉向今阿魯科爾沁旗西北，因此烏桓山應即烏遼山。但林幹認為烏桓山和赤山並非一山，赤山即烏桓人想像中的烏桓山（紅山、赤山），後來傳說流傳既久，遂逐漸以某山為赤山。[19]

支持曹廷傑說的學者則以馬長壽為代表。馬長壽也認為烏桓山與赤山並非一山，但贊同曹廷傑說，認為遼烏州在今松花江下游以西、洮兒河以下、西喇木倫河以北之地，烏桓山大約在今歸流河流域。[20] 在馬長壽的提倡下，此說漸成為學界的主流觀點。此外，呂思勉認為，"烏桓、鮮卑二山，蓋在今蒙古東部。蘇克蘇魯、索嶽爾濟等山是也"，[21] 也是對曹廷傑說的引申。[22]

近年來，個別學者又對烏桓山的地理位置提出了新的見解。張博泉認同顧祖禹赤山即烏桓山的說法，但認為完水（烏丸川）是今克魯倫河，而不是曹廷傑所說的歸流河，並根據赤山在遼東西北數千里的記載，認為烏桓山即克魯倫河發源的今蒙古國肯特山。[23] 賈敬顏認為，烏桓人對赤山的崇拜與契丹人對黑山的崇拜極其相似，烏桓人的赤山應即遼慶州黑山（又名望雲山）旁的赤山。[24] 鄭英德依據前人未曾注意的《舊唐書》卷一九九下《室韋傳》，"烏羅護之東北二百餘里，那河（今嫩江）之北，有古烏丸之遺人，今亦自稱烏丸國"，認為烏桓山必在嫩江以北，但他又對傳統觀點進行調和，認為："烏遼、烏蘭這兩座山俱在西拉木倫河以北，所以烏桓最初活動於西拉木倫河以北至額爾古納河流域。"[25]

二

自顧祖禹、張穆、丁謙以下，倡烏桓山即阿魯科爾沁旗烏遼山之說的學者皆受《遼史·地理志》影響，但問題是，有關遼烏州所在地的兩種觀點都是靠烏桓山定位，烏桓山即烏遼山是靠對音比附，不存在堅實的史料證據，而不是已經確定遼烏州所在地，再由此推求烏桓山所在地。這種研究方法是有問題的。另外，王沈《魏書》明確記載，赤山在"遼東西北數千里"，[26] 但漢遼東郡首府在今遼寧遼陽，其與阿魯科爾沁旗烏遼山一帶的距離，無論如何折算，也不足"數千里"之數，如認為烏桓山即赤山，則烏桓山為烏遼山之說明顯與《魏書》的記載矛盾。近年持此說的學者多認為烏桓山與赤山非一座山，實際上也就是為了解決此觀點與史料間的矛盾。

曹廷傑說雖然提出了新的研究思路，但說《遼史·地理志》烏州的烏丸川即古完水也僅由對音比附，並無堅實證據。而且古完水為今何水學界迄今並無定論，《中國歷史地圖集》認為完水指今額爾古納河及黑龍江上游；[27] 張博泉認為完水有二，與烏桓起源地相關的完水指今克魯倫河、額爾古納河，以及與松花江合流處以上的黑龍江。[28] 曹廷傑的歸流河說不過是諸說之一。即使完水確系烏桓水，烏桓山在其流域內，但完水為今何水難以確定，以此出發研究烏桓山的所在地自然具有不確定性。事實上，張博泉正是用其對完水的不同理解，定烏桓山為今蒙古國肯特山。

但是，如果認為烏桓山即肯特山，則烏桓人最初的居地竟在匈奴人分佈區之內，這顯然與史書的記載不符。通常認為匈奴單于庭在今蒙古國首都烏蘭巴托附近，烏桓人最初的居住地似不應如此接近單于庭。此外，賈敬顏說立論的基礎是烏桓人對赤山的崇拜與契丹人對黑山的崇拜相似，進而認為兩山在同一處，這種論證方法顯然也是有問題的。

上述諸說存在的共同問題是，都受包括《遼史》在內的後代史書影響，甚至是用後代史書的不確定記載以補前史之不足，因而才與漢魏史料存在不吻合之處。漢魏史料中雖然沒有對烏桓山具體位置的記載，但烏桓山的所在地也不是沒有一點線索可尋的。

《後漢書》卷九〇《烏桓鮮卑傳》："烏桓自為冒頓所破，眾遂孤弱，常臣伏匈奴，歲輸牛馬羊皮，過時不具，輒沒其妻子。及武帝遣驃騎將軍霍去病擊破匈奴左地，因徙烏桓於上谷、漁陽、右北平、遼東五郡塞外。"學界通常認為，此段記載中"五郡"僅提到四個郡名，是漏載了遼西郡。此記載透漏出的信息是，烏桓最初居於"匈奴左地"的範圍內。王可賓已指出，史書中的匈奴左地具有廣、狹二義，廣義的匈奴左地包括烏桓、鮮卑的分佈區，而狹義的匈奴左地指匈奴左方王將的駐地，也就是匈奴人的駐牧地，不包括烏桓、鮮卑分佈區。[29] 烏桓被漢遷居五郡塞外，即居於廣義的匈奴左地以南。《史記》卷一一〇《匈奴列傳》："左方王將居東方，直上谷以往者，東接穢、貉、朝鮮，右方王將居西方，直上郡以西，接月氏、氐、羌，而單于之庭直代、雲中。"西漢上谷郡、代郡緊鄰，說明此二郡以北是單于統轄區和匈奴左地的分界線，左地的匈奴人駐牧地自然與單于統轄區相接，因此上谷、代郡及與之相鄰的漁陽郡以北，不可能是烏桓人最初的居住地，烏桓山自然不會是尚在此以西的肯特山。

關於霍去病擊破匈奴左地之役，《史記》卷一一〇《匈奴列傳》記載："驃騎將軍之出代二千餘里，與左賢王接戰，漢兵得胡首虜凡七萬余級，左賢王將皆遁走。驃騎封於狼居胥山，禪姑衍，臨翰海而還。"有學者認為，狼居胥山、姑衍山應與匈奴左地有關，並由此推測烏桓山的所在地，或由對音出發，認為姑衍即烏延、烏丸、烏桓的不同譯寫，姑衍山即烏桓山。但是，學界通常認為狼居胥山為今蒙古國肯特山，姑衍山為今土拉河發源地的汗山，瀚海為貝加爾湖，總之，這些地名都在今烏蘭巴托附近或其正北，據前引《史記》所載匈奴三部的分界，正是單于統轄區，而不是左賢王統轄區，與匈奴左地無關。從上述《史記》的記載來看，霍去病是先破匈奴左地，遷徙烏桓人可能即在此時，而後自匈奴左地進軍單于庭，《史記》所載地名是其進軍的最終地點，以此判斷與匈奴左地相關的問題是不合適的。

烏桓人後遷至上谷、漁陽、右北平、遼東、遼西"五郡塞外"。從長城的走向來看，這裏所說的"塞外"大體是指西喇木倫河以及西遼河流域。阿魯科爾沁旗也好，遼代慶州所在的昭烏達盟巴林右旗也好，[30] 都距西喇木倫河過近，烏桓人最初的居住地不可能在這一帶。

史書記載烏桓人的葬俗："肥養犬，以采繩嬰牽，並取亡者所乘馬、衣服、生時服飾，皆燒以送之，特屬累犬，使護死者神靈歸乎赤山。赤山在遼東西北數千里，如中國人以死之魂神歸泰山也。"[31] 從中透漏出這樣一些信息：赤山應即烏桓山，烏桓人魂歸赤山的觀念與其發源地有關，但由於此時上距其最初遷離赤山已有三四百年之久，[32] 烏桓人自己也不知道祖先生活的赤山在何處，所以才需要狗來護送引路。由此看來，"赤山在遼東西北數千里"的說法，不僅"數千里"作為約數無法指實，更可能的情況是，烏桓人僅記得其發源地在遼東西北，已不清楚具體地點，距離更無從談起，以"數千里"為說，不過是為形容極遠而已。如果認為烏桓山在阿魯科爾沁旗或巴林右旗，那麼烏桓人遷居"五郡塞外"，不過是自西喇木倫河以北遷至河以南，顯然不會記不得烏桓山的所在地。

綜上，漢魏史籍透漏給我們的信息是，烏桓山在廣義的匈奴左地的範圍之內，並在遼東郡的西北。匈奴左地在漢上谷、漁陽、右北平、遼東、遼西五郡以北，烏桓山不可能在上谷、漁陽以北，又必在遼東的西北，則必在遼西與右北平之北。大體呈南北走向的大興安嶺山脈正在漢遼西郡和右北平郡正北，因此，烏桓山一定是指大興安嶺山脈中的某座山。

《舊唐書》卷一九九下《室韋傳》記載："烏羅護之東北二百餘里，那河之北，有古烏丸之遺人，今亦自稱烏丸國。"烏羅護即北魏時的烏洛侯，曾向北魏朝貢，並稱"其國西北"有拓跋鮮卑的"舊墟石室"，北魏"遣中書侍郎李敞告祭"，並"刊祝文於室之壁"，[33] 隨著李敞刻石發現于內蒙古自治區鄂倫春自治旗阿里河的嘎仙洞，為我們提供了準確的地理座標，可證《舊唐書》所說的烏丸遺人、烏丸國在今鄂倫春自治旗以東，嫩江以西，若認為烏桓山應在此區域內，則烏桓山當位於大興安嶺北段，那麼，居於烏桓以北的鮮卑人當置於何處？

需要引起我們注意的是漢代霍去病破匈奴之役的里程。《史記》卷一一〇《匈奴列傳》記載："驃騎將軍之出代二千餘里，與左賢王接戰。"霍去病自代郡出發，向匈奴左地進軍兩千餘里後與左賢王決戰，在打敗左賢王之後轉而向西進軍單于庭，故而遷徙烏桓人一定是在打敗左賢王之後、轉而西進之前，烏桓人的居住區應在霍去病與左賢王決戰處附近，也就是說，烏桓山與西漢代郡的距離大約是漢里兩千餘里。按 1 漢里合 325 米計算，[34] 漢代兩千里相當於今天的 650 公里，兩千餘里當在今 700 公里以上。草原行軍，當不存在太大迂回。因此，烏桓人最初的居住地當在西漢遼西郡和右北平郡以北，與西漢代郡距離在 700 公里以上，由此可以斷定，烏桓原居住地以今內蒙古自治區錫林郭勒盟東烏珠穆沁旗東部為中心，烏桓山應為東烏珠穆沁旗東北部的寶格達山。

寶格達山為大興安嶺餘脈，洮兒河南源歸流河即發源於此，從這個意義上講，曹廷傑對烏桓山的認識大體是正確的，可惜其論證與表述方法卻不無問題。

三

關於鮮卑山的所在地，較早的史書大多認為在柳城附近，即今遼寧朝陽附近。如，《太平寰宇記》："鮮卑山在今縣東南二百里。《十六國春秋》：慕容廆代居遼左，故號曰東胡，其後雄昌，與匈奴並盛。秦漢之際，為匈奴所敗，分保鮮卑山陰，復以山為號。棘城之東城塞外又有鮮卑山，在遼西之西北一百里，與此異山而同名。"[35] 但此地域在漢代屬遼西郡，鮮卑人顯然不可能發源于郡縣區內，該地域的鮮卑山都是鮮卑人南遷後將發源地的山名帶到遷入地的結果。至清代王先謙《後漢書集解》轉引《隋圖經》"山在柳城東南二百里"的記載，[36] 仍持此說。金毓黻認為鮮卑山，"不能實指其地，要不出今熱河省之北境"[37]，也是受此說影響的一種說法。但總體來說，此說早已為多數學者拋棄。

清乾隆間的官書多將鮮卑山定位於科爾沁右翼旗。如，乾隆《大清一統志》："鮮卑山在右翼西三十里，土人呼蒙格。"[38]《御批歷代通鑒輯覽》卷一七"東胡餘眾散保烏桓及鮮卑山"下注："（鮮卑山）在今喀爾沁右翼。"[39] 成書於乾隆五十三年（1788）的《乾隆府廳州縣圖志》："鮮卑山在右翼西三十里，土人呼蒙格。"[40] 但也有的持慎重態度稱不詳。如，《熱河志》卷六八《各屬有名無考諸山》稱："《一統志》原本據《後漢書》鮮卑以季春月大會于饒樂水上，謂遼之中京大定府在饒樂水南，則古鮮卑山當相去不遠。饒樂水為今英金河，流經赤峰、建昌、朝陽三縣地，則鮮卑山方位究難據以審定。"[41]《熱河志》這裏還為我們提供了另一條線索，即《大清一統志》主要是根據饒樂水來確定鮮卑山的位置。但饒樂水是否即英金河姑且不論，可以肯定的是，《後漢書》稱鮮卑活動于饒樂水，指的是鮮卑南遷後的居住地，而不是其發源地，在這裏尋找作為鮮卑起源地的鮮卑山肯定是錯誤的。

但是，張穆卻支持此說，其《蒙古遊牧記》於科尔沁右翼中旗提到："旗西三十里有鮮卑山，土人名蒙格。"[42] 建國後著名學者多受此說影響。如，馬長壽認為鮮卑山在科爾沁旗西哈古勒河附近；[43] 林幹、[44] 江應梁[45] 認為鮮卑山在今大興安嶺南段、科爾沁右翼中旗西；陳連開認為鮮卑山在霍林河沿岸，當大興安嶺南段中央。[46] 諸說雖各稍有變通，但皆本張穆說而來，使此說漸成為學界通說。

也有個別學者持不同意見。如，張博泉認為，後來隨著鮮卑族的遷徙，出現了一系列鮮卑山，而作為鮮卑人發源地的鮮卑山當在今黑龍江以南、額爾古納河以東、嫩江以西、洮兒河以北的大興安嶺北段地區。[47]

更有的學者干脆不承認存在一座作為鮮卑族發源地的鮮卑山，認為史書中稱東胡餘部"別保鮮卑山，因號焉"[48] 的記載有誤。最具代表性的學者是丁謙，他雖然贊同張穆對烏桓山的定位，但卻反對其關於鮮卑山的說法：

前《傳》謂東胡余種保烏桓山，因以為號，是矣。但此《傳》亦謂東胡之支別依鮮卑山，故因號焉，則不免臆說無據。蓋遼東塞外，別無鮮卑之山，不知鮮卑者，實東胡氏族之名。考《魏書·本紀卷一》言，魏之先，出自黄帝子昌意，昌意少子受封北國，有大鮮卑山，因以為號。此鮮卑之種所由來也。鮮卑為塞北三大種族之一（余別有考），族派繁衍，部落極多，東胡僅其一支而已。大鮮卑山，在俄屬伊爾古斯克省北、通姑斯河南。今外蒙古以北之地，西人皆稱為悉比利亞，悉比即鮮卑轉音，以其地皆鮮卑種所分佈故也。西儒談人種學者，以悉比利亞及東三省人為通姑斯種，通姑斯河即大鮮卑山所在，一以河為標識，一以山為標識，中西所考，若合符節。然則鮮卑之名，源出大鮮卑山，而非由後來之更改，彰明矣。惟拓跋氏為彼種貴族，世為君長，其南遷也，亦較後，此傳鮮卑，不過彼種中散姓，分徙甚早。[49]

但丁謙也承認："遼東塞外，即今奉天以北科爾沁、郭爾羅斯諸部境，鮮卑因避匈奴之鋒，遁居於此。"[50] 顯然是受清代官書與張穆的影響。與丁謙的觀點類似，馮家昇認為："鮮卑山乃具神話之意味，未必能指出今為何地。"[51]

在鄂倫春自治旗嘎仙洞發現北魏刻石以後，多數學者認為其所在的大興安嶺北段就是拓跋鮮卑的發源地大鮮卑山，鮮卑山應在大鮮卑山以南，這也進一步使鮮卑山位於大興安嶺南段、科爾沁右翼中旗之西的說法成為學界主流觀點。

目前在追溯鮮卑族的起源時，很多學者認為拓跋鮮卑與東部鮮卑同源，並將嘎仙洞作為其發源地，這實際上是認同前引丁謙的論述，認為東部鮮卑源於拓跋鮮卑，而在其論述中，往往還存在將鮮卑山與大鮮卑山相混同的趨勢，[52] 即認為鮮卑山在今鄂倫春自治旗。但是，《魏書》卷一《序紀》對拓跋鮮卑早期歷史的追述是靠不住的，拓跋鮮卑的信史始於成帝毛，依據《魏書》的記載認定拓跋鮮卑的歷史比東部鮮卑更為古老的觀點是不能成立的。[53] 因此，認為東部鮮卑源於拓跋鮮卑、鮮卑山在嘎仙洞的說法自然也是不能成立的。

漢魏史籍中關於鮮卑山的記載更為罕見，僅王沈《魏書》提到："自為冒頓所破，遠竄遼東塞外，不與餘國爭衡，未有名通於漢，而自與烏丸相接。"[54] 因此學者公認，鮮卑最初的居住地當在烏桓以北，鮮卑山自然也在烏桓山以北。我們既然認為烏桓山是今寶格達山，則鮮卑山最有可能位於寶格達山以北的大興安嶺中段，只是具體地點卻無從考究了。

注释

[1] 顧祖禹：《讀史方輿紀要》卷一八《北直九·附考·赤山》，北京：中華書局，2005年，第854頁。

[2]《三國志》卷三〇《魏書·烏丸鮮卑傳》裴松之注引王沈《魏書》。

[3] 顧祖禹：《讀史方輿紀要》卷一八《北直九·附考·廢烏州》，第851頁。

[4] 顧祖禹：《讀史方輿紀要》卷一八《北直九·附考·臨潢城》，第849頁。

[5] 顧祖禹：《讀史方輿紀要》卷一八《北直九·附考·兀良哈》，第848頁。關於兀良哈三衛的地理位置，

學界目前主要存在兩種不同觀點。其一，以譚其驤主編的《中國歷史地圖集》為代表，認為："福余衛在嫩江中游，今富裕爾河南北，西抵布特哈至大興安嶺。福余衛之南為朵顏衛，包括今安達市與綽爾河流域。泰寧衛又在朵顏衛之南，為今吉林省白城市與科左前旗、中旗等地。"（譚其驤主編：《〈中國歷史地圖集〉釋文彙編·東北卷》，北京：中央民族學院出版社，1988年，第237頁）其二，以張博泉等著《東北歷代疆域史》為代表，支持日本學者和田清的觀點，認為"泰寧衛設于洮安附近，福余衛設於齊齊哈爾附近，朵顏衛設于洮兒河上游"。（張博泉、蘇金源、董玉瑛：《東北歷代疆域史》，長春：吉林人民出版社，1981年，第273-274頁）概言之，第一種觀點認為三衛呈南北分佈，第二種觀點認為三衛呈"品"字形分佈，皆與顧祖禹認為三衛呈東西分佈不同。《東北歷代疆域史》認為，《明史》卷三二八《朵顏福余泰寧傳》所載為三衛在明後期的分佈，顧祖禹說同《明史》，也就是說，顧祖禹說為明後期的三衛分佈。

[6]《御批歷代通鑒輯覽》卷一七，影印文淵閣四庫全書本，臺灣商務印書館，1986年，第335冊第414頁。

[7] 乾隆《大清一統志》卷四〇四《舊藩蒙古統部·山川》，影印文淵閣四庫全書本，第407冊第483頁。

[8] 乾隆《大清一統志》卷四〇六《阿嚕科爾沁·山川》，第483冊第436頁。

[9]《盛京通志》卷二八《山川·古山川附考·烏丸山》，影印文淵閣四庫全書本，第501冊第560頁。

[10]《熱河志》卷六八《各屬有名無考諸山·赤山》，影印文淵閣四庫全書本，第496冊第124頁。

[11] 張穆：《蒙古遊牧記》卷三《昭烏達盟遊牧所在·阿嚕科爾沁》，同治六年壽陽祁氏刊本，第18頁a。

[12] 丁謙：《後漢書烏桓鮮卑傳地理考證》，《後漢書各外國傳地理考證》，民國四年浙江圖書館校刊本，第2頁b—3頁a。

[13] 田廣林：《釋烏桓山》，《昭烏達蒙族師專學報》1988年第1期。

[14] 史為樂主編：《中國歷史地名大辭典》（上冊），北京：中國社會科學出版社，2005年，第466頁。譚其驤主編《中國歷史地圖集》第六冊（中國地圖出版社，1982年，第6頁）亦繪烏州於今吉林雙遼一帶。

[15] 曹廷傑：《東三省輿地圖說·嫩江、陀喇河、喀魯倫河、黑龍江考》，影印遼海叢書本，瀋陽：遼沈書社，1984年，第2253頁。

[16] 張博泉、蘇金源、董玉瑛：《東北歷代疆域史》，第146頁。

[17] 丁謙：《後漢書烏桓鮮卑傳地理考證》，第3頁a。

[18] 陳漢章：《遼史索隱》卷三《營衛志》，綴學堂叢稿初集本，民國二十五年鉛印本，第17頁a。

[19] 林幹：《東胡史》，呼和浩特：內蒙古人民出版社，1989年，第32—34頁。

[20] 馬長壽：《烏桓與鮮卑》，上海：上海人民出版社，1962年，第114—115頁。

[21] 呂思勉：《中國民族史》，北京：東方出版社，1996年，第81頁。

[22] 呂思勉所說蘇克蘇魯山即曹廷傑所說歸流河的發源地瑚蘇圖山，索嶽爾濟山為曹廷傑所說洮兒河北源陀喇河的發源地，按呂思勉說，烏桓、鮮卑二山即分別在今洮兒河的南、北二源。

[23] 張博泉：《烏桓的起源地與赤山》，《黑龍江文物叢刊》1984年第2期。

[24] 賈敬顏：《烏桓赤山》，《東北古代民族古代地理叢考》，北京：中國社會科學出版社，1993年，第9—

11頁。法人閔宣化早已提出過類似觀點："烏桓之赤山，或即契丹之赤山，今日尚稱為巴顏五藍哈達(Bayan-olan-xata)，(《蒙古遊牧記》名巴顏烏蘭嶺，)華言赤山。蒙古人亦稱為五藍塔窪(olan-tawa)，亦赤山之義也。"但未作詳細論證。參見閔宣化：《東蒙古遼代舊城探考記》，馮承鈞譯，北京：中華書局，1956年，第57頁。

[25] 鄭英德：《東胡系諸部族與蒙古族源》，中國蒙古史學會編：《中國蒙古史學會論文選集》，呼和浩特：內蒙古人民出版社，1981年，第101頁。

[26] 《三國志》卷三〇《魏書·烏丸鮮卑傳》裴松之注引。

[27] 譚其驤主編：《〈中國歷史地圖集〉釋文彙編·東北卷》，第58—59頁。

[28] 張博泉：《烏桓的起源地與赤山》，《黑龍江文物叢刊》1984年第2期。

[29] 王可賓：《匈奴左地與姑夕王駐地》，《北方文物》1984年第2期。

[30] 遼慶州遺址在今內蒙古自治區昭烏達盟巴林右旗白塔子。參見張博泉、蘇金源、董玉瑛：《東北歷代疆域史》，第144頁。

[31] 《三國志》卷三〇《魏書·烏丸鮮卑傳》裴松之注引王沈《魏書》。

[32] 王沈卒於266年，其所著《魏書》反映的烏桓人葬俗應是3世紀上半葉的事情，上溯至烏桓人遷往五郡塞外的西元前119年，不少於320年。

[33] 《魏書》卷一〇〇《烏洛侯傳》。

[34] 楊寬《中國歷代尺度考》(商務印書館，1955年)認為，漢代1里相當於414米。陳夢家根據對居延地區漢代郵程的考證，認為"一漢里相當於325米的直線距離"，"用400米或414米折合則太大"。參見陳夢家：《漢簡考述》，《考古學報》1963年第1期。此據陳夢家說。

[35] 《太平寰宇記》卷七一《河北道》"營州柳城"條。

[36] 王先謙：《後漢書集解》卷九〇《烏桓鮮卑列傳》"別依鮮卑山故因號焉"條下注，北京：中華書局，1984年影印本，第1050頁。

[37] 金毓黻：《東北通史》上編，重慶：五十年代出版社，1981年，第96頁。

[38] 乾隆《大清一統志》卷四〇五《科爾沁·山川》，第483冊第419頁。

[39] 《御批歷代通鑒輯覽》卷一七，第335冊第414頁。

[40] 《乾隆府廳州縣圖志》卷五〇《外藩·科爾沁》，光緒五年授經堂重刊本，第12頁b。

[41] 《熱河志》卷六八《各屬有名無考諸山·鮮卑山》，第496冊第124頁。

[42] 張穆：《蒙古遊牧記》卷一《內蒙古哲里木盟遊牧所在·科爾沁·右翼中旗》，第4頁a。

[43] 馬長壽：《烏桓與鮮卑》，第175頁。

[44] 林幹：《東胡史》，第3、87頁。

[45] 江應梁：《中國民族史》上，北京：民族出版社，1990年，第154頁。

[46] 陳連開：《鮮卑山考》，《社會科學戰線》1982年第3期。

[47] 張博泉：《鮮卑新論》，長春：吉林文史出版社，1993年，第54頁。

[48] 《三國志》卷三〇《魏書·烏丸鮮卑傳》裴松之注引王沈《魏書》。《後漢書》卷九〇《烏桓鮮卑傳》

的記載與此相同。

[49] 丁謙：《後漢書烏桓鮮卑傳地理考證》，第 6 頁 a - 第 6 頁 b。
[50] 丁謙：《後漢書烏桓鮮卑傳地理考證》，第 7 頁 a。
[51] 馮家昇：《述東胡系之氏族》，《禹貢》第 3 卷第 8 期，1935 年。
[52] 米文平：《鮮卑源流及其族名初探》，《社會科學戰線》1982 年第 3 期；干志耿、孫秀仁：《關於鮮卑早期歷史及其考古遺存的幾個問題》，《民族研究》1982 年第 1 期。
[53] 楊軍：《拓跋鮮卑早期歷史辨誤》，《史學集刊》2006 年第 4 期。
[54] 《三國志》卷三〇《魏書·烏丸鮮卑傳》裴松之注引。

NEW RESEARCH ON THE WUHUAN AND XIANBEI MOUNTAINS

YANG Jun

The cradle of Wuhuan was Mount Wuhuan, which is today's Mount Baogeda 寶格達山 in the northeast of Eastern Wuzhumuqin 烏珠穆沁 County, Xilingol 錫林郭勒 Prefecture, Inner Mongolia Autonomous Region, while the ultimate homeland of the Xianbei should be in the middle part of Daxing'anling 大興安嶺 Range.

Byzantine-Turkic Relations and the Wider Eurasian Alliances during the Perso-Byzantine Wars

Stephanos Kordoses

In January 628, Emperor Heraclius entered the imperial Persian city of Dastagerde, causing the overthrow of Khusraw and forcing his heir, Seroes II, to sign a peace treaty (*αειπαγή ειρήνη*), whereby the frontiers of the two states reverted to those of 591.[1]

These events were preceded by Heraclius' epic wars (622-628), which commenced in 622 and can be divided in three periods: (1) From 622 to 624, Asia Minor was freed from the Persians. (2) In the next phase, which lasts until 627, Heraclius crossed the Taurus mountain range and the Tigris River, while Constantinople, the Byzantine capital, was under siege, simultaneously, by both the Persians and the Avars, in 626. At the same time, Heraclius tried to forge an alliance with the Khazars against the Persians. (3) The last phase started in the summer of 627, during which time the Khazars also participated in Heraclius' campaigns as his allies. In September 627, the Persian army was defeated in the battle of Nineveh.

Khazar participation in Heraclius' campaigns (during the last phase of his campaigns, 626-628)[2] and the simultaneous siege of Constantinople by the Persians and the Avars in 626 demonstrate that the Byzantino-Persian conflict was only a part, probably the most well-known and often cited, of a wider conflict, which most of the powers of the then known world had mobilized for, giving to the events a more Eurasian dimension. What is more, according to the sources, Khazar participation on Heraclius' side was the result of a previous, Byzantine-Turkic entente.

After the collapse of the efforts to establish trade relations between the Turkic khanate and the Persian empire,[3] the Sogdian vassals of the Turks prompted the Turk Khagan Silziboul (İstemi, Shidianmi 室點密) to establish trade relations with the Romans, to whom the Turks (and their vassals, the Sogdians) would sell their silk directly. At that time the

Romans were by far the bigger consumer of silk products.[4] The Turk Khagan agreed and a delegation was dispatched to the court of the Byzantine emperor, bringing along gifts and a letter (epistle-επιστολή) for the emperor.

It was at the beginning of Emperor Justin II's reign (end of 567 or beginning of 568) that the Turkic delegation arrived in Constantinople.[5] The Emperor was informed of the contents of the letter through his interpreters and accepted the delegation with great pleasure, for, amongst other things, it was a first class opportunity to obtain information regarding the nation and lands of the Turks.

The Turks requested peace and an alliance with the Emperor and pledged to fight against the enemies of the Byzantines. Their requests were granted by the Emperor, marking the beginning of diplomatic exchanges between the Turks and the Byzantines. Besides the establishment of trade relations regarding the commerce of silk, the establishment of a political alliance was also on the agenda of the delegation.[6] Obviously, the common objective was the Persian empire.[7]

In response to the Turkic delegation, Justin II sent a Byzantine delegation to the court of the Turk Khagan, led by ambassador Zemarchus from Cillicia, a general of the Byzantine army, before the end of the fourth year of his reign (i.e. shortly after the arrival of the Turkic delegation).[8] John of Ephesus mentions that it was the first time that a Roman delegation visited those "powerful and overpopulated tribes".[9]

The meeting between the Roman ambassador Zemarchus and the Turk khagan took place in the valley of the mountain Εκτάγ, a name which Menander Protector translates as "golden mountain" and which, when referring to Valentine's embassy, he calls Εκτέλ.[10] The Byzantine delegation, after saluting the Turk Khagan and offering the appropriate gifts, reported that they had been sent by their King to a friend of the Romans and of the Roman state, wishing him "felicitous and kind luck" and a victorious and glorious reign. Menander describes the events that took place during the official visit in great detail.[11] The fact that it was during this visit (and not during the visit of the previous delegation, sent by the Turks) that the foundations of the Byzantino-Turkic alliance were established becomes evident during the last Byzantine (under Vallentine's leadership) delegation to the Turks, in 576, when reference is made to the oaths made by both Turks and Byzantines.[12]

The Turk Khagan was determined to campaign against the Persians and for that reason he allowed Zemarchus, together with twenty of his men, to follow the campaign as observers.[13] Obviously, in this way he wanted to demonstrate his commitment regarding his position on Persia. Upon arriving at a place called Talas, between the rivers Chu and Jaxartes

(Syr-Darya), they were met by a Persian delegation. Silzaboul "staged" a diplomatic dinner, including the Byzantine ambassador as a guest, during which he made abundantly clear to the Persians that he deemed his relations with the Byzantines more important. The Persian ambassador overreacted and even crossed the lines set by the diplomatic protocol when Silziboul accused the Persians of forgery and animosity towards the Turks.

After the departure of the Persian delegation, Silziboul reaffirmed the Turkic friendship towards the Romans and allowed Zemarchus to return to Constantinople, accompanied by another Turkic delegation, led by a person named Taghma, who had the rank of "Tarkhan".[14]

Despite the fact that John of Ephesus states that Zemarchus' delegation was the first contact with the tribes of Asia, this is not confirmed by the eastern sources, since, in a Turkic inscription (postdating the events, erected at the beginning of the 8th century), the Byzantines (*Purum*) are mentioned among the peoples that had sent a delegation to attend the funeral ceremonies in honor of the first Turk Khagan, Boumin, in the year 553.[15] Besides that, the Byzantine chronicles record the arrival at Constantinople, in 563, of a delegation coming from the depths of the East. According to Theophanes the Confessor, the delegation came on behalf of Ἀσκήλ (Askil), king of *Ermichions*.[16] The identification of (K)ermichions with a tribe or nation has raised a great discussion amongst the scholars.[17] Some agree with Theophanes Byzantius, who clearly states that the name Kermichions is the Persian name for the Turks.[18] This is supported by a following phrase, in the same excerpt, which states that the aim of the delegation was to convince the Romans not to accept the Avars into their territory (although these events are placed within the reign of Justin and not Justinian). In conclusion, the delegation of 563 was probably Turkic. The Turks sent a reconnaissance delegation to Byzantium, the greatest power of Eurasia after the collapse of China, in order to assess the possibility of co-operation with the Byzantines, concerning the flight of their much hated enemies, the Avars, to the west. Besides, what is more important is the fact that from 563 (and not from 558, when the nearby Avars sent a delegation to Constantinople) the Byzantines came into direct contact with peoples living near the ocean, as Theophanes mentions, or on the ocean coasts, as Priscus states,[19] i.e. from the most distant parts of the East.[20]

Consequently, during the visit of the Turkic delegation of 563 and of the Byzantine delegation in 568, the foundations of an alliance between the Turks and the Byzantines were established, concerning the Balkans (Avars), Middle East, and Central Asia (Persia). The results of this alliance became apparent in the events that ensued despite the fact that the Turks had attacked and conquered the Byzantine city of Bosporus, in 576, in what proved to be a short breach in the Byzantino-Turkic alliance.[21] In 579, the Avars started the construction of a bridge between Sigidon and Sirmium and an Avar flotilla made its appearance on the river Sao.[22] At this difficult juncture the Byzantines, who had most of their army engaged in the east, tried to take advantage of the Turkic presence near the Avars. It was an awkward situation. The Byzantines would wield the threat of a Turkic raid in the Avars' rear, while the latter were raiding Byzantine territory.[23] But this strategy was unsuccessful and, in 582, Sirmium fell to the Avars.[24] Yet, in 584, during the reign of Maurice and despite the fact that he had signed a treaty with the Avars upon ascending the Byzantine throne,[25] things turned out differently. John of Ephesus mentions that as the Avars were raiding Aghialus and the capital of the Empire was readying itself to be besieged by them, they were forced to retreat because the Turks had attacked them in the rear, forcing them to pay tribute.[26]

The main target of the alliance, however, was the Persian Empire. It seems that the help that was provided to Emperor Heraclius by the Khazars, who entered the Byzantino-Persian war during its last phase (from 626 onwards), was given within the wider context of the Byzantino-Turkic alliance. The Khazars were, after all, vassals of the Turks, until the middle of the 7th century.[27] The Chinese believed that towards its end, the Persian Empire was a vassal of the Western Turks. *New Tang History* (Xin Tang Shu 新唐書) mentions that, at the end of Sui 隋 dynasty (581-618), Che-hou (Yabghu), Kagan of the Western Turks attacked and destroyed the kingdom (Persia); he killed the king K'ou-sa-ho (Khusraw). The latter's son, Che-li (Seroes) ascended the throne. Che-hou sent commanders to oversee and direct him. After Seroes' death, as the Persians were not willing to remain vassals of the Turks, they enthroned Khusraw's daughter, but she was also murdered by the Turks. Tan-kie, Seroes' son, who had taken refuge in Fulin 拂菻, was sought by the people of Persia and was enthroned. This person was I-ta-tche (Ardeschir). After his death, I-se-se (Yezdegerd) assumed power.[28]

This excerpt from *New Tang History* correctly mentions the names of three kings of Persia as well as the fact that one of Khusraw's daughters ascended the throne, but does not keep a chronological order. Byzantine, Syriac and Arabo-Persian chronicles also make many references to the events of that period but also contain many inaccuracies. Theophanes mentions Seroes, Ardeschir, Sharbaraz, Boran, and Hormizd, who reigned each for a few months and Nicephorus mentions Kavoe, Hormizd and possibly Sharbaraz. In Syriac and later Arabo-Persian sources (Tabari etc.),[29] more accurate information is provided. Ardaschir III ascended the throne, after Seroes (Kabor), who was considered a good king was possibly poisoned by Sirin. The latter was murdered in 27/4/630 by General Sharbaraz, who assumed power for 42 days. After his murder, due to a lack of male descendants, the Persian nobility brought to the throne Pourândokht (Theophanes calls her Voran and the eastern sources Bor or Boran), who died in the autumn of 631. She was succeeded by her sister Azermîdokht (amidst chaos, as more than one contender for the throne had appeared in various provinces of the empire), also put to death, after six months, by a Persian noble. The situation remained volatile for 6-9 months, while the empire was dissolving and many of its provinces were falling into Arab hands. In the end of 634, Yezdegerd III was enthroned, at the age of sixteen, shortly before the collapse of the whole empire before the Arab advance.

What is more important than the succession of Persian kings is that the Chinese source refers to the Persian vassalage to the Turks and, also, that in 618, or a little earlier, the Turk Khagan Che-hou invaded and destroyed Persia. This was repeated during the reign of the next Khagan, T'ong Che-hou Kagan (Tong Yabghu), who, according to the *New Tang History* conquered the Tölös, and subjugated Po-se (Persia) and Ki-pin (Kapissa).[30] Perhaps the use of "subjugate" (used for Persia and Kapissa) instead of "conquer" (used for the Tölös tribes) means that these countries were not incorporated into the Western Turkic khanate. This is also attested in the Sui chronicle, which states that the Turks were not able to reach the kingdom of Persia, but managed to impose their rule on it.[31] Tong Yabghu was both a great khagan and a conqueror. Xuanzang informs us of the vastness of his state, reaching as far as the Indus River. His son was king of Tockarestan and, consequently, Bactria must also have been part of his domain. So, the vassalage of Persia cannot be surprising especially at a time when the Persian Empire was crumbling.[32] The Khazar invasion in 630 within Persian territories, despite the fact that Heraclius had ended the war, must have had been decided together with their lords, the Western Turks.

To sum up, during the Byzantine-Persian wars (especially during Heraclius' reign) the Western Turks were also at war with the Persians. Theophanes mentions a separate peace treaty with the Khazars, who were actually vassals of the Turks. Moreover, according to another analysis of the sources, some scholars believe that the Khazars appeared near the Caspian Sea some three decades after the end of the Byzantino-Persian conflict. In that case, it is certain that the Turks were the allies of the Byzantines,[33] although it appears to be a far-fetched suggestion, since the Western Turks were at such a distance from the theater of hostilities that they probably acted through their agents there (be they Khazars or some other tribe).

Despite the fact that Persia was eventually defeated, it put up a fierce struggle by allying itself with the most natural ally, an enemy of its enemies, the Avar khanate in Eastern Europe. This is proven by the joint Perso-Avar operations in the siege of Constantinople in 626.

The entente between the Persians and the Avars came into existence either after Heraclius' efforts to ally with the Khazars, or more plausibly earlier (Heraclius' return from the front in 622 due to Avar attacks could be related to Avaro-Persian negotiations). The participation of one power in a coalition would lead to the participation of its opponent in the other. The basic strategy was to make the opponent divide his forces by opening a second front. These opposing coalitions covered a great part of Eurasia and most of the great powers participated in them, with the exception of China, which had not yet spread into Central Asia. The mobilization was so "ecumenical" that even peoples that did not participate in the conflict had knowledge of it. Evidence of this is provided by the example of the Indians, who sent congratulations to Emperor Heraclius accompanied with precious gifts, for his victory over the Persians.[34]

The division of the then known world into two opposing coalitions is best illustrated in the case of the tribes called Tarniah and Kotzagere by Theophylactus Simocattae, who joined the Avar khanate fleeing from the Western Turkic khanate, as they felt insecure due to their racial affinity with the Avars of Europe (pseudo-Avars, i.e. the tribes of War and Hunni).[35] Concurrent with Nicephorus' information that it was the Byzantines who instigated the revolt of the Bulgars against the Avars, in order to compromise Avar dominance, one can appreciate the scale of the mobilization.

Gumilev was one of the first to state that the "Ecumene" was divided into two coalitions and he even suggested that the whole of Eurasia, from the Far West to the Far East was engaged: one coalition including the Eastern Turks, Persians, and Avars as allies, and the other consisting of the Byzantines, Western Turks, and Chinese.[36] He also suggests that the coalitions were a result of intense diplomatic kneading.[37] But such an assumption is met with a lot of skepticism since there are no sources verifying it. It is certain that Byzantium had not yet contacted China. The Chinese chronicles mention that Emperor Yangdi failed to establish diplomatic contacts with Byzantium. The first contact Byzantium (as Fulin 拂菻 and not as Daqin 大秦) had with China is placed in the year 643.[38] Hence, it is safe to say that China abstained from the rivalry during the first half of the 7th century. Only after the establishment of the Chinese protectorate in Central Asia (with the capture of the city-states and the subjugation of the Western Turks) did China manage to become a "Eurasian player". The Arab advance, especially after 642, posed a serious threat not only to Byzantium (and its dominions in Asia Minor and Middle East) but also to the Chinese dominions in Central Asia and, as a result of that, China had to co-ordinate its efforts with the empire lying on the other side of the Arab dominion.[39]

The same also applies to the Eastern Turks. Allying themselves with Persia in order to strike the Western Turks is unlikely especially since the other Persian ally were the Avars, much hated by the Turks.

In general, only the power that ruled over the central network of trade routes crossing Eurasia could take the initiative for the creation of an "ecumenical" axis stretching from China to Byzantium. In the decades of the 620s and 630s the only power that has such characteristics was the Western Turkic Khanate. But, due to the lack of interest from the Chinese side in Central Asia and in the Byzantino-Persian war, the Western Turks had to "play" into two regional subsystems: one in the West (encompassing Persia, the Avars, and Byzantium) and the other in the East (encompassing Tibet, the Eastern Turkic Khanate and China).

NOTES

[1] Ζακυθηνού, Δ., *Βυζαντινή Ιστορία 324-1071*, Αθήνα, 1972 ζ1977 (reprint 1989), pp. 108-111. The crushing of the Persian army in Nineveh and the capture of Dastagerde were quickly followed by political developments within the higher ranks of the imperial Persian structure. Khusraw, sick and devastated, pressed by his wife, Sirin, decided to designate his son, Merdan-shah, as his successor. Cf. Christensen, A., *L'Iran sous les Sassanides*, (xerography of the 2nd edition), Otto Zeller, Osnabrück, 1971, p. 493. His first-born son, Seroes, was neglected in this process of succession, having the cooperation of some part of the nobility, mutinied and managed to ascend the throne. Khusraw was arrested and brought to Kavad (Seroes), and put to death shortly afterwards. The new Shah signed a peace treaty with the Romans, accepting all their terms.

[2] Chavannes, *Documents*, p. 252. Cf. Бартольд В. В., «Хазары», *Работы по Историй и Филологий Тюрских и Монголских Народов,* Москва, «Восточная Литература», 2002, pp. 597-601.

[3] The Turks, twice, tried to open the Persian market to their trade, mainly silk trade, by sending two delegations to the Persian court. Both of them were treated by animosity on the Persian part while most of the members of the second delegation were poisoned and murdered.

[4] Establishing friendly relations between the Byzantines and the Turko-Sogdians was a basic aim, on the part of the Turks and Sogdians, as confirmed several times in the Byzantine sources. Regarding the Sogdian delegation to the Byzantines, under the Sogdian Maniakh, see Parker, "The Origin", p. 439. Cf. *The Cambridge History of Iran,* T. 3, Cambridge University Press, 1983 (re-edition.1996), p. 617; Golden, P., *Khazar Studies: A Historico-philological Inquiry into the Origins of the Khazars (Bibliotheca Orientalis Hungarica)*, Akadémiai Kiadó, Budapest, 1980, p. 38; Beckwith, *Empires of the Silk Road*, p. 116-117; Zhang, Xu-shan, "The Northern Silk Route and its western terminus in the Balkans", *Ιστορική Γεωγραφία*.

Δρόμοι και Κόμβοι της Βαλκανικής από την αρχαιότητα στην ενιαία Ευρώπη, Διεθνές Συνέδριο Ιστορικής Γεωγραφίας, Thessaloniki, 1997, pp. 125-132, p. 127; Zhang, *Η Κίνα*, pp. 217, 218, 285; Vaissière, *Histoire*, p. 206; Vernadsky, *Ancient Russia*, p. 183;

[5] Chavannes, *Documents*, p. 235.

[6] See also Пигулевская Н. В., *Византия на путях в Индию*, Москва-Ленинград, 1951, p. 205.

[7] Chavannes, *Documents*, p. 239; Bury, J. B., *A History of the Later Roman Empire from Arcadius to Irene (395 A.D. to 800 A.D.)*, τόμ. I, II, London, 1889, Adolf M. Hakkert, (reprint Amsterdam, 1966), p. 97; Dickens, M., *Medieval Syriac Historians' Perceptions of the Turks*, Mphil Dissertation in Aramaic and Syriac Studies, Faculty of Oriental Studies, University of Cambridge, August 2004, p. 41; Vailhé, "Projet", 12 (1909), p. 210.

[8] Concerning Zemarchus' delegation see Chavannes, *Documents*, pp. 237 κ.έ; Sinor, D., "The Historical Role of the Turk Empire", Sinor, *Inner Asia*, p. 431; Grousset, *L' Empire*, p. 129; Vernadsky, *Ancient Russia*, p. 183; Zhang, *Η Κίνα*, pp. 127, 217-218, 285; Sinor-Klyashtorny, "The Türk Empire", p. 333; John of Ephesus, ch. VI, p. 22, mentions that the delegation was dispatched in the 7th year of Justin II's reign.

[9] Ιωάννης Εφέσου, ch.VI, 23.

[10] Theophylact Simocattae gives the Greek word for that mountain and places it 400 miles to the north of Ικάρ (Ikar) mountain. He believes that its name is due to the plenitude of fruits and vegetables it produces and of the animals that pasture around it. Finally, he provides us with the information that the mountain is given to the supreme Khagan, see Theophylacti Simocattae, p. 260. Cf. Haussig, "Theophylakts", pp. 381, 387; Menander Protector, p. 178; Moravscik, *Byzantinoturcica*, p. 122. Chavannes mentions that only the name Εκτέλ (Ektel) has the meaning of "golden mountain" and that it is different from Εκτάγ (Ektagh), which bears the meaning of "White mountain". See Chavannes, *Documents*, p. 235-236. Some scholars identify the Εκτέλ (Ektel) with the Altay (Altoun) mountain range, a name meaning "golden mountain". For the terms Εκτάγ/Εκτέλ (Ektagh/Ektel), also see Moravscik, *Byzantinoturcica*, p. 122. Chavannes rejects such an approach and suggests the mountains A-kie ή A-kie-t'ien, north of Koutcha, see Chavannes, *Documents*, pp. 236-237, 241. Blockley, even though believes that the term Ektel is a corrupted form of Ektağ (Menander Protector, p. 277, n. 232), and rejects Altay (Menander Protector, p. 264, n. 129). See also Baldwin, Menander, p. 118: "The repetition of effects, such as the two Golden Mountains, Ektag and Ektel, is not reasonable since they do seem to be quite different places". Also, Giraud, *L'Empire*, p. 181-182: « A propos d'un autre Äk-taγ, Chavannes (D.T.O., pp. 235-236 et 237) a ouvert une discussion fort intéressante. Il s'agit du mont où l'ambassade de Zémarque de Cilicie, en 568, trouve la résidence du quaghan Dizaboul (=Istämi). D' après Ménandre, qui a raison, le nom de la montagne est bien Äk-taγ (Εκτάγ) et signifie « la montagne d'or ». Tenant compte de la transcription chinoise A-kie-t'ien, Chavannes maintient la lecture Aq-taγ et la traduction « montagne blanche ». Si notre lecture de B.T. s'avère exacte, elle aurait l'avantage de confirmer par une source turque le témoignage du Ménandre. Chavannes a eu, en tous cas, le mérite de

localiser le séjour du qaghan turc occidental : au Nord de Koutcha, dans la vallée du Tekes. Grousset (*Empire*, 128 et 129) identifie l'Aktaγ avec les T'ien chan, ce qui rejoint le point de vue de Chavannes, mais place le campement du Qaghan, plus au Sud et à l'Est dans le vallée du haut Youldouz au N.O. de Karachar. Si l'on admet avec Grousset lui-même que le campement d'hiver des Turcs Occidentaux était situé soit sur les bordes de l'Issik Koul, soit dans la vallée du Talas, la localisation de Chavannes est plus vraisemblable, étant donné la distance considérable qui sépare le haut Youldouz de la vallée du Talas et même de l'Issyk Koul. » Cahun, *Asie*, p. 4, n. 2, mentions that: « L'étymologie ordinaire d'Altaï, *Altyn Dagh*, 'montagne d'or', est contraire à la phonétique turque. *Altaï*, dans les dialectes turcs du pays, se décompose en *Al-taïga*, 'la haute forêt'. Voir l'expilication et les exemples dans le dictionnaire général de Radloff, p. 402, au mot Altaï. *Altaï* correspond exactement à notre celtique *Morvan* et au *Hochwald* des Allemends ». Cf. Bury J. B., "The Turks in the 6th century", *EHR*, T. 12, N. 47 (1897), pp. 417, 420, 421, 426 ; Christian, D., *A History of Russia, Central Asia and Mongolia*, τόμ. 1, *Inner Eurasia from Prehistory to the Mongol Empire*, Blackwell, Oxford, 1998 p. 255; Пигулевская Н. В., «Византийская Дипломатия и Торговля Шелком в V-VII вв.», *Византйскии Временик*, Т. I (XXVI), Москва, 1947, p. 210-211.

[11] Menander Protector, pp. 118-120.

[12] Menander Protector, p. 172: "Which Silzabul and the Emperor Justin had made when Zemarchus first came there".

[13] The rest of the men of the Byzantine delegation would wait for Zemarchus to return in the country of Choliatai. Vaissière, *Histoire*, p. 251, identifies the Choliatai with the Khorazmians while Vailhé, "Projet", p. 211, with the Turkmens, north of Caspia. As Blockley observes (Menander Protector, p. 264-65, n. 135) such a location is too far north. Blockley rightly identifies them with a branch of the Western Turks. Logically speaking the Choliatai must have dwelled in the areas to the west or northwest of the river Talas, in the direction of Oxus River (Amu-Darya), since Zemarchus had to pass from that direction on his way to Constantinople.

[14] For this rank see Moravscik, *Byzantinoturcica*, T. II, p. 299; Chavannes, *Documents*, p. 239; Cahun, *Asie*, p. 58; The word derives from the Turkic root *tar* followed by the word *kaghan*. *Taramak* or *tarımak* means "to cultivate" and thus the rank Tarkhan was obviously a rank related to the administration of sedentary societies under Turkic rule.

[15] Talât, T., *A Grammar of Orkhon Turkic*, Indiana University, 1968, p. 232, 264 (translation); Golden, P., *An Introduction to the History of the Turkish Peoples: Ethnogenesis and State-Formation in Medieval and Early Modern Eurasia and Middle East (Turcologia)*, Wiesbaden, 1992, p. 76. Aalto, "Iranian Contacts of the Turks in Pre-Islamic Times", *Studia Turcica*, Budapest, 1971, p. 33; Haussig, *Die Geschichte*, p. 70; Κορδώσης, Σ., «Οι Πρεσβείες των Βυζαντινών και Ασιατών στους Τούρκους της Κεντρικής Ασίας, από τις Επιγραφές του Kül Tegin», *Ιστορικογεωγραφικά*, Τ. 10, (2004), p. 437.

[16] Theophanis Confessor, p. 239.

[17] Some scholars explain that the Pahlavi sources distinguish between Hephthalites in White (sped) Xyons and Red (karmir) Xyons = Kermichions, but, as Sinor points out the "Xyons" have to be identified with the Chionites, who, in the middle of the 4th century, caused problems to Sapur II and in 359 laid siege at Amida-this time as Persian allies. Cf. Sinor, "The Establishment", p. 301; Macartney, "On the Greek Sources", p. 271; Sinor relates Ασκήλ (Askel) with the Turks, Sinor, "The Establishment", p. 302: "Askel is the original form of the name of the first tribe of the confederation called by the Chinese Nushih-pi. This was the westernmost tribal group of the Western Türks, and the name Askel (A-shi-chieh in Chinese transcription) was applied indifferently to the tribe or to its ruler." See also Sinor-Klyashtorny, "The Türk Empire", p. 332. He suggests that Theophanes mentions the Turks by the Persian appellation because the interpreters were Persians, Sinor, D., "Languages and Cultural Interaction along the Silk Roads", *Studies in Medieval Inner Asia*, Variorum, 1997, p. 8. But in another work of his he states that the delegation of 567 was the first Turkic delegation, Sinor. D., « Réfléxions sur la présence Turco-Mongole dans le monde Méditerranéen et Pontique à l'époque pré-Ottomane », *Studies in Medieval Inner Asia*, Variorum, 1997, p. 489. Macartney rules out the Turks, the Jouan-jouan and the Hephthalites believing that delegation was either sent by the Oghors or the Chionites, see Macartney, "On the Greek Sources", p. 272: "The ambiguity, moreover, is probably less than we suppose. It will be noted that Theophanes describes the Kermichiones as the 'Turks, formerly called Massagetae', while Menander calls the Toue-Kioue 'Turks, formerly called Sakae'. The distinction is probably deliberate, and affords at the same time a valuable clue to the positions of the two nations. The Kermichiones lived in the homes of the old Massagetae, viz. on the Jaxartes and the Aral; the Toue Kioue further east, in the homes of the old Sacae". Cf. Parker, "The Origin", p. 439; Vernadsky, *Ancient Russia*, p. 182; Καρδαράς, *Βυζάντιο-Άβαροι*, p. 30-31.

[18] Theophanis Byzantius, p. 270. Haussig, "Theophylacts", p. 335. Baldwin, Menander, p 109. Chavannes is probably incorrect when he suggests as follows: "En premier lieu, il ne signifie pas que les Massagètes et les Turcs sont un seul et même peuple; il veut dire seulement que les Massagètes et les Turcs ont occupé successivement la même région".

[19] Priscus, p. 104.

[20] Distant-relative to the geographical knowledge of that era. This was not more than that of Strabo, who believed that the Earth was surrounded by the ocean and thought that the Asian continent did not extend far beyond the heights of India. Ptolemy (2nd century BCE), though, had knowledge of countries far more to the east, including China. Consequently, a large part of eastern Asia as well as Siberia were unknown and it was believed that the ocean began only slightly beyond the areas that were conquered by Alexander the Great. The ignorance of the ocean was such that, as Priscus mentions, it was believed that the peoples who lived near it were forced to leave, pressing in their path the Avars, due to poisonous vapours, which caused diseases. Concerning the belief in the existence of the ocean, see Κοσμάς Ινδικοπλεύστης, T. I, p. 333.

[21] The reason for that breach was the Byzantino-Avar treaty of 574, resulting in the payment of tribute to the Avars on the Byzantine part and in a ceasefire. Cf. Menander Protector, pp. 150, 216; Καρδαράς, *Βυζάντιο-Άβαροι*, pp. 40. Moreover there was also a Byzantine-Avar alliance, in 578, against the Slavs. Cf. Menander Protector, p. 192; Καρδαράς, *Βυζάντιο-Άβαροι*, pp. 39, 44-46. Another fact that has to be taken into account is that the Turks had managed to unify the whole steppe corridor under their political power and so there was a clash with the Byzantines who had a strong presence on the western edge of that corridor through their Crimean possessions; cf. Beckwith, *Empires of the Silk Road*, p. 117: "Between 567/571 the Western Turks took control of the North Caucasus Steppe, and in 576, the Western Steppe. Both regions apparently had already been populated at least partly by Turkic peoples, but now the Turks ruled over the entire Central Eurasian steppe zone. This was the second time in history that it had come under the control of a single ethno-linguistic group, though this time the unification was achieved by single family or dynasty. They were the political successors of the Avars, and before them the Hsiung-nu, but they far surpassed their predecessors". Having no real enemies, both in the West and East, the Turks were trying to assert control of the whole steppe route. This changed after the unification of China under the Sui dynasty and the subsequent pressure China exerted on the Eastern parts of the Turkic khanate. This fact made the Turks reconsider their policy towards the Byzantines and become more conciliatory in matters concerning the Avars and the Pontic Steppe, cf. Chavannes, *Documents*, p. 260.

[22] Καρδαράς, *Βυζάντιο-Άβαροι*, p. 48. Menander Protector, p. 222.

[23] Menander Protector, pp. 223-224.

[24] Browning, R., «Ο Αιώνας του Ιουστινιανού», Ιστορία Ελληνικού Έθνους, Τ. 7, p. 213. (There was also a failed attempt, on the Byzantine part, to engage the Lombards against the Avars). Cf. Καρδαράς, *Βυζάντιο-Άβαροι*, pp. 50, 51.

[25] Καρδαράς, *Βυζάντιο-Άβαροι*, p. 52.

[26] See the information taken from John of Ephesus in Καρδαράς, *Βυζάντιο-Άβαροι*, p. 53.

[27] Κραλίδης, Α., *Οι Χάζαροι και το Βυζάντιο. Ιστορική και Θρησκειολογική Προσέγγιση*, Σαββάλας, Αθήνα, 2003, p. 17, mentions that Khazar independence from the Turks came after 650 (i.e. when the Chinese advanced and subjugated the Western Turks). Dunlop, D., M., *The History of the Jewish Khazars*, Princeton, N. Jersey, 1954, p. 31.

[28] Chavannes, *Documents*, p. 171: « A la fin de (la dynastie) *Soei* (581-618), *Che-hou* (jabgou) kagan des *Tou-kiue* occidentaux, châtia et ruina ce royaume ; il tua le roi *K'ou-sa-ho* (Khosroû). Son fils, *Che-li* (Schîrôë), monta sur la trône. *Che-hou* envoya des gouverneurs le surveiller et le diriger. A la mort de *Che-li* (Schîrôë), (les Persans) ne voulurent plus se reconnaître sujets (des *Tou-kiue*) ; ils mirent sur le trône et proclamèrent reine la fille de *K'ou-sa-ho* (Khosroû). Les *Tou-kiue* la tuèrent elle aussi. *Tan-kie*, fils de *Che-li* (Schîrôë), se trouvait alors dans (le pays de) *Fou-lin* (Syrie) où il s'était réfugié ; les gens du royaume (de Perse) allèrent l'y

chercher et le mirent sur le trône ; ce fut *I-ta-tche* (Ardeshîr). A sa mort, *I-se-se* (Yezdegerd) prit le pouvoir ».

[29] In *Tabari*'s chronicle, *Tabari*, pp. 346. Seroes (7 months reign), Ardeschir (18 months reign), Sharbaraz (40 days reign), Pourândokht (Khusraw's daughter who also handed over the Holy Cross), Azermîdokht, another of Khusraw's daughters, together with Kesra, Khorzâd-Khosrau, Fîrouz, son of Mihrân, Ferroukhzâd-Khosrau (all of them either murdered or dethroned) and finally Yesdedjerd, are mentioned.

[30] Chavannes, *Documents*, p. 52.

[31] Chavannes, *Documents*, p. 171, n.1.

[32] Grousset, *L'Empire*, p. 140.

[33] Zuckerman, C., "Khazary I Vizantija: pervye kontakty. Materaly po Arkheologii, istorii i etnograffii", (Summary in English), *Proceedings of the International Colloquium on the Khazars (Jerusalem, 2001)*, p. 333: *The Khazars and Byzantium. The first encounter*, Tavrii (Simferopol), 8 (2001), pp. 312, 333: "A new analysis of the sources used by Moyses supports the identification of Heraclius' allies as Turks and eliminates the Khazars from the picture. A re-examination of another contemporary source, the Armenian Geography, suggests that the Khazars did not come anywhere close to the Caspian before the 660s-670s. What is more, the country of Barsilia from which the Khazars emerged on the way to their first conquests, is shown to be located not in the interfluvium of Sulakand Terek, where it is most often situated by scholars, but about 1000 km. to the north, on the Volga, in the region of the Samara Elbow."

[34] Theophanis Confessor, p. 814. One cannot tell if these Indians (*Ινδοί*) were of India or of the Red Sea, though the second seems more likely.

[35] Theophylacti Simocattae, p. 260, calculates their number at 10000 persons.

[36] Гумилев, *Тюрки*, p. 202: «Для западнотюркютских ханов оставились неразрешенными две внешнеполитические проблемы: нужно было покорить аваров и пробить сквозь Иран дорогу для караванов с шелком. Собственных сил им для этого не хватало, но их естественным союзником в обоих случаях была Византия, которую в это время громили персы». Also in Гумилев, *Тюрки*, p. 204: «Таким образом, Западнотюркютский каганат втянулся в борьбу Византии и Ирана, продалжая вместе с тем дружественные отношения с Китаем и, следовательно, враждебные с Восточнотюркютским каганатом. Цепь вражды замкнулась; создались две грандиозные коалиции: с одной стороны, Китай, Западнотюркютский каганат и Византийская империя, а с другой- Восточнотюркютский каганат, Иран и держава аваров».

[37] Гумилев, *Тюрки*, p. 204: «Возникает вопрос: были ли эти коалиции действительно плодом дипломатических переговоров или здесь имеют место военные выступления государств, просто совпадающие во времени? Подобно ситуации 589 г., тут наблюдается определенная связь между всеми членами обеих коалиций. Персы и авары были связаны военным союзом. Византия заключила союзный договор с наместником Западнотюркютского хана. Союз Западнотюркютских ханов

Шегуя и Тун-джабгу с Китаем, сначала Суйским, а после Танским, официально зафиксирован в китайских хрониках. Остается открытым вопрос о связи Византии с Китаем и Ирана с Восточными тюркютами. Документов, удостоверяющих такую связь, нет, но это reductio ad silentium, в логике недопустимое. Иран сносился с Дальним Востоком и до этого и после. По этому гораздо правдоподобнее предположить наличие дипломатических связей между Восточнотюркютским каганатом и Ираном в 20-е годы VII в., чем их отсутствие. К сожалению, арабское завоевание уничтожило сасанидские архивы, а китайцы могли не знать о секретной дипломатии их врагов.

Что же касается связь между Византией и Китаем, то только ее наличие объясняет сепаратный мир Ираклия с наследником Хосроя Парвиза, Кавадом Широе,-мир, странным образом совпадающий с последней активизацией восточных тюркютов. В сдучае успеха восточные тюркюти ударили бы на западных и лишили бы Ираклия единственного союзника в борьбе с Ираном. Вместе с тем победоносные действия западных тюркютов в Азербайджане были известны китайцам. Вероятно, согдийские купцы, постоянно передвигавшиеся между Востоком и Западом, своевременно оповещали своих союзников о всех перипетиях войны».

[38] Hirth, F., *China and the Roman Orient. Researches into their Ancient and Medieval Relations as Represented in Old Chinese records*, Leipzig, Munich, Shanghai, Hong-Kong, 1885, p. 55. Chen, Μελέτη, p. 71.

[39] Κορδώσης, «Η Κίνα των T'ang», p. 46.

Abbreviations-Bibliography

	Aalto, Penti, "Iranian Contacts of the Turks in Pre-Islamic Times", *Studia Turcica*, Budapest, 1971, pp. 29-37.
Baldwin, "Menander"	Baldwin, B., "Menander Protector", *Dumbarton Oaks Papers*, T. 32 (1978) pp. 99+101-125.
	Бартольд В. В., «Хазары», *Работы по Историй и Филологий Тюрских и Монголских Народов*, Москва, «Восточная Литература», 2002, pp. 597-601.
Beckwith, *Empires of the Silk Road*	Beckwith, C. I., *Empires of the Silk Road. A History of Central Eurasia from the Bronze Age to the Present*, Princeton University Press, Princeton, 2009.
	Browning, R., «Ο Αιώνας του Ιουστινιανού», Ιστορία Ελληνικού Έθνους, Τ. 7, pp. 150-221.
	Bury, J. B., *A History of the Later Roman Empire from Arcadius to Irene (395 A.D. to 800 A.D.)*, T. I, II, London, 1889, Adolf M. Hakkert, (reprint Amsterdam, 1966).
	Bury J. B., "The Turks in the 6th century", *EHR*, T. 12, N°. 47 (1897), pp. 417-426.
Cahun, *Asie*	Cahun, L., *L'histoire de l'Asie. Turcs et Mongoles des Origines à 1405*, Paris, 1896.
Chavannes, *Documents*	Chavannes E., *Document sur les Tou-Kiue (Turcs) occidentaux, recueillis et commentés, suivis des notes additionelles*, Paris, 1900 (réédition. 1969).
Chen, Μελέτη	Chen, Z.-Q., *Μελέτη της ιστορίας των βυζαντινο-λινεζικών σχέσεων (4ος-15ος αιώνας)*, PhD uned., 1994.
	Christensen, A., *L'Iran sous les Sassanides*, (xerography of the 2nd edition), Otto Zeller, Osnabrück, 1971.
	Christian, D., *A History of Russia, Central Asia and Mongolia*, τόμ. 1, *Inner Eurasia from Prehistory to the Mongol Empire*, Blackwell, Oxford, 1998.
Κοσμάς Ινδικοπλεύστης	Cosmas Indicopleustes, Topographie Chrétienne, ed. W. Wolska-Conus, T. I-III, Paris, 1968-1973 (Sources Chrétiennes, N° 141, 152, 197).
	Dickens, M., *Medieval Syriac Historians' Perceptions of the Turks*, M. Phil Dissertation in Aramaic and Syriac Studies, Faculty of Oriental Studies, University of Cambridge, August 2004.
	Dunlop, D., M., *The History of the Jewish Khazars*, Princeton, N. Jersey, 1954.

EHR	*English Historical Review.*
FHG	*Fragmenta Historicorum Graecorum.*
	Golden, P., *An Introduction to the History of the Turkish Peoples: Ethnogenesis and State-Formation in Medieval and Early Modern Eurasia and Middle East (Turcologia)*, Wiesbaden, 1992.
	Golden, P., *Khazar Studies: A Historico-philological Inquiry into the Origins of the Khazars (Bibliotheca Orientalis Hungarica)*, Akadémiai Kiadó, Budapest, 1980.
Golden, "The Turkic Peoples"	Golden, P., "The Turkic Peoples and Caucasia", *Nomads*, pp. 45-64.
Grousset, *L'Empire*	Grousset, R., *L'Empire des Steppes. Attila, Genghis-Khan, Tamerlan*, Payot, Paris, 1970.
Гумилев, *Тюрки*	Гумилев, Л. Н., *Древние Тюрки*, НАУКА, Москва, 1967.
Haussig, "Theophylakts"	Haussig, H. W., "Theophylakts Exkurs über die Skythischen Völker", *Byzantion* 23 (1953), pp. 275-462.
	Hirth, F., *China and the Roman Orient. Researches into their Ancient and Medieval Relations as Represented in Old Chinese records*, Leipsig, Munich, Shanghai Hong Kong, 1885.
John of Ephesus	Payne, S., *The Third Part of the Ecclesiastical History of John Bishop of Ephesus*, Oxford, University Press, 1860.
Καρδαράς, *Βυζάντιο-Άβαροι*	Καρδαράς, Γ., *Το Βυζάντιο και οι Άβαροι, Στ΄-Θ΄ αι.*, PhD dissertation, Ιωάννινα, 2007.
	Κορδώσης, Σ., «Οι Πρεσβείες των Βυζαντινών και Ασιατών στους Τούρκους της Κεντρικής Ασίας, από τις Επιγραφές του Kül Tegin», *Ιστορικογεωγραφικά*, Τ. 10, (2004), pp. 435-444.
	Κραλίδης, Α., *Οι Χάζαροι και το Βυζάντιο. Ιστορική και Θρησκειολογική Προσέγγιση*, Σαββάλας, Αθήνα, 2003.
Macartney, "On the Greek Sources"	Macartney, C. A., "On the Greek Sources for the History of the Turks in the Sixth Century", *Bulletin of the School of Oriental and African Studies*, T. 11, No. 2 (1944), pp. 266-275.

Menander Protector	Blockley, R., *The history of Menander the Guardsman*. Introductory Essay, Text, Translation and Historiographical Notes, Francis Cairns Ltd., Liverpool, 1985.
Moravscik, *Byzantinoturcica*	Moravcsik, G., *Byzantino Turcica*, 2nd edition, Berlin, T. I-II, 1958 (reprint Leiden 1983).
Nomads	*Nomads and their Neighbours in the Russian Steppe: Turks, Khazars and Qipchaqs (Variorum Collected Studies)*, Variorum, 2003.
Parker, "The Origin"	Parker, E. H., "The Origin of the Turks", *EHR*, 11 (1896), pp. 431-441.
	Пигулевская Н. В., *Византия на путях в Индию*, Москва-Ленинград, 1951.
	Пигулевская Н. В., «Византийская Дипломатия и Торговля Шелком в V-VII вв.», *Византийскии Временик*, Т. I (XXVI), Москва, 1947, pp. 184-214.
Priscus	Πρίσκος, Ιστορία Βυζαντιακή, *FHG* IV, pp. 71-110.
Sinor, *Inner Asia*	Sinor, D., *Inner Asia and its Contacts with Medieval Europe*, Variorum, London, 1977.
	Sinor, D., "Languages and Cultural Interaction along the Silk Roads", *Studies in Medieval Inner Asia*, Variorum, 1997.
	Sinor. D., « Réfléxions sur la présence Turco-Mongole dans le monde Méditerranéen et Pontique à l'époque pré-Ottomane », *Studies in Medieval Inner Asia*, Variorum, 1997, pp. 485-501.
Sinor, "The Establishment"	Sinor, D., "The Establishment and Disolution of the Türk Empire", *The Cambridge History of Early Inner Asia*, Cambridge University Press, 1990, pp. 285-316.
	Sinor, D., "The Historical Role of the Turk Empire", Sinor, *Inner Asia*, pp. 427-434.
Sinor-Klyashtorny, "The Türk Empire"	Sinor, D.-Klyashtorny, S. G., "The Türk Empire", *History*, pp. 327-347.

Tabari	*Chronique de Abou-djafar-Mo'hammed-Ben-Djarir-Ben-Yezid Tabari*, trad. Par M. Hermann Wotenberg, T. 2me, Editions d'art les heures claires-Maisonneuve et Larose, Paris, 1977.
	Talât, T., *A Grammar of Orkhon Turkic*, Indiana University, 1968.
	The Cambridge History of Iran, T. 3, Cambridge University Press, 1983 (re-edition.1996).
Theophanis Confessor	Theophanis, Chronographia, εκδ. Βόννης [and C. de Boor, I, Leipzig, 1883].
Theophanis Byzantius	Theophanis Byzantius: *Fragmenta*, FHG, IV, pp. 270-271.
Theophylacti Simocattae	Theophylacti Simocattae: *Historia*, ed. C. de Boor-P. Wirth, Stutgardiae, 1972.
Vailhé, "Projet"	Vailhé S., "Projet d'Alliance Turco-Byzantine au VIe Siécle", *Echos d' orient*, 12 (1909), pp. 204-214.
Vaissière, *Histoire*	Vaissière (de la) E., *Histoire des Marchands Sogdiens*, Bibliothêque de l' Institut des Hautes Études Chinois, Paris, 2002.
Vernadsky, *Ancient Russia*	Vernadsky G. V., *Ancient Russia*, New Haven, 1952.
	Ζακυθηνού, Δ., *Βυζαντινή Ιστορία 324-1071*, εν Αθήνας, 1972 ζ1977 (reprint. 1989).
Zhang, *H Κίνα*	Zhang, Xu-shan, *Η Κίνα και το Βυζάντιο. Σχέσεις-εμπόριο-αμοιβαίες γνώσεις, από τις αρχές του 6^ου ώς τα μέσα του 7^ου αιώνα*, Αθήνα, 1998 [reprint from *Ιστορικογεωγραφικά*, T. 6 (1996-97), pp. 155-343].
	Zhang, Xu-shan, "The Northern Silk Route and its western terminus in the Balkans", *Ιστορική Γεωγραφία. Δρόμοι και Κόμβοι της Βαλκανικής από την αρχαιότητα στην ενιαία Ευρώπη*, Συνέδριο Ιστορικής Γεωγραφίας, Thessaloniki, 1997, pp. 125-132.
	Zuckerman, C., "Khazary I Vizantija: pervye kontakty. Materaly po Arkheologii, istorii i etnograffii", ("The Khazars and Byzantium. The first encounter", Summary in English), *Proceedings of the International Colloquium on the Khazars (Jerusalem, 2001)*, σελ. 333: Tavrii (Simferopol), 8 (2001), pp 312-333.

漢籍所見拜占庭帝國地理、歷史與傳說

張緒山

在漢唐史冊中，羅馬帝國被稱為"大秦"，由羅馬帝國分裂而來的拜占庭帝國（即東羅馬帝國）被稱作"拂菻"。"拂菻"一名乃"羅馬"（Rum）一詞經中介語言如亞美尼亞語、波斯語（帕列維語、花拉子密語和粟特語）進入漢文典籍後的譯名。[1]在南北朝時代的漢籍中，"大秦"與"拂菻"有時混用，均表示拜占庭帝國；在隋唐時代的漢籍中，"拂菻"幾乎成為拜占庭帝國的唯一名稱，與拜占庭帝國相關的事物大多見於"拂菻"名稱之下。本文主要以漢籍史料為憑藉，勾勒南北朝末年及隋唐時期中國人所瞭解的拜占庭帝國地理、歷史與傳說。

一、漢籍所記拜占庭帝國地理與歷史

北魏末年（即西元六世紀初），漢末以來延續幾個世紀的分裂狀態雖未結束，但中國北部逐漸向統一政權發展，勢力有所增強；與此同時，拜占庭帝國經四世紀上半葉以來的嬗變，進入重新振興的黃金時代。這一時期的拜占庭帝國東部領土在規模上毫不遜色于鼎盛時期的羅馬帝國，其與東方的聯繫更是超邁前者，其表現之一是與中國北方的民間商貿交往。楊衒之《洛陽伽藍記》卷三記六世紀上半葉東都洛陽西域人雜居的情形：

> 永橋以南，圜丘以北，伊、洛之間，夾御道，東有四夷館，一曰金陵，二曰燕然，三曰扶桑，四曰崦嵫。道西有四夷里，一曰歸正，二曰歸德，三曰慕化，四曰慕義……西夷來附者，處之崦嵫館，賜宅慕義里。自蔥嶺以西，至於大秦，百國千城，莫不款附。商胡販客，日奔塞下，所謂盡天地之區矣。樂中國土風，因而宅者，不可勝數。是以附化之民，萬有餘家。……天下難得之貨，咸悉在焉。

商業交流之外，宗教交流也活躍起來，同書卷四又記載：

永明寺，宣武皇帝所立也，在大覺寺東，時佛法經像，盛於洛陽，異國沙門，咸來輻輳……百國沙門三千餘人。西域遠者乃至大秦國，盡天地之西陲。

來自大秦國的沙門當然不是佛教徒。這段記載使我們聯想到景教向東方的傳播。以明代出土的《大秦景教流行中國碑》，景教徒進入西安，受到隆重接待是在貞觀九年即西元635年，但它的勢力是否在六世紀初已經零星地滲透到中國境內，是值得注意的。[2] 不過，以此等晦暗曖昧的記載，我們還不能得出十分確切的斷論。

從六世紀下半葉到七世紀上半葉，歐亞大陸的交流因西突厥的崛起而呈現繁榮局面。《新唐書·西域傳》記昭武諸國之一何國的情況："何（國）或曰屈霜你迦，曰貴霜匿，即康居小王附墨城故地。城左有重樓，北繪中華古帝，東突厥、婆羅門、西波斯、拂菻等諸王。"[3] 婆羅門指印度、拂菻即拜占庭帝國、波斯即薩珊王朝統治下的波斯帝國。屈霜你迦在撒馬爾罕附近，其建築體上描繪四方國王形象，說明突厥主導下的中亞地區與周邊主要文明的交往已相當頻繁與密切。西突厥與拜占庭帝國及中國北方各政權（東魏、西魏，北齊、北周）的密切聯繫，成為中國獲取拜占庭帝國知識的重要管道。

589年，隋王朝一統江山，漢末以來數世紀的戰亂結束，域內至此再告安定。隋煬帝好大喜功，經營西域之心膨脹。當時西域商人多到張掖經商，隋煬帝的大臣裴矩秉承煬帝旨意，誘使他們述說其國山川地理及通達路線，寫成《西域圖記》三卷上奏。《隋書》卷六七《裴矩傳》：

煬帝即位……時西域諸蕃，多至張掖，與中國交市。帝令矩掌其事。矩知帝方勤遠略，諸商胡至者，矩誘令言其國俗山川險易，撰《西域圖記》三卷，入朝奏之。其序曰：……發自敦煌，至於西海，凡為三道，各有襟帶。北道從伊吾經蒲類海、鐵勒部、突厥可汗庭，度北流河水、至拂菻國，達於西海。其中道從高昌、焉耆、龜茲、疏勒，度葱嶺，又經鏺汗、蘇對沙那國、康國、曹國、何國、大小安國、穆國，至波斯，達于西海。其南道從鄯善、于闐、朱俱波、喝槃陀，度葱嶺，又經護密、吐火羅、挹怛、帆延、漕國，至北婆羅門，達于西海。其三道諸國，亦各自有路，南北交通。其東女國、南婆羅門國等，並隨其所往，諸處得達。故知伊吾、高昌、鄯善，並西域之門戶也，總湊敦煌，是其咽喉之地。

中西交通的三道中，南道經塔里木盆地南緣，越葱嶺，至阿富汗北部後南下，沿印度河至印度河口和印度西海岸；中道沿塔里木盆地北緣，越葱嶺西去，經伊朗高原到達地中海東岸；北道為"從伊吾，經蒲類海、鐵勒部、突厥可汗庭，度北流河水，至拂菻國，達于西海"。"北流河水"即錫爾河。這條道路的走向是，從伊吾翻越天山，出蒲類海（即巴里坤湖），沿天山北路西行，過突厥可汗庭，伊犁河，沿錫爾河（"北流河水"）繞鹹海北岸西行，經里海之北跨烏拉爾河和伏爾加河，到達黑海（"西海"）。

白鳥庫吉認為，《隋書·裴矩傳》記載從錫爾河以至拂菻國的歷程甚為簡略，是因為裴矩所獲得的有關這段行程的知識不多，此時中國人對錫爾河以遠地區不甚了了。[4] 白鳥此論未中鵠的。比較三道之記載，對中道穆國至西海之間的波斯全境，南道曹國至西海之間的北婆羅門（印度），著筆亦甚少。其原因在於，從略敘述的這三段路程，均為一族或處於統一的政權控制之下。六世紀末，錫爾河以西至黑海沿岸處於西突厥政權之下，故裴矩不將其治下各族詳細記述。可以說明這一點的，是《隋書》卷八四《鐵勒傳》對拜占庭帝國以東各民族的地理位置的準確記載：

拂菻東有恩屈，阿蘭，北褥九離，伏嗢昏等。

揆諸西史，恩屈即 Ongur（Ogur, Ugur），又作 Oγor，南北朝末期及隋代居於里海與黑海之間、伏爾加河下游流域以西地帶；阿蘭即 Alans，居於高加索山脈之北，里海西北部，其北鄰即恩屈；北褥九離即 Baskirs，居於烏拉爾河上游至卡馬河流域之間；伏嗢昏即 Bulgars，散佈於伏爾加河中游流域至卡馬河下游流域之間。[5] 可見，由於歐亞草原之路即裴矩所記北道的暢通，自鹹海經烏拉爾河至黑海各族以至拂菻國的地理位置，都進入了中國人的知識。

隋朝國運雖然短促，但對西域的準確認識超越以往。《舊唐書》卷二二一《西域傳·天竺國》："隋煬帝時，遣裴矩通西域諸國，獨天竺拂菻不至，為恨。"隋煬帝欲通使拜占庭，與中原對於拂菻國知識的增多大有關係。這種知識上的增長得益于突厥崛起於中亞地區後東西交流的加強。裴矩在敦煌的經營由此而奏大功。《隋書·裴矩傳》載，裴矩"訪採胡人，或有所疑，即詳眾口，依其本國服飾儀形，王及庶人，各顯容止，即丹青模寫，為〈西域圖記〉，共成三卷，合四十四國，仍別造地圖，窮其要害。從西傾以去，北海之南，縱橫所亙，將二萬里。諒由富商大賈，周遊經涉，故諸國之事罔不徧知"。可知《西域圖記》配有圖像。裴孝源《貞觀公私畫史》載，隋大臣楊素藏有拂菻人物器樣兩卷，此"拂菻人物器樣"畫像很可能是當時丹青妙手依照到達敦煌的東羅馬人儀形所作，或依裴矩所存圖像重繪。楊素為隋文帝創基功臣，並于文帝死後擁立楊廣踐祚，位高權重，有可能得此寶物。

唐太宗貞觀元年（627），著名僧人玄奘（600—664）動身往印度求法巡禮，遍游印度，歷時十七年。玄奘遊歷印度之時，正是阿拉伯崛起于西亞的初期。玄奘對於未履之地著墨甚少，對於拜占庭帝國只留下簡短的文字："波剌斯國西北接拂懍國，境壤風俗同波剌斯，形貌語言，稍有乖異。多珍寶，亦富饒也。"同時還記載了與拂菻國有關的"西女國"的傳說。[6]《大慈恩寺三藏法師傳》卷四記載大略相同："（波剌斯）國東境有鶴秣城，西北接拂懍國。"也是從地理方位角度提供拜占庭帝國（拂懍國）的消息。

七世紀三四十年代，歐亞大陸政治形勢驟然改變。在西亞方面，阿拉伯伊斯蘭勢力興起，迅速奪取拜占庭帝國在地中海東部和北非的領土，征服薩珊波斯，迫使抵抗失敗的薩珊波斯王廷及其大量波斯貴族向中國境內遷徙。同時，也使景教徒進入中國境內。景教徒是從拜占庭帝國的教會中分離出來，具有相當深厚的希臘—拜占庭社會知識背景，同時又長期活動于波斯境內，深染波斯色彩。景教傳入中國境內乃至中原地區的時間，以景教碑的記載，可推至貞觀九年（635），但這是景教徒進入長安、被官方正式承認的時間，景教入華的最初年限至少可推至六世紀前半葉。隨著對景教徒在中國的活動研究的深入，景教在傳播波斯和希臘—拜占庭文化中的作用更加清楚、明晰。[7]他們在中國境內的活動，增加了中國瞭解拜占庭帝國和波斯帝國相關知識的一個重要途徑。

《舊唐書》卷一九八記載阿拉伯的興起及其對拜占庭、波斯的征服：

> （隋）大業（605—617）中，有波斯胡人牧駝於俱紛摩地那之山，忽有獅子人語，謂之曰："此山西有三穴，穴中大有兵器，汝可取之。穴中並有黑石白文，讀之便作王位。"胡人依言，果見穴中有石及稍刃甚多，上有文，教其反叛。於是糾合亡命，渡恒曷水，劫奪商旅，其眾漸盛，遂割波斯西境，自立為王。波斯、拂菻各遣兵討之，皆為所敗。

此中知識不盡準確，所謂"波斯胡人"乃指先知穆罕默德；摩地那即 Medina，現通譯為"麥迪那"。摩地那山聞聽"獅子人語"的傳奇，乃由穆罕默德清修故事演化而來：傳說穆罕默德在四十歲時（610）離家到麥加東北的希拉山的洞穴隱修，據說他在冥思中聽得安拉命其以真主名義傳道的啟示，遂開始傳播宗教教義。由於受到麥加貴族的迫害，622年9月20日夜穆罕默德帶領其忠實信徒出走麥加，前往雅特里布，建立一個政教合一的國家。雅特里布改稱"麥迪那"，意為先知之城。在穆罕默德領導下，阿拉伯半島開始了統一的過程，這就是所謂"反叛"的含義。恒曷水可能是"達曷水"之誤，指底格里斯河（Tigris）。所謂"糾合亡命，渡恒曷水，劫奪商旅，其眾漸盛，遂割波斯西境，自立為王"，實際上說的是阿拉伯人在西亞崛起的過程；而所謂"波斯、拂菻各遣兵討之，皆為所敗"云云，則是指阿拉伯人對波斯、拂菻的戰爭：第二任哈里發奧默爾（634—644）時期，阿拉伯人的擴張大規模展開，638年8月於約旦河支流雅姆克河畔取得對拜占庭軍隊的決定性勝利，乘勢進取大馬士革、安條克、阿勒頗等，638年攻取耶路撒冷，旋即佔領巴勒斯坦全土。在波斯境內，636年阿拉伯軍隊在卡迭西亞擊潰波斯軍隊主力，次年佔領其首都泰西封，642年在尼哈溫徹底粉碎波斯的抵抗，波斯薩珊帝國覆亡。中國史書將哈里發時代的戰事一併歸於穆罕默德名下，或是史書作者在史料處理上的錯誤，但更有可能是消息提供者本身敘事混亂的結果。張星烺認為"此數語乃罝人之語，必非彼教中人所語，乃波斯人之口吻也"[8]，是很有道理的見解。

中國人獲悉新興起的阿拉伯與拜占庭帝國及波斯關係的消息，除了取諸波斯人之外，也取自拂菻國到達中土的使節。拜占庭使節帶來的也是與大食（阿拉伯）有關的消息。《舊唐書·拂菻傳》：

> 貞觀十七年（643）拂菻王波多力遣使獻赤玻璃、綠金精等物。太宗降璽書答慰，賜以綾綺焉。自大食強盛，漸陵諸國，乃遣大將軍摩栧伐其都，因約為和好，請每歲輸之金帛，遂臣屬大食焉。

這段史料所涉及的是，638年阿拉伯軍隊圍攻安條克，以及隨後完成的對敘利亞的征服。"波多力"一名不是哪位皇帝的名字，而是當時拜占庭帝國著名的皇帝希拉克略（Heraclius, 610—641）新啟用的稱號 βασιλεύς（拉丁文作 basileus）的譯音。在拜占庭帝國初期，這個稱號雖長期非正式地用作拜占庭皇帝的稱號，但作為正式稱號卻是由希拉克略於629年採用的；此前這個稱謂的意義相對低微，經希拉克略正式採用後，變成與 Imperator 即 "皇帝" 意義相同的稱號。貞觀十七年（643）的遣使，可能是希拉克略本人在641年2月死前不久所策劃，後由其他人實施。到達唐帝國朝廷的拜占庭使節，與主持外國事務的唐朝官員交涉時，可能多次提到 "吾皇陛下如何如何"，以強調這次外交行動的重要性，希望以此打動中國皇帝下定決心，與拜占庭帝國聯盟，共同抗擊新興阿拉伯勢力的攻擊，致使 βασιλεύς 一詞以 "波多力" 的譯音深印於中國史官的腦海，作為拂菻王的名稱保留下來。[9] 這是彌足珍貴的外交史材料，不獨對於拜占庭與中國的交往具有重要意義，[10] 而且對於阿拉伯初期的對外擴張以及與拜占庭帝國的關係史，亦具有重要價值。

唐代中國人還獲得了有關拜占庭宮廷習俗的消息。《舊唐書·拂菻傳》：

其王冠形如鳥舉翼，冠及瓔珞，皆綴以珠寶，著錦繡衣，前不開襟，坐金花床。有一鳥似鵝，其毛綠色，常在王邊倚枕上坐，每進食有毒，其鳥輒鳴。

有學者認為這些資訊來源於中國人對粟特人仿製的拜占庭金幣上皇帝圖像的觀察，其理由是："這段記載不見於前朝史書，唐代曾經到達西亞的中國人首推杜環，他的《經行紀》來自耳聞目睹，但是其中沒有任何拂菻王裝束的記載。另一方面，這段記載也不可能來自拜占庭人……粟特人製造的拜占庭金幣仿製品上的皇帝像同這段描述頗為接近，因為頭盔上方飾有羽毛，盔下的皇冠上連珠紋表現的是珠寶，皇冠兩側又有珠串垂下，因此，在不瞭解這些頭飾的內在結構的人看來，金幣仿製品上的羅馬皇帝胸像的確是 '王冠形如鳥舉翼，冠及瓔珞，皆綴以珠寶'。"[11] 如果說有關皇冠的資訊可以從粟特人的拜占庭金幣仿製品圖像上可以獲得，皇帝的衣著服飾可以想像的話，那麼，關於皇帝宮中習俗的敘述，則顯然不可能來自粟特人製造的錢幣仿製品上的圖像，而只能來自其他管道。

《舊唐書·拂菻傳》記載拂菻國王宮中養鳥事："有一鳥似鵝，其毛綠色，常在王邊倚枕上坐，每進食有毒，其鳥輒鳴。"由於不相信中國史料對異域事物記載的真實性，白鳥庫吉認為，關於鳥的這段故事也如同《舊唐書》中的其他事物一樣，是唐代中國人根據中國存在的事物杜撰出來的。在唐代，從宮廷到民間都盛行養鸚鵡。《明皇雜錄》記載楊貴妃養有一隻鸚鵡。《太平廣記》中收錄幾則鸚鵡故事。尤其是唐代王仁裕的《開元天寶遺事》中有鸚鵡助人破案故事：長安富戶楊崇義之妻與鄰居之子有情事，楊被此二人所害，屍體投入井中。官吏久不能破案，待查訪死者宅院時，鸚鵡說出兇手，卒使案情告破。玄宗皇帝聽說此事，名鸚鵡為 "綠衣大使"。鸚鵡破案故事，在中世紀的波斯、阿拉伯和印度廣為流傳。白鳥博引典例，證明早在西元前四世紀下半葉的印度孔雀王朝時期，就有識毒鳥的說法，這種說法一直流傳，而且喜馬拉雅山西部確有一種與毒蛇為敵的鳥，其體大如鵝。唐人相信"鵝不獨能警盜，亦能卻蛇。其糞蓋殺蛇。蜀人園池養鵝，蛇即遠去。"(《古今圖書集成》卷三七《鵝部》) 白鳥的結論是，《舊唐書·拂菻傳》中的這則記載："肯定是由唐代華人熟悉的寵物鸚鵡的故事與起源於印度而廣泛流傳於中亞的所謂識毒鳥故事加工而來，它不是基於東羅馬帝國的真實事實。"[12]

這段記載確有不確之處，但白鳥全盤否認這段記載中包含的史料價值，是沒有道理的。這裏需要弄清楚兩個問題：一是拜占庭皇帝身邊是否有"鳥"存在？二是如果有，這種資訊通過何種途徑傳入中國？

根據拜占庭帝國歷史，我們看到，拜占庭宮廷中確有與"鳥"有關的記載。我們知道，拜占庭帝國由於其地理位置而經常受到外族入侵的威脅，非常注意以外交手段化解面臨的危機，由此發展出一套行之有效的外交禮儀。其中最重要的環節之一是，極力渲染皇帝的威嚴，以豪華、宏大的帝國宮廷場面造成使節心靈的巨大震撼，坐收"不戰而屈人之兵"的功效。皇帝決定接見使節時，使節要有太監帶領，通過金碧輝煌的宮殿走廊，在兩邊威嚴的禁衛軍和衣著華麗的高官貴族前走向皇帝。皇帝端坐在寶座上一動不動，御座前擺著小樹，樹上的小鳥晃動翅膀，御座上也有小鳥（τά όρνεα τα έν τώ σένζω όμοίως τά έν τοίς δένδρεσι），使節走到一定位置時，小鳥們便發出唧唧喳喳的叫聲，兩旁的鍍金獅子翹著尾巴，以咆哮的姿態發出低沉的吼聲。[13]這種場面詳見於十世紀上半葉拜占庭皇帝君士坦丁七世（Constantine VII Porphyrogenitus, 905-959）授意編纂的《禮儀書》(De cerimoniis aulae Byzantinae libri duo, ii, 15)，[14]也為代表義大利國王兩次（948，966）出使君士坦丁堡的克里孟納主教留特普蘭（Liutprand, bishop of Cremona）的記述所證實。《禮儀書》收錄了此前拜占庭帝國接待外國使節的禮儀資料，從中既可以見到五世紀末帝國西部淪陷於蠻族之手後如何接待西部使者的規定，也可以見到547年接待波斯使者的儀式。查士丁尼一世（518—565）被公認為拜占庭帝國外交事業的奠基者，拜占庭帝國的後來的外交一直追隨查士丁尼的榜樣，可以說，皇帝接見外國使節的禮儀在這位皇帝統治時期基本形成。拜占庭皇帝宮中養"鳥"可謂歷史悠久，不是臆想出來的故事。

有關拜占庭宮廷鳥的故事，在唐代進入中國史書，顯然與唐代開拓西域，中西交流空前暢通有直接關係。中國史書所謂拜占庭宮廷之鳥"常在王邊倚枕上坐"，完全符合歷史實際；所不同的是它的"似鵝"的形狀及其辨識食物有無毒藥的功能，是拜占庭宮廷機械鳥所不具有的。識毒鳥與拜占庭宮廷聯繫起來，顯然並非如白鳥庫吉所說，只是出乎唐人的想像，而與此一時期拜占庭與中國的聯繫密切相關。這種訛誤的出現，說明這一資訊的來源並非拜占庭使節，其可能的傳播者，一是六世紀下半葉與拜占庭帝國保持密切外交往來的突厥—粟特人，突厥—粟特外交人員獲得的拜占庭宮廷消息經粟特商人轉輸後，為中國史官所獲得；二是在抗擊阿拉伯征服失敗而遁走中原的波斯人，這些人將外交人員獲得的拜占庭宮廷消息傳輸給中國史官。由於傳說過程中不可避免的加工，後人看到的是一個真假參半的傳說。

漢籍所載有關拜占庭帝國的史料也取自中國的旅外之人。這一時期為後世留下重要資料的旅行者有兩位：一是僧人慧超，一是杜環。八世紀上半葉阿拉伯勢力向印度和中亞的擴張進入一個高潮階段。710年，阿拉伯大將哈西姆率軍征服了馬克蘭後，繼續東進，711—712年征服信德，即印度河下游河谷和三角洲地區，713年征服地區北達旁遮普南部和木爾坦。[15] 與此同時，另一部阿拉伯軍隊由屈底波統率，兵鋒直指中亞地區，於705年征服吐火羅斯坦及其首府巴里黑，706—709年征服布哈拉及其周圍地區，710—712年征服撒馬爾罕和花喇子模，713—715年深入費爾幹納，建立政權。屈底波之後，奈斯爾被任命為河中地區的長官，于738—740年在中亞地區展開征服活動，751年擊敗高仙芝率領的唐朝軍隊，佔領撒馬爾罕東北的赭時（塔什幹），確立在中亞的霸權地位。[16] 慧超與杜環二人的記載見證了八世紀阿拉伯征服活動的高潮。

慧超是新羅人，大約於開元十一年（723）前往印度巡禮。《往五天竺國傳》是他在印度和中亞地區巡禮時所獲見聞的記錄。慧超印度巡禮之時，正是阿拉伯向印度和中亞的大規模征服活動結束不久，故所到之處能聽到與阿拉伯擴張有關的消息。727年他到達吐火羅國，記該地情況："又從此犯引[17]國，北行廿日，至吐火羅國，王住城名為縛底耶[18]。見今大寔兵馬，在彼鎮押。其王被（其王被）逼，走向東一月程，在蒲特山[19]住。見屬大寔所管。"《往五天竺國傳》所記見聞乃以旅行次第而為，慧超將"波斯國"、"大寔（食）國"和"大拂臨國"的消息，置於"吐火羅國"之後，中亞的"安、曹、史、石、米、康"等國之前，說明他是在吐火羅斯坦獲得未履其地的這三個國家的消息。也許正是大食（阿拉伯）人在此地的擴張活動引發了慧超的興趣，使慧超將獲聞的大食向波斯、拜占庭帝國這兩個主要鄰國擴張的歷史事實也一併記載下來。

在慧超的記錄中，拜占庭帝國以"拂臨"見稱。"拂臨"與"拂菻"乃一名異譯，由此一點我們即可斷言，慧超關於拜占庭帝國的知識來自中亞民眾，蓋拜占庭帝國以"拂菻"一名見於中國史籍，正是Rom一詞經由波斯、中亞語言轉變後的結果。[20] 慧超所記載拜占庭帝國的內容，也如同對於中亞各國記載，主要涉及它與阿拉伯的關係：[21]

> 從波斯國北行十日，入山，至大寔[22]國。彼王不住本國，見向小拂臨國住也。為打得彼國，彼國復居山島，處所極罕（牢），為此就彼……又小拂臨，傍海西北，即是大拂臨國。此王兵馬強多，不屬餘國。大寔數回討擊不得。突厥侵亦不得。土地足寶物，甚足駝、騾、羊、馬、疊布等物。衣著與波斯、大寔相似，言音各別不同。

慧超記載異乎其他記載之處，是他將拜占庭帝國區別為"小拂臨"和"大拂臨"。然而，對於"小拂臨"和"大拂臨"具體所指，學者尚有不同見解，原因是對於"彼王不住本國，見向小拂臨國住也。為打得彼國，彼國復居山島，處所極牢，為此就彼"一段的理解不同。夏德認為，大食王所不住的"本國"，乃是前期諸哈里發以麥迪那為都城的阿拉伯，現在居住的"小拂臨國"是倭馬亞王朝諸哈里發居住的以大馬士革為都城的敘利亞。所以他將"（諸王）為打得彼國，彼國復居山島，處所極牢，為此就彼"理解為："大食諸王由於已經征服那個國家，那個國家

— 319 —

已經撤退到（大陸）的山上和人所罕至的島嶼上"，他認為這段話的意思可能是指，拜占庭帝國被迫從敘利亞的亞洲領土撤退到了小亞細亞和歐洲。[23] 以夏德的見解，則"小拂臨"指敘利亞，而"大拂臨"則是拜占庭帝國仍然控制的小亞和歐洲領土。

白鳥庫吉認為，"為打得彼國"的意思是指阿拉伯軍隊對敘利亞的佔領，此處的"彼國"指"敘利亞"，但接下來的"彼國復居山島……"中的"彼國"是指大食；塞浦路斯此時是在阿拉伯穆斯林勢力範圍之內，但鑒於大食王從來沒有駐紮在那裏，文中的"山島"也許是指阿拉伯半島的麥迪那地區，"處所極罕（牢），為此就彼"中的"牢"是"窄"字之誤；此段文字的意思是，麥迪那地方狹窄，所以大食王長居於"小拂臨"。白鳥認為，慧超說"小拂臨，傍海西北，即是大拂臨國"，從敘利亞經由小亞細亞西北行可以到達君士坦丁堡，這裏的"大拂臨"顯然是指君士坦丁堡。這是中國史籍首次記載君士坦丁堡。[24]

《往五天竺國傳》箋釋者張毅認為，慧超書乃殘卷，如許多敦煌卷子一樣，存在許多敦煌俗字及不少錯字衍文，以往學者的校釋存在問題，如"為打得彼國，彼國復居山島，處所極罕（牢）"一句，第二個"彼國"乃衍文，"罕"為"牢"，該句實應校為："為打得彼國，復居山島，處所極牢。"理由是，"山是指大食人進攻拜占庭時的前進基地陶魯斯（Taurus）山而言。這一前哨線上堡壘林立，大食人稱內線堡壘為關隘（awa-sim），外線堡壘為要塞（thughur）。陶魯斯山的隘口更是有名的'西里西亞之門'。這些都是防衛堅固的軍事要塞，原卷所用'極牢'二字形容並未錯誤。但改為'窄'與'罕'均十分不妥，因為大食國王所處之地既非'極罕'，更非'極窄'，就是小拂臨（Al-rum，即小亞細亞）也非極狹小的地方。"張毅認為，慧超書中的"大拂臨"指東羅馬本部，小拂臨指小亞細亞。[25]

這一見解雖有合理之處，但難通之處在於：其一，將"小拂臨"釋為小亞細亞，"大拂臨"為東羅馬本部，則其前的"彼（大食）王不住本國，見向小拂臨國住也"一句如何理解？歷史上，阿拉伯的任何哈里發都未駐紮於小亞細亞，這種情況直到塞爾柱突厥人佔領小亞時才有改變；其二，將"為打得彼國，彼國復居山島，處所極罕（牢）"校釋為"為打得彼國，復居山島，處所極牢"，則"為打得彼國"中的"彼國"，無論解為"小拂臨"還是"大拂臨"，都難以自圓其說，如解為"小拂臨"，則無以照應"見向小拂臨國住也"，如解為拜占庭帝國本土，則無以對應慧超行文尚未涉及"大拂臨"的事實。

我認為，慧超所謂"彼王不住本國，見向小拂臨國住也。為打得彼國，彼國復居山島，處所極罕（牢），為此就彼"，應校釋為"彼王不住本國，見向小拂臨國住也。為打得彼國，彼國復居山島，處所極牢，為此就彼。"意思是："大食國王並不在本國居住，而是住在小拂臨國。因為小拂臨國已被征服，且該國有山地和海島，地勢險峻牢固，因為這一點，國王在那裏居住。"大食王住在小拂臨國，並不意味著住在形勢險峻的山地或海島。這裏的山應是陶魯斯山，而海島應指672年佔領的羅德島和674年佔領的克里特島。"為此就彼"之"此"指小拂臨地勢險峻這一特點，而"彼"則指"小拂臨"。因此，"小拂臨"是指阿拉伯人奪取的以敘利亞為中心的拜占庭帝國領土，而"大拂臨"則是指以君士坦丁堡為中心的領土，尤其是小亞細亞。[26]

這段文字所反映的是阿拉伯人征服敘利亞後，將政治重心轉往敘利亞的歷史。

"又小拂臨，傍海西北，即是大拂臨國"一語，似可斷為："又小拂臨，傍海，西北即是大拂臨國。"既然"小拂臨"是敘利亞，則所"傍"之"海"為地中海，其西北的大拂臨國，正是以陶魯斯山為界與阿拉伯對抗的拜占庭帝國統屬的小亞及歐洲部分。"此（大拂臨國）王兵馬強多，不屬餘國。大寔數回討擊不得，突厥侵亦不得"，指的是這一時期拜占庭帝國在阿拉伯軍隊進攻面前所進行的成功的自衛戰爭：662年和672年摩阿維亞兩次圍攻君士坦丁堡，而717年、718年哈里發蘇萊曼也兩次圍攻君士坦丁堡，均損兵折將，無功而返。"突厥"是指西突厥的一支，以Khazars見稱於西方歷史。杜環《經行紀》稱之為"可薩突厥"，《新唐書》稱"突厥可薩部"。這一族群活動於高加索以北地區，與拜占庭帝國保持著敵對和聯盟的複雜關係，慧超說他們對拜占庭帝國"侵亦不得"，並不為錯。概言之，慧超從中亞地區所獲聞的拜占庭相關知識，大致反映了此前的歷史事實。

杜環是《通典》作者、唐代著名歷史家杜佑的族子，他隨唐將高仙芝出征中亞，在751年怛邏斯一戰中被阿拉伯軍隊俘虜，在地中海東部遊歷十餘年後，[27]於寶應元年（762）乘商船經海路返回中國，著成《經行記》，記述他在被阿拉伯人征服的原拜占庭帝國領土上旅行時的見聞，真實度很高。但《經行記》不幸失傳，僅有部分存留于杜佑《通典》：

> 杜環《經行記》云："拂菻國在苦國西，隔山數千里，亦曰大秦。其人顏色紅白，男子悉著素衣，婦人皆服珠錦。好飲酒，尚乾餅，多淫巧，善織絡。或有俘在諸國，守死不改鄉風。琉璃妙者，天下莫比。王城方八十里，四面境土各數千里。勝兵約有百萬，常與大食相禦。西枕西海，南枕南海，北接可薩突厥……又聞西有女國，感水而生……其大秦善醫眼及痢，或未病先見，或開腦出蟲。"

就存留片段，《經行記》對於拜占庭帝國重要知識的貢獻包括：第一，拜占庭的地理。《經行紀》稱："拂菻國在苦國西，隔山數千里，亦曰大秦。"苦國即Sham國，乃阿拉伯人對敘利亞的稱呼。此時敘利亞早已被併入阿拉伯帝國版圖，但除了向哈里發繳納賦稅表示臣服外，行政上仍有當地人管理，保持原貌，且文化仍有別於其他地區，故被視為一"國"。拂菻相對于敘利亞應為西北，此點杜環的說法稍欠精確。"隔山數千里"，二者所"隔"之"山"乃陶魯斯山，其基點應是大馬士革與君士坦丁堡。[28]

《經行紀》又云：拂菻"西枕西海，南枕南海，北接可薩突厥。"杜環遊歷西亞之前，阿拉伯哈里發帝國對拜占庭帝國的戰爭，以717—718年的失敗而告終，此後停止了一個時期，726年以後又捲土重來，每年都發動對小亞細亞的進攻，這種騷擾性的戰爭持續到740年，這一年雙方在小亞的阿克羅伊農（Acroinon，今土耳其的阿克薩萊）進行戰略決戰，拜占庭軍隊取得對阿拉伯十萬騎兵的決定性勝利。從此拜占庭帝國完全控制了小亞，並利用倭馬亞王朝被阿拔斯王朝（750—1258）取代之際發動進攻，將邊界推進到兩河流域的上游。這種進攻勢態保持到782年才有所改變。[29] 換言之，杜環在阿拉伯世界遊歷期間，正是拜占庭帝國控制小亞細亞後向東推進的時期。他對拂菻國"西枕西海，南枕南海，北接可薩突厥"的記載，其觀察點顯然是阿拉伯人此時控制的敘利亞或阿拔斯王朝的伊拉克地區，因此杜環的"西海"應指達達尼爾海峽到愛琴海的一片水域，而"南海"應指小亞細亞以南的地中海水域，雖然此時的拜占庭帝國在希臘半島和義大利半島還有領土。[30]

《經行紀》提到拂菻"北接可薩突厥"，同時也提到："苫國在大食西界，周廻數千里。其苫國有五節度，有兵馬一萬以上，北接可薩突厥。"《新唐書·大食傳》："大食之西，有苫者，亦自國，北距突厥可薩部，地數千里，有五節度，勝兵萬人。"顯然取材于杜環《經行紀》。[31]又《新唐書·西域傳》云，"波斯國……北鄰突厥可薩部"。杜環稱可薩在拂菻之北，同時又稱可薩在苫國之北、波斯之北，實際上，皆指大略方位。可薩即 Khazars, 是西突厥西遷的一支，七世紀初已經移居到里海以西、高加索以北地區，七至八世紀間可薩突厥人對阿拉伯人進行了一系列戰爭。685 年前後，可薩人越過高加索山脈南下，佔領格魯吉亞、亞美尼亞和阿塞拜疆大部。八世紀二十年代阿拉伯人反攻可薩人，737 年再次打敗可薩人，將其逐回高加索山以北。阿拉伯人雖取得對可薩人的勝利，但不能越過高加索而深入北進，可薩人成為阻擋穆斯林勢力向高加索山以北擴展的障礙，而可薩人也沒有力量跨越高加索向南推進，高加索山成為邊界。同時，可薩突厥向西擴張到克裏米亞和黑海北岸，甚至達第聶伯河。從拜占庭帝國控制的東方領土，斷言可薩突厥汗國位於北方，是沒有問題的。

第二，民俗。"其人顏色紅白，男子悉著素衣，婦人皆服珠錦。好飲酒，尚乾餅，多淫巧，善織絡。或有俘在諸國，守死不改鄉風。琉璃妙者，天下莫比。王城方八十里，四面境土各數千里。"此時的拜占庭帝國規模已大為縮小，居民主要是以希臘人為主的白種人，稱其"顏色紅白"，可謂名實相副；希臘人自古就以善飲酒著稱，所以杜環的"好飲酒"描述完全符合事實；所謂"有俘在諸國，守死不改鄉風"大概是指拜占庭帝國的戰俘在外國拒絕放棄基督教信仰；而君士坦丁堡的馬賽克玻璃製造術也稱得起"琉璃妙者，天下莫比"的稱譽；"王城方八十里，四面境土各數千里"，符合君士坦丁堡和拜占庭帝國疆域的實際。[32]

第三，與新崛起的阿拉伯帝國的關係："勝兵約有百萬，常與大食相禦。"這裏的"百萬"似應理解為軍隊數量龐大，不可執著於具體數字。這一記載顯然是指七世紀下半葉以來綿延於八世紀上半葉的阿拉伯帝國對拜占庭帝國的戰爭。其真實性可與稍前的慧超的記載相印證："此王兵馬強多，不屬餘國。大寔數回討擊不得，突厥侵亦不得。"

第四，對拜占庭傳統技藝的記載："大秦善醫眼及痢，或未病先見，或開腦出蟲。"杜環這裏記錄的是流行於地中海東岸希臘世界具有悠久傳統的開顱療盲術。這種醫術在唐代隨著景教徒入華而傳入中原。[33]

最後需要指出，杜環《經行紀》最終澄清了"大秦"與"拂菻"兩個名稱的關係。貞觀九年景教徒達到長安以後的活動，無疑有助於澄清"拂菻"與漢魏史冊中"大秦"的關係。天寶四年（745）九月玄宗頒佈詔令，改兩京"波斯寺"為"大秦寺"，並令天下諸府郡照改，說明唐人已經明曉景教本源，同時也意味著，官方承認了拂菻即古代大秦的認定。將拂菻等同于大秦的認識並非始于杜環,而在杜環回國之前13年即天寶四年(745)已經完全確立,[34] 但以親身經歷肯定"拂菻"即古之"大秦"的認識,則是杜環做出的獨特貢獻。

二、漢籍所載希臘—拜占庭傳說

南北朝時代的南朝各代與中亞及其以遠地區交往較少,其獲得的西方知識包括有關拂菻的傳說多取自海路。其中包括有關寶石的傳說。《太平廣記》卷八一引唐張說《梁四公記》載,梁武帝蕭衍大同年間(535—545),四川名士顒傑與梁武帝的儒士談論四方奇聞時提到:

> 西至西海,海中有島,方二百里。島上有大林,林皆寶樹。中有萬餘家。其人皆巧,能造寶器,所謂拂林國也。島西北有坑,盤拗深千餘尺。以肉投之,鳥銜寶出。大者重五斤,彼云是色界天王之寶藏。

張說(667—730)在唐睿宗至玄宗時三度為相,封燕國公,詩文皆顯名。《梁四公記》為小說體裁,但涉及中外交往的內容並非面壁虛構。有關拂菻("拂林"即拂菻)的內容不見於《梁書》,可能是取自民間筆記。其原型見於拜占庭帝國文獻。塞浦路斯島康斯坦提亞(Constantia)地方的主教艾比法紐斯(Epiphanius,約生活於315—403之間)記載一個故事:[35]

> 在大斯基泰(Great Scythia)沙漠中,有一高山環繞的幽谷,幽谷中煙霧彌漫,深不可測。尋寶之人為得到谷中寶石,殺羊剝皮,自山岩投諸谷中。寶石粘附在羊肉上。空中飛行的雄鷹聞到羊肉味,潛翔于谷中,將羊肉銜出吃掉,寶石留在雄鷹駐留處。尋寶者在雄鷹落地處尋得寶石。這些寶石色彩各異,均為價值連城之寶,並具有特殊效能:投諸烈火中,烈火自滅而寶石無損;還能助女人分娩,驅除妖魔。

艾比法紐斯記載的內容只是當時流行的故事形式,不是故事最初的形態。類似的傳說在希臘羅馬世界的流傳已相當悠久。希羅多德(約前484—前425)記載,在阿拉伯沙漠,一些大鳥將肉桂枝以泥土固定在人們無法企及的山岩上,搭造巢穴。阿拉伯人為了得到肉桂,殺死馱獸將肉放置在鳥穴下面,大鳥飛下將肉塊銜入巢窩,因肉塊大,巢穴被弄破落到地上,於是阿拉伯人得到這些肉桂。[36] 希羅多德所記故事,實際已包含後來發展諸因素:一是寶物(肉桂枝);二是探寶地點(山岩);三是獲取寶物的手段:以獸肉為誘餌勞動大鳥為之效勞而達到目的。

後來故事流傳過程中發生的變化在於:探寶地點由山岩轉為峽谷,寶物則由肉桂轉為寶石。後一因素的變化似與希臘羅馬世界對寶石的信仰有關,如相信鷹巢中的石頭具有助產的功能。普林尼(23—79)記載,這種石頭保持懷孕狀態,當搖動一塊石頭時,就會聽到其內部另一塊石頭響動的聲音,好似包裹在子宮中。人們發現,鷹巢中總是有陰陽兩塊石頭,沒有石頭,鷹子就不能蕃息。[37] 不過,希羅多德所記故事與艾比法紐斯所述故事相隔時間太長,更具體的演化過程似很難說清。白鳥庫吉認為，艾比法紐斯所述故事傳說並非起源於希臘世界，而是起源於印度，然後傳播到西方。[38] 我們不能排除這個傳說在它最初的演化中吸取了印度傳說的元素，正如希臘神話故事中許多母題其實並非希臘本土元素一樣。[39] 但似可以肯定的是，這個傳說趨於定型，是在艾比法紐斯時代拜占庭帝國境內，即希臘—羅馬世界的東部。

中國和拜占庭兩個方面記載在時間上的接近和故事的大同點（深谷；投肉作餌；鳥將寶石銜出），使人無法懷疑其聯繫性。[40] 二者之間的不同點僅在於，故事發生的地點有所變化：在早期艾比法紐斯的記載中是大斯基泰沙漠，即中亞沙漠，而在《梁四公記》中故事的發生地是拂菻國的西北某地。可見此類神秘故事總是與遙遠而具有神秘色彩的地區相聯繫。對早期的艾比法紐斯和他的同胞來說，大斯基泰沙漠即中亞沙漠無疑具有神秘色彩，自從亞歷山大東侵以後，很多神秘傳說都是跟中亞聯繫在一起的；當這個故事傳至中國時，則不能不與故事流行的那個遙遠的神秘國度（拂菻）發生聯繫。這種變化在文化傳播中屢見不鮮，幾乎是一個定則。中國典籍將這個傳說與拂菻聯繫起來，一方面表明了它與拜占庭帝國的密切聯繫，同時也表明了當時拂菻國在中國人心目中仍然具有神秘色彩。

就文獻而論，《梁四公記》之後，這個傳說見於九世紀中葉偽託亞里斯多德之名的阿拉伯礦物學著作對"金剛石"的記載："除了我的弟子亞歷山大，無人可達金剛石山谷。此谷在東方呼羅珊（Khorasan）的極邊，谷底深不可測。谷中有蛇，視人而人必死。亞歷山大至此，為群蛇所阻，不能前進。亞歷山大乃命人製造鏡子，群蛇鏡中視己而死，而部眾安然無恙。亞歷山大又出一計：命人屠羊剝皮，投之谷底，金剛石粘附於肉上。覓食之鳥銜肉若干而出，部眾追逐鳥後，得其棄物。"[41] 這一時期的傳說又增加一個元素：山谷之蛇的出現，更增加傳說的動聽情節。這種情形符合故事演變的"累層積累"規則。

這個流行傳說也見於阿拉伯故事集《一千零一夜》。航海家辛巴達第二次歷險故事提到這個傳說：辛巴達出海經商，被遺忘在一個荒無人煙的島上，遇見一隻大鳥落在島上，遂決定將自己縛在鳥腿上飛走。大鳥飛行一段時間後，落在一處高地上。辛巴達解開束縛後發現自己處在懸崖邊上，由於無路可走，便走向山谷，發現谷底竟然遍是鑽石和巨蛇。他正在谷中行走間，空中落下一塊肉來，這使他想起一個傳說："據說出產鑽石的地方，都是極深的山谷，人們無法下去採集。鑽石商人卻想出辦法，用宰了的羊，剝掉皮，扔到山谷中，待沾滿鑽石的血淋淋的羊肉被山中龐大的兀鷹攫著飛到山頂，快要啄食的時候，他們便叫喊著奔去，趕走兀鷹，收拾沾在肉上的鑽石，然後扔掉羊肉餵鷹，帶走鑽石。據說除了用這種方法，商人們是無法獲得鑽石的。"於是他撿足寶石，將羊肉片捆綁在身上，由兀鷹將他叼出山谷，由尋寶石的人救出。這個歷險故事的巧妙在於，它將辛巴達的歷險經歷和聽到的傳說糅合在一起，將以往傳說的所有因素（山谷、寶石、大鳥、蛇）都納入其中，使故事情節更為曲折而逼真，但從總體上，新舊版本並無二致，後者可謂前者的翻版。[42]

此後，這一傳說進入了馬可·波羅的《行紀》。在《行紀》中，故事的背景轉移到了印度，在馬拉巴以北約千里的木夫梯里（Muftili），此國"境內多有高山，冬降大雨；水自諸山流下，其聲甚大，構成大溪。雨過山水流下之後，人往溪底尋求金剛石，所獲甚多。及至夏季，日光甚烈，山中奇熱，登山甚難，蓋至是山無點水也。人在此季登山者，可得金剛石無算。山中奇熱，由是大蛇及其他毒蟲頗眾。人在山中見有世界最毒之蛇，往者屢為所食。如是諸山尚有山谷，既深且大，無人能下。往取金剛石之人擲最瘦之肉塊于谷中。山中頗有白鷺，以蛇為食，及見肉擲穀中，用爪攫取，飛上岩石食之。取金剛石之人伏於其處者，立即捕而取其所攫之肉，可見其上粘結谷中金剛石全滿，蓋深谷之中金剛石多至不可思議。然人不能降至谷底，且有蛇甚眾，降者立被吞食。尚有別法覓取金剛石，山中多有鷺巢，人往巢中鷺糞中覓之，亦可獲取不少，蓋鷺食人擲谷底之肉，糞石而出也。彼等捕鷺時，亦可破腹求之，可得石無算，其石甚巨。"馬可·波羅記載的傳說，增加了鷺糞中尋覓寶石的情節；而且，還增加了當時的歷史因素以賦予傳說以真實感，說："攜來吾國之石乃是選擇之餘，蓋金剛石之佳者以及大石大珠，皆獻大汗及世界各國之君王，而彼等獨據有世界之大寶也。應知世界各國除此木夫梯里國之外，皆不出產金剛石。"[43] 將傳說置於當時人們所知道的地理與歷史中，賦予傳說以真實感，這與辛巴達歷險故事如出一轍。

可見這是流傳於歐亞大陸的通俗故事，在拜占庭人艾比法紐斯時代（四世紀）已經成型，故此後的傳說大致沒有大的變化。在時間上，艾比法紐斯的版本與《梁四公記》版本最為接近，前後銜接，其淵源關係非常明顯。

這個故事傳說如何傳入中國？有學者認為粟特人可能為中間媒介，其根據是，蘇聯學者對粟特文獻的研究證明，一些間接證據表明，偽加利斯特尼（pseudo-Callisthenes）作的《亞歷山大傳奇》（*Romance of Alexander the Great*）曾有粟特文譯本。粟特人既與拜占庭的希臘人有過使節往來，那麼粟特人很有可能接受和翻譯過西方流傳甚廣的《亞歷山大傳奇》。粟特人是文明開化的經商民族，他們有可能將這個故事與商品一起傳輸給中國人。而且，《亞歷山大傳奇》也為波斯人所熟悉，他們有些人到訪過中國，或者在錫蘭的港口與中國水手有過接觸。換言之，通過粟特人或波斯人，中國都有可能接觸到這個故事。[44]

不過，還要考慮另一種更大的可能。最早與這個故事聯繫在一起的是南梁人物。梁朝地處南方，與西方的聯繫幾全賴於海路。五世紀初法顯由海路自錫蘭乘商船返回中國，說明自印度到中國的海上航線早已暢通。《宋書》卷九七："若夫大秦天竺，迥出西溟；二漢銜役，特艱斯路。而商貨所資，或出交部，泛海陵波，因風遠至……山琛水寶，由茲自出，通犀翠羽之珍，蛇珠火布之異，千名萬品，並世主之虛心，故舟船繼路，商使交屬。"從羅馬—拜占庭方面，通過波斯灣或紅海與印度西部保持著聯繫。這種聯繫自希臘羅馬時代就已開始。《後漢書·西域傳》記載中天竺與羅馬帝國的貿易，"其西與大秦交市海中，多大秦珍物"，而大秦從它與印度的絲綢貿易中獲利豐厚："與安息、天竺交市海中，利有十倍。"這裏的"海"主要是指印度西部的海。五世紀末六世紀初，拜占庭與印度和斯里蘭卡的聯繫空前繁榮。拜占庭商人在這一地區非常活躍。五世紀末六世紀初出生在埃及亞歷山大里亞的希臘人科斯馬斯（Cosmas），在印度洋遊歷、經商，到過錫蘭，晚年寫的書中特別提到錫蘭島作為海運中心的地位："這個島

（錫蘭）處於中心位置，所以經常有來自印度各地和波斯、埃塞俄比亞的船隻，同時也派出很多自己的船隻。從最遠處——我指的是秦尼斯達（Tzinista，即中國。——引者）——和其他商埠，它接受的是絲綢、蘆薈、檀香木和其他產品……"可見此時海路上印度、斯里蘭卡與拜占庭和中國兩個方面都保持繁榮的商貿交往。[45]

《梁四公記》所記故事中增加的"寶樹"、"色界天王"諸語均為佛教術語，表明這個故事經由印度或錫蘭東傳而來。《梁四公記》在記載這個故事的之後還記載另一故事，扶南（現柬埔寨）大船自西天竺國來，攜碧玻璃鏡在梁朝境內出售，鏡"廣一尺五寸，重四十斤。內外皎潔，置五色物於其上，向明視之，不見其質……其商人言：'此色界天王，有福樂事，天澍大雨，眾寶如山，納之山藏，取之難得。以大獸肉投之藏中。肉爛粘寶，一鳥銜出，而即此寶焉。'"（《太平廣記》卷八一）扶南商人所述拂菻故事與顏傑所說幾乎完全相同。事實上，扶南商人所兜售的碧玻璃鏡並非山中寶石，可能是背面嵌入玻璃（頗黎）作為裝飾的一面大銅鏡。[46] 羅馬所產玻璃在中原各朝久負盛名，中土視之為寶貨。五世紀初，羅馬帝國的玻璃製造技術已傳入中國北方。[47] 但南方尚未掌握這種製造五色玻璃的技術。扶南商人既在印度西部或錫蘭獲知拂菻傳說，[48] 在與南梁朝廷打交道時自然樂於以玻璃器皿與此傳說相比附，故弄玄虛，將其說成寶石，使物品變得神秘而致貴重以謀求高利。這是古往今來商人慣用的伎倆。

這一時期見諸漢籍記載的還有"女人國"傳說。《法苑珠林》卷三九云：

案《梁貢職圖》云，（拂菻）去波斯北一萬里，西南海島有西女國，非印度攝，拂懍年別送男夫配焉。

《貢職圖》亦作《職貢圖》，乃南梁元帝蕭繹所作。"拂懍"即"拂菻"，無須贅言。梁朝處於南方，此傳說顯然由海路傳來。與此相應的是，玄奘（600-664）西域求法途中在北印度也聽到了類似的"女人國"傳說：

波剌斯國西北接拂懍國……拂懍國西南海島，有西女國，皆是女人，略無男子。多諸珍貨，附拂懍國，故拂懍王歲遣丈夫配焉。其俗產男，皆不舉也。[49]

《大慈恩寺三藏法師傳》卷四記載大略相同：

（波剌斯）國東境有鶴秣城，西北接拂懍國，西南海島有西女國，皆是女人，無男子，多珍寶，附屬拂懍，拂懍王歲遣丈夫配焉，其俗產男例皆不舉。[50]

《新唐書》卷二二一：

拂菻西，有西女國，種皆女子，附拂菻。拂菻君長歲遣男子配焉，俗產男不舉。

《大慈恩寺三藏法師傳》與《新唐書》所記"女人國"事，均取材於玄奘《西遊記》，故所記與《西域記》完全一致。顯然，在印度和中亞都流傳著與"拂菻"相聯繫的"西女國"故事。

有學者認為女人國傳說源出於印度，最初在印度西海，後來傳說廣泛流傳，女國的位置向西移到東羅馬的西南海島上。[51]其實不然。將女人國故事與拂菻聯繫起來，是這一時期東方各國民間傳說的突出現象。夏德指出："我們必須假定，這些記載並非基於真實；他們只是西方民間傳說的一些片段，與其他國家的記述一起傳輸到了中國，而介紹者不管是中國人還是羅馬人，都沒有親自訪問過這些國家。"[52]這是不錯的見解。《西域記》所記內容多取自梵文典籍或玄奘親身見聞。玄奘《西遊記》將拂懍國與女人國的記載附於"波剌斯國"條下，且明言"非印度之國，路次附見"，說明女國故事乃玄奘在中亞或印度所獲聞。

夏德注意到玄奘關於女人國的記載多與斯特拉波著作關於女人國（Amazons）的記載相合，似乎在提示人們注意二者之間的淵源關係，不過，他對此似乎有些猶豫不決，難以斷定，原因是兩種記載中女人國位置的不同："斯特拉波筆下的女人國據說位於麥奧提斯湖（Lake Maeotis，即亞速海）岸邊，而不是在拂菻西南，他們也不是生活在島上，派遣男子與她們相配的鄰人不是敘利亞人而是居於高加索山下的加加爾人（Gargareans）。"[53]

不管夏德態度如何優柔寡斷，他聯想到玄奘所記故事與希臘世界的"女人國"傳說的關係，確實顯示了他思維的敏銳。其不足之處在於：首先，他對希臘羅馬世界有關"女人國"傳說的考察僅上溯至斯特拉波，未能從根源上看到它的原型；正如下文所要討論，希臘神話中的"女人國"故事，不僅遠比斯特拉波更為古老，而且在傳播範圍上也比想像的更為廣闊。其次，夏德不太瞭解民俗傳說在不同地區傳播的規則，所以要向人們指出兩種記載顯示的地點的差異。實際上，從民間傳說顯示的傳播規則看，將故事發生地與講述者母邦混為一談，這一現象在世界各地的民間傳說交流中十分常見，是一種普遍現象。由於當時的"拂菻"在歐亞大陸是有相當知名度而又充滿神秘感的國家，將一種帶有神秘色彩的傳說附會於其上，是完全可以理解的。再次，夏德似乎沒有注意到，在六世紀下半葉，西突厥與拜占庭帝國沿南俄草原之路保持了長期的友好關係，[54]人員交往的順暢也有利於希臘傳說傳播到中亞地區。

在希臘世界，"女人國"的傳說可能產生于希臘人向黑海地區殖民時期，所以，在地理範圍上，古希臘神話傳說將"女人國"置於黑海（亞速海）沿岸或小亞細亞地區。根據希臘神話，女人國的女人們崇尚武藝，驍勇異常。為繁衍後代，她們與鄰近的部落男子婚配，然後將男子送走，生下女嬰便留下由母親撫養，訓練其狩獵和戰爭本領，培養成勇猛的女將，男嬰則交還其父，或將其殺掉。女人國的婦女自認為是戰神阿瑞斯的後裔，熱衷於戰爭，經常對他族發動戰爭。為便於使用弓箭，她們燒掉右側乳房。女武士使用的武器有雙面斧、弓、矛和半月形盾等。[55]早期"女人國"傳說有三個元素：一是女人國婦女的尚武；二是女人國婦女與鄰近群體的男子婚配以繁衍後代；三是所生後代只留養女嬰而不留男嬰。在這三個元素中，又以後兩個元素為基本核心元素。

與早期女人國傳說相關的神話人物有赫拉克利斯等。在大力神赫拉克利斯建立的十二功勳中，其中之一是他從女人國取得金腰帶。在赫拉克利斯神話中，女人國位於黑海邊本都地區的特爾莫冬河兩岸，國王擁有戰神阿瑞斯贈送的金腰帶。赫拉克利斯到達女人國後，女王對大力神很有好感，打算獻出金腰帶，不料大力神的敵人天后赫拉從中挑起事端，致使赫拉克利斯與尚武好戰的女人國戰士發生戰爭。赫拉克利斯打敗女人國的軍隊，女王被迫交出金腰帶。由於赫拉克利斯以力大勇武著稱，所以大力神傳說突出的是女人國婦女的強悍和好戰。

"女人國"主題除了見於神話傳說，也進入歷史著作。夏德提到的斯特拉波的記載，顯然延續了傳統的說法。其實，最早提到這個神話傳說的歷史家並非斯特拉波，而是遠在此前的希羅多德。希羅多德在其著作《歷史》(IV, 110—117)記載，女人國的女子曾與黑海沿岸的希臘人作戰，希臘人打敗了她們，準備把大量俘虜運到雅典，船到海上航行時，女人國戰士殺死了押運她們的希臘人。但她們不會操縱船隻，任船漂流到黑海東北部的亞速海（麥奧提斯湖）岸邊，由此與該地的斯基泰人發生戰爭。斯基泰人從戰死的女人國戰士屍體上發現她們是婦女，決定不再以戰爭手段對付她們。他們派出大約數量相等的年輕男子，在她們的駐地附近安營紮寨，並模仿女人國戰士的一切動作。如果女戰士們前來交戰，斯基泰男人並不迎戰，而是逃跑；待女戰士停止追擊，則仍回到女戰士駐地附近安營。當女戰士看到斯基泰人並無傷害自己的意圖時，就不再主動發起攻擊，雙方的營地也逐漸接近起來。起初，單個的斯基泰男子與單個的女戰士的交往，隨後帶來各自身邊的夥伴彼此交往，最後雙方的營帳合併在一起，每個斯基泰男子娶最初交往的女戰士為妻，彼此結合在一起。新形成的群體並沒有回到斯基泰男子原來的群體，也沒有定居于女戰士佔領的土地，而是遷移到一個新的地區開始生活，這個地區位於塔奈斯河以東三日路程，從麥奧提斯湖向北三日路程。[56] 在希羅多德的記載中，我們確實可以看到斯基泰人"遣丈夫配焉"這個情節，但不是每歲都派遣，而是派遣的男子與女戰士結合成一個新團體；而且，希羅多德也沒有提到"產男不舉"的風俗。實際上包含了女人國婦女尚武和他族派遣男子婚配這兩個元素。這體現出歷史著作的的特點：神話傳說母題在與歷史事實結合時，只保留與歷史實際相符合的細節，並加以突出和強調，而改變或略去一些具體細節，一些人們熟悉的細節。正如在中國的帝王神話中，與"龍"的關係及由此獲得的神聖性是不可缺少的核心元素，但如何表現"龍"與帝王的關係則形式各異。[57]

"女人國"故事，在歐亞大陸各地經久流傳，地點隨時代不同而有所變化。阿拉伯故事集《天方夜譚》中，女人國位於第聶伯河中的若干島嶼上。馬可·波羅遊記中，女人國是印度轄下的一個島嶼，與男人島相對，位於克思馬克蘭南海行五百哩，兩島相距約三十哩，每年第三月，諸男子盡赴女島，居住三個月，與女子歡處，然後返回。"彼等與諸婦所產之子女，女則屬母，男則由母撫養至十四歲，然後遣歸父所。"[58] 十五世紀初葉出使帖木兒汗廷的西班牙人克拉維約（Klavuyo）則將女人國置於中亞以東地區："由撒馬爾罕向契丹行十五日里程，有女人國（Amazons），迄今仍保持不與男人相處之俗，只是一年一度與男人交往。她們從首領們那裏獲得准許，攜女兒前往最近的地區與男人交會，每人得一悅己之男人，與之同居住、共飲食，隨後返歸本土。生女後則留下撫養，生男則送其生父養育。女人國現屬帖木兒統治，但曾經歸轄于契丹皇帝。信仰基督教，屬希臘教會。她們是守防特洛耶城的女戰士的後裔，希臘人攻取特洛耶城後，乃移居於此地。"[59] 克拉維約所述顯然是久已流行的版本，但仍突出了希臘淵源。

西班牙人門多薩（Juan Gonzalez De Mendoza，1545—1618）根據此前相關人員的東方消息，於1585年出版《大中華帝國史》，其中也有"女人國"的記載，不過，他筆下的"女人國"是在東亞海中："距離日本不遠，近頃發現有女人島，島中僅有女人，持弓矢，善射，為習射致燒其右乳房。每年一定月份，有若干日本船舶，載貨至其島交易。船至島後，令二人登岸，以船中人數通知女王。女王指定舟人登岸之日，至日，舟人未登岸前，島中女子至港，女數如舟中男數，女各攜繩鞋一雙，鞋上皆有暗記，亂置沙上而退。舟中男子然後登岸，各著繩鞋往就諸女，諸女各認鞋而延之歸。其著女王之鞋者，雖醜陋而亦不拒。迨至限期已滿，各人以其住址告女而與之別。告以住址者，如次年生子，男兒應送交其父也。"這位西班牙人明言"此事乃諸教士聞諸兩年前曾至此島某人者，但日本之耶穌會士，對於此事毫無記錄，余尚疑而未信云。"[60] 很顯然，這裏的東方"女人國"，是歐西人將希臘淵源的"女人國"傳說移植到了東方背景中，雖其細節有所變化，而其整體面目仍是西方傳統的。這是民間傳說隨時代、地域變動而發生時空轉化的又一例證。

類似的例證還有一例。波迪埃引《傳教信劄》載1697年法國某傳教士在Manille寫成的書信："此種外人（假擬在Mariannes群島南方某島中之外人），謂彼等島中有一島，僅有女子住在其中，自成一國，不許男子羼入。女子多不婚，惟在年中某季許男子來會，聚數日，攜其無需乳哺之男孩而歸，女孩則留母所。"[61] 其核心仍是與外部男子婚配、生男不舉的內容。

自古希臘以降，"女人國"傳說的一個特點是婚配繁衍。希臘傳統的"女人國"傳說中，幾乎看不到無性繁殖的實例。羅馬傳說中出現無性繁殖的實例，但似不佔據主導地位。如西元一世紀的羅馬作家梅拉（Pomponius Mela）曾記載一地"女子獨居，全身有毛，浴海而孕，其俗蠻野，為人所捕者，用繩縛之，尚虞其逃走。"杜環《經行記》說："又聞（拂菻國）西有女國，感水而生。"依夏德的看法，杜環所說的意思可能是"生於水"，如塞浦路斯島流行的維納斯崇拜（Venus Anadyomene of Cyprus）。[62] 如此，則與女人國無關。

在中國，女人國（或女兒國）傳說也是歷史悠久，連綿不絕。《山海經》記載的女人國故事：女子國無男子；成年女子到黃池洗澡而致使懷孕，生育男嬰，至多活三歲而死，唯女嬰才能長大成人。就正史論，《後漢書·東夷列傳》最早提到"女國"，其位置在東海，"海中有女國，無男人，或傳其國有神井，窺之輒生子云。"《梁書·東夷傳》記"女國"："慧深又云：'扶桑東千里，有女國，容貌端正，色甚潔白，身體有毛，髮長委地。至二、三月，競入水則任娠，六七月產子。女人胸前無乳，項後生毛，根白，毛中有汁，以乳子，一百日能行，三四年則成人矣。見人驚避，偏畏丈夫。'"宋代趙汝適《諸蕃志》多採前輩周去非《嶺外代答》材料，其於"沙華公國"之後記"女人國"："又東南有女人國，水常東流，數年水一泛漲⋯⋯昔常有舶舟飄落其國，群女攜以歸，數日無不死。有一智者，夜盜船亡命，得去，遂傳其事。其國女人遇南風盛發，裸而感風，即生女也。"[63] "沙華公國"不可定考。有人認為在加里曼丹島。[64] 南宋末年建州崇安（今屬福建）人陳元靚撰《事林廣記》記女人國："女人國，居

— 329 —

東北海角，與奚部小如者部抵界。其國無男，每視井即生也。"宋代的兩位作者的作品中都貫穿無性繁衍的母題。而作為明代文學作品的《西遊記》，其中的女人國的故事，也突出女人喝過子母河的河水而懷孕的主題。可以說，無性繁殖是"女人國"傳說中遠東系統區別於西方系統的最重要、也最明顯的元素。[65]

需要指出的是，中國"女國"傳說系統中的"女王國"，其實並非嚴格意義上的"女人國"，那裏只是盛行女子掌權而已。《北史·女國傳》記女國："其地五男三女，貴女子，賤丈夫，婦人為吏職，男子為軍士。女子貴者則多有侍男，男子不得有侍女。雖賤庶之女，盡為家長，有數夫焉。生子皆從母姓。"《隋書·女國列傳》："女國，在葱嶺之南，其國代以女為王，王姓蘇毗。女王之夫號為金聚，不知政事。國內丈夫唯以征伐為務。山上為城，方五六里，人有萬家。王居九層之樓，侍女數百人，五日一聽朝。復有小女王，共理國政。其俗貴婦人，輕丈夫，而性不妒忌。"《舊唐書》："東女國，西羌之別種，以西海中復有女國，故稱東女焉。俗以女為王。東與茂州、黨項接，東南與雅州接，界隔羅女蠻及白狼夷。其境東西九日行，南北二十日行。有大小八十餘城。……王號為'賓就'。有女官，曰'高霸'，平議國事。在外官僚，並男夫為之。"《通典》"女國，隋時通焉。在葱嶺之南，世以女為王，因以女為國"，顯然取自《隋書》。

可見，玄奘《西域記》中的"女人國"傳說屬於希臘傳說系統，是希臘淵源的"女人國"傳說的翻板。玄奘《西域記》記載中"拂菻"與"女人國"的聯繫，暗示著拜占庭帝國在這個傳說流播過程中的作用；同時也反映了此一時期拜占庭帝國在歐亞大陸文化交往中的重要地位。阿拉伯伊斯蘭勢力興起以後，女人國傳說演化為伊斯蘭教文化的一個內容了。

注释

[1] 參見張緒山：《"拂菻"名稱語源研究述評》，《歷史研究》2009 年第 5 期，第 143-151 頁。

[2] 沈福偉認為，"5、6 世紀之際，景教已在洛陽正式傳教……所謂大秦國，不一定來自拜占庭，而是以敘利亞僧侶為骨幹的景教徒。景教的傳教似乎最初就利用了佛法的外衣和犍陀羅美術的宣傳手法"。見氏著：《中西文化交流史》，上海：上海人民出版社，2006 年，第 155 頁。林梅村也認為，"這裏說的大秦國'沙門'應即混跡與洛陽佛寺的東羅馬或敘利亞景教徒。" 見林梅村：《中國基督教史的黎明時代》，《西域文明》，北京：東方出版社，1995 年，第 451 頁。

[3]《新唐書》卷二二一下《西域傳》。

[4] K. Shiratori, "A New Attempt at the Solution of the Fulin Problem", in *Memoir of the Research Department of the Toyo Bunko*, 15, Tokyo: The Toyo Bunko, 1956, pp. 215-216.

[5] K. Shiratori, "A New Attempt at the Solution of the Fulin Problem", pp. 210-246; 張星烺：《中西交通史料彙編》，第一冊，北京：中華書局，2003 年，第 169-181 頁。

[6] 玄奘、辯機：《大唐西域記校注》下，季羨林等校注，北京：中華書局，2000 年，第 942-943 頁。

[7] 榮新江：《一個入仕唐朝的波斯景教家族》，《中古中國與外來文明》，三聯書店，2001 年，第 238-257 頁；張緒山：《景教東漸及傳入中國的希臘—拜占庭文化》，《世界歷史》2005 年第 6 期。

[8] 張星烺：《中西交通史料彙編》，第二冊，北京：中華書局，2003 年，第 685 頁。

[9] 張緒山：《唐代拜占庭帝國遣使中國考略》，《世界歷史》2010 年第 1 期，第 110-116 頁。

[10] 齊思和：《中國和拜占庭帝國的關係》，上海：上海人民出版社，1956 年，第 16 頁。

[11] 林英：《唐代拂菻叢說》，北京：中華書局 2006 年，第 87-88，90-91 頁。

[12] K. Shiratori, "A New Attempt at the Solution of the Fu-lin Problem", pp. 322-325.

[13] 這種機械設計，主要是利用空氣動力原理，以空氣鼓動相應機械發出類似鳥類或獅子的聲音。相關研究，見 Gerard Brett, "The automata of the Byzantine 'Throne of Solomon' ", *Speculum*, vol. XXIX (1954), pp. 477-487。波將金等編：《外交史》，北京：三聯書店，1979 年，第一卷，第 134-135 頁；陳志強：《拜占庭學研究》，北京：人民出版社，2001 年，第 292 頁；Franz Tinnefeld, "Ceremonies for Foreign Ambassadors at the Court of Byzantium and Their Political Background", p. 203.

[14] Constantine Porphyrogenitus, *De cerimoniis aulae Byzantinae libri duo*, (Corpus Scriptorum Historiae Byzantinae), Bonnae 1829-1830.

[15] 希提：《阿拉伯通史》上冊，馬堅譯，北京：商務印書館，1979 年，第 243-244 頁。

[16] 希提：《阿拉伯通史》上冊，第 241-243 頁。

[17] 即隋唐史冊之"帆延"。

[18] 即 Bactria,《魏書·嚈噠傳》作"拔底延"。

[19] 即巴達克尚。

[20] 張緒山：《"拂菻"名稱語源研究述評》，《歷史研究》2009 年第 5 期，第 143-151 頁。

[21] 慧超：《往五天竺國傳》，張毅箋釋，北京：中華書局，2000 年，第 108、116 頁。

[22] 舊、新《唐書》、《經行紀》與《諸蕃志》均作"大食"。

[23] F. Hirth, "The Mystery of Fu-lin", *Journal of American Oriental Society*, XXXIII (1913), p. 205.

[24] K. Shiratori, "A New Attempt at the Solution of the Fu-lin Problem", pp. 266-268.

[25] 慧超：《往五天竺國傳箋注》，張毅箋注，"前言"第 8-9 頁；第 112-115 頁。

[26] 張星烺：《中西交通史料彙編》，第一冊，第 211 頁。

[27] 宋峴：《杜環遊歷大食國之路線考》，謝方主編《中西初識》，鄭州：大象出版社 1999 年，第 232-250 頁。

[28] 白鳥庫吉：《大秦國與拂菻國考》，《塞外史地論文譯叢》第一輯，王古魯譯，長沙：商務印書館，1938-1939 年，第 27-28 頁。

[29] 喬治·奧斯特洛格爾斯基：《拜占庭帝國》，陳志強譯，西寧：青海人民出版社，2006 年，第 133-134 頁；希提：《阿拉伯通史》上冊，第 234-235 頁；陳志強：《拜占庭帝國史》，北京：商務印書館，2003 年，第 206-209 頁，徐家玲：《拜占庭文明》，北京：人民出版社，2006 年，第 85 頁。

[30] 白鳥庫吉認為:"杜環《經行紀》所記拂菻國西枕的'西海',當然是指地中海,但'南枕南海'一語,可作兩解。裕爾(Yule)氏目之為普洛滂的(Propontis)固屬有理,但亦可解釋,這是在小亞細亞與埃及間的地中海一部(即阿拉伯人所謂顯姆海或露姆海)。"見氏著:《大秦國與拂菻國考》,第 29 頁。

[31] 倭馬亞王朝佔領下的苫國,哈里發政府只限於徵收賦稅,實際管理權仍歸當地權力機構,五節度是指五個軍區,即:Kinnasrin、Hims (Emesa)、Damascus、al-Urdum (Jordania)、Palestine。見 K. Shiratori, "A New Attempt at the Solution of the Fu-lin Problem", p. 272. 張星烺認為:"《新唐書》苫國……就其地理位置而言,或為卓支亞(Geoorgia)也。"見《中西交通史料彙編》,第二卷,第 698—699 頁。認為苫國為卓支亞即今之格魯吉亞,此說非是。

[32] H. Yule, *Cathay and the Way Thither*, vol. I, London: The Hakluyt Society, 1915, p. 46.

[33] 張緒山:《景教東漸及傳入中國的希臘—拜占庭文化》,《世界歷史》2005 年第 6 期,第 82-84 頁。

[34] K. Shiratori, "A New Attempt at the Solution of the Fu-lin Problem", pp. 284.

[35] B. Laufer, "The Diamond: a Study in Chinese and Hellenistic Folk-lore", *Anthropological Series*, vol. XV, no. 1, Chicago 1915, p. 9.

[36] 希羅多德:《歷史》,王嘉雋譯,北京:商務印書館,1962 年,第 409 頁。

[37] B. Laufer, "The Diamond", pp. 9, 15.

[38] K. Shiratori, "The Mu-na-chu 木難珠 of Ta-chin and the Cintāmani of India", *Memoirs of the Research Department of Toyo Bunko*, 11 (1939), pp.15-24.

[39] 舉例言之。半人半鳥的海妖形象最早源自兩河流域,但卻見於《荷馬史詩》中;獅身人面的斯芬克斯原本源自埃及,但關於斯芬克斯的故事卻以完整的故事形式見於希臘神話(如俄狄浦斯故事)。參見 M. H. 鮑特文尼克等:《神話辭典》,北京:商務印書館,1985 年,第 132、275 頁。

[40] B. Laufer, "The Diamond", p. 10.

[41] B. Laufer, "The Diamond", p. 10.

[42] 《一千零一夜故事選》,納訓譯,北京:人民文學出版社,1995 年,第 77 頁;《一千零一夜》(五),李維中譯,銀川:寧夏人民出版社,2006 年,第 1960-1963、1973 頁。

[43] 馬可·波羅:《馬可波羅行紀》,馮承鈞譯,党寶海新注,石家莊:河北人民出版社,1999 年,第 635-636 頁。

[44] L. Boulnois, *The Silk Road*, trans. by D. Chamberlin, London: George Allen & Unwin Ltd., 1966, p. 162-163.

[45] Cosmas Indicopleustes, *The Christian Topography of Cosmas, an Egyptian Monk*, trans. by J. W. McCrindle, New York: The Hukluyt Society, 1897, pp. 365-366; F. Hirth, and W. W. Rockhill, *Chau Ju-kua, His Work on the Chinese and Arab Trade in the Twelfth and Thirteenth Century, Entitled Chu-fan-chi*, Taipei, 1970, p. 3.

[46] 宮崎市定:《中國南洋關係史概說》,《宮崎市定論文選集》下卷,中國社會科學院歷史研究所翻譯組編譯,北京:商務印書館,1965 年,第 191 頁。

[47] 玻璃是希臘羅馬世界輸入中國的重要產品。在整個古代,亞歷山大裏亞、梯爾和西頓是重要的玻璃產地。中國人珍視玻璃,史書中對它有明確的記載。東晉(317-420)時玻璃與金剛石、瑪瑙等同

列為貴族的陪葬品。五世紀上半葉（424）彩色玻璃製造術才傳入中國北方。《魏書》卷一〇二記載："（北魏）世祖（424-452）時，其人（大月氏）商販至京師，自云能鑄石為五色玻璃，於是採礦山中，於京師（平城）鑄之。既成，光澤乃美於西方來者。乃詔為行殿，容百餘人，光色映澈，觀者莫不驚駭，以為神明所作。自此中國遂賤，後不復珍之。"

[48] B. Laufer, "The Diamond", p. 20.

[49] 玄奘、辯機：《大唐西域記校注》下，第 942-943 頁。

[50] 慧立、彥悰：《大慈恩寺三藏法師傳》，孫毓棠、謝方點校，北京：中華書局，2000 年，第 93 頁。

[51] 玄奘、辯機：《大唐西域記校注》下，第 943 頁。

[52] F. Hirth, *China and the Roman Orient：Researches into Their Ancient and Medieval Relations as Represented in Old Chinese Records*, Leipsic & München, Shanghai-Hongkong, 1885, p. 200.

[53] F. Hirth, *China and the Roman Orient*, p. 202.

[54] 見張緒山：《6—7 世紀拜占庭帝國和西突厥的交往》，《世界歷史》2002 年第 1 期，第 81-98 頁。

[55] 鮑特文尼克等：《神話辭典》，第 25-26 頁。

[56] 希羅多德：《歷史》，第 473-476 頁。

[57] 《史記·封禪書》："黃帝采首山銅，鑄鼎于荊山下，鼎既成，有龍垂胡髯下迎黃帝。黃帝上騎，群臣後宮從上者七十余人，龍乃上去。"在漢高祖劉邦的傳說中，以其母與龍發生關係出現。東漢光武帝劉秀有"四夷雲集龍鬥野，四七之際火為王"的受命之符。北齊高歡臥睡時，被人附會"見赤蛇蟠床上"。唐太宗被人贊稱"龍鳳之姿，天日之表"。 洪秀全言志詩，"風雪鼓舞三千浪，易像飛龍定在天"，表明自己是"真龍天子"。

[58] 馬可·波羅：《馬可波羅行紀》，第 667-668 頁。

[59] 羅·哥·克拉維約：《克拉維約東使記》，楊兆鈞譯，北京：商務印書館，1997 年，第 160 頁；H. Yule, *Cathay and the Way Thither*, vol. 1, pp. 266-267.

[60] 馬可·波羅：《馬可波羅行紀》，第 669-670 頁。

[61] 馬可·波羅：《馬可波羅行紀》，第 670 頁。

[62] F. Hirth, *China and the Roman Orient*, p. 204.

[63] 趙汝適：《諸蕃志校釋》，楊博文校釋，中華書局，1996 年，第 130 頁。

[64] 趙汝適：《諸蕃志校釋》，第 129 頁。

[65] 關於唐代"女國"的討論，見 Jennifer W. Jay, "Imagining Matriarchy: 'Kingdom of Woman' in Tang China", *Journal of the American Oriental Society*, 116. 2 (1996), pp. 220-229.

KNOWLEDGE OF THE GEOGRAPHY, HISTORY AND LEGENDS OF THE BYZANTINE EMPIRE IN CHINESE SOURCES

ZHANG Xushan

In the period from the late Southern and Northern Dynasties to the Sui and Tang Dynasties, Chinese sources contain much knowledge about the Byzantine Empire under the name of "Fulin", including the routes from the Byzantine Empire to China, the geography of the Byzantine Empire in relationship to neighboring countries such as Persia and Arabia, and its wars with the newly-rising power of the Islamic Arabs. Byzantine social customs, such as court etiquette, and in particular Graeco-Byzantine legends such as tales of the "diamond" and the "Amazons", were also mentioned in the Chinese sources. This information was introduced to the Chinese by three agents: intermediary traders, Nestorians, and Persian exiles; Byzantine emissaries to China; and Chinese travelers in the Western Regions. This kind of information in the Chinese sources testifies to the prosperous interchange between the two empires during that period.

THE "HAN" IN THE THREE MIRRORS OF HISTORY, FOREIGNERS AND MINORITIES: AN INDEXICAL-EMBODIMENT INTERPRETATION

Naran Bilik

The fluid meaning of "Han" beats attempts by those who try to trace its origins to antiquity. In the Yuan period (1271-1368), for example, the "Han" included the Jurchen, Khitan (Qidan), and Koreans; now "Han" mostly overlaps with Chinese (*Tangren*, *Huaren*) by default. The connotation of "Han" in modern discourses took shape as a result of encounters between Chinese and foreigners, on the one hand, and through interactions between majority Chinese and minorities in the process of nation-state building on the other. "Han" denotes a complex semiotic continuum of icons, indexes, and symbols;[1] "Han" is a virtual reality that is dialogical, negotiated, performed, and manufactured, signifying the multiple boundaries of cultures, "races" and civilizations.

Who Are the Han?

The question evokes Moerman's "Who are the Lue?" (Moerman 1965); it highlights ethnic self-identification with the statement: "they are who they say they are". However, identity is no longer so simple; asking "who are the Lue?" today is as much clarifying as begging for "the ambiguity and contradictions that Moerman thought he cleared up" (O'Connor 2008). Putting side by side Moerman's concern for ethnic distinctions and self-identification, Leach's wet rice adaptation model for Tai identity, and Condominas' political model emphasizing conquest and assimilation that help spread a Tai identity, we can find a synesthetic basis that they all share. "All three assume the Tai are…one thing" (O'Connor 2008). One interpretive alternative is proposed by O'Connor who brings contradiction and power into his model, equates "culture with the openness of discourse rather than the closure of a code or text", grounds his constructs empirically and historically, and keeps culture open by stressing "the interaction of semi-autonomous complexes within a regional tradition rather than the integration of a single timeless ethnic whole" (O'Connor 2008). Similarly, the answer to the question of who the Han are lies in our adequate understanding of the interplay between history, power, and contextualized negotiation processes. However, as yet most discourses on the Han in Mainland China have been based on the synchronic model that assumes a perfectly integrated, timeless whole. 'Han", "Hanren", "Hanzu" and "Han minzu" have been indiscriminately used in academic publications and scholarly communications, disregarding the historical complicity and notional ambiguity of this terminology.

Fluidity of "Han Chinese" and Other

The Chinese character *guo* ("state", as used in "Zhongguo" [Central State(s)], now referred to as "China" in English) appeared as early as the Zhou Dynasty (1046 BCE-256 BCE) (Yu 1981). There were three states at the time: the "Xia" Dynasty (2070 BCE-1600 BCE); the "Zhou" that had evolved to the west (of Xia); and the "Shang" (1600 BCE-1046 BCE) that had originated to the east of Xia (Fu 1935). At the time of the Zhou Dynasty the concept of the "Central States" ("Zhongguo") started to take shape based on the identity of "Xia" (Chen 1989). Geographically positioned between the Zhou and Shang, the Xia took great pride in their graceful language, and their culture had become the core of early "Chinese" civilization (Chen 1989). In the late Zhou Dynasty warring states were contending for supremacy, creating a situation in which some "Yi Di" ("less-than-civilized" groups) were assimilated into "Xia"; the Qin and Chu, for example, the two previously despised "Yi Di", became two of the seven warring states, all of whom claimed to have inherited Xia culture and thus appropriated the title "Zhongguo" (Chen 1989). Thus the "Central State" stood out with its topographic symbolism and territorial-cultural centrality in classical Chinese literature. Such semantic evolvement and delicacy, however, is hardly discernable in its English equivalent "China".

Apparently, beginning from the Kingdom of Wei (220-65), an extra term "Han" had to be used in addition to "Zhongguo". According to Chen (1989), those "Yi Di" peoples who were beyond the confines of "civilization" also had a territorial stake in the "Central State". That is, "Zhongguo" had been a territorial container for Xia and non-Xia peoples and cultures from the outset. The non-"Xia" used the term "Han" to designate the descendants of the Han Dynasty who also lived in the "Central States".

While the term "Zhongguo" was used by multiple cultures as a toponym that denoted a multi-ethnic land, some ethnonyms were also used by various peoples, both inside and outside the "Central State", to designate "Zhongguo". The Tuoba, a subgroup of the Xianbei (a non-Xia people), ruled what is now Northern China for quite some time and were so well-known to the Turkic speaking world that the latter used "Tabghach" and "Taughast" to refer to China (Jia 1989). Actually, while it is believed that the term "Han" comes from the Han Dynasty (206 BCE-CE 220), people who inhabited the Han territory were actually known as the "Qin" to the people in India and Persia, rather than "Han". The word "Qin" ("Cin" or "Chin") is believed to be the root from which the word "China" derives (Jia 1989: 138). The Khitan ("Qidan") conquered Northern China and established the Liao Dynasty (907-1125). Their military might (*wuwei*) has left their ethnonym "Cathay" (Khitan), which had become equivalent to the "Central State" in several European languages (Lathan 1958: 10; Jia 1989). Even now Mongols refer to China and the Chinese as Khitad.

Moreover, the term "Han" was used in different senses in different contexts. The "Han" of the Northern Wei Dynasty were different from the "Han" of the Jin Dynasty (1115-1234), the latter being a generic term covering the "Han" (people from Henan and Shandong), as well as "Bohai" and "Qidan", the latter inhabiting what had been the Liao territory (Jia 1989). Again, the Mongols of the Yuan Dynasty (1271-1368) included in the category of "Han" not only "Han" but also Jurchen, Khitan (Qidan), and Koreans, excluding the Han subjects of the Southern Song, who were called "Nanggiyad" or "Nanren" ("southern people") (Jia 1989). The Manchu word "Nikan" shares the same root "Nankia" (Nanggiyad, cf. Wu Lan 2000: 787) with Mongolian "Nanggiyad", and both refer to Southern Han.

That the notion of "Central State" was understood quite differently in the meaning systems of Chinese, Japanese, Manchu, and other languages led to "polyphonic" (Bakhtin 1981) narrations that produced contextually structured remembrance and amnesia (Halbwachs 1992; Connerton 1989). The Qing Dynasty (1636-1911) was established by the Manchus who were mostly Jurchen, a northeastern minority, and "who organized themselves around the mission of ruling China between the seventeenth and twentieth centuries" (Guy 2002:162, 163). For the Chinese, however, to be conquered "by a foreign people whom they considered below themselves was a bitter pill to swallow" (Elliott 2001: 21). In 1730, a native scholar of Hunan, Zeng Jing, acquired a copy of a secret treatise "exposing the unworthiness of the Manchus to rule", authored by a deceased scholar Lü Liuliang from Zhejiang who claimed that the ancestors of the Manchus were described as barbarians as early as the Zhou Dynasty of classical times, and therefore "the Manchus themselves must still be barbarous in character" (Crossley 1997: 110). Interestingly, the Yongzheng Emperor rebutted Lü's accusation by writing the *Dayi Juemi Lu* (Record of Great Righteousness to Dispel Confusion), insisting that the Manchus had been civilized through centuries of exposure to Confucianism (Spence 2001; Crossley 1997: 110-12; Elliott 2001: 347). The Manchu rulers were clearly fighting to define "Central State" as a domain open to non-Han and to maintain their dominance. In the late Qing period, Chinese revolutionaries used *shina* (Zhina), the same term used by Japanese nativist *(kokugaku)* scholars in the modern period to separate Japan from "the barbarian/civilized or outer/inner implication of the term *chuugoku*", to distinguish themselves from the Manchus; and in early-twentieth-century Japan, *shina* signified China as a troubled place mired in its past, in contrast to Japan, a modem Asian nation" (Tanaka 1993: 3-4).

The failure of the Qing government in Sino-foreign wars provided momentum for Han nationalists such as Sun Yat-sen and Zhang Taiyan who were devoted to "throwing out the Tartar caitiffs and reviving China". According to Sun Yat-sen defeating foreign imperialist forces was secondary to ousting the Manchus. Zou Rong stated in his popular pamphlet *Geming Jun* (The revolutionary army): "Unjust! Unjust! What is more unjust and bitter in China today is to have to put up with this inferior race of nomads with wolfish ambitions, these thievish Manchus, as our rulers" (Tsou 1968: 65). The rise of Han nationalism reached its apex at the moment of the 1911 Revolution that brought into being the Republic of China. "In a China so defined, the Manchus, simply because they were non-Han, had no rightful place; they should be, according to the manifesto of the revolutionary alliance, 'expelled'" (Rhoads 2000: 293). At first Republicans identified China as the Han nation with common descent, common territory and culture, "which was also politically sovereign" (Harrell 2001: 29). In order to lay claim to the frontier territory inhabited by non-Han peoples, which had been under imperial rule, Sun Yat-sen and his comrades had to include, rather than expel, the Manchus and other non-Han, to form a "Republic of Five Nationalities" (*wuzu gonghe*) of Han, Manchu, Mongolian, Muslim, and Tibetan (Zhao 2004: 67-68). Sun Yat-sen planned to relocate 10 million Han people over a span of 10 years in Southwest China, Inner Mongolia and Xinjiang.[2] This long-term plan for colonizing Mongolia and Xinjiang was designed for demobilized soldiers in the future (Sun 1998: 175-176). In Sun's vision ethnic minorities in China could not stand alone and should be assimilated into the Han, forming a big *minzu* and therefore a homogenous nation-state (Sun 1994: 272).

Communist Nation-Building: The Soviet Moment

Stevan Harrell points out that since 1949 the Chinese Communist Party has "inherited both the remnant cultural nationalism of the Republic and the very different Marxist-Leninist views" on nationality issues (Harrell 2001: 30-31). In 1957, the Editorial Department of *Historical Research* (*Lishi yanjiu*) journal published a collection of papers on debates over the origin of the Han. At issue was the interpretation and application of Joseph Stalin's "four common features" that define a nation with relevance to the chronological order that molded the Han into a nation or *minzu*.[3] Fan Wenlan insisted that the Hanzu was formed during the transitional period between the Qin and the Han Dynasty; he argued that at that time the Stalin's "four common" features took shape. Others believed that what Fan was talking about was actually *Hanzu* not *Han minzu* (narodnost'); *minzu* (*natsia*/nation) had not been known in history until capitalism was on the rise. They put the formation time of the *Han minzu* at a period between 17th and 19th century.

Modeling on the Soviet experience and accepting (in a quite modified way) Stalin's "four-common" definition of *natsia* (nation),[4] the CCP reclassified the non-Han from four to fifty-five nationalities. However, the CCP did not follow the Soviet evolutionary ethno-taxonomy and made no distinction between pre-feudal and post-feudal community—they were all lumped together as *minzu*. The Contemporary Chinese Dictionary, for example, makes no distinction between "Han nationality" and "Han ethnic group" (Bianjishi 2002:765, 766).

Though *minzu* sounds onomastically equal, Chinese speakers can still distinguish *yuanshi minzu* (primitive *minzu*) from *xiandai minzu* (modern *minzu*), *luohou minzu* (underdeveloped *minzu*) from *xianjin minzu* (advanced *minzu*), and *yeman minzu* (barbarous *minzu*) from *wenming minzu* (civilized *minzu*). Generally speaking the Han are the *xiandai*, *xianjin* and *wenming minzu* and most non-Han peoples are either *yuanshi minzu*, *luohou* or *yeman minzu*. The concept of Han was greatly substantiated after this engineering of enthonyms. It will be highly interesting to see how Taiwan's changing ethnicity will redefine Han; how the internationalization of ethnic identities of the Manchus, the Mongols, the Uygurs, the Hui, the Yao, the Miao and so on, will redefine Han; how the transforming Sino-foreign relationship will redefine Han; and how the organization and manipulation of historic memories will redefine Han.

The intended denotation of "Chinese nation" that sounds synonymous with "Han" contradicts a diversified linguistic and cultural landscape, a situation that retrospectively agrees with the statement by Franz Boas and Edward Sapir that the boundaries of language, culture and race do not coincide (Boas 1966: 3-4, Sapir 2007: 163-172). No better instance that serves to display nomenclatural differences and to testify denotational plurality than the Mongolian translation of *Zhonghua minzu* ("Chinese nation"), which is *dumdadu yin undusuten-nuud* ("roots of the middle"). While in Chinese "*Zhonghua minzu*" usually refers to the singularity of the nation, in Mongolian *dumdadu yin undusuten-nuud* denotes the plurality of the nation. Here we have two types of *Zhonghua minzu*; one centers on linguistic-cultural plurality and the other focuses on political singularity.

Western Encounters and *Zhonghua minzu* (the Chinese Nation)

"Han" has also been defined along the processual interface between Western-centric and Sino-centric views and practices before, during, and after the Opium Wars in the 19th century; "[F]ive foreign wars, five domestic upheavals, and dozens of imposed treaties later- this proud and comfortable world had been shattered". (Cohen 2003:25) Through the plural interpretation of modern history, such as "The Boxers as Event, Experience, and Myth" (Paul A. Cohen 1997), the Chinese realized that they are not only different from the Manchus and others but also different from, say, the English and Americans, and apparently more so. They are Han when they rose to drive out the Manchu in an attempt to restore *Zhonghua*; they are Chinese when they fought the Eight-Power Allied Forces.

The rise of Chinese-cum-Han nationalism coincides with the globalization of the nation-state system. On the one hand there are humiliating Sino-foreign wars and resultant unequal treaties signed by China; on the other, an increasing number of students are sent overseas to study Western science and technology in order to save China's civilization by adopting Western material civilization (Cohen 2003: 35). In the 19th century, Western technologies of typography, printing presses, and printing machines were introduced to Shanghai (Reed 2004). With the increased flow of Western objects and technology "trans-lingual practice" also strengthened and underscored the "translated modernity" (Liu 1993). Yan Fu introduced Darwin and Spencer to China; Liang Qichao regarded human history as the "development and strife of human races" (Dikötter1992: 68). Wang Tao was the first to make use of the term *minzu* (Peng 1985: 8), a loanword from Meiji-era Japan (Lin Yaohua 1963: 175, Han and Li 1985: 21, Liu 1995:292 [Appendix B]). Liang Qichao started to write of China as *minzu* (nation) in its modern sense, which was defined as a community "with a common geographic origin, a common bloodline, common physical characteristics, common language, common writing, common religion, common customs, and a common mode of livelihood" (Harrell 2001: 29, Peng 1985: 9, Han and Li 1985: 53-54). Assisted by Chinese colleagues, W.A.P. Martin (Ding Weiliang) translated and published T.D. Woolsey's *Introduction to the Study of International Law*, J.C. Bluntschli's *Das Moderne Völkerrecht der Civilisierten Staten als Rechtsbuch dargestellt,* and W. E. Hall's *Treatise on International Law (1903)* (Liu 2004:114). Martin was also responsible for publishing the Chinese translation of Henry Wheaton's *Elements of International Law* (1864) (Wanguo Gongfa) "under the official auspices of Prince Gong and his newly established foreign affairs office" (Liu 2004:114). The concept of "sovereign right" also found its Chinese equivalent, the neologism *zhuquan* (Liu 2004:109). The techno-material availability and Western ideological accessibility cries for the coinciding of the political boundary and that of the national (Gellner 2006:1). The double task of resisting the Western aliens and driving out the Manchu "barbarians" in order to build a Chinese nation-state, as envisaged by Dr. Sun Yat-sen in his early political career, finalized the core notion of Han.

After China opened up to the West and entered a largely English-speaking world in the late 1970s, the word "nationality" that was used as the equivalent for *minzu* (as applied to the 55 national minorities and the Han) became problematic although it had been praised for its originality that brought nomenclatural equality to all communities, in sharp contrast with the Russian hierarchical terminologies.[5] In the latter half of the 1990s the Chinese government replaced 'nationality' with 'ethnic(ity)' in its translation of "*minzu*". The English version of Guojia Minzu Shiwu Weiyuanhui, which was State Nationalities Affairs Commission of the People's Republic of China, has officially been changed to State Ethnic Affairs Commission of the People's Republic of China, and the journal *Minzu Tuanjie*, the official journal dedicated to *minzu* affairs, has also changed its English title from 'Nationalities Unity' to 'Ethnic Unity'. A professor based at Peking University calls for 'depoliticising' *minzu* and insists that *minzu* (which he translates as 'nation') and *zuqun* (which he translates as 'ethnic group') are very different concepts: *minzu* purportedly involves nationalism and national movements of self-determination. Confusing a 'multinational state' with a 'polyethnic state' (Kymlicka 1995; Bulag 2002),[6] Ma believes that the national minorities in China are largely similar to racial and ethnic minorities in the United States, thereby necessitating a terminological rectification. Ma calls his newly named ethnic groups in China 'subcultural groups' (*ya wenhua qunti*), meaning they are not even autonomous cultural groups but are branches of "the culture of the Chinese nation" (*Zhonghua minzu*). This nomenclatural change, he hopes, "will help avoid misunderstandings due to the close connection of 'nationalities' (the old translation of *shaoshu minzu*) with nationalism and rights of national self-determination, which will bring instability and separatism" (Bilik 2007).

Indexicality and Embodiment: a Semiotic Analysis of Han

Researchers like Ma would embrace the Saussurean idea of arbitrariness of sign-object relations when they deal with nomenclatural use of "*minzu*". They would argue that whether a community was called "*minzu*" or "*zuqun*" (ethnic group) is arbitrary and could be "managed" for political purposes. However, the American semiotician Peirce pointed out that sign-object relation is not that arbitrary: Many interpretants predict real relations between signs and their objects. He called such signs indices, and one of his favorite examples was the interpretation of a weathercock as accurately signifying the direction of the wind because of its having a real relation with the wind (James Hoopes 1991:12). Such indexical signs bear a family resemblance to Merleau-Ponty's phenomenal body, further developed by Csordas.[7] Since embodiment is "the existential ground of culture and self" and "culture is grounded in the human body" (Csordas 1994:6), it fits nicely Peirce's triadic formula of human cognition: "According to Peirce, the triadic nature of thinking is exemplified in the process through which the concept of the self is, itself, created. An infant, inferring no self, knows no distinction between its body and the body of a hot stove. The child may therefore touch the stove. From the resulting feeling (sign), the child arrives at the conclusion (interpretant) that there is such a thing as error and that it inheres in its self (object)" (Hoopes 1991: 8). This bodily sign (the resulting feeling) is a kind of embodiment. The stove is touched by the infant resulting in his/her body a haptic sign, which produces the interpretant that "there is such a thing as error and that it inheres in its self (object)". The relation between the body of the hot stove and the body of the infant self is one of mutual embodiment facilitated by the "touch", finalized by the formation of interpretant. It is through touching the body of the hot stove that the infant starts to know its own body. To the infant, the stove has become "embodiment-by-proxy"-"the process of embedding oneself in a meaningful array of symbols" (Rouse 2004). The embodiment connects the self as object on one end, and interpretant on the other, in the same way the interpretation of a weathercock is signifying the direction of the wind because of its real relation with the wind. This indexical, contiguous relationship is vital for understanding and interpreting the culture, society, and history of human beings.

The interpretant of Han has been evolving by pointing to the indexical relationships between Han and non-Han, which include China's national minorities and foreigners; it also points to the memory of historic encounters between the Han and non-Han. By touching the stove and through the resulting feeling (sign), the Peircean child "arrives at the conclusion (interpretant) that there is such a thing as error and that it inheres in its self (object)"; analogically, the "pre-Han" realized that they were "Han" by "touching" those "non-Han" by way of war, trade, marriage, imagination, and so forth. Indexical embodiment of ethnicity and nationality does not imply primordialism or structural stagnancy; it is an open process and acquires negotiated meaning of "bodily experience in the indeterminate space between the analytics of representation and being-in-the-world" (Csordas 1994:16). To further understand the power of indexical embodiment that works to strengthen Han identities in China, it is beneficial to look at how majorities are made via interacting with minorities (Gladney 1998, 2004), and vice versa (Schein 2000). According to Hsieh (1998: 97), the majority Han in Taiwan could be defined in three ways: How Han politicians look at the Han; how indigenous intellectuals view the Han; how Han humanists define Han.

Again we need to emphasize, however, that Han is created not only by "thinking" but also by "doing", not only by cognitive classification but also by interethnic physical violence. The creation of "Han" is not possible without embodiment and without "letting the child touch the stove and feel the pain". Peircean realistic idealism can shed new light on the notion of "Han".

Politico-Culutural Communities of Inquireres

In the quote "We are Han", as a shifter "we" points to the presence of another shifter "you".[8] Shifters in use occupy time and space ("here", "there", "then"...); when "we" call ourselves "Han" "we" are engaged in a dialogue with "you" at a moment in time and a locality in space. Such dialogue about "Han" is an open process, which is necessitated by the trichotomic relationship of signs. While icon is of resemblance relationship and index of contiguity, symbol depends on arbitrariness and convention, which makes any dialogue an open process and "more vulnerable to destabilization and change" than iconicity and indexicality. "Han" as a sign is not a closed, completed entity; it is ready and open to conceptual renegotiation between politico-cultural communities of inquirers.[9] In the same way that a semiotic sign ("man") is always virtual and never actual, "Han" is a negotiated, dialogical, manufactured virtual reality. Though confined in the hierarchy of power relationship, the politico-cultural communities of inquirers are reproducing and modifying the image and the notion of "Han" in daily traffic of multilingual signs and corporeal encounters of identity politics. This is a question we cannot and will not stop asking: Who are the "Han"?

NOTES

[1] An analyst may view a culture as "a system of symbols and meanings;" but the natives conceptualize their culture in terms of the triads of indexical, iconic and symbolic signs. (Daniel 1984: 32)

[2] Sun Zhonghsan, *The International Development of China,* written between 1918 and 1919, became the second part of *Jianguo Fanglüe* (Nation-building Strategies 1998).

[3] "The nation is a historically evolved, stable community of language, territory, economic life, and psychological make-up". (Stalin 1942: 12)

[4] Such a "nation" is based on one important precondition, that is, the nation takes shape only at the prime stage of Capitalism, which has created a huge army of proletariat, thus laying the class foundation for building a modern state. Those pre-capitalism people should better be called nationality or narodnast' according to the Soviet nationality theory. This Identification Project, however, does not always follow linguistic criterion; instead, it sometimes switches to other parameters, either in lump sum or individually, such as history, ethnic origin, or self-other identities. (Dru 1998, Harrell 1999) For example, the Zhuang and Buyei, which belong to the same language branch, were classified into separate ethnicities; the Western Yugur speaking a Turkic language, and the Eastern Yugur speaking a Mongolian language, were merged into one Yugur ethnicity.

[5] According to the Stalinist Soviet nationality theory, the formation of *natsia* (nation) is based on one important precondition, that it evolves only at the prime stage of capitalism, which has created a huge proletarian army, thus laying the class foundation for building a modern state. The pre-capitalist people should, in this theory, better be called *narodnast'* (pre-capitalist) or *plemia* (pre-class). Chinese communists, however, deviated from this hegemonic theory in their nationality policy. All the 56 official *minzu*, large or small, developed or underdeveloped, modern or 'primitive', with or without writing systems, are equally called "nationalities", and are not discriminated by terms like, in Russian, *narodnast'* or *plemia*. Cf. Bilik 2007.

[6] According to Kymlicka (1995) and Bulag (2002), a 'multinational state', involving 'previously self-governing, territorially concentrated cultures' which were incorporated into 'a large state' and as a result of which cultural diversity was created, is fundamentally different from a 'polyethnic state', in which case 'cultural diversity arises from individual and familial migration.

[7] "If embodiment is an existential condition in which the body is the subjective source or intersubjective ground of experience, then studies under the rubric of embodiment are not 'about' the body per se. Instead

they are about culture and experience insofar as these can be understood from the standpoint of bodily being-in-the-world (Csordas 1999)."

[8] It is a kind of sign that demands "the copresence of a symbolic and an indexical mode of signification"; also known as "duplex sign" (Daniel 1984: 39; Jakobson 1957; Silverstein 1976).

[9] For Charles Peirce "the community of inquirers" is "for the most part a community of truthfully, faithfully, charitably, and open-mindedly communicating scientists" (Daniel 1984: 17); my "politico-cultural communities of inquirers" can also have members who are political speculators, cultural manipulators, and identity imitators.

BIBLIOGRAPHY OF WORKS CITED

Bianjishi (Editorial Institute), The Institute of Linguistics, Chinese Academy of Social Sciences. 2002. *The Contemporary Chinese Dictionary (Chinese-English Edition)*. Beijing: Foreign Language Teaching and Research Press.

Bilik, N. 2007. "Names Have Memories: History, Semantic Identity and Conflict in Mongolian and Chinese Langauge Use", *Inner Asia*, 9(1): 23-39.

Boas, Franz. 1966. Introduction to *Handbook of American Indian Languages*. In Preston Holder ed. *Franz Boas' Introduction to Handbook of American Indian Languages; J. W. Powell Indian Linguistic Families of America North of Mexico*. pp. 1-79. Lincoln: University of Nebraska Press.

Bulag, Uradyn E. 2002. *The Mongols at China's Edge: History and the Politics of National Unity*. Lanham (MD): Rowman & Littlefield Publishers.

Chen, Liankai. 1989. *zhongguo, huayi, fanhan, zhonghua, zhonghuaminzu* (China, Huayi, Fan Han, Zhonghua, Chinese Nation). In Xiaotong Fei et al. *Zhonghua minzu duoyuan yiti geju* (The Configuration of Plurality and Unity of the Chinese Nation). pp. 72-113. Beijing: Central Institute of Nationalities Press.

Cohen, Paul A. 1997. *History in Three Keys: The Boxers as Event, Experience, and Myth*. New York: Columbia University Press.

Cohen, Paul A. 2003. *China Unbound: Evolving perspectives on the Chinese past*. London and New York: RoutledgeCurzon.

Connor, Walker. 1984. *The National Question in Marxist-Leninist Theory and Strategy*. Princeton: Princeton University Press.

Daniel, Valintine. 1984. *Fluid Signs: Being a Person the Tamil Way*. Berkeley: University of California Press.

Dikötter, Frank. 1992. *The Discourse of Race in Modern China*. Hong Kong: Hong Kong University Press.

Editorial Department of *Historical Research* 1957. *A Collection of Papers on the Formation of the Han Minzu*

(*Han minzu xingcheng wenti taolun ji*). Beijing: Joint Publishing.

Fu Zhengyuan. 1994. *Autocratic Tradition and Chinse Politics.* Cambridge University Press.

Gellner, Ernest. 2006 (1983). *Nations and Nationalism.* 2nd ed. Malden, Massachusetts: Blackwell Publishing Ltd.

Gladney, Dru C., ed. 1998. *Making Majorities.* Stanford: Stanford University Press.

Guy, R. Kent. 2002. Who Were the Manchus? A Review Essay. *The Journal of Asian Studies* 61 (1): 151-164.

Han, Jinchun, and Li Yifu. 1985. *Hanwen "Minzu" Yi-Ci Kaoyuan Ziliao* (Etymological Data on Minzu in Chinese). Beijing: Department of Nationality Theory Research, Institute of Nationality Studies.

Harrell, Stevan. 1999 The Role of the Periphery in Chinese Nationalism. In *Imaging China: Regional Division and National Unity.* Shu-min Huang, and Cheng-Kuang Hsu, eds. Pp. 133-160. Taipei: Institute of Ethnology, Academia Sinica.

Harrell, Stevan. 2001. *Ways of Being Ethnic in Southwest China.* Seattle: University of Washington Press.

Hirsch, Francine. 2005. *Empire of Nations: Ethnographic Knowledge and the Making of the Soviet Union.* Ithaca and London: Cornell University Press.

Hsieh Shih-Chung. 1998. "On Three Definitions of Han Ren-Images of the Majority People in Taiwan". In Dru C. Gladney ed. *Making Majorities—Constituting the Nation in Japan, Korea, China, Malyasia, Fiji, Turkey, an the United States,* pp. 95-105. Stanford: Stanford University Press.

Jakobson, Roman. 1957. *Sifters, Verbal Categories, and the Russian Verb.* Cambridge, Massachusetts: Department of Slavic Languages and Literature, Harvard University.

Jia, Jingyan. 1989. "Hanren" kao (Textual analysis of "Hanren"), in Fei Xiaotong et al. *Zhonghua minzu duo yuan yiti geju* (Plurality and Unity in the Configuration of the Chinese People): 137-152. Beijing: *Zhongyang minzu xueyuan chubanshe.*

Kymlicka, Will. 1995. *Multicultural Citizenship.* Oxford: Clarendon.

Lin, Yaohua (Lin, Yueh-hwa). 1963. Guanyu "minzu" yi ci de shiyong he yiming de wenti (About the use and translation of the term *minzu*). *Lishi yanjiu* 1963 (2): 171-190.

Liu, Lydia H. 1993. *Translingual Practice: Literature, National Culture, and Translated Modernity China, 1900-1937.* Stanford: Stanford University Press.

Liu, Lydia H. 2004. *The Clash of Empires: The Invention of China in Modern World Making.* Cambridge, Massachusetts: Harvard University Press.

Moerman, Michael. 1965. Ethnic Identification in a Complex Civilization: Who Are the Lue? *American Anthropologist* (67)5: 1215-1230.

Peng, Yingming. 1985. *Guanyu wo guo minzu gainian lishi de chubu kaocha* (A preliminary investigation concerning the idea of *minzu* in our country). *Minzu yanjiu* 1985 (2): 5-11.

Reed, Christopher A. 2004. *Gutenberg in Shanghai: Chinese Print Capitalism, 1876-1937.* Vancouver: UBC

Press.

Rhoads, Edward J.M. 2000. *Manchus and Han: Ethnic Relations and Political Power in Late Qing and Early Republican China, 1861-1928.* Seattle: University of Washington Press.

Sapir, Edward. 2007. *Language: An Introduction to the Study of Speech.* Charleston: BiblioBazaar.

Siverstein, Michael. 1976. "Shifters, Linguistic Categories, and Cultural Description". In Keith H. Basso and Henry A. Selby eds. *Meanign in Anthropology*, pp. 11-55. Albuquerque: University of New Mexico Press.

Stalin, J. 1942. *Marxism and the National Question.* New York: International Publishers.

Tsou, Jung. 1968. *The Revolutionary Army: A Chinese Nationalist Tract of 1903.* Trans. John Just. The Hague: Mouton.

Sun, Zhongshan. 1998. *Jianguo fanlüe* (The International Development of China). Henan: Zhongzhou Guji Chubanshe.

Sun, Zhongshan. 1994. *Junren jingshen jiaoyu* (Spiritual education for soldiers). In Cao Jinqing ed. *Sun Zhongshan Wenxuan* (Selected Works of Sun Yat-sen). pp.257-287. Shanghai: Shanghai Yuandong Chubanshe.

Zhao, Suisheng. 2004. *Nation-State by Construction: Dynamics of Modern Chinese Nationalism.* Stanford: Stanford University Press.

ON THE ORIGINS OF THE PLACE-NAME BUXĀRĀ

Shamsiddin S. Kamoliddin

There are several ancient place-names in Central Asia such as Āmū, Chāch, Xīwa, Samarqand, Chaghāniyān, and some others, the origin of which till now remains unknown. The name of Buxārā, which is one of largest cities of the region, also belongs to this group. This name was mentioned for the first time on the earliest copper coins of Buxārā (4th-5th centuries CE) [Наймарк, 1995, с. 37] with Sogdian inscriptions in the forms Puɣar (*pwɣ'r*) and Puxar (*pwx'r*) [Смирнова, 1981, с. 34 (792-796); Смирнова, 1982, с. 143]. In the Sogdian sources (early 8th-9th centuries) it is mentioned in the forms Puɣar (*pwɣ'r*) and Puxar (*pwx'r*) [Согдийские документы, с.182; Henning, 1940, p. 10], and in the inscription of Kül-tegin (early 8th century)-in the form Buqar (*buqar*) [Малов, 1951, с. 19-20].

It is supposed, that this name originated from the Sanskrit word *vihara*, which means "a Buddhist monastery" [Frye, 1956, p. 106-119]. However, according to the norms of the Sogdian language, this name could not have been transformed from the word *vihara* which in the Sogdian used the word *βrx'r* [Лурье, 2004, с. 20]. In New Persian this word is transferred in the form فاخر *farxār* [Баевский, 1980, p. 88] or بهار *bihār* [Худуд ал-'āлем, f. 27A; Hudud al-'Alam, p. 108], and in Arabic-in the form البهار *al-bahār* or *al-buhār* [al-Khowarezmi, p. 34]. Consequently, the written *pwx'r* transcribes the name's sound as *buxar* (*buɣar, buqar*) or *puxar* (*puɣar, puqar*), formed on the basis of a word of non-Sogdian [Tremblay, 2004, p. 122], probably Hephthalite, origin [Лившиц, Кауфман, Дьяконов, 1954, с. 155, 157]. There is a place-name Puxar in Siberia which originated from the word (*puxar*), which in the Yeniseic languages (*hanty*) means "an island" [Мурзаев, 1984, с. 470].[1]

In this connection the data of some sources which can throw light on the true origin of this word are of interest. According to Juwayni, the word بخار (*buxār*), underlying the name

Buxārā (بخارا), meant in the language of the Mughs (*ba-luġ'at-i muγān*) "the assembly of a science" (*majma' 'ilm*), and in the language of the Buddhists (*ba-luġ'at-i but-parastān*), the Uighur and the Chinese, it was used for a designation of their temples where their idols (*ma 'ābid ishān ke mawzi'-i butān*) were located. Therefore this city was named Buxārā, and its former name was Banuğkath بنجكث [Juwayni, vol. 1, p. 76; Бартольд, 1963, c. 214]. In the old Uighur language the word بخار (*buxār*) had the meaning of "a temple" or "a chapel" [Будагов, 1869, т. 1, c. 285]. In Old Turkic the Sanskrit word *vihāra* was used in form *viχār*, and the Sogdian word *βry'r*-in the form *vrχar* [Древнетюркский словарь, c. 634]. Consequently, the word *buxār* might be a Turkic form of the Sanskrit word *vihāra*. Mahmūd Kāšgharī remarked that the city of Buxārā was so named because of the Buddhists' temple which was located there [Kašgarli, p. 111].

From these data it follows that the name of the city of Buxārā could have derived from the word *buxār*, which was not a Sogdian, but a Turkic (Uighur), transfer of the Sanskrit word *vihara* (a Buddhist monastery). Consequently, it is possible to assume that the occurrence of this name was connected with the activity of some Turkic ruler who reigned in the pre-Islamic period in the Bukhara oasis.

It is known, that, in the 6th century CE the oasis of Buxārā was a property of Tardu-kagan (Sāwa-shāh, Shīr-i Kishwar), who was the son of the Supreme Turkic kagan Istami (Qarā Chūrīn). He was the uncle of the Sassanid *šāhanšāh* Xurmazd IV Turkzāda in his mother's line [Bel'ami, vol. 2, p. 248, 265; Firdousi, vol. 6, p. 656-657], because he was the native brother of the daughter of Istami-kagan who married the Sassanid *šāhanšāh* Xusraw I Anūshirwān. According to Narshakhi, Shīr-i Kishwar ruled in Buxārā for twenty years and resided in Baykand. He built the fortress of Buxārā, and also established some settlements in the oasis of Buxārā such as Mamastin, Sakmatin, Samtin, and Farab. His son El-tigin (Parmūda, Nili-xān) had also established some settlements in the oasis of Buxārā, such as Iskijkath, Sharg, Faraxsha, and Rāmitan. He was married to a Chinese princess who brought from China "a temple of idols" and it was established in Rāmitan (Rāmtin) [Frye, 1954, p. 8]. Rāmitan was more ancient than the city of Buxārā; formerly it was a residence of the kings, and after building the city of Buxārā they moved there. In some books Rāmitan was also named Buxārā [Frye, 1954, p. 16].

In the region of medieval Nasaf was mentioned a settlement named Nawqad Sāwa نوقد ساوه [an-Nasafī, Arabe, f. 59V; as-Sam'ānī, Marg., f. 571R] which name can be connected with a name Sāwa ساوه . The Supreme Turkic kagan Tardu (Shīr-i Kishwar) is mentioned in the Arabic sources as Shāba شابة [Ibn Khordadhbeh, p. 40], and in the Persian sources as Sāwa-shāh ساوه شاه [Firdousi, vol. 6, p. 656-658]. The word *sawa* or *šāwa* is a Baktrian title, which meant "a king" [Frye, 1956, p. 122; Harmatta, Litvinsky, 1996, p. 371]. From these data it follows that Shīr-i Kishwar had established settlements not only in the region of Bukhara, but in the region of Naxshab as well.

To the southeast from the remains of Farabr on the hill named Qiz-qir near the Amu-Darja river are the remains of a watchtower known as the Ding of Arslān-khān. This is the most ancient of the archaeological remains in the region of Farabr [Массон, 1966, p. 167]. If we take into account the information of Narshkhī, that Farabr had been established by Shīr-i Kishwar (Tardu-kagan) [Наршахий, с. 17], referred to also as El-Araslan, it is possible to assume that this tower was constructed at the end of 6th- early 7th centuries by him or by his son El-tegin, who reigned here after him.

Among the coins of the pre-Islamic rulers of Bukhara (6th-8th centuries) there is a coin with a portrait of a ruler with Mongoloid features (AV) and *tamgha* in the form ⚯ (RV) without any inscriptions.[2] It is possible to assume that this coin had been minted by Tardu-kagan (Shīr-i Kishwar) or his son El-tegin.

In the 10th century the city of Buxārā was also referred to as Numijkath نمجكث or Bumijkath بمجكث as it was formerly named [al-Istakhri, p. 313; Ibn Haukal, p. 463; al-Moqaddasi, p. 40, 289]. Consequently, the name Buxārā was not so ancient and appeared in the early medieval period. Therefore some settlements of the Buxārā oasis, such as Baykand, Waraxshā, Wardān, Nūr, Rāmitan, and Rāmush, were mentioned as "villages more ancient than the city of Bukhara" [al-Moqaddasi, p. 282; Frye, 1954, p. 16-20).

El-tegin (Parmūda, Nili-khan) who was married to the Chinese princess, had established a Buddhist temple in Rāmitan, where he resided. It is known, that in 590 the Chinese queen, who belonged to the house Chžow (Zhou), led a rebellion against the emperor of the Sui Dynasty. With the aim of getting support among the Turks, she made a treaty with Nili-khan (Parmūda), the governor of Buxārā [Бичурин, 1950, т. 1, с. 240; Гумилев, 1967, с. 136]. It seems that the marriage and arrival of the Chinese princess in Buxārā and the further construction of the Buddhist temple in Rāmitan took place at the same time.

The Chinese princess, whose name was Sian-shy (Xianshi), gave birth to Nili-khan (Yil-teguin) the son named Daman (Taman). Soon afterwards, Nili-khan died, and she married his younger brother named Poshi dele (teguin). Around the year 600, Poshi together with Sian-shy arrived at the Chinese court and was left there as a hostage. The Chinese princess Sian-shy did not return to Bukhara and stayed in China to the end of her life. After the death of Nili-khan on the throne of Bukhara, the son of Sian-shy named Daman (Taman) with the title

Nigyu Chulo-khan ascended the throne. In 614, Chulo-khan married the Chinese princess named Sin-I (Xinyi), and went to do military service for the Chinese emperor. In 618 he was lost in a war with the Eastern Turks [Бичурин, т. 1, с. 279-283].

On the basis of the above mentioned data, it seems that the name of Buxār originally belonged to the temple in Rāmitan, and it was later transferred to the entire area and its new capital on the site of modern Buxārā. On a map of Buxārā made in the mid-19th century,[3] the tomb of the Chinese prince (*qabri-i pīsar-i pādishāh-i Xitā*) is mentioned [Мухамеджанов, 1965, с. 31-42], from which it follows that the Chinese princess in the late period of her life lived in the city of Buxārā, where her "temple of idols" was also situated.

In this connection the mausoleum of the Samanids in Bukhara,[4] construction of which was undertaken in the 9th-early 10th centuries, is of interest. The planning structure of the mausoleum's building represents the cubic volume topped with a dome and having a centric composition-four entrances with completely identical facades [Пугаченкова, 1968, с. 119]. The architectural image of this building represents an embodiment of a cosmogram: a square and a circle [Булатов, 2005, с. 36]. It was supposed that the mausoleum of the Samanids repeated the form of a Sogdian lock [Пугаченкова, Ремпель, 1958, с. 67] or a pre-Islamic memorial *kedh*, widespread in Sogdian architecture [Пугаченкова, 1962, с. 52]. However, according to another view, the mausoleum building represents a Sabian (Manichean) temple-an observatory devoted to a cult of the Sun, from which supervision over the movement of the sun was conducted [Булатов, 1976, с. 71-77; Булатов, 2005, с. 36]. Near the mausoleum of the Samanids there are archeological remains of more ancient buildings the floors of which has been decorated with figures in the form of concentric circles made from the brickwork. It was supposed that this building was connected with a solar cult [Булатов, 1976, с. 91].

In our opinion, the mausoleum of the Samanids was an exact copy of that temple which had been constructed by El-tegin for the Chinese princess. The rest of that temple is the foundation of an ancient cultic building, which was discovered near the mausoleum of the Samanids. The general layout of the mausoleum from the top view is an exact reproduction of a Buddhist mandala [Mandala, p. 140].

Another indication, specifying a connection of this monument with Buddhism, are similar symbols represented on the outside walls of the mausoleum.[5] This symbol represents the complex geometrical composition consisting of squares built within each other and a circle in the middle [Пугаченкова, Ремпель, 1960, с. 67; Пугаченкова, 1968, с. 121; Булатов, 1976, с. 85], exemplifying a cosmogram of the decreasing and increasing Universe [Булатов, 2005, с. 36]. The symbol of the entered squares and disks is presented also in the wall paintings of the early medieval palace in Varakhsha [Ремпель, 1961, с. 152]. Precisely the same symbol is represented in the wall paintings with subject images from Buddhist legends in the cave complex of Dunhuang, which was one of the largest Buddhist cult centers of Central and East Asia in the early Middle Ages [Арапов, 2002, с. 120-125]. In antiquity the ornamentation could furnish buildings with a magical character, and serve as symbols of the durability of a building and the well-being of the inhabitants [Алпаткина, 2004, с. 32].

El-tegin (Parmūda) was a follower of Buddhism and with him was connected penetration of this religion to Buxārā [Ставиский, 1960, с. 115]. In 588 he had been sent as a governor to Kashmir, where he established two Buddhist temples [Chavannes, 1903, p. 157]. The Chinese traveler U-kun, who visited Kashmir and Gandhara between 759 and 764, saw among the Buddhist relics there some temples built in the 6th-7th centuries by Turkic governors, including the temple of Ve-li-tele, i.e., Ve-li-tegin or El-tegin, who was a son of the king of the Turks. This building had been constructed one hundred years previously [Chavannes, 1903, p. 198, 242-245; Литвинский, Зеймаль, 1971, с. 120]. In the 11th century some Turks who worshipped Buddhism still lived in the northern and eastern parts of Kashmir [Бируни, 1963, с. 202-203].

However, the place name Buxārā was for the first time mentioned on the coins of the 4th- 5th centuries [Смирнова, 1982, с. 143; Мусакаева, 1985, с. 82; Мусакаева, 1990, с. 33-37; Наймарк, 1995, с. 37]. Consequently, there was a Buddhist temple, established in the period of the Xionits or Hephthalites, and the oasis of Buxārā was named after it. However, the date on the issue of the earliest coins of Bukhara is not certain and, considering paleographical data of their inscriptions, it is also supposed that they were issued in the early 6th century.[6] This lends weight to the hypothesis of Narshakhī that the appearance of the name Buxar (Puxar) in the period of the Turkic qaghanate was connected with the foundation of a Buddhist temple for the Chinese princess in Rāmitan.

Among the nobles who arrived in 732 in the Orxon Horde of the kagan to participate in the funeral of Kul-tigin, is mentioned Ogul-tarxān, who represented the *ulus* of the Buqara people (*buqaraq ulus budun*) [Малов, 1951, с. 19-20]. Although the word *buqaraq* here refers to the name of the people, rather than the name of the country, it might be the ancient Turkic form of this place-name *(buqar)*. The word *ulus*, accompanying the word *buqaraq* in the Turkic text, means also "a residence of Buddha" [Мурзаев, 1984, с. 575].

Buddhism, probably, was not widely spread in the oasis of Buxārā, because the Chinese pilgrim Xuanzang, who passed through the lands of Pu-ho (Buxārā) in the year 630, has not mentioned existence of any Buddhist relics or followers of Buddhism there [Beal, 1990,

p. 45]. Most of the population of early medieval Sogdiana were followers of Mazdaism. However, data from other textual sources testifies to the existence of the followers of other religions in Bukhara. According to Narshakhī, the inhabitants of pre-Islamic Bukhara were idolaters (*būt parast būdand*). In the 10th century in Bukhara was the market named Bāzār-i Māh, where twice annually idols were sold, and these were in great demand among inhabitants of the city. This market was established in pre-Islamic times by the king of Bukhara named Māh (Moon) which sat there during the fair on the throne to encourage the trade in idols [Наршахий, с. 26-27].

From these data it would seem that in pre-Islamic times the inhabitants of Bukhara were idolaters (*būt parast*). Idols were also found in temples of Paykand, Varakhsha, and other cities of Sogd. When Qutayba ibn Muslim entered Paykand, he found in one of its temples of idolaters *(butxāna)* a silver idol worth as much as 400 dirhams [Наршахий, с. 45].

Idolatry, described in writings as the earliest form of religion in Bukhara [Зуев, 2002, с. 195], was one of the main distinctive features of Manichaeism. Followers of Mānī considered anthropomorphic idols to be symbols of divine stars—the Sun and the Moon, the last stations on the way to Light Paradise [Бируни, 1963, с. 479]. The name of king Māh can be compared with Mānī, who in Manichaean texts was also called the god of the Moon (*Aj tängri*) [Зуев, 2002, с. 194]. Hence, in pre-Islamic times the majority of inhabitants of Bukhara were Manichaeans.

Manichaeism in Central Asia long coexisted with Buddhism, and the influence of Buddhism on the eastern branch of Manichaeism was so strong that Mānī in the Manichaean texts was called the Buddha or Mānī-Buddha [Восточный Туркестан, 1992, с. 526]. Hence, the prototype of the mausoleum of the Samanids was, most likely, not Buddhist, but a Manichaean temple, and the king of Bukhara named Māh (El-tegin, Parmūda) was also not Buddhist, but Manichaean.

Some data show that the Supreme qaghans of the Western Turkic qaghanate were Manichaeans. The second name of Tardu-qaghan, Sāwa-shāh (Shāwa, Shāba), incorporates the Middle Persian word *syava* ("black") or the Sogdian *s'w* ("black") [Зуев, 2002, с. 195]. Among the Turk-Manichaeans of the Yetisū region the legend about a Turkic king named Shū (from the Sogdian *s'w*, meaning "black") was widespread [Kāšγarī, vol. 3, p. 419, vol. 1, p. 117]. In Turkic Manichaeism *qara* ("black") indicated a rank and religious post of a person who oversaw the education and training of young pupils in Manichaean schools [Зуев, 2002, с. 201]. Another name of Tardu-qaghan-Shīr-i Kishwar (the lion of the country) or El-Arslan (the lion of the people), also specifies that he was a Manichaean. An image of a lion (Persian *shīr*, Turkic *arslān*) and its symbols occupied a special place in Turkic Manichaeism whereas in Zoroastrianism and Buddhism it was almost not used [Зуев, 2002, с. 188, 192-193, 203]. The second name of Istami-qaghan (Dizavul) was Qarā Chūrīn [Наршахий, с. 16], and the name-title Qarā-čor is also widely known from the Manichaean texts of East Turkestan [Зуев, 2002, с. 200-201].

On the basis of the above mentioned data, it might be supposed that the name of Buxārā originated from a Turkic word *buxar*, which means "a Buddhist temple". In such a case it would be impossible to explain the formation of the form *pux'r*, fixed in Sogdian sources, from the Sanskrit word *vihara*, which, in turn, testifies that the name of the city (Buxārā) was not formed on the basis of the Sogdian lexicon, but on the basis of the Turkic one. In that case the Sogdian form Puxar *(pwx'r)* was a transformation not of the Sanskrit word *vihara*, but the Turkic *buxar* with the same meaning.

The occurrence of this name might be connected with the construction of a Buddhist temple there in the period of the Xionits or Hephthalites. In the 6th century the Turkic governor of this region Yil-tigin (Barmūda, Nili-xān), the son of Tardu-kagan (Shīr-i Kishwar, Sāwa-shāh), who was a follower of Buddhism, established another Buddhist temple there for the Chinese princess. This temple has been located not in the city of Buxārā, but in Rāmitan, where the residence of El-tigin was located, and the idols of the Chinese princess, who had brought them from China, had been placed. From the temple of that time the city and its area came to be known by the Turkic name Buxār, which was alien to the Sogdian language. After transferring a residence of governors to the city of Numijkath (Bumijkath), this name began to be applied to the new city, where a new temple for idols was probably built. At the same time, the old Sogdian name of the city Numilkath or Bumijkath remained in use until the 10th century.

NOTES

[1] There is a hypothesis that many ancient place names of Central Asia have a Yenisei origin, and carriers of the Yeniseic languages made up a significant part of the pre Indo-European population of Central Asia. See: Яйленко, 1990, с. 37-49.

[2] This coin was found at the historical city site of Qanqa in the oasis of Tashkent and at present it is kept in the private collection of Andrey Kuzneysov in Tashkent.

[3] The author of this map, which was stored in the private archive of the Russian Orientalist P. I. Lerx

(1827-1884), is unknown. It is supposed that it was made by the Uzbek scholar and writer Ahmad Dānish (1827-1897). See: Сухарева, 1976, с. 132-148.

[4] Pre-Islamic ancestors of the Samanids were descendants of Bahram Chubin from his marriage with the daughter of Parmuda (El-tegin).

[5] In all there are eight, with two symbols on each side of the building, located on the right and left sides above the entrances.

[6] This information was provided by Dr. A. Musakaeva (Museum of the History of Uzbekistan of the Academy of Sciences), who first investigated these coins.

REFERENCES

Textual Sources

Бируни, Абу Рейхан. Индия / Перевод с арабского А.Б.Халидова и Ю.Н.Завадовского. Комментарии В.Г.Эрмана и А.Б.Халидова // Избранные произведения. Т. 2. Ташкент: Изд-во АН УзССР, 1963.

Бичурин Н.Я. (Иакинф). Собрание сведений о народах, обитавших в Средней Азии в древние времена. В 3-х томах. М.; Л.: Изд-во АН СССР, 1950-1953.

Кошгарий, Махмуд. Туркий сўзлар девони (Девону-луғот ит-турк) / Таржимон ва нашрга тайёрловчи С.М.Муталлибов. 3 томлик. Тошкент: Фан, 1960-1963.

Малов С.Е. Памятники древнетюркской письменности. Тексты и исследования. М.; Л.: Изд-во АН СССР, 1951.

Наршахий, Абу Бакр Мухаммад ибн Жаъфар. Бухоро тарихи / Форс тилидан А.Расулев таржимаси, мухаррир А.Уринбоев. Тошкент: Шарк баёзи, 1993.

ан-Насафи, Абу Хафс 'Умар ибн Мухаммад. Мунтахаб Китаб ал-Канд. Сокращенная версия Абу-л-Фадла Мухаммада ибн 'Абд ал-Джалила ас-Самарканди. Ркп.

Национальной библиотеки в Париже: Инв. № Arabe, 6284. Л. 1 V-75 R.

Согдийские документы с горы Муг. Чтение, Перевод. Комментарий. Вып. 2.

Юридические документы и письма / Чтение, перевод и комментарии В.А.Лившица. М.: Изд-во вост. лит-ры, 1962.

Худуд ал-'āлем. Рукопись Туманского. С введением и указателем В.Бартольда. Л., 1930.

Beal R.S. *The Life of Hiuen Tsiang Shaman Hwui Li*, Translated with an introduction containing an account of the works of I-Tsing, new edition with a preface by L.Cranmer-Byng, 2-reprint, Delhi, 1990.

Bel'ami, Abou-'Ali Mohammed, traduite sur la version persane de Chronique de Abou-Djafar Mohammedben-Djarir-ben-Jazid Tabari, d'apres les manuscrits de Paris, de Gotha, de Londres et de Canterbury par H.Zotenberg, t. I-IV, Paris, 1867-1874.

Firdousi, *Le livre des rois*, ed. J.Mohl, vol. I-VI, Paris, 1868.

Frye R.N. *The History of Bukhara*, translated from a Persian abridgement of the Arabic original by Narshakhi, Cambridge, 1954.

Hudud al-'Alam, *The Regions of the World, a Persian Geography*, translated and explained by V. Minorsky. London, 1970.

Hudūd al-'ālem. Rukopis Tumanskogo, S vvedeniem i ukazatelem V. Bartol'da, Leningrad, 1930 (Facsimile edition).

Ibn Haukal, Abu-l-Kasim an-Nasibi, *Opus geographicum*, ed. M.J. de Goeje, Bibliotheca Geographorum Arabicorum, pars 2, Lugduni-Batavorum: E.J.Brill, 1967.

Ibn Khordadhbeh, Abu-l-Kasim 'Obaydallah ibn 'Abdallah, Kitab al-Masalik wa-l-mamalik / ed. M.J. de Goeje, Bibliotheca geographorum Arabicorum, pars 6, Lugduni-Batavorum: E.J.Brill, 1967.

al-Istakhri, Abu Ishak al-Farisi, *Viae regnorum*, ed. M.J. de Goeje, Bibliotheca Geographorum Arabicorum, pars 1. Lugduni-Batavorum: E.J.Brill, 1967.

Juwayni, 'Ala'u 'd-Din 'Ata Malik, The Ta'rikh-i Jahan-gusha (composed in A.H. 658=A.D. 1260, ed. with an introduction, notes and indices from several old MSS by Mirza Muhammad ibn 'Abdu'l-Wahhab-i-Qazwini, Leiden-London: Brill, Luzac, 1912 (Part 1); 1916 (Part 2), 1937 (Part 3) (GMS, Old series, XVI, 1-3).

Kašgarli, Mahmūd, *Dīvānu Lug'āt it-Türk*, ed. Rifat, Istanbul, 1915-1917.

al-Khowarezmī, Abū ' Abdallah Mohammed ibn Ahmed ibn Jūsof al-Kātib, *Liber Mafatih al-'Olum*, ed. G. van Vloten, Lugduni-Batavorum: E.J.Brill, 1968.

al-Moqaddasī, Abū 'Abdallah Mohammad ibn Ahmad Shamsaddīn, *Descriptio Imperii moslemici*, ed. M.J. de Goeje, Bibliotheca Geographorum Arabicorum, pars 3. Lugduni-Batavorum, 1967.

Narshakhī, Abū Bakr Muhammad ibn Ja'far. *Buxārā ta'rīxī*, Uzbek translation from the Persian text by A.Rasulev and A.Urunbayev, Tashkent: Sharq bayazī, 1993.

an-Nasafī, Abu Hafs 'Umar ibn Muhammad ibn Ahmad, *Muntaxab Kitab al-Qand*, Abridged version by Abu-l-Fadl Muhammad ibn 'Abd al-Jalīl al-Samarqandī. MS of the Bibliothèque Nationale (Paris), Arabe, 6284, f. 1 V-75 R.

al-Sam'ānī, Abū Sa'd 'Abd al-Karīm ibn Muhammad, *The Kitab al-Ansab*, reproduced facsimile from the manuscript of British Museum with an introduction of by D. S. Margoliouth, Leiden-London, 1912.

Research Literature

Алпаткина Т. Свастика в резном декоре дворца правителей Термеза // Transoxiana: История и культура.

Ташкент, 2004. С. 31-35.

Аманжолов А.С. История и теория древнетюркского письма. Алматы: Мектеп, 2003.

Арапов А. Космограммы ранних исламских мавзолеев Центральной Азии // Ежегодник Московского отделения Международной Академии архитектуры. М., 2002. С. 120-125.

Баевский С.И. Географические названия в ранних персидских толковых словарях (XI-XV вв.) // Страны и народы Востока, вып. 22, книга 2. М., 1980. С. 83-89.

Бартольд В.В. История культурной жизни Туркестана // Сочинения в 9 томах. Т. 2. Часть 1. М., 1963. С. 169-433.

Будагов Л.З. Сравнительный словарь турецко-татарских наречий, с включением употребительнейших слов арабских и персидских и с переводом на русский язык. В 2-х томах. СПб., 1869. [М., 1960].

Булатов М. Мавзолей Саманидов-жемчужина архитектуры Средней Азии. Ташкент: Изд-во лит-ры и искусства им. Г.Гуляма, 1976.

Булатов М.С. Храмы Солнца в древней Трансоксиане // Архитектура и строительство Узбекистана, 2005, № 2-3-4. С. 35-36.

Восточный Туркестан в древности и раннем средневековье. Этнос, языки, религии. Под ред. Б.А.Литвинского. М.: Наука, 1992.

Гумилев Л.Н. Древние тюрки. Л.: Наука ЛО, 1967.

Древнетюркский словарь. Л.: Наука ЛО, 1969.

Зуев Ю.А. Ранние тюрки: очерки истории и идеологии. Алматы: Дайк-Пресс, 2002.

Лившиц В.А., Кауфман К.В., Дьяконов И.М. О древней согдийской письменности Бухары // Вестник древней истории, 1954, 1 (47). С. 150-163.

Литвинский Б.А., Зеймаль Т.И. Аджина-Тепа. Архитектура. Живопись. Скульптура. М.: Искусство, 1971.

Лурье П.Б. Историко-лингвистический анализ согдийской топонимии. Диссертация . . . кандидата филологических наук. СПб., 2004.

Массон М. Е. Средневековые торговые пути из Мерва в Хорезм и в Мавераннахр // Труды Южно-Туркменистанской археологической комплексной экспедиции. Т. 13. Ашхабад, 1966. С. 139-145.

Мурзаев Э.М. Словарь народных географических терминов. М., 1984.

Мусакаева А. К типологии монет Бухары с изображением верблюда // Из истории культурного наследия Бухары. Ташкент: Узбекистан, 1990. С. 33-37.

Мусакаева А. Монета с изображением верблюда из коллекции Музея истории народов Узбекистана // Творческое наследие народов Средней Азии в памятниках искусства, архитектуры и археологии. Ташкент, 1985. С. 82.

Мухамеджанов А.Р. Историко-топографический план Бухары Ахмада Дониша // Общественные науки в Узбекистане, 1965, 5. С. 31-42.

Наймарк А.И. О начале чеканки медной монеты в Бухарском Согде // Нумизматика Центральной Азии, вып. 1. Ташкент, 1995. С. 29-50.

Пугаченкова Г.А. Архитектурный генезис мавзолея Саманидов // Общественные науки в Узбекистане, 1962, 2. С. 47-52.

Пугаченкова Г. А. По древним памятникам Самарканда и Бухары. Издание второе дополненное, М.: Искусство, 1968.

Пугаченкова Г.И., Ремпель Л.И. Выдающиеся памятники изобразительного искусства Узбекистана. Ташкент: Изд-во художественной литературы, 1960.

Ремпель Л.И Архитектурный орнамент Узбекистана. Ташкент, 1961.

Смирнова О.И. Загадочная надпись на монетах Варахши // Письменные памятники и проблемы истории культуры народов Востока. XVI годичная научная сессия ЛО ИВ АН СССР. Часть 2. М., 1982. С. 143-145.

Смирнова О.И. Сводный каталог согдийских монет. Бронза. М.: Наука, 1981.

Ставиский Б.Я. О международных связях Средней Азии в V-сер. VIII вв. (в свете данных советской археологии) // Проблемы востоковедения, 1960, № 5. С. 108-118.

Сухарева О.А. Квартальная община позднефеодального города Бухары (в связи с историей кварталов). М.: Наука, 1976.

Яйленко В.П. Енисейцы-кеты в этнической истории древней Средней Азии // Проблемы этногенеза и этнической истории народов Средней Азии и Казахстана. Вып. 1. М., 1990. С. 37-49.

Frye R. Notes on the history of Transoxiana, in: *Harvard Journal of Asiatic Studies* 19, Cambridge, Mass., 1956, pp. 106-122, reprinted in: Islamic Iran and Central Asia (7th-12th centuries), London: Variorum Reprints, 1979, XV.

Gharib B. *Sogdian Dictionary. Sogdian-Persian-English*, Tehran, 1995.

Harmatta J., Litvinsky B.A. Tokharistan and Gandhara under Western Turk Rule (650-750), part 1, "History of the regions", in: *History of Civilizations of Central Asia*, vol. 3, Paris, 1996, pp. 367-401.

Henning W.B. *Sogdica*, London: The Royal Asiatic Society, 1940.

Mandala, in. *Brockhaus die Enzyklopädie in vierunzwangzig Bänden*, Leipzig: E.A.Brockhaus Mannheim, 1998, p. 140.

Tremblay X. La Toponymie de la Sogdiane et le traitement de *xoet foen* Iranien, in: *Studia Iranica*, t. 33, 2004, fascicule 1, pp. 113-149.

《西域圖記》考

李錦繡

　　隋大業初年裴矩撰寫的三卷《西域圖記》，是西域歷史地理領域里程碑式著作，尤因記載由敦煌至西海的三條交通路線，長期以來受到重視。[1]但《西域圖記》原書已佚，僅存保存在《隋書·裴矩傳》、《北史·裴矩傳》中的序文。日本學者內田吟風先生《隋裴矩撰〈西域圖記〉遺文纂考》[2]一文，根據《通典》、《太平寰宇記》、《玉海》、《史記正義》等，輯錄了除《西域圖記序》外的六條遺文，為一窺《西域圖記》面貌做出了貢獻。我也曾以《太平廣記》卷四三五"馬"條《洽聞記》引《圖記》為線索，結合《冊府元龜》、《唐會要》、《通典》的記載，復原了《西域圖記》"吐火羅"條。[3]但這些文字的輯錄，距再現《西域圖記》的原貌，還相差太遠。

　　《西域圖記》的復原是一項艱巨的工作，需要我們對唐宋西域史籍文獻進行全盤梳理，逐一溯源。其中，《西域圖記序》顯然是復原工作的指南，具有舉足輕重的意義。因此，對《西域圖記序》的解讀無疑更為重要。本文即以《西域圖記序》為線索，結合唐、宋、元代文獻記載，試圖對裴矩《西域圖記》的結構、形式、內容與作用等提出淺見，請讀者指正。

一、《西域圖記》的結構

　　顧名思義，《西域圖記》顯然是包括"圖"與"記"兩部分內容。我們需要首先明確的是，《西域圖記》中的"圖"是怎樣的？"圖"與"記"的關係如何呢？

　　《隋書》卷六七《裴矩傳》引《西域圖記序》云：

> 臣既因撫納，監知關市，尋討書傳，訪採胡人，或有所疑，即詳眾口。依其本國服飾儀形，王及庶人，各顯容止，即丹青模寫，為《西域圖記》，共成三卷，合四十四國[4]。

仍別造地圖，窮其要害。從西頃以去，北海之南，縱橫所亙，將二萬里。諒由富商大賈，周遊經涉，故諸國之事罔不徧知。

可見裴矩之書中，有畫著西域諸國國王及庶人"容止"的人物圖，也有"窮其要害"的地圖。這兩種圖，顯然以"丹青模寫"的人物圖為主，《西域圖記》因這種圖而得名。地圖只是另行別造的，"從西頃以去，北海之南，縱橫所亙，將二萬里"，可能只是附上了一幅萬里地圖。地圖的重要性遠遠不能與按四十四國"服飾儀形，王及庶人，各顯容止"的人物圖相比。值得注意的是，《西域圖記》中四十四國的人物圖，不是使臣，而是"王及庶人"。也就是說，《西域圖記》的"圖"描繪的是各国国王和庶人的容貌、服飾，這是《西域圖記》的顯著特色。

需要說明的是，中國古代也有《西域圖》指繪製的地圖。如宋代盛度所上《西域圖》就是地圖。《宋史》卷二九二《盛度傳》略云：

奉使陝西，因覽疆域，參質漢、唐故地，繪為《西域圖》以獻……度嘗奏事便殿，真宗問其所上《西域圖》。度因言："酒泉、張掖、武威、燉煌、金城五郡之東南，自秦築長城，西起臨洮，東至遼碣，延袤萬里。有郡、有軍、有守捉，襟帶相屬，烽火相望，其為形勢備禦之道至矣。唐始置節度，後以宰相兼領，用非其人，故有河山之險而不能固，有甲兵之利而不能禦。今復繪山川、道路、壁壘、區聚，為《河西隴右圖》，願備上覽。"真宗稱其博學。

自安史之亂後，唐朝勢力逐漸退出西域，貞元中形成了"平時安西萬里疆，今日邊防在鳳翔"[5]的局面。延至宋代，西北邊境更為萎縮，唐代的西域指安西以西，而盛度《西域圖》所謂的西域只是"酒泉、張掖、武威、燉煌、金城五郡之東南"，即唐河西、隴右之地。河隴地區的唐代文獻、地志及圖經留存較多，因而盛度能據之繪制地圖。盛度的《西域圖》不論范圍還是內容，都不能與裴矩《西域圖記》同日而語。不能因盛度《西域圖》是地圖，影響我們對裴矩《西域圖記》描繪的是人物肖像圖的認識。

繪制域外人物圖，在中國古代外交領域，是一種歷史悠久的傳統。如《舊唐書》卷一九七《西南蠻傳》略云：

（東謝蠻）其首領謝元深，既世為酋長，其部落皆尊畏之……貞觀三年，元深入朝，冠烏熊皮冠，若今之髦頭，以金銀絡額，身披毛帔，韋皮行縢而著履。中書侍郎顏師古奏言："昔周武王時，天下太平，遠國歸款，周史乃書其事為《王會篇》。今萬國來朝，至於此輩章服，實可圖寫，今請撰為《王會圖》。"從之。

為前來朝貢的外國使者繪制朝貢圖和王會圖，遠宗周制，"遠國歸款"，成為天下太平的景象之一。在這種思想指導下，歷代的職貢圖、王會圖，史不絕書。南北朝以來，職貢圖更為普遍。以裴子野《方國使圖》為底本而繪制的《梁職貢圖》[6]，就是最為著名的一件。宋摹本《梁職貢圖》

殘卷今存於中國歷史博物館，殘卷有(滑國)、波斯國、百濟國、龜茲、儴國、狼牙修國、鄧至國、周古柯國、呵跋檀國、胡蜜丹國、白題國、末國等十二國使者的畫像，像側有簡短的題記。這種肖像圖加題記的形式，應該就是中國古代《王會圖》、《朝貢圖》的基本模式。

從《西域圖記序》"依其本國服飾儀形，王及庶人，各顯容止，即丹青模寫，為《西域圖記》"的記載看，《西域圖記》的格式當一仍《梁職貢圖》之舊。結合《梁職貢圖》與《西域圖記序》，可知《西域圖記》以"圖"為主，"記"只是圖上的題記。《西域圖記》雖然圖文并茂，但圖無疑占更重要的地位。

正因為《西域圖記》以圖為主，其書名經常被省稱為《西域圖》。如《冊府元龜》卷五五四《國史部·恩獎》云：

> 裴矩，為吏部尚書。大業初，西域諸蕃塞與中國互市，煬帝遣矩監其事。矩撰《西域圖》三卷，入朝奏之。帝大悦，賜物五百段。

同書卷九九〇《外臣部·備禦三》又云：

> 又西域諸藩，多至張掖，與中國交市。帝令吏部侍郎裴矩掌其事。矩知帝方勤遠略，諸商胡至者，矩誘令言其國俗、山川險易，撰《西域圖》三卷，入朝奏之。

這裏，裴矩所撰皆被省稱為《西域圖》。在隋、唐、宋代的書籍目錄中，裴矩之書也多被著錄為《西域圖》。如《隋書》卷三三《經籍志》云："《隋西域圖》三卷。(裴矩撰。)"這體現了隋末唐初之人對裴矩之書的認識。之後，《舊唐書·經籍志》無著錄，《新唐書》卷五八《藝文志》云："裴矩又撰《西域圖記》三卷。"歐陽修著錄為《西域圖記》，可能是根據裴矩的傳記資料概括著錄的。鄭樵的著錄最能體現《西域圖記》特色。在《通志》卷六六《藝文略》中，鄭樵記載為："《西域圖》三卷。(裴矩撰。)"可見宋人更傾向將此書稱為《西域圖》。更值得注意的是，在《通志》卷七二《圖譜略》"記無"門"地理"條，有"裴矩《西域圖》"[7]。這表明，鄭樵直接把這部著作放在"圖譜"類。以圖譜作為裴矩之書屬性，是對《西域圖記》特點的最好概括。在鄭樵著錄時，《西域圖》已經佚失了，鄭樵只存其名，未能親見，故而將《西域圖》列於"記無"的門類中。

內田吟風先生也注意到了《宋史·藝文志》沒有著錄《西域圖記》，而《通志》記錄了《西域圖》的現象。他解釋說，可能在宋代《西域圖記》已經佚失，只存圖的部分。這種解說顯然是未解《西域圖記》與《西域圖》的內涵所致。這也從一個側面證明了理解《西域圖記》中"圖"與"記"關係的重要性。

《西域圖記》繼承了周代以來，尤其是南北朝以來繪制萬國朝貢王會圖的傳統，但它又不僅僅同於此前的《職貢圖》等。裴矩在繪制圖時採用了突破傳統、嚴整一致的形式(詳見下論)，同時又在《西域圖記》的布局謀篇中繼承《漢書·西域傳》及漢魏以來的游記按交通路線排序的傳統，將兩種傳統的綜合貫通，融為一體，才形成了《西域圖記》這部前無古人的著作。

二、《西域圖記》中的"圖"

現今遺留唐宋史籍中徵引《西域圖記》文字是其書"記"的部分，而《西域圖記》更為重要的"圖"的部分，僅根據唐代史料，無從窺見一鱗半爪。我們似乎只能等待天降奇跡或今後新的考古發現了。但《西域圖》是否在此後千年的歷史中，完全無蛛絲馬跡可尋呢？現存文獻中是否存在對裴矩《西域圖》內容的描述呢？我認為現存的宋元史料，還是留下了一些裴矩《西域圖》流傳線索和蹤跡的。[8]

元代戴表元所著《剡源文集》卷四中，有《唐畫西域圖記》一文，乃探尋裴矩《西域圖記》內容的重要資料。《全元文》收錄戴表元文時，以"宜稼堂叢書"本為底本，并據孫鏘校刻本、四庫全書本、明鈔本、萬曆本、馬思贊校本、何焯校本等進行了校勘，今引之如下。《全元文》卷四二八云：

> 唐畫《西域圖》一卷。卷凡四則，每則各先書其國號、風土不同。而同為羌種，畫者又特舉其梁。每國畫一王，而一二奴前後夾侍之。王皆藉皮坐於地，侍者皆立。一王掀掌倨語，員皮頭帽如鉢，項組鐵，下垂至藉皮，服皮裘，牛腳靴，胸懸一員金花。一奴小員皮帽，斂袂受事；一奴曳幕羅，手上下奉酒壺，若俟而進，裘靴與王同者：蜀郡西北二千餘里附國，良夷也。
> 一王皮韜，小髻，餘髮垂，雙辮如縷，皮裘玄靴，微解袘，交手按膝。一奴皮[9]韜，髮餘垂，獨辮，朱裘玄靴者：吐谷渾之南，白蘭之北，彌羅國也。
> 一王烏氈冠如首絰，上標白犛牛尾，旁䍁二雕翎，皮裘朱帶，玄履綠襪。二奴，一冠飾、裘帶、履、襪與王同，而紺縪；一紺帶素襪，而朱鞾者：又西於白蘭數千里，佇貶欲歸國也。
> 一王二奴皆椎[10]髻，王白皮裘，黃毛靴，坐而僂，指數曲。奴青襦黃屨者，拍手為節而歌，面有酒色；丹襦皮束項者，與王目同右注而盼，衣皆反領者：又党項之西，千碉國也。
> 所藉皮或毛、或不毛，色或素、或淡紫、或絢緂、或紅波。人物膚肉，溢生紙面，顧揖向背、動止遲速諸態，觀之變然如生。餘器藻鏤精潤，功參神鬼，不可探度。
> 余考唐史，諸國名俱不經見，當由史官追書，不能諳知當時事。而當時來朝，此鬼瑣者混居羌中，亦無特出名字，故若是泯泯不著。此可以見唐治之盛，而為國大體正，不必當然也。今人常恨生世不如太古，生太古時，風氣不嘗如是而已：無官府而能不亂，無城郭而能不危，無宮室玉帛、魚肉葷籥，而能不害。其為生，誠可比於不雕之朴，未散之質。[11]

除末尾部分乃作者將圖中諸羌比作太古之人的感慨外，全文所記錄的圖及文字均值得細緻分析。

戴表元之文記載其所見唐畫《西域圖》有四則，即有附國、彌羅國、佇貶欲歸國及千碉國。[12]戴表元詳細描繪了畫面上的人物形象，文字生動，敘述細致，四國王及奴之形象，栩栩如生。但對"每則各先書其國號、風土不同"的說明文字，則著錄簡略，只存四句："蜀郡西北二千餘里附國，良夷也"；"吐谷渾之南，白蘭之北，彌羅國也"；"又西於白蘭數千里，佇貶欲歸國也"；"又党項之西，千碉國也"。其間有漏字及錯訛，如"佇貶欲歸國"，就不知是傳刻還是抄寫時的錯誤。但不能據此否認此文的價值。

幸而在元代見到并記錄了這四則《西域圖》的，尚有鮮于樞（伯機）。在《困學齋雜錄》（知不足齋叢書本）中，他也為我們留下了寶貴資料。其文云：

> 杭士王子慶收《西域圖》，閻中令畫，褚河南書。丹青翰墨，信為精絕。意當時所畫甚多，今止存四國。前史皆逸而不書，今錄於此：
>
> 附國者，蜀郡西北二千餘里，即漢之西南夷也。有嘉良夷，即其東部，所居種姓，自相率領，土俗與附國同，言語少殊，不相統一。其人並無姓氏。附國王子（字）宜僧。其國南北八百里，東西千五百里，無城柵，近川谷，傍山險。俗好復讎，故壘石為巢而居，以避其患。其巢高至十丈，每級丈餘，以木隔之。基方三四步，巢上方二三步，狀似浮屠。於下級開小門，從內上通，夜必閉關，以防盜賊。國有二萬餘家，號令自王出。嘉良夷政令繫之酋帥，重罪死，輕罰牛。人皆輕捷，便擊劍，用矛。漆皮為甲，弓長六尺，以竹為弦。妻其群母及嫂。兄弟死，父兄亦納其妻。好歌舞，鼓簧，吹長笛。有死者，無服制，置屍高床之上，沐浴衣服，被以牟甲，覆以獸皮。子孫不哭，帶甲舞劍，而呼云："我父為鬼所取，我欲報冤殺鬼。"其餘親戚哭三聲而止。婦人哭，必以兩手掩面。死家殺牛，親屬以豬酒相遺，共飲啖而瘞之。死後十年而大葬。

鮮于樞所記錄的王子慶藏《西域圖》，與戴表元記錄的唐畫《西域圖》是一個，鮮于樞詳於抄錄文字，戴表元詳於描繪圖畫內容，二者各有詳略，適可互相補充。鮮于樞抄錄的是四則《西域圖》中的第一則，即戴表元所謂"蜀郡西北二千餘里附國，良夷也"者，鮮于樞并未描寫畫卷，只是抄錄了部分文字。正是有鮮于樞的抄錄和戴表元的描述，我們對《西域圖記》的認識才能夠取得突破性的進展。

鄭天挺先生最早注意到《困學齋雜錄》中的這條史料，并做了詳細考證。在《〈隋書·西域傳〉附國之地望與對音》[13]一文注14中，鄭先生指出：

> 附國尚見於閻立本《西域圖》，《新唐書》二二二下《南蠻南平獠傳》，《太平御覽》七八八卷，《通志·都邑略西南夷》，《文獻通考》三二九卷，但文字相若，事無所增，蓋皆用《隋書》為本者也。《西域圖》唐閻立本繪，褚遂良書，見元鮮于樞（伯機）《困學齋雜錄》，錄稱，"杭士王子慶收《西域圖》，閻中令畫，褚河南書。丹青翰墨，信為精絕。意當時所圖甚多，今止存四圖，前史逸而不書今錄於此。附國者……"云云，其文略同《隋書》。鮮于樞精鑒別，審定當不差，惟謂"前史逸而不書"則非也。《困學齋雜錄》收入《畿輔叢書》，其所稱《西域圖》，張政烺先生以為當是《職貢圖》之

— 363 —

殘本，其說甚是。兩圖均不見於《新書·藝文志》，惟《宣和畫譜》卷一載御府所藏閻立德畫四十有二，其中有《西域圖》二《職貢圖》二。案唐張彥遠《歷代名畫記》卷九《閻立本》條稱："時天下初定，異國來朝，詔立本畫《外國圖》。"《宣和畫譜》卷一《閻立德》條稱："唐貞觀中，東蠻謝元深入朝，顏師古奏言，昔周武時遠國歸款，乃集其事為《王會圖》，今卉服鳥章，俱集蠻邸，實可圖寫，因命立德等圖之。……故李嗣真云：'大安博陵，難兄難弟，'謂立德立本也。"謝元深即東謝蠻，《舊唐書》一九七、《新唐書》二二二下有傳。《舊書》傳稱："貞觀三年元深入朝……中書侍郎顏師古奏言昔周武時，天下太平，遠國歸款，周史乃書其事為《王會篇》，今萬國來朝，至於此輩章服實可圖寫，今請撰為《王會圖》，從之。"是則圖寫之始，初無定稱，職貢、西域、外國、王會，其實一也。伯機所見之四圖，當即宣和時內府所藏之兩西域兩職貢也。圖作於貞觀三年，其時吐蕃未始貢，故仍沿附國舊稱。宋李廌 (方叔)《德隅齋畫品》謂"《番客入朝圖》梁元帝為荊州刺史日作，粉本，魯國而上三十有五國，閻立本所作《職貢圖》亦相若，得非立本摹元帝舊本乎"(《顧氏文房小說》本第一頁)。其說與諸家不同。竊疑李氏所稱摹元帝舊本，蓋舉其大體，或指其章法氣韻而言，非必卉服鳥章之異一一從舊本而來。惜其目不傳，無從斷定。

鄭先生出入唐、宋、元史料，指出《困學齋雜錄》記錄"前史逸而不書"的文字出自《隋書》，并考證閻立德、立本兄弟"圖寫之始，初無定稱，職貢、西域、外國、王會，其實一也"，誠為卓識。本文的考釋，也正是在鄭先生的基礎上展開。《困學齋雜錄》的著錄與《隋書》卷八三《西域傳》"附國"條及《北史》卷九六《附國傳》略同。《北史》及《隋書》文字略有不同之處，正可藉此校勘。然此非關本文主旨，在此不贅論。

再回到戴表元和鮮于樞所記之《西域圖》上來。戴表元只稱其是"唐畫"，并沒說是何人所畫，但鮮于樞言之鑿鑿，稱"閻中令畫，褚河南書"，鄭先生據此分析了閻立本兄弟繪制《西域圖》始末。閻立本兄弟畫《王會圖》，見於《宣和畫譜》，而《舊唐書》卷一九七《西南蠻傳》只記載貞觀三年顏師古因東謝蠻來朝而請求繪制《王會圖》事，并沒提到繪制之人。據《宣和畫譜》，顏師古因蕃客入朝，"今卉服鳥章，俱集蠻邸，實可圖寫"，表明所《王會圖》所畫影圖形的對象是蕃客，描繪的是其入朝情況。《宣和畫譜》卷一《道釋一》在"因命立德等圖之"之後，又寫到："其序位之際，折旋規矩，端簪奉笏之儀，與夫鼻飲頭飛、人物詭異之狀，莫不備該毫末。"可見閻立本兄弟《王會圖》或《西域圖》所描繪的是蕃客朝貢的形象，蕃客"端簪奉笏"，立於朝堂，這與戴表元所描寫《西域圖》中的王及奴的形象，還是大相徑庭的。

對宋人收藏的閻立本《西域圖》，同一時代的著名書畫家米芾已辨其為假托者。在《畫史》中，米芾指出：[14]

王球 (璥) 夔玉收《西域圖》，謂之閻令畫，褚遂良書，與馮京家同假名耳。

大觀年間，此《西域圖》進入御府，民間只有摹本。宋人吳曾撰《能改齋漫錄》卷一二《記事》"閻立本畫"[15]條云：

> 右伯時跋閻立本《西域圖》，廬陵王方贄侍郎家有之，其孫瓌夔玉寶藏之。大觀間，開封尹宋喬年言之省中，詔取以上進。時廬陵令張達淳、郡法掾吳祖源被檄委焉。因竊摹之，于是始有摹本。

但戴表元、鮮于樞所見《西域圖》，并不是據王方贄家藏而摹寫者。[16] 米芾稱王方贄家藏為假托，當有所據。實際上，戴表元、鮮于樞所見所題非但不是閻立本《西域圖》摹本，而且根本就不是閻立本繪制的《西域圖》。

前論閻立本兄弟繪畫之《王會圖》等內容與戴表元記載的圖畫繪及王及奴形象不符，是一個證據，另一證據來源於鮮于樞和戴表元的文字。在二人所見《西域圖》中，明確無誤地題寫著："蜀郡西北二千餘里附國……"此條與《隋書·西域傳》記載相同，可無疑義。需要考證的是，"蜀郡西北二千餘里附國"一句，是否符合閻立本兄弟繪圖時間（可能是貞觀三年）的實際狀況？顯而易見，答案是否定的。因為《通典》卷一七二《州郡二·序目》明確記載，"大唐武德初，改郡為州。"這裏的"武德初"，即武德元年，如《元和郡縣圖志》卷一《關內道·京兆府》云："煬帝改為京兆郡。武德元年，復為雍州。"貞觀初，天下各道之下的基本單位是州，而不是郡，閻立本繪制的《西域圖》上，褚遂良所書的也應該是"益州"，而不是"蜀郡"，作為國家中樞機構官員的褚遂良不會犯這樣常識性的錯誤。稱"蜀郡"，只能在大業三年改州為郡[17]到大業末這一段時間。據此可知，所謂閻立本《西域圖》不但不是閻立本所繪，而且其底本也不是唐代的，而是隋代的。戴表元稱"唐畫《西域圖》"，不妨理解為唐代摹寫的《西域圖》。也正因為《西域圖》所畫所寫不是唐代的外蕃，戴表元及鮮于樞在唐代史籍中尋找證據，忽略隋代史料，才一無所獲，以致有二人有"余考唐史，諸國名俱不經見"、"前史逸而不書"的錯誤感嘆。

排除了"唐畫《西域圖》"為閻立本繪《西域圖》的可能性，我們可以展開更進一步的推測。我認為，唐代摹寫（或者是隋代原本）的這份《西域圖》殘卷，就是裴矩的《西域圖》。首先，在裴矩《西域圖》之外，并未見隋代還有其他《西域圖》的記載。其次，戴表元，尤其是鮮于樞所引與《隋書·西域傳》驚人的相似，也昭示了畫卷的時間性。再次，也是更為明顯的證據，即戴表元描繪的《西域圖》中王及二奴的形象，與裴矩在《西域圖記序》中所說的"依其本國服飾儀形，王及庶人，各顯容止，即丹青模寫"的情形完全符合。嚴格說來，"庶人"與"奴"，在社會地位上有區別的，戴表元稱圖畫中國王旁邊的人為奴，可能是對國王之下的侍者、眾臣、平民和奴隸的統稱，與《西域圖記》稱"庶人"并不矛盾。從現存《職貢圖》看，繪及"王及庶人"的，只有裴矩的《西域圖》，其餘所繪，均是使臣等形象。繪"王及庶人"，是《西域圖記》的顯著特徵，而這一特徵，在戴表元的描寫中不但得到證實，也隨著戴表元的文字，清晰再現出來。

戴表元文字的意義還不止於上論。根據其描繪，我們知道附國國王及庶人的形象是這樣的：

> 王掀掌倨語，員皮頭帽如鉢，項組鐵，下垂至藉皮，服皮裘，牛腳靴，胸懸一員金花。一奴小員皮帽，歛袂受事；一奴曳幕羅，手上下奉酒壺，若俟而進，裘靴與王同者。

《隋書·西域傳》"附國"條（《北史·附國傳》略同）下還有一段文字，鮮于樞沒有抄錄。其文如下：

> 其俗以皮為帽，形圓如鉢，或帶羃䍦。衣多毛毷皮裘，全剝牛腳皮為靴。項繫鐵鎖，手貫鐵釧。王與酋帥，金為首飾，胸前懸一金花，徑三寸。

戴表元的描述，與《隋書·西域傳》合若符契，不禁令人擊節贊嘆。[18]這也說明了三點：其一，戴表元所描繪、鮮于樞所著錄的，正是裴矩的《西域圖記》的殘片。其二，《西域圖記》分圖與記兩部分，圖是對"王及庶人"的畫影圖形，記是題在圖側的補充說明文字。其三，戴表元所謂"一奴小員皮帽，歛袂受事；一奴曳幕羅"，正是《隋書·西域傳》所記"其俗以皮為帽，形圓如鉢，或帶羃䍦"的服飾，戴表元稱作"奴"的衣帽，是附國尋常百姓之服，"其俗"如此。這也證明了戴表元稱為王及奴的人物，即《西域圖記》所謂的"王及庶人"。其四，《隋書·西域傳》"附國"條自"蜀郡西北二千餘里"至"胸前懸一金花，徑三寸"一段，完全照抄《西域圖記》，《北史》照抄《隋書》。這不但使我們在復原《西域圖記》時增加了新的內容，而且為我們探討《隋書·西域傳》與《西域圖記》的關係[19]，也提供了新的資料。

從戴表元的描述看，裴矩的《西域圖》，"人物膚肉，溢生紙面，顧揖向背、動止遲速諸態，觀之變然如生。餘器藻鏤精潤，功參神鬼，不可探度"，繪畫水平顯然極高的。裴矩並未說《西域圖》是由誰"丹青模寫"，但從裴矩在張掖，"訪採胡人"看，繪圖者可能是西域胡人。隋時，西域及中亞地區繪畫技藝超群，能工善畫者代有其人。如隋唐時期最為著名的西域畫家尉遲跋質那、尉遲乙僧父子，張彥遠《歷代名畫記》卷八、卷九記載：[20]

> 尉遲跋質那，西國人，善畫外國及佛像。當時擅名，今謂之大尉遲。（《六番圖》、《外國寶樹圖》，又有《婆羅門圖》，傳於代。）
>
> 尉遲乙僧，于闐國人，父跋質那。乙僧國初授宿衛官，襲封郡公，善畫外國及佛像，時人以跋質那為大尉遲，乙僧為小尉遲。畫外國及菩薩，小則用筆緊勁如屈鐵盤絲，大則灑落有氣概。僧悰云："外國鬼神，奇形異貌，中華罕繼。"（竇云："澄思用筆，雖與中華道殊，然氣正迹高，可與顧、陸為友。"）

尉遲跋質那、尉遲乙僧父子在畫外國人物上，水平顯然高於隋唐王朝同輩畫家，因為被贊為"中華罕繼"。尉遲跋質那、尉遲乙僧父子繪畫造詣，是西域畫家之翹楚，其出色的繪畫成就，也顯示了西域胡人在繪製外國人物上的整體水平。

裴矩的《西域圖》可能不是尉遲跋質那所畫。而且由於《西域圖記》涉及四十四個國家，其國王有的遠在萬里之外，中原人難睹其廬山真面目，只能"諒由富商大賈，周遊經涉，故諸國之事罔不徧知"，聽商賈傳聞，由胡人涂影摹寫。裴矩撰寫"記"時，依賴胡人；繪圖時，也依賴胡人。我推測，繪圖的胡人可能不是一個，而是有一批來自不同國家和地區的胡人參與其中，各盡所能，描摹親見或接近或想象的諸國國王之"容止"。可以肯定的是，這些參加繪圖的西域胡人均具有高水平繪畫造詣。從這個角度看，《西域圖記》不但是記敘西域諸國風土人情、展示西域文化的多姿多彩的畫卷，而且由於裴矩親赴張掖、招致胡人、采訪胡人，并由胡人直接繪畫，《西域圖記》本身也正是隋與西域諸國文化交流的產物。

《西域圖記》"記"的部分，結合唐宋史籍，尚能復原一些段落，但其"圖"的部分，似乎已成了"廣陵散"。幸賴戴表元的文字，我們能夠窺見《西域圖》的精彩畫面。不知元時戴表元和鮮于樞所見的殘片，是否還存於天壤？

三、西域與西戎

戴表元和鮮于樞關於《西域圖記》的記載，在豐富我們對《西域圖記》"圖"的部分的感知之外，也促使我們更進一步理解《西域圖記》的內容。

中國古代正史《西域傳》濫觴於《史記·大宛列傳》，《漢書·西域傳》確立了正史《西域傳》的編寫格局。在《漢書》所列五十四個西域諸國中，分為五大部分，基本按照交通路線排序。[21]此後，《後漢書·西域傳》、《魏略·西戎傳》、《魏書·西域傳》、《晉書·西戎傳》、《周書·異域傳》、《梁書·西北諸戎傳》等大體如此，《晉書》以下，略欠嚴格。易言之，南北朝以前編纂的正史《西域傳》，最重交通路線，記述諸國之先後取決於各國在交通路線的位置。[22]也正因為如此，《漢書·西域傳》以下，首先記敘交通道路。《西域圖記》沿襲了漢魏以來的西域文獻編纂體例，即按地理位置，亦即交通路線上的國家順序排列。這種排序規則裴矩在《西域圖記序》中有詳細說明，即：

> 發自敦煌，至于西海，凡為三道，各有襟帶。北道從伊吾，經蒲類海鐵勒部，突厥可汗庭，度北流河水，至拂菻國，達于西海。其中道從高昌，焉耆，龜茲，疏勒，度葱嶺，又經鏺汗，蘇對沙那國，康國，曹國，何國，大、小安國，穆國，至波斯，達于西海。其南道從鄯善，于闐，朱俱波、喝槃陀，度葱嶺，又經護密，吐火羅，挹怛，帆延，漕國，至北婆羅門，達于西海。其三道諸國，亦各自有路，南北交通。其東女國、南婆羅門國等，並隨其所往，諸處得達。故知伊吾、高昌、鄯善，並西域之門戶也。總湊敦煌，是其咽喉之地。

《西域圖記》記載了北道從伊吾至拂菻國，達于西海；中道從高昌，至波斯，達于西海；南道從鄯善至北婆羅門，達于西海的道路。《西域圖記》即按照這三條路線排列，《序》文所列國家，正是其書每卷內排列順序。據《序》文,《西域圖記》記錄的主幹國家有：北道：伊吾、鐵勒、突厥、拂菻；中道：高昌、焉耆、龜茲、疏勒、鏺汗、蘇對沙那國、康國、曹國、何國、大小安國、穆國、波斯；南道：鄯善、于闐、朱俱波、喝槃陀、護密、吐火羅、挹怛、帆延、漕國、北婆羅門。而《西域圖記》的三卷，也是按路線劃分，北、中、南三道各一卷。

《西域圖記序》中提到的這些三道主幹國家只有二十七個，與四十四國還相距甚遠。即使加上《隋書·西域傳》在記載諸國里程時提到的"米國"、"史國"、"那色波國"、"烏那曷國"、"劫國"等五國，也只有三十二國，距《西域圖記》的全貌，還有一定距離。那麼，這剩餘的十數個國家，究竟是哪些國家呢？

據戴表元所記,《西域圖》還包括了蜀郡西北二千餘里附國，吐谷渾之南、白蘭之北的彌羅國，白蘭西數千里的佇貶欲歸國，党項西的千碩國。戴表元見到的《圖》只殘存四國，但從其所引文字看，吐谷渾、白蘭、党項諸國，既然在殘卷上出現國名，根據《西域圖記》的撰寫體例，也應該有其國的圖與記。也就是說，戴表元之文為我們補充了至少七個應列入《西域圖記》中的國家。這也使我們對《西域圖記》內容提出了新的疑問，即裴矩的《西域圖記》是只記載西域諸國，還是也同時包括屬於"西戎"的諸國呢？

回答應該是肯定的。詳繹《西域圖記序》，我們可以看到，在嚴格按照東西交通路線排序之外，裴矩還為自己著錄非交通幹線上的國家確定了靈活的、富於彈性的原則，此即《序》文所謂："其三道諸國，亦各自有路，南北交通。其東女國、南婆羅門國等，並隨其所往，諸處得達。"對於非東西幹道國家，如東女國、南婆羅門國等，裴矩採取"並隨其所往，諸處得達"的方針，也靈活著錄。這樣，既嚴守按三道排序的原則，又兼顧西域諸國縱橫交錯的面貌，嚴謹而有彈性。據此可知,《西域圖記》不僅發展繼承了中國古代《王會圖》、《職貢圖》的傳統，而且發展完善了漢魏以來西域地理著作的編纂原則，體例嚴整，其布局謀篇，井然有序，因此成為自漢以來集大成的西域著述總結之作。

《西域圖記序》提到的"東女國"，與我們的疑問有直接關係。隋、唐及宋代史籍中，"女國"、"東女國"多處提及，且記載混亂，治史者多有解說，論考日漸深入。[23] 本文在此不詳論。具體涉及到《隋書·西域傳》與《西域圖記》，本文同意任乃強先生的觀點，即《隋書·西域傳》"女國"條取自《西域圖記》"東女國"條,《隋書·西域傳》不收西海女國，故單稱雪山女國為"女國"，而《西域圖記》尚記載海西女國，故將葱嶺之南的女國稱為"東女國"。[24]《隋書·西域傳》所記女國如下：

女國，在葱嶺之南。其國代以女為王……恒將鹽向天竺興販，其利數倍，亦數與天竺及党項戰爭。

此處的"天竺",《西域圖記序》中作南北婆羅門,《隋書·西域傳》中的"天竺"二字，應是魏徵所改。值得注意的是,《隋書·女國傳》提到党項，根據《西域圖記》編纂體例，可知裴矩書中是有党項的。

中國古代將邊疆之民，分為東夷、南蠻、西戎和北狄四類，西域屬於西戎的一部分。正史中為外夷列傳，肇始於《史記》，如《匈奴列傳》、《南越列傳》、《東越列傳》、《朝鮮列傳》、《西南夷列傳》、《大宛列傳》等。司馬遷從政治作用及影響的角度為一些外族立傳，在編纂及書寫時無四夷畢書的觀念。《漢書》在書末列四夷傳，分匈奴、西南夷、兩粵、朝鮮、西域諸傳。《後漢書》因之，大別為東夷、南蠻西南夷、西羌、西域、南匈奴、烏桓鮮卑列傳。其中"西域"為地理概念，與西戎（即西南夷、西羌等）是分開的。《魏略》別出心裁，不但記載了"中道"、"新道"、"南道"三道，而且首敘益州之西諸羌，將西戎與三道西域諸國編纂在一起。其後諸史，《魏書》、《北史》有《西域傳》，其他南北朝正史因資料不足，或無嚴格意義上的《西域傳》，或不區分"西域"與"西戎"，將西戎與西域混編，以西域入《西戎傳》或《西北諸戎傳》。

比較裴矩《西域圖記序》與《魏略·西戎傳》，可知裴矩深受《魏略·西戎傳》之影響。其列舉"三道"，以"三道"次序排列西域諸國，顯係模仿《魏略·西戎傳》，而首敘益州（蜀郡）以西的西戎諸國，也是繼承了《魏略·西戎傳》的編纂傳統。只不過《魏略》是將西域并入西戎，而裴矩則是將西戎歸入西域而已。

唐初史家對西戎和西域有明確區分。如李延壽在編著《南史》中，西戎、西域並列，二者截然有別；尤其是其所著之《北史》，在東夷、南蠻、西戎傳之後，單列《西域傳》，體現了對西域的清晰認識。但值得注意的是，同是唐初編纂的史書，《隋書》卻與《南史》、《北史》不同。魏徵以四夷分類，分東夷、南蠻、西域（包括吐谷渾、党項、高昌、康國、安國等）、北狄四傳，但名之為《西域傳》，實際卻包括西戎。結合上文所引《隋書·附國傳》完全照抄《西域圖記》看，魏徵在編纂《隋書·西域傳》時，不僅在文字上抄錄《西域圖記》，而且在援西戎入西域、首敘西戎這一點上，也與《西域圖記》同出一轍。此點又被之後的《新唐書·西域傳》所延續。

四、《西域圖記》在隋末唐初的作用

雖然有《魏略》的影響，但以西戎入西域，畢竟還是裴矩首創。《西域圖記》為什麼要記載西戎？我認為，除了《魏略》等傳統影響外，裴矩在《西域圖記》中首先記載西戎，是因為當時經營西域的軍事、政治需要。易言之，西戎諸羌，核心在吐谷渾。裴矩首列諸羌，意在吐谷渾。

《隋書》卷六七《裴矩傳》略云：

時西域諸番，多至張掖，與中國交市。帝令〔裴〕矩掌其事。矩知帝方勤遠略，諸商胡至者，
矩誘令言其國俗、山川險易，撰《西域圖記》三卷，入朝奏之。其序曰：

以國家威德，將士驍雄，汎濛汜而揚旌，越崑崙而躍馬，易如反掌，何往不至！但突厥、吐渾分領羌胡之國，為其擁遏，故朝貢不通。今並因商人密送誠款，引領翹首，願為臣妾。聖情含養，澤及普天，服而撫之，務存安輯。故皇華遣使，弗動兵車，諸蕃既從，渾、厥可滅。混一戎夏，其在茲乎！不有所記，無以表威化之遠也。

帝大悅，賜物五百段。每日引矩至御坐，親問西方之事。矩盛言胡中多諸寶物，吐谷渾易可并吞。帝由是甘心，將通西域，四夷經略，咸以委之。

據《西域圖記序》，可知裴矩記載了"突厥、吐渾分領羌胡之國"的具體情況。魏徵記載裴矩對隋煬帝的影響主要有"矩盛言胡中多諸寶物，吐谷渾易可并吞"兩點。關於西域寶物，《西域圖記序》明確寫到："今者所編，皆餘千戶，利盡西海，多產珍異。"而關於吐谷渾可并吞，也體現在《西域圖記序》中。西域"多諸寶物"，《西域圖記》諸國條有詳細記載，而"突厥、吐渾分領羌胡之國，為其擁遏，故朝貢不通"的現狀，必然也體現在《西域圖記》的行文中。正因為《西域圖記》中要貫徹"吐谷渾可并吞"之旨，因此，裴矩首列吐谷渾，在名為"西域"的圖記中，添加進西戎的內容。戴表元的《唐畫西域圖記》一文正為裴矩撰著《西域圖記》之宗旨，提供了佐證。

隋煬帝不但將"四夷經略"委任裴矩，而且對裴矩通過《西域圖記》所表達的經營西域思想，言聽計從。平定吐谷渾，是隋煬帝經營西域的開始。大業五年，隋出兵大破吐谷渾，"其故地皆空，自西平臨羌城以西，且末以東，祁連以南，雪山以北，東西四千里，南北二千里，皆為隋有"。[25] 通過平定吐谷渾，隋勢力伸向西域。平吐谷渾，是隋經營西域的第一步，奠定了隋經營西域的基礎。[26]

邁出這一步後，緊接著的舉措是占領西域門戶。據《西域圖記序》，"伊吾、高昌、鄯善，並西域之門戶也。"因此，大業五年，因平吐谷渾，煬帝設鄯善郡，掌控了南道門戶。接著，在大業六、七年間，薛世雄"與突厥啓民可汗連兵擊伊吾"，[27] 隋在漢舊伊吾城東築新伊吾城，占領了西域北道門戶。對於中道門戶高昌，隋煬帝則采取了積極加強聯繫的方式。"煬帝大業五年，高昌王麴伯雅來朝，拜左光祿大夫、車師太守，封弁國公"[28]。麴伯雅接受隋朝官封，確立了高昌臣屬於隋的關係。大業八年十一月，又"以宗女華容公主嫁于高昌王"[29]，通過和親，使高昌更加心向隋朝。

據上所論，隋煬帝經營西域，每一步驟，均遵循裴矩的設計，皆以《西域圖記》為準繩。從這個角度說，《西域圖記》不但是西域地理文獻，而且是隋煬帝經營西域的指導性著作。[30] 與裴矩同時代的魏徵對此有清晰認識。《隋書》卷六七《裴矩傳》、卷八三《西域傳》後的"史臣曰"，皆魏徵評論，其論云：

使高昌入朝，伊吾獻地，聚糧且末，師出玉門。關右騷然，頗亦〔裴〕矩之由也。

自古開遠夷，通絕域，必因宏放之主，皆起好事之臣……煬帝規摹宏侈，掩吞秦、漢，裴矩方進《西域圖記》以蕩其心，故萬乘親出玉門關，置伊吾、且末，而關右暨於流沙，騷然無聊生矣。

師出玉門（平吐谷渾）、聚糧且末（設鄯善郡）、伊吾獻地、高昌入朝，正是隋煬帝經營西域的四步，裴矩不但主謀設計，而且身體力行，參與其中。隋煬帝之所以能"親出玉門關"，是因為裴矩"進《西域圖記》以蕩其心"。隋代西域經營，肇始於《西域圖記》。這是對《西域圖記》影響隋煬帝經營西域方略的準確概括，雖然魏徵顯然是貶斥而不是稱贊。

隋煬帝按《西域圖記》的方略，經營西域，平吐谷渾，取鄯善、伊吾，并設郡，恩撫高昌，但由於鐵勒力量尚強，高昌未徹底變成隋領地，西域的三道門戶尚缺其一。這關鍵的一步，只能留待唐太宗完成了。貞觀四年（630），突厥頡利破滅，伊吾首領降唐，唐列其地為西伊州，六年（632）更名為伊州，同於編戶，[31] 鑿通西域北道伊吾路；八年（634），李靖征討吐谷渾，清除了唐向西域發展的主要障礙；十四年（640），大軍討擊高昌，太宗不顧朝臣的反對，力排眾議以其地為西昌州，又改為西州，[32] 真正掌握了西域中道門戶。至此，唐完全建立了經營西域前沿基地。唐太宗擊吐谷渾，建伊州，平高昌之舉，亦均沿襲《西域圖記》的規劃。

裴矩卒於貞觀元年，不及見唐廷控制西域軍事體系的建立，但《新唐書》卷一〇〇《裴矩傳》云：

年八十，精明不忘，多識故事，見重于時。

裴矩能獲得唐太宗的推重，是否也有其《西域圖記》主旨與太宗雄才大略相符的原因呢？或許裴矩在太宗手下恩寵不衰，也有《西域圖記》之功。因為《西域圖記》并不僅僅是一部歷史地理著作，還是隋唐兩朝經營西域的指導綱領。

注釋

[1] 詳見史念海：《隋唐時期域外地理的探索及世界認識的再擴大》，《中國歷史地理論叢》1988年第2期，第73-110頁；余太山：《裴矩〈西域圖記〉所見敦煌至西海的"三道"》，《西域研究》2005年第4期，第16-24頁，收入其著《早期絲綢之路文獻研究》，上海人民出版社，2009年，第72-86頁。

[2] 內田吟風：《隋裴矩撰〈西域圖記〉遺文纂考》，《藤原弘道先生古稀記念史學佛教學論集》，內外印刷株式會社，1973年，第115-128頁。

[3] 李錦繡：《〈通典·邊防典〉"吐火羅"條史料來源與〈西域圖記〉》，《西域研究》2005年4期，第25-34頁。

[4]《北史》卷三八《裴矩傳》作"四十五國"。參見《北史》點校本《校勘記》九，中華書局，1983年，第1409頁。

[5]《白居易集》卷四《新乐府·西涼伎》，顧學頡點校，中華書局，1979年，第76頁。

[6] 詳見余太山:《〈梁書·西北諸戎傳〉與〈梁職貢圖〉——兼說今存〈梁職貢圖〉殘卷與裴子野〈方國使圖〉的關係》，《燕京學報》新5期，北京大學出版社，1998年，第93-123頁；收入其著《兩漢魏晉南北朝正史西域傳研究》，中華書局，2003年，第26-64頁。

[7]《通志》，中華書局影印，1987年，第783、839頁。

[8] 關於宋元史籍中記載的《西域圖》，湯開建先生有細緻論考，見其著《閻立本〈西域圖〉在宋元著作中的著錄及其史料價值》，《文史》第31輯，中華書局，1988年，第143-157頁。

[9] "皮"，四部叢刊影印明萬曆本作"布"。

[10] "椎"，四部叢刊本作"垂"。

[11] 李修生主編:《全元文》，江蘇古籍出版社，1999年，第12冊，第382-383頁。本文所引，標點或有改變，個別文字，據《四庫全書》本進行了校改。

[12] 湯開建對此四國均有考證考，見注8所引文，第149-154頁。

[13] 載《國學季刊》第6卷4號，收入《清史探微》，北京大學出版社，1999年7月，第233-242頁。

[14] 于安瀾編:《畫品叢書》，上海人民美術出版社，1982年，第192頁。

[15] 上海古籍出版社，1979年，第354-356頁。

[16] 詳見拙著:《閻立本〈西域圖〉考》。

[17]《隋書》卷三《煬帝紀》，大業三年四月"壬辰，改州為郡"。見中華書局點校本，第67頁。

[18] 此點湯開建已指出，見注8引文，第150頁。

[19] 日本學者白鳥庫吉、嶋崎昌等都指出《西域圖記》是《隋書·西域傳》編纂的重要材料，詳見白鳥庫吉:《大秦國及び拂林國に就きて》，《白鳥庫吉全集·西域史研究（下）》，東京：岩波書店，1971年，第125-203頁；嶋崎昌:《〈隋書·高昌傳〉解說》，《隋唐時代の東トゥルキスターン研究》，東京大學出版會，1977年，第311-340頁。

[20] 俞劍華注釋，上海人民美術出版社，第164、172頁。

[21] 詳見余太山:《〈漢書·西域傳下〉要注》，《兩漢魏晉南北朝正史西域傳要注》，第152-232頁，esp. 219-220頁。

[22] 詳見余太山:《兩漢魏晉南北朝正史"西域傳"的體例》，《兩漢魏晉南北朝正史西域傳研究》，中華書局，2003年，第95-108頁。

[23] 詳見周維衍:《隋唐兩女國——兩〈唐書東女國傳〉辨證》，《歷史地理》1990年第8期，第204-211頁；呂思勉:《呂思勉讀史劄記（下）》，上海古籍出版社，1982年，第1079-1084頁；楊正剛:《蘇毗初探（一）》、《蘇毗初探（續）》，《中國藏學》1989年第3期，第35-43頁，第4期，第136-144頁；李紹明:《唐代西山諸羌考略》，《四川大學學報》1980年第1期，第83-95頁；達熱澤仁:《蘇毗社會狀況述論》，《西藏研究》1988年第2期，第31-37頁；周偉洲:《蘇毗與女國》，《邊疆民族歷史與文物考論》，黑龍江教育出版社，2000年，第18-36頁；石碩:《女國是蘇毗嗎？——論女國與蘇毗之差異及女國即蘇毗說之緣起》，《西藏研究》2009年第3期，第19-27頁。

[24] 任乃強:《隋唐之女國》,原刊《康藏研究月刊》第6期,收入《任乃強民族研究論文集》,民族出版社,1990年,第212-235頁。

[25] 《隋書》卷八三《吐谷渾傳》,中華書局點校本,第1845頁。

[26] 伊瀬仙太郎:《中國西域經營史研究》,東京:岩南堂,1968年,第147-155頁。

[27] 《隋書》卷六五《薛世雄傳》。隋并伊吾的時間,詳見松田壽男:《古代天山の歷史地理學的研究》,早稻田大學出版社,1970年,第454-456頁;余太山:《隋與西域諸國關係述考》,《文史》69輯,2004年,第49-57頁。

[28] 《冊府元龜》卷九六三《外臣八·封冊一》,周勛初等校訂,鳳凰出版社,2006年,第11冊,第11165頁。

[29] 《元和郡縣圖志·隴西道·西州》(卷四〇)云:"伯雅來朝,隋煬帝以宇文氏女玉波為華容公主,妻之"。《隋書·蘇夔傳》:"其年,高昌王麴伯雅來朝,朝廷妻以公主。夔有雅望,令主婚焉"。

[30] 齊陳駿《裴矩功過述評》一文已指出,裴矩的《西域圖記序》分析了西域的形勢和提出了經營西域的方略,裴矩的方略,得到了以煬帝為首的楊隋最高統治集團的極大賞識,並逐步付諸實施。見《敦煌學輯刊》1983年創刊號(總第4輯),第98-105頁。

[31] 《通典》卷一九一《邊防七·西戎總序》,中華書局點校本,第5198頁;《舊唐書》卷四〇《地理志》,中華書局點校本,第1643頁。

[32] 《資治通鑒》卷一九四、一九五,貞觀八年十二月、九年五月、貞觀十四年九月條,中華書局點校本,第6108、6110-6113、6154-6156頁。

A STUDY ON *XIYU TUJI* (*ILLUSTRATED RECORD OF THD WESTERN REGIONS*)

LI Jinxiu

Xiyu Tuji (*Illustrated Record of the Western Regions*), in three fascicles, composed by Pei Ju in the Daye reign period of the Sui Dynasty, was a monumental work treating the geo-historical domain of the Western Regions. It has been recorded as a significant work for some time, in part because of its accurate documentation of three routes to the Western Sea (Mediterranean) from Dunhuang. However, the original version of *Xiyu Tuji* has long been lost, with only a preface preserved in "Biography of Pei Ju" in *Sui Shu*. The Japanese scholar Uchida Ginpū 內田吟風 has gathered and compiled six fragments of the work, thus providing a glimpse of *Xiyu Tuji*. I subsequently restored the section titled "*Tuhuoluo*" of

Xiyu Tuji. However, it will be a long time before these materials which we have gathered and compiled enable us to reproduce the existing appearance of the *Xiyu Tuji*.

Following clues provided in "Preface of *Xiyu Tuji*", and combining literary records from the Tang, Song and Yuan periods, I have proposed some new views on the formal structure and content of Pei Ju's *Xiyu Tuji*, and point out that two sections, namely portraits and inscriptions, were included in *Xiyu Tuji*. The portraits depicted monarchs and their attendants, and the inscriptions provided explanations of the portraits. Because the portraits were primary content, the book was also titled *Xiyu Tu*. *Xiyu Tuji* described various states of the Western Rong, such as Tuyuhun and Dangxiang, in addition to documenting those states which lay along the three routes through the Western Regions mentioned above.

CRIMINAL LAW PRACTICES AMONG TURFAN UIGURS ACCORDING TO CIVIL DOCUMENTS

A. Melek Özyetgin

Introduction

We have very limited information about the history of pre-Islamic Turkic laws, in particular, the written rules regulating law in ancient Turkic eras, given that no rule books are available at the present day. Most of the information we have comes from indirect sources. Today, one of the major sources about the ancient Turkic law system is Uigur (Uighur, Uygur) civil documents, which date back to a period between the 13th century and 14th century. These documents from the most eminent representative of the culture of the settled Turkic tribes during their middle period, namely the Turfan-Uigurs, show us legal processes not only between people, but also between people and the government.[1]

In this paper, I will discuss criminal law practices in Uigur civil documents. The reason why I have chosen this topic is that criminal law is the oldest branch of law and a field closely related to social culture. In a sense, criminal law is an expression of social culture. It is appropriate to say that, in terms of resources and practices, more comprehensive research in the future should cover this topic, which I will look at here on the basis of the Turfan-Uigur state. As just mentioned the written rules or rule books on which Uigur criminal law was based are not available today. From the period of the Huns, the origins of Turkic-Uigur law certainly lay in the ancient Turkic official and customary rules. On the other hand, in civil documents, it is possible to find clues about the Uigurs' understanding of the law of the Chinese, who lived together with the Uigurs for centuries. Similarly, the influence of the Mongols should also be considered.

In the Uigur contract tradition, it is generally agreed that Chinese contracts were taken as models and that many words of Chinese origin were used in the Uigur documents. Similarities in form and content between Uigur civil documents and ancient Chinese contracts are remarkable. Masao Mori (1961: 113),[2] the Japanese Uigurist, has recognized these Chinese influences, but stated that the Uigurs created their tradition of correspondence on the basis of their own culture mixed with some Chinese elements in the Turkic style. In other words, it is not incorrect to say that the Uigurs, inspired by Chinese practices, had their own customs and habits which became authentic and peculiar to their own language. On the other hand, we should not forget that the Uigurs and the Chinese may have developed similar legal viewpoints as they lived together for centuries within the broader Asian cultural context, while considering Chinese influences on the Uigur-Turkic understanding of law (Ayiter 1952: 418).

When the Uigur documents treating criminal law practices are examined in terms of content, it is seen that they are composed of land contracts, slave sale contracts, adoption contracts, emancipation of slave contracts, and loan contracts, as well as of personal and family declarations which are fundamental to wills and censuses. In those contracts, including agreements between people or between people and the government, there are some penalty clauses that serve as dissuasive precautions against unjustifiable protests and they are intended to protect legality by providing securities. Similarities between these penalty clauses in most of the contracts show us that Uigur society had an understanding of systematic criminal law.

It is possible to find some clues about the official rules on which criminal laws were based, although the actual rules of the system are not available today. For example, the following statement, in a document treating tax payments (no. Mi04), is noteworthy:

"yasa-taqï qïyïn-qa tägir-män". män oz-miš togrïl kin öngdün basa togrïl-qa kim-ning
qayu-ning küčin tutup čam čarïm kïlsar-män yasa-taqï qïyïn-qa tägir-män.

I, Ozmış Togrıl, consent to penalty if I am to raise a subsequent objection against Basa Togrıl, relying on someone else's power. (Yamada 1993)

A similar use is observed in adoption contract no. Ad01:

män čintso ayag-qa tägimlig-ning inim ičim oglum qam qadašïm ilmäzün tartmazun
apam birök ilgli tartïglï saqïnsar savlarï yorumazun yasa-taqï qïn-qa tägsünlär

I, respectable Çintso, let not my brother, my uncle, my son and relatives interfere, not take by force; if so, let not their word be acceptable, and demand that they be punished by law.

(Yamada 1993)

Here, it is clear that the application of penalty has a certain basis in rules. The rules on which the law is based in contracts are called *yasa*, a word of Mongolian origin. At the same time, the term *yosun*,[3] another word of Mongolian origin, is also used in contracts.

There are two sources on which impositions of penalties in Uigur civil documents are based. The first source is official rules drawn up by state authorities. These specify the imposition of a penalty for crimes against the state and various property rights between people. The second source is customary rules. As it is known, customary rules consist of accepted practices in traditions which regulate social life. Among Uigurs, penalties in contracts on interpersonal dealings, leasing, and loans are mostly based on customary rules. Such an understanding of law, whereby both official rules and customary rules are found together, was the most significant organizational factor in Uigur social and economic life.

In Uigur contracts, penalty clauses specified according to customary rules are stated using the following phrase: "*il yangïnča*", meaning "according to provincial rules". Thus, in a sense, the term "*il yangïnča*" corresponds to customary rules. For example, a penalty clause in a loan contract is specified to be "*il* yangïnča" or in accordance with customary law:

Yïlan yïl üčünč ay (iki yangïq-a) manga qïryaquz-qa böz kärgäk bolup vaptu-dïn iki [iki] bag böz aldïm yangïd-a iki šïg tarïg birürmän birmädin käčür[sär]-sär-män il yangïnča tüši bilä köni birürmän

I, Qïryaquz, needed *böz* on t he 2nd of the 3rd month of the snake year, and bought two bunches of *böz* from Vaptu. First, I will give two 2 *şıg* of corn. If time is overdue, I will give the complete amount back with interest according to provincial rules". (Yamada Lo15 TM 212 U5257 US p. 29, Clark 13)

A statement in another document (P.102), a pledging contract, is remarkable:

män samboqdu tutung birtke ... bolmïšqa ton ätük adaq baš birmäz-män äv täg yogun iš šlätsär män il-ning tutug y(a)ngïnča birürmän qalmïš turušï yangï tutug y(a)ngïnča bolzun

I, Samboqdu, will not give Bolmış clothes or shoes as *Tutung birt* [the tax]. If I make him work busily at home, I will give according to the provincial [country] pledging rule. Let the rest of his life be according to the new hypothecation rule.

The phrase "*ilning tutug yangïnča*" in this contract shows us that there were special rules about pledging specified by customary law.

"*Yang*" in the phrase "*il yangïnča*" is of Chinese origin and it basically means "a pattern, model" and, abstractly, "kind, sort, manner" (Giles 12, 854; see ED940b). The word appeared in the Uigur language, as well as in the literature of the post-Islamic period: DLT *yang* "center or pattern of something" (III, 361); KB *yang* "custom, habit, style"; Kİ *yong* (< *yang*) "customary law"; Chag. *yangla* "alike"; Ott. *yang* "shape, form, kind" (Caferoğlu: 17). The concept used with the word *İl* was used to mean "customary law" in Uigur society. Similarly, the phrase "*İl yangïnča*" is found in DLT and KB.

Reşit Rahmeti Arat, the eminent Turkologist and Uigurist, divides the imposition of penalties in Uigur civil documents into five categories (1964: 49-51):

1. Death penalty
2. Corporal punishment
3. Financial/property penalties
4. Penalties in law
5. Penalties by accepted practices and judgments

In this paper, I will discuss every type of penalty according to documents and based on Reşit Rahmeti Arat's classification. In the study, I will examine the commitment of crimes that lead to a penalty; persons to whom a penalty directly relates; powers (state, society, etc.) with penal sanctions; different impositions of penalty in various law procedures; and, the role and power of the state as lawmaker.

The *death penalty*, the most severe sentence, comes at the top of the list of penalties. In civil documents, we come across the death penalty only in the personal declarations which served as a basis for censuses. In the past, censuses were fundamental in organizing personal responsibilities towards the government, so it was essential that censuses should be recorded properly. When the role of the declarations in regulating the social, economic, and military structure of the state is taken into account, the state had to introduce dissuasive penalties in order to ensure that such declarations were correct and to prevent false representations:

[Iduq] qut t(ä)ngrikäni[m(i)zkä] ülcäy tümän ilči beglär-kä tümän ilči beg[lärkä] m(ä)n yïgmïš bitig birürmän ulug däptär-tä bititmiš nägü kimimtin taš nägü m-ä yoq bar tip ayïg ünüp sözi (ayaq ürüp sözi) čïn bolsar öz bašïm ölürm(ä)n

May his royal highness, Iduk-Kut, be blissful! I, Yıgmış, give the Tümen ilçi rulers written certification. If there is a rumor that there is someone else apart from the ones recorded in *Ulug depter* and if it is proved to be true I am to consent to my own death [USp.40 (T.I.T.M. 224 (101/016/R.40)]

In these documents, it is striking that people consent to the death penalty in case of false representation. This case shows us that population reports [4] and birth records were seriously and meticulously kept. There is no record of the death penalty for a committed crime among the current examined documents. As far as it is known, among Uigurs, the death penalty applied only when there was crime against national security and the economy, etc.

There are documents in which we find examples of the second type of penalty: *corporal punishment*. We also find an example of corporal punishment [5] in a detailed declaration (entry made in the register) by a Uigur family. In the declaration, the names and ages of a person called Yölek and his family members are listed. In the same section, two people called Yoluga and Çerig, who were probably acquaintances or neighbors, bear witness for confirmation of the information. If there is false representation, they will consent to "57 whippings", as well as financial penalty. The declaration is then sealed by Yölek:

... [al]tï k[iši ärür] [m(ä)n] yöläk beš al[tmïš yašar] · [k]išim arïg-a otuz yašar · [q]ïzïm b[aq]šal üč y(i)g(i)rmi yašar·... oglum [qut]lug sï[nggur] on yaš[ar]...än oglum buyan sïnggur [sä]kiz yaš[ar] ... n o[glu]m baraq sïnggur beš yašar · [munča] kiši-lär-im-ning barï čïn · munča yaš-lïg ärür-i čïn · bu [kiši]-lär-im-ni yolug-a · čärig ekägü bilir bu sözlär čïn äzük [bo]lup ayïg ünsär 'älig yeti qamčï yip manga tägir yastuq-tïn qurug qalïr-m(ä)n...

... includes six people. I, Yölek, am 55. My wife, Arıga, is 30. My daughter, Bakşal, is 13... My son, Kutlug Sıŋgur, is 10. ... my son, Buyan Sıŋgur, is 8.... my son, Barak Sıŋgur, is 5. I certify that they are my family and their ages are right. Both Yoluga (and) Çerig know them. My words are all true, if there is wrong information I will be punished by 57 whippings and not get my *yastuq*.

In the second part of the document, Yoluga and Çerig testify that all the information Yölek mentions above is correct and declare that they consent to a penalty that Yölek would be given if the information is proved to be incorrect. Similar impositions of penalties are found in censuses in the Chinese tradition. For example, Sangha (Sang-ko), a Tibetan Buddhist monk, held a census in 1289 in South China, which was under the control of the Yuan Empire. All the residents in South China were asked to go to a suitable local governmental office and register themselves and all the recorded families were given sealed certificates (*hutie*). The registered ones were responsible for controlling their neighbors in order to avoid any kind of mistakes and false representation. According to the command, those who did not get registered were sentenced to death, whereas those who knew that their neighbor had made a false representation were beaten with a stick 107 times, and those who made a false representation concerning their income were whipped 77 times (Tadashi 1983: 61; Ikeda On 1973: 121-150).

Another whipping penalty is seen in document WP04. The document is a will which divides someone's wealth between their children and stipulates that everyone equally profits from possessions for joint use. Generally, penalties in Uigur wills were paid to the government as possessions or money. However, in this document (WP04), the one to object to the will was mentioned and it was asked that this person should not to take an interest in the will and be whipped:

...bu bitig-ni qayu-sï taplamadïn čatiš-//////y-lar //////////////-nï yorïtmamïš yazuq-qa tgip ülüš almadïn kiši-si ///////////////////// yiti qamčï berge yip yitzün.

If there is a conflict over this will without confirmation…let it not be valid [let them not be influential]. Regarding the crime they commit by preventing something from being valid, let them not take an interest and his wife ... be whipped for seven times" (WP04$_{31-34}$). (Yamada 1993-II: 138-139)

The third type of penalty in the Uigur civil documents is *financial penalty and property penalty*. These penalties as dissuasive penalties served to prevent any contracts being broken and were always applied as a financial compensation. The history of financial penalties goes back to ancient times. In such impositions, financial compensation means fixation and payment of the amount of money and possessions as blood money in return for the committed crime. This compensation was given to the victim or his relatives. However, the state took a certain part of the payment in different law systems (Arık 1996: 20-21; Arsal 1947: 207).

Among the Uigurs, we see that financial penalties and property penalties were paid to the government in the case of land contracts, slavery sale contracts, adoption contracts, emancipation of slave contracts, wills and miscellaneous contracts that show certain legal procedures. Yet, in the Uigur documents, it is striking that there are different practices in terms of the creditor of the financial or property penalty. In Uigur contracts that have the same content but were drawn up at different dates, we see different impositions of penalties.

For example, for a sale contract, if a contract is broken, it is common to punish the person who has broken the contract with double pay of the item for sale to the buyer and the government takes no interest in the penalty. In other sale contracts probably made at a later time, the amount specified as the penalty is paid not to the aggrieved, but to the government, as either cash or property.

In the Uigur civil documents we examined, it is observed that financial penalties and property penalties are paid in two ways according to the type of the contract. The first one is the institution of compromise which has played an important role in the history of criminal law. The institution is based on an agreement between the offender and the aggrieved. Among Uigurs, particularly in land sale contracts, there was a guarantee that the offender would provide the aggrieved with the goods of the same kind in the proportion of one to one or generally two to one. In most of the land sale contracts examined, penalty pays are based on such compromise. The second method in some of the documents examined is that the state institution is more closely involved with impositions of penalties and that financial or property penalties are paid directly to the government.

A. Financial and property penalties in sale contracts

a. Impositions of penalties in land sale contracts

Among Uigurs, penalties are clearly stated in contracts in order to guarantee clauses of land sale contracts and to ensure their dissuasive and enforcement nature against protests. Impositions of penalties as a guarantee by the seller to prevent the buyer from any damage or unfair practices caused by the third person's intervention are found in the documents.

We clearly see that there are various penalties available for those who are to object to clauses of land sale contracts and those who are to bring suits. Contrary to modern legal procedures, among Uigurs, quiet enjoyment (a case where others cannot claim any rights over property) is different. In today's sale contracts, the seller is liable for this debt. That is, the seller is held responsible for a third person divesting the buyer of his property by assertion of a right or preventing the buyer from using his property (Zevkliler 2007: 123). Moreover, the seller is liable to compensate any damages of the buyer caused by this case. In Uigur contracts, although the seller verbally reassures the buyer of sale rights, we see that the protesting third person is liable to the payment of quiet enjoyment debt, not the seller, and that again the third person is held responsible for any damages. In the contracts, it is observed that the seller is not directly responsible for the compensation of the buyer's loss and that there are warnings against possible third persons breaking the contract. In sale contracts, the sections where these impositions of penalties are mentioned are generally similar:

Sa04

> ...män šabi-nïng ogulum qïzïm ičim inim qam qadšïm ygänim tagayïm aytmazun istmäzün aytglï istgli sqïnsr savlarï yorïmazun taqï birök ärklig bäg iši küč-in tutup alayïn yulayïn tisär-lär bu oq ögän üzä suvaq-lïg iki tanču yir yaratu birip yulup alzun yultačï kiši qor-lug bolzun basmïl qor-suz bolzun

> I am Şabi; let my son, my daughter, my elder brother, my younger brother, my relatives, my nephew, and my uncle not tell (anything) or want anything (let them not protest)! If they intend to tell or want (to protest), let their words not be influential (and) even if the powerful ruler and his wife use their influence and take it back, they are to buy two pieces of watering land in this carrier. Let the buyer end up a loser! Let Basmıl not be damaged.

Sa08

> ...biz ikägü-ning inimiz ičimiz qamïz qadaš-ïmïz čamlamazun kim ärklig bäg iši küčün tutup čamlasar bu oq yir tänglig iki yir birip alzun-lar yulzun-lar yulgučï qorlug bolzun toyïnčog qorsuz bolzun

> We both; let our younger brother, our elder brother, and relatives not protest. Whoever uses the influence of the powerful ruler (and) (his) wife and protests, he is to buy two pieces of land equal to this one! Let the buyer end up a loser. Let Toyınçoq not be damaged.

Sa15

> ...män sinsidu-nung aqam inim on-luqum... qïlmazun-lar 'ärklig bäg iši küčin tutup... yir birip sözlär-i yorïmazun yuldačï... kök buqa qorsuz bolzun

> I am Sinsidu; let my elder brother, my brother, *onluk* (arbat)... not protest! The powerful ruler and his wife use their influence ... let their words not be influential. The seller ... let Kök Buqa not be damaged.

In these documents, for those who protest, the terms "*yultačï*" (Sa04, Sa15, Sa06, Sa07, Sa09), "*yulgučï*" (Sa08) and "*čamlagučï*" (meaning "protester", Sa16) are used. These people are to be given the penalty fixed by contract because of their intervention and loss. On the other hand, the buyer is mentioned and prevented from any damages. Here, the person who is referred to by the terms "*yultačï*", "*yulgučï*" and "*čamlagučï*" is the one responsible for the payment of the quiet enjoyment in case of contract breakings.

In the sale contracts we have, there are two observed ways for the compensation of damages caused by a third person's intervention in the favor of the buyer. The first and the common one is that the person who breaks the contract doubles the payment and gives the buyer two parcels of land, or vineyards, etc., for sale. Therefore, the penalty clause requires the proportion of one to two. Only in Sa01 and Sa02 is it conspicuous that protesters give only one parcel of land equal to the one for sale for the compensation of the buyer's loss. Except for this, in the land sale contracts no. Sa03, Sa04, Sa05, Sa06, Sa07, Sa08, Sa09, Sa10, Sa13, Sa15 and Sa16, the protester is responsible for providing the aggrieved with two parcels of land in return for the one for sale as a penalty.

As well as land sale contracts, in a land exchange contract, we see that if the clauses of the contract are violated, the aggrieved is provided with a compensation of the proportion one to two as is the case in some of the same land contracts. In document Ex01, sections of which are missing, it is stated that two people who have exchanged a piece of land with a vineyard will give the aggrieved two parcels of land of the same kind as a penalty, in case of protests by their relatives and elder or younger brothers.

In Uigur land sale contracts, another imposition of a penalty for the compensation of losses is penalty payment, called by different names and given to the top authorities of the government.[6] In the land sale contracts nos. Sa11 and Sa12, it is striking that contract breakers pay the penalty directly to the top governmental authorities:

Sa11

…bu borluq yolïnta män tärbiš-ning aqam inim yigenim tagayïm kim kim m-ä bolup čam čarïm qïlmazun-lar apam birök ärklig bäg iši yat yalavač küčin tutup čam čarïm qïlsar-lar ulug süü-kä bir altun yastuq ičgär-i agïlïq-qa bir bir kümüš yastuq bägät-lär-kä birär ädär-kä yarašu at qïzgut birip söz-lär-i yorïmazun

I, Terbiş, concerning this vineyard, let my elder brother, my younger brother, my nephew, and my uncle or others not protest. But if they use the powerful ruler and (his) wife's influence or that of strangers and protest, let them pay the Great Majesty (Great Khan) one golden *yastuk*, the royal treasury one silver *yastuk*, give rulers fine horses as a penalty (payment), and let their words not be influential!

Sa12

...bu kün-tin mïnča tapmïš-nïng aqa-sï ini-si yigän-i tagay-ï kim kim m-ä čam čarïm qïlmazun-lar apam birök ärklig bäg iš-i küčin tutup čam čarïm qïlsar-lar ulug süü-kä bir altun yastuq basïp il bäg-lär-ingä ädär-kä yaragu at birip sözlär-i yorïmazun čamlagučï kiši qoor-lug bolzun vapso tu qoor-suz bolzun

From now on, let Tapmïş's elder brother, younger brother, his nephew, his uncle or anyone else not protest! If they protest, using the influence of the powerful ruler and his wife let them pay the Great Majesty (Great Khan) one golden *yastuk*, and give the provincial rulers fine horses. Let their words not be influential! Let the protester end up a loser. Let Vapsotu not be damaged.

These documents are significant in that they show penalties were the monopoly of the state at that time. In both of the documents, there is a clause stipulating that *ulug süü* [7] (the Great Majesty) shall be given one golden *yastuq* as a penalty. In addition to the penalty pay, only in Sa11 is it demanded that one silver *yastuq* be paid to *ičgärü agïlïq* or "the royal treasury". Apart from that, in both of the documents, it is required that provincial rulers be given fine horses. Also, in the contract, the wish is expressed that protesters be heavily fined by paying the specified amounts by contract and their words not be influential. The reason why the penalty is paid not to the aggrieved, but to the state authorities is that penalties as dissuasive factors are socially accepted and they reveal the power, the control and the lawmaking function of the government. Money and properties which are submitted to important people in the hierarchy of the state, starting at the top, are also revenues or gains for the government as penalty payments. We can consider the case among Uigurs in the same way.

In Sa03, another land sale contract, a different penalty payment is found:

Sa03

...män yrp yanga-nïng ädgününg ičimiz inimz qamïz qadašïmïz ogulumïz qïzïmz ayïtmaz-un istämäzün ayïtglï istäglï saqïnsar-lar savlarï yorïmazun-lar birök 'ärklig bäg iši küčin tutup alayïn yulayïn tisär-lär bu'oq ögän-tä bu yir tngin-čä iki yir birip alzunlar bu sav-ta qayu-sï agïsar-biz üčär yüz bišär otuz qu(a)npu ičrä quvpar birüšür-biz

We are Yrp Yanga and Edgü; let our elder brother, younger brother, our relatives, sons and daughters not tell (anything) or want anything (or protest)! If they intend to tell (something) or want something (or protest) let their words not be influential. If they tend to take it back, using the influence of the powerful ruler and (his) wife, they are to buy two pieces of land in this carrier equal to this land. Whoever goes back on his words, he will pay 325 *quanpu* to the palace as a penalty.

In this contract, it can be seen that the protester pays penalties both to the buyer and to the government. In the contract, it is stated that if the protester or the seller with a joint responsibility goes back on his words, he will pay 325 *qu(a)npu* to the palace or the official authorities as a penalty, as well as providing the buyer with two pieces of land financially equal to the land he has bought. In the case of no compensation for losses caused by contract violation, third persons as protesters get the financial penalty in order to prevent the buyer from being aggrieved. The document is crucial in that it indicates the control and enforcement of the official institutions in impositions of penalties. However, we unfortunately have no other documents for comparison.

In the contract, the following statement takes place: *bu sav-ta qayu-sï agïsar-biz üčär yüz bišär otuz qu(a)npu ičrä quvpar birüšür-biz*. The word "*quvpar ~ quvar*" is of Chinese origin (< 口罰): "Whoever goes back on his words, he will pay 325 *quanpu* (25) to the palace as a penalty"; "Penalty pay means punishment" (Bussgeld, Bestrafung) (Yamada 1993-II: 278). The word is found in a land sale contract and a slavery trade contract: Ad02 *qayusï bu sav-tïn agïš-sar-biz birer yasduq quvar birüšürbiz* "Whoever goes back on his words, he will pay one *yastuq* as a penalty". This word must be a technical term which means "official financial penalty" in sale contracts. It is noteworthy that the word "*qïzguť*" [8] of Turkic origin corresponds to the Chinese word "*quvpar*" used in the Uigur civil documents. The word "*qïzguť*" in Sa11 might be compared to *quvpar ~ quvar* in Sa03. In the Uigur civil documents, "*qïzguť*" is used in documents Mi01 and Em01, which means "financial penalty, penalty" (Yamada 1993-II: 276).

b. Penalty clauses in slavery trade documents

Slavery trade documents are similar to land sale documents. In some of the contracts we examined, it is understood that an agreement of compromise is made in the event of a case which demands a penalty. For example, in contracts Sa21, Sa22, Sa23, Sa24, Sa26, Sa28, and

Sa29, which all treat trade in slaves, there are statements stipulating that protesters will give the aggrieved two slaves, instead of one, who are equal to the referred slave:

Sa22

...bu qarabaš yolïnta män yrp togrïl ...ičim inim tugmïšïm qadašïm yigänim tagayïm kim qayu čam čarïm qïlmazunlar apam birök čam čarïm qïlsarlar bu qarabaš tänginčä iki qarabaš yaratu birip yulup alzun

About this slave; I am Yrp Togrıl ...let my elder brother, younger brother, my relatives, my nephew, my uncle or anyone else not protest; if they do so let them prepare and give two slaves equal to this one.

Sa24

...män atay tutungnung ičim inim tugmïşïm qadašïm ygänim tgayïm kim kim mä ärsär čam čarïm qïlmazunlar apam birök ärklig bäg iši yat yalavač küčin tutup yulayïn alayïn saqïnsarlar bu qrabaš tänginčä iki qrabaš birip yulup alzunlar

I am Atay Tutung, let my elder brother, younger brother, my relatives, my nephew, my uncle or anyone else not protest; if they intend to buy and sell, using the influence of the powerful ruler and his wife, let them trade two slaves equal to this one"

It is clear that the method of compromise is not applied to the imposition of penalty in the slaver trade document no. Sa27 and protesters pay the penalty to the government and the top authorities:

...kim kim mä bolup čam čarïm qïlsar ulug süükä aq yastuq bäglärkä ädärkä yaragu at birip sözleri yorïmazun

...Whoever protests, let him pay the Great Majesty one *aq* (silver) *yastuk,* and give provincial rulers fine horses and let their words not be influential!

B. Impositions of penalties in emancipation of slave contracts

In contract no. Em01, which shows a slave is set free by his master, it is stated that protesters, especially the master and his relatives, will pay a penalty to the government and those in the state hierarchy:

Em01

...bu bitigtäki söztin öngi bolsar biz ulug suuqa bir altun yastuq aqa ini tägitlär birär kümüš yastuq ïduqqutqa bir yastuq šazïn aygučïqa bir at qïzgut ötünüp sözläri yorïmazun

In case of any contradicting situation with the words here, let them pay *Ulug Süü* one golden *yastuq*, princes and princelings one silver *yastuq* each, and İdikut (the Uigur emperor) one *yastuq*, *şazın ayguçı* (counsellors) one *at qızgut* (penalty pay) and let their words not be influential.

This document in particular gives us more clues than other penalty documents about penalties paid to the government. The document shows that there is a more systematic imposition of a penalty available, which is not seen in other official financial-property penalty contracts. In other words, it is remarkable that the penalties in the document are more advanced and comprehensive. We should certainly consider the fact that the dates of the documents where we see the official financial-property penalties might be different. This document is probably one from the period when the government took a larger interest in penalties. It is seen that as well as the Great Khan (*Ulug Süü*), the Uigur Khan İdiqut, under the control of the Great Khan, is paid penalties. Given the hierarchical order here, penalties are paid as one golden *yastuq* to the Great Khan, who is in the center, one silver *yastuq* each to princes as his successors, then one *yastuq* to the Uigur khan (*İdiqut*) and one horse each to the official counselors. In another contract, Mi01, we see that the official penalty is paid to İdiqut (see below).

C. Imposition of penalties in adoption documents

Two of the three adoption contracts we examined include the official penalties paid to the government, whereas in one contract (Ad03), unlike the others, the penalty is demanded to be paid according to accepted practices.

We see that in the adoption contracts Ad01 and Ad02, penal sanctions depend on the government's initiative. Among the documents we examined, in Ad01, which might be considered to be one of the oldest documents, it is stated that a penalty can be applied within the framework of the rules the government introduces:

Ad01

...män čintso ayag-qa tägimlig-ning inim ičim oglum qam qadašïm ilmäzün tartmazun apam birök ilgli tartïglï saqïnsar savlarï yorumazun yasa-taqï qïn-qa tägsünlär

I, respectable Çintso, let my brother, my uncle, my son and my relatives not intervene, or juggle me out of what is mine; if they do so, let their words not be influential and let them be punished by law.

In this adoption contract, the following penalties will be paid according to the above mentioned law against protesters among the relatives of the adopted:

Ögödäy süüsingä iki yürüng atan ötünüp ambï balïq tarugalarïnga ädärkä yarašu at birip čintso ayagqa tägimligkä birkä iki birip agïr qïnqa tägirbiz
We consent to pay our majesty Ögödey two white camels, give the *darugas* of Ambı Balıq fine horses and respectable Çintso two (adoptees) instead of one, so we will be heavily punished.

It is understood that the document was arranged during the time of the Great Khan Ögödey. In this document, it can be seen that the official penalty was not paid in cash but as properties. It was demanded that Ögödey, as the representative of the state, be paid two white camels, and *darugas*, as the administrative representatives of the state in provinces, and governors, one horse each.

Here, another striking point is that in case of violation of the contract, the loss of the aggrieved is compensated in the proportion of two to one. This statement is not found in the documents where other official penalties are paid to the government.

In another adoption document, no. Ad02, although the high state officials are not directly mentioned, it is stated that those who protest the *quvar* (~ *quvpar*), which is the official penalty paid to the government, will pay one *yastuq* each: *...qayusï bu savtïn agïššarbiz birär yastuq quvar birüšürbiz*; "Whoever goes back on his words, he will pay (the government) one *yastuq* as a penalty".

D. Imposition of penalties in wills

It is understood that the imposition of penalties concerning family law matters are the official penalties paid to the government.

Among Uigurs, the specified penalties are clearly stated in wills in order to guarantee clauses in wills and to ensure their dissuasive and enforcing nature against possible protests. The imposition of penalties in case of protests and personal statements of the inheritor are presented in documents in order to prevent particular successors from any damages or unfair practices because of the clauses of the will. It is possible to see that there are financial penalties, property penalties, and corporal punishments available for those who protest against clauses of wills and bring suits.

In will WP01, the following imposition of penalties are mentioned in case the sons of the family protest against the house which the family man vests his wife with as an inheritance:

...oglum qošang 'äsän qay-a olar ögäy anamïz biz-kä tgir alïr-biz tip almazun qatïl-mazun-lar apam birök alïr-biz tip čamlasar-lar ulug süü-kä bir altun yastuq oglan tigit-lärkä birär kümüš yastuq ičgärü agïlïg-qa bir yastuq ičgärü agïlïg-qa bir at birip agïr qïyn-qa tgip sözläri yorïmazun

Let my sons Koşan, Esen Kaya not intervene, claiming that this belongs to them and she is their step-mother. If they bring a suit to take it back, let them pay the Great Majesty one golden *yastuk*, and princes one silver *yastuk* each, the royal treasury one *yastuk*, and a horse. Let them be heavily punished. Let their words not be influential" (WP01[7-17]).

In another will (WP02), similar impositions of penalties for those who could protest against the person the inheritor grants an emancipation document:

...äv-täki qatïnlarïm mning tugmïš-larïm kim ymä čmlamazun-lar čmlasar-lar ičgärü agïlïg-qa bir altun yastuq qočo bägingä bir at balïg bägingä bir ud birip agïr qïyn-qa tägzün

Let my wives and my relatives or anyone else not protest. If they do (or bring a suit), let them pay the royal treasury one golden *yastuk*, the Koço ruler a horse, and the provincial ruler a cattle. Let them be heavily punished. (WP02[11-16])

It is striking in wills that the institutions to which penalties are paid directly are top state institutions. In the documents, there is a stipulation that *Ulug Süü* [9] "the Great Majesty" (the

Great Khan) be paid one golden *yastuq*. In addition to this penalty pay, it is demanded that princes be paid one silver *yastuk* each, and *ičgerü agïlïq* or "the royal treasury" one *yastuq* and a horse. Also, it is the expressed wish that they will be heavily punished by paying these amounts and their words will not be influential. In another will, protesters are heavily punished by paying the treasury one golden *yastuk* and the Koço rulers a horse and cattle each.

Apart from financial and property penalties, in document WP04 the protester of the will is mentioned and it is demanded that he take no interest in the will and be whipped (see corporal punishment mentioned above).

E. Impositions of penalties in miscellaneous contracts

Among the civil documents, we see financial and property penalties paid to the government in securities that we call miscellaneous contracts in terms of content. For example, in a security (Mi01), a girl is given as security for a loan and then she is taken back. After that, it is demanded that there should be no protests for the girl's clothes and personal belongings. In case of protests, the protester will give the Great Majesty five golden *yastuq*, *shahzadahs* one golden *yastuq* each, İdik-Kut one golden *yastuq*, and the counselor of Koçu province one silver *yastuq*. The imposition here in this document is noteworthy. When it is compared to the penalty proportions paid to the government in other documents, the proportion in this document is much higher and heavier:

Mi01

> ...*kim qayu kiši inäčikä čam... qïlmazunlar apam čam čarïm qïlsarlar ulug süükä biš altun yastuq aqa ini tigitlärkä birär altun yastuq qïzgut ötünüp iduqqutqa bir altun yastuq kögürüp qočo balïq aygučïqa bir kümüš yastuq birip agïr qïynqa tägzünlär*

> Let no one protest against İnäçi... If they do, let them pay the Great Majesty five golden *yastuq*, princes and princelings one golden *yastuq* each, İdikut (the Uigur emperor) one golden *yastuq*, and the counselor of Koço one silver *yastuq*. Let them be heavily punished.

This document must have been arranged later than the others. In another miscellaneous contract (Mi03), a slave disappears. Someone finds the dead body of the slave and takes his clothes for himself. Thus, there is a bargain between the master of the slave and the borrower of the clothes. As a result of the bargain, it is decided that if the master protests he will pay the Great Majesty two *yastuk*, the *miŋ* ruler one *yastuq*, the *daruga* of Lükčüng a half *yastuk*:

Mi03

> ...*ulug süükä 2 yastuq ötünüp ming bägikä 1 yastuq lükčüng targuïnga yarïm yastuq birip agïr qïn tgirmän*

> ... I will pay the Great Majesty two *yastuq*, the ruler of the troop one *yastuq*, and the *daruga* of Lükčüng province a half *yastuq*. I will be heavily punished.

Penalties according to accepted practices and judgments

In Uigur contracts, there are penalties according to accepted practices and judgments based on customary rules, as well as the official penalties. In case of any damage of personal interests, such penalties require compensation for the financial loss. Penalties according to accepted practices and judgments are seen in loan documents, pledging documents, and exchange documents. In these contracts where there is an *İl yangïnča* statement, the penalty rate is given according to accepted practices in a certain province. In such impositions, it is seen that the government does not take any interest in the penalty. Although penalties in loan contracts, pledging contracts and exchange contracts are generally similar, there are some exceptions. For example; in one of the adoption documents which generally include the official impositions of penalties, it is demanded that the penalty be according to accepted practices. In contract Ad03, there is the following regarding those who protest against adoption: *törü yargu yosunï birle ata yazmïš yazuqqa tegsün*, "be punished according to accepted practices and judgments inherited from ancestors".

Penal practices and sources may vary according to the type of the contract. For example, interests are striking as an imposition of a penalty in loan contracts concerning special borrowings.

a) Loan contracts

Among Uigur civil documents, loan contracts are the most numerous. In almost all of the thirty loan contracts we examined, we can see that penalties are imposed according to provincial rules and accepted practices. There are impositions in this contract as dissuasive precautions to prevent the lender from being damaged in case of no return of borrowed things. In the loan contracts we examined, there are penalty payments including various interest rates over the same kind of goods or different products according to customary rules:

Luu yıl ekinti ay beš *otuz-qa manga torčï-[q]a süč[üg]-kä böz [kär]gäk bolup q(a)yïmtutïn bir y(a)rïm böz aldïm küz y(a)ngï-ta otuzar tänbin süčüg-ni bir qap berürmän bermädin käčür-sär-män il yangïnč-a asïgï bilä köni berürmän*

I, Torçı, needed cotton cloth in return for wine on the 25th of the second month of the dragon year and bought one and a half rolls of cotton cloth from Kayımtu. In autumn, I will give thirty *tenbin* of wine as a bowl. If time is overdue, I will give it back directly with interest according to the provincial rules.

In the contracts, it can be seen that interest rates are high in the case of the return of borrowed things. There is no clear statement about penalty interests in the contracts. These probably vary according to the related provincial rules concerning the contract. Examples are given in the following table:

Document no.	Borrowed unit	Back payment and imposition of penalties
Lo06	Sheepskin rug	For every sheepskin rug, 6 *böz*, for every month the interest is 1 *böz*
Lo07	6 *stır kümüş*	Every month, for the interest of a half *baqır kümüş*
Lo13	3 halves of *böz*	Will give 7 bowls of *böz*. In case of no payment, the amount will be given at interest *İl yanıŋça*
Lo20	4 *küri yür*	8 *küri yür*. In case of no payment, the amount will be given at interest *İl yanıŋça*
Lo27	12 *batır künčit*	22 *batır künčit*. In case of no payment, the amount will be given interest *İl yangïnča*
Lo28	1 *küri künčit*	2 *küri künčit*. In case of no payment, the amount will be given interest *İl yangïnča*
Lo29	4 *teng kepez*	7 *teng kepez*. In case of no payment, the amount will be given at interest *İl yangïnča*

b) Pledging documents

It is understood that impositions of penalties are arranged according to customary rules in pledging documents as well. In document Pl01, interest payment is demanded as a penalty. In another pledging document (Pl02), the interesting point is that there is a special law on pledging:

...män samboqdu tutung birtke ...bolmïšqa ton ätük adaq baš birmäz-män äv täg yogun iš išlätsär män il-ning tutug y(a)ngïnča birürmän qalmïš turušï yangï tutug y(a)ngïnča bolzun

I, Samboqdu, will not give Bolmış clothes or shoes as *Tutung birt* (tax). If I make him work busily at home, I will give according to the provincial (country) pledging rule. Let the rest of his life be according to the new pledging rule.

Conclusion

Generally, the imposition of penalties in the Uigur civil documents are encountered as compensation for financial loss with interest or special compensation paid to the government in cases where personal interests are damaged. Heavier penalties such as the death penalty and corporal punishments are given when there is an offense against the government. We understand that, at first, customary law practices applied concerning personal property rights and then impositions of penalties under the monopoly of the state were introduced. In a sense, different practices in contracts show us the history of the development of Uigur penal law.

When considered in terms of penal law, it is seen that financial indemnification is generally made through a process of compromise between individuals. In addition to one-to-two proportional values, there are back payments at various interest rates in Uigur contracts. In these contracts, the payer is a third person who would like to break the contract. Such penalties in the contracts have directly preventive and dissuasive functions, so the responsible party gives a guarantee to the other party.

Before Islam, the government was the only authority in Turkic states in terms of penal law. However, we see that unwritten customary rules formed by people have a functional role in the penal law system. It is noteworthy that when contracts between people are broken, the process of compromise is effective and penal indemnifications are presented not to the government, but to the aggrieved.

In some of the Uigur documents, it is seen that penalties are paid not to the aggrieved, but to governmental institutions. The state must have had a source of revenue in this way. Given the fact that the contracts we obtained belong to different political periods and have different dates, it is possible to see various impositions of penalties for the same situation. In other words, penalties originally paid to the aggrieved were later paid to the government.

The state interest in penalties among Uigurs must have been introduced after the reign of Chinggis Khan. As it is well known, Uigurs came under the control of the Chinggisid Empire in 1209. The Chinggisid Empire developed states over the region which extended and became stronger, and the power to impose penalties was made a state monopoly. The Great Khan (Ulug Süü) at the center was the first to be paid official penalties. In several documents, the Great Khan and his rulers are followed by the Uigur emperor İdikut in terms of penalty payments, and we see that the Great Khanate had a source of revenue thanks to these penalty payments. Accordingly, we can suggest that impositions of penalties among Uigurs changed after Chinggis' reign.

We have stated that the origin of the Uigur law system, including penalties, is a topic to be studied in future research. It is not wrong to think there was an influential common law system which included all Asian people (Chinese, Indians, and Mongols) as well as Turkic customary rules which shaped this understanding of law and the official rules introduced by state authorities. Regardless of the source, the related documents clearly indicate that Uigurs as a settled civilized society applied their legal system successfully in social life.

NOTES

[1] For the publication of these documents, see: W. Radloff, *Uigurische Sprachdenkmäler: Materialien nach dem Tode des Verfassers mit Ergänzungen von S. Malov herausgegeben*, Leningrad 1928, 305+8 pp., 3 tables, reprint, Osnabrück: Biblio Verlag, 1972; N. Yamada, *Sammlung uigurischer Kontrakte*, tr. by Juten Oda, Peter Zieme, Hiroshi Umera and Takao Moriyasu, 1-3, Osaka, 1993; Li Jingwei, *Tulufan Huiguwen Shehui Jingji Wenshu Yanjiu* (Research on Uighur Socio-economic Manuscripts from Turfan), Ürümçi: Xinjiang Renmin Chubanshe, 1994; Muhemmetrehim Sayit, İsrapil Yusup, *Qadimqi Uygur Yeziqidiki Vesiqiler*, Urumçi: Şincan Halk Neşriyatı, 2000; Geng Shimin, *Studies of Uighur Civil Documents,* Beijing, 2006.

[2] Also see Masao Mori, "A study on Uygur documents of loans for consumption", *Memoirs of the Research*

Department of the Toyo Bunko, Vol. 20, 1961; Masao Mori, "The clause of warrant in the Uigur documents of sale and purchase", *Toyo Gakuho*, vol. 44, no. 2, Tokyo, 1961, 1-23.

[3] ED 975b *yosun* "manner, custom" < Mo. *yosun* "habit, accepted practice, system, social order" (Kovalevskiy III, 238). Also see: TMEN IV 408, *yosun* "habit, accepted practice". RSl. III, 441, *yosun* "rule, method". The word is available in various Turkic languages today: Yak. *çoşun*, Soy. *yozu*, Kzk. *çozuq* "habit, custom, accepted practice", Şor. *çozak* "trust, faith, religion, rule", Tat. *yusuq* "eligible, proper" (VEWT 202). The word is frequently used in the Golden Horde yarliqs (Özyetgin 1996: 169).

[4] As stated before, we have a limited number of documents about the Turkic censuses. The four documents (121/R41, 101/R40, 140a/055, 215/67) mentioned by Reşit Rahmeti Arat in his notable extensive article titled "In the Ancient Turkic law documents" are the only documents we currently have. The two documents, no. 121/R41, 101/R40 in Arat, appeared in Radloff's *Uigurische Sprach-denkmäler* (1928: 57-59). The texts of the two other documents whose top parts are missing were first completed and published by Osman Fikri Sertkaya (1992: 131-148).

[5] The first publication of the document whose top part is missing (TM 111, U5298; R 153/4) was by Peter Zieme (1982: 263-267). Zieme put a date on the declaration as 1275.

[6] See Hiroshi Umemura, "İyaku-batsu nôkan mongon no aru Uiguru monco; tokuni sono sakusei ciki to nendai no kettei ni tsuite", *Tôyo Gaku-hô* 58/3-4, 1977, pp. 1-40.

[7] Reşit R. Arat suggests that the word *süü* (< Chinese *dz'uo* < *tsu*, Mo. *su* ~ *sü*, Kalmuk sū) corresponds to the Turkic word 'kut' and points out that the word means "happiness and majesty". See Arat (1991: 389); Clark (1975:14).

[8] Qïzgut < Turkic *qïz*-"get annoyed, get angry". As well as the civil documents, it is seen in U. II 26, 14 as qïn qïzgut (ED681b). In DLT, the word can be traced: *qïzgut* "penalty; torture, penalty or torture before others for making an example of one" (I, 451). *qïzgut* (Erdal I, 313), which means "penalty", is given in U II 20, 1 and 26,14, U III 56, 7, BT II 1095, Maitr 81v2 together with the word kıyın. Erdal suggests *qïzgut* is about the verb *qïzgur*-"to inflict exemplary punishment" (1991-II, 749). If we try to explain the word with the verb root *qïz*-, Erdal says-g is not inexplicable, yet relates the word with bışgur-,bışgut, yapgur-yapgut in terms of word formation.

[9] See footnote 5 for the word *ulug süü*.

BIBLIOGRAPHY

Allsen, Thomas T. (1983). "The Yüan Dynasty and the Uighurs of Turfan in the 13th century", M. Rossabi ed., *China among Equals: The Middle Kingdom and its Neighbours, 10th-14th Century,* 243-280.

Arat, R.R. (1937). "Uygurca Yazılar Arasında", İstanbul, 14s.+1 levha.

Arat, R.R. (1964). "Eski Türk Hukuk Vesikaları", *JSFOu*, No.65, Helsinki, 11-77 (= Türk Kültürü Araştırmaları, I-1, Ankara, 1964, 5-53.

Arat, R.R. (1979). *Kutadgu Bilig III İndeks*, Haz.: Kemal Eraslan, Osman F. Sertkaya, Nuri Yüce, İstanbul: Türk Kültürü Araştırma Enstitüsü Yayınları.

Arat, R.R. (1991). *Eski Türk Şiiri*, Ankara: Türk Tarih Kurumu Yayınları.

Arık, Feda Şamil (1996). "Eski Türk Ceza Hukukuna Dair Notlar, I. Suçlar ve Cezalar", *Tarih Araştırmaları Dergisi 1995*, C. XVII, Sayı: 28, A.Ü. DTCF Tarih Bölümü, Ankara, 1-50.

Arsal, Sadri Maksudi (1947). *Türk Tarihi ve Hukuk*, İstanbul: İ.Ü. Hukuk Fakültesi Yayınları.

Atalay, Besim (1985-1986). *Divanü Lugati't-Türk Tercümesi*, C. I-IV, Ankara: Türk Dil Kurumu Yayınları.

Ayiter, Ferit, (1950). "Eski Türk Hususî Hukukuna ait bazı notlar", *İstanbul Üniversitesi, İktisat Fakültesi Mecmuası*, 11 (1949-1950), 417-436.

Caferoğlu, Ahmet (1993). *Eski Uygur Türkçesi Sözlüğü*, İstanbul.

Clark, Larry V. (1975). *Introduction to the Uyghur Civil Documents of East Turkestan (13th-14th centuries)*, Ph.D. dissertation, Bloomington: Indiana University.

Clauson, Sir Gerard (1972). *An Etymological Dictionary of Pre-Thirteenth-Century Turkish*, Oxford.

DLT: See Atalay (1985-1986).

Doerfer, G., (1963-75). *Türkische und Mongolische Elemente im Neupersischen*, I-IV, Wiesbaden.

ED: see Clauson (1972).

Erdal, Marcel (1991). *Old Turkic Word Formation, A Functional Approach to the Lexicon*, Vol. I-II, Wiesbaden.

Giles, H.A., (1912). *Chinese-English Dictionary*, London.

Ikeda On (1973). "T'ang household registers and related documents", Arthur F. Wright, Dennis Twitchett eds., *Perspectives on the T'ang*, New Haven-London, 1973, 121-150.

İzgi, Özkan, (1987). *Uygurların Siyasî ve Kültürel Tarihi (Hukuk Vesikalarına Göre)*, Türk Kültürünü Araştırma Enstitüsü Yayınları: Ankara.

JW: see Li Jingwei (1994).

Li Jingwei (1994). *Tulufan Huiguwen Shehui Jingji Wenshu Yanjiu*, Ürümçi: Xinjiang Renmin Chubanshe.

Kovalevskiy, J.E. (1844-49). *Mongol'sko-Russko-Frantsuzskiy Slovar'* (Dictionnaire Mongol-Russe-Français), 3. t., Kazan.

Mori, Masao (1961), "The clause of warrant in the Uigur documents of sale and purchase", *Toyo Gakuhô*, vol. 44, no. 2, Tokyo, 1-23.

Mori, Masao (1961). "A study on Uygur documents of loans for consumption", *Memoirs of the Research Department of the Toyo Bunko*, vol. 20.

Özyetgin, A. Melek (1996). *Altın Ordu, Kırım ve Kazan Sahasına Ait Yarlık ve Bitiklerin Dil ve Üslûp İncelemesi*

(İnceleme-Metin-Tercüme-Notlar-Dizin-Tıpkıbasım), Ankara: Türk Dil Kurumu Yayınları.

Özyetgin, A. Melek (2005), *Orta Zaman Türk Dili ve Kültürü Üzerine İncelemeler*, Ötüken Yayınevi: Ankara.

Radloff, W., (1928). *Uigurische Sprachdenkmäler, Materialien nach dem Tode des Verfassers mit Ergänzungen von S. Malov herausgegeben*, Leningrad 1928, S. VIII + 305, mit 3 Tfln.

Räsänen, M., (1969). *Versuch eines etymologischen Wörterbuchs der Türksprachen*, Helsinki.

Sertkaya, Osman Fikri (1992). "Eski Uygur Türklerinden Hukuk Belgeleri Örnekleri", *Türklerde İnsanî Değerler ve İnsan Hakları (Başlangıcından Osmanlı Dönemine Kadar)*, Türk Kültürüne Hizmet Vakfı Yay., İstanbul, 131-148.

Tadashi, Uematsu (1983). "The control of Chiang-nan in the early Yuan", *Acta Asiatica*, 45, Tokyo.

TMEN: See Doerfer.

Umemura, Hiroshi (1977). "İyaku-batsu nôkan mongon no aru Uiguru monco; tokuni sono sakusei ciki to nendai no kettei ni tsuite", *Tôyo Gakuhô* 58/3-4, 01-40.

USp.: See Radloff (1928).

VEWT: see Räsänen (1969).

Yamada, Nobuo (1964). "Uigur document of sale and loan contracts brought by Ôtani Expeditions", *Memoirs of the Research Department of the Toyo Bunko*, no. 23, Tokyo 1967, 71-118.

Yamada, Nobuo (1965). "The form of the Uighur documents of loan contracts", *Memoirs of the Faculty of Letters*, Ōsaka University, XI, 1965, 87-216.

Yamada, Nobuo (1972). "Uighur documents of slaves and adopted sons", *Memoirs of Faculty of Letters, Ōsaka University*, XVI, 161-268.

Yamada, Nobuo (1981). "An Uighur document for the emancipation of a slave, revised", *Journal Asiatique* 269: 1-2, 373-383.

Yamada, Nobuo (1993). *Sammlung uigurischer Kontrakte*. Hrsg. von Juten Oda, Peter Zieme, Hiroshi Umemura, Takao Moriyasu,. v.1-3. Osaka.

Zevkliler, Aydın, Ayşe Havutçu, (2007). *Borçlar Hukuku, Özel Borç İlişkileri,* Ankara: Seçkin Yayınevi.

Zieme, Peter (1982), 'Ein Uigurischen Familienregister aus Turfan,' *Altorientalische Forschungen*, IX (1982), 263-267.

蒙元時期蒙古文書中的"威懾語"

青格力

　　"威懾語"（*sürdegülülge üge*）是蒙元時期官方文書程式構成諸要素之一。尤其在帝王頒發的聖旨文書中位置明顯，用語獨特，威懾禁戒色彩突出，使國家公文和外交文書顯得更加莊重威嚴，給人深刻印象。作為蒙元時期公文程式研究的一個環節，本文以帝王聖旨資料為中心，試對文書"威懾語"內部結構、與主體之間的關係以及刑罰意義等方面的基本特徵作一些綜合分析。

一、"威懾語"資料特徵

　　留存至今的蒙元時期蒙古文書資料中，相對較完整的是帝王所頒發的聖旨文書。其中，頒發給宗教人士的聖旨文書出現最早，其形成和發展影響了整個蒙元帝國時期文書制度，是觀察蒙古文書程式特徵的最基本資料。

1. 頒發給宗教人士的聖旨

　　蒙元帝王給宗教人士頒發過大量免除賦稅並保護寺產的聖旨（*jarliγ-un bičig*）。據史料記載，1219 年成吉思汗曾給中觀和海雲禪師聖旨，命"達里罕行者"（*darqalatuγai*）[1]。"達里罕"為蒙古語 *darqan*，專指享受特殊待遇或多種特權的人。這可能是蒙元帝王頒發給宗教人士享有類似"達里罕"（*darqalaqu*）待遇的聖旨的開端，而頒發給宗教人士的聖旨是蒙元時期蒙古文書之基礎。至忽必烈汗時期，頒發給宗教人士的聖旨結構已趨於完整嚴謹，成為元朝文書之典範，影響到整個王朝典章，對於研究蒙元文書制度具有重要意義。

　　頒發給宗教人士的聖旨資料有兩種。一種是以八思巴字（*dörbeljin üsüg*）和回鶻式蒙古字（uyiɣurjin mongɣul üsüg）寫成的蒙古文聖旨，至今發現約有 40 餘件。另一種是相當數量的漢文和少量的藏文[2]等其他語種的譯文聖旨。其中漢譯聖旨大量散見於碑銘、地方誌和《元史》、《元典章》、《通制條格》、《憲台通紀》等元代史料。尤為可貴的是，漢譯聖旨所採用的準確表現原文語法形態及語氣的翻譯方法，能夠一定程度上復原蒙古文聖旨原貌，可彌補蒙古文聖旨數量的不足。

這種翻譯例規的產生，與當時蒙古人的"語言敬畏"意識和文化心理有關。在蒙古遊牧社會，帝王們的言語、命令叫做"聖言"（jarliɣ）或"口諭"（aman jarliɣ）[3]，被認為是在傳達天神的旨意。傳達"聖言"，謂之"持聲音"（daɣu bariɣulqu）或"送言語"（kele kürgekü）[4]，不可任意增減或改變詞語，必須依照原樣復述。不寧唯是，若譯成其他語言，還要經得起還原或"返譯"的考驗，否則將以違反天神之意志而受到懲罰。

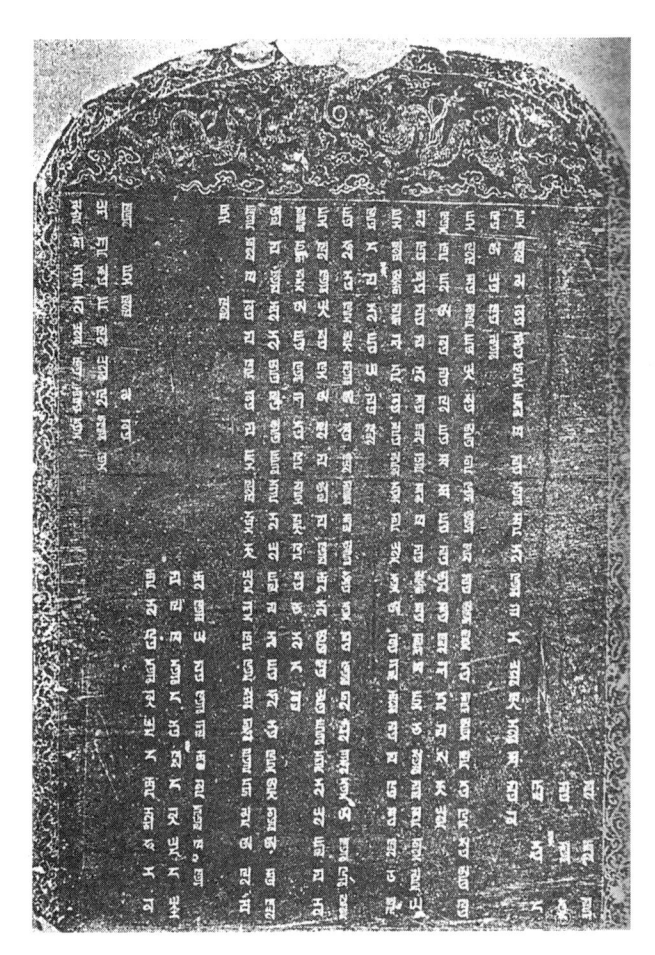

圖一：山西省交城縣石壁山玄中寺的八思巴文蒙古語碑

正因為對傳達"聖言"的要求如此苛刻，所以聖旨譯文忠實地保持著蒙古語語法和修辭的特點，而於譯文語言本身則顯得"不倫不類"。以往的研究將這種對譯歸咎於翻譯水準或蒙古文書本身的發展程度問題，被稱作"白話體"[5]、"粗俗體"[6]、"硬譯體"[7]、"直譯體"[8]、"蒙式漢語"[9]等等，這些顯然不足以體現其宗教信仰和語言表現形式高度結合的內在因素。因此，筆者曾用"忠實翻譯"（sidurɣu orčiɣuly-a）來表現這種翻譯體[10]，現予修正，改稱為"敬譯體"（kündütgel orčiɣuly-a）。本文將這部分聖旨視為准蒙古文書資料來加以利用。

2. "威懾語"在聖旨程式中的位置

筆者曾概括頒發給宗教人士的聖旨程式基本結構如下[11]：

①祈禱語（daɣadqal-un üge）—②頒發者（jarliɣ baɣulɣaɣči）—③宣諭對象（jarliɣ daɣulɣaqui eteged）—④先帝聖旨之引用（uridaqi qaɣad-un jarliɣ-un duradqal）—⑤遵從先帝聖旨之意志（uridaqi qaɣad-un jarliɣ-i daɣaqu čiqulčilay-a）—⑥頒發對象（jarliɣ küliyegči）—⑦禁令

(*jorbuslaysan čaɣaja*)—⑧威懾語（*sürdegülülge üge*）—⑨確定語（*batulaburi*）—⑩頒發年（*jarliɣ baɣulɣaɣsan on*）—⑪頒發月（*jarliɣ baɣulɣaɣsan sar-a*）—⑫頒發日（*jarliɣ baɣulɣaɣsan edür*）—⑬頒發地點（*jarliɣ baɣulɣaɣsan ɣajar orun*）—⑭印璽文（*tamaɣ-a*）

①—③為前文，④—⑧為正文，⑨—⑭為結尾。在聖旨程式整體結構中，"威懾語"處於第八位，也是正文的最後一個要素。這一狀況基本貫穿於整個蒙古帝王頒發給宗教人士的聖旨當中。可以忽必烈皇帝牛年的蒙漢（八思巴字和敬譯體漢文）合璧聖旨[12]為例，觀察"威懾語"及其位置（見圖一）。八思巴字蒙古文轉寫：

1	*monŋga dėŋri-yin kʻüčʻü-dür yeke su jail-yin ihēn-dür*
2	*qān jarliq manu*
3	*čʻeriʻüd-ün noyad-da čʻerig haran-a balaqad-un daruqas-da noyad-da yor- čiqun yabuqun ėlč ʻin-e dūlqaquė jarliq*
4	*jiŋgis qan-u ba qān-u ba jarliq-dur doyid ėrkʻeʻüd sėnšhiŋuŋ\<d\> dašmad aliba alba qubčʻiri ülü üjen dėŋri-yi jalbariju hirüʻer ögün atʻuqai gēkʻdegsed ajuʻuė*
5	*ėdüʻe ber böʻesü uridan-u jarliq-un yosuʻar aliba alba qubčʻiri ülü üjen dėŋri-yi jalbari-ju hirüʻer ögün atʻuqai gēn*
6	*tʻay-ven-fu-dur büküʻün ši-bi-zhi-dur aqun an-shiŋ-leu-da bariju yabuʻai jarliq ögbeė*
7	*ėden-ü sümes-dür geyid-dür anu ėlčʻin bu baʻutʻuqai ulā šiʻüsü bu baritʻuqai tsʻaŋ tʻamqa bu ögtʻügeė qajar usun baq tʻegirmed yaʻud kʻej\<d\>-i anu buliju tʻatʻaju bu abtʻuqai*
8	*ėde basa doyid jarliqtʻu gējü yosu ügeʻüė üėles bu üėleddügeė üėlėdüʻesü ülüʻü ayuqu mun*
9	*jarliq manu*
10	*hükʻer jil*
11	*qabur-un tʻeriʻün zara-yin*
12	*qorin tʻabun-a*
13	*taydu-da bügüė-dür bičibeė*

蒙元時期蒙古文書中的"威懾語"

漢譯文[13]：

1	長生天氣力裏 大福蔭護助裏
2	皇帝聖旨
3	管軍的官人每根底軍人每根底 城子達魯花赤官人每根底 往來的使臣每根底 宣諭的 聖旨
4	成吉思皇帝聖旨裏和尚每也裏可溫每先生每答失蠻每不揀什麼差發休交當者拜天祝壽者麼道有來
5	如今呵 依著在聖旨裏不揀什麼差發休當拜天祝壽者麼道
6	太原府裏石壁寺有的安僧錄根底執把聖旨與了也
7	這寺院房子裏使臣休□安下者鋪馬祗應休要者稅糧休納者地土園林水碾不揀什麼物件他每的休奪要者麼道
8	更這（和）尚每聖旨與了也沒體例的勾當休做做呵他每不怕那什麼
9	聖旨了也
10	牛兒年
11	正月
12	二十五日
13	大都有時分寫來

按照從左向右轉行的蒙古文書寫格式，上述聖旨碑文的結構圖為：

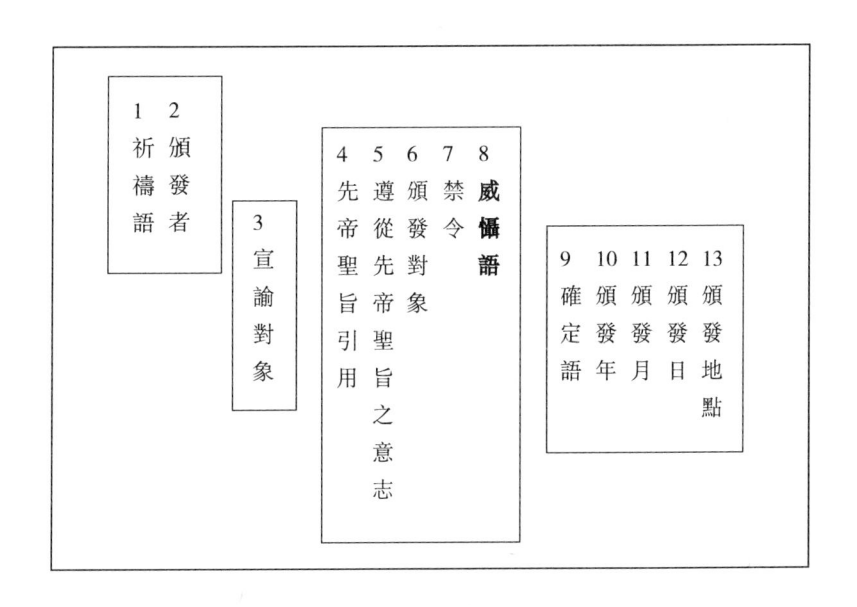

1 2 祈 頒 禱 發 語 者	3 宣 諭 對 象	4 5 6 7 8 先 遵 頒 禁 **威** 帝 從 發 令 **懾** 聖 先 對 **語** 旨 帝 象 引 聖 用 旨 之 意 志	9 10 11 12 13 確 頒 頒 頒 頒 定 發 發 發 發 語 年 月 日 地 　 　 　 　 點

首先，"威懾語"包含具有明顯威嚇義的詞語，如"不怕那什麼"、"無罪過那什麼"、"斷

按答奚死罪者"等等。其次，"威懾語"具有完整的內容和形式，在文書程式中可獨立對其結構構成進行更細緻的分析。

二、"威懾語"結構特徵

作為文書程式結構的一要素，"威懾語"有一定的獨立性。但在不同情況下，其內容和形式又有所差異。那麼，這些究竟是同一內容的不同表現形式，還是不同內容的相同表現形式呢？仔細觀察其結構特徵，也許是探其究竟的一個有效途徑。

（一）"單一式威懾語"和"重疊式威懾語"

如果把一個帶有完整威懾禁戒語氣的句段視為一個"威懾語"，那麼，根據聖旨中的構成形式，可將"威懾語"分為"單一式威懾語"（*dang sürdügülülge üge*）和"重疊式威懾語"（*dabqur sürdügülülge üge*）兩類。

1. "單一式威懾語"

一件聖旨文書要素裏，只包含一個"威懾語"，可叫做"單一式威懾語"。如，

（1）　ėde　basa doyid　jarliqt'u gējü yosu üge·üė üėles bu üėleddügeė
　　　　這　（和）尚每　聖旨與了也　沒體例的勾當　休做

üėledü·esü ülü·ü ayuqu mun.
做呵，　他每不怕那什麼。
現代漢語譯文：他們不得因持有聖旨而做無理的事。如做，他們豈不怕？[14]
（忽必烈汗1277—1289年蒙漢合璧聖旨，《彙編》，第7—10頁）

（2）　ėne basa li t'i-dėm　t'üšigdebe ėle gējü yosu üge·üė üėles bu üėleddügeė
　　　　這　李提點　倚付來　麼道　無體例勾當　　休行者

üėledü·esü bidan-a öč'idk'ün　k'er　ber　gėrün bida uqad je.
行呵，俺每根底　奏者。不揀　說什麼呵，俺每識也者。
現代漢語譯文：李提點也不要因有權勢而做無理的事。如做，向我們起奏，是非如何，我們將明察。（1280—1292年忽必烈汗蒙漢合璧聖旨，《彙編》，第44—47頁）

"單一式威懾語"有四個基本要素：

第一要素——"警告對象"。如，"這和尚每"（ėde basa doyid）、"這先生每"（ėde basa senshingud）、"這李提點"（ėne basa li tʻi-dėm）、"陀羅尼僧"（dharničʻin）。這些"警告對象"是接受聖旨的主體，在聖旨整體程式結構中與"頒發對象"一致。

第二要素——"前提條件"。如，"聖旨與了也"（jarliqtʻu gejü），"倚付來麼道"（tʻušigdebe ėle gejü）等。交代一種前提條件，其中心詞是隨聖旨頒發者身份的變化而變化的。如：

皇后所發懿旨："說有懿旨"（ijitʻen ėle kʻējü）

太子、王子所發令旨："令旨麼道"（bičigtʻen ėle gējü）

教主所發法令："道有法旨"（fajitʻu kʻējü）

第三要素——"禁止句"。如，"沒體例的勾當休做"（yosu üge·üė üėles bu üėleddügeė）、"無體例勾當休行者"、"沒體例的公事休做者"等等。其基本用語是"休……"。"單一式威懾語"的這一要素的表現形式最穩定，敬譯體表現差異也不大。如：

無體例公事休行者（1261年聖旨，《白話錄》，第22頁）

沒體例的公事休做者（1267年聖旨，《靈巖寺聖旨碑》）[15]

無體例勾當休行者（1268年聖旨，《白話錄》，第23頁）

休倚做沒體例勾當者（1276年聖旨，《白話錄》，第25頁）

無體例勾當休做者（1293年聖旨，《白話錄》，第35頁）

沒體例的事休做者（1296年聖旨，《白話錄》，第39頁）

第四要素——"警告句"。如，"做呵，他每不怕那什麼"（üėledü·esü ülü·ü ayuqu mun），"行呵，俺每根底奏者。不揀說什麼呵，俺每識也者"（üėledü·esü bidan-a öčʻidkʻün kʻer ber gerün bida uqad je）等等。其基本用語是"做呵……"、"行呵……"等。

2. "重疊式威懾語"

一件聖旨裏，出現兩個或兩個以上的"威懾語"時，可稱作"重疊式威懾語"。如下例中A代表的是第一個"威懾語"，B代表的是第二個"威懾語"。

（1）*ėyin gē·ülü·ed burun buši bolqaqun haran ülü·ü ayuqun*（B），

現代漢語譯文：如此　講明瞭，　違者　　　豈不怕？

ėde basa ijitʻu gējü yosu üge·üė üėles bu üėledtʻügeė,

他們　　也　　　　　不得因持有懿旨而做無理的事，

üėledü·esü ülü·ü ayuqu mud（A）

如做，　　　他們豈不怕？　　（答吉皇太后蒙文懿旨（1320）《彙編》，第 357—358, 361 頁）

（2）*ėyin gē·ülü·ed burun buši bolqaqun haran ülü·ü ayuqun*（B），
　　　這般宣諭了，別了的人，不怕那甚麼

ėde basa　senšiŋud ijit'en ėle kējü yosu üge·üė üėles üėledü·esü
更這　　　先生每　　說道有懿旨　若無體例的勾當做呵，

mud ülü·ü ayuqu（A）
他每不怕那甚麼

現代漢語譯文：如此講明瞭，為這豈不怕？先生們如果因持有懿旨而做無理的事，他們也豈不怕？（《答吉皇太后雞年（1321）懿旨》，《彙編》，第 368—369、370 頁）

不難看出，A 與前面看到的"單一式威懾語"相一致。而構成"重疊式威懾語"的方式是在 A 之前嵌入一個"威懾語"B，從而形成 B+A 重疊的威懾語結構。在早期的聖旨文書中還能看到兩個以上的"威懾語"重疊形式，如 1255 年蒙哥汗聖旨[16]。但現存聖旨資料裏出現的基本為 B+A 構成的雙重重疊形式。如：

（1）<u>這般宣諭了呵，違別了的人每，不怕那甚麼（B）。更這先生每、這般宣諭了麼道、不屬自己的影占，行無體例的勾當呵，他每不怕那甚麼（A）</u>。（1318 年鰲屹重陽萬壽宮聖旨碑，《白話錄》，第 76 頁）

（2）<u>這般宣諭了呵，別了的人每，要罪過者（B）。更這的每有聖旨麼道、做沒體例勾當呵，他每更不怕那（A）</u>。（1335 年重編百丈清規聖旨，《白話錄》，第 109 頁）

"重疊式威懾語"的 B 部分也是一個完整的"威懾語"表現形式。從結構上看包括以下三個基本要素。

第一要素——"前提條件"。如，"這般宣諭了呵"（*ėyin ge·ülü·ed burun*）、"這般教諭了呵"、"這般曉諭了呵"等等。

第二要素——"警告對象"。如，"違別了的人每"（*buši bolqaqun haran*）、"法旨別了的人每"等等。在聖旨整體程式結構中，這些"警告對象"是宣諭聖旨的對象，即與聖旨程式整體結構中的"宣諭對象"一致，不同於 A 中的"警告對象"。有些宗教人士是作為"宣諭對象"而納入"警告對象"裏的。如，"別了的管民官、和尚每"（《通制條格》卷二十九《僧道·詞訟》）。

第三要素——"警告句"。如，"不怕那甚麼"（*ülü·ü ayuqun*）、"要罪過者"（*ėre·üt'en boltuqai*）、"斷按答奚死罪"（*aldaqu ükükü*）等等。

（二）"宣諭對象性威懾語"和"頒發對象性威懾語"

同樣是"威懾語"，A和B之間存在較明顯區別。比較：

A：①威脅對象—②前提條件—③禁止句—④警告句

B：①前提條件—②威脅對象—③警告句

兩者在要素數量以及順序安排上都有所不同。B類缺少"禁止句"，且"前提條件"和"威脅對象"的位置也和A類不同。顯而易見，兩者在基本結構上存在差異。

出現這種差異的根本原因在於"警告對象"的不同。A類的警告對象是"和尚每"（*doyid*）、"先生每"（*senšingud*）或具體某人，與聖旨整體結構中的第六部分"頒發對象"（*jarliɣ küliyegči*）相一致。B類的警告對象則是"人每"（*haran*）、"管民官"等泛指對象，與聖旨整體程式結構中的第三部分"宣諭對象"（*jarliɣ dayulɣaqui eteged*）相一致。與"警告對象"之間的內在聯繫決定了"前提條件"、"警告句"、"禁止句"等諸要素的出現與否以及表現方式。換言之，A類和B類"威懾語"的結構樣式和內容，是和"警告對象"這一要素的內容緊密相關的。從這一特點出發，可以把A類歸納為"頒發對象性威懾語"（*jarliɣ dayulɣaqui eteged-tü qanduɣuluɣsan sürdegülülge üge*），把B類歸納為"宣諭對象性威懾語"（*jarliɣ küliyegči-dü qanduɣuluɣsan sürdegülülge üge*）。從兩者的相互關係而言，前者是後者出現的必要條件，是不可缺少的。所以，"單一式威懾語"一般都是"頒發對象性威懾語"。

在具體聖旨資料中由於詞語形態變化或內容伸縮，甚至是筆誤等原因，其構成要素可能出現用語或表現不盡相同的現象。敬譯體也忠實地體現著蒙古文原文之間或者對譯文之間的類似差異。如在"頒發對象性威懾語"裏，蒙古文 "*mun*"（複數為 *mud*），原義為"這個"、"那個"，指示代詞，可在句末或句首出現。而在敬譯體裏固定以人稱代詞"他"、"他每"來表現，其位置也都固定在句首。還有些是意義相同，表現形式相似，但存在細微的形態差異的情況。如，"聖旨與了也"與"有聖旨麼道"，"俺每根底奏者"與"俺根底說將來者"，"行呵"與"做呵"，"無體例"與"沒體例"，"勾當"與"公事"、"事"等等。若表現形式出現較大的出入或差異，那很可能是一些書寫錯誤所致。例如，"做呵，不怕那"（《白話錄》，第37頁）一句，少了結尾的"甚麼"。又，"行的"（1326年，《白話錄》，第80頁）為"行呵"之誤。再如"他每根底那甚麼"（1314令旨，《白話錄》，第70頁）一句，用法也較少見，其中的"根底"[17]應當是"不怕"或"更不怕"等之誤。同樣，"宣諭對象性威懾語"裏也存在類似的問題。

不過，不論"宣諭對象性威懾語"還是"頒發對象性威懾語"，即使出現一些細微的偏差，但前述基本結構形式不會有根本性的改變。

"頒發對象性威懾語"基本要素：

	蒙古文	敬譯體漢文
警告對象	ėde basa doyid	這和尚每
	ėde basa	更這的每
	senšhingud	這先生每
	dharničʻin	陀羅尼僧
	ėne basa li tʻi-dėm	這李提點
前提條件	jarliqtʻu (jarliqtʻen) gejü	聖旨與了也 / 有聖旨麼道
	ijitʻen ėle kʻējü	說有懿旨
	bičigtʻen ala gējü	令旨麼道
	fajitʻu kʻējü	道有法旨
	tʻüšigdebe ėle gējü	倚付來麼道
禁止句	bu üėleddügeė	休行者 / 休做者
警告句	yosu ügeˑüė, yosu ügeˑün	無體例 / 沒體例 / 沒體例的
	üėles	公事 / 勾當 / 事
	üėledüˑesü	行呵 / 做呵 / 若做呵
	ülüˑü ayuqu	不怕那甚麼 / 更不怕那甚麼 / 那甚麼
	bidan-a öčʻidkʻün	俺每根底奏者 / 俺根底說將來者
	kʻer ber gerün	不揀說什麼呵 / 怎生行底 / 不揀怎生呵
	bida uqad je	俺每識也者 / 咱每識也者
	mun, mud	他 / 他每 / 他每是 / 他每根底

"宣諭對象性威懾語威懾語"基本要素：

	蒙古文	漢文
前提條件	ène jarliq èyin dūlqaqdād burun	俺每的這聖旨宣諭了呵 / 俺每底聖旨省諭，聽了呵
	èyin gē·ülü·ed burun	這般宣諭了呵 / 這般教諭了呵 / 這般宣諭了 / 這般曉諭了呵
警告對象	buši bolqaqun haran, ülü k'üyič'i·ek'ün haran, jük-iyer ülü k'üyič'i·ek'ün haran,	違別了的人每 / 別了的人每 / 別了的人 / 見了法旨別了呵 / 法旨別了的人每 / 別了的管民官、和尚每 / 已前斷了的言語別了呵
警告句	ülü·ü ayuqun	不怕那甚麽 / 他更不怕那甚麽
	ère·üt'en boltuqai	要罪過者
	aldaqu ükükü	斷按答奚死罪

三、"威懾語"主體特徵

"威懾語"的核心是"警告句"。"警告句"語氣的輕重決定著"威懾語"的威脅程度。而在聖旨文書中"警告句"往往與某個控制其性質、狀態和作用的主體相聯繫。觀察"威懾語"中的"警告句"，可發現有以下幾種與主體相關聯的類型。

（一）"無主體性威懾語"

"警告句"中出現頻率最高的是"做呵，他（每）不怕那什麽"（üèledü·esü ülü·ü ayuqu mun/mud）。句中的反詰疑問詞"ülü·ü"（豈不……）與句末的主語"mun（mud）"相呼應，加強了警告語氣和威脅程度。然而，威脅氣氛之所以很濃厚，原因不僅在於這種特殊句型，還在於隱晦的主體和懲罰手段不可預知的神秘性。這種隱藏主體的威懾語可稱作"無主體性威懾語"（ejen bey-e ügei sürdegülülge üge）。這種"無主體性威懾語"一般出現在"頒發對象性威懾語"裏，即"單一式威懾語"和"重疊式威懾語"的A類中，主要針對的是宗教人士。

"無主體"並非真正意義上的無主體。按照古代蒙古人的世界觀和思維方式，一切神秘力量都來自"天神"（tengreri），所以，"無主體性威懾語"的神秘主體即是"天神"。而宗教人士與天神之間存在著內在的"聯繫"。因為，在蒙古人薩滿信仰世界裏，各個主體之間的主次關係是以"諸天神—諸薩滿—帝王們—普通人"的體系來聯結的。薩滿與天神是可直接"聯繫"的，為蒙古帝王進行"告天祝壽"的所有神職人員，即宗教人士都屬於薩滿階層。故，能夠給與宗教人士獎懲的主體自然也是"天神"了。因此，有些種類的聖旨文書中會明確提到"威懾語"的這一"天神"主體，我們將在下一節談到。在一些牌符、印璽等簡短命令式文書形式中，也能見到"*büsiretügei ayutuyai*"（要服從，要懼怕）[18]這樣的更簡潔的命令式"威懾語"，也應一併看作是"無主體性威懾語"。

（二）"有主體性威懾語"

明確指出其主體的"威懾語"可稱作"有主體性威懾語"（*ejen beyetü sürdegülülge üge*）。根據主體的不同身份可細分如下：

1. "'天'主體威懾語"

這類"威懾語"的標誌為帶有"天識者"（*tenggeri medetügei*）詞語。"如違反——我們無從知曉——只有天知道"是這種句子的模式。如前所述，這種形式實際上與"無主體性威懾語"性質相同，只是明確了"天"主體，使"威懾語"更具有恐嚇性，稱之為"'天'主體性威懾語"（*'tenggeri' ejen beyetü sürdegülülge üge*）。不過，在聖旨文書裏出現次數極少，屬於較特殊類型，主要見於外交文書中，與頒發對象有一定的關係。頒發給宗教人士之聖旨裏的"'天'主體性威懾語"，目前僅見於1243年闊端太子給草堂寺的令旨中。如：

"如你每我底令旨不肯聽從時分，將來說底。理落底，天識者。"（《白話錄》，第8頁）
（如你們不遵從我的令旨，將奏來，作如何處理，天知道。）

外交文書有1246年貴由可汗給英諾森四世的拉丁文和波斯文書信和1247年7月蒙古大將拜住給教皇的書信：

（1）如果那樣，我們就不知道將會發生什麼事情，只有長生天才知道。[19]
（2）倘如你們不聽從上蒼和那受命擁有全世界的人的永恆旨意，此情我們不知道，上蒼是知道的[20]。

2. "'俺每'主體威懾語"

標誌為"俺（咱）每識也者"（*bida uqad je*）。"如違反—告知俺每—如何處置—俺每知道"是這種句子的模式。因其主體是"俺每"，可稱之為"'俺每'主體威懾語"（*'bida' ejen beyetü sürdegülülge üge*）。"俺每"，自然是指帝王們自身，而威脅對象是聖旨程式結構中的"宣諭對象"，即一般人們。如：

（1）*üiledbesü biṭa-a jiyaṭuyai, ker be kemer-ün biṭa uqad j-e*（1261年少林寺回鶻蒙文聖

旨碑）[21]

行呵，俺每根底奏説者。怎麼般道底，俺每識也者。

（2）aldal üge·ün hara alan alda·ulun yabu·asu bidan-a öč'idk'ün
現代漢語譯文：處死、懲罰無罪的人，要上奏我們。

k'ed ber k'ērün bida uqad je.
如何處置，由我們決定。（妥歡帖睦爾可汗聖旨（1328），《彙編》，第237-238、第240頁）

（3）行呵，俺每根底奏者。不揀説什麼呵，俺每識也者。（1268年聖旨，《白話錄》，第23頁）

（4）行呵，俺根底説將來者。怎生行底，咱每識也者。（1280年勢都兒大王令旨，《白話錄》，第27頁）

（5）做呵，咱每根底奏者。不揀怎生呵，咱每識也者。（1314年聖旨，《白話錄》，第69頁）

"'俺每'主體威懾語"也有"這裏説來者"（《白話錄》，第16頁），"俺每根底説來者"（《白話錄》，第20頁），"俺不問那什麼"（《白話錄》，第49頁）等"俺（咱）每識也者"的省略形式。但是，更多的時候我們可不必拘泥於這些標誌性用語，而是看它所針對的對象是誰來進行判斷。也就是説，即使沒有"俺（咱）每識者也"一句，若果針對的對象是"宣諭對象"，那麼其主體一般都是"俺每"，屬於"'俺每'主體威懾語"。

3. "'你'主體威懾語"

標誌是 "…你識者"（ta medütügei）[22]、"八合只你識者"（bayši medütügei）、"交那摩大師識者"等等。這種明確第二和第三人稱為主體的，稱之為"'你'主體威懾語"（'ta' ejen beyetü sürdegülülge üge）。所謂的"你"或者第三人稱是聖旨整體結構中的"頒發對象"，即宗教人士。而"威脅對象"則是一般人，即"宣諭對象"。如：

（1）仙孔八合識你不揀擇出來那什麼,你底言語不信底人你識者。（《白話錄》,第3頁）

（2）basu šuui čanglao tiling tüsigdebe eele kemejü yosu ügegü:n üyi:les
又　肅長老　提領　特委付來　麼道　沒體例　公事

buu üyi:ledtügei. üyi:ledbe:sü bagisba bayši-ta jiyatuyai.
休行者，　行呵，　拔合思把八合失識根底説者。

ani barilduyulju ker ber eeregüi elgür-ün.
怎生問當道不是

bagisba bayši medütügei. [23]
拔合思把八合失識者。(1268年少林寺回鶻蒙文聖旨碑文)

(3) 斷事官前立下證見，交那摩大師識者。(1255年蒙哥汗聖旨，《白話錄》，第101頁)

四、"威懾語"刑罰特徵

"威懾語"之所以具備威脅禁戒性質，與"警告句"所起的作用分不開。而"威懾"的程度是和"警告句"所顯示的實質內容之威脅手段，即刑罰特徵（*čayajalaquončaliy*）緊密相連的。明確與不明確，輕與重等，刑罰特徵也呈現其多樣性，在現有聖旨文書材料範圍之內，可指出以下六類。

（一）"天識者"類（*tenggeri medetügei*）

"天識者"類，表述形式是以"不怕那甚麼"（*ülü·ü ayuqu mud*）、"天識者"（*tenggeri medetügei*）等"警告句"結尾。此類"警告句"大多屬上述"無主體性威懾語"或"'天'主體性威懾語"，如上所指出，其主體就是"天神"。在頒發給宗教人士的這類以"天神"為主體的聖旨"威懾語"，一般沒有明確其威脅的具體手段，但通過參照對外文書，可以看到它所暗示的內容或懲罰手段。如，1231年窩闊台汗給高麗國王的信中寫道：

天道將來底言語，所得不秋[24]底人，有眼瞎了，有手沒了，有腳子瘸了[25]。

這句話的意思是，"得到來自天神的命令而不理睬者，將失去眼睛、手和腿的功能"，是在"告知"異國君主若違反天神之命令，將會有何種後果。1254年7月，蒙哥汗致法國國王聖路易和英諾森四世的拉丁文信中也有相似的威懾語：

不相信而跟我們打仗的人，均將得知和發現，他們是有眼無珠，取物而無手，行路而無腳；這是神的永久訓誡。[26]

從殘害肉體的特點來看，這種"天識者"類具有明顯的身體刑罰特徵。但這只是一種詛咒或者是道義上的譴責，它暗示將由某種超自然的力量來實施完成這些懲罰。所以，與法律意義上的刑罰有著本質的區別。

（二）"有罪過"類（eregüten boltuγai）

"有罪過"類，表述形式是以"要罪過者"（ere·üt'en boltuqai）、"無罪過那甚麼"等等"警告句"結尾。根據1314年仁宗普顏篤汗蒙漢合璧聖旨對譯以及《蒙古秘史》總譯，敬譯體"要罪過者"與蒙古文的"ere·ü-"相對應，意為實行懲罰。如：

（1）henlegč'in qudalduqč'in senšhiŋud-i ere·üt'en boltuqai.
施獻的人、典賣的人根底要罪過者。（1314年普顏篤汗聖旨，《彙編》，160—161）

（2）kü'ün-i ere'üleye
旁譯：人行罪咱。
總譯：要罪過者。（《蒙古秘史》，第228節）

由此可大致推測出"有罪過"類"警告句"不同表現的蒙漢用語對應。如，"不怕罪過那甚麼"、"不有罪過那甚麼"、"無罪過那甚麼"等等當為"ülü·ü ere·üt'en bolqun"；"有罪過者"當為"ere·üt'en boltuqai"；"有大罪過者"當為"yeke ere·üt'en boltuqai"；"要重罪過者"當為"kundü ere·üt'en boltuqai"等等，其中有無"大"、"重"等修飾語，其實際刑罰程度可能也有所不同。如果那樣的話，"有罪過"類中還可分"有罪過"、"有大罪過"、"要重罪過"等幾種類型。不過，"究治施行"[27]不太像獨立的類型，可能是"有罪過者"一語的純粹漢語表述形式。

"有罪過"類適用於"頒發對象性威懾語"，也適用于"宣諭對象性威懾語"。因此，其針對的可以是"頒發對象"，也可以是"宣諭對象"。針對"頒發對象"的，如：

（1）又這和尚每，有聖旨麼道，已前斷了的已外，不屬自己的寺院田地水土爭呵，不怕罪過那甚麼。（1261年忽必烈可汗聖旨，《白話錄》，第104頁）

（2）先生不得隱藏者，若有隱藏的，或人告首出來，那先生有大罪過者。（1258年忽必烈可汗聖旨，《白話錄》，第102頁）

（3）別了這言語的和尚，先生要重罪過者。（《通制條格》卷二九《僧道·寺觀僧道數目》）

（4）更和尚每，俺有聖旨麼道，在前斷定底別做呵，不幹自己底寺院田地水土爭呵，他每不怕那不有罪過那甚麼。（1280年聖旨，《白話錄》，第29頁）

（5）更這般高秀才等有聖旨麼道，沒體例不是秀才的人秀才麼道影占來呵，他每不怕那，無罪過那甚麼。（《通制條格》卷第三《戶令·儒人被虜》）

針對"宣諭對象"的，如：

（1）亦依前體例，要罪過者。（1255年蒙哥皇帝聖旨，《白話錄》，第101頁）

（2）這般省諭了呵，咱的言語別了的，不有罪過那甚麼。（《通制條格》卷二八《雜

令·圍獵》）

（3）這聖旨宣諭了呵,聖旨裏的言語別了的畏兀兒每,有罪過者。（《通制條格》卷四《戶令·畏兀兒家私》）

（4）俺底這聖旨,這般宣諭了呵,別了在前斷定底言語,寺院並田地水土不肯囬與,相爭底人每,有罪過者。（1280 年忽必烈可汗聖旨,《白話錄》, 第 102 頁）

（三）"斷按答奚罪過"類（aldaltan/ aldangkitu/ eregüten boltuγai）

"斷按答奚罪過"類,表述形式是以"斷按答奚罪過者"、"斷按打奚罪過者"、"斷按答奚罪戾"、"不斷按答奚那甚麼"等等"警告句"結尾。"斷按答奚罪過者"為"（斷按答奚）+（有罪過）"結構,與單一"斷按答奚"有區別。由此可推測,"斷按答奚罪過"類,包含"斷按答奚"和"斷按答奚罪過"兩種類型。

"按答奚"（按打奚、案答奚）的詞幹"按答-"為蒙古語"alda-，aldal-"（丟失、喪失、損失）無疑。"按答+奚"的蒙古語語音對應可能是"aldanggi"[28],見於十六至十七世紀《樺樹皮法典》。《蒙古秘史》出現有"aldal"、"alda"、"aldaltan"、"aldatuγai"等,旁譯為"罰"、"罰有",總譯為"有罪"、"犯罪"、"要罰者"。如：

（1）*ese sonosqabasu kesig-üd-ün ötögüs aldaltan boltuγai*
旁譯：不曾教聽呵,班每的為長的每罰每教做者。（第 227、203、205 節）
總譯：若不省會,則掌管的有罪。

（2）*yesün aldal alda'asu bu aldatuγai*
旁譯：九次罰罰阿,休罰者。
總譯：九次犯罪休要罰者。（第 211、214 節）

"aldal-"（alda-）與"ere'ü-"相比較,兩者的邏輯關係是"aldal-"在先,具有可數性,"ere'ü-"在後,具有不可數性。"aldal-"具有可量化或可積累的特點,而"ere'ü-"具有程度和性質或可操作性方面有進一步深化和推進"aldal-"的特點。如：

（1）*yesün aldal alda'asu ere'ü-dür bu orotuγai*
旁譯：九次罰罰阿,罪裏休教入者。
總譯：九次犯罪休罰者。（第 203、211、219 節）

（2）*čerig medekü-deče inu ere'ülejü bau'ulba*
旁譯：軍管的行他的罪著削了。
總譯：只重責罰,不許管軍。（第 257 節）

（3）*bidan-u dergede yabuqui-ban berkesiye'esü busu-yi oro'ulju tere kü'ün-i <u>ere'ülejü</u> nidün-ü ečine qolo γajar-a ileye*

旁譯：那人行罪著眼的背行遠地行教去。（第 224 節）

總譯：（沒有相應的）

故，認為 "*aldal*"（*alda*）意為犯罪、罪過、違法，所以構成 "*aldaqun*"、"*aldaltan*"、"*aldatuγai*" 等動詞時，即表示斷罪，與確定犯罪性質有關，"*ere'ü*" 意為處罰、懲罰，與具體實施刑罰的過程有關。"斷按答奚罪過"，正是這兩種意義的結合，並非簡單的疊加形式。現代蒙古語中的 "*aldaγa*"（錯誤、過失·）和 "*eregüü*"（刑罰）仍具有這種基本義。

在敬譯體裏，"斷按答奚" 一語可能對應 "*aldal-*"、"*alda*"、"*aldaqu*"、"*aldaqun*"、"*aldaltan*"、"*aldatuγai*" 等所有 "*alda-*" 類蒙古語詞。因為，這些詞雖存在形態差異，但意義相同，均用 "斷按答奚" 一語來對譯，不會出現偏差[29]。而且，在聖旨文書裏，語法形態較為固定。因而按照敬譯體對應原則，"斷按答奚" 的原型當為 "*aldatuγai*" 或 "*aldaltan*（*aldangkitu*）*boltuγai*" 等，而 "斷按答奚罪過"，也就能與 "*aldatuγai eregültügei*" 或 "*aldaltan*（*aldangkitu*）*boltuγai eregüten boltuγai*" 等相對應。"斷按答奚" 類針對的對象都是 "宣諭對象"，而不涉及 "頒發對象"。如：

（1）俺每的這聖旨宣諭了呵，已前斷了的言語別了呵，寺院的田地不可與呵，爭底人有呵，**斷按答奚罪過**者。（1261 年忽必烈可汗聖旨，《白話錄》，第 104 頁）

（2）這般道了呵，做道場的、夜頭動燒鈸作鬧行的、燒鈸藏著不收拾的人每，**斷案答奚罪過**者。（《通制條格》卷二九《僧道·俗人做道場》）

（3）如是主人識認者，**斷按答奚罪戾**。（1234 年聖旨《通制條格》卷二《戶令·戶例》）

（4）不揀是誰，但是有性命的背地裏偷殺的人每，不**斷按答奚**那甚麼。（蒙哥汗聖旨《元典章》卷五七《刑部十九·禁刑》）

（5）已上如有違犯者，並**斷按答奚罪戾**。（《通制條格》卷二九《商稅地稅》）

單獨 "斷按答奚" 一語可能是一種省略。在伊利汗國的文書中出現有：

bidan-a eyin kemegülüged daberiγsad čerigüd iregenü daruγas
現代漢語譯文：如此被我們教做之後，若經過的軍人們的達魯花赤們、

noyad küčü kürgejü yaγud kedi anu buliju tataju abubasu
諾顏們依仗權勢，搶奪他們的任何東西的話，

yeke jrlγ（*jarliγ*）*-un yosuγar ülükü ayuqun aldaqun.*[30]
難道不怕依照大聖旨體例斷罪嗎。

從 "aldaqun" 的出現看，這自然歸 "斷按答奚" 一類，而 "yeke jrly（jarliγ）-un yosuγar… aldaqun"（依照大聖旨體例斷罪／依照大聖旨體例斷按答奚），應當是 "斷按答奚" 一語的完整意義。

（四）"斷按答奚死罪" 類（aldaqu ükükü）

"斷按答奚死罪" 類，表述形式是以 "斷按答奚死罪者"、"斷按答奚罪戾·仍処死" 等 "警告句" 結尾。"斷按答奚死罪者" 為 "（斷按答奚）+（死罪者）" 結構，指以 "斷按答奚" 論處，並實行死刑。《黑韃事略》稱："有過則殺之，謂之按打奚"。單獨的 "斷按打奚" 一語，不包含死刑。彭大雅的解釋不夠完整，遺漏了 "死罪" 兩個字。蒙古文聖旨資料中不見與 "按打奚" 相對應的詞。不過，符牌等簡短命令文中的 "aldaqu ük'ügü" 完全能夠對應敬譯體 "斷按答奚死罪者" 一語。如：

（1）k'en ülü büširegü aldaqu ük'ügü（八思巴字金質長牌，《彙編》，第 456—457 頁）
現代漢語譯文：誰若不從，論罪處死。
（2）ken ülü büsir·ekü kümün aldaqu ükükü（回鶻文銀質長牌，Dobu, p. 415）[31]
現代漢語譯文：誰若不從，論罪處死。
（3）如有別使欲騎，給者，受者並斷按答奚死罪。（《永樂大典》所引《經世大典·站赤》）
（4）委係朝廷差去使命，有牌子文字者，若不聽從之人，亦斷按答奚罪戾，仍処死。（《永樂大典》所引《經世大典·站赤》）
（5）我每的聖旨不依的，不揀甚麼人，斷按答奚死罪者。（1238 年窩闊台可汗聖旨，《白話錄》第 5 頁）

（五）"斷案主" 類（anjultuγai）

表述形式是以 "斷案主"、"財產沒官" 等 "警告語" 結尾。"案主" 無疑是蒙古語 "anju"，見於 16—17 世紀《樺樹皮法典》（üisün degereki čaγaja-yin bičig），17 世紀編年史《蒙古源流》（erdeni-yin tobči），18 世紀初《喀爾喀集日姆》（qalq-a jirum）等文獻，曰 "anju"、"anjuntai"、"anju abqu"、"anju ögkü" 等等，有賠償（mal-un anju）和抵命（kümün-ü anju）兩大類型，重可 "處死本人，剝奪全部家產"（qar-a bey-e-i alaγ-a, qaruyiqu baruyiqu-yi-ni talaγ-a），輕則罰幾百或上千頭牲畜[32]。所以，"斷案主"（anjutai）之基礎為處治財產刑。《通制條格》"斷案主戶" 曰："斷沒家屬並戶下人"[33]，意義相同。而《吏學指南·雜刑》"斷按打奚罪戾" 曰："謂斷沒罪過也"，用來解釋 "斷按打奚罪戾"，顯然不準確，卻更符合解釋 "斷案主"。有 "本人處死，財產沒官" 等漢語表述，其敬譯體雖不見資料，想必應當是"斷案主死罪者"，蒙古語可還原為"*anjultuyai ükütügei*"、"*anjutai boltuyai ükükü boltuyai*"等等。如：

（1）其外詐推出家影占差發底人每，告到官司治罪，斷案主者。（1223年成吉思汗聖旨，《白話錄》第1頁）

（2）俺每底聖旨省諭，聽了呵不俙，差發、鋪馬、祗應不當，元住處不去；躲避隱藏底人，本人[處]死，財產沒官。（《通制條格》卷第二《戶令·戶例·五投下軍站戶》）

（六）"違札撒治罪"類（*jasaylatuyai*）

表述形式是以"以依故違札撒治罪施行"、"照依先□皇帝聖旨治罪施行者"、"照依故違札撒治罪施行"等"警告句"結尾。"札撒"（*jasay*），帝王所制定的法律，始於成吉思汗。"大札撒"（*yeke jasay*），專指成吉思汗所制《札撒》，《蒙古秘史》旁譯為"法度"，其副動詞"*jasaylaju*"為"法度著"（第81，199節）。"違札撒治罪"類，其對應蒙古語也不見於文書，但還原為"*jasaylatuyai*"、"*jasay bolyatuyai*"，不會有錯。

（1）如有違犯□人，照依先□皇帝聖旨治罪施行者。（1245年懿旨，《白話錄》，第10頁）

（2）如有違犯之人，照依故違札撒治罪施行，無得違錯。（1244年茶罕官人言語，《白話錄》，第9頁）

（3）如有違犯之人，具姓名申來，以依故違聖旨治罪施行。（1252年蒙哥皇帝聖旨，《白話錄》，第17頁）

那麼，"俺每識也者"有什麼具體涵義呢？《蒙古秘史》（第278節）中的一段話可謂最貼切的表現：

jasay könde'esü bidan-a ja'atuyai ükü 'üldekü yosutu bö'esü bida
法度　動呵　咱每　告者，　可死的　理有的　有呵　咱每

mököri'ülüd je kese'egdekü yosutu bö'esü bida söyüd je
斬也　者，可懲戒的　理有的　有呵　咱每　教道　者。

現代漢語譯文：若有違札撒者，稟告於我們，當處死者，朕處斬之，該懲戒者，朕教訓之。[34]

結束語

　　以上，從資料、結構、主體、刑罰等幾個方面對蒙元時期聖旨文書"威懾語"特徵作了分析歸納。為便於論述，本文也試用了一些新的術語或概念。總結所述，其主要部分可用圖解方式進行概括（如下表）。當然，這些不會是"威懾語"的全部特徵，這種研究方法也不過是在現有材料範圍之內識別蒙古文書或敬譯體文書"威懾語"要素的一途徑而已。

　　總之，蒙元時期，"威懾語"之所以成為文書程式的固定要素，與古代蒙古人的宗教信仰和思維方式分不開。蒙古人信奉天神（*tenggeri / tegri*），相信其創造力，也相信其毀滅力，從而敬仰天神，恐懼天神。祭司薩滿（*böke /böö, uduyan*）和帝王（*qaan / qayan noyad*）被看作是天神的代言人，也成為人們尊崇和畏懼的對象。另一方面，蒙古人賦予語言以極大魔力，相信天神通過代言人發出指令（*jarliɣ*），也相信祈禱、起誓、避諱、祝福、表敬和詛咒等能夠起到影響天神意旨的作用，因而產生各種語言儀式，語言儀式成為人們日常生活中不可或缺的行動模式。因此，"祈禱語"（*dayatqal üge*）、"表敬語"（*kündüdgel üge*）"威懾語"（*sürdegülülge üge*）等語言儀式方式自然延伸到了文書程式當中，被帝王們所利用，也使蒙元時期蒙古文書具有了鮮明的時代與民族特色。不言而喻，這些文化特徵是決定文書程式要素"威懾語"存在的關鍵所在，是我們今後深入研究的課題。

威懾語										
結構特徵		主體特徵			刑罰特徵						
單一式威懾語	重疊式威懾語	無主體性威懾語	有主體性威懾語			"天識者"類	"有罪過"類	"斷按答奚罪過"類	"斷按答奚死罪"類	"斷案主"類	"違札撒治罪"類
宣諭對象性威懾語 / 頒發對象性威懾語 / 頒發對象性威懾語		"天"主體威懾語	"俺每"主體威懾語	"你每"主體威懾語		有罪過 / 有大罪過 / 要重罪過	斷按答奚 / 斷按答奚罪過			
				第二人稱	第三人稱						

注释

[1] 念常:《佛祖歷代通載》卷三二,《至元辯偽錄》卷三。"-者",對應古蒙古語詞尾 -tuγai,表示命令,"達里罕行者",即 darqalatuγai,意為任"達里罕"或封"達里罕"。

[2] *Krung go'i bod sa gnas kyi lo rgyus yig tshang phyogs btus*, bod ljongs dmangs dpe skrun khang,1986.《西藏歷史檔案薈萃》,文物出版社,1995 年。陳慶英:《夏魯的元朝帝師法旨》,《西藏民族學院學報》1988 年第 4 期,第 38-44+51 頁,1989 年第 1 期,第 73-79+86 頁。

[3] aman jarliγ 一詞出現在蒙哥汗聖旨裏(見中村淳、松川節:《新発現の蒙漢合璧の少林寺聖旨碑(第一截回鶻蒙文碑文)》,《内陸アジア言語の研究》,中央ユーラシア学研究会,1993 年,第 32 頁)。

[4]《蒙古秘史》旁譯為"教把話"、"聲話教把著"(第 177 節、第 181 節)。稱"把持聲音"。這種口傳"聖旨"的傳統帶到元朝之後引起了混亂,不得不採取"禁口傳敕旨""不得口傳言語""諸人臣口傳聖旨行事者,禁之"措施(《元典章》卷一四《吏部八·案牘》,明立案驗不得口傳言語。《元史》卷五《世祖紀二》,至元元年八月乙巳。《元史》卷一百二《職制》)。

[5] 馮承鈞:《元代白話碑》商務印書館民國二十二年;蔡美彪:《元代白話碑集錄》,科學出版社,1955 年。

[6] 閔庚堯稱"俗體",其中包括"粗俗體"和"白話體"(《中國公文研究》,中國社會科學出版社,2000 年,第 195-201 頁)。

[7] Aradnagarba, yuwan ulus-un üy-e-yin kitad güjir orčiγulγ-a, *öbür mongγul-un yeke surγaγuli-yin erdem sinjilegen-ü sedkül*,1978. 2,亦鄰真:《元代硬譯公牘文體》,《元史論叢》第一輯,中華書局,1982 年。

[8] 日本學者普遍採用的名稱,較早的有田中謙二:《蒙文直譯体における白話について》《東洋史研究》19 卷 4 期,1961 年,第 51-69 頁。近來國内也有學者使用此名稱。

[9] 祖生利:《〈元典章·刑部〉直譯體文字中的特殊語法現象》,《蒙古史研究》第 7 輯,第 138 頁。

[10] 拙作:"13-14düger jaγun-u mongγul alban bičig-ün kündüdkel-ün orun ba abiyan-u toγtalčaγ-a", *mongγul kele bičig*, 1992, 4, pp.40-49.

[11] 拙作:"13-14düger jaγun-u šasinten-du baγulγaγsan jarliγ-un bičig-un keb kelberi-yin sinjilel", *jou uda-yin mongγul ündüsüten-ü baγsi-yin tusqai mergejil-ün surγaγuli-yin erdem sinjilegen-ü sedkül*,1994 年,3,pp.30-37. 有關蒙元時期的公文程式結構方面的研究,筆者之後又有松川節:《大元ウルス命令文の書式》(載日本《待兼山論叢》史學篇,29, 1995 年),祖生利、舩田善之《元代白話碑文的體例初探》(《中国史研究》2006 年,3,第 117-135 頁)等。

[12] 胡格吉勒圖、薩如拉:《八思巴字蒙古語文獻彙編》(以下簡稱《彙編》)內蒙古教育出版社,2004 年,§01。

[13] 簡體錄文見《彙編》,第 2-9 頁;繁體見小澤重男:《山西省交城縣石壁山玄中寺の八思巴文字蒙古語碑文の解読》,《東京外国語大学論集》9,1962 年,第 30-32 頁。

[14] 關於威懾語的漢譯問題,見芳齡貴:《為不怕那甚麼進一解》,《雲南師範大學學報》第 31 卷,1999 年,第 1 期。蔡美彪:《長安竹林寺碑譯釋》,《中國蒙元史學術研討會暨芳齡貴教授九十華誕慶祝會

文集》，民族出版社，2010 年，第 23-24 頁。

[15] 舩田善之撰，宮海峰譯：《蒙元時期硬譯公牘文體的格式化》，《元史論叢》第 11 輯，2009 年，第 368 頁。

[16]《辯證偽錄》卷四（《白話錄》，第 101 頁）。

[17] 在文書中 "... 每根底" 一般對應蒙古語的與格 "-a /-e" "-du /-tu"。"根底"，根據具體語言環境，漢語可譯作 "在, 向, 從, 同, 把" 等介詞（可參照亦鄰真:《元代硬譯公牘文體》,《亦鄰真蒙古學文集》，第 591 頁）。

[18] 1246 年，貴由汗致英諾森四世之信所加蓋印璽之文字。

[19] [英] 道森編、呂浦譯、周良宵注：《出使蒙古記》，中國社會科學出版社，1983 年，第 100-103 頁。伯希和撰、馮承鈞譯：《蒙古與教廷》，中華書局，1994 年，第 13-14 頁。

[20] 伯希和撰、馮承鈞譯：《蒙古與教廷》，中華書局，1994 年，第 140-141 頁。馮承鈞譯：《多桑蒙古史》，商務印書館，1934 年，上册，第 256-257 頁。

[21] 中村淳、松川節：《新発現の蒙漢合璧の少林寺聖旨碑（碑文第二截文字）》，《内陸アジア言語の研究》，中央ユーラシア学研究会，1993 年，第 37-39 頁。

[22]《蒙古秘史》"ta medegtün"，旁譯為 "您自知者"（第 167 節）。

[23] 中村淳、松川節：《新発現の蒙漢合璧の少林寺聖旨碑（碑文第三截文字）》，《内陸アジア言語の研究》，中央ユーラシア学研究会，1993 年，第 44-47 頁。

[24] "秋"，"偢" 字之誤。類似的用法見《通制條格》,卷二《户令》曰："俺每底聖旨省諭，聽了呵不偢……本人處死，財產沒官"。

[25]《高麗史》卷二三，高宗十八年十二月條。

[26] 佐口透譯注：《モンゴル帝国史》2, 1968 年，第 321-323 頁，《モンゴル帝国と西洋》1980 年，第 69-71 頁。護雅夫訳《中央アジア蒙古旅行記》1985 年，第 124-125 頁。海老沢哲雄：《モンゴル帝国の対外文書をめぐって》，《加賀博士退官紀念中國文史哲學論集》1979 年，第 732-733 頁。馮承鈞譯：《多桑蒙古史》上，商務印書館，1935 年，第 280 頁。耿昇、何高濟譯：《柏朗嘉賓蒙古行紀·魯布魯克東行紀》中華書局，1985 年，第 309-310 頁。另有 [英] 道森編，呂浦譯，周良宵注：《出使蒙古記》，中國社會科學出版社，1983 年，第 222 頁。

[27] 1245 年闊端太子令旨,《白話錄》第 13 頁。

[28] Takashi Matsukawa, In Regards to *alday-situ* on the Sino-Mongolian Inscription of 1240,《西域歷史語言研究集刊》第 1 輯, 第 297-301 頁。有關 "按答奚" 研究近況還可參照納斯圖：《釋蒙元時期長方形聖旨牌文字》，《民族研究》2007 年第 4 期，第 65-69 頁；劉曉：《蒙元早期刑罰用語 "案答奚" 小考——兼論 "斷案主" 與斷沒罪的關係》，《中國社會科學院歷史研究所學刊》第 5 集，第 229-241 頁。

[29] "按答奚" 一詞，最早出現於《析津志輯佚·學校》中所錄窩闊台汗 1233 年聖旨（"... 好底孩兒隱藏下底，並斷按答奚罪戾"）。

[30] Doerfer, G. "Mongolica aus Ardabīl." *Zentralasiatische Studien* 9. 1975, p.243.

[31] Dobu, *uiγurjin mongγul üsüg-ün durasqaltu bičig-üd*, ündüsüten-ü keblel-ün qoriy-a, 1983,p.415.

[32] Х.Пэрлээ, Монгол ба төв Азийн орнуудън соелън туухэнд холбогдох хоер ховор сурвалж бичиг. *Monumenta Historica*, Tom.VI, fasc.1-2, Улаанбаар, 1974.

[33]《通制條格》卷第二《斷案主戶》。

[34]《蒙古秘史》沒有相應的總譯文，現代漢語譯文引自余大鈞譯注：《蒙古秘史》，河北人民出版社，2001年，第487頁。

"*SÜRDEGÜLÜLGE ÜGE*" ("THREATENING WORDS") IN ANCIENT DOCUMENTS OF THE MONGOL EMPIRE AND THE YUAN DYNASTY

Qinggeli (Khoshut Tsengel)

The linguistic element designated "*sürdegülülge üge*" was one of the essential elements in official document forms of the Mongol Empire and Yuan Dynasty. With the imperial edict materials as central documentation, this article presents a comprehensive study of the structure, warning subjects, and punishment effects of "*sürdegülülge üge*" in documents:

1. Materials. The imperial edict documents issued to the religious constitute basic materials for examining the characteristics of Mongol documents of the time since they were the first to appear and achieve completion, as well as which they exist in a rich variety. The materials contain written Mongolian imperial edicts in 'Phags-Pa script (*dörbeljin üsüg*) and Uyghur script (*uyiγurjin mongγul üsüg*) styled Mongolian words, as well as versions of translation into Chinese and other languages. The Chinese translations serve to supplement inadequacies of the Mongolian materials since they are true to the original texts. "*Sürdegülülge üge*" often appear at the end of the main body in the whole structure of the forms and formulas of imperial edicts.

2. Structures. "*Sürdegülülge üge*" contain "single" *sürdegülülge üge*, as well as "overlapping" *sürdegülülge üge*. The "single" forms are as follows: 1. the warned object; 2. preconditions; 3. prohibition words; and 4. warning words, while "overlapping" forms depend on: 1. preconditions; 2. warned objects; and 3. warning words. In accordance with the different objects, the "overlapping" forms can be further divided into two categories:

"*sürdegülülge üge*" in the document-specific general objects, and "*sürdegülülge üge*" to the specific objects who accept the document.

3. Warning words as the core of the essential factor of *sürdegülülge üge* are often related to the warning subjects who control the nature, status, and functions of the essential elements. Whether or not the subjects are clearly known, there are "*sürdegülülge üge* without warning subjects" and "*sürdegülülge üge* with warning subjects". The mysteriously unrevealed subject in the former form is the "God" in whom the Mongols of the time believed. The "*sürdegülülge üge* with warning subjects" include: 1. "*sürdegülülge üge* with 'Heaven' as the warning subject", "*sürdegülülge üge* with 'We' as the warning subject", and "*sürdegülülge üge* with 'You' as the warning subject".

4. The deterrent and prohibitive force of *sürdegülülge üge* relates to the deterrent means expressed by the essential factor of the warning words, namely the punishment. With the characteristics of the punishment, there are six categories: "Heaven known guilt", "*aldangki'* guilt", "*aldangki* death guilt", "*anju* guilt", and "violation *jasaɣ* guilt". All five contain punishments severe or light except for the category of "Heaven known guilt".

In conclusion, the ancient Mongolians were awed by and venerated God, and concomitantly endowed language with magical force. The combination of belief-in-God and the mystique associated with language produced various linguistic forms. "*Sürdegülülge üge*" was an expression of the forms in the ancient documents of the Mongol empire and the Yuan Dynasty. The study of "*sürdegülülge üge*" will help deepen our understanding of the ways of thought and action of the ancient Mongols.

『集史』第一巻「モンゴル史」校訂における
アラビア語版写本 Ayasofya 3034 の価値

赤坂恒明

はじめに

　イル汗国の宰相（wazīr）ラシードッディーン rašīd al-dīn が編纂した『集史』*jāmi' al-tawārīx* の第一巻「モンゴル史」は、モンゴル帝国史、及び、モンゴル帝国成立以前のモンゴル高原とその周辺に分布した諸集団の歴史を研究するために不可欠の重要な史料であり、既に複数種の校訂・訳注が存在する。それらは、専門研究に裨益すると同時に、研究の裾野を広げる上でも大きな役割を果たしている。しかし、それら既存の校訂・訳注には、学術的な面で不完全な点がある。即ち、本文の校訂に、所謂「テヘラン本」（JT/Tm）とアラビア語版の写本 Ayasofya 3034 が全く用いられていない、という点である[1]。

　本稿では、現在、存在が知られている唯一のアラビア語版『集史』第一巻「モンゴル史」写本である Ayasofya 3034 を取り上げ、その、『集史』「モンゴル史」本文を校訂する上での重要性を明らかにしたい。

一、アラビア語版『集史』「モンゴル史」写本 Ayasofya 3034（JT/S3034）について

　イラン地域（īrān zamīn）において編纂された『集史』はペルシア語によって著述されたが、編者ラシードによる写本作成事業の一環としてアラビア語に訳された版も存在している。ラシードが、『集史』をも含む自身の編著の写本をペルシア語だけでなくアラビア語でも作成させていたことは、夙に周知の事実であろう。現に、アラビア語版『集史』の写本は、華麗な挿画――所謂「ミニアチュール」――によって飾られたものをも含め、少な

からず伝存している。しかし、アラビア語版『集史』の写本は、そのほとんどが第二巻「世界史」の写本であり、第一巻「モンゴル史」のアラビア語版写本は、現在、一写本の存在が知られているに過ぎない。即ち、トルコ共和国イスタンブル İstanbul のスレイマニエ図書館（Süleymaniye kütüphanesi）に所蔵されるアヤソフィヤ旧蔵の写本、Ayasofya 3034（以下、JT/S3034 と略す）である[2]。

　JT/S3034 に関する書誌情報については、スレイマニエ図書館のカードに、「Yz: Sülüs. H.785. 416 y. 13 str.」と記されている。即ち、スルス書体の手写本でヒジュラ暦785年（西暦1383年3月6日～1384年2月23日）に書写、416葉、行数13行、である。本写本の表紙（f.1a）には、「tārīx jinkīz xān bi-l-'arabiyyat」即ち「アラビア語によるチンギス・ハンの歴史」と表題が記されているが、明らかに後世の加筆によるものである。

　本写本の料紙は、厚手というほどでもないがしっかりとした感じでやや光沢がある。中には、赤味がかった紙（やや光沢あり）もある（ff.72ab,75ab,78ab）が、一見して、質の良い紙を使用していることは明らかである。

　写本の冒頭、第一葉の裏と第二葉の表（ff.1b,2a）には、神への賛辞を伴った装飾・挿画がある。f.2a の挿画は、金泥で塗りつぶされているが、紙を透かせば、両脇に人が侍立している様子を見て取ることができる。第七葉まで（ff.2b-7b）は本文の四方に朱色の枠が付いているが、第八葉以降には枠がない。

　スルス書体の文字は丁寧に書写されており、読み易い。文字色は、黒字に朱字を交えたものが基本であり、黒褐色の字で発音を示す符号が補われ、ときに本文の訂正をも行っている。黒字と朱字の使い分けは、読みやすいようにとの工夫であると考えられるが、モンゴル王族の名が朱字で書かれているわけでもなく、特別の規範は無いように思われる。f.157a 以降は、黒字と赤字と薄い緑字の三色となる。f.209a からは鈍い青緑字、f.211b からは蒼字も加わるが、しばらくするとまた黒字と朱字の二色に戻る。f.379b から f.396a までは、黒字と朱字と鈍い黄緑字の三色、f.397a からは、黒字と朱字と煉瓦色字の三色である。これらの文字色の使い分けにも、特に規範は無いようである。いずれにせよ、本写本は、複数色の文字によって彩られており、書写には、一定の注意が払われていたことが窺われる。

　以上より、JT/S3034 は、外見的には良質な写本であるように見做すことができる。では、文献学的に重要な、本文証跡の質については如何であろうか。

　JT/S3034 の内容構成をまとめたのが、表1である。一見して明らかなように、本写本は、記載の排列順が乱れており、また、記載が欠脱している部分も少なからず、さらに、若干の本紀については表題のみが残されているに過ぎず、全般的に見ると不完全な抄出本であると評価せざるを得ない。

　従って、JT/S3034 は、写本そのものは比較的丁寧に作成されていると考えられるものの、構成上の混乱や、本文の残存状況における大きな偏りがあり、本文証跡については質的に良いとは言い難い写本である、と言わざるを得ないのである。

　おそらく、JT/S3034 の書本（写本の書写のもととなった写本）自体に、既に錯簡があり、また、欠落箇所が含まれていたものと推測される。

二、アラビア語版 JT/S3034 写本に関する先行研究

　次に、JT/S3034 に関する先行研究について述べる。

　そもそも、JT/S3034 を対象とした書誌学的研究は、甚だ少ない[3]。古いものとしては、オスマン朝期に作成されたアヤソフィヤ図書館の写本目録に本写本に関する記載があるが、ごく簡単なものに過ぎず、特に述べるべきこともない。Bregel 1972, p.311 には、『集史』第一巻「モンゴル史」のアラビア語版として本写本が挙げられているが、「Айа София, 3034（Tauer, p.93, 注を参照）」とあるに過ぎず、そこに引用された Tauer 1931 においても、「Āya Sofya 3034 est la version arabe du Ğāmi'u-t-tawārīh」即ち「Āya Sofya 3034 は『集史』のアラビア語版である」と記されるのみである（Tauer 1931, p.93, n.1）。尤も、Bregel 1972 と Tauer 1931 が対象とするのはペルシア語文献であるので、アラビア語で書かれた本写本について最低限の紹介にとどまっているのは、蓋し当然のことであろう。

　JT/S3034 を最初にヨーロッパの学界に本格的に紹介したのはＥ．Ｇ．ブラウンである。彼は、『集史』諸写本の所在情報の報告（Browne 1908, p.36, No.(25)）において、「In the Catalogue of the Mosque Library of St. Sophia, No.3034, mention is made of a volume of the *Jámi'u' t-Tawárikh* which appears to contain the history of Chingíz Khán, i.e. in all probability the whole or the greater part of vol. i of the *Jámi'u't-Tawárikh.* ‥‥‥」と述べ、アヤソフィヤ図書館の写本目録の記載に基づき、本写本について「『集史』第一巻の、多分、全体または大部分」を含むと指摘した。尤も、本写本に本文の欠脱が少なくないことは既に確認したとおりである。

　トルコでは、バシキール（バシコルト）人出身の碩学、ゼキ・ヴェリディ・トガン A.Zeki Velidi Togan が、本写本の重要性を認識しており（Togan 1962, p.60）、トガンに親炙した小林高四郎によって、1940 年代、本写本の写真が日本にもたらされた。そして、その後まもなく、遠峯四郎〔榎一雄〔補〕〕「小林学士将来東洋学書目録（一）ペルシヤ文古鈔本撮影目録」に、次のように本写本が紹介された。[4]

三、ラシード＝ウ＝ディーン「集史」アラビヤ語訳本

Rashīd ud-Dīn Fradlullāh【ママ】: Jāmi'ut-Tawārīkh. a) Fol.414. b) Ayā Sūfiyah, no.3034. c)？

ラシード＝ウ＝ディーンが諸著書の散佚を防止するために、彼の収入中より毎年一定の金額を割いて、アラビヤ語ペルシヤ語の両本を幾通りか作り、これらを回教諸国の各主要都市に寄贈したことは、カトルメール（ブラウン・バルトーリド）諸書の記述に詳かであるが、右の摂影本もその一つである。而も小林氏が将来された前記ペルシア語原本[5]が〔第一部の中の〕部族考、太祖、及び太宗殂落の部分にすぎない[6]のに反し、本アラビア語訳本は〔第一部の〕全部を含み[7]、書中の固有名詞には母音符号を附してあるので読方の上に大いに参考となる。因みにアラビア語訳の所在に関しては、ストーリイの詳細な報告[8]を参照せられ度い。著録 Tauer, p.93, note.〔参考 E.Quatremère, Histoire des Mongols de la Perse, Paris, 1836. p.cxxxiv ff. Browne, III, pp.68-86; W.Barthold, Turkestan down to the Mongol Invation, Oxford, 1928. p.46; Storey, II, p.75.〕

　ここには、JT/S3034 が、『集史』中にあらわれる固有名詞を解釈する上で有用であると述べられ、本写本に史料的価値があることが指摘されている。しかし、小林高四郎氏が日本にもたらした当該の写真は、1990 年代に至るまで学術研究に使用されることはなかったようである。

　　一方、トガンは、ワシントン大学の極東研究所（The Far Eastern Institute of the Unoversity of Washington）に提出した学術論文「ラシードッディーンによるモンゴル人の歴史の構成」（Togan 1962）において、『集史』「モンゴル史」部族篇「タタル族 qawm-i tātār」におけるアラビア文字によるモンゴル語表記「ū sūtū mūnkqūn」、「alāqjīn ādūtān munkkū balāūrtān」の部分（JT/Az-1-1, p.160）が、「アラビア語版（Manuscript of Ayasofya, no.3130, f.46a）」においても見出されると述べ[9]、アラビア語版『集史』「モンゴル史」写本について言及した。トガンは写本番号を「no.3130」とするが、「no.3034」とあるべきであることは、JT/S3034 の f.46a に「ū sūtū sūnkiqūn(SWN。KiQuWn)」、「alāqjīn ādūtān mankkū(MaN。KW) balāūrtān」とあり、若干の綴形の違いはあるものの、該当箇所の写本の葉数が一致していることから、明らかである。

　　それはともかく、更にトガンは次のように述べて、JT/S3034 の重要性を強調している（Togan 1962, p.72. 下線：引用者）。

> 　In regard to the problem of the composition of the history of the mongols by Rashīd al-dīn, <u>the Arabic version will play an important role in the future</u>.
>
> 　I have brought with me a microfilm of this version from <u>the only copy of Ayasofya Museum</u>, in the hope that you here in America have better possibilities, with your Mongolists, Turkologues and Sinologists, to study the culture of the Mongol and the Central Asiatic Turks than we have in Istanbul, where we have excellent material but no Mongolists. In closing I would like to mention that new Russian edition of the first volume of the *Jāmiʻal-tavārīx*[10] does not consider the possibility of the influence of the Mongolian

original upon the Persian context. Nor was the *Shu'ab-i panjgāne* considered. For this reason the new Russian translation of the parts about the Mongol and Tatar tribes and the history of Chingiz-Khān is very poor in comparison with the translation of the part of the same book concerning Ghāzān Khān and his organization. The translation of the first volume has to be redone, with reference to the Arabic version of Jāmi'al-tavārīx and to the Shin-Yüan-Shih of K'o-shao-min.[11]

トガンは、「優れた素材はあるがモンゴル学者がいないイスタンブルで持つ以上の、モンゴルと中央アジア＝テュルク人の文化を学ぶためのより良い可能性を持つという期待をもって」（Togan 1962, p.72）、JT/S3034 のマイクロフィルム（microfilm）を米国にもたらした。

カール・ヤーン Karl Yahn は、1962 年 6 月にインディアナ大学（Indiana University）で開かれたＰＩＡＣ（The Permanent International Altaistic Conference）の第五回会議において、トガンの指摘を紹介した（Jahn 1963, p.198）。しかし、その後、トガンの期待に反し、このマイクロフィルムも日の目を浴びないまま埋没してしまったが如くであり、Ｗ．Ｍ．サクストン Thackston が、アラビア語版『集史』第一巻「モンゴル史」の存在は知られていない（No copies of the Arabic version of Tome One are known to exist）とまで述べている（Thackston 1998, p.xiii, n.6）ように、学界においても、その存在はほとんど認識されていないという有様であった。

一方、日本においては、1990 年代に至り、ようやく本写本を利用した研究が現れるようになった。

まず、志茂碩敏 1995 において、部族篇における、フレグ家の王族イリ yīrī の出自に関する独自の情報（JT/S3034, f.40a）が使用された（志茂碩敏 1995, p.158; p.227, n.(71)）。

また、私は、ジュチ裔の系譜情報に関する「ジュチ紀」第一部の記載（文章系譜）を、固有名詞の校訂のため補助的に使用し（赤坂恒明 2000; 赤坂恒明 2003）、さらに、自著において「ジュチ紀」第一部の単色写真を掲載した（赤坂恒明 2005, pp.311-330）。

このように、日本では、本写本の研究上の重要性、即ち、他の諸本には見られない独自の情報を含む場合があること、及び、固有名詞の表記を校訂する際、有益に用いることができることが、ある程度までは認識されている。

以上より、JT/S3034 には、書本に由来する本文証跡上の問題点が存在しているにもかかわらず、現在 存在が知られている唯一のアラビア語版『集史』第一巻「モンゴル史」の写本であるという点で、『集史』「モンゴル史」のペルシア語本文を校訂する上で無視し得ない重要性を有していると考えられており、現に、一部のモンゴル帝国史研究者によって既に使用されているということが確認された。

四、ラシード区におけるアラビア語版『集史』の書写

　本章では、アラビア語版『集史』「モンゴル史」写本が、『集史』「モンゴル史」のペルシア語本文を校訂において重要性を持っていると考えられている根拠について、主に先行研究の成果に基づきつつ、簡潔に確認しておきたい。

　ラシードによる自身の編著の写本作成については、今は亡き岩武昭男氏による、ラシード区（rabʻ-i rašīdī）のワクフ文書（al-waqfiyya）の詳密な分析によって、その具体的な様相が明らかにされた（岩武昭男 1995; 岩武昭男 1997）。そこで、岩武昭男氏の研究に基づきつつ、ラシードの編著のアラビア語版写本の作成に関する問題について確認しておきたい。

　パリのフランス国立図書館（Bibliothèque Nationale de France）に所蔵されている、ラシードの神学著作集『ラシード集成』majmūʻa al-rašīdīya のアラビア語写本（de Slane 2324）には、所謂「ラシード著作目録」が付載されている。その内容は次のとおりである（岩武昭男 1995, p.279）。

(1) 導入部分

(2)『ラシード著作全集』jāmʻ al-tasānīf al-rašīdī 目次（fihrist）

(3) 写本作成指示書

　これは、神学著作集『ラシード集成』を構成する四著作 ── 第一神学著作集『注釈の書』kitāb al-tawḍīhāt、第二神学著作集『解釈の鍵』miftāh al-tafāsīr、第三神学著作集『スルターンの諸益』fawāʼid-i sulṭāniyya、第四神学著作集『真理の精妙』laṭāʼif al-haqāʼiq ── の個別の諸写本の一部（TD/S, FS/S, LH/AS）にも付けられている（岩武昭男 1995, pp.278-280）。

　上記 (1)・(2)・(3) のうち、(2)『ラシード著作全集』目次には、『集史』目次に記されている『集史』の構成（JT/Az-1-1, pp.28-39）── 第一巻「モンゴル史」、第二巻「世界史」と「オルジェイトゥ史」、第三巻「地理志」── とは異なり、『集史』が四巻構成 ── 第一巻「モンゴル史」、第二巻「世界史」と「オルジェイトゥ史」、第三巻「系図」、第四巻「地理志」── であると記載されている[12]ことで、学術上、甚だ有名であるが、ここで問題となるのは、(3) 写本作成指示書である。

　この、『ラシード集成』に付載のアラビア語版の写本作成指示書[13]の中には、当該指示書がラシード区のワクフ文書からの写しであることが明記されている（MR/Qtr, p.clxiv; 岩武昭男 1995, pp.278-280）。岩武昭男氏によると、ラシード区ワクフ文書には、写本作成指示書が二通、「ワクフ文書本体」にではなく、「本体とは別に」収められている（これを岩武氏は「ラシード区ワクフ文書補遺」と称す）。これら二通の写本作成指示書はペルシア語によるものであり、本文は概ね一致しているが、両者の作成年代に起因する若干の差異が認められる。そして、パリ本『ラシード集成』に付載のアラビア語版の写本作成指示書は、そのうち

の一通と内容的に「ほぼ完全に一致」している（岩武昭男 1995, p.288）。

　さて、ラシード区ワクフ文書補遺の写本作成指示書二通には、「『集史』の書（kitāb-i jāmi' al-tawārīx）」の「アラビア語版」と「ペルシア語版」の各写本を、ワクフ全権管理者（mutawallī）が「よいと考えた巻数で」、「毎年、完全な写本一部を、極めてよい上質の、バグダード紙大判の紙に、美しく正しい字で書く。それをラシード区のドーム（gunbad）／図書室（kutubxāna）[14]に置かれた元になる写本と、誤りや文字の点を変えることがないように照合する」ことが指示されている（岩武昭男 1995, p.293）。

　また、上記の所謂「ラシード著作目録」における、(2)『ラシード著作全集』目次と (3) 写本作成指示書とをつなぐ箇所にも、「上述の著者‥‥‥は、上述のこれらの諸書の、個別およびまとめてのアラビア語とペルシア語での書写を命じていた」と記されている（岩武昭男 1997, p.527）。

　以上より、アラビア語版『集史』の写本系統樹上の祖本は、ラシード区内に安置されていた「元となる写本」にまで遡らせることが可能である。従って、現在 存在が知られている唯一のアラビア語版『集史』「モンゴル史」写本である JT/S3034 についても、もし、そのアラビア語訳がラシードの写本作成事業のもとでの翻訳に由来するものであれば、仮令それが後世に転写された不完全な写本であるとしても、そこに伝えられているアラビア語の本文証跡は、ペルシア語で書かれた『集史』「モンゴル史」の原本を復元する上で、比較資料として非常に重要な価値を持つものである、と考えることが可能となるのである。

　しかし、先行研究においては、JT/S3034 のアラビア語本文が、ラシードの編纂・写本作成事業の一環として翻訳されたものに由来するのか、それとも、ラシードとは無関係に翻訳されたものであるか、全く検討が行われていない。

　そこで、次章では、JT/S3034 が、ラシード区内に安置されていた「元となる写本」の系統を引く写本であるか否かを、検討してみたい。

五、アラビア語版 JT/S3034 写本と他の諸本との、本文証跡の比較・検討

　『集史』第一巻「モンゴル史」のうち所謂「部族篇」の部分は、Ａ．Ａ．アリー＝ザーデの校訂本があり、また、諸写本間の本文証跡の比較・検討について、先行研究による一定の蓄積がある。よって、JT/S3034 の本文証跡を他の諸本のそれと比較する上でも、具体的にどの部分を取り上げればよいかが既に明らかにされている。そこで、本章では、アラビア語版『集史』「モンゴル史」JT/S3034 写本の本文証跡が、ラシード区内に安置されていた「元となる写本」にまで遡り得るか否かを判断するために、「部族篇」における諸本群分類の規準となる部分が、JT/S3034 においてはどのような形態となっているか、検討を行う。

そもそも、『集史』「モンゴル史」の諸写本のうち、所謂イスタンブル本（JT/S）と所謂テヘラン本（JT/Tm）については、これら両写本の本文証跡が、他の諸本群に属する諸写本と比較して、『五族譜』——ラシードによる『集史』編纂事業の一環として編纂された——における『集史』対応部分と合致しており、両写本が属するそれぞれの諸本群の祖本は相対的に『集史』原本に近いことが明らかにされている（赤坂恒明 1998）。そして、JT/Tm の祖本は、『集史』「モンゴル史」の、比較的早い編纂段階における形態を伝えており、JT/S の祖本は、地理情報などが増補された、比較的遅い編纂段階における形態を伝えている（赤坂恒明 1998．宇野伸浩 2002, 宇野伸浩 2003 をも参照せよ）。

　これら両写本の間に、諸本群の祖本に由来すると考えられる相違がある部分を、JT/S3034 における対応部分と比較したのが、表2である。

　これを見ると、JT/S3034 は、概ね JT/S と内容的に合致していることが確認される。しかし、その一方で、部族篇の「表（fihrist）」における諸族の配列、「オイラト部」における地理関係情報、「バヤウト氏」における地理関係情報の三箇所については、JT/S とではなく JT/Tm と一致しており、また、「ジャライル諸部」については、どちらとも合致していない。

　部族篇「表」と「オイラト部」の事例については、記載内容の根本的な相違ではなく、記載の排列順の違いに過ぎないので、JT/S が書写されるまでの転写段階において排列順が崩れて変化したものである可能性が高いであろう。また、「ジャライル諸部」の事例については、JT/S3034 に至るまでの転写段階において、本来 JT/Tm と同様に欄外に書かれていた記載が、書写の際に脱落した可能性が高いように思われる。「バヤウト氏」の場合についても同様である可能性が高い。

　いずれにせよ、JT/A3034 が、記載内容の上で、基本的には所謂「テヘラン本」（JT/Tm）と同族の諸本群よりも、所謂「イスタンブル本」（JT/S）と同族の諸本群と共通する点が多い、という事実に変りはない。これは、JT/S3034 の記載内容が、『集史』「モンゴル史」の比較的遅い編纂段階における状態を保持しているということに他ならない。そして、これは、JT/S3034 のアラビア語の本文証跡が、ラシード区内に安置されていた「元となる写本」にまで遡り得るという推測とも矛盾しないのである。

　既述のように、『集史』「モンゴル史」における JT/Tm と JT/S の記載内容に相違があるのは、JT/Tm の祖本に増補が加えられて JT/S の祖本が成立したという事情によるものであるが、『集史』「モンゴル史」における記載の増補と諸本群との関係は、写本の欄外に書き込まれた増補記事が転写の際に本文中に取り込まれるという増補の手順のあることが宇野伸浩氏によって明らかにされており（宇野伸浩 2002; 宇野伸浩 2003）、表2に示された JT/S3034 に関する本文の異同の諸事例も、基本的には、その増補の状況と矛盾していないように思われる。

　ここで注目に値するのは、「ノヤキン・ウルウト・マングト氏」における増補部分である。当該の記述は、JT/S と同族の諸本と JT/S3034 とに存在するのみであるが、それぞれにおいて、増補部分の挿入箇所が異なっている。即ち、JT/S と同族の写本 JT/A を底本としたアリーザーデ校訂本には、次のように記されている（JT/Az-1-1, pp.501-504）。

ノヤキン・ウルウト・マングト族

トンビナ・ハン tūmbina xān の九人の子息のうちから、最年長の子息には、名前がジャクス jāqsū であった。

そして、彼の子供たちから、三つの分支が現れた。一つをノヤキン nūyāqīn 族と [人々は] 呼ぶ。そして、もうひとつをウルウト ūr'ūt 族と。そして、第三をマングト mankqūt 族と。★

ノヤキン・ウルウト諸族は、チンギス・ハン jīnkkīz xān の時代において、タイチウト tāyjyūt 族と一つになった。そして、チンギス・ハンに対する数多くの敵対・反対をしていた。

そして、それらの諸族から、今日、この国【引用者注：イラン】には、誰もいない。

チンギス・ハンの時代において、ウルウト族の指導者は、知られているものは、ウドゥト ūdūt [と] バルドゥト bardūt であった [が、彼らは] 敵対している。

☆そして、ある伝承を [人々は] 次のように述べている。即ち、[彼らは] 昔からずっと互い互いの親族 [であり]、そして、一つの血統から [の出身である] 諸氏族は、詳述される次の集団である。

  コンゴタン qūnkqutān

  スニト sūnīt

  カラカス qaraqas

  バルラス barūlās

  バーリン bārīn

  イリンキト īlīnkit

  イルジト īljit

  ククメン kukūmān

  ウルート ūr'ūt

  マングト mankqūt

  オルナウト ūrnāwūt

  アルラト arlāt

  ベスート bīs'ūt ☆

そして、チンギス・ハンのもとにいた権威あるアミールたちのうちから、ジェデイ・ノヤン jaday nūyān [がいた]。[我々は] 彼の歴史をこの章において述べる。

そして、ノヤキン族の権威あるアミールは知られていない。そして、マングト族出身 [の権威あるアミール] も [知られていない]。

この「☆～☆」の部分が、増補部分にあたる。

増補部分は父系同族諸集団に関する異伝であり、JT/S においてウルート氏の指導者や部将（アミール）に関する叙述中に挿入されているのは、聊か不自然である。これに対し、JT/S3034 では、当該の増補部分は、「★」の箇所に挿入されている（JT/S3034, ff.91a-91b）。文脈から明白であるように、JT/S3034 の方が適切である。

ここに、『集史』「モンゴル史」原本の本文を復元・確定する上で、現在 存在が知られているペルシア語諸本における不適切な箇所を JT/S3034 が是正することができる、という事例が存在することを確認することができた。

以上より、アラビア語版『集史』「モンゴル史」写本 JT/S3034 は、錯簡・脱落のある書本から写されたために本文の残存状況の上で大きな偏りがあり、部分的にしか使用できないという限界があるにもかかわらず、『集史』「モンゴル史」諸本の系統樹の構築や、本文の異同の比較・検討、本文の確定の上で、他のペルシア語諸写本にはない重要性をも有している、という事実が明らかになったものと思われる。

おわりに

以上より、JT/S3034 は、ラシードッディーンによる『集史』写本作成事業のもとで翻訳されたアラビア語版『集史』「モンゴル史」の系統を引く、現在 存在が知られる唯一の写本である可能性が極めて高いことが確認された。そして、本写本は、『集史』「モンゴル史」のペルシア語本文を校訂する上で、大きな価値を有している、と評価することができる。

JT/S3034 の重要性は、既述のように、既にトガンによって指摘されて久しいが、先行研究においては、本写本における本文と、他の『集史』「モンゴル史」諸本のそれとの比較・検討は、管見の限り、トガンが部族篇「タタル部」におけるモンゴル語表記について、ごく簡単に言及した以外には、未だ行われていないようである。今後、JT/S3034 は、固有名詞の綴形を他写本と比較・検討する以外にも、ペルシア文では解釈が分かれる部分について、本写本ではどのようにアラビア語訳されているかを確認する、また、ペルシア語本文における術語が、本写本ではどのように扱われているかに着目するなど、さまざまな分析が行われ、モンゴル帝国史研究のために積極的に使用されることが望まれよう。

注釈

[1]『集史』第一巻「モンゴル史」の校訂諸刊本における諸写本の校訂に関する問題については、宇野伸浩 2006 等を参照せよ。

[2] 本写本は、カラーによるデジタル影像（カラー）化が済んでいる。ＣＤ番号は 16159。

[3] 白岩一彦 2000, p.17, No.(20) を参照されたい。なお、同氏は、JT/Tm を「オルジェイトゥ・ハンに捧げられた「ガザン史」【引用者注：『集史』第一巻「モンゴル史」】の献呈本と考えられる」と主張している（白岩一彦 2000, p.10）。これが誤りであることは既に先行研究においても指摘されている（宇野伸浩 2003, p.57 他）が、ここで新たに別の根拠を示しておきたい。即ち、JT/Tm には、部族篇「タタル部」の、f.19b の 25 行目から f.20a の 2 行目にかけての複数箇所において、JT/Tm の書本における本文の破損を空欄にしたり、単語の残闕部のみを書写したと考えられる部分が存在する。このような欠陥がある JT/Tm が献呈本であるとは、到底、考えられない。この問題については、機会があれば詳細に論じたい。

[4] 遠峯四郎 1948, pp.107-108. 旧字は新字に改めた。a) は葉数、b) は所蔵所、c) は書写年代である。

[5] 所謂「イスタンブル本」（JT/S）。

[6] これは、JT/S のうち、小林高四郎氏が「將來」した部分である。

[7]『集史』第一巻「モンゴル史」の全てを含むとあるが、既述のように、本文の欠脱が少なからず存在している。

[8] 尤も、ストーリイが「詳細」に述べるアラビア語版『集史』とは、第二巻「世界史」である。

[9] Togan 1962, pp.65-66. 但し、トガンは「*Usūtū Mankūn alaqchin adūtān; mangū bilavurnān*」と表記している。

[10] JT 露訳 -1-1, JT 露訳 -1-2。

[11] 柯劭忞の『新元史』。尤も、このトガンの所言は適切ではない。

[12] 当該の部分については、赤坂恒明 1994, pp.54-55（但し、p.55, 下段 2 行目の「二派（bābāni）」は「教皇たち（bābān）」の誤訳である）, 白岩一彦 1997, p.6 をも参照されたい。

[13] この写本作成指示書は、カトルメール E.Quatremère によって紹介されている。MR/Qtr, pp.clxiv-clxxiv. なお、Browne 1928 は、これに基づいて検討を行っている。

[14] 二通の写本作成指示書に、「ドーム」／「図書室」とそれぞれ異なって書かれているが、これは、ワクフが設定された A.H.709.3.1（A.D.1309.8.9）から、写本作成指示書の一方が成立した日付 A.H.713.12（A.D.1314.3. 下旬）までの間に、「元になる写本」の架蔵場所が「ドーム」から「図書室」に変更されたためであると岩武昭男氏は指摘している。岩武昭男 1995, pp.289-299,300。

教育部哲學社會科學重點研究基地内蒙古大學蒙古學研究中心重大項目資助（項目批准號 08XZS008）

文献

1. ラシードッディーン rašīd al-dīn の編著

○『集史』 *jāmi' al-tawārīx*.
・MS., İstanbul, Topkapı Sarayı Müzesi Kütüphanesi, Revan 1518. [JT/S]
・MS., Taškent, Institut vostokovedeniya Akademiya nauk RUz., sobranie vostochnïx rukopisey, inventarnïy No.1620.（未見）[JT/A]
・MS., Tehrān, ketāb-xāne-ye majles-e šourāy-e mellī, 2294. 足利惇氏・田村実造・恵谷俊之『京都大学イラン・アフガニスタン・パキスタン学術調査報告 イランの歴史と言語』京都大学, 1968, pp.69-172. [JT/Tm]
・MS., Sankt-Peterburg, National Library of Russia, PSN 46. (旧 Publičnaya biblioteka im. Saltïkova-Ščedrina, šifr v,3,1). [JT/C]
・MS., Paris, Bibliothéque Nationale, Supplément persan 1113. [JT/P]
・MS., İstanbul, Süleymaniye Kütüphanesi, Ayasofya 3034. [JT/S3034]
・Фазлаллах Рашид ад-дин, *Джами' ат-таварих*. том I, часть 1. Критическии текст А.А.Ромаскевича, А.А.Хетагурова, А.А.Али-заде. Москва, 1965. [JT/Az-1-1]
・Рашид-ад-дин, *Сборник летописей*, том I, книга первая, Перевод с персидского Л.А.Хетагурова, редакция и примечания Проф.А.А.Семенова. Москва, 1952. [JT 露訳 -1-1]
・Рашид-ад-дин, *Сборник летописей*, том I, книга вторая, Перевод с персидского О.И.Смирновой, примечания Б.И. Панкратова и О.И.Смирновой, редакция Проф. А.А.Семенова. Москва, 1952. [JT 露訳 -1-2]

○『ラシード集成』 *majmū'a al-rašīdiyya*.
・MS., Paris, Bibliothèque Nationale, de Slane 2324, Ancien fonds persan 107. (E.Quatremère, *Histoire des Mongols de la Perse*. Paris, 1836). [MR/Qtr]

○『注釈の書』 *kitāb al-tawḏīhāt*.
・MS., İstanbul, Topkapı-Sarayı Müzesi Kütüphanesi, Ahmet III 2300. [TD/S]

○『スルターンの諸益』 *fawā'id-i sulṭāniyya*.
・MS., İstanbul, Nuru Osmaniye Kütüphanesi, 3415. [FS/S]

○『真理の精妙』 *laṭā'if al-ḥaqā'iq*.
・MS., İstanbul, Süleymaniye Kütüphanesi, Ayasofya 3833. [LH/AS]

2．二次文献

・W.Barthold, *Turkestan down to the Mongol Invasion.* T.Minorsky(tr.). 1968.

・Bregel 1972 : Брегель, Ю.Э.(пер), Стори, Ч.А. *Персидская литература: Био-библиографический обзор.* в трех частях. Москва, 1972.

・E.G.Browne, *A Literary History of Persia*, Vol. Ⅲ, Cambridge, 1956.

・岩武昭男「ラシード区ワクフ文書補遺写本作成指示書」『アジアの文化と社会（関西学院大学東洋史学専修開設30周年記念論集）』京都, 法律文化社, 1995.6, pp.277-310.

・岩武昭男「ラシード著作全集の編纂——『ワッサーフ史』著者自筆本の記述より」『東洋学報』第七八巻第四号, 1997.3, pp.01-031.

・Karl Yahn, "The Still Missing Works of Rashīd al-Dīn", *Central Asiatic Journal*, vol.IX, No.2, 1964. pp.113-122.

・志茂碩敏『モンゴル帝国史研究序説——イル汗国の中核部族——』東京, 東京大学出版会, 1995.2.

・志茂智子「ラシード・ウッディーンの『モンゴル史』——『集史』との関係について——」『東洋学報』第七六巻第三・四号, 1995. pp.93-122.

・白岩一彦「歴史家ラシード・ウッディーンの生涯と著作」『アジア資料通報』第35巻第2号, 国立国会図書館, 1997.4, pp.1-12.

・白岩一彦「ラシード・ウッディーン『歴史集成』現存写本目録——Rashid al-Din's Compendium of Chronicles: a bibliography of the extant manuscripts」『参考書誌研究』第五三号, 国立国会図書館専門資料部, 2000.10, pp.1-33.

・C.A.Storey, *Persian Literature, A Bio-bibliographical Survey.* 1927-1939, reprinted 1970.

・Felix Tauer, Les manuscrits persans historiques des bibliothèques de Stamboul, 1, *Archiv Orientalni*, vol.3, No.1, Prag, 1931, pp.87-118.

・Thackston 1998: *Rashiduddin Fazlullah's Jami'u't-tawarikh: Compendium of Chronivles. A History of the Mongols.* Part One. English Translation & Annotation by W.M.Thackston. Harvard University, Department of Near Eastern Languages and Civilizations. 1998, pp.xi-xviii, Translator's Preface.

・Togan, A.Zeki Velidi "The Composition of the History of the Mongols by Rashīd al-dīn". *Central Asiatic Journal*, vol.VII, Nr.1. 1962.3, pp.60-72.

・遠峰四郎〔榎一雄〔補〕〕「小林学士将来東洋学書目録（一）ペルシヤ文古鈔本攝影目録」『東洋学報』第三十二巻第一号, 1948.10, pp.102-114.

・宇野伸浩「『集史』イラン国民議会図書館写本の欄外の加筆」『碑刻等史料の総合的分析によるモンゴル帝国・元朝の政治・経済システムの基礎的研究究（研究課題番号

12410096）平成 12 ~ 13 年度科学研究費補助金基盤研究 (B)(1) 研究成果報告書』, 研究代表者 松田孝一, 平成 14 年（2002）3 月, pp.129-149.

・宇野伸浩「ラシード・ウッディーン『集史』の増補加筆のプロセス」広島修道大学人間環境学会『人間環境研究』第 1 巻第 1・2 号合併号, 2003.2, pp.39-62.

・宇野伸浩「『集史』第 1 巻「モンゴル史」研究の現状と課題」『中央民族大学蒙古文文献國際研討會 論文提要』北京, 中央民族大学, 2004.5.2.

・宇野伸浩「ラシードッディーン『集史』第 1 巻「モンゴル史」の諸写本に見られる脱落」広島修道大学人間環境学会『人間環境研究』第 5 巻第 1 号, 2006.9, pp.95-113.

・赤坂恒明「『五族譜』と『集史』編纂」『史観』第百三十冊，1994.3, pp.47-61.

・赤坂恒明「『五族譜』モンゴル分支と『集史』諸写本」『アジア・アフリカ言語文化研究』55 号, 1998.3, pp.141-164.

・赤坂恒明「系譜史料におけるジュチの諸子に関する記載」『史観』第百四十二冊, 2000.3, pp.38-57.

・赤坂恒明「トカ＝テムル裔の系譜情報の復元」黒田卓・高倉浩樹・塩谷昌史編『中央ユーラシアにおける民族文化と歴史像』(東北アジア研究センター叢書 第 13 号) 仙台, 東北大学東北アジア研究センター, 2003.9, pp.7–46.

・赤坂恒明『ジュチ裔諸政権史の研究』風間書房, 2005.2.

表1 アラビア語版『集史』「モンゴル史」写本 Ayasofya 3034 の内容

f.1b ~ f.14a	「モンゴル史」序文（JT/Az-1-1, p.67, l.4 対応箇所あたりまで）
f.15b,l.1 ~ f.18b,l.3	部族篇 2「オイラト部」
f.18b,l.4 ~ f.19b,l.2	部族篇 2「タルグト・コリ・トレス諸部」
f.19b,l.3 ~ f.20a,l.1	部族篇 2「トマト部」
f.20a,ll.2-6	部族篇 2「ボルガジン・ケレムジン部」
f.20a,l.7 ~ f.21a,l.14	部族篇 2「ウラスト・テレングト・ケステミ部」
f.21b,l.1 ~ f.22b,l.13	部族篇 2「森林ウリャンカト部」（前半部）
f.23a,l.1 ~ f.24b,l.3	部族篇 序
f.24b,l.4 ~ f.27a,l.4	部族篇 表
f.27a,l.5 ~ f.39a,l.2	部族篇 1「オグズ伝」
f.39a,ll.3-11	部族篇 2 序
f.39a,l.12 ~ f.44b,l.5	部族篇 2「ジャライル諸部」
f.44b,l.6 ~ f.46b,l.5	部族篇 2「スニト部」
f.46b,l.6 ~ f.52b.	部族篇 2「タタル部」（前半部。JT/Az-1-1, p.185,l1 対応箇所まで）
f.53a ~ f.55b,l.10	部族篇 3「ナイマン部」（途中から。JT/Az-1-1, p.291,l9 対応箇所より）
f.55b,l.11 ~ f.58a,l.8	部族篇 3「オングト部」
f.58a,l.9 ~ f.60b,l.5	部族篇 3「タングト部」
f.60b,l.5 ~ f.62b,l.11	部族篇 3「ウイグル部」
f.62b,l.11 ~ f.63b,l.1	部族篇 3「ベクリン部」
f.63b,l.2 ~ f.64a,l.3	部族篇 3「キルギス部」
f.64a,ll.3-9	部族篇 3「カルルク部」
f.64a,ll.10-12	部族篇 3「キプチャク部」
f.64a,l.13 ~ f.64b,l.7	部族篇 4 序（JT/Az-1-1, p.354, l.9 対応箇所より）
f.64b,l.8 ~ f.68b,l.1	部族篇 4 - 1 序
f.68b,l.1 ~ f.70b,l.12	部族篇 4 - 1「ウリャンカト氏」
f.70b,l.12 ~ f.76a,l.1	部族篇 4 - 1「コンギラト氏」
f.76a,l.1 ~ f.80a,l.12	部族篇 4 - 1「オロナウト氏」
f.80a,l.12 ~ f.80b,l.13	部族篇 4 - 1「フーシン氏」
f.80b,l.13 ~ f.83b,l.10	部族篇 4 - 1「スルドス氏」

(续)

f.83b,l.10 ~ f.84a,l.2	部族篇 4 - 1「イルドルキン氏」
f.84a,l.3 ~ f.85b,l.8	部族篇 4 - 1「バヤウト氏」
f.85b,l.9 ~ f.86a,l.1	部族篇 4 - 1「ゲネゲト氏」
f.86a,ll.1-10	部族篇 4 - 2 序
f.86a,l.10 ~ f.86b,l.2	部族篇 4 - 2「カタギン氏」
f.86b,l.2 ~ f.87b,l.13	部族篇 4 - 2「サルジウト氏」
f.87b,l.13 ~ f.90b,l.1	部族篇 4 - 2「タイチウト氏」
f.90b,ll.1-10	部族篇 4 - 2「ホルテゲン・シジウト氏」
f.90b,l.11 ~ f.91a,l.5	部族篇 4 - 2「チノス氏」
f.91a,l.6 ~ f.93b,l.9	部族篇 4 - 2「ノヤキン・ウルウト・マングト氏」
f.93b,l.9 ~ f.94a,l.4	部族篇 4 - 2「ドゥルベン氏」
f.94a,l.4 ~ f.95a,l.1	部族篇 4 - 2「バーリン氏」
f.95a,l.1 ~ f.95b,l.9	部族篇 4 - 2「スクヌト氏」
f.95b,ll.9-13	部族篇 4 - 2「バルラス氏」
f.95b,l.13 ~ f.96a,l.5	部族篇 4 - 2「ハダルキン部」
f.96a,l.5 ~ f.98b,l.11	部族篇 4 - 2「ジュリヤト氏」
f.98b,ll.11-13	部族篇 4 - 2「ブダート氏」
f.99a,l.1 ~ f.100a,l.2	部族篇 4 - 2「ベスート氏」
f.100a,ll.2-5	部族篇 4 - 2「スケーン氏」
f.100a,ll.5-8	部族篇 4 - 2「キンギヤト氏」
f.100a,l.9 ~ f.100b,l.9	部族篇 末尾
f.100b,l.9 ~ f.102a,l.2	チンギス列祖紀 序
f.102a,ll.3-4	「ドブン=バヤン紀」
f.102b,l.4 ~ f.106a,l.4	「アラン=ゴア紀」
f.106a,ll.4-5	「ボドンチャル紀」
f.106b,l.1 ~ f.108a,l.5	「ドトン=メネン紀」
f.108b,ll.1 ~ 13	「カイド=ハン紀」序
f.109a,l.1 ~ f.111a,l.9	「トンビナ=ハン紀」
f.112a,l.1 ~ f.126a,l.4	「カブル=ハン紀」
f.126a,l.5 ~ f.129b,l.5	「バルタン=バハドル紀」
f.129b,l.6 ~ f.136b,l.7	「イェスゲイ=バハドル紀」第一部

『集史』第一巻「モンゴル史」校訂におけるアラビア語版写本 Ayasofya 3034 の価値

(続)

f.136b,*ll*.8-13	「イェスゲイ゠バハドル紀」第二部
f.137a,*l*.1 ~ f.139a,*l*.2	「チンギス゠ハン紀」序
f.139a,*l*.3 ~ f.139b,*l*.2	「チンギス゠ハン紀」目次
f.139b,*l*.3 ~ f.143b,*l*.4	「チンギス゠ハン紀」第一部
f.143b,*l*.5 ~ f.144a,*l*.5	「チンギス゠ハン紀」第二部 序
f.144a,*l*.6 ~ f.150b,*l*.13	「チンギス゠ハン紀」第二部第一章
f.151a,*l*.1 ~ f.168a,*l*.9	「チンギス゠ハン紀」第二部第二章
f.168a,*l*.9 ~ f.188a,*l*.8	「チンギス゠ハン紀」第二部第五章
f.188a,*l*.9 ~ f.246a,*l*.13	「チンギス゠ハン紀」第二部第六章
f.246b,*l*.1 ~ f.249b,*l*.6	「チンギス゠ハン紀」第二部 編年史
f.249b,*l*.7 ~ f.269a,*l*.1	「チンギス゠ハン紀」第三部
f.269a,*ll*.2-9	「オゴデイ紀」序
f.269b,*ll*.1-13	「オゴデイ紀」目次
f.270a,*l*.1 ~ f.280b,*l*.6	「オゴデイ紀」第一部
f.280b,*l*.6 ~ f.298a,*l*.3	「オゴデイ紀」第二部第一章(第二節以下)
f.298a,*l*.3 ~ f.317a,*l*.4	「オゴデイ紀」第二部第二章
f.317a,*l*.5 ~ f.333a,*l*.10	「オゴデイ紀」第三部
f.333a,*l*.11 ~ f.333b,*l*.11	「ジュチ紀」表題・目次
f.333b,*l*.11 ~ f.353a,*l*.13	「ジュチ紀」第一部
f.354b,*ll*.1-13	「ジュチ紀」第二部
f.355a,*l*.1 ~ f.360a,*l*.5	「チンギス゠ハン紀」第二部第四章
f.360a,*l*.6	「チャガタイ紀」第一部(系図)
f.361a,*l*.1 ~ f.364a,*l*.7	「チャガタイ紀」第二部第一節
f.364a,*l*.7 ~ f.373a,*l*.6	「チンギス゠ハン紀」第二部第四章
f.373a,*l*.6 ~ f.377a,*l*.8	「チャガタイ紀」第二部第二節
f.377a,*l*.8 ~ f.379b,*l*.1	「チャガタイ紀」第二部第三節
f.379b,*ll*.2-5	「チャガタイ紀」第三部
f.379b,*l*.6 ~ f.380b,*l*.5	「チャガタイ紀」第一部
f.381a,*l*.1	「チャガタイ紀」第二部 表題の一部
f.381b,*l*.1 ~ f.385b,*l*.10	「ジュチ紀」第二部
f.385b,*ll*.10-13	「ジュチ紀」第三部

（续）

f.386b,l.1 ~ f.389b,l.5	「トルイ紀」第一部
f.389b,l.5 ~ f.390a,l.11	「トルイ紀」第二部第三節
f.390a,l.11 ~ f.390b,l.8	「グユク紀」表題・目次
f.390b,l.9 ~ f.391a,l.12	「グユク紀」第一部
f.391a,l.12 ~ f.396b,l.4	「グユク紀」第二部
f.397a,ll.1-13	(抄)「ジュチ紀」
f.397b,ll.1-8	(抄)「チャガタイ紀」
f.397b,l.9 ~ f.398a,l.10	(抄)「トルイ紀」
f.398a,l.11 ~ f.398b,l.4	(抄)「グユク紀」
f.398b,l.5 ~ f.399a,l.7	(抄)「モンケ紀」
f.399a,l.8 ~ f.399b,l.12	(抄)「フビライ紀」
f.399b,l.13 ~ f.400a,l.8	(抄)「テムル紀」
f.400a,l.9 ~ f.400b,l.12	(抄)「フレグ紀」
f.400b,l.13 ~ f.396a,l.10	(抄)「フレグ紀」と「アバガ紀」（排列順に混乱あり）
f.402a,l.11 ~ f.402b,l.3	(抄)「アフマド紀」
f.402b,ll.4-13	(抄)「キハト紀」
f.403a,l.1 ~ f.403b,l.13	(抄)「アルグン紀」
f.403b,l.14 ~ f.408b,l.13	(抄)「ガザン紀」
f.409a,ll.1-13	「オルジェイトゥ即位紀」第一節
f.409b,ll.1-13	「オルジェイトゥ即位紀」第二節
f.410a,l.1 ~ f.414b,l.2	『集史』総序文
f.415b,l.1 ~ f.417b,l.2	「トルイ紀」第二部第二節
f.417b,l.3 ~ f.421b,l.13	「トルイ紀」第二部第三節（内容の増補あり）
f.422a	「アルグン紀」
f.422b	「キハト紀」第一部
f.423a	「ガザン紀」第一部
f.423b,l.1 ~ f.424a,l.13	「オルジェイトゥ紀」第一部

表2 『集史』「モンゴル史」部族篇におけるアラビア語版 JT/S3034 JT/S と JT/Tm に本文の異同がある箇所

	JT/Az-1-1 の対応箇所	JT/S3034	JT/S	JT/Tm	志茂智子 1995, p.114, 表5	備考
部族篇「表」: 諸部族の配列	pp.82-83	Tm と同じ f.24b, *ll*7-10	Tm と異なる	S と異なる	—	宇野伸浩 2002; 2003「ジャライル族の牧地についての記事」
「ジャライル諸部」	p.132, n.4	なし（f.38b）	あり	欄外にあり	1	宇野伸浩 2002; 2003「ジャライル族の牧地についての記事」
「タタル部」	p.160, n.4; p.161, n.1	あり f.45b, *l*.12 ~ f.46a, *l*.11	あり	欄外にあり	2	宇野伸浩 2002; 2003「タタル族と南シベリアについての記事」
「タタル部」	注なし（p.180, *l*.2 ~ p.184, *l*.5）	あり f.50b, *l*.8 ~ f.51b, *l*.11	あり	なし	3	（クトク・ノヤンの物語）
「オイラト部」	p.221, n.19（p.221, *l*.2 ~ *l*.8）	Tm と同じ位置に配置 f.14b *l*.4-*l*.10	Tm と配置位置が異なる	S と配置位置が異なる	18	（地理関係情報）
「オイラト部」	p.225, n.21	あり f.15b右, *l*.12 ~ f.16a右, *l*.5	あり	欄外にあり	4	宇野伸浩 2002; 2003「オイラト族のブカ・テムルの4姉妹についての記事」
「ナイマン部」	p.289, n.3	あり f.52a, *l*.1 ~ *l*.3	あり	なし	9	（地理関係情報）
「ウイグル部」	p.342, n.26	あり f.61b, *l*.9 ~ *l*.11	あり	なし	10	（最末尾）
「コンギラト氏」	p.388, n.17	あり f.70a, *l*.6 ~ *l*.7	あり	なし	11	（地理関係情報）
「バヤウト氏」	p.458, n.14; p.459, n.7	なし（f.83a, *l*.7）	あり	なし	12	（地理関係情報）
「タイチウト氏」	p.480, n.1	あり f.87a, *l*.4 ~ *l*.10 S と異なる配置	あり	なし	13	（ナチンの系譜）（S3034 の配置は C, P と同じ）
「タイチウト氏」	p.488, n.8	あり。※但し錯簡により完全には未確認（f.88a, *ll*.2-5）	あり	なし	14	（ジェベの物語）
「タイチウト氏」	p.490, n.14	あり f.88a, *l*.10 ~ f.89a, *l*.5	あり	なし	15	
「ノヤキン・ウルウト・マングト氏」	p.503, n.9	あり f.90a, *l*.8 ~ *l*.11 S と異なる配置	あり	なし	16	（C, P もなし）→ S3034 の配置が妥当
「ジュリヤト氏」	p.541, *ll*.1-7	あり f.96b, *ll*.6-9	あり	なし	17	（ジャムカ処刑の話）（C, P あり）

ON THE SIGNIFICANCE OF MS. AYASOFYA 3034 FOR TEXTUAL CRITICISM OF "HISTORY OF THE MONGOLS" IN *JAMI' AL-TAWARIKH*

AKASAKA Tsuneaki

MS. Süleymaniye Kütüphanesi (Ayasofya 3034) which is the only manuscript of the Arabic version of "History of the Mongols" in *Jāmi' al-Tawārīkh* is descended from the manuscript which was translated into Arabic from Persian under the auspices of Rashīd al-Dīn's project to make manuscripts of *Jāmi' al-Tawārīkh* in Rashīdiyya. The contents of the manuscript are closer to MS. Topkapı Sarayı Müzesi Kütüphanesi, Revan 1518 than MS.Ketāb-xāne-ye Majles-e Šourāy-e Mellī 2294. Although the text of MS. Ayasofya 3034 is not complete, the manuscript is significant for the restoration and revision of the Persian original text of "History of the Mongols" in *Jāmi' al-Tawārīkh* as a comparable text for textual criticism.

朝鮮時代的長白山踏查記與《白山圖》

李花子

　　1712年（康熙五十一年）清朝派烏喇總管穆克登到達長白山，調查鴨綠江、土門江（今天的圖們江，以下同）水源及劃分兩江之間的邊界，距今已有三百年時間了。其間雖然經歷了1885、1887年兩次勘界（見圖1），然而此次定界的諸多細節仍在迷霧中，比如穆克登立碑的位置，指定的水源，以及朝鮮設柵的位置等，在學界存在很大的爭議。有人認為碑一開始就立在天池東南邊（約十餘里），也有人認為碑原來立于小白山頂，後來被朝鮮人暗移到了天池附近，即所謂的"界碑暗移說"。[1] 至於穆克登指定的水源，有人認為定的是松花江上流，也有人認為原來打算定圖們江水源卻誤定了松花江上流，也有人認為定的是小白山東麓發源的紅丹水，也有人認為定的是長白山東麓發源的紅土山水等等。[2] 此外，有關此次踏查活動的性質也存在分歧，有人認為是清朝單方面的查邊，也有人認為是中朝兩國的定界。[3]

　　本文試利用親歷1712年長白山定界的三位朝鮮人的踏查記，結合當時繪製的《白山圖》，對於穆克登立碑的位置，查得的鴨、圖二江水源及定界的結果等，再做深入探討，以求接近歷史真實。

一、從三部踏查記看1712年長白山定界的經過

　　1712年清朝派烏喇總管穆克登到長白山調查鴨綠江、圖們江水源和在分水嶺上立碑，隨行的朝鮮接伴使朴權和譯官金指南寫有踏查記，如朴權寫了《北征日記》，金指南寫了《北征錄》。金指南的兒子金慶門也是隨行譯官，他陪同穆克登登上長白山頂，親歷查水源、定界的全過程。因其父親已寫有記錄全程的踏查記，所以他托友人洪世泰寫了一部反映登山、查水源過程的《白頭山記》。這三部踏查記，加上當時繪製的《白山圖》，是瞭解1712年長白山定界的重要資料，特別是在中方的檔案資料因清朝內閣大庫失火而消失殆盡的情況下，這三位朝鮮

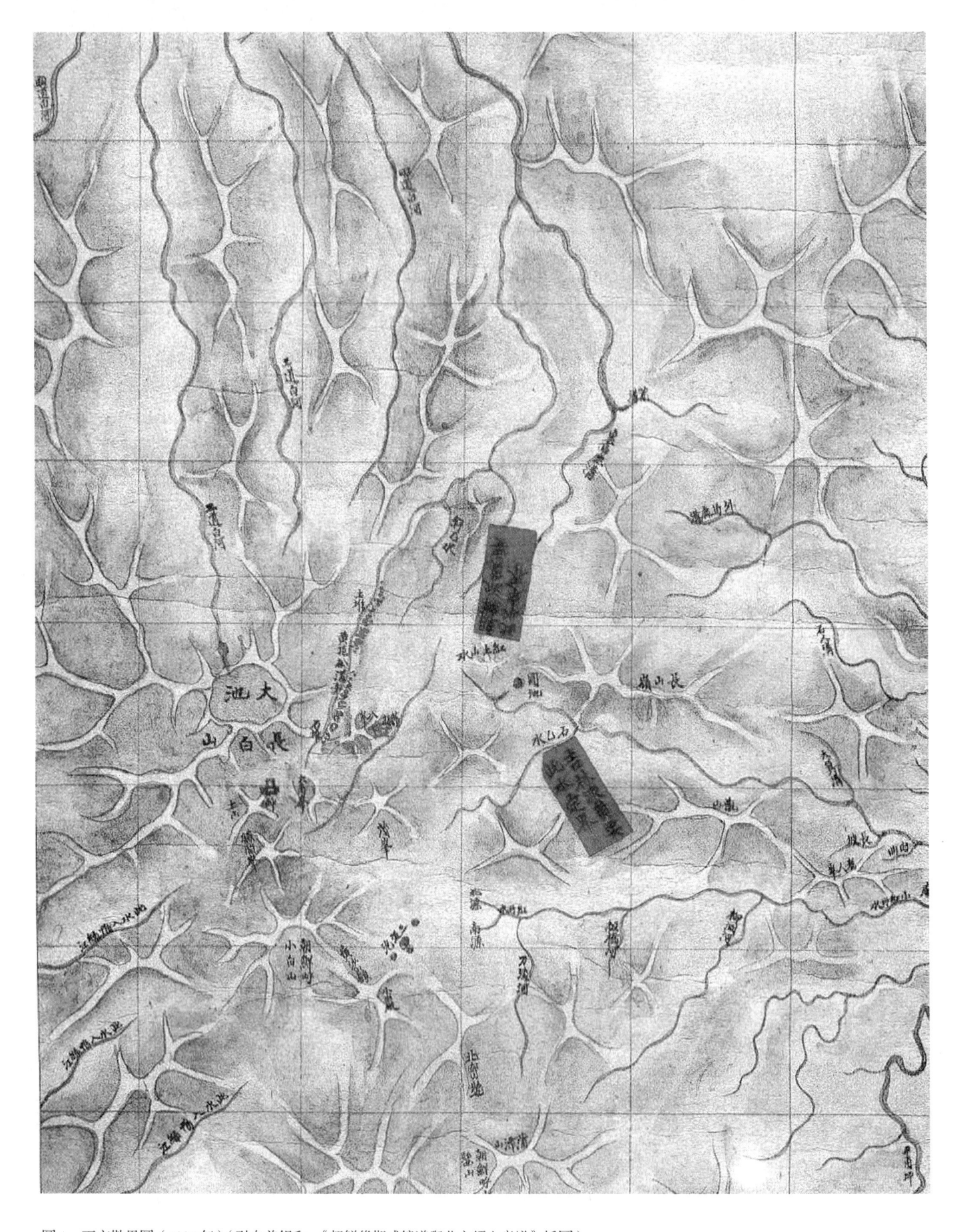

圖1　丁亥勘界圖（1887年）（引自姜錫和：《朝鮮後期咸鏡道與北方領土意識》插圖）

人親歷的踏查記和《白山圖》，成為瞭解這一段史事的彌足珍貴的資料。

在這三部踏查記中，金指南的《北征錄》內容最豐富。他以日記體的形式記錄了從首爾出發，一路跋山涉水，到鴨綠江邊的厚州與清使穆克登等見面，再溯鴨綠江而上到達長白山，查水源、定界以後，順圖們江而下，一直走到下游入海口的全過程。朴權的《北征日記》也是以日記體的形式記錄了陪伴穆克登查界的過程，但是內容比金指南的《北征錄》要簡略得多。在此次踏查中，朝鮮接伴使朴權和譯官金指南因年老的關係，未能陪同穆克登登上長白山頂，也沒有參與查水源、立碑的過程，所以二人的踏查記缺少這部分最重要內容的親歷的記錄。不過金指南大量轉載了陪伴穆克登登山、查水源、立碑的朝鮮軍官、譯官、差使員的報告書，因此他的书的史料價值仍很高。其子金慶門托友人洪世泰寫的《白頭山記》，多少彌補了這一缺陷。

據《北征錄》、《北征日記》記載，穆克登此行由盛京出發，到達鴨綠江邊的頭道溝，然後水陸並進，逆江而上前往長白山。穆克登帶着許多人馬從陸路行走，侍衛布蘇倫乘着馬尚船溯江而上，每晚會於一道溝，目的是為了勘查鴨綠江上游的十三道溝。"道溝"是指"兩山間水流處"，[4]是鴨綠江上游眾多支流匯入而形成的一道道溝子，反映了這裏獨有的山形水貌特徵。正因為有了這次水陸並進的踏查，若干年後完成的《皇輿全覽圖》及後來編纂的清朝輿圖中，才出現了鴨綠江上游的頭道溝、二道溝直至十幾道溝的支流名稱。

4月26日布蘇倫率領十艘馬尚船，到達廢四郡盡處的厚州即鴨綠江八道溝一帶，29日穆克登到達此處與他會合，朝鮮接伴使朴權及譯官、軍官等早已在此迎候他們。之後布蘇倫繼續乘馬尚船前行，穆克登則與朝鮮接伴使朴權等一起從鴨綠江南岸朝鮮境內行走，5月4日到達惠山，繼續向長白山前進。經過鴨綠江上游的三條支流即吾時川、申大新川、劍川以後，一行人由陸路分作兩路行走，一路由穆克登帶領年輕的譯官、軍官、指路人、斧手等，沿着鴨綠江幹流溯江而上直上長白山天池；一路包括朝鮮接伴使朴權和咸鏡監司李善溥、清朝侍衛、譯官金指南等年老體弱者，由甫多會山北路，經過臨淵水（朝鮮今稱鯉明水）、虛項嶺、三池淵、長坡、魯隱東山、紅丹水、魚潤江、朴下川，到達茂山等候。[5]這樣一來，負有接伴和定界任務的朝鮮使臣朴權和李善溥被排除在查水源、定界的過程中，後來朴、李二人不願意在穆克登立的碑上刻下名字，與此有關。[6]

在惠山，朴權和李善溥曾勸阻穆克登不要親自上山，選擇"矯捷明敏者數人與朝鮮譯官及知路人偕往看審"；如若上山，則在朝鮮二使中務必帶上一人，使其不辱"儐接欽差之行"的使命，然而穆克登堅持自己是奉皇旨看審，"不得不躬往"，而二位使臣"高年有壽，決不可隨行"。[7]當一行人來到鴨綠江自浦水邊將要分行的時候，朝鮮老譯官金指南向穆克登提出了令畫師繪出"山圖"以贈的要求，穆克登答應了他的請求。[8]金指南之所以提這個要求，是為了免去他本人和朝鮮二使不能一同上山查水源的責任，這樣便有了現收藏于首爾大學奎章閣的《白山圖》（參見圖2）。

從《北征錄》、《北征日記》及《朝鮮王朝實錄》所載朴權、李善溥的狀啓內容看，在穆克登查水源、定界的過程中，朝鮮譯官金慶門、金指南和當地土人起了很大的作用。譯官金指南、金慶門父子向穆克登轉達了長白山天池以南為朝鮮界的定界主張；[9] 而朝鮮土人則使穆克登瞭解到圖們江發源于長白山天池向東流，中間斷流百餘里後湧出地面。這些不僅影響了穆克登立碑的位置及確定圖們江源，同時對定界結果也產生了重大影響。

朴權於4月30日給國王上的狀啓，記錄了穆克登和金慶門之間有關中朝邊界的對話，詳細內容如下：

> 總管（穆克登）曰："爾能明知兩國界耶？"（金慶門）答以"雖未目見，而長白山巔有大池，西流為鴨綠江，東流為豆滿江，大池之南即我國界。上年皇帝招問時，亦以此仰對矣。"又問："有可據文書耶？"答以"立國以來，至今流傳，何待文書耶？"又問："白山之南，連有把守耶？"答以"此地絕險，人跡不至，故荒廢無把守，有同大國柵門外之地耳。"[10]

洪世泰的《白頭山記》也記錄了穆、金二人有關中朝邊界的對話，內容如下：

> 先是，克登在燕京，語我使曰："得一知山南路者待我。"及是，克登問之，慶門對曰："是在惠山。公之此行，必欲審定疆界。然白頭山頂有大池，東流為土門，西流為鴨綠，此即北南界也。而自惠山沿流至源，其間山水險阻，從古不通，間有獵夫攀木猱升，而亦未有至山頂者，公何得窮之哉？"克登曰："吾奉皇命而來，安所憚險？爾言爾國界在此，此豈奏聞皇上而定之歟？"曰："小邦自古以此為界，婦孺皆知之。此豈可上請，而亦何用文字為證也？昨年皇上在暢春苑招我使，問西北之界，實以此對，公必與聞之矣。蓋二江發源此池，為天下大水，此天所以限南北也。公今一見決矣。"[11]

此外，金指南的《北征錄》也記錄了過惠山之後，5月5日穆克登向金慶門的父親金指南追問中朝邊界的對話，內容如下：

> 總管（穆克登）招余（金指南）謂曰："我們此行，專為看審邊界而已。雖上天入地，當依你們所指示而往。你今明說你國邊界，果何如耶？"余答曰："長白山巔大池之南，是吾邊界之意，當初有訴，今何改說。"總管曰："然則勢將登山以去。"[12]

由以上穆克登和金指南父子的對話可知，金指南父子將鴨、圖二江發源于長白山天池，天池以南為朝鮮界的朝方的定界主張，向穆克登做了充分的表述。金慶門還把長白山以南地區比做清朝柳條邊外空地，雖"荒廢無把守"卻屬於朝鮮，回答得可謂巧妙之極。面對朝鮮譯官的此番對答，穆克登只好決定登上長白山頂查看水源。

此外，朝鮮土人有關圖們江發源于長白山天池向東流，中間斷流百餘里後湧出地面的說法，對穆克登查找圖們江源起了很大的作用。穆克登從長白山天池下來後，很快找到了鴨綠江源。據《白頭山記》記載，一行從長白山天池下來後，穆克登"即引下向東行"，"從崗脊冉冉而下，約三、四里，而始得鴨綠之源"。[13] 這個位置大概在天池東南麓十餘里，這裏就是鴨綠

— 444 —

江東源的發源地（參見圖2《白山圖》）。從這裏開始，穆克登向東行過百餘里，尋找朝鮮土人所說的圖們江湧出處，而未及湧出處十餘里他發現了一條東流之水，於是定此水為圖們江源，他還向隨行的朝鮮人誇耀說，此水要比朝鮮人"所謂湧出處，加遠十餘里"，以朝鮮"多得地方為幸"。[14]

從今天我們已知的地理知識看，從長白山發源的三大水系只有松花江是從天池落下形成瀑布形成水源的，其他兩大水系都不是以天池水形成水源的。鴨綠江發源于長白山天池東南麓約四十里，[15] 圖們江發源地距離天池更遠，無論是初源紅土山（赤峰）水，還是其下的紅丹水，距離天池都有一百多里。[16] 實際上，圖們江源無所謂"入地伏流"不伏流，當地土人所謂東流之水伏流百餘里湧出地面的說法，不過是地理知識貧乏年代的不實傳言，卻影響了穆克登查找圖們江源的過程。尽管如此，我們不能據此就認為穆克登定界完全盲從了朝鮮土人的說法。他在長白山天池以東尋找東流之水，這與中國歷代地理志的記述不無關係。無論是《元一統志》、《明一統志》，還是清代的《盛京通志》（康熙二十三年），均記載土門江（今圖們江）發源于長白山天池向東流或東南流。此外，1711年康熙帝命令穆克登查界的諭旨也指出："土門江自長白山東邊流出，向東南流入於海"。[17] 這同樣成為穆克登查找圖們江源和定界的依據。

此外，《北征錄》、《北征日記》還記載了朴權和穆克登之間有關"真豆江"的一番爭論，也就是圍繞哪一條水是真正的豆滿江源展開的爭論，二人的對話如下：

> 伴相（朴權）以為："臨江台近處，有一水來合于大紅丹水，明是白山東流之水，此是真豆江。而大人所得之水，乃大紅丹水上流云。"則總管（穆克登）即出山圖（《白山圖》），一一指示曰："我與鮮人在山時，詳察形勢，下山後遍尋水源，此水之外，實無他水云。"伴相又以為："臨江台上邊來合之水，此地之人，皆稱為豆江。自此相距不過十餘里，大人若暫時往見，則可知其實狀矣。"總管曰："我在惠山時，詳問于爾國指路人。則以為東流之水，斷流過百餘里後，始為湧出云。今我所得水源，與此言相符。"[18]

從上面的二人對話可知，朴權所謂"真豆江"是指在臨江台（魚潤江南邊十里、距離茂山七十里）[19] 附近與大紅丹水會合的圖們江上源。從今天我們已知的圖們江水系看，這似乎是指今天的紅旗河，它距離臨江台、魚潤江（今西豆水）均不遠。

一番爭論之後，朴權要求穆克登溯流而上重新查水源，然而事已晚矣。穆克登露宿野外多日查找圖們江水源，刻石立碑後，[20] 已經馬不停蹄地派出筆帖式帶著奏本前往厚春（琿春），再轉往北京了。於是穆克登只得回答："我若誤尋水源，而果有真豆江自白山流下者，則國王具奏于皇上，然後可以更審，我則決難變改前見。"[21] 穆、朴二人有關"真豆江"的爭論至此結束。如果此時穆克登按照朴權的建議，溯流而上重新查水源，或許能夠避免誤定松花江上流為圖們江源的錯誤。[22] 然而穆克登堅持己見，又急於求成，錯過了修正錯誤的一次好機會。

經過此次定界，朝鮮達到了預期的目標，從前模糊不清的天池以南大部分空地歸屬了朝鮮。朴權在《北征日記》中，對此記述如下：

> 自吾時川至魚潤江，長白山（朝鮮鏡城的一座山）以北、白頭山以南，周圍千餘里之地，本是我國之土，而以《輿地勝覽》及《北關志》中，皆以"彼地"懸錄之。故我國人之采獵者，恐犯潛越之禁，不敢任意往來是白如乎。今則界限既定，沿邊之人，皆知此之明為我境，其間西水羅德、虛項嶺、緩項嶺等地，及甫多會山左右前後，皆是參田是白遣，貂鼠則在在產出是白乎於。白頭山下，所謂天坪、長坡等地，樺木簇立，一望無際，三甲（三水、甲山）、茂山三邑之民，若許采於此中，則衣食自可饒足是白在果。[23]

如上文，從鴨綠江上游的吾時川至圖們江上游的魚潤江，長白山（鏡城）以北、白頭山以南，在朝鮮初期地理志《東國輿地勝覽》和《北關志》裏，均記載為"彼地"，即女真人的領地。然而此次定界以後，朝鮮人在這些地方采獵，也不會犯下潛越之罪。此外，長白山東南麓的西水羅德、虛項嶺、緩項嶺、甫多會山等處的參田、貂鼠，都可以由朝鮮人任意採取。天坪、長坡等地的樺木，同樣可以任由三甲、茂山人採取。這表明以上地方都劃歸了朝鮮。

如其所言，在以後的歷史長河中，茂山及其周邊地區的朝鮮流民，不斷越過朴下川、魚潤江、紅丹水，在其以北地區開墾和居住。到了光緒年間勘界時，朝鮮在紅丹水北面的長坡設置了社倉，這裏的朝鮮村落已有了百餘年歷史。[24] 有鑒於此，中方代表不得不從一開始力主以紅丹水為界，後來退主以紅丹水北面的石乙水為界了。

二、1712年的定界成果《白山圖》

《白山圖》又稱"山圖"，收入韓國首爾大學奎章閣收藏的《輿地圖》（古4709-1）中。如圖2所示，該圖右上角有如下題記："康熙五十一年我肅宗三十八年 壬辰穆胡克登定界時所模朴權定界使"。這表明該圖是康熙五十一年穆克登定界時模製的，題記估計是後來朝鮮人加上去的。文中所謂"穆胡"指穆克登，反映了朝鮮人視清人為"胡"或"夷狄"，自認為是中華的"華夷觀念"。

該圖（圖2）是一幅彩圖，圖的左上端畫有長白山天池，標有"白頭山"。從天池流出的三條河流分別是北流的松花江，西南流的鴨綠江，東南流的圖們江。這其中，松花江做了簡化處理，鴨綠江、圖們江上游各派水系標示得很詳細。鴨綠江上游主要標示惠山以上的水流，圖們江上游主要標示茂山以上的水流。顯然，主要表現了長白山天池以南鴨綠江、圖們江上游水系。該圖在天池東南還標有"江源碑"的字樣，與其正對的右側標有"土門"，左側標有"鴨綠江源"。這與碑文所記"西為鴨綠，東為土門，故於分水嶺上勒石為記"相符。鴨綠江源又分為東、西二源，與"江源碑"正對的是鴨綠江東源，其西邊是鴨綠江西源，西源與天池相

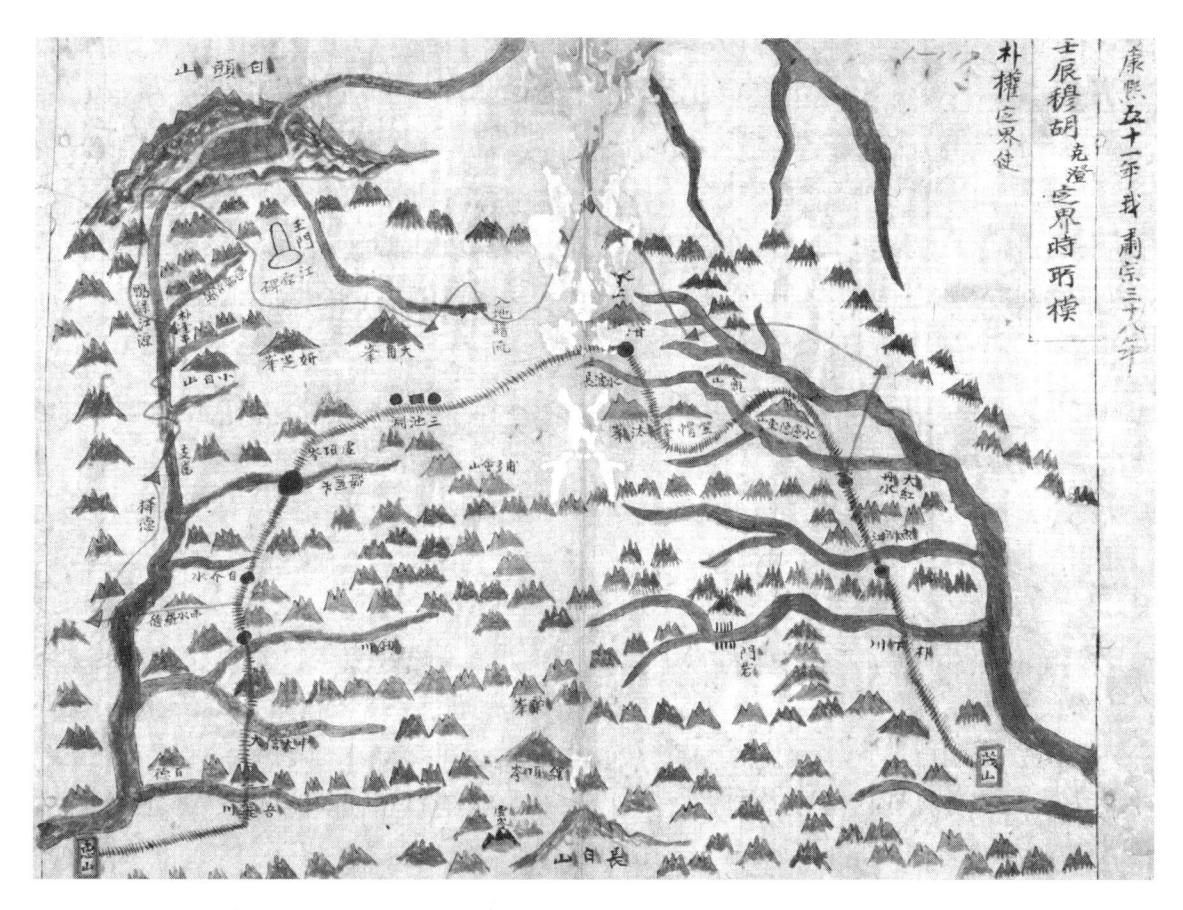

圖2 白山圖〔收入奎章閣收藏《輿地圖》（古4709-1）〕

連。土門江源自天池流出後，中間有斷流的地方，標有"入地暗流"，相隔一段後，在右側的甘土峰下有三派水流與之相連。這大概表現了土門江入地伏流後湧出地面之意，這裏就是朝鮮人所說的土門江湧出處。其下有紅丹水流入，再下有魚潤江、朴下川流入，再下有茂山。該圖還標有從鴨綠江邊的惠山，到達土門江邊的茂山的兩條登山路線，如果把它和三部踏查記進行對照，那麼其中一條是穆克登的登山路線，另一條是朴權、金指南等前往茂山的路線，這兩條路線分別用小三角形和圓圈標注一行人的住宿處。

　　無論是《北征錄》、《北征日記》，還是《朝鮮王朝實錄》所載朴權、李善溥的狀啓，都有關於這幅《白山圖》的記載。如前述，朝鮮之所以能得到這張圖，是譯官金指南和穆克登周旋的結果。5月8日當中朝人員來到鴨綠江自浦水邊，準備分作兩路行走時，朝鮮譯官金指南向穆克登提出想得到一張《白山圖》，以了卻他平生一登覽長白山的素志。這實際上是為了免去他本人和朝鮮二使不能和穆克登一同登山的責任，穆克登答應了他的請求。此時穆、金二人圍繞長白山（朝鮮稱白頭山）有一番對話，內容如下：

余（金指南）起而言曰："小官是朝鮮之人，白山亦是朝鮮之地。而傳稱宇內之名山，故願一登覽，平生素志。而道里絕遠，無由遂願。今行又因大人憐憫小官之老病，不許同行，白山真面，一見之願，未免墮空想。大人必令劉畫師圖出山形，倘以一件畫本見惠，則猶可以償小官平生之願。大人恩德，何可量哉？"總管（穆克登）曰："大國山川，雖不得圖畫以給，白山既是你國之地，則畫給一本，有何難哉？"余又曰："如其大國之山，則何敢生意仰請乎？"曰："唯。"余不勝喜幸，而退及抵宿舍，告於兩使前曰："今日始聞喜報矣。"[25]

如上文，金指南指出自己是朝鮮人，長白山也是朝鮮之地和宇內名山，要求清朝畫員圖出山形回贈一件，以了卻自己平生一見長白山的素願。在這裏，金指南把長白山說成是朝鮮之地，這恐怕與朝鮮人對長白山的宗山意識有關，即認為長白山是朝鮮山脈之祖。[26] 對此，穆克登回答："大國山川，雖不得圖畫以給，白山既是你國之地，則畫給一本，有何難哉？"穆克登這句話是一個反問句，語氣顯得不太順。意思是說，既然你說長白山是"你國之地"，那麼畫給一本有什麼難的。正因為穆的語氣不順，所以金指南才又小心地確認一次："如其大國之山，則何敢生意仰請乎？"穆克登"唯"了一聲，應允了金指南的請求。

上引文內容在5月13日接伴使朴權、咸鏡監司李善溥的狀啓中再度出現，但是意思已經完全走了樣，記載如下："譯官願得《白山圖》一件，總管曰：'大國山川，不可畫給，而白山乃爾國也。何難畫給？'以此觀之，白山以南，似無爭地之慮。"[27] 在這裏，穆克登的話由原來的"白山既是你國之地，則畫給一本，有何難哉？"的反問句，變成了"白山乃爾國也"的肯定句。不僅如此，這份狀啓還略掉了金指南先前說的一大段話，顯然有斷章取義之嫌。然而穆克登再糊塗，也不至於把清朝奉為祖宗發祥地的長白山說成是朝鮮地。而朴、李二人的狀啓之所以如此表述，是因為二人作為負有接伴和定界任務的朝方重臣，未能與穆克登一同上山查水源，他們一方面以得到《白山圖》來為自己開脫責任，另一方面以長白山以南為朝鮮地恐無大礙來安撫朝廷。

這張《白山圖》，還出現在5月21日朴權、穆克登圍繞"真豆江"爭論時，以及5月23日二人討論在圖們江斷流處設柵問題時，穆克登指着山圖說明自己定的水源無誤，還告訴朴權朝鮮應設柵的位置等。比如5月23日這一天，穆克登拿出山圖，"令二使離席近前，親手一一指示，其間道里遠近，斷流與否，縷縷言說，不啻千百。其意概以為所見極其明的，少無可疑。與差員、軍官、譯官等，終始目見，萬無差誤之理。"朴、李二使出去後，穆克登又指着山圖對金指南說："此是白山以南朝鮮地方圖本也。畫出二本，一則歸奏皇上，一則當送國王。而繕寫未完，完後出給。你告重臣，歸達國王前可也。"[28]

5月24日中朝兩國人員離開茂山到達豐山鎮，穆克登正式將《白山圖》交給了朝方。朴權細看後，發現其上有破綻，鴨綠江二源中，只有東源書"鴨綠江源"，而與天池相連的西源沒有書"鴨綠江源"。他命令金指南向穆克登提出西源一並書"鴨綠江源"四個字。《北征錄》

對此有如下記載：

> 伴相（朴權）細觀，則鴨江之源，有兩派。一自白山巔南邊流下，一自白山之西北流下，會合為一。而南邊之派，與豆江之源不遠而相對，故書"鴨綠江源"之名，西北之派，則不書其名。伴相謂余（金指南）曰："此派亦書江源，極其要緊。君可措辭善諭，必受書名而來。否則君之前仕，盡削於此矣。"余覆曰："此是當初定界立碑時，李宣傳義復與金應瀗、金慶門等，爭之總管曰：'此亦鴨江之源，一體立碑，以明境界'云，而終不能得者也。今以小人之齟齬，何可必得乎？"曰："第往言之。"余袖其圖而進館所。[29]

如上文，朴權之所以要求在《白山圖》的鴨綠江西源上一併書"鴨綠江源"四個字，是因為如圖2所示，西源是和天池相連的，西源能否寫上"鴨綠江源"四個字，關係到長白山天池以南是否全部為朝鮮所有，因此他強令金指南"必受書名而來，否則君之前仕，盡削於此矣"，即如果不能受書而來，那麼金指南先前的功勞都將一筆勾銷。如文中所記，穆克登還在山上時，隨行的朝鮮譯官金慶門、金應瀗及軍官李義復等，曾要求穆克登在鴨綠江西源上"一體立碑"，估計出於同樣的理由。然而穆克登沒有答應他們的請求，可能考慮到一江不可以有二源，穆克登認定的鴨綠江正源是東源，更何況其對面是圖們江源開始的地方，即圖們江"入地伏流"處。換言之，這裏就是穆克登指定的鴨、圖二江之源的分水嶺。

按照朴權的命令，金指南帶着《白山圖》來到了穆克登住的館所，他指出鴨綠江源有二派，只一派書江源，另一派不寫，則有違奉使者之道，無以向國王交待。穆克登最初不肯答應，金指南再三懇求，提出只有朝鮮這一本寫"鴨綠江源"，而呈覽給皇帝的那一本可以不寫，使朝鮮官員"得免問責之歸"。無奈之下，穆克登只好答應西源寫上"鴨綠江源"四個字。書給之後，穆克登感覺不釋然，他戲謔金指南道："此山有何寶貝之產耶？"顯然他明白朝鮮人的意圖在長白山。一江不可以有二源，穆克登千辛萬苦地查找水源，就是為了查明哪一條水是正源，以確定兩國界線，然而到頭來他竟然做出如此令人費解的舉動。此時，同在一旁的清朝侍衛嘲弄金指南道："明日再來，我給你一個山。後日再來，主事（指鄂世）該給你一個山。共通三個山，白白的得了。"於是，大家大笑而罷。正當清朝官員妄自尊大時，金指南則出色地完成使命，回到了朴權的住處。[30]

接下來，更有趣的是，穆克登自覺迫于金指南的再三懇求而書給"鴨綠江源"以後，第二天便"懊悔其錯了，達夜不寐"。他不是懊悔一江不可以有二源，而是想到只有朝鮮那一本書"鴨綠江源"，而呈覽給皇帝的這一本不書，則顯得不誠實，有欺瞞皇上之嫌。他獨自口誦道："只書於留此者，而不書歸奏之本，則便為欺瞞皇上之歸。既已書給之物，還推抹削，亦非體面之所可為。百而思，惟終不如從實直為之，為愈也。"於是，穆克登取出圖本又書'江源'而藏之。也就是說，他在準備奏聞皇帝的那一本《白山圖》上，也寫上了"鴨綠江源"四個字。[31] 我們通過《皇輿全覽圖》可以看出，連接長白山的鴨綠江源，的確有東、西二源（如

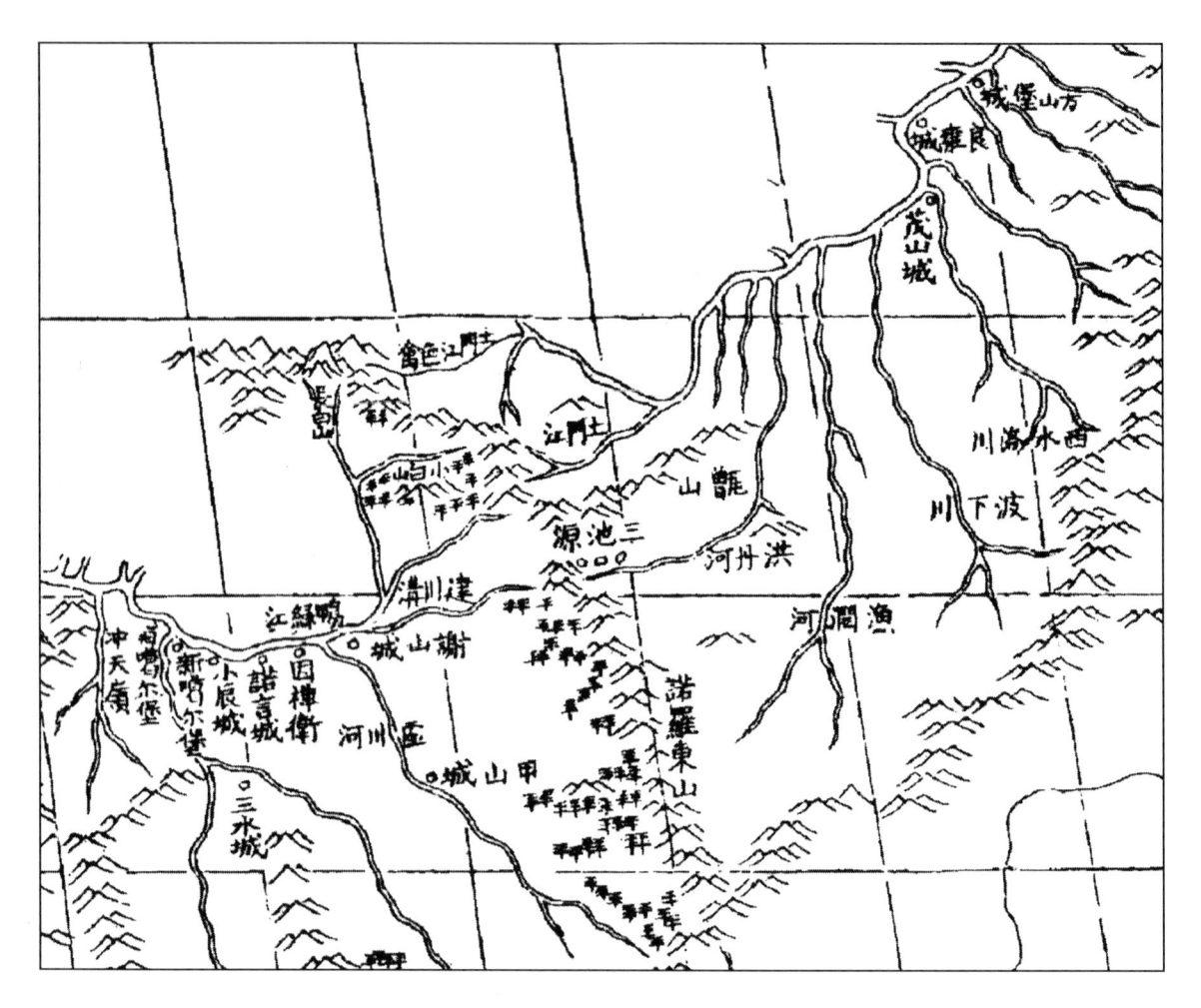

圖3　康熙《皇輿全覽圖》的一部分（1943年福克司影印本）

圖3），這大概反映了穆克登調查水源的結果。

　　《白山圖》（圖2）還有一個值得我們關注的地方，那就是立于長白山天池東南邊（約十餘里）的那塊碑，標有"江源碑"的字樣。表明這裏就是鴨、圖二江的發源地，同時也是標記兩國分界的地方，朝鮮後世稱這塊碑為"定界碑"不無道理。我們不妨看一下，此碑為何立於此處。據洪世泰的《白頭山記》記載，穆克登登上長白山天池，從崗脊緩緩下來，約走三、四里，便找到了鴨綠江發源地，這就是鴨綠江東源。鴨綠江東源並非立馬見水，要從碑的西邊順着溝子向南行走約三十里才有水。1908年劉建封等踏查長白山時，將此溝命名為"大旱河"，就是因為這裏是無水的幹溝，雨季時才有水，其他季節無水。[32] 而與西邊的溝子正對着的東邊也有一溝，光緒勘界時稱之為"黃花松溝子"（今稱"黑石溝"）。穆克登沿着此溝一直向東行，行走約百餘里，才到達朝鮮人所指圖們江湧出處（甘土峰下），並指定未及湧出處十餘里的一派東流之水為圖們江源。這個碑東邊的黃花松溝子，就是穆克登所指圖們江斷流處，在

— 450 —

該圖（圖2）標為"入地暗流"。之後穆克登在前述東、西二溝之間的分水嶺上立了碑，碑文記載："西為鴨綠，東為土門，故於分水嶺上勒石為記"。這就是天池東南邊立着的那塊"江源碑"的來歷。正因為"江源碑"和圖們江湧出處之間，相隔較遠，所以穆克登才要求朝鮮在斷流處設柵以做為標記。

最後，這幅《白山圖》還有一個另人費解的地方。穆克登通過親身踏查，明明發現鴨綠江、圖們江水源並不是從長白山天池流出的，如前述，鴨綠江發源地距離天池以南約四十里，圖們江發源地距離天池更遠，位於天池以東百餘里。然而在這幅《白山圖》上，鴨、圖二江之源仍和長白山天池連在了一起，這是為什麼？這說明穆克登沒有勇氣打破前人的成見嗎？因為無論是《元一統志》、《明一統志》及清代《盛京通志》（康熙二十三年），均記載鴨、圖、松三大江發源于長白山天池。再者，穆克登迫於朝鮮人堅持鴨、圖二江發源于長白山天池，天池以南為朝鮮界，故不得已才把鴨、圖二江之源與長白山天池連在了一起嗎？也許二者兼而有之。

三、穆克登錯定圖們江源的原因分析

依據三部踏查記和《朝鮮王朝實錄》的有關記載，來分析穆克登錯定圖們江源的原因，可以總結出以下四點：第一，作為主導此次定界的清朝官員，穆克登沒有對鴨、圖二江水系複雜，特別是圖們江上游水系複雜做充分的心理準備，他也不具備這方面的專門知識。他依據自己所瞭解到的圖們江發源于長白山東邊向東流的地理知識，結合朝鮮土人所講的"東流之水，斷流百餘里後，始為湧出"的說法，在距離長白山天池以東百餘里的地方尋找圖們江水源，確定一條東流之水為江源。然而這裏也是松花江上流五道白河水系的發源地，結果他誤定五道白河的一支為圖們江源。而當朝鮮接伴使對水源提出質疑，要求溯流而上重新查水源時，他堅持己見，錯過了修正錯誤的機會。另外，從查水源、立碑的過程看，穆克登有些急於求成。5月15日他在分水嶺上立碑之後，當即派出筆帖式馳往北京奏報。21日當朴權對江源提出質疑時，筆帖式已經離開厚春（琿春）轉往北京了。[33] 於是穆克登只得回答，若修改江源，需由國王奏聞皇帝，可見他沒有多少迴旋的餘地了。

第二，作為定界另一方的朝鮮事先也沒有做出充分的準備。在穆克登到來之前，朝鮮雖派出咸鏡北道兵使和咸鏡南道兵使查看水源，然而他們"或以路絕，或以雪塞，但登高遙望"，未能查清江源。不久，咸鏡監司又派出魚山僉使、仁遮外萬戶調查水源，查得的結果鴨綠江源與南、北兵使基本一致，而"豆滿江源流"則不一致。[34] 後來穆克登結束行查來到魚潤江邊時，朴權所說的"真豆江"，也不是調查的結果，而是從茂山土人那裏聽來的。穆克登尚在山上時，朴權曾派茂山土人前往"真豆江"與紅丹水匯流處查看，後來又趁軍官、譯官給穆克登送糧的機會，讓他們導引穆克登從"真豆江"匯流處下來。然而還沒有等他們到達匯流處，穆克登已經結束行查派出了筆帖式。[35]

　　第三，穆克登調查圖們江水源的方法有問題，他沒有溯江而上尋找水源，而是沿着圖們江順流而下查看水源，結果誤定了江源。其過程大致如下：穆克登先派朝鮮差使員等到長白山以東百餘里的所謂湧出處等候（B：朝鮮人所指圖們江第二派水），隨後他自己也追往。未及湧出處十餘里，他看到了一派東流之水（A：初派水，五道白河的一支）。他認為此水必入圖們江，指定此東流之水（A）為圖們江源。[36] 他派清朝大通官、朝鮮軍官、譯官等往審水道六十餘里，這些人回來後報告"明有水道，似無可疑"。[37] 之後，穆克登順着朝鮮人所指的湧出處的水（B：第二派水）繼續向下走，看到一派自北而來的水（C），以為這就是他看到的初派水來合者。[38] 這裏，穆克登犯了一個致命的錯誤，他沒有沿着這條自北而來的水（C），溯流而上窮尋江源。如果他做到了這一點，就可以發現這個自北而來的水（C），並不是他指定的那條東流之水（A：初派水），因為流入圖們江的水是不可能與松花江上流接流的。

　　第四，當朝鮮發現圖們江水源錯誤後，沒有即時通告清朝，因而錯過了糾正錯誤的機會。朝鮮在設柵時發現了穆克登定的水向北流，而不流入圖們江。儘管如此，當時負責在圖們江斷流處設柵的朝鮮北評事洪致中，仍下令自江源碑開始沿着斷流處（黃松花溝子）設柵，因為這是穆克登指定的。至於連接到哪一派水源，待他向朝廷報告後再做決定。然而差使員朴道常等不顧洪致中的命令，擅自將木柵連接到了第二派水源（B），這就是朝鮮人從一開始認定的圖們江湧出處。[39] 同年12月在廷議的過程中，雖有一些朝臣建議通告清朝重新審查水源，但是以領議政李濡為首，擔心此次定界時多得的天池以南空地得而復失，因而反對通告清廷。於是朝鮮默認了朴道常等擅自移柵于第二派水源的做法。[40] 同年11月前往北京的朝鮮冬至使，並不知道朝鮮變更水源和移柵的情形。他們只是把朝鮮正在斷流處設柵一事，按照之前穆克登和朴權的約定，通過清朝通官轉達給穆克登，穆克登又奏聞了皇帝。接下來，穆克登以皇旨傳言道："白頭山事，今已了當，更無往審之舉，須勿為慮。立標之役，亦以農時，徐徐為之，毋或傷民。"[41]

　　第二年，穆克登以副使的身份，為慶賀康熙帝六十壽辰頒詔而出使朝鮮。此行，穆克登有一個重要使命，就是要得到朝鮮宮廷內藏"朝鮮全圖"，這與清朝製作《皇輿全覽圖》有關。此前一年，穆克登已經親自踏查了長白山，確定了鴨、圖二江水源和兩國邊界，繪製了《白山圖》。然而長白山南邊的水派、山脈伸入半島的形勢，仍沒有把握，於是借此機會想得到一張"朝鮮全圖"。然而朝鮮不願意透露本國的地理信息，最初拒絕了穆克登的索圖要求，後來耐不住他的再三請求，拿出了一張"不詳不略"的地圖。此圖的長白山水派有明顯的錯誤，於是朝鮮不得不拿出定界時繪製的《白山圖》加以說明。[42] 這兩幅圖估計就是《皇輿全覽圖》"朝鮮圖"（參見圖3）的底本，而朝鮮擅自變更水源的事實仍被掩蓋着。

小結

　　陪伴穆克登參與定界的三位朝鮮人的踏查記，加上當時繪製的《白山圖》，是瞭解1712年長白山定界過程和結果的重要史料。特別是在清朝内閣大庫失火導致相關資料蕩然無存的情況下，這三位朝鮮人的踏查記和《白山圖》顯得彌足珍貴。

　　通過這三部踏查記、《白山圖》及《朝鮮王朝實錄》相關記載可以看出，穆克登定界是從中朝兩國以鴨綠江、圖們江為界的事實和二江發源于長白山天池的地理認識出發的。與此同時，穆克登還參酌和聽取了朝鮮人對於邊界的想法和所持地理認識。基於此，他決定登上長白山天池查看水源，在天池以南、以東尋找二江之源，並立碑于天池東南十餘里的分水嶺上。由於中朝雙方事先並不瞭解鴨、圖二江上游的水流狀況，這樣一來，生活在當地的朝鮮土人的看法就成為查找水源時的重要的參考依據。比如朝鮮土人認為圖們江"東流之水，斷流百餘里，始為湧出"，這對穆克登查找圖們江源起了很大的作用。在當時繪製的《白山圖》上，圖們江源自長白山天池流出向東流，中間斷流一段，在斷流處標有"入地暗流"字樣，之後在甘土峰下復流為三派水流，就是這種地理認識的反映。

　　穆克登通過實地踏查，明明發現鴨、圖二江之源並不是從長白山天池流出的，鴨綠江發源地距離天池東南約四十餘里，圖們江發源地距離天池更遠，位於天池以東百餘里。然而在《白山圖》上，鴨、圖二江水源仍和長白山天池連在了一起。這一方面說明穆克登沒有勇氣突破前人的成見，另一方面迫於朝鮮人堅持此二江發源于長白山天池，天池以南為朝鮮界。總之，此次定界以後，朝鮮人心安理得地接受了長白山天池以南為朝鮮界的定界成果，這就為以後朝鮮人自由地靠近長白山天池，以及朝鮮流民在長白山以南地區開墾和居住提供了便利條件。

　　我們結合三部踏查記和《白山圖》可以瞭解到，立于長白山天池東南邊的那塊碑，首先是"江源碑"，也就是標記西邊為鴨綠江源、東邊為圖們江源的碑。同時它也是標記兩國分界的碑，穆克登要求朝鮮在碑東邊的圖們江斷流處設柵，就是為了明確彼此之間的界限，朝鮮後世稱這塊碑為"定界碑"不無道理。如果按照江源碑所處的位置來看，兩國應以江源碑（分水嶺）——西邊的鴨綠江源——東邊的圖們江源為界線，此線以南屬於朝鮮，以北屬於清朝，天池位於此線以北，當屬清朝。然而如果從這張《白山圖》來看，鴨、圖二江發源于長白山天池，以長白山天池為界，其南邊屬於朝鮮，北邊屬於清朝。這也許是此次定界的矛盾所在，也是不夠嚴謹的地方。

　　康熙年間的長白山定界最大的失誤就在於錯定了圖們江源，穆克登指定了一條向東流過一段後繼續向東北流入松花江的水。其責任首當其衝在於清使穆克登身上，他尋找圖們江源的方法有問題。他沒有做到溯流而上窮尋江源，而是順流而下查看水源，結果出了差錯。不僅如此，他還急於求成，錯過了修正錯誤的機會。而朝鮮的責任似乎不亞於此，當朝鮮發現水源錯誤後，沒有即時通告清朝，而是掩蓋事實擅自變更了水源，並移設木柵于此水。而后一段木柵朽爛，造成了朝鮮后世土門非豆滿，土門、豆滿為二江的錯誤認識。

注释

[1] 主張碑從一開始就立在天池東南邊的學者：張存武：《清代中韓邊務問題探源》，《近代史研究所集刊》第 2 期，1971 年；楊昭全、孫玉梅：《中朝邊界史》；李花子：《清朝與朝鮮關係史研究——以越境交涉為中心》，延邊大學出版社，2006 年。主張碑被朝鮮人從小白山頂移至天池東南邊的學者：徐德源：《長白山東南地區石堆土堆築設的真相》，《中國邊疆史地研究》1996 年第 2 期；徐德源：《穆克登碑的性質及其鑿立地點與位移述考——近世中朝邊界爭議的焦點》，《中國邊疆史地研究》1997 年第 1 期；刁書仁：《康熙年間穆克登查邊定界考辨》，《中國邊疆史地研究》2003 年第 3 期；陳慧：《後世所見的穆克登碑》，中國朝鮮史研究會、延邊大學朝鮮·韓國歷史研究所編：《朝鮮·韓國歷史研究》第 10 輯。

[2] 日本學者篠田治策認為，穆克登定穆克登的水是松花江上流，他稱之為"土門江"，並與豆滿江（今圖們江）區別開來。韓國學者姜錫和認為，穆克登原打算定圖們江卻誤定了松花江上流。光緒年間勘界時中方代表認為，穆克登定的是小白山東麓發源的紅丹水，朝方代表則認為定的是紅土山水。

[3] 光緒年間勘界時，中方代表認為穆克登踏查長白山為清朝單方面的查邊，朝方則堅持認為它是中朝兩國共派代表進行的定界。當今中國學者中，徐德源主張清朝單方面"查邊說"，張存武、楊昭全、刁書仁、李花子等主張"定界說"，韓國學者則一直主張"定界說"。

[4] 朴權：《北征日記》，東北亞歷史財團編：《白頭山定界碑資料集》，2006 年，第 118 頁。

[5] 金指南：《北征錄》，朝鮮總督府"朝鮮史編修會"1945 年 3 月抄本，第 59-95 頁。朴權前引書，第 114-119 頁。

[6] 金指南前引書，第 129 頁。

[7] 金指南前引書，第 108-114 頁。

[8] 金指南前引書，第 117 頁。

[9] 康熙五十一年二、三月間，當朝鮮接到清朝禮部有關穆克登查界的咨文時，經過一番廷議，決定以長白山以南為朝鮮界作為此次定界的目標，詳見李花子：《清朝與朝鮮關係史研究——以越境交涉為中心》，延邊大學出版社，2006 年，第四章"康熙年間中朝查界、定界交涉"。

[10]《朝鮮肅宗實錄》卷五十一，肅宗三十八年五月丁亥。

[11] 洪世泰：《白頭山記》，引自梁泰鎮：《韓國國境史研究》，法經出版社，1992 年，第 34-38 頁。

[12] 金指南前引書，第 101 頁。

[13] 洪世泰前引書，第 37 頁。

[14]《朝鮮肅宗實錄》卷五二，肅宗三十八年十二月丙辰。

[15] 據張鳳臺、劉建封記載：長白山天池三奇峰的南麓有"大旱河"，"壑底無水，多沙石"，一直向南，至南阜約三十里始出水，這就是鴨綠江源。參見張鳳臺：《長白匯征錄》，李澍田主編：《長白叢書》初集，吉林文史出版社，1987 年，第 55 頁；劉建封：《長白山江崗志略》，《長白叢書》初集，第 360、365 頁及插圖"天池附近形勢一覽圖"。

[16] 光緒勘界時查得紅丹水與天池南北相距一百三十里，紅土山水與天池東西相距一百二十里。參見李重夏：《問答記》、《照會謄抄》，《白山學報》1968 年第 4 號，第 272-278 頁；金魯奎：《北輿要選》，

梁泰鎮:《韓國國境史研究》附錄，第 358 頁。

[17]《清聖祖實錄》卷二四六，康熙五十年五月癸巳，中華書局 1986 年影印本。

[18] 金指南前引書，第 150-151 頁。

[19]《朝鮮肅宗實錄》卷五三，肅宗三十九年正月庚子。

[20] 1712（康熙五十一）年 5 月 11 日穆克登登上長白山頂天池，當日從天池下來，15 日刻石立碑，這其間他一直在尋找圖們江水源。

[21] 金指南前引書，第 151 頁。

[22] 有關穆克登錯定圖們江源，詳見於李花子:《穆克登錯定圖們江源及朝鮮移柵位置考》，復旦大學韓國研究中心編:《韓國研究論叢》第 18 輯，2008 年。

[23] 朴權前引書，第 131-132 頁。

[24] 全國圖書館文獻縮微複製中心編:《國家圖書館藏清代孤本外交檔案續編》第 5 冊，"吉朝分界案"，照錄吉林將軍來文，2005 年，第 1853 頁。

[25] 金指南前引書，第 119 頁。

[26] 中國的長白山朝鮮稱"白頭山"，1712 年定界以後朝鮮對此山的關注度提高，然而之前從很早開始朝鮮人已將此山看作是半島諸山的祖宗山。參見楊普景:《我們民族的傳統山地觀和白頭大幹》，《白頭大幹的自然和人》，山嶽文化，2002 年，第 19-62 頁。

[27]《朝鮮肅宗實錄》卷五一，肅宗三十八年五月丁酉。

[28] 金指南前引書，第 156-161 頁。

[29] 金指南前引書，第 162-163 頁。

[30] 金指南前引書，第 163-165 頁。

[31] 金指南前引書，第 166 頁。

[32] 參見張鳳臺:《長白匯征錄》，第 55 頁；劉建封:《長白山江崗志略》，第 360、365 頁。

[33] 據記載，筆帖式蘇爾昌帶着奏本於 5 月 17 日到達茂山，20 日到達慶源，當日越往厚春（琿春），參見金指南前引書，第 133、160-161 頁。

[34]《朝鮮肅宗實錄》卷五一，肅宗三十八年三月己丑、四月乙未。

[35] 金指南前引書，第 131-132、136、145 頁。

[36]《朝鮮肅宗實錄》卷五二，肅宗三十八年十二月丙辰。

[37] 金指南前引書，第 129-130 頁。

[38]《朝鮮肅宗實錄》卷五二，肅宗三十八年十二月丙辰。

[39]《朝鮮肅宗實錄》卷五二，肅宗三十八年十二月丙辰。

[40]《朝鮮肅宗實錄》卷五二，肅宗三十八年十二月丙辰。

[41]《朝鮮肅宗實錄》卷五二，肅宗三十八年十月庚申、十一月壬午；卷五三，三十九年三月壬辰；《承政院日記》第 467 冊，肅宗三十九年三月十五日。

[42]《朝鮮肅宗實錄》卷五三，肅宗三十九年五月壬辰；卷五十四，閏五月甲子、癸酉、六月丁丑、己卯。

CHANDBAI MOUNTAIN IN THE LIGHT OF NOTES BY KOREAN EXPLORERS AND *PAINTING OF THE WHITE MOUNTAIN* OF THE JOSEON (CHOSŎN) ERA

LI Huazi

This article investigates the location of the tablet erected by Mukedeng by using the exploratory notes of three Koreans personally engaged in both demarcating the frontier between China and Korea on Changbai Mountain in the 51st year of the Kangxi reign period and in locating the source of the Yalu and Tumen Rivers. The tablet was located more than 5 kilometers southeast of Tianchi. The tablet serves to denote the source of the waters of the two rivers, as well as serving as the merestone that marks the boundary between China and Korea. Although Mukedeng found that the Tianchi of Changbai Mountain was not the source of the Yalu and Tumen Rivers after his exploration of the site, the water source of the Yalu and Tumen Rivers is still shown to be joined with Tianchi of Changbai Mountain in *Painting of White Mountain*. From the position where the tablet was located, the boundary line between China and Korea should be indicated. In other words the land south of the line running through the source of the Yalu River in the west and the source of the Tumen River in the east should belong to Korea, while the land north of the line should belong to China. However, *Painting of White Mountain* shows the Yalu River and Tumen River originating in the Tianchi of Changbai Mountain, which forms the boundary between China and Korea; Korea possessed the land south of the Tianchi of Changbai Mountain and China possessed the land north of it. This resulted in contradictions and imprecision. The demarcation was convenient for the Korean side, ensuring that Korea possessed the lands south of the Tianchi of Changbai Mountain, enabling Koreans to move freely in the vicinity of Changbai Mountain while Korean migrants could develop and inhabit land south of Changbai Mountain.

OFFICIAL GENEALOGIES AND PRIVATE GENEALOGIES OF THE EIGHT BANNERS IN THE QING DYNASTY

DING Yizhuang

I. Official genealogies in the early Qing Dynasty

Genealogies (*pudie*) are documents recording family blood relationship, which are mainly written privately. The composition of genealogies in Chinese traditional society required two preconditions, one being that the patriarchal family system (*zongfazhi jiazu* 宗法制家族) had fully formed, and the other being that the family had someone able to write up its genealogy. Neither of these two preconditions was available in Hou Jin (Latter Jin) society before 1644. Although the Nüzhen and their successors in the Manchu Bannermen both attached importance to lineage and the handed down memory about their own clans, tribes and ancestors might exist, the traditional ethnic Han concept of the "household" did not exist in Nüzhen society prior to 1644, and we never found any written genealogies from before 1644 in Manchu, Han, or any other language.

After the Qing army entered Beijing in 1644, members of the Eight Banners were heavily restricted by the Eight Banner system, and were neither allowed to engage in business activities nor work or farm. The restrictions were especially onerous for ordinary Eight Banner soldiers, who lost their land soon after gaining it in early 1644. This meant that in Manchu society households lacked a dependable material basis. Since the conditions for forming households in Eight Banner society were lacking, there was no demand for the composition of genealogies for the purposes of respecting ancestors and connecting families (*jingzong-shouzu* 敬宗收族). Although many genealogies composed by later Bannermen trace the family lineage back to the early Qing, these genealogies were not genealogies in the traditional Han sense, but merely genealogies composed by the government for members of the Eight Banners.

Before 1644, the Qing began to record the Eight Banner population, as determined by of the unique Eight Banner system. Firstly, the Banner *beile* chiefs (*nirui ejen beile* 旗主貝勒) sought to expand the strength of the people under their domination, which necessitated that they strictly control and manage the population. This was why the Eight Banners established the population registration system. Secondly, the Eight Banners governed their members in accordance with a strict ranking system, which was based on various factors, including the time and method of joining the Banner, the place of residence prior to joining the Banner, and ethnic affiliation. Having joined the Banner, the member's position within it was largely confirmed, and very difficult to alter later. For instance, the descendants of soldiers who died in battle or contributed to a victory were entitled to an official position; those soldiers who surrendered to or were included within Banners as slaves because they were criminals, even though their descendants might excel in battle, could only later either leave their masters (*kaihu*) at best; in other words, they could only be classified somewhere between commoners and servants, described as "servants who had left their masters" (*kaihuren*). In the Eight Banner system, most *kaihuren* and the lowest servants were ethnic Han. In the many battles of the early Qing, the Manchus had a shortage of soldiers and so servants often went into battle as commoners of the Eight Banners, many of them winning honors. In order to prevent the descendants of these people changing their social position and becoming commoners after several generations and to avoid contradictions between servants and their masters, the Qing government attached great importance to the blood lineage of the members of the Eight Banners and formulated rules to check the family lineage when following the official position, so that the "Eight Banner hereditary genealogies archives" 八旗世襲譜檔 emerged.

Although the Eight Banner household registration booklets (*hukouce* 户口册), soldier registration booklets, and hereditary booklets of Eight Banner officials had appeared at an earlier date, they differed from the family genealogies of the ethnic Han. They were composed with specific official requirements and in accordance with strict rules. In the Qing, such documents were called "Banner booklets", and Bannermen genealogies were one of these booklets which were composed by the government, the main purpose being to record the origins, generations, official positions of ancestors, and reasons for becoming Bannermen. These Banner booklets were originally collected by the government, and can be described as "official genealogies".

The composition of such official genealogies was, however, not initiated by the Eight Banners. Officials in the Liaodong Weisuo 衛所 in the Ming Dynasty had prepared similar hereditary booklets (*chengxice* 承襲册), and these were largely the same as the genealogies among the Qing Banner booklets in both character and function. The way in which the Eight Banners composed their official genealogies most likely followed the precedents set by their Nüzhen ancestors who held positions in the Liaodong Weisuo in the Ming Dynasty. They were not concerned with Han family genealogies, and no one would consider these documents to be "family genealogies".

II. The normalization of the official registration booklets and genealogies

Although the Manchu governors established the registration system before 1644, the normalization of all household registered names was initiated during the Yongzheng reign (1723-1735). They were improved in the early years of the Qianlong reign, when each Banner composed soldier registration booklets; the Banners sought to identify each different position, record the resume of three generations under each person's name, and compose the booklets with different positions. The registration booklets of the Eight Banners had different names, but the format remained the same until the end of the Qing Dynasty.

The Qing rulers emphasized the different origins of the Eight Banner members and recorded three generations because, by this time, Qing governance had stabilized and Bannermen were entitled to various rights as a privileged group. Many ethnic Han people also became Bannermen by "adoption". In order to keep the Manchu bloodline pure and to prevent Han people from sharing Bannermen's privileges, the Qing government was neither willing nor able to expand the Eight Banner groups. Internally, this was because the soldiers' numbers and payments were fixed. In order to ensure that Manchu Bannermen received more payment and greater opportunities and to ease tensions regarding "Eight Banner living conditions", the government needed to separate the servants who had left their masters (*kaihuren*) and the adopted Han people from the Manchu Bannermen. The genealogies were thus the most important evidence used to identify Bannermen.

At this time, the most important measure which the Qing government adopted for tracing the origins of many Manchu clans, was the 80-volume *General Genealogy of the Eight Banner Manchu Clans* (Baqi Manzhou Shizu Tongpu 八旗滿洲氏族通譜), on which the government expended much labor and money to compile over a ten-year period. The compilation of the genealogies was initiated in 1735 and completed in 1744; the genealogies included 654 Manchu surnames apart from Aisin-Gioro 愛新覺羅, and 521 names of Mongolian, Korean and Han provenance, totalling 1175 surnames. Some scholars regard this as a major assertion of ethnic identity and consciousness on the part of the Manchu rulers after entering central China where the majority of the population was ethnic Han.

General Genealogy of the Eight Banner Manchu Clans was a typically official work, not only because the emperor authorized its composition and the service it provided for governance, but especially because of its content. Firstly, the first ancestors of most clans were included since they were under the Hou Jin (Qing). Secondly, much of the essential content of Han genealogies, such as the number of males in each generation and the number of children each man had, were not recorded in the *General Genealogy*; only the people who had positions in the Qing government were recorded. Thirdly, although we do not know the source materials used in the compilation of the *General Genealogy*, from the content we know that the materials would probably have been selected from the official hereditary booklets (*chengxice* 承襲册), and other related booklets. Of course, these latter materials help us understand the formation of the Eight Banner organization, the distribution of each ethnic group in the Northeast, and the story of each Manchu surname, information that cannot be provided by other documents.

III. The popularity of private composition of genealogies by Bannermen

The private composition of genealogies by Bannerman became popular from the mid-Qianlong reign. The reasons for this were threefold:

Firstly, those Manchu Bannermen who had lived for a long time in the Central Plains and had accepted a greater measure of Han Confucian culture, became familiar with and emulated the ethnic Han family system. Some officials of the Eight Banners, who had held high positions for generations, as well as their descendants, were also influenced by Confucian culture, and they had all the necessary preconditions for forming households.

Secondly, ordinary Eight Banner officials and soldiers were distributed as a result of military deployment and garrison duties, and it was impossible for them to live together as they had previously. Nor could they remember the oral histories of their own clans. To ensure that their descendants did not forget their own clans and surnames over the passage of time, they sought to imitate the Han practice of recording their ancestors' names, origins and development through genealogies.

Thirdly, many Bannermen understood that the purpose and function of the official population records and of family genealogies were different. The official genealogies could not meet the demand to "respect ancestors and connect families".

However, there were obvious connections between the private genealogies of Bannermen and the official registration booklets, and these constitute the major differences between the genealogies of the Bannermen and of the Han. Much of the content of these genealogies was based on registration booklets and official books, especially when recording the ancestors prior to the Qianlong reign. Some genealogies of the Bannermen of lower status were obviously compiled from registration booklets. For example, we can see that in the very simple genealogies preserved in Xiapo village (Shunyi county, Beijing), which was deregistered as a Banner in the 57th year (1792) of the Qianlong reign, there is little order after that date, with incomplete details of names and generations, and no information about farmers (zhuangtou 莊頭). The huge difference in one set of genealogies, with the earlier sections much fuller than the later section, makes it obvious that the first part of these genealogies was copied from the official books, and the second part was composed by the family.

Of course, the fact that Bannermen composed these genealogies by copying from the official book does not reduce the value of these Banner genealogies, because on the one hand many of the early official booklets were lost and on the other hand there were differences in concerns and records between official and private genealogies. The chaos of the official registration management and the migration of the members of the Eight Banners make the private genealogies the most important source for the revisions and makeup of official books and thus they are valuable for research.

IV. Banner society and population questions viewed through the comparison between official genealogies and household genealogies

The population of the Eight Banners in the Qing Dynasty was almost all registered in official booklets, regardless of position, which means there is a file for almost the entire Eight Banner population. Although more than half of the Banner booklets have been lost in the century following the demise of the Qing, many complete booklets have been preserved. The private genealogies composed by Bannermen, which became popular after the mid-Qing, provide a source which can be compared with the population recorded in official booklets and this provides a unique channel and perspective for conducting research on the population and social affairs of Bannermen. Although the Bannermen's private genealogies are not comparable with

Han genealogies in quality or quantity, or even in terms of history and richness of content, they were nevertheless based on official registration booklets. Comparative research with Han genealogies, which are difficult to utilize, highlights their research value, and connects the seemingly meaningless booklets hidden in archives with actual people and their lives in given locations and times, endowing these books with meaning.

Over the past decade, I have been attempting to conduct such research in the suburbs of Beijing with scholars from Liaoning province. This research is bidirectional; not only can we find the related ethnic groups according to the official registration booklets, with the names of people and places, and so find their genealogies, but we can also check their registration booklets in archives after meeting with a Manchu family and seeing their genealogies. These two approaches have proved successful. In addition, every success has led to other unexpected, and even outstanding, developments. We have achieved success in what might seem like looking for a needle in a haystack on several occasions, but of course Banner society was relatively limited in region and population, and government controlled this population relatively strictly, as underscored by the unique character of the Bannermen's registration booklets and genealogies.

The search for people through official booklets began with a survey conducted by Professor Guo Songyi, Professor James Z.Lee, Professor Cameron Campbell and myself in Liaoning province ten years ago. My students and I also conducted field work from another direction in Manchu settlements in the suburbs of Beijing, in which we could locate private genealogies and then check for their record in official booklets, and this also led to meaningful discoveries.

Checking for official registration booklets enhanced the value of Bannermen genealogies, enabling the two types of document to play greater roles in research. However, this required certain preconditions. Firstly, we needed to have a greater understanding of the quality, function and character of these two types of documents, especially in order to discern the differences between them. However, some scholars continue to confuse the genealogies of the Bannermen with those of the Han. Secondly, in comparing official registration booklets with private genealogies, one must have a basic understanding of the Eight Banner system and to which organization groups of people belong, otherwise it is difficult to know where to begin when confronted by such a large archive of files, even when one has the genealogies in hand. Thirdly, this archival work needs to be combined with field work. My experience from many years of field work has shown that it is the field work that invariably reveals the connection between official books and private genealogies.

圖書在版編目(CIP)數據

歐亞學刊：國際版／余太山，李錦繡主編.—北京：商務印書館，2011
ISBN 978-7-100-08518-2

I.①歐⋯ II.①余⋯ ②李⋯ III.①東方學－叢刊
IV.①K107.8-55

中國版本圖書館CIP數據核字(2011)第170435号

所有權利保留。

未經許可，不得以任何方式使用。

歐亞學刊（國際版）

余太山　李錦繡　主編

商　務　印　書　館　出　版
（北京王府井大街36號　郵政編碼　100710）
商　務　印　書　館　發　行
三河市尚藝印裝有限公司印刷
ISBN 978-7-100-08518-2

2011年10月第1版　　開本889×1194　1/16
2011年10月北京第1次印刷　印張29 5/8　插頁40
定　價：88.00圓